Gerard Clauson's

Skeleton Tangut (Hsi Hsia) Dictionary

A facsimile edition

CORPUS TEXTORUM TANGUTORUM

Volume 1

To Asher

Best wishes,

Andrew West

2021-10-01

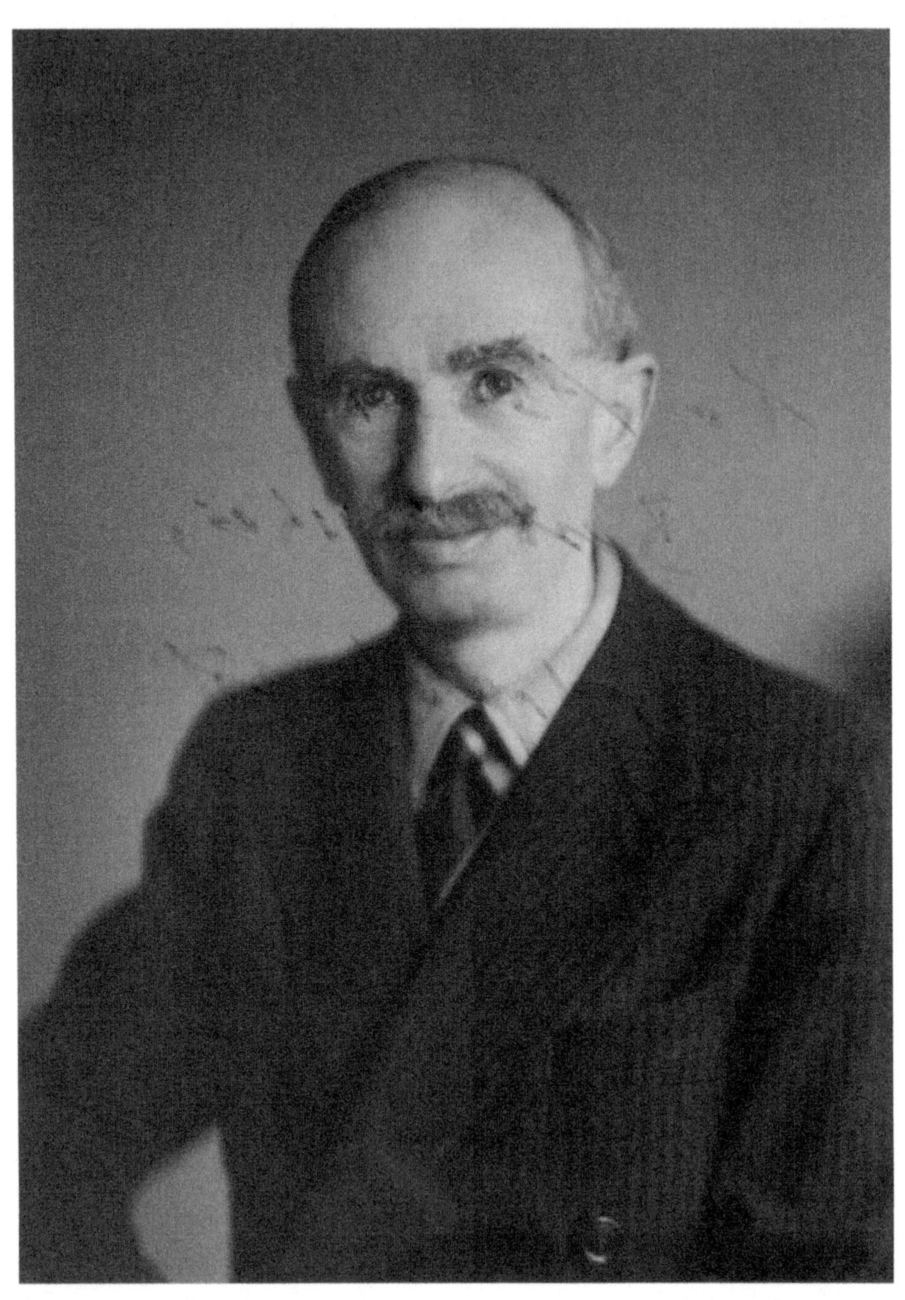

Sir Gerard Leslie Makins Clauson, KCMG, OBE, FSA (1891–1974)

CORPUS TEXTORUM TANGUTORUM
Volume 1

Gerard Clauson's
Skeleton Tangut (Hsi Hsia) Dictionary

A facsimile edition

With an Introduction by
Imre Galambos

With Editorial notes and an Index by
Andrew West

Prepared for publication by
Michael Everson

2016

Published by Evertype, 73 Woodgrove, Portlaoise, R32 ENP6, Ireland. *www.evertype.com*.

This edition © 2016 Michael Everson.
Introduction © 2016 Imre Galambos.
Editorial notes © 2016 Andrew West.
Dictionary © 1974 Estate of Gerard Clauson.

First edition 2016.

All rights reserved. No part of this publication may be reproduced, stored in a retrieval system, or transmitted, in any form or by any means, electronic, mechanical, photocopying, recording, or otherwise, without the prior permission in writing of the Publisher, or as expressly permitted by law, or under terms agreed with the appropriate reprographics rights organization.

A catalogue record for this book is available from the British Library.

ISBN-10 1-78201-167-6
ISBN-13 978-1-78201-167-5

Typeset in Baskerville by Michael Everson.

Cover design by Michael Everson. The cover image is folio 53b of the *Homophones* (*Tóngyīn* 同音) edition B collected from Khara-khoto by Aurel Stein in 1914. © The British Library Board. Or.12380/3116.

The frontispiece photograph of Gerard Clauson was taken in June 1945 by Walter Stoneman (1876–1958). © National Portrait Gallery, London.

Printed and bound by LightningSource.

Table of contents

INTRODUCTION

Sir Gerard Clauson and his *Skeleton Tangut Dictionary*

Sir Gerard Leslie Makins Clauson (1891–1974) worked most of his life as a civil servant and conducted academic research in his spare time.[1] Only after retiring in 1951 at the age of 60 was he able to devote his full attention to scholarly endeavours, which were primarily focussed on Turkic languages. Thus as a scholar, today he is primarily remembered for his contribution to Turkic studies, and his *Etymological Dictionary of Pre-Thirteenth-Century Turkish* is still an essential reference tool in the field.[2] Yet in addition to his study of Turkic and Mongolian linguistics, he also worked on a number of other Asian languages, including Tangut. Even though his extensive list of publications includes only a small number of items related to Tangut studies,[3] he devoted an incredible amount of time and effort to studying the language and to compiling a dictionary. He never finished the dictionary but deposited a draft version along with his notes in seven large volumes at the Library of the School of Oriental and African Studies (SOAS), so that they would be available to anyone who wished to study Tangut and perhaps continue his research. Eric Grinstead, who used the dictionary when working on the Tangut manuscripts at the British Museum, called it "a paragon of excellence" in comparison with high level of errors in dictionaries available at the time.[4] Indeed, the erudition of Clauson's dictionary is obvious even upon a cursory look at the manuscript version and had it ever been published, it would have undoubtedly made a major impact on scholarship. This introduction presents the available material in an attempt to shed some light on an unknown episode in the history of Tangut studies, a promising start that due to a variety of reasons never reached its potential.

1. The Tangut collection in London

The Tangut material in London originates from the third Central Asian expedition of Sir Aurel Stein (1862–1943), who visited the ruins of Khara-khoto in 1914. Although the site had been excavated in 1908–1909 by the Russian team led by Pyotr Kuz′mich Kozlov (Пётр Кузьми́ч Козло́в, 1863–1935), Stein was still able to gather a considerable amount of material, including

1 I would like to thank the staff of SOAS Archives for their assistance in working with Clauson's papers. I am also grateful to Mr Oliver Clauson who kindly related some of his memories concerning his father's work on Tangut in a telephone interview on 23 March 2015. Special thanks to Nathan Hill, Sam van Schaik, and Kirill Solonin who helped to locate archival sources and gave useful comments on earlier versions of this paper. I also thank Ruben de Jong for alerting me to Berthold Laufer's involvement in the initial attempts to catalogue the Stein material. Research on this Introduction was kindly supported by the Centre for the Study of Manuscript Cultures, Hamburg University.

2 Clauson 1972. Clauson advocated against the word "Turkic"—preferring "Turkish" for the entire family—but here the more common term has been used.

3 Clauson 1940 and 1964, and 1969 and 1973, respectively.

4 Grinstead 1972, 30. Grinstead was referring to the index of characters to the Russian edition of the *Sea of Characters* (Keping et al. 1969) or the index in Vol. 1 of Sofronov's *Grammatika Tangutskogo Iazyka* (Sofronov 1968), both of which, according to Grinstead, had numerous errors.

fragments of manuscripts and printed books, and a variety of art objects. Following the expedition, the results of the excavations were deposited at the British Museum from where some items were shipped to India on account of the Government of India having sponsored part of Stein's expedition. But the majority of the textual materials remained at the Museum and with the establishment of the British Library was subsequently transferred there. Today, the 6,000 plus Tangut fragments in London represent one of the most important Tangut collections in the world. Unfortunately, the collection remained almost entirely unstudied until the 1960s.

The first inventory of the texts obtained from Khara-khoto was completed by Stein himself. In Volume 1 of the scientific report of his third expedition, published in 1928 in four folio-size volumes under the title *Innermost Asia*, he elaborates on his visit to the site at great length, giving an exhaustive account of everything he saw or excavated at the ruins, from traces of irrigation channels to discarded shards of pottery.[5] To supplement his description of the site, Stein also included a number of photographs and maps. Naturally, fragments of manuscripts and printed books occupy a prominent place in Stein's narrative, not the least because they helped to date the site and establish its cultural identity. The 90-page detailed list of objects found at the ruins is in fact the first catalogue of the Stein collection from Khara-khoto, even though it primarily focuses on books with illustrations and allocates a considerable amount of space to various artefacts. The reason for highlighting the non-textual aspect of manuscripts was probably that at this time Tangut was still largely undeciphered and even though Stein had secured a promise from Berthold Laufer (1874–1934) to examine and describe the fragments, Laufer in the end gave up on the project.

Despite Stein's meticulous description of Tangut items found at the ruins of Khara-khoto, the collection seems to have received little attention. It is somewhat surprising that the fragments in London remained dormant and nobody consulted them, even though there was an obvious interest in Tangut materials worldwide during the pre-war period. While it is true that the Russian collection was much richer and appeared to have an inexhaustible supply of exciting texts, these only became accessible once Russian scholars studied and published them. Under such circumstances, it would have been sensible for European scholars to turn to the fragments kept in London, had this been possible. Yet it seems that the collection was either not easily accessible or largely unknown to contemporary scholars.

Initially, the person in charge of the Chinese material in the British Museum was Lionel Giles (1875–1958), a sinologist by training who catalogued the Chinese manuscripts from Dunhuang.[6] Along with the Chinese language material, the Tangut fragments would have technically also been under his care, although he never published anything related to this part of the collection. There is indication that in his dealings with Chinese scholars, Giles was at times reluctant to facilitate access to the Dunhuang manuscripts.[7] Yet the situation with the Tangut collection must have been different and there is no record of any requests to see the fragments during Giles's time at the Museum.[8] Perhaps researchers believed that it was too fragmentary to be of practical use.

5 Stein 1928, v. 1, 429.

6 Giles 1957.

7 In a Chinese-language article Frances Wood (Wu 2011) writes about Giles's reluctance to show the manuscripts to Chinese scholars. See also Rong 2012, 212.

8 There is in fact correspondence among Clauson's papers (Letter dated 5 November 1935, SOAS Archives, MS 84335) in which F. W. Thomas suggests to him that they should solicit Giles's help to assign more specific meanings to the Chinese glosses published in Nevsky 1926. This reveals that neither Thomas nor Clauson regarded Giles as a difficult person who would hinder their attempts to work on Tangut.

Whatever the reasons for the neglect of the collection may have been, the situation changed following the retirement of Giles. From 1957 onward, the person in charge of the Chinese collections was Eric Grinstead, who became the first person to do research on the Tangut fragments. It is no coincidence that this was also the time of the revival of Tangut studies in Russia, one the first steps of which was the posthumous publication of the works of Nikolai Aleksandrovich Nevsky (Никола́й Алекса́ндрович Не́вский, 1892–1937). Nevsky's research on Tangut was published in 1960 in two large volumes under the title *Tangutskaia Filologiia* (*Тангутская Филология*, 'Tangut Philology'), the bigger part of which comprised a facsimile version of a handwritten Tangut dictionary.[9] The Russian publications triggered Grinstead's interest in Tangut and Nevsky's dictionary provided a practical means for reading the fragments at the British Museum.

As a result of Grinstead's publications, scholars in Russia and Japan took notice of the Stein fragments in London. Archival documentation related to the collection (currently held at the British Library) includes correspondence from the 1960s with Russian and Japanese scholars who showed interested in the collection. Thus a letter from 1966 by the Russian Tibetologist Bronislav Ivanovich Kuznetsov (Бронисла́в Ива́нович Кузнецо́в, 1931–1985), addressed to A. F. Thompson of the India Office Library, enquired whether their collection had "Tangut books" recovered by Stein, as he was particularly interested in the Tibetan transcriptions of Tangut words.[10] To this Miss Thompson replied that all of these were at the British Museum and Eric Grinstead was in the process of compiling a vocabulary, also pointing out that the Library of SOAS had "some unpublished material deposited some time ago by Sir Gerard Clauson". To this, she added that "[y]ou probably know that Sir Gerard has done a good deal of work on Tangut".[11]

Two more letters are from Hashimoto Mantarō (橋本萬太郎, 1932–1987), a linguist who worked both in Japan and the United States. While still in Japan, until 1962 he had studied Tangut phonology together with Ishihama Juntarō (石濱純太郎, 1888–1968), who had been Nevsky's colleague during the1920–1930s. According to the letters, after having left Japan, Hashimoto had no chance to converse with colleagues on Tangut matters and so reading Clauson's article in *Asia Major* was "a great encouragement" for him, although he was also sad to learn that this article was Clauson's "swan song" with regard to Tangut studies.[12] In the next letter, Hashimoto thanked Grinstead for sending him offprints of his two articles published in the *British Museum Quarterly*.[13]

From 1963, Nishida Tatsuo (西田龍雄, 1928–2012) of Kyoto University visited the British Museum with the aim of studying the Tangut fragments. He remembers in a later publication that at this time the materials in the Stein collection were "preserved in bags, sealed and stored away, as yet unclassified and practically in the state in which they were first excavated".[14] He later made additional visits and helped Museum staff with renumbering some of the fragments. He also assisted in the conservation of the collection, providing conservators detailed instructions as to which fragments belonged together and how they should be aligned and positioned in relation to each other.

9 Nevsky 1960.

10 Handwritten letter dated 29 January 1966 (British Library). These letters are not catalogued but form part of the documentation attached to the Tangut collection.

11 Typescript letter dated 10 February 1966 (British Library).

12 Typescript letter dated 17 January 1965. The article referred here is Clauson 1964.

13 Typescript letter dated 19 May 1966. The articles in question are Grinstead 1961 and 1962.

14 Nishida 1964–1966, v. 2, 512.

These activities show that after Grinstead became the person in charge of the collection, the fragments became well-known in the academic community and there was considerable interest in them. It would have been around the beginning of his tenure at the Museum that Grinstead learned about the existence of a dictionary compiled by Clauson which had been deposited at the Library of the SOAS by the author sometime in the second half of the 1950s. This impressive work, referred to by its creator as a "skeleton dictionary", was the result of intensive labour over the course of many years. In a letter to James Douglas Pearson (1911–1997), Librarian of SOAS, Clauson wrote about the reasons for discontinuing work on the dictionary and depositing it along with his notes at SOAS the following way:[15]

> As regards to the MS material, Simon's idea, which I am very willing to adopt, is that I should present it to the Library, subject to the right to reborrow it in the (very unlikely) event of wishing to do so. The stuff is frankly in a bit of a muddle, but it represents a very large quantity of work & would be a great help if anyone ever wished to embark on Hsi-hsia studies. He would do so with my blessing & I would gladly explain to him what the stuff all represents. It includes inter alia a skeleton dictionary of the whole language. I stopped work on it partly because of other distractions but mainly because the job could not be done properly without getting access to further material which is known to exist in Russia. At the time I stopped, communications with Russia were impossible & it was believed that the stuff was hopelessly mislaid. However an article by Z. I. Gorbacheva in *Uchëniye Zapiski Instituta Vostokvedeniya* Vol. IX shows that it has now been located & put in order & very likely photographs of the other material required could be got.
>
> You might like to put this letter with the material so that this clue is not lost.

One of the interesting points in the letter is that Clauson considered the possibility of taking the dictionary back from the SOAS Library and resuming work on it, which indicates that he did not keep a copy to himself, even if by this time this would not have posed a challenge from a technical point of view. In fact, Clauson himself mentioned in a publication that he had sent a microfilm copy of his dictionary to Mikhail Viktorovich Sofronov (Михаил Ви́кторович Софро́нов) in Moscow.[16] Thus it seems that he considered the volumes deposited in the SOAS Library an official master copy which functioned very much like a publication, albeit an unofficial one.

In the letter to Pearson, Clauson identifies the reason for discontinuing his work on the dictionary as not being able to access to the Tangut material kept in Russia. The fact that he never raises the possibility of looking at the collection in the British Museum demonstrates that he not only did not have access to the Stein collection but possibly was unaware of the amount of Tangut material there. Apparently, Clauson was working with the Tangut materials published before World War II in Russia, and possibly Japan and China, and with time these became insufficient for his purposes. He notes that the material in St Petersburg may have been "mislaid", even though a recent publication showed that the situation may not have been as hopeless. The publication he

15 Letter dated 29 June 1956 (SOAS Archives, MS 84335).

16 Clauson 1964, 55. In his monograph on Tangut grammar, Sofronov expresses his gratitude for having received a microfilm version of the dictionary and mentions Clauson's research on the Tangut language in his overview of Tangut studies (Sofronov 1968, v.1, 4 and 26, respectively).

mentions in the letter is Zoya I. Gorbachëva's short catalogue of texts identified in the Kozlov collection, which came out in 1954.[17]

2. Clauson's research on Tangut

Clauson's name is seldom mentioned with regard to Tangut studies because his publications on the topic are few and cursory.[18] By far the greatest part of his research remain unpublished and his actual impact on the field was primarily through personal contact and correspondence. Clauson began studying Tangut around 1935, which coincides with the time other scholars around the world were also engaged in Tangut studies. Among the main figures of this scholarly trend at that time were Nevsky, Aleksandr Aleksandrovich Dragunov (Алекса́ндр Алекса́ндрович Драгуно́в, 1900–1955), Ishihama Juntarō and Wáng Jìngrú (王靜如, 1903–1990), to whose publications Clauson had access.[19] Stuart N. Wolfenden (1889–1938), the American linguist at the University of California, Berkeley, who normally worked on Tibeto-Burman dialects, also wrote a couple of short studies on Tibetan and Chinese transcriptions of Tangut words and Clauson would have naturally read these.[20] Especially Nevsky's progress on the original collection looked promising and it was known that he was compiling a dictionary of the Tangut language, which was expected to advance the field forward.

Clauson corresponded with Frederick W. Thomas (1867–1956), professor of Sanskrit at the University of Oxford, who at the time was working on the decipherment of the Nam and Zhangzhung languages, manuscripts of which had been discovered in Dunhuang. In a couple of letters from November 1935, Thomas commended Clauson for his progress in reading the Tangut script, noting that he himself had also tried his luck with Tangut but had to lay it aside indefinitely in order to be able to finish his study of Tibetan documents. Although we do not have Clauson's side of the correspondence, Thomas's letters make it clear that Clauson was exploring the idea whether the Nam language was related to Tangut, and tried to use, without much success, the list of Tangut words published by Nevsky to verify the hypothetical connection.[21] As Thomas was interested in proving a different identity to the Nam language, he was less excited about such a possibility, writing that "I have been hoping that my language is not Si-hia, though of course related to it more or less, as I have something else to do with it".[22] In another letter three days later, Thomas wrote:[23]

> Many thanks for your letter. We will see further about the identity of the two languages! In the meanwhile you are attacking the major problem of the script, the solution of which would be a real triumph.

17 Gorbacheva 1954.

18 See, for example, Nie Hongyin's review of *Tangut studies* (Nie 1993), which makes no mention of Clauson.

19 E.g. Dragunov 1929; Lóng, Niè and Wáng 1930; Wáng 1930 and 1932–1933; Nevsky 1926 and Nevsky 1931. We should also note that Clauson began studying Japanese only during WWII (Bosworth 2001, 92) and so at this time he would not have been able to rely on Japanese scholarship.

20 Wolfenden 1931 and 1934.

21 This must have been a reference to Nevsky's *Brief Manual of the Si-hia Characters with Tibetan Transcriptions* published in Osaka (Nevsky 1926).

22 Letter dated 5 November 1935 (SOAS Archives, MS 84335).

23 Letter dated 8 November 1935 (SOAS Archives, MS 84335).

> I have not doubted that the language would be related to the Hsi-hsia; but if the Hsi-hsia is the language of the Tang-hsiang & went into Kansu only in the XIth century, that would be less welcome to me, though I really have no serious ground for hoping otherwise.

Thus Thomas was dubious about such a connection and regarded Tangut and Nam distant relatives at best. But Clauson remained optimistic and believed that a thorough study of Tangut might help to identify it with one of the languages written with the Tibetan alphabet (but not in the Tibetan language), which had been found among the Dunhuang manuscripts. He periodically returned to this idea even in publications written later in his life.[24]

World War II interrupted Clauson's work on Tangut and it was more than two decades later that he was able to return to it. By this time, however, as we have seen above in his letter to SOAS Librarian Pearson, he had already given up the idea of completing his dictionary because of the dearth of texts accessible to him as a result of the long hiatus in Russian scholarship following the political events of the late 1930s and World War II. His son Mr Oliver Clauson also points out that as some of his colleagues had seen their research papers destroyed during the war, Clauson was anxious about the possibility of losing his Tangut notes and wanted to deposit them in a public collection.[25] Yet it is clear that he did not stop his research until much later. In fact, his son remembers that the Tangut language and the dictionary remained a major part of their life during the post-war period, and that his father brought his research with them to family vacations to work on.[26]

In 1960 Clauson attended the International Congress of Orientalists in Moscow where he presented a paper in which he identified the recently excavated site of Ak-Beshim with the city of Suyab known from Chinese sources.[27] While in Russia, he also travelled to Leningrad where he visited the exhibition of manuscripts from the collection of the Institute of Oriental Studies (predecessor of the current Institute of Oriental Manuscripts). The exhibition also included material from Khara-khoto and one of the staff members in charge of welcoming foreign visitors was the young Evgeny Ivanovich Kychanov (Евгéний Ивáнович Кычáнов, 1932–2013) who had recently defended his doctoral dissertation on the Xixia state and been granted access to the Kozlov collection.[28] Many years later Kychanov remembered that his meeting with Clauson had been significant from the point of view of чис career because Clauson praised him in *Asia Major*, and this made his name widely known in academic circles in the West.[29] Kychanov also pointed out that Clauson had studied Tangut earlier but by the time they met he was already working on

24 See, for example, Clauson 1964, 73 and 1969, 419.

25 Interview, March 23, 2015.

26 Mr Oliver Clauson also remembered that his father collaborated with a Czech scholar who was also interested in the Tangut language. This must have been Kamil Sedláček, a linguist mainly working on Tibetan. In fact, Clauson's papers at the SOAS Archives, include a sheet of paper with the name Sedláček on one side and some Tangut characters and radicals on the other. In his article on the origin of the name of the Tanguts, Sedláček (1964, 184, n.14) refers to a letter from Clauson dated 26 November 1961, showing that the two of them indeed corresponded around this time.

27 Garufov et al. 1962–1963, v. 3, 126–127.

28 Kychanov 2012, 10.

29 *Ibid.*, 20. The article Kychanov is referring to is Clauson 1964, which cites quite a few works of Kychanov.

Central Asia, which suggests that by 1960 Clauson had only a passive interest in Tangut studies and had given up hope of ever finishing his dictionary.

In 1964, in the same *Asia Major* article where he praised the research of Kychanov, Clauson wrote in general about the future potentials of Tangut studies, closing it with some personal remarks that relate the reasons why he decided to abandon his research in this field:[30]

> So far as Tangut studies are concerned this is, I hope, my swan song. When I embarked upon them over thirty years ago I regarded them as a fascinating exercise in cryptography, with a little mathematics thrown in. But I very soon found that a profound study of Tangut was impossible without, if not a profound, at any rate a good knowledge of Chinese, Tibetan and, if possible, some Hsifan languages. To have described my knowledge of any of these languages as better than inadequate would have been gross flattery, and so I retired from the field, I thought for ever, and returned to the Turkish studies on which my interests are now concentrated. I have returned momentarily to this subject only because I am perhaps the only survivor from an earlier and less scientific age, and felt it my duty to put my own experience at the disposal of the new and vigorous generation of young students of this fascinating language before it is too late...

This note gives the impression that Clauson felt that his linguistic capacities were inadequate for pursuing the study of Tangut at the level he aspired to. Yet his Tangut notes and dictionary at the SOAS Archives by far surpass contemporary scholarship, with perhaps the sole exception of the results of Nevsky. Along the same line of thought there is no question that the linguistic requirements Clauson mentioned in the article are hard to meet for anyone. A "profound" knowledge of Chinese, Tibetan, and other Xifan languages is simply not that common. In fact, the lack of a good knowledge of Tibetan on the part of researchers working on Tangut today is widely recognized as a problem in the field, which is heavily dominated by a Sino-centric approach. In any case, Clauson's reasons for withdrawing from active research may reflect his perfectionism, rather than his actual skills and potential in the field.

3. The *Skeleton Dictionary*

The catalogue of the SOAS Archives describes Clauson's Tangut material with the following words:

> Papers of Sir Gerard Leslie Makins Clauson, comprising preliminary studies in the decipherment of the Hsi-hsia language, a skeleton dictionary and other manuscripts concerned with Hsi-hsia studies. 7 folders and an envelope containing miscellaneous manuscripts. (MS. 84335).[31]

The same description also appears as typewritten notes glued onto the inner cover of each large volume. In reality, there are more papers because in addition to the seven relatively well organized large volumes, which contain the dictionary and research notes, there are several smaller notebooks

30 Clauson 1964, 77.

31 This entry matches verbatim the description in Matthews and Wainwright 1977, 83.

with miscellaneous materials, including numerous word lists and incomplete notes. There are also envelopes which contain four letters from F. W. Thomas and one from the French Tibetologist Marcelle Lalou (1890–1967), all written during the period of 1935–1938.

The seven thick manuscript volumes contain more organized material. All volumes are titled "Hsi-hsia language", two of them also carrying the subtitles "Dictionary Part I" and "Dictionary Part II". The material in the volumes is diverse and includes linguistic notes on the language, lists of transliterations, summaries of secondary literature (e.g. Luo Fuchang's introduction to the Tangut language). The dictionary has a note added in 1963, claiming that Clauson began working on it in 1938.[32] The two volumes of the dictionary represent a monumental work that would have made a significant impact on Tangut studies had he decided to publish it. In terms of their breadth and erudition, the dictionary and the accompanying studies could only be compared with Nevsky's *Tangutskaia Filologiia*. In a way, Clauson's seven unpublished volumes parallel Nevsky's opus which was published posthumously by later scholars who edited his papers following his rehabilitation in 1957. Yet even in its current unauthorized form, *Tangutskaia Filologiia* became a milestone in the history of Tangut studies, inspiring a new generation of scholars and laying down the foundations for an entire field.

At the beginning of the first volume (i.e. Part I) of the *Skeleton Dictionary* we find a leaf inserted subsequently, probably when Clauson deposited the material in the Library of SOAS. This leaf contains a short description of the conventions of the dictionary, with the aim to elucidate for future users the notation and the principles of arrangement.[33]

> Skeleton Tangut (Hsi Hsia) dictionary in two volumes, by Sir Gerard Clauson.
> The arrangement of the characters is based on the assumption that each character can be analysed either as a "component", that is a fixed pattern of strokes, or as a combination of a component & a "sub-component", that is a stroke or combination of strokes placed above a component & forming an integral whole with it, or as a combination of two or more components, each with or without sub-components attached. The analysis starts at the top left hand corner, & moves downwards and to the right.
>
> The following is a table of the sub-components and components in the order in which they are arranged. A simple asterisk × indicates that a component occurs both in its simple form & with sub-components, a dotted asterisk ※ that it occurs *only* with sub-components.
>
> Sub-components
>
> Components
>
> Covers
>
> Verticals
>
> Rectangles

32 Elsewhere he claims that he began compiling the dictionary in 1937–1938 (Clauson 1964, 55).

33 The leaf, the recto and verso of folio i, is given in facsimile on pp. 1–2 below.

Curves [illegible] & [illegible] & [illegible]

Miscellaneous [illegible]

References in Roman & Latin numbers, e.g. I.1. are to Chapters & sections in the *Homophones*, i.e. Part I of each Chapter, references like IA1 are to the "unique sounds" in the second part of each Chapter.

References starting with *B.* are to the special volume of the *Bulletin of the National Library at Peiping* (or some such title) devoted to Hsi Hsia. References starting with *W.* are to Wang's *Hsi Hsia Studies* (3 volumes). *CCC* is the Chinese-Tangut handbook "The Handful of Pearls". *X* means the Tangut explanation just quoted.

(Note added on 29/7/63)

Gerard Clauson

My copies of B, W & CCC are now in the Library of the School of Oriental and African Studies

Right at the beginning of the main text of the dictionary a short note says that it was begun in October 1938. At the very end of the second volume, after the last character another note says that it was finished on 27 March 1939, which is followed by a line of text added in different ink, claiming that the cross references were completed on 14 September 1946. Accordingly, Clauson compiled the dictionary itself in 1938–1939 in about six months time but made corrections to it later on, on several occasions. This is also seen from the fact that although the main body of the dictionary is written in the same black (slightly faded) ink, there are additions and notes in different shades of blue and in pencil. Sporadic references in blue ink signify page numbers in Nevsky's *Tangutskaia Filologiia* (1960), which show that Clauson continued adding notes to the dictionary as late as the 1960s.

The dictionary consists of a total of 441 numbered folios, divided equally between the two volumes (1–221 and 222–441, respectively), with pagination running continuously. The folios are written on one side only but many of the empty pages contain supplementary notes with reference to entries on facing pages. As a result, the dictionary is in reality larger than the total count of folios indicates. Each page is divided into two columns, thereby forming a traditional dictionary layout. The characters are numbered from 1 to 5724, which represents the total number of main entries in the dictionary.[34]

In terms of its source material, the dictionary heavily relies on the monolingual Tangut dictionary *Homophones* and the Tangut-Chinese glossary *Handful of Pearls*. Each entry has references to these sources, showing that Clauson was largely working from lexicographic sources, rather than actual texts. Of course, this is understandable because only a few texts had been published by 1938 and he could only rely on the material available to him. To illustrate the form and composition of individual entries in the dictionary, let us look at two sample entries, selected randomly. The first is No. 78 with the word *ɣji* [illegible] ("diamond"):[35]

34 In reality, Clauson (1964, 75) mentions that there are some added characters and a small number of repeated ones and thus the entries in the dictionary need to be re-numbered.

35 See p. 17 below, *f* 7r. In order to maintain a consistency of notation, I added quotation marks to those English definitions which did not have these. This is surely in accord with the author's intent because in most cases he

78. [Tangut] *γi* VIII 6 [Tangut] | 637

(a) I 6 ditto

(b) IX 48 | [Tangut] "stone" 0601

(i) | [Tangut] C.C.C. 21[a] W.I. 208[II] 218[I]

金剛 *rdo.rje* "diamond".

(ii) [Tangut] | C.C.C. 13[a] W.II 24[6] 瑠(or 琉)璃 "crystal". 5157

The vertical line next to Tangut characters (|) stands for the main character in the entry, similar to the tilde (~) used in modern dictionaries. The numbers on the far right are the cross-references with other entries in the same dictionary (added to the entries subsequently), which greatly facilitate using it. We can see that under this entry Clauson lists different compound words and gives the meaning for these: [Tangut][Tangut] ("stone"); [Tangut][Tangut] ("diamond"); [Tangut][Tangut] ("crystal"). In addition to the Chinese words adopted from the *Homophones* and the *Handful of Pearls*, whenever attested, he also includes Tibetan equivalents.

The same Tangut word appears in Kychanov's dictionary (4347-0) with definitions in three languages (i.e. Russian, English and Chinese) as follows:[36]

"алмаз; ваджра (*санск.*)"
"diamond; vajra (*Skt.*)"
"金剛; 金剛石"

While the Russian and English match each other, the Chinese is slightly different. Considering that the focus of the dictionary is on Tangut and the other three languages are meant to define the meaning of the Tangut word, we would expect that all three modern languages say the same thing. Accordingly, the English word "diamond" should match the Chinese *jīngāng* 金剛, and "vajra" (unitalicized) in the English should match *jīngāngshí* 金剛石 in the Chinese definition. This, however, is not entirely so and the paranthetical indication that *vajra* comes from Sanskrit (present in both the English and Russian definitions) is omitted. In fact, the first word in the Chinese definition (i.e. 金剛) would be a better match for Sanskrit *vajra*,[37] whereas the standard word for "diamond"—at least in modern Chinese—is *zuànshí* 鑽石. There is no question that the editors used Chinese 金剛 because it matches the word commonly translated from Chinese Buddhist texts into Tangut with the Tangut word in question, yet the hybrid use of classical vs. modern Chinese definitions creates an occasional mismatch with the two other modern languages of the dictionary.

In terms of compound words under the same head entry, Kychanov's dictionary has the following items:[38]

supplies the quotation marks.

36 Kychanov 2006, 613. Here I only use the dictionaries of Kychanov and Lǐ Fànwén for the sake of comparison, as these are the ones that have been published as separate dictionaries. There are, however, several other, less comprehensive, Tangut dictionaries and vocabularies, which form part of larger works (e.g. Nevsky 1960, Nishida 1964–1966, Sofronov 1968, Grinstead 1972).

37 Indeed, the editors of the dictionary apparently were of the same opinion because they translate the first compound word [Tangut][Tangut] as "ваджра (*санск.*)", "vajra (*Skt.*)", "金剛."

38 In this place I refrain from analysing the phonetic reconstructions of the words in question and limit myself to comparing their lexical meaning.

[illegible] “ваджра (*санск.*)”, “vajra (*Skt.*)”, “金剛”.
[illegible] “*будд.* жезл ваджра”, “*Budd.* vajra pest”, “〈佛〉金剛杵”.
[illegible] “каменные изваяния животных у могил”, “stone animals near the tomb”, “獸像”.
[illegible] “алмаз; руда”, “diamond; ore”, “金剛石；礦石”.
[illegible] “руда”, “ore”, “瓦礫”.

Once again, we have some problems with the modern definitions of the items in three different languages. Just to note the more serious issues, the phrase “vajra pest” (!) is an obvious mistake for “vajra pestle”, as it is clear from the Russian and Chinese definitions. A more standard way to call the “stone animals near the tomb” would have been “tomb guardian animals” or *zhènmùshòu* 鎮墓獸 in Chinese. Finally, the Chinese word *wǎlì* 瓦礫 means “debris, gravel”, rather than “ore” as listed in the English and Russian definitions.

In comparison, Clauson’s dictionary has fewer examples of compound words but it is certainly more precise in its definitions. Whenever it provides Chinese or Tibetan terms, it is clear that these are not meant as modern definitions but contemporary equivalents used in parallel texts or identical context. In addition, it includes not only compound words which begin with the head entry but also some where the word is in second or third place, which is of obvious benefit for the user.

The other Tangut dictionary compiled relatively recently is Lǐ Fànwén’s 李範文 Tangut-Chinese dictionary, which came out in print in 1997.[39] This is essentially a bilingual dictionary but the head word usually has an English gloss, even if this is often imprecise. The advantage of the dictionary, in contrast with Kychanov’s is that it gives the source for its examples, enabling the user to track down the example or at least ascertain whether it comes from a medieval dictionary, a Buddhist text or a translation of a secular work. In fact, this dictionary is more like an index because the definitions are either adopted from surviving Tangut lexicographic works or consist of words that correspond to the Tangut word in parallel texts. Thus under the entry for the word [illegible] (“diamond”), we first find the following list of glosses:[40]

礦、金剛、石、琉璃、明、瓦也。(名)
Ore, diamond, stone, crystal, bright, clay tile. (noun)

While the inclusion of the part of speech in parantheses at the end of the line is useful, the definitions contain the word *míng* 明 “bright, wise” which is not a noun. We could of course translate it as “brightness, wisdom” but that would not match the example given further below where it occurs in the name of Bodhisattva *Míngwángshǒu Púsà* 明王手菩薩 and has an adjectival use. As for the definitions, they are not based on a linguistic understanding of the Tangut word but are extracted from the examples listed underneath and show the variety of Chinese words this Tangut word was used to translate.

To compare another word appearing in Clauson’s dictionary, let us look at the verb *tjwi* [illegible] (“to beat”), which is listed in the *Skeleton Dictionary* under entry No. 3812:[41]

39 Lǐ 1997.

40 *Ibid.*, 4.

41 See p. 591 below, *f* 292r.

3812. 緵 IIIA76 | 㣲 x(3778), 1954
(a) III 72 ditto
(b) I 33 | 𗤶 5550
(c) I 139 繎 | 4711
(d) VII 22 | 𗥃 1801

This word means broadly "to strike", but represents various Chinese words
(i) By itself C.C.C.32[a] W.I.136[18]
W.I.138[2] 侵 "to invade"
(ii) (b) above W.I.134[16] 打撲 "hit, squash" (flies)
(iii) | 𗗙 C.C.C.31[a2] 打拷 "to beat & strike"

On the facing page on the left side, we find a supplementary note attached to this entry, most likely added at a later time. The note contains the cross-reference numbers (which also occur to the right side of the original entry) and two additional Chinese meanings with their English translations:

3812
1954-3778
1801
4711
5550

(b)
W.I.136[6]? 掠打 "plunder & beat"
打擲 "beat & throw down"

In Kychanov's dictionary, the same word appears as No. 3168, and has the following trilingual definitions:[42]

緵 "бить", "beat", "打".

In this case, the Chinese definition matches perfectly well the meaning of the Russian and English definitions. Under the same head entry, Kychanov cites the following compound words:

緵𗤶 "прихлопнуть; придавить; бросать; метать", "slap; hold down; throw; cast", "撲打; 擲".
緵𗗙 "бить; пытать", "beat, torture", "拷打".
緵𗿀 "ковать железо", "forge", "打鐵".
緵緵𗧊𗪘 "драка", "fight; brave", "毆".
緵𗥃 "ковать (железо)", "forge iron", "打鐵".
緵㣲 "хлестать плетью; избивать", "lash, whip", "捶打".

42 Kychanov 2006, 465.

Once again, there is some inconsistency between the definitions in the different languages. This is especially true for the entry 𘃡𘃡𗠁𘕿, which is explained in Russian as *драка* ("a brawl, fight") and *ōu* 毆 ("to beat, hit") in Chinese. The fact that the Russian word is a noun and the Chinese a verb is reflected in the English definition (i.e. "fight; brave") which seems to consist of a noun and an adjective. In either case, the meaning "brave" does not appear in Russian and Chinese. In comparison, Clauson also lists the meaning "to invade", which is absent from Kychanov's dictionary.

Turning to Lǐ Fànwén's dictionary, the entry begins with the English gloss "flog; beat". But then we have two main definitions:

3679.

1. 打、拷、撻也 (動)
   to beat, flog/torture, flog (verb)
2. 築也
   to build/construct

While the second definition is based on a single reference, there are quite a few examples for the first one, coming from various sources, including lexicographic works and Buddhist texts. As mentioned before, the definitions are merely extracts from the examples and the reason why several close synonyms are listed as glosses is because the Tangut word in question is used in context for all of them.

These two examples show the basic format of Clauson's *Skeleton Dictionary*. The fact that the definitions are in English is useful not only because this way the dictionary can be used by scholars who do not read Chinese but are nevertheless interested in Tangut but also because English offers a linguistic system independent of the complex system of Tangut translating and glossing the languages of China and Tibet. With a modern Tangut-Chinese dictionary there is inevitably the difficulty of separating modern definitions from medieval glosses and word-to-word correspondences, which also tends to bring about the confusion of classical Chinese with the language of today's China. Despite all of these advantages of the *Skeleton Dictionary*, we should note that there are entries which do not have definitions but are included nonetheless because they form part of the overall system. It is this system that most interested Clauson, as the numerous draft word lists among his Tangut material reveal. He believed that he succeeded in devising a logical system that was superior to that of others, including Nevsky's dictionary arrangement. In fact, although he valued Nevsky's dictionary greatly and considered it "full of valuable information", he thought that it was "better compared to a gold mine rich in precious nuggets than to a finished product of the goldsmith's art".[43] In the same place, he explains the merits of his own dictionary the following way:

> Before I began to write it [i.e. the dictionary] out in October 1938, by an odd coincidence at about the date of Nevsky's death, I had carried out a detailed analysis of the structure of Tangut characters and compiled a list of the components and sub-components which seem to have been used in building up the individual characters. I had arranged these in a logical order starting with the simplest and most regular and

43 Clauson 1964, 75.

> proceeding from them to the more complicated and irregular. My arrangement of the characters was based on the assumption that every character could be regarded either as itself a component (few are), or as having been built up of a series of sub-components and components, and that the predetermined order of these sub-components and components could be used to determine the order of characters in the dictionary. It may not be the best arrangement which could be devised, but it has at any rate stood the test of time to the extent that, coming back to my Tangut studies after an interval of nearly twenty-seven years, I found no difficulty in locating a character in the dictionary in a very brief space of time. It is not of course in its present state suitable for use as more than a working dictionary; like Nevsky's it is a mine not a finished product.[44]

These words show his pride in devising a logical order for the characters, which made it possible to look them up with relative ease. He considered it the best available system and hoped that others would adopt it when compiling new dictionaries.[45] Despite his confidence in the arrangement of characters, Clauson was obviously dissatisfied with the dictionary itself, which was the reason why he did not try to publish it. He felt that he could not complete the dictionary without having access to more texts and at the time when he gave up the project, it was very improbable that new texts would become accessible. Surely, access to Tangut translations of Chinese and Tibetan works would have provided enough linguistic data to fill the structural framework of the dictionary with concrete examples, thereby adding substance to the "skeleton". This would have enabled him to complete the work and have it published. Yet by the time such texts started to become available, he was engaged in research on Turkic languages and did not have time to resume work on Tangut. Still, he felt that the dictionary had a sound framework and wanted to make it accessible to others working on the language. With this view in mind, he deposited it at the SOAS Archives where it was indeed consulted by several researchers working on Tangut.

In fact, Grinstead compiled an index to Clauson's dictionary, the sole copy of which is now held at the Oriental Reading Room of the British Library. The list includes the Tangut characters, the entry number in Clauson's dictionary, the number in Nevsky's dictionary and in the *Homophones* dictionary, followed by an English gloss. When Grinstead published his monograph on the Tangut script, he incorporated this index with the English glosses into the book.[46] But the compilation of the original index shows that he used Clauson's dictionary on a regular basis and wanted to make it more accessible to others.

4. Conclusions

Since the 1960s, there have been significant advances in the study of Tangut and today we know much more about the language and the script than in Clauson's time. We now have access to a great variety of Tangut texts, partly because of new archaeological discoveries and partly due to the publication of photographic reproductions of existing collections. In addition, most of the major texts written in Tangut have been transcribed, edited, translated and published so that they are readily available in a conveniently annotated form. Thanks to the work of scholars such as

44 *Ibid.*

45 *Ibid.*, 76.

46 Grinstead 1972, 70–151. In this version, however, Grinstead omitted the reference numbers to the three dictionaries (i.e. Clauson, Nevsky, and the *Homophones*).

Nishida, Sofronov, and Kepping, we today have a much better grasp of Tangut grammar and lexicon than a few decades earlier. There are also several Tangut dictionaries in existence, which raises the question whether Clauson's *Skeleton Dictionary* is of any practical use today, or is it merely a memento of the extraordinary efforts of a great scholar and a reminder of what Tangut studies in Britain could have become, had the dictionary been published sometime in the late 1930s.

In Clauson's view, the dictionary to a significant extent comprised a skeleton structure, that is, a framework which still awaited to be populated with lexical data extracted from real texts. Yet it is important to point out that a substantial amount of lexical information is already in place. The two sample entries shown above are not exceptional but representative of a significant portion of the total number of entries. In other words, the dictionary is perfectly usable in its current form, even though there are some entries that do not have semantic glosses assigned to them. The data already in place was primarily derived from native Tangut dictionaries and essentially originated from the same sources Nevsky used for his dictionary. Clauson considered the task of populating the dictionary with lexical data "simply a matter of sheer hard work".[47] In contrast with this relatively uninteresting task, what he took pride in was the structure and arrangement of the dictionary, as well as the ability to design a lookup method which allowed finding characters with ease. In this regard he considered his system superior to those of others, not only in the 1930s but even in the 1960s, when he briefly returned to working on it. Indeed, Clauson had a great interest in lexicography and it is also clear that he had an unusual talent for it. In 1960 he published a facsimile edition of an eighteenth-century Persian dictionary of Chagatai, prefixed with a critical introduction and indices.[48] But most important in this respect is his *Etymological Dictionary of Pre-Thirteenth-Century Turkish*, published in 1972. In effect, the vast amount of research invested in the Tangut dictionary was eventually put to good use when compiling the *Etymological Dictionary*. It is no coincidence that this dictionary, like the Tangut one, also has a unique arrangement and lookup system designed specifically for a language and dialects which came down to us in manuscripts written in several different alphabets. In order to avoid the hassle of looking up the same word in several different places (depending on how it is spelled in different scripts) and to circumvent the necessity of double or multiple entries, Clauson designed a completely new arrangement based on focussing on the "significant sounds" in a word, forming a system in which, despite its initial unfamiliarity, the user "needed only a few minutes to find his way about".[49]

Similarly, Clauson arranged the Tangut dictionary using a novel system which he designed on the basis of his analysis of the graphical composition of characters. Today, we have several Tangut dictionaries at our disposal and their lookup systems can be learned relatively quickly, regardless whether they are based on the left or right component, or use the four-corner system. As a result, looking up characters does not pose a major challenge to users anymore, even if most researchers have their own preferences. What makes Clauson's dictionary unique is its general framework and structure, which was the result of a careful arrangement and referencing of the material available to him. On the most basic level, it represents an only partially filled shell of a potentially comprehensive dictionary which could not be completed with the material available to him in 1938. This shell or, as he called it himself, "skeleton", was constructed with extreme care and accuracy and may indeed be superior to other Tangut dictionaries available today. This echoes

47 Clauson 1964, 76.

48 Clauson 1960.

49 Lewis 1973, 171.

the minimalist approach seen in Clauson's etymological dictionary of Turkic, where entries and glosses are carefully referenced and double-checked, and doubtful items are either not included or explicitly marked as such.

In this respect, the *Skeleton Dictionary* has not lost its pertinence and applicability and is a perfectly useful tool for reading Tangut texts. Its accuracy and reliability makes it especially useful today, when scholars are increasingly trying to leave behind the obsolete method of mechanically transcribing Tangut with Chinese characters on the basis of parallel texts and are willing to understand the language itself. In addition, because of the presence of precise and consistent English glosses, the dictionary can be consulted for researchers who work on Tibeto-Burman or other languages but do not read Chinese. Considering the wealth of Tangut texts that have become available during the past decades, it would be suitable to update the entries and populate them with additional layers of lexical data derived from these texts, thereby completing the work envisaged by Clauson.

Imre Galambos

References

Bosworth, C. Edmund. 2001. *A Century of British Orientalists*, 1902–2001. Oxford: Oxford University Press.

Clauson, Gerard. 1940. "A programme of Hsi Hsia studies", in *Actes du XXe Congrès international des orientalistes: Bruxelles, 5-10 septembre 1938*. Louvain: Bureaux du muséon, 218–219.

———. 1960. *Sanglāx: A Persian Guide to the Turkish Language , by Muhammad Mahdī Xān. Facsimile Text with an Introduction and Indices*. London: Luzac.

———. 1964. "The future of Tangut (Hsi Hsia) studies", in *Asia Major* (New Series) 11.1: 54–77.

———. 1969. "Ocherk istorii tangutskogo gosudarstva by Ye. I. Kychanov; Grammatika tangutskogo yazyka by M. V. Sofronov", in *Bulletin of the School of Oriental and African Studies* 32.2: 416–419.

———. 1972. *An Etymological Dictionary of Pre-Thirteenth-Century Turkish*. Oxford: Clarendon Press.

———. 1973. "Analysis of the Tangut script", in *Bulletin of the School of Oriental and African Studies* 36.3: 696–698.

Dragunov, Aleksandr A. (Драгунов, Александр А.) 1929. "Binoms of the type 尼+卒 in the Tangut-Chinese dictionary", in *Академия Наук, Доклады* (*Akademiia Nauk, Doklady*), Series B, 145–148.

Garufov, B. G. (Гаруфов, Б. Г.) et al., eds. 1962–1963. *Труды двадцать пятого Международного конгресса востоковедов: Москва, 9-16 августа 1960* (*Trudy dvadtsat' piatogo Mezhdunarodnogo kongressa vostokovedov: Moskva, 9–16 avgusta 1960*). Moscow: Izdatel'stvo vostochnoy literatury. 5 vols.

Giles, Lionel. 1957. *Descriptive Catalogue of the Chinese Manuscripts from Tunhuang in the British Museum*. London: Trustees of the British Museum.

Gorbachëva, Zoya I. (Горбачёва, Зоя И.) 1954. "Тангутские рукописи и ксилографы Института востоковедения Академии наук СССР" ("Tangutskie rukopisi i ksilografy Instituta vostokovedeniia Akademii nauk SSSR"), in *Учёные Записки Института Востоковедения АН 9* (*Uchënye Zapiski Instituta Vostokovedeniia AN 9*), 67–89.

Grinstead, Eric D. 1961. "Tangut fragments in the British Museum", in *The British Museum Quarterly* 24, 3/4: 82–87.

———. 1962. "The General's Garden, a Twelfth-Century Military Work", in *The British Museum Quarterly* 26, 1/2: 35–37.

———. 1972. *Analysis of the Tangut Script*. Scandinavian Institute of Asian Studies Monograph Series. Lund: Studentlitteratur.

Kepping, Kseniia B., Vsevolod S. Kolokolov, Evgenii I. Kychanov, and Anton P. Terent'ev-Katanskii (Кепинг, Ксения Б., Всеволод С. Колоколов, Евгений И. Кычанов, & Антон П. Терентьев-Катанский). 1969. *Море Письмен: Факсимиле Тангутских Ксилографов* (*More Pis'men: Faksimile Tangutskikh Ksilografov*). Moskva: Nauka.

Kychanov, Evgenii I. (Кычанов, Евгений И.). 2006. *Словарь Тангутского (Си Ся) Языка: Тангутско-Русско-Англо-Китайский Словарь* (*Slovar' Tangutskogo (Si Sia) Iazyka: Tangutsko-Russko-Anglo-Kitaiskii Slovar'*). Kyoto: Faculty of Letters, Kyoto University. With the collaboration of S. Arakawa.

———. 2012. "Интервью с Кычановым Е. И." ("Interv'iu s Kychanovym E. I."), in *Китаеведение—Устная История* (*Kitaevedenie—Ustnaia Istoriia*), http://politics.ntu.edu.tw/RAEC/comm2/ra27.pdf, last accessed 7 July 2014.

Lewis, G. L. 1973. "Review of *An Etymological Dictionary of Pre-Thirteenth-Century Turkish*, by Sir Gerard Clauson", in *Journal of the Royal Asiatic Society of Great Britain and Ireland* 2, 171–172.

Lǐ Fànwén (李範文). 1997. 夏漢字典 (*Xià-Hàn zìdiǎn*). Beijing: 中國社會科學出版社 (Zhōngguó shèhuì kēxué chūbǎnshè).

Lóng Guǒfū (龍果夫; Dragunov), Niè Lìshān (聶歷山; Nevsky) and Wáng Jìngrú (王靜如). 1930. "蘇俄研究院亞洲博物館藏西夏文書籍目錄二則" ("Sū'é yánjiùyuàn Yàzhōu bówùguǎn cáng Xīxiàwén shūjí mùlù èrzé"), in 國立北平圖書館館刊 (*Guólì Běipíng túshūguǎn guǎnkān*) 4.3, 367–368.

Matthews, Noel and M. Doreen Wainwright. 1977. *A Guide to Manuscripts and Documents in the British Isles Relating to the Far East*. Oxford; New York: Oxford University Press. Edited by J. D. Pearson.

Nevsky, Nicolas. 1926. *A Brief Manual of the Si-hia Characters with Tibetan Transcriptions*. Osaka: The Osaka Asiatic Society. (Japanese title: 西夏文字抄覧: 西蔵文字対照 (*Seika moji shōran: Chibetto moji taishō*).

Nevsky, Nikolai A. (Невский, Николай А.) 1931. "Очерк истории тангутоведения" ("Ocherk istorii tanguto-vedeniia"), in *Известия Академии Наук СССР* (*Izvestiia Akademii Nauk SSSR*), VII.1, 7–22.

———. 1960. *Тангутская Филология: Исследования и Словарь* (*Tangutskaia Filologiia: Issledovaniia i Slovar'*). Moskva: Nauka. 2 vols.

Niè Hóngyīn (聶鴻音). 1993. "Tangutology during the past decades", in *Monumenta Serica* 41, 329–347.

Nishida Tatsuo (西田龍雄). 1964–1966. 西夏語の研究 (*Seikago no kenkyū*). Tokyo: Zauhō Kankōkai. (English title: *A Study of the Hsi-hsia Language, Reconstruction of the Hsi-hsia Language and Decipherment of the Hsi-hsia Script*.)

Róng Xīnjiāng (榮新江). 2013. *Eighteen Lectures on Dunhuang*. Leiden & Boston: Brill. Translated by Imre Galambos.

Sedláček, Kamil. 1964. "New light on the name of the Tangut people of the Hsi-Hsia dynasty", in *Zeitschrift der Deutschen Morgenländischen Gesellschaft*, Band 114, Heft 1, 180–185.

Sofronov, M. V. (Софронов, М. В.). 1968. *Грамматика Тангутского Языка* (*Grammatika Tangutskogo Iazyka*). Moskva: Nauka. 2 vols.

Stein, M. Aurel. 1928. *Innermost Asia: Detailed Report of Explorations in Central Asia, Kan-su and Irān*. Oxford: Clarendon Press, 4 vols.

Wáng Jìngrú (王靜如). 1930. 西夏番漢合時掌中珠補及西夏民族語言與夏國史料 (*Xīxià Fān-Hàn héshí zhǎng zhōng zhū bǔ jí Xīxià mínzú yǔyán yǔ Xiàguó shǐliào*). Beiping: Institute of History and Philology, Academia Sinica.

———. 1932–1933. 西夏研究 (*Xīxià yánjiū*). Beiping: Institute of History and Philology, Academia Sinica. Parts I-III. (English title: *Shishiah Studies*.)

Wolfenden, Stuart N. 1931. "On the Tibetan transcriptions of Si-hia words", in *Journal of the Royal Asiatic Society* (New Series) 63.1, 47–52.

———. 1934. "On the prefixes and consonantal finals of Si-Hia as evidenced by their Chinese and Tibetan transcriptions", in *Journal of the Royal Asiatic Society* (New Series) 66.4, 745–770.

Wú Fāngsī (吳芳思; Frances Wood). 2011. "向達在英國" ("Xiàng Dá zài Yīngguó"), in 樊錦詩 (Fán Jǐnshī), 榮新江 (Róng Xīnjiāng) and 林世田 (Lín Shìtián), eds., 敦煌文獻考古藝術綜合研究——紀念向達先生誕辰110周年國際學術研討會論文集 (*Dūnhuáng wénxiàn kǎogǔ yìshù zōnghé yánjiū: Jìniàn Xiàng Dá xiānshēng dànchén 100 zhōunián guójì xuéshù yántǎohuì lùnwénjí*). Beijing: 中華書局 (Zhōnghuá shūjú).

EDITORIAL NOTES

Organization

Clauson's *Skeleton Tangut Dictionary* consists of two large notebooks. Part I (pp. 1–446 in this edition) originally comprised 222 folios: an originally unnumbered folio headed "Table of number of characters in the 'Homophones'" followed by 221 folios numbered 1 through 221. A blank folio and a folio for Clauson's introductory note were inserted at the beginning of the notebook at a later date, presumably in 1963 when he wrote the introductory note, and the folio with the introductory note and the following folio with the table of number of characters were numbered as i and ii.[50] Part II (pp. 447–892 in this edition) comprises 222 folios numbered 222 through 441, with folios 284A and 284B, two folios numbered 315 (numbered 315A and 315B in this edition), two folios numbered 321 (321A and 321B here), and no folio 323, as well as an extra sheet inserted after folio 247 (the two being numbered 247A and 247B here). Folios originally numbered 352–370 in ink (preceded by 350, and followed by 370) were renumbered as 351–369 in faint pencil; in the headers the pencil numbers have been used. The dictionary entries are written on the recto side of each folio only; on the verso of each folio, supplementary data relevant to the following recto is given.

Clauson wrote out the draft of his dictionary into these two notebooks between October 1938 (note in top margin of *f.* 1r) and 27 March 1939 (note on *f.* 441r). Six months is surely far too short a period of time for him to have written the dictionary from scratch, and the fact that the entries appear to have been written out sequentially in component order with no gaps between them strongly suggests that there must have been earlier rough drafts or a set of index cards which allowed him to order the characters to be included in his dictionary before he wrote the entries for them into his notebooks. As discussed below, the major sources for Tangut characters used by Clauson were published in 1935 (and none of his sources are later than this date), so it is likely that he did preliminary work on the compilation and ordering of characters for two or three years before he started to write up the actual dictionary entries in October 1938.

The system for ordering Tangut characters that Clauson devised for his dictionary uses a set of components that occur on the top or left side of characters, similar to the radicals used in ordering Chinese characters. Characters sharing the same top or left side component are grouped together as described in his introductory note dated 29 July 1963 (see pp. xvi–xvii above and p. 1 below). Clauson lists 70 main component types: 12 covers, 16 verticals, 12 rectangles, 12 curves, and 18 miscellaneous. These components are listed in the table below.

50 The unnumbered blank and folio i both have 24 rules, while the rest of the pages in the volume have 25. Both sheets are somewhat cleaner than the other sheets, as well.

Components used for ordering characters in Clauson's dictionary

Nº	Component type	Entries	Actual components
1		1–522	
2		523–536	
3		537–558	
4		559–689	
5		690–695	
6		696–1222	
7		1223–1264	
8		1265–1282	
9		1283–1293	
10		1294	
11		1295–1302	
12		1303–1316	
13		1317–1519	
14		1520–1656	
15		1657–1736	
16		1737–1749	
17		1750–1823	
18		1824–1868	
19		1869–1892	
20		1893	
21		1894–1899	
22		1900–2241	
23		2242–2250	
24		2251–2333	
25		2334–2347	
26		2348–2382	
27		2383–2410	
28		2411–2417	
29		2418–2727	
30		2728	
31		2729–2733	
32		2734–2738	
33		2739–2923	
34		2924–2927	
35		2928–3143	

36	[illegible]	3144–3169	[illegible]
37	[illegible]	3170–3174	[illegible]
38	[illegible]	3175–3186	[illegible]
39	[illegible]	3187–3211	[illegible]
40	[illegible]	3212–3244	[illegible]
41	[illegible]	3245–3254	[illegible]
42	[illegible]	3255–3256	[illegible]
43	[illegible]	3257–3648	[illegible]
44	[illegible]	3649–3661	[illegible]
45	[illegible]	3662	[illegible]
46	[illegible]	3663–3664	[illegible]
47	[illegible]	3665–4620	[illegible]
48	[illegible] + [illegible]	4621–4704	[illegible]
49	[illegible]	4705–4711	[illegible]
50	[illegible]	4712–4841	[illegible]
51	[illegible] + [illegible]	4842–4882	[illegible]
52	[illegible]	4883–4898	[illegible]
53	[illegible]	4899–5083	[illegible]
54	[illegible]	5084–5097	[illegible]
55	[illegible]	5098–5266	[illegible]
56	[illegible]	5267–5422	[illegible]
57	[illegible]	5423	[illegible]
58	[illegible]	5424–5534	[illegible]
59	[illegible]	5535–5561	[illegible]
60	[illegible]	5562–5569	[illegible]
61	[illegible]	5570–5607	[illegible]
62	[illegible]	5608–5619	[illegible]
63	[illegible]	5620–5646	[illegible]
64	[illegible]	5647–5660	[illegible]
65	[illegible]	5661–5663	[illegible]
66	[illegible]	5664–5716	[illegible]
67	[illegible]	5717–5718	[illegible]
68	[illegible]	5719–5721	[illegible]
69	[illegible]	5722–5723	[illegible]
70	[illegible]	5724	[illegible]

There are a few anomalies in the component types listed in Clauson's notes:

Component type 14 (|=). In his introductory note, Clauson inserts |= after the component |, but this does not seem to be a concrete component type. It is perhaps intended to represent components [Tangut] through [Tangut] where the vertical stroke is the leftmost part of a more complex component.

Component type 19 ([Tangut]). The component [Tangut] is not found as a component on the left side of any Tangut character, and I think it must be a mistake for the component [Tangut] or [Tangut], as there are 24 characters with either of these components at the end of the entries for characters with the preceding component type ([Tangut] or [Tangut]).

Component type 30 ([Tangut]). The component [Tangut] only corresponds to a single character in the dictionary ([Tangut]), which does not include the component as written by Clauson.

Component type 62 ([Tangut]). The component [Tangut] corresponds to characters with [Tangut] or [Tangut] on their left, and it would seem to be a mistake.

Each component type corresponds to one or more actual components, as listed in the above table. In some cases, the actual components include additional interpolated components. For example, there are 53 characters corresponding to the component [Tangut] (5267–5316), but these include three characters with [Tangut] on the left (5286–5288), and one character with [Tangut] on the left (5306). In the table above, such interpolated components are given in parentheses.

The component ordering method used by Clauson is well-designed, and it prefigures the various radical systems used in all later works of Tangutological scholarship. However, there are a few problems caused by Clauson's incomplete knowledge of the correct glyph forms of Tangut characters. Clauson carefully distinguishes some minor glyph differences, such as those between [Tangut] and [Tangut] and between [Tangut] and [Tangut], which are not always distinguished in the works of later scholars. Unfortunately, some significant glyph differences that should be distinguished are not. The most serious issue is that Clauson treats the elements [Tangut] and [Tangut] as being the same, both when they occur as top components and when they occur as elements of left side components (such as [Tangut] and [Tangut]) and elements of right side components (such as [Tangut] and [Tangut]). Clauson uniformly writes [Tangut] as [Tangut], and only distinguishes them in a few cases where two characters are otherwise identical (e.g. 2538 [Tangut] and 2539 [Tangut]). Another pair of components that Clauson conflates together are [Tangut] and [Tangut], which are both written as [Tangut]. In the table above, a component that has been conflated with another component by Clauson is given in square brackets after the component form used by Clauson for both components.

Numbering

Main entries in the dictionary were numbered sequentially from 1 through 5724 in the first draft completed on 27 March 1939. In addition to these main entries, the first draft included about 200 subsidiary entries for characters that Clauson considered to be uncertain or mistaken. These subsidiary entries are mixed in with the main entries, but are not given a unique sequential number. Instead, a subsidiary entry has the same number as the preceding main entry, followed by the letter A. Where there are two or three subsidiary entries in succession, then they share the same number, followed by the letter A, B, or C. For example, on *f.* 64r the main entry 849 [Tangut] "cork" is followed by the subsidiary entries 849A (noted as an error for 1240 [Tangut]), 849B (noted as an error for 1242 [Tangut]), and 849C (noted as doubtful, possibly an error for 857 [Tangut], although actually it is a miswritten form of [Tangut] which is unclear in the original *Homophones* text).

Clauson continued to work on the dictionary sporadically for many years after the completion of the first draft in 1939. He notes on the final page that he finished cross-referencing entries on

14 September 1946, and his final introductory note was added on 29 July 1963. During this time Clauson made many corrections, additions, and deletions to the original entries, and renumbered many entries to account for additions and deletions. The draft in its final form consists of main entries numbered 1 through 5724, with two entries for 1438 (1438 [illegible] is the last entry on *f.* 108r, and 1438 [illegible]—given here as 1438* in the header—is the first entry on *f.* 109r), and no entries for seven numbers:

224 is crossed out as a duplicate of 179 [illegible];
2388 is missing;
3363 [illegible] is crossed out as a mistake for 4688 (3363 is actually the correct form);
3833 is crossed out as a mistake for 3764bis [illegible];
4689 (first entry on *f.* 362r) is crossed out as a duplicate of 4688 [illegible] (last entry on *f.* 361r);
5018 is crossed out as a mistake for 3423 [illegible];
5688 (mistake for [illegible]) is renumbered as 5674A.

Additional main entries, added in the upper or lower margin, take the number of the preceding entry suffixed by *bis*. There are seventeen *bis* entries, of which sixteen are additions in the margins (267bis [illegible], 330bis [illegible], 781bis [illegible], 832bis [illegible], 962bis [illegible], 1473bis [illegible], 2083bis [illegible], 2203bis [illegible], 3271bis [illegible], 3764bis [illegible], 3782bis [mistakenly written as 3872bis] [illegible], 4269bis [illegible], 4581bis [illegible], 4939bis [illegible], 5103bis [illegible], and 5202bis [illegible]), while one entry (695bis [illegible]) is an original main entry to which Clauson added a *bis* suffix at a later date because renumbering had inadvertently resulted in two entries numbered 695. There is also one deleted *bis* entry on *f.* 14r (158bis, which is a duplicate of 422 [illegible]). Most of the *bis* entries are for variant forms of characters listed elsewhere in the dictionary, but seven of the entries are for main characters in the *Homophones* that Clauson must have missed the first time round. There are also a few inserted main entries with a unique number due to renumbering of adjacent entries (e.g. 771 [illegible] which is inserted in the bottom margin of *f.* 59r).

During Clauson's revisions he added about 56 additional subsidiary entries suffixed A or B in the margin or on the facing page. He also demoted a few main entries by adding an A suffix and renumbering adjacent entries (e.g. 138 was renumbered as 136A, and the reader directed to the correct form of the character at 611 [illegible]). In the final draft there are a total of 258 subsidiary entries:

237 numbers suffixed A;
2 numbers suffixed AA (5306AA before 5306A; and 4545AA after 4545A);
18 numbers suffixed B;
1 number suffixed C (849C).

In addition to the numbered entries, there are also seven unnumbered entries in the top margin, which are all errors for characters listed elsewhere:

f. 57r: mistake for 738 [illegible];
f. 82r: mistake for 1060 [illegible];
f. 89r: mistake for 685 [illegible] (Clauson suggests it is a mistake for 1222 [illegible], but the meaning *qiān* 慳 "avarice" indicates that 685 is correct);

- *f.* 172r: mistake for 2123 [Tangut];
- *f.* 304r: mistake for 4649 [Tangut];
- *f.* 427r: mistake for 5547 [Tangut] or 5578 [Tangut] (neither character fits the meaning, *xīn* 辛 "pungent", although Lǐ Fànwén gives the character [Tangut] in the same source quotation);[51]
- *f.* 436r: mistake for 5701 [Tangut].

As he revised the dictionary, Clauson crossed out quite a few entries which are duplicates or mistakes for characters listed elsewhere, and with one exception these deleted entries are not included in the radical index. The one exception is 779A [Tangut], which was added in the upper margin on *f.* 59r. Clauson glosses this character as "chisel" based on *Handful of Pearls*, but he crosses out the entry, noting that it is an error for 798 [Tangut], which he glosses as "a chisel, punch". In fact, the definition of 798 is wrong (it means "to hold"), and despite only differing by one stroke, it is not the same character as 779A.

In total Clauson's dictionary comprises 5,993 numbered entries (5,718 main numbered entries, 17 *bis* entries, 237 A entries, 18 B entries, 1 C entry, and 2 AA entries). These represent a total of approximately 5,744 distinct Tangut characters (including the one crossed-out entry 779A for [Tangut]).

The numbered dictionary entries are written on the recto side of each folio. The verso side of each folio is used to list pairs and chains of characters for the entries on the facing recto page, as well as supplementary information for which there was no room on the recto page.

Pairs of characters are two characters that mutually gloss each other in the *Homophones*. So for example, on the page facing folio 1r (*f.* ii v) is a note for 10 that states "0010 5342 pair", which means that the *Homophones* entry for 10 [Tangut] "foolish" (*H.* 54B13)[52] has the gloss character [Tangut] (5342), and the *Homophones* entry for 5342 [Tangut] "foolish" (*H.* 10B24) has the gloss character [Tangut] (10). In fact, unknown to Clauson at the time he wrote his dictionary, the gloss character is not a gloss *per se*, but should be read together with the main character to form a single word, starting with the gloss character if it is below right of the main character (as is the case for [Tangut]), or starting with the main character if the gloss character is below left of it (as is the case for [Tangut]). Thus, in this case the entries for [Tangut] and [Tangut] in the *Homophones* both give the word [Tangut][Tangut] meaning "foolish".

Chains of characters are a chained list of main characters and corresponding gloss character in the *Homophones*. As an example, on the facing page of folio 2 is the following chain of characters for 22 [Tangut] "snake":

0022		
	2444	3661
	1063	1168
		2056
	3036	
	3666	
	4841	
	5117	5121

51 Lǐ Fànwén 李範文, *Xià-Hàn zìdiǎn* 夏漢字典 (Beijing: Zhōngguó shèhuì kēxué chūbǎnshè, 2008) entry #1079.

52 References with *H.* in this format are to the A edition of the *Homophones*.

This means that:

22 [Tangut] is a gloss character for 2444 [Tangut] "frog" (*H.* 9A45)
2444 [Tangut] is a gloss character for 3661 [Tangut] "turtle" (*H.* 48A77)

22 [Tangut] is a gloss character for 1063 [Tangut] "dragon" (*H.* 9B37)
1063 [Tangut] is a gloss character for 1168 [Tangut] "dragon" (*H.* 52B42) and for 2056 [Tangut] "dragon" (*H.* 27A41)

22 [Tangut] is a gloss character for 3036 [Tangut] "to crawl" (*H.* 14B17)

22 [Tangut] is a gloss character for 3666 [Tangut] "snake" (*H.* 46A64)

22 [Tangut] is a gloss character for 4841 [Tangut] "snake" (*H.* 26B47)

22 [Tangut] is a gloss character for 5117 [Tangut] "fish" (*H.* 52B25)
5117 [Tangut] is a gloss character for 5121 [Tangut] "tortoise" (*H.* 31B56)

Sources

Clauson's sources for his dictionary were of necessity very limited, and with no access to the Tangut material from Khara-khoto that was held in Leningrad (or indeed, it seems, to the Tangut material brought back by Aurel Stein, and held at the British Museum), he had to rely on a very few published editions and studies of Tangut texts that had been published during the 1920s and 1930s. The major sources used by Clauson are listed below.

Xīxià Guóshū Zìdiǎn Yīntóng (西夏國書字典音同). [Lüshun], 1935. This is a lithographic edition of the *Homophones* published in China by Luó Fúchéng (羅福成, 1885–1960), eldest son of Luó Zhènyù (羅振玉, 1866–1940). It reproduces a hand-copied facsimile made by Luó Fúchéng from photographs of a woodblock edition held at the Asiatic Museum in Leningrad. *Homophones* (Tangut title: [Tangut][Tangut]) is the largest surviving source of Tangut characters, listing nearly 5,800 Tangut characters by rime, with all characters sharing the same pronunciation grouped together. Each entry consists of a single Tangut character with one or two small-sized gloss characters beneath it. There are two known editions of *Homophones*: Edition A, which only survives as a single, incomplete copy (missing most of folios 37B and 38A, and parts of folios 54A through 56B); and Edition B, which survives as several incomplete copies of at least two printings from different printing blocks. The 1935 edition used by Clauson represents the A edition of *Homophones*.

Fān-Hàn Héshí Zhǎngzhōngzhū 番漢合時掌中珠. [Tianjin]: Yí'āntáng jīngjípū (貽安堂經籍鋪), 1935. This is a lithographic edition of the Chinese-Tangut glossary, *Handful of Pearls*, published in 1935 by Luó Fúchéng. It is not the same as the lithographic edition of *Handful of Pearls* that was published by Luó Fúchéng in 1924. The earlier edition reproduces a hand-copied facsimile made by his father, Luó Zhènyù, from photographs of a woodblock edition held at the Asiatic Museum in Leningrad, and provided to Luó in 1922 by Aleksei Ivanovich Ivanov (Алексéй Ивáнович Ивáнов, 1878–1937). However, the 1935 edition states that the text was hand-copied by Nikolai

Nevsky, and it includes an appended table of corrections not found in the 1924 edition. There are some significant differences between the text of the 1924 and 1935 editions, and in some cases (as discussed below) the text of the 1935 edition is inferior to that of the 1924 edition. Clauson's copy is now held at SOAS library (CL495.49 / 84332). *Handful of Pearls* (Tangut title: [illegible]) is the only surviving bilingual Chinese-Tangut glossary, and was the main key to the decipherment of the Tangut language. There are several incomplete copies of *Handful of Pearls*, representing two slightly different editions, and the 1924 and 1935 editions are both composites of several different copies. In Clauson's dictionary *Handful of Pearls* is referenced as "C.C.C." (standing for the Wade-Giles transliteration *Chang Chung Chu* 掌中珠).

Bulletin of the National Library of Peiping (國立北平圖書館館栞) vol. 4 May–June 1930 (issued January 1932) No. 3: "A volume on Tangut (Hsi Hsia) Studies" (西夏文專號). This is a collection of articles by Wáng Jìngrú (王靜如, 1903–1990) and others on Tangut texts discovered at Khara-khoto and elsewhere in China. In Clauson's dictionary this work is referenced as "B".

Luó Fúcháng (羅福萇, 1896–1921), *Xīxià Guóshū Lüèshuō* (西夏國書略説). Kyoto: Higashiyama gakusha (東山學社), 1914. Introductory handbook on Tangut script written by Luó Fúcháng, second son of Luó Zhènyù. Clauson's copy is now held at SOAS library (CL495.49 / 84331). In Clauson's dictionary this work is referenced as "Lo Handbook".

Nicolas Nevsky, "A Brief Manual of the Si-Hia Characters with Tibetan Transcriptions" (西藏文字對照西夏文字抄覽); *Research Review of the Osaka Asiatic Society* No. 4 March 15, 1926. This is a list compiled by Nikolai Aleksandrovich Nevsky (Никола́й Алекса́ндрович Не́вский, 1892–1937) of 334 Tangut characters with corresponding Tibetan phonetic glosses. In Clauson's dictionary this work is referenced as "T".

Wáng Jìngrú (王靜如, 1903–1990), *Hsi Hsia Studies* (*Xīxià yánjiū* 西夏研究). Beiping: 1932. This is collection of articles on Tangut studies by Wáng Jìngrú, in three volumes. Clauson's copy is now held at SOAS (CL495.49 /28564). In Clauson's dictionary this work is referenced as "W. I", "W. II" and "W. III" for vols. I through III respectively.

In his latest revisions of the dictionary in the early 1960s, Clauson also adds a few references in blue ballpoint to Nevsky's draft manuscript Tangut dictionary that had been published posthumously in 1960 under the title *Тангутская Филология: Исследования и Словарь* (*Tangut Philology: Research and Dictionary*). However, this work was not used as a source for any additional entries to Clauson's dictionary. Actually, Nevsky's dictionary, with 5,237 entries, only includes about sixty distinct characters that are not present in Clauson's dictionary, of which about half are from the B edition of *Homophones* that are missing in the extant A edition.

The two major primary sources for Clauson's dictionary were the facsimile editions of the *Homophones* and the *Handful of Pearls*. However, as these were both based on hand-written copies of the original xylograph editions rather than being photographic reproductions, they were not entirely reliable. Characters that were unclear or damaged in the original text were commonly written incorrectly in the hand-written facsimile, and even clearly-written characters were sometimes miswritten in the facsimile edition. This means that, through no fault of his own, the character forms given in Clauson's dictionary are not always exactly correct, although in most cases the correct form is not difficult to determine. Another issue with his sources is that the character forms used in *Homophones* and *Handful of Pearls* sometimes differ from what modern scholars consider to be the standard forms, so even where a character is clearly written in the original xylographic edition, correctly copied in the hand-written facsimile, and carefully transcribed by Clauson, it may not exactly match the form given in modern Tangut dictionaries. As an example, Clauson's entry 275 [Tangut] faithfully reflects the character form given in *Homophones* A folio 16A53. The form of this character in modern dictionaries is [Tangut] (e.g. Lǐ Fànwén 2008 #4849), which reflects the form given in Homophones B folio 17A33.

The *Homophones* is the main source for the repertoire of Tangut characters listed as main entries in Clauson's dictionary, and most main entries start with a reference to the position of the character in the *Homophones*, and list the gloss character(s) given under the character in the *Homophones*. The A edition available to Clauson would originally have listed between 5,778 and 5,784 main characters, but between 133 and 139 characters are partially or wholly missing in the extant copy (see Clauson's summary at the start of the dictionary). Clauson includes all of the 5,645 surviving complete main characters, as well as two partial characters (4363 [Tangut] which is the left side of [Tangut], partially legible on *H.* folio 54A; and 0821 (*f.* 62r) which is a mistaken reconstruction of [Tangut], partially preserved on *H.* folio 38A). These characters form the bulk of the 5,718 main entries in Clauson's dictionary, although seven were added later as *bis* entries (781bis [Tangut], 962bis [Tangut], 3271bis [Tangut], 3764bis [Tangut], 4269bis [Tangut], 4939bis [Tangut], and 2203bis [Tangut]), and three are subsidiary entries: 3195A [Tangut] (which Clauson mistakenly considered to be a misspelling of 3192 [Tangut]), 3991A [Tangut], and 5674A [Tangut] (renumbered from 5688).

There are about 80 main entries in Clauson's dictionary which do not have a reference to a main character in the *Homophones*, most of which are found in *Handful of Pearls*, or occur as gloss characters in the *Homophones*, or are sourced to *Bulletin of the National Library of Peiping* or *Hsi Hsia Studies*. Some of these characters are actually variants of main characters in the *Homophones* that are listed under a different entry (e.g. 1189 [Tangut] = 675 [Tangut], and 1748 [Tangut] = 3250 [Tangut]). Eight main entries give no source and no details of their usage or meaning, and it is not clear where Clauson found them:

595 [Tangut]: occurs as a gloss character for 679 [Tangut] in the *Homophones*.
1205 [Tangut]: occurs as a phonetic gloss character in *Handful of Pearls*.
1247 [Tangut]: a rare transliteration character that does not occur in *Handful of Pearls* or as a main character in the *Homophones*. The original entry for 1247, which was later crossed out, gives the same glyph, but defines it as a main character in *Homophones* glossed with 4561 [Tangut], which would actually be 1230 [Tangut].
4344 [Tangut]: occurs as a phonetic gloss character in *Handful of Pearls*.
4706 [Tangut]: occurs as a phonetic gloss character in *Handful of Pearls*.
5272 [Tangut]: This is an error for 5292 [Tangut], which occurs as a phonetic gloss in *Handful of Pearls* folio 21b. The character is written correctly in the original text and in the 1924 lithographic edition, but [Tangut] has been miswritten as [Tangut] in the 1935 lithographic edition used by Clauson.
5276 [Tangut]: Clauson does not give a source or meaning for this character, but Nishida Tatsuo gives this character in his Tangut dictionary, where it is glossed as "lamp wick" *dēngxīn* 燈心, and sourced to *Handful of Pearls* folio 23 6th column (i.e. last

column of folio 23b).[53] This character does not occur in *Handful of Pearls*, but the penultimate entry on folio 23b gives the Tangut word [Tangut][Tangut] "grass wick" against the Chinese word *dēngcǎo* 燈草 "lamp wick", and the unknown character [Tangut] is composed from the left side of [Tangut] "grass" and the right side of [Tangut] "wick". The 1924 lithographic edition of *Handful of Pearls* correctly shows [Tangut][Tangut] for "lamp wick", but in the 1935 lithographic edition this word is miswritten as [Tangut][Tangut]. Therefore, 5276 [Tangut] is a mistake for 5271 [Tangut] in both Clauson's and Nishida's dictionaries, due to them both relying on the 1935 edition of the *Handful of Pearls*.

5426 [Tangut]: occurs as a phonetic gloss character in *Handful of Pearls*.

As to the 258 subsidiary entries in Clauson's dictionary, most are variant, mistaken or corrupt forms of characters listed elsewhere in the dictionary, but a significant number are gloss characters attested once in the *Homophones*. Some of these are variant or mistaken forms of a character with a main entry in the dictionary, but 35 are distinct characters that are not listed elsewhere (13A [Tangut], 13B [Tangut], 92A [Tangut], 359A [Tangut], 629A [Tangut], 710A [Tangut], 792A [Tangut], 977B [Tangut], 1009A [Tangut], 1029A [Tangut], 1054A [Tangut], 1546A [Tangut], 1550A [Tangut], 2026A [Tangut], 2118A [Tangut], 2123A [Tangut], 2123B [Tangut], 2133A [Tangut], 2380A [Tangut], 2745A [Tangut], 2888A [Tangut], 3316A [Tangut], 3386A [Tangut], 3519A [Tangut], 3697A [Tangut], 4304A [Tangut], 4308A [Tangut], 4502B [Tangut], 4510A [Tangut], 4610A [Tangut], 4620A [Tangut], 4712A [Tangut], 4788A [Tangut], 5174B [Tangut], and 5345A [Tangut]), and probably correspond to a main character that was in the damaged part of the A edition of *Homophones*. Characters that were used as gloss characters in at least two place in the *Homophones*, or which were also attested in another source, are usually given as main entries by Clauson, but in most cases where a character was only attested in a single place as a gloss character he errs on the side of caution, and gives it as subsidiary entry. The only other subsidiary entries that are for known characters not listed elsewhere in the dictionary are: 677A [Tangut] and 1164A [Tangut], which are both transliteration characters that Clauson sourced to secondary sources; and 4235B [Tangut], which Clauson mistakenly considered to be the correct form of 4176 [Tangut], when they are actually two distinct characters.

For most subsidiary entries for variant, corrupt, or mistaken character forms, Clauson provides a cross-reference to the main entry with the correct character form, although occasionally the character form in the subsidiary entry is actually the correct form. For example, 4779A [Tangut] is noted as an error for 3315, when in fact 4779A is the correct form, and the form given under 3315 has an incorrect left side component ([Tangut] instead of [Tangut]). Some 52 subsidiary entries for characters with incorrect or variant glyphs either have no cross-reference to the correct character, or the cross-reference is doubtful. These are listed below.

437A: Error for 442 [Tangut]. Gloss character for 3191 [Tangut] in the *Homophones* (*H.* 4A17).

471A: Error for 464 [Tangut]. Gloss character for 4432 [Tangut] in the *Homophones* (*H.* 50B53.

596A: Error for 528 [Tangut]. Gloss character for 947 [Tangut] in the *Homophones* (*H.* 44A13).

686A: Unidentified error in Nevsky's *Manual* (#331 *dbi'*).

735A: Error for 872 [Tangut]. Clauson's misinterpretation of the character as given in *Bulletin of the National Library of Peiping*.

849C: Error for 730 [Tangut]. Gloss character for 726 [Tangut] in the *Homophones* (*H.* 41B28).

870A: Probably an error for 926 [Tangut]. Sourced to *Hsi Hsia Studies*.

889A: Unidentified error in Nevsky's *Manual* (#317 *ko*).

53 Nishida Tatsuo 西田龍雄 (1928–2012), *Seikabun Shōjiten* 西夏文小字典 (Tokyo, 1966) entry 185-065.

1234A: Unidentified error in Nevsky's *Manual* (#318 *g.yi*).
1353A: Error for 1487 [Tangut] in *Bulletin of the National Library of Peiping*.
1383A: Error for 1401 [Tangut]. Gloss character for 3284 [Tangut] in the *Homophones* (*H.* 5A15).
1425A: Possibly an error for 1455 [Tangut] (as a transliteration of Chinese *guāng* 光). Sourced to *Hsi Hsia Studies*.
1598A: Error for 1598 [Tangut]. Gloss character for 3293 [Tangut] in the *Homophones* (*H.* 6A73).
1686A: Probably an error for 1691 [Tangut]. No source given.
2153A: Error for 2151 [Tangut]. Gloss character for 2159 [Tangut] in the *Homophones* (*H.* 36A71).
2428A: Error for 2427 [Tangut]. Gloss character for 3303 [Tangut] in the *Homophones* (*H.* 6B72).
2529A: Error for 2439 [Tangut] in *Hsi Hsia Studies*.
3018A: Error for 3107 [Tangut] in *Hsi Hsia Studies*.
3105B: Error for 2339 [Tangut]. Gloss character for 2159 [Tangut] in the *Homophones* (*H.* 19B17).
3137A: Error for 3134 [Tangut]. No source given.
3147A: Unidentified error in Nevsky's *Manual* (#329 *bla'*).
3274A: Error for 3281 [Tangut]. Gloss character for 2571 [Tangut] in the *Homophones* (*H.* 22B57).
3324A: Error for 3331 [Tangut]. Gloss character for 617 [Tangut] in the *Homophones* (*H.* 18A18).
3343A: Probably an error for 3870 [Tangut]. No source given.
3574A: Unidentified error in Nevsky's *Manual* (#232 *'dzwa*).
3575A: Unidentified character in *Bulletin of the National Library of Peiping*. Probably not 3580 [Tangut] as suggested by Clauson.
3614A: Error for 3454 [Tangut]. Gloss character for 3864 [Tangut] in the *Homophones* (*H.* 40A71).
3674A: Error for 4216 [Tangut]. Gloss character for 4673 [Tangut] in the *Homophones* (*H.* 39B58).
3700A: Error for 3709 [Tangut]. Gloss character for 329 [Tangut] in the *Homophones* (*H.* 52A78).
3758A: Unidentified error in Nevsky's *Manual* (#308 *ni*).
3769A: Clauson glosses this character as *zàng* 藏 "Tibet", and sources it to Luó Fúcháng's 1914 *Handbook* (*Xīxià Guóshū Lüèshuō* 西夏國書略説). On folio 20a of the *Handbook* there is indeed a list of five languages: Sanskrit ([Tangut][Tangut] = *fàn yǔ* 梵語), Chinese ([Tangut][Tangut] = *hàn yǔ* 漢語), Tibetan ([Tangut][Tangut][Tangut] = *xīzàng yǔ* 西藏語), Khitan ([Tangut][Tangut][Tangut] = *qìdān yǔ* 契丹語), and Tibetan ([Tangut][Tangut] = *fān yǔ* 番語). 3769A [Tangut] occurs as the middle character in the first term for Tibetan, but this term is problematic as Tibet was not known as Xīzàng during the Western Xia period. In fact, Luó Fúcháng's list of languages derives from a fragment of a Tangut manuscript collected by Count Ōtani Kōzui 大谷光瑞 (1876–1948), which lists the following seven languages on one line: Sanskrit ([Tangut][Tangut]), Uighur ([Tangut][Tangut][Tangut]), Tangut ([Tangut][Tangut]), Tibetan ([Tangut][Tangut]), Chinese ([Tangut][Tangut]), Khitan ([Tangut][Tangut][Tangut]), and Jurchen ([Tangut]□[Tangut]). Luó's "Tibetan" ([Tangut][Tangut][Tangut]) is evidently a misreading of "Uighur" ([Tangut][Tangut][Tangut]), so 3769A is an error for 4048 [Tangut].[54]
3884A: Error for 3839 [Tangut]. Gloss character for 1147 [Tangut] in the *Homophones* (*H.* 10B27).
3887A: Error for 3846 [Tangut] in *Hsi Hsia Studies*.
3935A: Error for 3284 [Tangut]. Gloss character for 4977 [Tangut] in the *Homophones* (*H.* 10B18).

54 The Ōtani fragment is held at the library of Ryūkoku University (龍谷大学図書館) in Kyoto, and is reproduced in *Rìběn Cáng Xīxiàwén Wénxiàn* 日本藏西夏文文獻 ['*Xixia documents collected in Japan*'] (Beijing: Zhōnghuá shūjú, 2011), vol. 1: 不明論典 03-03 (the list of languages is on column 3 of folio 8a). I am grateful to Viacheslav Zaytsev for helping to explain this error.

3948A: Error for 3702. Gloss character for 578 in the *Homophones* (*H.* 51A13).
4188A: Error for 4677 "hump" [of a camel] in *Bulletin of the National Library of Peiping*.
4201A: Error for 4197. Gloss character for 2925 in the *Homophones* (*H.* 26B18).
4227A: Error for 4132. Gloss character for 3922 in the *Homophones* (*H.* 22A44).
4235A: Error for 4694. Gloss character for 5167 in the *Homophones* (*H.* 40A72).
4249A: Error for 4692. Gloss character for 125 in the *Homophones* (*H.* 49A48).
4311A: Error for 4302. Gloss character for 3698 in the *Homophones* (*H.* 23A12).
4412A: Error for 4528. Gloss character for 4529 in the *Homophones* (*H.* 45A14).
4430A: Error for 4494. Incomplete gloss character for 3569 in the *Homophones* (*H.* 56A21).
4441A: Variant of 4468. Gloss character for 4410 in the *Homophones* (*H.* 54A24).
4545AA: Probably an error for 4546. No source given.
4545B: Error for 4555. Gloss character for 5496 in the *Homophones* (*H.* 40B23).
4571A: Error for 4578. Gloss character for 4583 in the *Homophones* (*H.* 46A36).
4697A: Error for 4626. Gloss character for 4675 in the *Homophones* (*H.* 19A51).
4985A: Probably an error for 4899 in *Bulletin of the National Library of Peiping*. Second *fǎnqiè* character for 3793.
5306AA: Error for 5309 or 5323 in *Bulletin of the National Library of Peiping*.
5491A: Error for 5458. Gloss character for 5118 in the *Homophones* (*H.* 44A74).
5697A: Error for 5694 in *Bulletin of the National Library of Peiping*.

Andrew West

i

Skeleton ~~Hsia~~ Tangut (Hsi Hsia) Dictionary in two volumes, by Sir Gerard Clauson.

The arrangement of the characters is based on the assumption that each character can be analyzed either as a "component", that is a fixed pattern of strokes, or as a combination of a component & a "sub-component", that is a stroke or ~~pattern~~ combination of strokes placed above a component & forming an integral whole with it, or as a combination of two or more components, each with or without sub-components attached. The analysis starts at the top left hand corner, & moves downwards and to the right.

The following is a table of the sub-components and components in the order in which they are arranged. A simple asterisk × indicates that a component occurs both in its simple form & with sub-components, a dotted asterisk ⁂ that it occurs only with sub components.

Sub-components. [illegible]

Components

Covers [illegible]

Verticals [illegible]

Rectangles [illegible]

Curves [illegible]

Miscellaneous [illegible]

References in Roman & ~~Latt~~ Latin numbers, e.g. I.1. are to Chapters & sections in the Homophones, i.e. part 1 of each Chapter, references like IA1 are to the "unique sounds" in the second part of each Chapter.

References starting with B. are to the special volume of the Bulletin of the National Library at Peiping (or some such title) devoted to Hsi Hsia.

References starting with W. are to Wang's Hsi Hsia Studies (3 ~~vo~~ volumes). CCC is the Chinese-~~Hsi~~ Tangut handbook "the Handful of Pearls". X means the Tangut ~~translation~~ explanation just quoted.

(Note added on 29/7/63)

Gerard Clauson

My copies of B, ~~&~~ W [& CCC] are now in the Library of the School of Oriental & African Studies

S.-H. Soothill & Hodous Dict. of Chinese Buddhism

ii

SCHOOL OF ORIENTAL & AFRICAN STUDIES LONDON

Table of number of characters in the "Homophones" (1) chapter headings

	characters per page 56	characters per line 8	1	Total	
Chapter I	11 pages	7 lines	6 characters	678	[written 996] + 206
IA				112	
II	2	12	6	214	
IIA				34	[written 264] + 16
III	12	7	4	732	
IIIA				137	[written 885] + 16
IV				15	
IVA				5	[written 20] -
V	13	5	2	770	
VA				141	[written 923] + 12
VI	9	1	7	519	
VIA				129	[written 664] + 16
VII.	10	.	1	561	
VIIA				143	[written 738] + 34
VIII	6	7	3	395	
VIIIA				111	[written 518] + 12
IX	15	7	-	896	
IXA				186	+ up to 6
	78	46	29	5778	+ up to 6.

90 in Ch. VII
9 in Ch. IX
34 in Ch. IXA

312 Missing 133 + up to 6

6090
43
6133

5645

78
56
468 368
390
4368
368
29
4765
998
15
5778

112
34
137
5
141
129
143
111
186
998

996
264
885
20
923
664
738
518
5008
1125
6133

0001 0001 0008 0017
0003 0003 0009 0018
0004 0002 0010 0019
0033 0004 0011 0021
0035 0005 0012 0022
0036 0007
0037 0008
0038 0009 0002
0039 0011
0005 0012
0006 0014
0007 0015

The order of pairs requires revision down to p. 48

3523

6 |𗀀 B. 104 cat. under "women's clothing"
0006 0036 chain

0007 0042 chain

7A 𗀀 W.I.170? 塡 to barricade, block up" ? same as 7.

0001 – ~~0051~~ 0049 0051 chain

0008 ≠ 3941 pair

0009 0271 chain

0002 ≠ ~~0052~~ 0050 chain

0010 ≠ 5342 pair

0003 ~~no chain~~ 3802

0011 3354 chain

0004 ≠ 4011 chain

0012 5465 chain

0005 4208 chain

Begun October 1938

1.

1. [Tangut] .... III 153 [Tangut] | 51 ? 0051
 (a) III 152 ditto
 (b) III 151 [Tangut] | ? 0049
~~Apparently a theme from verb;~~
? meaning. cf. 2.
~~No clue to sound exc. III 151 is b'T'i~~

0031-2
2. [Tangut] .... III 153 [Tangut] | ? 0052
 (a) III 152 ditto
 (b) III 151 [Tangut] | ? 0050
~~Apparently a theme from verb~~
? meaning. See 36 II (ii) cf. 1.
~~No clue to sound exc. III 151 is b'T'i~~

3. [Tangut] K'a V. 155 | [Tangut] ? 3802
 (a) III 58 ditto.
 ? meaning ? right form v. 1362 A

Note. [Tangut] is to be distinguished from [Tangut], & [Tangut] from [Tangut] & [Tangut]

4. [Tangut] Nu V1. | [Tangut] 3760
 ? meaning (a) III 47 | [Tangut] ? see 0759 4011 chain

5. [Tangut] ... V A 12 [Tangut] | 5688 "body, limb."
 ? meaning

6. [Tangut] .... IX A 94 [Tangut] | 0036
 ? meaning

7. [Tangut] ... IX 131 | [Tangut] 0042
 W. II 54[11,12], 78[7] 障 "screen, barricade" hindrance,
 [Bud. t.t. varaṇa] See 1318

8. [Tangut] Nu V1 [Tangut] | q.v. 3941
 (a) VIII 1 ditto
 ? meaning

9. [Tangut] ... V A 41 [Tangut] | "ear" 0271
 ? meaning

10. [Tangut] ti IX A 11 [Tangut] |
 (a) II 14 ditto
 I. (ccc. 31a; W. II 60[4] The di-syllable "stupid" (small man) B. 196[1]
 II As a monosyllable ccc. 35[b]; W. I 132[11]
 癡 Bud. t.t. moha "delusion"; one of the three poisons "desire, dislike, delusion".

11. [Tangut] .... IX 57 [Tangut] | "dog" 3354
 W. I. 134[16] 蚊 gnat ~~"louse, flea"~~
 N.B. 虫 "insect" + [Tangut] Phonetic.

12. [Tangut] Lu IX 41 [Tangut] | "fire" 0972
 W. I. 136[1] II 84[9] 燒 "to burn".
 B 217[1] 焚 (W. I. 136[1] [Tangut])

0013 0024
A 0025
B 0027
0014 0028
0014A 0030
0015 0029 X

0016 0031 X
0017 0032
0018 0034
0019 0035
0020 0037

0021 0038
0022 0039
0023 0041 + 0036

0013A – 1427 – chain
0013B – 1436 – chain

0013 – 1385?
– 0282
– 1797

W.II 80[5] 誘 to lead on B.188' 引 to lead,

0019 – 3090

0020
– 3803
– 1393

0014 chain 0270 chain
– 0270 – 0122
– 0822
– 0764
– 1915

0021 2149 chain

0022
– 2444 – 3661
– 1063 – 1168
– 2056
– 3036
– 3666
– 4841
– 5117 – 5121
turn to 2444

14A
v.1479

0015 chain
– 0921
– 1816

0016 chain
– 0018 – 2862
– 4624
– 0017

0023 – 4739

0017 0016 chain

0018 0016 chain

+2

2.

13A [Tangut] V 31 × of [Tangut] | 1427

13B [Tangut] V 31 × of [Tangut] | ? 1436

13. [Tangut] VII 59-60 (c) I 60 1385

(a) VII 18 [Tangut] |

(b) VII 76 [Tangut] | v.1797

W. I 132[14] II 20[4] 將 ; W. II. 6[6] 70[4] 導

"to lead, leader". B 246[9] 𨗴 q.v.

W. I 146[17] [Tangut] | = 將衆

"Universal leader". Name of Buddha

14. [Tangut] .... V A 29 [Tangut] | "confused"

(a) V 34 ditto v.270

(b) I A 91 [Tangut] | v.1915

(c) VII 61 | [Tangut] "to stand up on end (of hair)". 0822 0761

Actual word not traced, but general meaning clear.

14A v.1479

15. [Tangut] V 66 | [Tangut] ? 0921

(a) II. 6 ditto

(b) IX 84 | [Tangut] × of [Tangut]

? meaning

16 [Tangut] bWa II 20 | [Tangut]

(b) VII 99 | [Tangut]

(a) IX A 59 ditto

(? meaning) See 17, 18

17. [Tangut] .... VII. 99 [Tangut] |

? meaning See 16.

18. [Tangut] .... IX A 59 [Tangut] |

(a) II 20 ditto

(b) VI 57 | [Tangut]

(c) IX A 48 | [Tangut] ? pitfall

? meaning. See 16

19. [Tangut] Kwa V 77 | [Tangut] ?

(a) IX 79 ditto

? meaning.

20. [Tangut] .... I.138 | [Tangut]

(a) V 22 ditto

(b) VII 22 | [Tangut] "to cross the eyes" v.1393

B. 168[4] 171[2] 級 step, grade

21. [Tangut] Č'a VII.12 | [Tangut] "to make" 2149

?

22. [Tangut] mo I. 116 [Tangut] | [illegible]

(a) I A 93 ditto

(b) II 1 | [Tangut] 'dragon'

(c) III 57 | [Tangut] ?

(d) V. 157 [Tangut] × by [Tangut] [Tangut]

C.C.C. 6[b] 16[a] W. I. 208[18] 蛇 sbrul ~ "snake, serpent".

C.C.C. 10[a] 巳 6th horary character.

23. [Tangut] I 138 | [Tangut]

(a) VI 74 [Tangut] ditto

?

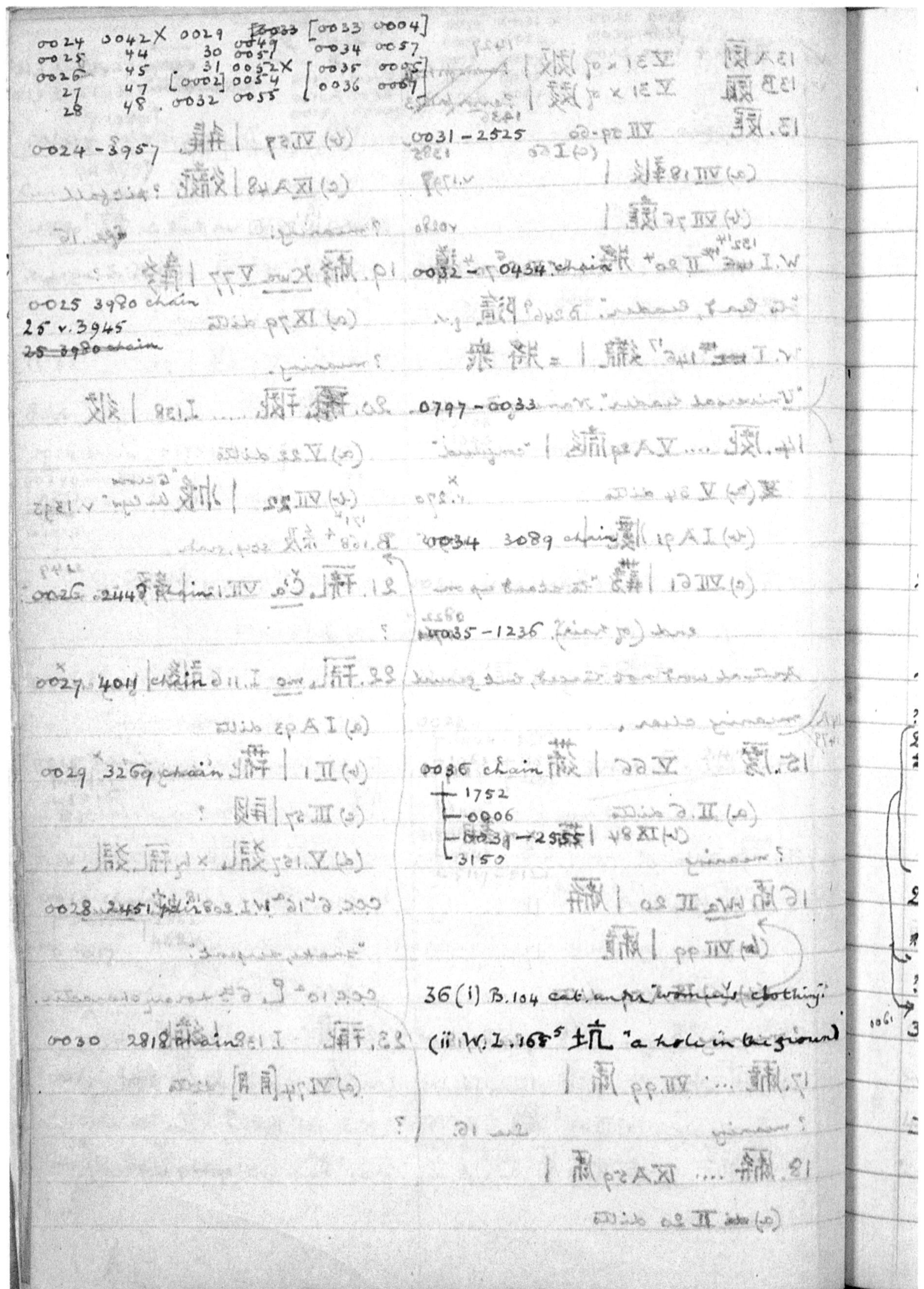

3.

24. [Tangut] č'a VII 12 | [Tangut]

(a) III 20 ditto

As di-syllable W I 190[13] nar. ba

'strong, violent'. Name of Nāgarājā.

25. [Tangut] č'a VII 12 [Tangut] | high, supreme

(a) V 59 [Tangut] |

(b) V A 1 [Tangut] | ? v.1983

(c) IX 84 | [Tangut]

W.I. 102[2] 168[3] 194[13] 218[12] = 上 -na

Postposn 'on, upon'. B. 180[5]

26. [Tangut] č'a VII 12 [Tangut] | ? 0222

?

27. [Tangut] gZe III 61 [Tangut] | 'head' [Tangut] 4011

?

4011 chain

28 [Tangut] .... IX 103 [Tangut] | 'to see, appear'.

W. II 4[8] 經 to endure? pass through

29. [Tangut] .... I 110 [Tangut] |

(a) VII 112 ditto.

? ?B. 176[3] part of J.H.

30. [Tangut] na III 47 | [Tangut] 1061 2818

I. The disyllable W. I. 132[10] 毒 'poison'

II By itself, W. I 134[3], 208[17] etc. 毒 dug

'poison' B. 232[5]

0002 here

31. [Tangut] I A 28 | [Tangut] 2525

(a) I 72 ditto

W. I. 206[8] sba. ba 'to conceal'.

32. [Tangut] VI 94 | [Tangut]

(a) V 19 ditto

? Nevsky "incomplete"

33. [Tangut] IX 17 [Tangut] |

(a) I 8 ditto

?

34. [Tangut] IX 34 [Tangut] |

?

35. [Tangut] nu VI [Tangut] |

(a) VII 64 ditto See 1236

?

36 [Tangut] ňu V 1. | [Tangut]

(a) VI A 70 ditto v.1752

(b) I 45 [Tangut] | 3150

(c) VIII A 29 | [Tangut] 0039

(d) IX A 94 See 6. 0006

I The disyllable C.C.C. 25[a] 領襟

'a collar for the neck'.

II By itself (i) C.C.C. 13[a] [Tangut] |. 地程

'a measure of land' (?)

(ii) C.C.C. 30[b] | [Tangut] 出氣

頭字 "an aspirated principal character (?)

0042 chain goes over to 4683

4683 — 5373 — 2337

0007

(a) III 2a ditto

(a) I 72 ditto

W. I. 206[3]

'strong, valiant'. Name of Nagaraja. 32. VI 94

25. VII 12 | high, supreme (a) VI 19 ditto

(a) V 59 |

0644 ?

0037 4000 chain IX 17 33. 0043 chain Transfer to 0056.

0056 — 0711 — 4783

0054 — 4882 — 4815 — 5448

(a) I 8 ditto

0038 -3201

W. I. 102[2] 168[3] 194[13] 218

34. IX 90 |

26. VII 12 |

35. VI |

27. III 61

0039 - 0036 chain (a) VII 64 ditto

0044 5708 chain

28. IX 103 | 36 VI. | 0040 - 0699

0045 - 0448

(a) VI A 70 ditto

(b) I 45 |

29. I 110 |

(a) VIII A 29 |

(a) VII 112 ditto

(a) IX A 94

30. III 47 0046 3918 chain

'a cotton for the rich.'

W. I. 152[10] 'cotton'

0041 2485 chain

0047 2149 chain

ccc. 30[b] | (iii)

'cotton' B. 232

頭字 "an aspirated principal character (?)"

AN 2

4.

36 cont.

(iii) W.I.168

(iv) 𘄴 | B.p.256 yidgñis

"doubt".

Most obscure; ? meaning

37. 𘄵 V 29. | 𘄶

?

38. 𘄷 ... VI 𘄸 |

(a) IX 131 ditto

?

39. 𘄹 VIII A 29 𘄺 | See 36(c)

(a) VII A 105 | 𘄹

?

40. 𘄻 VII 2 | 𘄼 chariot

(a) V 75 ditto [𘄼]

chariot, cart.

Analysed at B.p.93.:-

𘄽 above 𘄾 below

| has the same sound as the

Chinese word 車. The Hsi-hsia word

means 𘄼 "chariot".

41. 𘄿 V 19 𘅀 | 'leg, foot'.

?

42. 𘅁 IX 109 𘅂 | 4683 (4683)

(a) IX A 93 [𘅂] ditto

(b) See 7. (0007A) 0007

No clue except that it is used in (b) to translate 'screen, barricade'.

43. 𘅃 III 118 𘅄 | ? bird

(a) II A 3 ditto

(b) I A 92 | 𘅅

(c) VII 26 | 𘅆 0111

~~Possibly something to do with a bird, or some kind of bird.~~ W.I.134[14] 卵 'egg'

44. 𘅇 IX 148 𘅈 | 'only, alone'

(a) IX 39 | 𘅉 "final particle" v.2153

'One' passim. Follows noun to which it refers.

45. 𘅊 III 28 | 𘅋

(a) I 5 ditto

?

Often used as a phonetic for ta

46. 𘅌 III 13 𘅍 | disease

?

47. 𘅎 III 13 | 𘅏 "to make"

ccc. 31[b] | 𘅐 ... 謀矢 "pure man".

0048 1608 pair (d) W.I.132[18] [illegible] fowls.

0049 0051 chain

0050 0052 chain 0057 – 0658

0051 ~~0001 chain~~ 0058 chain ~~4919~~
⊥0001–0049
- 4919 takes over
- 4915
- 4918

0052 0002 chain
⊥0002–0050

0053 – 0203

0054 0043 chain

0059 3086 chain

0055 2596 chain. 0060 3334 chain

0061 5188 chain

~~0062~~ – 1866 pair

take over
0056 ~~0043~~ chain

~~0063 chain~~ Transfer to 0277
- 0277
- 0064
- 1576

48A v. 54 1608 5.

48. [Tangut] VII 33 [Tangut] |
(a) VIII 61 ditto v. 1608
?
49. [Tangut] III 151 ? See 1 0051 chain
50. [Tangut] III 151 See 2
See 36 II (ii)
51. [Tangut] III 152 See 1.
52. [Tangut] III 152 See 2
53. [Tangut] IA 47 | [Tangut]
(a) IX 103 ditto
54. [Tangut] IX 118 [Tangut] | [error for [Tangut]] 0056
I The disyllable C.C.C. 16b W.I. 126[15] 190'ct. W II 46[12] 寒 "cold" B 220[5] 雹 hail
孔雀 rma. bya Mayūrā "peacock"
(or rather 'peahen'.)
55. [Tangut] V 124 [Tangut] | 'breast'.
(a) II 38 | [Tangut] 'shoulder'
(b) IX 9 | [Tangut] 0987
'Back' 背 C.C.C. 18b (a) reversed
"shoulder & back: 24a | [Tangut] = 椅子
"chair": (b) above 24b | [Tangut] = 襯 心
"pasteboard heart"?
56. [Tangut] II A 3 | [Tangut] egg
(a) III 118 ditto. See 43
(b) I. 16 [Tangut] | "mandarin duck & drake" 4082
(c) VII 75 [Tangut] | ? 4815

(d) VIII 76 | [Tangut] "cock" 5448
(e) IX 118 See 54 "peacock" 0054
Some kind of bird. So far only traced in compounds.
57. [Tangut] IX 30 | [Tangut] 658
(a) IX A 154 ditto
?
58 [Tangut] [Tangut] VII A iii [Tangut] | 4919
(a) VII 92 ditto
(b) I. 61 | [Tangut] ? 4915
(c) V 174 | [Tangut] ? 4918
59. [Tangut] III 73 [Tangut] | 4604 Particle
60. [Tangut] VI A 64 [Tangut] | 3661A 3334
?
61. [Tangut] III 173 | [Tangut] See 1271
B 344[4] ?
62. [Tangut] kā·ta VII 21 [Tangut] | 1866
(a) V 2 ditto
The disyllable: C.C.C. 7a 16a W I 94[16]
101[3] 獅子 W.I. 194[11] seng. ge "lion". 0277
63. [Tangut] [Tangut] IX 14 [Tangut] | TO-Ri
(a) III 18 ditto
(b) III 95 | [Tangut] v. 1576

Dissyl. reversed. B.230[4]

0067 independent

0068 = 2189 chain

B.165[2] dissyl.

0065 # 2099 pair

0069 = 2531 chain

B.233[2] tr. 值

64. By itself. B.346[4] (sing.?)

0064 ~~0063~~ 0277 chain

0066 independent

6.

63 cont.

(c) V 14 | [Tangut] See 64

This is one of several words meaning 'all' which are difficult to distinguish; it seems always to be used with the full meaning of 'all' & not as a plural prefix.

I. The dissyllable. C.C.C. 20a W.I. 196³ 皆, 悉 "all".

II (a) By itself. W.I. 220² B.p. 249 皆. t'ams.cad W.I. 224⁷ kun II 6⁶ 悉 "all"

(b) In phrase | [Tangut] C.C.C. 27a 28b 34a,b 盡 皆 "all, completely"

65 [corrected from 64]. [Tangut] IX 15 [Tangut] | 2099

(a) V 157 ditto

64 [corrected from 65]. [Tangut] no V 14 [Tangut] See 63 (c)

(a) VIII 4 x [Tangut] | [Tangut] See [Tangut]

The word by itself is very rare; but the reduplicated form | |, 一切, Sarwa t'ams.cad, kun.gyi "altogether, one & all, universal" is very common W.I. 90⁵, 220⁷ etc. B 253²

66. [Tangut] IX A 119 [Tangut] 3685

'A man's name. B. 177¹ P.N. 萬

In C.C.C. 16a it seems to be used as a phonetic 兒 zi. See [Tangut] 532

67. [Tangut] IX A 120 [Tangut]

'Name of country'.

68. [Tangut] VII 35 [Tangut] | "a, one". v. 1891

(a) III 60 [Tangut] | "wish, vow." Verb

A very common verb representing 生 (B.p. 249 & passim) 起 (C 35b W.I. 98⁴ & passim) 發 (W.II. 116¹¹) byun.ba (W.I. 192¹⁷) hgyur.ba (B.p. 249) bskyed.pa (B.p. 254)

"to arise, to be born, to emerge; ?to raise, to bring forth".

(ii) (a) B. 347¹ 心 + [?發]

69. [Tangut] I A 107 [Tangut] | 2523

(a) VII 109 ditto.

A rather common verb; governs [Tangut]. (W.I. 108¹²) 遇 "to meet, experience" (II 32¹²) 遭 to meet) 36⁸ ditto. 蒙 I 136¹² II 130² "to receive (from a superior)".

~~70~~ 69A. [Tangut] IX A 88 [Tangut] |

(a) I A 54 ditto

This word sh^d have — — not

0070–0380

Take over 0076 1130 chain

0071 1361 chain

(ii W.II 130⁵ 勇健 'brave'.

0072 1538 chain

0077 3889 chain

transfer to 0637

0073 chain
├ 0566
└ 2460

~~0078 chain~~
├ 0637
└ 0601 ┬ 0590 ┬ 0589
          │   └ 5151
          └ 0667

0074 4561 chain

0079 0899 chain

0075 1080 chain

7

70. [Tangut] VII 35 | [Tangut]
(a) II 15 ditto
Nevski 1257

71. [Tangut] IX 125 [Tangut] | 'brave' 1361
(a) V 128 ditto See 1361
(i) W. II 80[5] 樂 joy (sic!)
(ii) W. I. 214[8] [Tangut] | spar.ldan 'brave'? B.125[4]

72 [Tangut] či VII 10 [Tangut] |
(a) IX 40 ditto [[Tangut]] v. 1538
B. 127[4] tr.
Phonetic W. II 22[7] 月氏 [Tangut] chih 'hoof'

73. [Tangut] VII A 81 | [Tangut] 0566
(a) VIII 30 ditto See 566
(b) VI A 112 | [Tangut]
W. I. 212[16], 218[15] [Tangut] | srul.po
a sort of devil.

74. [Tangut] II 5 [Tangut] | 4561 (particle instrumental) v. 1968
(a) IX A 100 [Tangut] | to fall etc.
W. I. 196[6] me.ons.pa "not to come,
to stay".

75. [Tangut] VII A 83 [Tangut] | 'way, path' 1080
(a) IX 28 | [Tangut] 4068
C.C.C. 7[a] [Tangut] 2364 | 巨蟹 name of a
constellation "the great crab."
B. p. 100 [Tangut] 1806 | catalogued under

"horse"

76. [Tangut] V 108 | [Tangut] rie. Gi 1130
(a) V 141 ditto
I The dissyllable C.C.C. 4[b] W. I 220[7] 222"
星宿 B. 230[7] rgyu. skar. A lunar
mansion, fixed star.
The second half is frequently found
by itself, but the first has not so
far been traced

77. [Tangut] VII A 141 [Tangut] | 'night' 3889
?

78. [Tangut] ri VIII 6 [Tangut] |
(a) I. 6 ditto
(b) IX 48 | [Tangut] 'stone' 0601
(i) | [Tangut] C.C.C. 21[a] W. I 208[11] 218[1]
金剛 rdo. rje "diamond".
(ii) [Tangut] | C.C.C. 13[a] W. II 24[6] 琉(or 瑠)
璃 'crystal'. [Tangut] transfer to 67 bis A

79 [Tangut] IX 41 [Tangut] | 'to sit' 4185
(a) III 34 | [Tangut]
W. II 24[8] 38[7] 座, 坐 gdan
"throne, seat". B. 163[4] 172[5]
N.B. In III 34 this character is
written with [Tangut] but this seems
to be an error.

0080 4083 chain

0081 5690 chain

0088 0087 pair

0082 0899 chain

0089 duplicate of [1520]
~~1535 bis — 4664~~

0083 (= 1896
3233A)

0090 v 2464 chain

00844 1253 pair
~~(3233A)~~

0091 v 0097

0092 chains
- 0357
- 1917
- 2672
- 3085
v.1968

0085 ~ 0086

B.175' part of ?.N.

0086 0085 pair

0087 - 0088

80. [Tangut] VI 103 [Tangut] | v. 3186

?

81. [Tangut] gne III 96 [Tangut] | 'emperor, king'

Passim 王 rgyal "king" rājā

82. [Tangut] III 34 [Tangut] | See 79(a)

?

83. [Tangut] VII 71 | [Tangut]

(a) I 20 ditto

?

v. 3233 A

84. [Tangut] II 12 [Tangut] |

(a) I 18 ditto

I. The dissyllable C.C.C. 34^a 奉送 'to receive & escort'

II By itself C.C.C. 34^b 送 "to escort".

85. [Tangut] IX 41 [Tangut] |

(a) VII 112 ditto

?

86. [Tangut] VII 112 See 85.

?

C.C.C. 30^a ? Phonetic 只 chih.

87. [Tangut] V 9. | [Tangut]

(a) IX 41 ditto

?

8

~~88. [Tangut] I 11 [Tangut] Error [Tangut]~~

~~[Tangut] does not otherwise exist, but [Tangut] VIII 82 is defined as "family or clan". Possibly a dissyllable name~~

88. [Tangut] IX 41 See 87

89
~~90.~~ [Tangut] III 103 [Tangut] |

?(a) III 86 ditto

90. [Tangut] VII 10 | [Tangut]

(a) VIII A 5 ditto

91
~~92.~~ [Tangut] X VII 112 [Tangut] |

Possibly VII 59-60

?

92
~~93.~~ [Tangut] VII 59-60

D (a) | [Tangut] III A 123

C (b) [Tangut] | V 99

B (d) [Tangut] | IX A 104 v. 1917

A (c) [Tangut] | VI 56

C.C.C. 9^b 行 a planet

C.C.C. 28^a 巡 to circumambulate

W.I. 118^9 游 to ramble, travel;

136^3 行 to walk; 190^10 hgro to go;

194^5 rgyu to walk, wander

194^12 | [Tangut] 3003 hgro. Idiin P.N. Dramila

0092 A 4485 chain

0093 1183 pair II.1

0094 1076 chain

0095 2514 chain

0096 4221 4232

0097 (0091) # 0107 (0120) pair

0098

0099 3918 chain

0100 5708 chain

0101 5106 ~~0216~~ chain

0102

0103 3974 chain

0104 0786 chain

0105 4326 chain

0106 - 1890

0107 - (0097 pair) chain

0108 - 1543

0109 - 3529

0092A [Tangut] I 136 X of 4485

9

93 ~~94~~. [Tangut] III 85 | [Tangut] 1183

(a) IX 53 ditto

?

94 ~~95~~. [Tangut] III 85 [Tangut] | "gold" 1096

?

95 ~~96~~ [Tangut] III 85 | [Tangut] 'ulcer' 2614

?

96 [Tangut] VII 112 [Tangut] | 4221

(a) I.14 ditto reversed

(b) I.30 [Tangut] | 4232

W.I.192[1] | [Tangut] rtogs.pa 'understanding, knowledge' 2649

II 6[5] 悟 'to apprehend',

97 ~~98~~ [Tangut] VIII 9 [Tangut][Tangut] | 0107

(a) VII 112 [Tangut] | ← 2120 v. 91

?

98 [Tangut] III 139 *

Family or clan name

~~99~~ [Tangut] VIII 44 [Tangut] | disease 3916

A sort of disease.

100 [Tangut] III 38 [Tangut][Tangut] 1099 5694

'to give .. ?

101 ~~102~~ [Tangut] Yu VIII 44 | [Tangut] 0216

W.I.138[12] 油 oil

102 ~~103~~ [Tangut] VIII 44

Family or clan name

B 344[1] 姚 Yao

W.I 27,[16]

103 ~~104~~. [Tangut] IX ~~44~~ 41 [Tangut] | 3974 ~~0103~~

C.C.C. 34[b] [Tangut] | 沁房 .... woman 3379

104 ~~103~~ [Tangut] III 82 [Tangut] | river TE 0786

(a) V 162 ditto

(b) V A 34 dissyllable is X of [Tangut]

I The dissyllable C.C.C. 16[b] 頑羊 "stupid sheep." B.p.100 catalogued under "wild animals."

105 ~~106~~. [Tangut] VI A 7 [Tangut] | man

?

106 ~~107~~ [Tangut] VII 112 | [Tangut] 1890

(a) IX 72 ditto

The dissyl. B.164[5]

107 ~~108~~ [Tangut] × VIII 9 see ~~98~~ 97

Not traced elsewhere, but pretty obviously authentic.

108 ~~109~~ [Tangut] V A 75 [Tangut] |

(a) VII 68 ditto V. 1543

?

109 ~~110~~ [Tangut] I.14 | [Tangut][Tangut] tail, end 3929

(a) III 96 ditto

?

0110 2395 chain

0111 0043 chain

0119 5078 chain

0112 - 0612

0113 - 4074 pair

0120

0121 1992 chain

0114 3587 chain

0115 44838 pair

0122 - 0014 chain

0116 2494 ~~2306~~ chain

0123 - 0032

0117 0148 chain

0124 41264 pair

0118 0752 chain

0125 - 4249 4868

Correct ... Minus 2

10

110. [Tangut] V 98 | [Tangut] male 2530

?

111 ~~112~~. [Tangut] VII 26. [Tangut] | See 43(c) 0043

?

112 ~~113~~. [Tangut] I.14 | [Tangut] 0612
(a) I 85 ditto

?

113 ~~114~~. [Tangut] lai IX 66 [Tangut] | 4074
(a) IX 53 ditto

?

v. 304

114 ~~115~~. [Tangut] lai IX 66 [Tangut] [Tangut]
X means "wine vessel"

115 ~~116~~. [Tangut] III 15 [Tangut] | 4838

?

116 ~~117~~. [Tangut] IX 77 | [Tangut] 2307
C.C.C. 24[a] [Tangut] | 褥子 mattress 3702

117 ~~118~~. [Tangut] II 12 [Tangut] | 0148
(a) VII ~~8~~14 ditto

?

118. [Tangut] rMS I.5 [Tangut] | people, every one. 0752
(a) [Tangut] | II 18 to decide ? 4132
(b) [Tangut] | V 25 . 4448
(c) VI 22 [Tangut] | . 3839
(d) VI 32 [Tangut] | . 5072

(e) VII 34 [Tangut] | . 4676
Passim. A participial suffix comparable to 者 + T. po

119 ~~120~~. [Tangut] X VIII A 40 [Tangut] 5078
A doubtful character, possibly non existent.

120 [Tangut] VII ~~XV~~ 112 | [Tangut] See VII
See 91 Possibly error for 107

121 ~~122~~. [Tangut] I 86 [Tangut] [Tangut] 1992 2462
B. 188[3] q.v. 極 utmost, very
W.I. 218[3] | [Tangut] 4194 bigs. byed "piercing" (name of a Parvatarāja)
cf. [Tangut] "spear" 1175

122 ~~123~~. [Tangut] IX A 51 [Tangut] | confused 0270

?

123 ~~124~~. [Tangut] VI 48 | [Tangut] 0132
(a) VI 93 ditto

?

124 ~~125~~. [Tangut] IV 112 [Tangut] | [Tangut]
(a) IV A 3 ditto See 1264

?

125 ~~126~~. [Tangut] IX 45 | [Tangut] 4692 [Tangut]

?

There is no appreciable difference between 12~~4~~ + ~~126~~ 125

10

0126 'Transfer to 2203

2203 – 0335 – 0334

0332

1167

0132 0128 pair

0134 0148 chain

0133

4762

2643

0127 2575

0128 2482 chain

0129 1130 chain

0135 0148 chain

0130 #2723 pair

0136 3783 chain

0131 #4980 pair

11

126. 𘟙 IX A8 𘟙 | 2243

(a) IX A 66 ditto

(b) V 34 [illegible] | 0332

(c) V. 42. [illegible] | v. 1167

W. I. 108[13], 168[6] II 76[9] 82[4] 墮 "to fall"

with or without [illegible] for "into".

B. p. 252[4] 流 ltan. ba "to fall, shoot"

(of a star.) B 227[2] 拭 to wipe off

127. [illegible] IX 93 | [illegible] 2575

(a) IX 125 ditto, but [illegible]

?

128. [illegible] Râ IX 86 | [illegible] "black" 2482

(a) VI A 60 | [illegible] 3605

W. I. 136[14] B. p. 181 影 "shadow".

129. [illegible] La IX 93 [illegible] | ? 2515

CCC. 8[a] 11[a] B. p. 186 北 W. I. 222[8] by air "north".

130. [illegible] III 44 [illegible] | 2723 [illegible]

(a) IX 131 ditto

?

131 [illegible] III 44 [illegible] | 4980

(a) III 34 ditto [but [illegible]]

?

132. [illegible] VI 93 [illegible] |

(a) ditto VI 48 See 124

134. [illegible] V 2 [illegible] [illegible] "past...." 5159

(a) VII 19 [illegible] | 0499

?

133. [illegible] V 2 | [illegible] 4762

(a) VII 19 ditto

(b) III 82 | [illegible] is x of [illegible] 2643 1694

(N.B. [illegible] is "butterfly"

I The disyllable CCC. 17[a] 老鴟 "old owl"

~~136 [illegible] VII 17 [illegible] |~~

134A [illegible] error for:-

135. [illegible] VII 17 [illegible] | 1940

(ii) The disyllable CCC. 35[6] W. I. 138[2] II 66[3] 72[4] 纏 縛 "to tie, bind".

(i) By itself I. 164[5] 縛 "to bind".

136. [illegible] I. 125 [illegible] | not 6, 3783

(a) I. 21. ditto

W. II 64[4] 無 "non-existence" B. 229[3]

I 178[1] ditto v. 4911 : I 168[11] B 161[5] not having 1871

136A. [illegible] I. 85 | [illegible] 2790

(a) VI 99 ditto, but [illegible] See 0611

? N.B. [illegible] is almost certainly correct.

0137-3388

0143 0422 pair (~~0158~~)

0138 2954 chain

0139 ~~2892~~ 2989 chain

B.230[5]

0144 ~~2013~~ 2635 chain

0145

0140
- 0816-3168
- 3755

0146 2778 chain

0147-0150

0141-0158

0142-3202 chain
(44 entries)

0148
- 0117
- 0149-4415
- 1441-1311
  - 1563-3103
  - 2726-4042-4580-3894
    - 5159
      - 0134-0499
      - 0592-2145
        - 4317
      - 1611-1466
      - 2543-3072
      - 3022
      - 3279
      - 3323
      - 4013
      - 4827-2984
  - 4937-4936
- 1940-0135
  - 2921
- 2848
- 4501-0172-0173-0672
  - 1160
    - 4050

0148
- 0117
- 0149-4415
- 1441-1318
  - 1563-3103
  - 1940-0135
  - 2921
- 0502
- 2251
  - 1440-2557
  - 2295

Minus 2

12

137 ~~138~~. VIII 35 | 3388

(a) I.73 ditto

?

138 III A 54 | pure?

(a) III 179 ditto v.2954

?

139 ~~140~~. La IX A 88 | 2989

(a) I A.54 ditto

(b) 5175 (I.50)

(i) ccc.36b W.I.130[3], 140[18] 惑, 迷 B161[2]

"Moha, Māyā, illusion, delusion

(ii) W.I.196[5] | myos.pa 5126

140. possibly VII A 59-60 145A v.140

(a) | VII A125 3755

(b) IX A 45 | 0816

Nevsky I 270

141 ~~142~~. VI 36 | 0158

(a) III 45 ditto [ ]

?

142 ~~143~~. IX 59 | to transgress

I The trisyllable W.II.64[11] 158[3] 過失

"transgression & error."

3202 chain

~~144 V 44 | 'a drop'~~

~~(a) IX 4 |~~

?

143 ~~144~~ V 44 | 0422

(a) IX 4 ditto

?

N.B. In the Dict. the word is mis-written as 144 in V 44, but the true form appears in IX 4.

144 ~~145~~ V 44 | 'a drop' 3523

?

145 ~~146~~ IX 66

Family or clan name

N.B. Form not absolutely certain. Might be | or even |

146 V 18 | 'turtle' 3309

?

147. VIII 65 | 0150

(a) IX 5 ditto

?

148 VII 14 | 0117

(a) II 12 ditto. See 117

(b) I.87 | 'to tie' 1940

(c) I.144 | 4501

(d) VI 85 | See 1441

(e) VIII 3 | 2846

(f) IX 110 | 0149

(i) ccc.24b | 腰繩 'waist-band'

+B p.103

12

0156 0233 chain

0157 transfer to 3689

3639 - 4951
3332
4176
4443 - 0494
1465
3184

0149 0148 chain

0150 0147 pair

0151 1106 chain
1106
0176 - 4932 - 5112
5250

0152 3430 chain

0153 4153 chain

0154 - 1288

0155 - ? 0604 chain

13

148 (cont.)

(ii) W.II 74[4] | 綪 逸 放 "loose, unrestrained."

The word by itself seems to mean 'cord, belt.'

149 ~~150~~. [Tangut] IX 110 [Tangut] | See 148(b)

(a) IX 73 [Tangut] | 4415

?

150 [Tangut] IX 5 See 148

(a) VIII 65 ditto

?

151 ~~152~~. [Tangut] IX 115 [Tangut] | 'summer'

(a) VII 96 ditto See 1106

(b) VI 108 [Tangut] | 'winter' 0176

CCC 9[b] [Tangut] | 白日 "early dawn".

152 ~~153~~ [Tangut] V 47 | [Tangut] 3430

?

153 ~~154~~. [Tangut] VIII A 22 [Tangut] | 4153

(a) VII A 7 ditto

?

154 ~~155~~ [Tangut] V 2 [Tangut] | [Tangut]

(a) VII 27 ditto See 1288

?

155 ~~156~~ [Tangut] V 47 [Tangut] |

? v. 169 A

156. [Tangut] VI 90 | [Tangut] s.v. 5380

?

157 ~~158~~. [Tangut] V 2 [Tangut] |

(a) VII 7 ditto v. 3639

(b) I.A 12 [Tangut] | 4443

(c) V 8 [Tangut] | 3332

(d) VII A 10 [Tangut] | 4176

CCC 36[a] [Tangut] | 遠離 viviz- to be far removed from: W.I. 90[15], 132[1] (135[11]) 離 to abandon: W.I. 134[2] (avoid B. 232[1], 168[14])

[Tangut] | 分離 "to tear asunder" = (d): 214[6] [Tangut] | ši.ba hdzin "overcoming death" (name of a Nadirājā): 214[12] [Tangut] | dri dral "tearing asunder filth" (ditto): 214[12] [Tangut] | skyon bral bral "tearing asunder guilt (doṣa)": II 66[1] 背 "to turn the back on."

The basic meaning seems to be "apart, away"; hence come two parallel meanings "to go apart" i.e. "to abandon" & "to make apart" i.e. to tear asunder.

(ii) The disyllable W.II 18[5] 分離 "to separate, tear asunder"

13

0158 bis 0143 pair

0158 0141 pair

0163 3918 chain

0159 transfer to 2227

+2227 – 5164 – 1141
  └ 5161
– 0160 – 0542 – 0546
– 3254
– 4346 4927
└ 5509

0165 – 3076

0166 2141 chain

0160 2227 ~~0159~~ chain

0167 | 0168

0161 take over 4083 chain

0168
+3257
└ 0167

0162 – 5420

0169 – 4063

159.

159
~~160~~.

(e)

(f)

(ii) C.C.

(i)

(iii) B.

160

(a)

161
~~162~~.

(a)

162

(a)

B. 229[4]

~~158 bis 𗁅 IX 4 | 𗁆 0143~~ Minus 2

14

158. 𘟂 III 45 See 141. ?
0141.0158 VI 36 III 45

159 ~~160~~. 𗁇 II 4 𗁈 | 2227
(a) IX 95 ditto (d) V 159 | 𗁉
(b) V 31. 𗁊 | 0160 ?
(c) V 60. 𗁋 | 𗁌 cake 3509
(e) ~~(d)~~ VII 89. 𗁍 | persimmon 3254
(f) ~~(e)~~ VIII 16. | 𗁎 4346 ?
(ii) C.C.C. 33a (c) above 油餅 "rich pastry"
~~(ii) By itself W.I. 98[9] 124[10] 134[4]~~
(i) The dissyllable W.I. 98[9] 味 "rasa (sweet) taste"
(iii) By itself W.I. 124[10] 134[4] B.194[2] B.221[5] 味 "rasa taste", one of the 6 senses 170[18] do.

160 𗁊 V 31 See 159(b)
(a) VII A 2 | 𗁏 0542
?

161 ~~162~~. 𗁐 I.1. | 𗁑
(a) VIII 52 ditto
?

162 𗁒 IX 9 𗁓 |
(a) VII 35 ditto
B.229[4] [?]

163 ~~164~~. 𗁔 III 14 𗁕 | 'disease' 3918
?

164 ~~165~~. 𗁖 III 76 𗁗 | 'usnisa'
(a) VI 54 ditto
?

165 ~~166~~. 𗁘 VI 33 | 𗁙 'sin'
(a) VI A 93 ditto.
?

166 ~~167~~ 𗁚 III 76 𗁛 |
(a) VI 56 ditto v.2141
I ~~(i)~~ The dissyllable C.C.C. 20b 21b 脩葢, 脩造 'to repair & build'
II By itself, (i) C.C.C. 30a 醫 W II 8[6] 療 "to cure" (disease)
(ii) W.I. 144[6] 𗁜 | 巖調 "controlling cliffs" (Name of Buddha)

167. 𗁝 VII 25 𗁞 |
Nevski I 269 (?) 'to undress'

168. 𗁞 IX A 130 𗁟 | 3257
(a) IX 37 ditto
(b) See 167
?

169 ~~170~~. 𗁠 IX 109 | 𗁡 family name 4063
?

0174 41397 pair

0170 4226 chain

0175 5190 chain

B.232 離 to leave, apart.

0171 5096 chain

0176 0151 chain

0172 0148 chain

0177 3071 chain

0178 - 4925

0173 0148 chain

0179 4926 chain

15

169 ~~170~~ A [Tangut] ~~N. 36 rki. ? = 159~~ 0259

170 [Tangut] VII A 40 [Tangut] |

(a) IX. 163 ditto

I. The ~~disyllable~~ No. one C.C.C. 31a 淩 [:: 淩] 持 "to grasp profoundly"?

II By itself (i) W. I. 132[14] II 22[12] 害 "to injure"

(ii) [Tangut] | I 134[3,15] 220[3] "to injure & destroy (?)" 134[3]? 切横 cut & harm

171 ~~172~~. [Tangut] IX 26 [Tangut] | [5096]

?

172 ~~173~~ [Tangut] IX 26 [Tangut] | 4501

(a) I. 63 [Tangut] | 4050

(b) IX 40 | [Tangut] 0173

(i). (a) above W. I 90[14] 解脫 "release, salvation moksa, mukti, vimoksa vimukti." II 66[3] I 112[8] 136[13] 140[3]

(ii) By itself I 194[8] t'ar ditto II 122[10] 脫 B. 132[2]

173 ~~174~~ [Tangut] IX 40 See 172 (b)

(a) II 10 [Tangut] | 0672

?

174 ~~175~~ [Tangut] IX 20 [Tangut] |

(a) VIII 94 ditto See 1397

?

175 ~~176~~ [Tangut] VI A 44 | [Tangut] 5190

(i) I 90[4] [Tangut] | 寂滅 "silence calmness & destruction", nirvāna (Name of Buddha)

(ii) I 94[11] [Tangut] | 垢滅 "destroying defilement (Name of Buddha)

I 220[2] sel. ba "to wash away" B. 163[1] 終 to end

I 122[9], 134[13], 136[15], 208[7] II 18[1], 52[6]

A common word, the general meaning seems to be "to destroy, abolish"

176 ~~177~~ [Tangut] VI 108 | [Tangut] See 152 (b)

(a) VIII 43 | [Tangut] 4932

(i) C.C.C. 9a 冬 "winter"

(ii) C.C.C. 25a | [Tangut] 煖帽 "warm hat" lit. "winter hat".

177 ~~178~~ [Tangut] IX 48 | [Tangut] 3071

?

178 [Tangut] V 92 [Tangut] |

(a) V 119 ditto reversed

?

179 ~~180~~ [Tangut] V 152 [Tangut] |

(a) V 159 ditto

?

15

5025
0180 take over
5025-2062
5520

0186
0104
1481

180

0187 5465 chain

0181-2135

181
~~182~~

0188 interpretant?

182
~~183~~

0182 40662 pales

183
~~184~~

0183 5034

0189 3086 chain

184
~~185~~

0184-1812

0190 0424 chain

185
~~186~~

0185-2195

Kinus 2

16

180 [Tangut] III 131 [Tangut] | .. Ne 5025

(a) IX A 99 ditto

(b) VIII 49 | [Tangut]

I The dissyllable W I.226[7] dmod.pa

II 68[8] [Tangut] "to curse"

181 ~~182~~. [Tangut] VI A 65 | [Tangut]

(a) VI 37 ditto

Nevski I 269

182 ~~183~~ [Tangut] III 53 [Tangut] |

(a) III 5 ditto 0662

?

183 ~~184~~. [Tangut] VI 36 | [Tangut] 5034

?

184 ~~185~~ [Tangut] V 65 | [Tangut] 1812

(a) VI 68 ditto

I The dissyllable B.p.100 cat. under ~~186~~ "wild animals"

185 ~~186~~ [Tangut] V 65 | [Tangut] 2195

(a) VI 99 ditto

I The dissyllable B.p.100 cat. under "horse."

(a) VII.82 ditto

186 ~~187~~ [Tangut] V.162 | [Tangut] 0104

(b) V A 34 | [Tangut] x of [Tangut] v.1481

See 104 "a sort of sheep" 0186.0104 1481

187 ~~188~~ [Tangut] IX 119 [Tangut] | "fire" 0972

?

187 ~~189~~A [Tangut] = [Tangut] 0510

~~189. [Tangut] III A 62 [Tangut] |~~

188 [Tangut] ?

W II 78[6] 倒 "to fall" etc. (Soot p.320)

The word is no doubt authentic.

Wang gives the value la.

189 ~~190~~. [Tangut] III A 62 [Tangut] | 4246

?

190 [Tangut] I.61 [Tangut] | 3620

(a) I.31 | [Tangut] 3691

(b) I A.7 | [Tangut] 0307

(c) IV 5 | [Tangut] 3613

(d) V 41 | [Tangut] "younger sister" 3899

(e) VI 24 [Tangut] | female 3377 (1028)

CCC 20[a,b] 34[a] 女 "woman"; as "female" as opposed to "male"

[Tangut] 男 B.124[5] tr. 妃 (imperial) concubine

(f) IX 83 [Tangut] | 0377

0191 #2497 pair

0192 = 4880

0193 3240 chain

0194 ┌ 4745
└ 3537

0195 0252 chain

0196 #3340 p.

0197 2149 chain

0198 1506 chain

0199 – 2284

0200 – 0558

201 怒 anger, wrath I.164[13]

0201 ┌ 0385
└ 0201 1615

The Hsiang. B.216[2] 奮怒 rouse anger

W.J.132[11] 瞋 anger B.X.439

0202 #1589 p.

0203 0053 pair

0204 2412 chain

0205 3086 chain

0206 0752 chain

191
~~192.~~

I.I

192

?

193

?

194

?

195.

B 125

196

C.C.C.

197.

?

198

?

minus 2

17

191 ~~192~~. [Tangut] IX 162 [Tangut] | 2497
(a) VIII 62 ditto ([Tangut])

I. The disyllable C.C.C. 34a
[Tangut] [Tangut] | | : 諸處爲婚
0568.
"all ~~virgins~~ marry"

192 [Tangut] I.11 | [Tangut] [Tangut]
(a) III A 80 ditto [[Tangut]] 4880
?

193 [Tangut] I 27 [Tangut] | back teeth 3240
(a) VII 100 | [Tangut] ? 5608
?

194 [Tangut] V 86 | [Tangut] 4745 [Tangut]
(a) I 29 [Tangut]
(b) IX 145 | [Tangut] 3537
?

195. [Tangut] III A 73 [Tangut] | "terrace" ~~"eminent"~~ 0262
(a) V 99 [Tangut] | 5684
B 125[5] (twin) 126[1] (twin) ? Phon. 126[3] q.v.

196 [Tangut] k'ü V 86 [Tangut] | "1,000" 3340
(127?)
(a) III 128 ditto
C.C.C. 36b 27b W.II 2[6], 4[6] 萬 "10,000"

197. [Tangut] V 93 [Tangut] | sing? 3955 [Tangut]
?

198 [Tangut] IX A 162 [Tangut] | v. 1506
?

199 [Tangut] I 14 | [Tangut] 2284
(a) VI 93 ditto
Nevski I 323 "10,000"

200 [Tangut] III 170 | [Tangut] 0538
(a) III A 134 [[Tangut]]
[Vars. of 0538]
?

201 [Tangut] VI 129 | [Tangut] 0385
(a) V 153 ditto (nil)
(b) VI 115 [Tangut] | (nil) v. 1615
C.C.C. 30a (q.v.) 35b 嗔 W.II. 196[9]
~~anger~~, k'ro.ba "anger, wrath".
W.I 132[4] II 18[5] 瞋 ditto

202. [Tangut] V 48 [Tangut] |
(a) VII 90 ditto v. 1589
? cf. 203

203. [Tangut] IX 103 [Tangut] | 0053
(a) I.A 47 ditto cf. 202
?

204 [Tangut] III 80 [Tangut] | 'statue' v. 1285
?

205. [Tangut] VII 104 | [Tangut] 'to strike' [[Tangut]] v. 1468
(a) V 44 | [Tangut] 5023
?

206. [Tangut] VII 104 [Tangut] | 3996
?

0207 1891 chain

0208 Independent

0209 1846 chain

0210 4208 chain

0211 5685 pair

0212 0211 chain

0213 – 3399

0214
- 5004 – 4397 – {3363, 4864} – 2188
- 5103
- 0212
- 0426
- 2390
- 3378
- 0618 – 0616
- 5107
- 5125

0215 3402 chain

0216 5106 chain

207

208

209

210

211

212

213

minus 2

18

207 [Tangut] III 114 [Tangut] | "a, one" V.1891
(a) IX A 111 | [Tangut] ×(0924) 2965
?

208 [Tangut] ... 256
(i) By itself W II 2[7] ? Nevski I 325
(ii) [Tangut] | W.I. 198[9] ... "to give tranquillity". B. 220[1]

~~209 [Tangut] × VIII 57 | [Tangut]~~

208 A [Tangut] See [Tangut] 0242

209 [Tangut] IX A 60 [Tangut] | 4412
?

210 [Tangut] IX 13 [Tangut] | "bone" 4206
(a) V 10 [Tangut] | "limb" 5688
(b) VII 54 [Tangut] | ? 3697
(c) IX A 18 | [Tangut] q.v. 3873
C.C.C. 19[a,b] 27[a] etc. W I 98[11] 身 I 218[15] lus "body"

211 [Tangut] V 16 [Tangut] | 5685
(a) V 63 ditto
?

212 [Tangut] IX 7 | [Tangut] See 214
?

213 [Tangut] IX 13 | [Tangut] 3399
(a) I 40 ditto
I. The dissyllable C.C.C. 25[b] 米分 "rice-flour, powder".

214. [Tangut] VI A 13 | [Tangut] × 5004
(a) V A 90 ditto
(b) II 9 | [Tangut] × 5107
(c) V 106 | [Tangut] × 3378
(d) VI 7 | [Tangut] 0426
(e) VI 20 [Tangut] | nil 5125
(f) VI 90 | [Tangut] × See 618 (0618)
(g) VIII 97 | [Tangut] (nil) 2390
(h) IX 7 [Tangut] | See 212 0212
C.C.C. 27[b] W I 90[14] 92[9,11] W I 192[6] 224[9]
B. p. 254 etc. etc.
(i) 樂 dgah "joy, pleasure [Soot. p. 438]
(ii) 愛 sred kāma, rāga, tṛṣṇā love, passion, desire
(iii) 喜 mos.pa joyful B 254[4] W II. 156[9]

215 [Tangut] II 1 | [Tangut] "adorned" 3402
?

216 [Tangut] IX A 68 [Tangut] | 5106
(a) IX 101 ditto
(b) I. 97 | [Tangut] 0694
(c) VII A 137 | [Tangut] 5214
(d) VIII 44 [Tangut] | "oil" See 101
I The dissyllable B. p. 99 cak. under sheep
II By itself (i) [Tangut] | W.I. 214[8] sbran. rtsi "honey" 5161

0217 2071 chain

0218 0445 chain

0219 4208 chain

0220 4285 chain

0221 2662 chain

0222 2448 chain

0223 5677 chain

0224 does not exist ~~4996 chain~~ IX

0225 5155 chain

0226 0236 chain

0227 2395 chain

0228 1903 chain

0229-3198

0230 ~~4965 chain~~

0231 0233 chain

0232 1389 ~~0249~~ chain

0233
- 4576-1408
- 0231
- 0371
- 0819
- 3197
- 5278
- 5359
- 5380
  - 0156
  - 1137

B.192³ q.v. (name of a country?)

217. ?

218 ?

219 ?

220 ?

221. ?

222. (a) ?

223 (a) ?

224 (a) ?

225- ?

226. (a) ?

minus 2

19

217. [Tangut] III A88 [Tangut] | 2071
(a) | [Tangut] (III.155) 4941
?

218 [Tangut] V 76 [Tangut] | 6445
(a) VII 80 ditto
?

219 [Tangut] VIII 52 [Tangut] | "measure"? 4942
?

220 [Tangut] VII 64 | [Tangut] 4285
?

221. [Tangut] III 12 | [Tangut] 3612
?

222. [Tangut] VII 30 | [Tangut] "to flow." 3971
(a) VII 12 | [Tangut] See 26
?

223 [Tangut] I.51 | [Tangut] "bright" 1090
(a) III 103 | [Tangut] 5222
?

~~224 [Tangut] V 152 [Tangut] | 4925~~
~~(a) V 159 ditto~~ duplicate of 0179
?

225 [Tangut] IX 80 [Tangut] | "confused" 5155
?

226. [Tangut] VII A 106 [Tangut] | 0236
(a) I 27 ditto
?

227. [Tangut] V.182 " | [Tangut] 'nali' 2530
B125[5] [illegible] 126[1] [illegible] 2? [illegible]

228 [Tangut] VII 80 [Tangut] | v.1903
?

229. [Tangut] IX 30 [Tangut] | 3198
(a) I.128 ditto
?

230 [Tangut] VI A 37 [Tangut] | 4965
(a) VI A 76 ditto
?

231. [Tangut] VI A 19 [Tangut] | See 233.
?

232 [Tangut] II 41 [Tangut] | 4098
?

233. [Tangut] VIII 4 [Tangut] | × 4576
(a) I.14 ditto
(b) III 26 [Tangut] | [Tangut] 0819
(c) III 126 | [Tangut] each ~~"to be born"~~ × 5380
(d) V A 41 | [Tangut] 5278
(e) V A 67 | [Tangut] "pride" See 371 ~~[illegible]~~
(f) VI 13 | [Tangut] 3197
(g) VI 38 | [Tangut] 5259
(h) VI A 19 | [Tangut] See 231

CCC 35[a] 36[a] 37[a] W.I.94[9], 108[5] etc 自 + 己
"self" : I.118[6] | [Tangut] "svabhāva"

19

0234 3948 chain

0242 5030 chain

0235-4085

0243
3697 A chain

0236
0226
3868

0237 4098 chain

0244 2197 chain

0238 5708 chain

0245 2204 chain

0239 4011 chain

0246 1873 chain

0240 5678 chain

0241 40507 pair

0247 2778 chain

234

235

W.I.16

236

237

238

239

240

241

minus 2

20

234 [Tangut] IX A 58 [Tangut] | 0578

?

235 [Tangut] III A 19 | [Tangut] 4085 "who, which?"

(a) VI 25 ditto I'E. 650

W.I. 168 (a) II 28 (b) 30 (d) 34 (c) 44 (a) 78 (b)

I. The Dissyllable (a) 何以故 "why?" (b) 云何 "what means?" (why?) (c) 所以者何 "why?" B 225 如何

II By itself (d) ? W.I. 170 v. 2169

236. [Tangut] I. 27 | [Tangut] See 226

(a) VII A 106 ditto

(b) I. 70 [Tangut] | 3868

?

237. [Tangut] III A 77 [Tangut] | 0668

?

238 [Tangut] VII 44 | [Tangut] ? 3693 有

?

Used as Phonetic

239 [Tangut] I 131 [Tangut] | 4011 "heat"

?

[[Tangut]] 4011 chain

240 [Tangut] V A 21 | [Tangut] 3983 'I'

?

241 [Tangut] IX 17 [Tangut] | 0507 [Tangut]

(a) VII 21 ditto

?

242 [Tangut] II 8 [Tangut] | compassionate 5030

(a) II 18 | [Tangut] 4962

(b) VIII 57 | [Tangut] v. 1947

(i) By itself W I. 112 (172) 悲 (Soot. p. 371)

"karuṇā, kṛpā sympathy, pity":

I 130 哀 "to mourn"; B 272 慈

(ii) [Tangut] (5030) | W II 6 慈悲 "compassion & pity" (20, 42, 70) see above

243. [Tangut] VII 13 [Tangut] | "ten" 2490

(a) IX 38 | [Tangut] 2491

B. p. 93. | is [Tangut] without the [Tangut]

It is the same as [Tangut], [Tangut] & [Tangut] & is a numeral.

W.I. 96 B p. 252 十 "ten" W.I. 204 ben

244 [Tangut] II 40 [Tangut] | 2197

I The dissyllable: ḥe'i. bdag "the lord of death".

245 [Tangut] I 20 [Tangut] | 1293

?

246. [Tangut] I 20 [Tangut] | "to tie"

(a) VI 30 ditto [[Tangut]] v. 1673

?

247 [Tangut] II 19 [Tangut] | 2778

?

0248 ≠3357 pair

0249 ~~1389 chain~~
- 1389
  - 3037
  - 3787
  - 4872
  - 5668
- 4098
  - 0232
  - 0331+
  - 0668 – 0237
  - 4003
  - 5397

0250 ≠1586 pair

0251 – 4144

251 W.I.168[6] ? but cis. 勸 "to admonish, request" II.116[8] B.212[5]

(ii) | 絹勸請 "to request" W II 98[4,12] ditto

0252 4276 chain II

0253 ≠2336 pair I 20

0254 – 2532

0255 4734 chain

0256 2149 chain

0257 4276 chain

0258 transfer to 3875
- 3875
- 0260
- 0318
- 0458
- 1242
  - 0317
  - 3070 – 1243
  - 3429
- ~~3028 – 4581 bis~~
- 3872 – 3028 – 4581 bis
  - 3627

0259
- 0731 – 0964
- 2901
- 0927

0254 0259 0731 chain
- 0731 – 0964
- 2901

248 ~~247~~

(a)

Presu…

249 ~~248~~

W.2.13

250 ~~249~~

B.p.1

251 ~~250~~

Dict.1[a]

252

?

253 ~~252~~

?

254 ~~253~~

(a)

?

N.B.

minus 2

21

248 ~~247~~. [Tangut] II 19 [Tangut] | 3357

(a) V 97 ditto

Presumably a kind of plant

249 ~~248~~ [Tangut] I 105 | [Tangut]

(a) IX 44 ditto Su 1389

(b) IX 153 [Tangut] | 4098

W. I. 132[18] ?

250 ~~249~~ [Tangut] I 105 [Tangut] | [Tangut]

(a) III 32 ditto v. 1586

[Tangut] | B. p. 100 cat. under "wild animals".

2634A [prob. same as 1586.]

251 ~~250~~. [Tangut] I. 83 | [Tangut] to save 4144

(a) V 157 ditto

Dict. 1a 7 1b 4 (ii) disyllable [Tangut] B 161[5] tr. 勸救 "exhort & save" B 174[2]

252 [Tangut] VIII 3 | [Tangut] 5316

(a) V 17 | [Tangut] 4233

?

253 ~~252~~. [Tangut] V 4 [Tangut] | 2336

(a) I 3 ditto

?

254 ~~253~~ [Tangut] V 4 | [Tangut] (earth 2532

(a) I 34 ditto

?

N.B. [Tangut] is sometimes found in error for [Tangut]

255 ~~254~~. [Tangut] V A 123 [Tangut] | 4727

~~C.C.C. 9a 節 (the eight) "division of the year"~~ W I 108[1] II 4[8] 劫

I 194[17] bskal. pa. 'kalpa, aeon'.

~~255~~

256. [Tangut] III 2 | [Tangut] "to make" 2149

? W. II 2[7] 能 to be able to 善 well'

257 ~~256~~ [Tangut] VII 77 | [Tangut] 5570

C.C.C. 20b 21b B. p. 253[4] W. I. 218[16]

或 "if"

258 ~~257~~. [Tangut] VIII 10 [Tangut] | 3875

(a) VIII 19 ditto

(b) V 3 | [Tangut] 0458

(c) VI 29 | [Tangut] 0318

(d) VI 36 [Tangut] | 0260

(e) VI 69 [Tangut] | 5295

(f) VII 108 | [Tangut] Su 1242

(g) VIII A 21 [Tangut] | 3872

I. The disyllable C.C.C. 29b 鬪爭 "to fight, quarrel" with [[Tangut]]

II By itself. W. I. 196[1] ditto?

259 ~~258~~. [Tangut] Ru IX 27 [Tangut] | 0731 (0964)

(a) IX 52 ditto

(b) III 86 [Tangut] | 2901

C.C.C. 13b W. I. 138[11] 竹 "bamboo"

B. 172[3]

0268 – 0278

B.162[4]

268 (B.344[4] 劫 kalpa error for 0423) W.I 266

0260 0258 chain

0261 independent

0262 transfer to
2958
– 2958
– 0195
– 0320 – 5684

B.227[2] 臺 'platform'

0269 3084 chain

0270 ~~0014 chain~~
0014 0822
0122 1915

0263 2377 chain

0264 3446 chain

0271 chain
– 2583 – 1151
– 2911
– 0387 – 0420 – 0327
– 0386
– 3057 – 1958 – 5031
– 0391
– 2926 2935
– 3044
– 4322
– 4906
– 4308 – 1351
– 1430
– 3700 – 3249
– 4601 – 3819 – 3766 – 3619
– 5042
– ?3284 – 1617
– 5657

0255 0284 pair

0256 – 0352

0267 – 0339

0267 bis 0899 chain

260
~~259~~
B 221
261
~~260~~
262
2372
W.I.142
164[15]
263
~~262~~
264
~~263~~
265
~~264~~
0392
0393
266
267
~~266~~
0267 bis

minus 2

22

260 259. [Tangut] VI 36 See 258 (d)

B 221[1]

261 260 [Tangut] VIII 30 Family or clan name.

262. [Tangut] III 174 [Tangut] | 2958

(a) III 42 ditto

(b) II 13 | [Tangut] 0320

(c) III A 73 | [Tangut] ? See 195

2372 W.I.142[9] [Tangut] | 法台 "platform (or terrace) of the Law (Name of Buddha) 164[15] 台 "terrace". B 260[2] 341[3] W I 270[20] 窟 'cave'

263 262 [Tangut] III 126 [Tangut] | 2377

(a) I 26 | [Tangut] ? 2263

?

264 263 [Tangut] III 126 [Tangut] | 3445

?

265 264 [Tangut] VIII 23 [Tangut] |

(a) VI 64 ditto

0392? 0393 268 cf. 269

266 [Tangut] V 87 | [Tangut] 0352

(a) V 21 ditto

?

267 266 [Tangut] V 15 | [Tangut]

(a) V 37 ditto

? moved from

0267 bis [Tangut] IX 41 [Tangut] | 4185 — see 0079

268. [Tangut] VI 64 [Tangut] | [Tangut] 0278

(a) VIII 23 ditto 265 cf. 264 (278)

By itself. CCC. 9[a] 節 (eight) divisions (of the year) 19[a] 節 joints (of the body) W.I.134[2]

269 268. [Tangut] V 144 | [Tangut] 3084

?

270 269. [Tangut] V 34 | [Tangut]

(a) V A 29 ditto v.14

(b) IX A 51 | [Tangut] 0722

W.I.98[13] 亂 confused (thoughts) 120[7] 散 'distracted' 196[17] e.g. 'absence of mind etc.' W.II 70[1]

271 270 [Tangut] ndu III 98 | [Tangut] 'nose'

(a) III 16 ditto v.2585

(b) I 14 [Tangut] | 5657

(c) I 30 | [Tangut] 'hear' 0387

(d) I A 49 | [Tangut] 'deaf' 4601

(e) III 122 | [Tangut] ? 3044

(f) V 160 | [Tangut] ? 5042

(ff) VI 89 2935

(g) V A 47 | [Tangut] ? See 9. 0009

(gg) VI 108 2926

(h) IX 39 | [Tangut] ? 0391

(i) IX 70 | [Tangut] 'hear' 'listen' 4308

CCC. 18[62] 25[a2] W.I.98[5] 218[7] 耳 'ear'

v.1383 A

0272-0274

0279 · 0586 chain

0280 0013 chain

0273
2913—4771

0281 4200 chain

0274 0272 pair

0275 ~~intipendent~~

0282-0538

0276 intependent

take over

0277 0063 chain

0283 3334 chain

~~0265 pair~~ 0284-0265

0278 0268 pair

272

I. Th

"bran

273
~~272~~.

?

274
~~273~~.

"bra

275
~~274~~.

name

276
~~275~~

name

277
~~276~~

(a).

See 63.

meanin

I. The

皆, 悉

"altoge

II By itself

278
~~277~~

(N.B. not a

minus 2

23

272 [Tangut] IA6 [Tangut] |

(a) VI 72 ditto

I. The dissyllable C.C.C. 21ª 鐃鈸

"brass cymbals".

~~272~~ 273 [Tangut] III 96 [Tangut] [Tangut]

(a) I 84 [Tangut] × by | [Tangut] 4771

(b) IX 48 [Tangut] × by | [Tangut] v. 2913

?

~~273~~ 274 [Tangut] VI 72 See 272

"brass cymbals"

~~274~~ 275 [Tangut] III 98 Family or clan name

~~275~~ 276 [Tangut] VII 78 Family or clan name.

~~276~~ 277 [Tangut] III 18 | [Tangut] 0063

(a) IX 14 ditto

See 63. This is one of several words meaning "all".

I. The dissyllable C.C.C. 20ª W.I. 196³ 98¹134⁵

皆, 悉 "all": 198⁷ 220⁵ kun, gyi "altogether".

II By itself, not yet traced.

~~277~~ 278 [Tangut] VIII 23 See 267 268 [Tangut]

(N.B. not a dissyllable)

~~278~~ 279 [Tangut] III 98 [Tangut] [Tangut] (sic)

(a) I.16 [Tangut] × by [Tangut] |

Some kind of vegetable

~~279~~ 280 [Tangut] VII 76 [Tangut] [Tangut] 'to live' 0013

See 13; possibly a 2-root verb.

~~280~~ [Tangut]

~~280~~ 281 [Tangut] III 27 | [Tangut] 3813

?

N.B. Written 攵: 文 is probably right.

~~281~~ 282 [Tangut] III 27 [Tangut] | 6538

(a) IX 25 ditto

By itself C.C.C. 28ᵇ 群牧

"Herdsman" (Name of a shrine)

~~282~~ 283 [Tangut] [Tangut] IX 108 | [Tangut]

(a) III A 125 ditto reversed

(b) V 65 | [Tangut] "secret" 4120

C.C.C. 11ª B. 185 南 W.I. 220¹⁶ Cho

South

~~283~~ 284 [Tangut] VI 64 | [Tangut] See 265

(a) VIII 23 ditto

By itself.

W.I. 134³ 裂 "to crack, split"

0285 1690 chain

0286-4045

0827-0511

287 Φ(i) | 殺羅剎 Rākṣasa W.I.170[10]

0288 4469 pair

0289 4276 chain

0290 0518 chain

0291-0988

0292 5708 chain

0293-0889

0294 3663 chain

294 | 'Sea of characters' (Title of dictionary.

0295 2652 chain

~~W.I.138~~

0296 5375 chain

0297 4889 chain

286
~~283.~~

Possi

286
~~284.~~

287
~~285.~~

I 222[14]

A ve

288
~~286.~~

289
~~288.~~

290
~~289~~

I. The

k'ams

II. By

I 206[17]

291.

(a)

minus 2

24

285 ~~283~~. [Tangut] VIII A 76 [Tangut] | 2756

Possibly a kind of grain.

286 ~~285~~. [Tangut] III 96 | [Tangut] 4045

(a) III 175 ditto

287 ~~286~~. [Tangut] IX 20 | [Tangut] 0511

(a) V 111 ditto

I 222[14] 170[10] W.I 266[5] (proper name)

A very common Phonetic

288 ~~286~~. [Tangut] I 80 [Tangut] | "to display"

(a) IX 80 ditto v. 1469

289 ~~288~~. [Tangut] V 100 [Tangut] [Tangut]

(a) VIII 20 [Tangut] 0397

290 ~~289~~. [Tangut] V 41 [Tangut] | 0518

(a) IX 79 ditto

I. The dissyllable 世 界 loka "the (finite) world" hjig. rten. kyi k'ams B. 249

II. By itself C. 35[b] W.I. 96[8] II 2[5] 界 B. 196[3]

I 206[17] mi. mjed "world" S.-H. dhātu

291. [Tangut] V 100 | [Tangut] 0988

(a) VI 23 ditto

?

292. [Tangut] V A 109 | [Tangut] 2158

Nevski I 278

293. [Tangut] V 98 | [Tangut] 0889

(a) IX 81 ditto

?

294. [Tangut] VIII 68 | [Tangut] 3663

(a) III 136 ditto

I. The dissyllable. CCC 27[a] 文 字 "written character"

II By itself CCC. 19[b] 文 "literature"

W.I. 124[14] 典 "canon." [0470 / 1002]

295. [Tangut] VII 41 | [Tangut]

(a) VIII 53 [Tangut] | "break" v. 2064

I. The dissyllable W.I. 96[11] 138[5] wrong "4"

296 [Tangut] VII 39 [Tangut] [Tangut] 5375 1975

The X at CCC 15[a] is translated 鹽 "salt"

W.I. 132[13] 池 "lake" ~~pond~~

297 [Tangut] I 27 | [Tangut] v. 1590

?

0298-1641

0304-1775 [2684 VIII
[5583 [3970
[4247

B.134[1]

0299 1313 chain

0305 independent

B224[3] φ v.5039

0306-0515

0300 3685 chain

0301 [0470
[1005]

0307 0424 chain

0308 0322 chain

0309 independent

0310 4326 chain

0302 independent

0303 4011 chain

0312-1001

298

299.

I

cata

3.00.

301.

(a)

(b)

I Th

"a co

II (b)

"a can

302.

nam

303.

c.c.c. 28[4]

受

受用

WI.19

奉持

B.165[5]

minus 2

25

298 [Tangut] VII 75 | [Tangut]
(a) VI 80 ditto v.1641

299. [Tangut] VII 42 [Tangut] | v.1867
I The dissyllable B.103 catalogued under "men's clothing"

300. [Tangut] VII 21 | [Tangut] "name" 2438

301. [Tangut] III 35 | [Tangut] 0470
(a) VI 23 ditto
(b) VI 53 | [Tangut]
I The dissyllable C.C.C. 23a 梳 "a comb"
II (b) above C.C.C. 23a 檠子 "a stand for bending a bow"

302. [Tangut] II 1 Family or clan name. 之 + [Tangut]

303. [Tangut] VIII A 35 [Tangut] | 3760
C.C.C. 28b W.I. 108b 190[3] etc.
受 "to receive": C.C.C. 36a [Tangut] |
受用 "received for use":
W.I. 190[3] | [Tangut] zuins "receive"
奉持 "to receive & grasp": W.II 4[7]
B. 163[5]

304 [Tangut] [IX 524]
(a) VIII 63 [Tangut] | v.1775
[(b) VII A 134 [Tangut] | X of [Tangut] 542]
: W.I. 138[9]: B 347[3] 亡 to lose, forget

305 [Tangut] VI 68 Family or clan name 之 + [Tangut] B.177[4] P.N. 孫

306. [Tangut] V 81 | [Tangut]
(a) V 19 ditto [[Tangut]]
?

307 [Tangut] I A 7 [Tangut] | "woman" 0190
= 190 (b) :

308. [Tangut] III A 5 [Tangut] [Tangut] "eye"
Nevski I 282 to protrude in anger

309 [Tangut] V.154 "Man's name"

310 [Tangut] VI 103 [Tangut] [Tangut] "musical instrument" 0485
C.C.C. 32b S.424 [Tangut]
C.C.C. 32b | [Tangut] is translated 拍板 "to strike a plank".
Probably a musical instrument of some kind.

312 [Tangut] VI A 104 [Tangut] |
(a) VI 19 ditto See 1001
?
311 See over

311 B.346[5] 塞 Spir. Monastic in P.N.

0311 2519 chain

0313 – 3176

0314 0322 chain

0316 2149 chain

W.I.134[8] q.v.

316 (ii) | [Tangut] 鬥戰 'to fight' W.I.154[13]

諍訟 II 108[3]

0317 0258 chain

0315 – 1391

0318 0258 chain

0319 independent

0320 0262 chain

B.246[1] 壇 altar

0321 2519 chain

0322

- 4174
- 0314
- 0480
- 0308
- 0664-0663
- 1675
- 3387-5207
- 3074
- 3484
- 3642
- 3643
- 3645-3045
- 3646
- 4890
- 4943
- 5196
- 5216
- 5322-5321
- 5325
- 5009

311
~~312~~

I T

清

II By

CCC.13

"lotu

ts'ain

313. [Tangut]

(a) I

?

314. [Tangut]

?

316. [Tangut]

W.I.134[8]

317
~~316~~ [Tangut]

? Nevsk

315. [Tangut]

(a) I

?

318. [Tangut]

?

26

311 ~~312~~. [Tangut] VI 66 [Tangut] | 2519
(a) V 42 ditto
(b) I 20 [Tangut] | silence ~~[illegible]~~ 2075
(c) V 103 | [Tangut] 0321
I The dissyllable W.I.100³ 116³
清淨 "pure" v. 2519
II By itself W.I.94⁹ etc 淨 "pure": ?
CCC.13⁶ [Tangut] | W.I.214¹¹ 蓮花 pad.ma "lotus": W.I.190⁴ 208¹¹ etc | [Tangut]
ts'ans.pa "pure":

313. [Tangut] VI 122 | [Tangut] (misspelt)
(a) III 46 ditto 3176
?

314. [Tangut] V 136 [Tangut] | "eye"
?

316. [Tangut] VIII 10 | [Tangut] "to make"
W.I.134⁸ ? war
317 ~~316~~ [Tangut] IX 64 | [Tangut] "enemy" See 1242
? Nevski I 224 "[illegible]"

315. [Tangut] V 99 [Tangut] |
(a) V 4 ditto See 1381
?

318. [Tangut] VI 29 [Tangut] |
? See 258(c)

319. [Tangut] VI 66 Family or clan name [Tangut] + [Tangut]

320. [Tangut] II 13 [Tangut] | "platform ÷ 262(b) W.I.194¹³ dkyil.hk'or "circle (of earth)"

321. [Tangut] V 103 [Tangut] | "pure" 311
See 311(c)

322. [Tangut] I 57 [Tangut] | "eye" 4174
(a) V A 36 ditto
(b) I.17 | [Tangut] "see" ×(3045) 3645
(c) I.73 | [Tangut] "eye-brow" ×(5207) 3387
(d) I 81 | [Tangut] ? 5216
(e) I 98 | [Tangut] "to look" 3643
(f) I A 89 | [Tangut] "blind" ×(5321) 5322
(g) II 32 | [Tangut] "mist" 0480
(h) III 122 | [Tangut] ? 3646
(i) III 147 | [Tangut] ? 5325
(j) III A 5 | [Tangut] × of [Tangut] 0308
(k) V 33 | [Tangut] ? v.1675
(l) V 132 | [Tangut] low rich × of [Tangut] 3484
(m) V 136 | [Tangut] ? 0314
(n) V A 6 | [Tangut] ? 3642
(o) VI 134 | [Tangut] ~~[illegible]~~ 3074 4890
(p) VIII 51 | [Tangut] "eye-lashes" × of [Tangut]
(q) IX 132 [Tangut] | ? See 664
(pp) VIII A 93 | [Tangut] misspelt

0330 vis 2147 chain

0327 0271 chain

0328 4326 chain

0323 1781 chain

0329 take over 3700A chain

0324 independent

[0330 independent]

0325 independent

0331 0249 chain

0326 independent

0332 0126 chain

0333 1528 pairs

minus 2

322 (cont)

(r) IX 154 | 缾 5196

(s) IX 169 | 衣 4943 ?

C.C.C. 14[a] 眼 (18[b]) W I 98[2] 124[11] "pupil of eye": C.C.C. 18[a] 目 W.I.192[15] mig "eye"

This word seems to be "pupil", 𘂋 being "eye". It is significant that 𘂋 appears in more compound characters.

323. 𘟀 V 110 | 𘟁 v.1689 ~~[illegible]~~

I ~~C.C.C. 7~~ The disyllable C.C.C. 7[b] 陽 [illegible] "the sun's rays"?

324. 𘟂 VIII 69 "Family or clan name"

325 𘟃 VIII 69 "Name of country" X

[(a) VIII A 93 | [illegible] (~~possibly~~ certainly an error for 𘟃.)]

? B.174[3]

326 𘟄 VIII 69 Family or clan name.

B. p. 93. "𘟂 and after it 𘟄: a Chinese family or clan name An 安: also used ~~with the proper significance of the word~~ as a Phonetic (?) 安 "(?) ~~in peace~~". B.186[1]

0330 bis 𘟅 IX 42 | [illegible] 2147

27

B.186[1] used as a proper name "Emperor An of the E. Tsin Dynasty".

327. 𘟆 I. A 9 [illegible]

[illegible] is "to hear" & also a common phonetic for M.I. [illegible] is a [illegible] "phonetic". The word is ~~possibly a phonetic~~ Min

328. 𘟇 VII. 41 [illegible] | "man" 4964

(a) III 19 3709

?

329. 𘟈 IX 114 [illegible] | 3700 A [illegible]

(a) VIII. 2 | [illegible] v.2960

?

330. 𘟉 probably error for 0338

Found only in III A 133 [illegible] | X of [illegible] a phonetic group

331. 𘟊 IX 42 | [illegible] 4098

[~~(a) III 56 | [illegible] v. 2147~~]

? See 1318

332 𘟋 V 34 | [illegible] "to fall" 1266(b) 0126

~~W II 8? 畢 "complete"~~

333. 𘟌 V A 125 [illegible] | [illegible]

(a) V A 127 ditto v.1528

Probably a Phonetic like [illegible].

0335 2179 ~~1992~~ chain

0336 0126 chain

336 中 | 龍 綏. 耆闍崛

Gṛdhrakūṭa W.II 2[4] B.199[3]

0337 [illegible]

0338 2231 chain

0339 0267 pair

B.1173[5]

0340 -2269

0341-4008

341 衣 "clothing" W.I.102[3] II 84[9]

(ii) | 㼝 衣服 "clothing" W.II 96[7]

0342 1305 chain

0343 -0415

0344 2306 chain

0345
- 0348
- 0347-4820
- 0349
- 1071
- 3521

0346 ~~0??~~ 0259 chain

0347 0345 chain

334.

A p

335.

"An

336.

?

Frequ

cf. 334

337.

name

338.

(a)

(b)

(c

I The

目眼 "

339.

(a) I

340.

(a) I

341

(a) II

W.I. 98[12]

Sos "clo

minus 2

28

334. 𗎭 K'YAU V A130 𗎮 𗎯 0336 2203

A phonetic.

335. 𗎰 𗎱 K'an K-V A124 [illegible] 𗎲

"An Indian word" i.e. Phonetic

336. 𗎳 V 29 𗎴 | 2203
(a) V A130 0334

? cf. 126

Frequently used as a Phonetic

cf. 334.

337. 𗎵 V 3 Family or clan name. [illegible] + 𗎵

338. 𗎶 I.130 𗎷 | 2331
(a) III 59 | 𗎸 2233
(b) V A7 | 𗎹 2232
(c) v. 0330 w

II The dissyllable I.196[6] II 18[7] 睡眼 "to sleep"

339. 𗎺 V 37 𗎻 |
(a) V 15 ditto See 267.

340. 𗎼 III 1 𗎽 | 2269
(a) VI 132 ditto

By itself W.I.98[9] 肥 "fat"

341 𗎾 IX A146 𗎿 | 0250
(a) III 15 ditto

W.I.98[12] B.103 W.II 18[8] 24[9] 服 W.I.224[16] gos "clothing". cf. 343

342. 𗏀 I.135 [illegible] | "brocade"

Nevsky I 300 "[illegible]" See 1315

343. 𗏁 I.27 | 𗏂 0415
(a) IX A155 ditto

I. The dissyllable CCC.24[b] 褐衫 "serge shirt"

344. 𗏃 VII 36 𗏄 | v.1598

?

345. 𗏅 VI 36 𗏆 | 0348
(a) VI 25 ditto
(b) II 2 | 𗏇 3521
(c) II 15 | 𗏈 1071
(d) VI A103 | 𗏉 1145 X of 𗏊 0349
(e) VIII 89 | 𗏋 See 347

?

(d) is a "phonetic rendering"; See 349

346 𗏌 VI 36 𗏍 0417 | "wood"

~~Presumably a kind of tree.~~

I The dissyllable CCC.24[a] 櫃子 "wardrobe, box"

347. 𗏎 VIII 89 𗏏 | 0345
(a) II 12 | 𗏐 4820

W.I.90[13] 96[2] 110[17] II 8[1] etc. 藏 "Treasury, basket, pitaka". A frequent element in names of Buddhas B179[4] etc.

0348 0345 chain

0349 0345 chain

0350 independent

0351 independent

0352 0266 chain

0353-3440

0354 v. 3654 sub-chain

0355 0582 chain

B.191[5] tr. 正

0356-4509

0357 0092 chain

0358 0598 chain

0359 2193 chain

0359A 2441 pair

0360-2123 A

348.

349.

A

350

A

351

cla

352.

(a

353.

(a

?

354

?

355

(a

(

(Ⅸ

A1)

(ⅨA116

(Ⅸ

(1) By its

etc 真 I

real"

29

348. [Tangut] VI 25 [Tangut] |

(a) VI 36 ditto See 345

349. [Tangut] VI A 103 [Tangut] [Tangut]

A phonetic character

350 [Tangut] VII A 75 [Tangut] |

A name. B.177¹ part of P.N.

351 [Tangut] IX A 165 Family or clan name Nevski I 313 (Chinese)

352. [Tangut] V 21 [Tangut] |

(a) V 87 ditto See 266.

353. [Tangut] VIII 28 [Tangut] |

(a) V 168 ditto

?

354 [Tangut] VIII 28 [Tangut] | 3797

?

355 [Tangut] VIII 28 [Tangut] | 0679 [Tangut]

(a) IX A. 98 [Tangut] | See ×1292

(b) [Tangut] (2342) | is X of [Tangut] (V 39) [Tangut] (I 112)

[Tangut] (V A 80) [Tangut] (V A 81) [Tangut] (VII A 1) [Tangut] (VIII A 3) [Tangut] (VIII A 17) [Tangut] (VIII A 32) (1894) [Tangut] (VIII A 36) [Tangut] (IX A 116) [Tangut] (IX A 117) [Tangut] (IX A 133) [Tangut] (IX A 141) [Tangut] (IX 103)

(i) By itself. W.I.96⁴ C.C.C. 17ᵇ II 52¹ etc [Chinese ×2] I.222¹⁸ dai.pa etc "true, real"

(ii) (b) = 眞言 "true word, i.e. mantra, mystical sound". It is to be noted that nearly all these characters contain [Tangut] or [Tangut], i.e. parts of [Tangut] "sound".

356. [Tangut] VIII 28 [Tangut] |

(a) III 176 ditto

I. The dissyllable B.101 cat. under "wild animals".

357. [Tangut] VI 56 | [Tangut] See 92 (c)

I. The dissyllable W.I. 220⁷ rgya.ba "to wander, move about"

358 [Tangut] VIII 20 | [Tangut]

(a) I.11 ditto

?

359. [Tangut] VII 30 | [Tangut] 2253

(a) III 57 [Tangut] | See 1267

?

359A [Tangut] X of [Tangut] | I.1. 3604, poss 2441

A doubtful form; probably incorrect

360 [Tangut] VII 30 [Tangut] | 2123A

?

29

0361 0809 chain 言 真 = (ii) 0368 error for 330 bis

0369 imperfect

0362 – 3590

0370 5690 chain

0363 5106 chain

0371 0233 chain

0364
├3817 – 5592
└1039 [0771]

| (“great Rep”) W. I, 269[15] 玄奘 0372 5623 chain

(the monk) Shyuan Jvang.

0373 2710 chain

0365 – 3182 pair Double family name 0374 1085 pair

0366 1501 chain

0375 3226 chain

0367 2531 chain 0376 1128 chain

361.
?
362
(a
?
363
?
364
(a
(b
I. The
"shall
II By i
"deep
N.B. Al
phoneti
365.
clan n
disyllab
366.
W.II 94"
367
B 211[2] 遇

minus 2

30

361. [Tangut] VIII 6 [Tangut] | 2843

~~(a) III 36 [Tangut] | –~~

?

362 [Tangut] V 99 [Tangut] |

(a) V 4 ditto (probably: written [Tangut])

?

(cf. 364)

363 [Tangut] VII A 74 [Tangut] | 5106

?

364 [Tangut] III 1 [Tangut] | 3817

(a) III 164 ditto

(b) ~~? See 362 (a)~~ III 36 [Tangut] | 1039

I. The dissyllable C.C.C. 12[6] 淺 深 "shallow & deep".

II By itself I 94[14] 深 B.255 zab.mo "deep", W.II 2[5] B.193[5]

N.B. Also frequently used as a phonetic NAn. e.g. B.179[4]

365. [Tangut] IX 9 | [Tangut] "Family or clan name" [VI 33]. Clearly a dissyllabic name: [Tangut] + [Tangut]

366. [Tangut] I 89 | [Tangut] 3268 + 2518

W.II 94" 蒙 "to receive (from above), deceive"

367 [Tangut] III 97 [Tangut] | 2531

B 211[2] 遇 to meet 212[4] cf. 69

368 [Tangut] IX 42 | [Tangut]

?

369. [Tangut] IV 1 "Family or clan name" [Tangut] + [Tangut]

370. [Tangut] IX 104 [Tangut] |

?

~~370 A [Tangut] Error for 330~~

371 [Tangut] V A 67 [Tangut] | "self"

W.I 132" II 68[12] 慢 "pride, arrogance"

B.187[3]

372. [Tangut] I 132 | [Tangut] 5623

(a) I.A 95 [Tangut] | ? 4658

(b) V 84 [Tangut] | ? 2713

?

373 [Tangut] I 79 | [Tangut] foot 5440

(a) I 94 [Tangut] | ? 4036

?

374 [Tangut] IX 49 | [Tangut] "to see" 1085

(a) IX 109 ditto

?

375 [Tangut] V 109 [Tangut] | 0577

?

376 [Tangut] III A 67 [Tangut] | 5646

0377 0424 chain

0378 1357 chain

0379 = 5044

0380 0070 part

0381 – 2903

0382 important

0383 0809 chain

377.

?

378

?

379

?

380.

~~See 7~~

~~381.~~

381.

?

382

country

382. A

383.

(a)

(b)

[(c)

(d)

(e)

(f)

minus 2

31

377. [Tangut] IX 83. | [Tangut] 0190 "woman"

?

378 [Tangut] VI 30 | [Tangut]

(a) VI 73 ditto See 1357

?

379 [Tangut] VI 30 | [Tangut] 5044

(a) VI 18 ditto

?

380. [Tangut] II 15 [Tangut] | 70

~~See 70~~ (a) VII 35 ditto

~~381.~~ See 70

381. [Tangut] IX 74 | [Tangut] 2903

(a) II 37 ditto

?

382 [Tangut] I A 8 Name of country. A common phonetic

382A [Tangut] Error for 265

383. [Tangut] III 134 [Tangut] | 0809

(a) I. 89 [Tangut] | v. 1911

(b) V 4 [Tangut] | 2852

[(c) V 95 [Tangut] | × of [Tangut]]

(d) V 134 | [Tangut] 4870

(e) VI 84 [Tangut] | 3704

(f) VI 136 [Tangut] | 3457

(g) VII 7 [Tangut] | × {0361 0442} 2843

(h) VII 88 [Tangut] | 0675

[(i) VII 105 [Tangut] | × of [Tangut]] 2274

(j) VIII 57 [Tangut] | 2225

(k) VIII 58 [Tangut] | 3923

(l) IX 1 [Tangut] | 3969

(m) IX 49 [Tangut] | 5479

(n) IX 151 [Tangut] | "leek" × v. 1942

This is the word for "vegetables" in general, as opposed e.g. to "fruit" W. I. 134[18], 138[11] 菜 & is the origin of [Tangut], the common determinative for vegetable names. It is frequently found as the second member of dissyllabic compounds (i) the main dissyllable C.C.C. 14b 菜蔬 "vegetarian food."

(ii) (a) C.C.C. 14b 菠薐 "spinach" + ..

(iii) (c) C.C.C. 15a [Tangut] [Tangut] | 半春菜 "half spring vegetable" 1110

(iv) (e) C.C.C. 14b 芥菜 "mustard"

(v) (f) C.C.C. 14b 茄子 "egg-plant"

(vi) (i) C.C.C. 15a [Tangut] [Tangut] | 馬齒菜 "horse's teeth vegetable"

0190

0388 – 0399

0389 2167 chain

0390 – [1148]

0384 – 1731

0391 0271 chain

0385 0201 chin

0392 4082 6 pair

0386 0271 chin

0393 2658 chain

0387 0271 chain

φ(i) | [Tangut] B.223' 彌勒 Maitreya

394 φ(i) | [Tangut] 摩訶薩

Mahāsattva W II 4[6] etc.

0394
+4180
L3251

φ(ii) B.224[5] Mahākāśyapa

φ(iii) B.225[2] Mahāprajāpati

φ(iv) B 230[5] Mahāya...?

383 (

(vii)

(viii)

vegeta

(ix)

"tun

(x)

error

(xi)

kinds of

384.

(a)

?

385.

See 20

386

compoun

387.

(b

(c

ccc. 31[6]

in vent

·minal

B 45[7]

minus 2

32

383 (contd)

(vii) (k) C.C.C. 14b 茵蔯

(viii) (m) C.C.C. 14b 香菜 "fragrant vegetable"

(ix) (n) C.C.C. 14b 蔓菁菜 "turnip"

(x) C.C.C. 14b 菁 | [possibly an error for (h). 薄荷 "small lotus?"

(xi) C.C.C. 14b 䉷 | 百菜 "all kinds of vegetables"

384. 𗹙 III 134 𗹙 |

(a) VI 104 ditto v.173

?

385. 𗹙 V 153 𗹙 | "anger"

(a) VI 129 ditto

See 201

386 𗹙 I.A 81 Phonetic compound 𗹙 𗹙

387. 𗹙 I 30 𗹙 | "ear" 0271

(b) I.15 𗹙 | "to hear" 0420

(c) III 65 𗹙 | 3057

C.C.C. 31b W.I. 108[5] 聞 "to hear" in sentences in which the pronominal subject comes first.

B 245[7] B.188[5] B 211[2]

I A 9 0327

I A 81 0386

When a pronominal subject follows the verb, the form used seems to be 𗹙. B 237

Also used as a phonetic, see ~~388~~ e.g. 386.

388. 𗹙 I 40 | 𗹙

(a) III 134 ditto

?

389. 𗹙 V 107 𗹙 | 3118

?

390. 𗹙 V 107 𗹙 | [1148]

(a) V 162 ditto

?

391 𗹙 IX 39 𗹙 | "ear" 0271

?

392 𗹙 IX 107 𗹙 | 0826

(a) IX 161 ditto ?

393. 𗹙 V 108 | 𗹙 2658

?

394 𗹙 I 78 | 𗹙 4180

(a) I 130 ditto

(b) VII 89 | 𗹙 3251

C.C.C. 21b 塗 "mud" B.216[4]

32

0395
3223 chain

0396-3406

0403 0518 chain

0404-3402 chain

0397 4276 chain

0405 interpretant

0398 - 2434

0406 4431

0399 0388 pair

0407 3577

0400 3346

0408 interpretant

0401 interpretant

0409 -3572

0402 -3383

0410 3628 chain

395.
?
396
I. The
397
?
398.
(a)
?
399
(a)
?
400
(a)
?
401
clan
402.
(a)
(i) W.I.130[2]
202[3]
pāla:
(ii)

minus 2

33

395. [Tangut] VI 121 | [Tangut] 3223
?
396 [Tangut] VII 10 | [Tangut] 3406
(a) VIII 59 ditto
I. The dissyllable C.C.C. 25b 火回 火旨

397 [Tangut] VIII 20 [Tangut] | 0289
? See 289
398. [Tangut] III 134 [Tangut] | 2434
(a) IX 1 ditto
?
399 [Tangut] III 134 [Tangut] | 0388
(a) I 40 ditto
?
400 [Tangut] IX A 4 [Tangut] |
(a) III A 46 ditto
?
401 [Tangut] V 106 Family or clan name. [Tangut] + [Tangut]
402. [Tangut] γwe VIII 33 [Tangut] | 3383
(a) VII A 71 ditto
(i) W.I. 130[2] 護 I 192[9], 214[3] etc. srun 202[8] skyob. "to protect, protector, pāla:' B.122[4] 守 'to protect.'
(ii) [Tangut] | C.24b B.903 (cat. under

'clothing) 汗衫 "sweat-shirt", 'sweater' lit. 'sweat protector'.
N.B. Not to be confused with 406.
403. [Tangut] VI 7 [Tangut] | "family"
?
404. [Tangut] IV 5 ~~VI 9~~ [Tangut] | glorious 3402
?
405. [Tangut] VIII 11 'Family or clan name.' [Tangut] + [Tangut]
406. [Tangut] III 83 [Tangut] | 4401
(a) III 176 ditto (Contrast 402.
Passim 若, 或. "If", Sometimes |....| is practically "either...or".
407. [Tangut] I 74 | [Tangut] 3577
(a) I 43 ditto
?
408 [Tangut] IX 94 'Family or clan name.' [Tangut] + [Tangut]
409. [Tangut] IX 105 | [Tangut] 3752
(a) IX A 109 ditto
?
410. [Tangut] IX 111 | [Tangut] ? 3628
?

0411 – 0632

0412 3259 chain

0413 2149 chain

0414 independent

0415 0343 pair

0416 independent

416. B.246³ 夷 I (part of name) (a)

0417 3655 chain

| [Tangut] B.215³ 秘密 secret

0418 – 0634

0419 4775 chain

0420 0271 chain

0421 2381 chain

0422 – 0143 pair

0423 3241

0424
- 3608
- 1111
- 1924 – 0537 [= 0577A] – 5476 – 1580
  - 3389
- 3620 – 0190
  - 0377
  - 0307
  - 3379 – 1028
  - 3613
  - 3691
  - 3899 – 1434

0425 3771 chain

? [Tangut] W.II 150 ? 攞 to collect, gather together ? own fr 3918

0426 0214 chain

411. [Tangut]

?

412. [Tangut]

?

413. [Tangut]

至 W. II

The ch…

sound]

414. [Tangut]

nam…

415. [Tangut]

(a) I …

See 3432 …

416. [Tangut]

nam…

417. [Tangut]

C.C.C. 29⁶

g-sai

418 [Tangut]

(a)

?

419. [Tangut]

Probabl…

minus 2

34

411. [Tangut] III 40 [Tangut] | 0632

(a) IX 79 ditto

?

412. [Tangut] I 77 | [Tangut] 3259

?

413. [Tangut] V 51 [Tangut] | "clothing" 3550

W. II 18^8 46^{12} 著 "to put on, wear"

The character is [Tangut] "clothing" [same sound] turned into a verb by [Tangut]

414. [Tangut] V 4 "Family or clan name." [Tangut] + [Tangut]

415. [Tangut] IX A 155 [Tangut] |

(a) I 27 ditto

See 343. "Shirt".

416. [Tangut] VIII 7 "Family or clan name." [Tangut] + [Tangut]

417. [Tangut] III A 47 [Tangut] | (a) VI 125 ditto

CCC. 27^b W. II 6^7 密 II 20^5 秘 I 206^4

gsan "secret, esoteric". B 125^4

418 [Tangut] VI 100 | [Tangut] 0634

(a) VII 25 ditto

?

419. [Tangut] IX 57 [Tangut] | "bird" 2657

Probably some kind of bird.

420 [Tangut] I 15 | [Tangut] "hear" 0387

See 387. W. II 2^4 44^7 聞, 聽 "to hear." | [Tangut] "I have heard"

0387 [Tangut] "hear" + 0271 [Tangut] "ear"

421. [Tangut] III 42 [Tangut] | 2381

?

422. [Tangut] IX 4 | [Tangut] 0143

(a) V 44 ditto

? 0143 See 105.

423. [Tangut] [VII 59-60]

(a) IX 98 | [Tangut] 3241

(i) CCC. 34^b 齒 "back teeth" q. 3240

(ii) B. 99 [Tangut] | cat. under "cattle"

424. [Tangut] II 30 | [Tangut]

(a) II 4 ditto

(b) I A 29 | [Tangut] maternal uncle 3620

(c) III 148 | [Tangut] See 1111

(d) VI 8 [Tangut] | v. 1924

CCC. 31^a W. II. 34^7 父 "father"

B. 124^4

425. [Tangut] III 137 [Tangut] 4718

?

426 [Tangut] VI 7 [Tangut] | 0214

?

N.B. There is no discoverable difference between 425 & 426 but 425 might be [Tangut] or [Tangut]

0427 3323 chain

0428 4773 chain

0429 2445 chain

0430 5690 chain

0431 3086 chain

0432 1222 chain

0433 – 1888

0434 [0032, 4525]

0435 independent

0436 – 3946

0437 independent

0437A 3191 pair

0438 2138 pair

0439 0460 chain

0440 0680 chain

B.224[4]
440(ii) W.I.130[8] 眷屬 "family, relations"

0441 1128 chain

427.

?

428

? found

429

?

430

(a)

(b)

W.I.96

"to sa

431

?

432.

?

433

(a)

?

434.

(a)

(b)

?

435

clan

minus 2

35

427. [Tangut] IX 4 [Tangut] | 38100
?
Phon. v. 5701

428 [Tangut] V 12 | [Tangut] 2968
? fourth son Nevski I 293

429 [Tangut] VII A 84 [Tangut] | 2445
?

430 [Tangut] gen V. 49 [Tangut] | 5690
(a) III 3 [Tangut] | 4192 ?
(b) III 70 [Tangut] | 3544 ?
W.I. 96[13] 98[6] 語 224[13] dag: II 26[7] 言
"to say, speak" B. 160[2] 176[1] 201[4] 232[1]

431 [Tangut] VI 100 [Tangut] | [i.e. [Tangut]]
?

432. [Tangut] IX 173 | [Tangut] to disrespect v. 1886
~~(a) V 117 [Tangut] |~~
?

433 [Tangut] IX 4 [Tangut] | v. 1888
(a) V 117 ditto
?

434. [Tangut] V 19 [Tangut] | 10032
(a) VI 94 ditto
(b) V A 105 | [Tangut] 4525 ?
?

435 [Tangut] VII A 82. Family or clan name.

436 [Tangut] VII A 65 | [Tangut]
(a) VII A 64 ditto
Nevski I 293

437. [Tangut] VIII A 10. Family or clan name.

437A [Tangut] X of I. 22 [Tangut] |
Not otherwise located. Possibly incorrect. v. 1205

438 [Tangut] IX 173 [on torn page]
(a) IX 39 [Tangut] | 2133
?

439 [Tangut] III A 63 [Tangut] | v. 2244
(i) The disyllable B. 99 cat. under "sheep".

440. [Tangut] II 4 | [Tangut] 0680
(a) VII 43 ditto
(i) W.I. 144[4] 友 214[10] bées "friend"
(ii) The disyllable W.I. 100[5] where meaning is not quite clear 164[15] 朋友 "friend"

441. [Tangut] VI 67 [Tangut] |
(a) V. 5 ditto
(i) The disyllable C.S.C. 21[a] W.I. 96[1] 112[11] 138[8] II 22[8] 46[4] 供養 "to make offerings of food".

0442
0809 chain?

0443–1214

0444
4434
0504
1533

0445
0218
2788

0446 2928 chain

0447 0680 chain

0448 0045 pair

0449 0627 chain

0450 1891 chain

0451 2167 chain

0452 2231 chain

442.
of t
of t
like
but
which
443.
(
?
444
(
(
(
?
(c) is
445.
(a)
(b)
c.c.c.
446
(a)
(b)
?

minus 1

36

442. [Tangut] VII 27 [Tangut] | "Name of family or clan" (I.22). In spite of the wrong position this looks like a double name, the characters being [Tangut] + [Tangut] (same group); but there is also a word [Tangut] 2843 ("India") which might be the X here. B185[6] 竺

443. [Tangut] V 7 [Tangut] |
(a) IX 68 ditto see 1214
?

444 [Tangut] II 17 | [Tangut] 4434
(a) VI 32 ditto
(b) III 52 [Tangut] | v. 1533
(c) II A 28 | [Tangut] X of [Tangut] 0504
?
(c) is possibly a phonetic.

445. [Tangut] VII 80 | [Tangut] 0218
(a) V 76 ditto see 218
(b) III 74 | [Tangut] [[Tangut]]
C.C.C. 20[b] 祇 "(earth) spirits"

446 [Tangut] IX 173 | [Tangut] 2928
(a) V. 171 | [Tangut] x(4492) 4591
(b) VIII A. 73 [Tangut] | 4907
?

447. [Tangut] IX 4 [Tangut] |
C.C.C. 29[b] W.I. 98[13], 100[14] II 2[6] 34[9], 48[9] etc.
A common postposition meaning "in, with, at", corresponding to Chinese 與, but sometimes is not represented in the Chinese original.
| [Tangut] W.I 269" tr. 合順

448. [Tangut] I. 5 [Tangut] |
(a) III 28 ditto
?

449. [Tangut] V 22 | [Tangut] 4230
?

450. [Tangut] VII 40 | [Tangut] 3876
?

451. [Tangut] VIII 34 [Tangut] | 5069
?

452. [Tangut] IX 4 [Tangut] |
(a) VIII A. 16 ditto v. 2231
?

0453 -4950

0462-2333

0454 4276 chain

0463 5461 chain (4561)

0455 3446 chain

0456 1650 chain

0464 -3727
+3727
+0487
L4432-1970-4460

0457
+1127-4987-4989
L2394

B. 204[2] 希 to hope for

0458 0258 chain

0465 5461 chain

0459-3318

0466 3587 chain

0460
+2422
L2244-0439

0467 4276 (chain)

0468 5461 chain

0468 interpinent

0469 5461 chain

453

?

454.

elder

Nevs

455.

?

456

?

457.

(a)

(b)

B122[5]

W.I.138

458.

?

459.

(a)

?

460.

(a)

(b)

The Hsixll

B.99 ca

461.

clan na

minus 1

37

453 [Tangut] V 3 | [Tangut] 4950
(a) IX 76 ditto
?

454. [Tangut] II 31 [Tangut] [Tangut] "an elder sister" 1838
Nevski I 297

455. [Tangut] VII A 72 [Tangut] | 3446
?

456 [Tangut] V 104 | [Tangut]
?

457. [Tangut] V 26 [Tangut] | 1127
(a) II 23 ditto
(b) IX 72 [Tangut] | 12394
B 122[5]
W.I. 138[2] 領 "to receive", Dict 56[a] 5

458. [Tangut] V 3 [Tangut] | "to fight."
? See 258 (b)

459. [Tangut] V 3 | [Tangut]
(a) III 81 ditto
?

460. [Tangut] V 109 | [Tangut] 2422
(a) VII 62 ditto
(b) III 107 | [Tangut] 2244
The Disyllable
B. 99 cat. under "sheep" cf. 439.

461. [Tangut] VIII 70 Family or clan name. [Tangut] + [Tangut]

462 [Tangut] II 31 | [Tangut]
(a) I 37 ditto
~~ditto~~

463. [Tangut] VII A 77 [Tangut] | 4561
(a) VII A 130 | [Tangut] [?] x of [Tangut]
(b) VII A 132 | [Tangut] x of [Tangut]
C.C.C. 25[a] [Tangut] | 月完 劍
bracket.
(a) & (b) are phonetic groups.

464 [Tangut] VIII A 30 [Tangut] |
(a) VII 52 ditto
(b) VIII 89 [Tangut] | vehicle 0487
(c) IX 74 v. 471A
C.C.C. 22[b] [Tangut] | 運土
"the wheel of ~~revolving~~ earth"

465. [Tangut] VII A 130 [Tangut] [Tangut] 0463
Phonetic character

466 [Tangut] III 59 [Tangut] | 5131
? cf. 469

467 [Tangut] I 34 | 亦 "also"
?

468 [Tangut] VII A 132 [Tangut] [Tangut]
Phonetic character

469 [Tangut] III 67 [Tangut] | 5131
? cf. 466

37

0470 0301 chain

0471 – 4575

0471A = 0464

0472 4615 chain

0473 4651 chain

0474 – 0957

0475 4619 chain

0476
1024
4792

0477 4657 chain

0478 – 0536

0479 + 0535

0480 0322 chain

0481 2149 chain

0482 3893 chain

0483 3226 chain

0484 2149 chain

0485 4326 "chain"

470.

471.

?

471A

? (do

472

?

473

C.C.C. 6

474

?

475

?

476

(a)

(b)

?

minus 1

38

470. [Tangut] VI 23 [Tangut] | 0301
(a) III 35 ditto
See 301 "comb" (as dissyllable)

471. [Tangut] I.130 [Tangut] | 4575
(a) IX 115 ditto
?

471A [Tangut] IX 74 X of [Tangut] |
? (doubtful if authentic).

472 [Tangut] V A 99 [Tangut] | 4615
?

473 [Tangut] VI 24 [Tangut] | "earth" 4651
(a) | [Tangut] 1124
CCC. 6a 神 "spirit": [Tangut] |
食 | "food spirit": [Tangut] |
祿 | "prosperity spirit".

474 [Tangut] VIII 31 | [Tangut]
(a) VI 21 ditto See 957
?

475 [Tangut] VII 33 [Tangut] | dawn 4619
?

476 [Tangut] IX.151 | [Tangut]
(a) VI 24 ditto See 1024
(b) III 37 [Tangut] | 4792
?

477. [Tangut] I.16 [Tangut] | "earth" 4651
?
N.B. W. I.198[10] Phonetic B-

478 [Tangut] I.16 | [Tangut] 0536
(a) I.29 ditto
?
cf. 479

479 [Tangut] I.16 | [Tangut] 0535
(a) I.29 ditto cf. 478
(i) the dissyllable ([Tangut] W. I.116[8]) "floss-silk, cotton wool."

480. [Tangut] II 32 [Tangut] | "eye" 0322
W. II 10[4] [Tangut] "mist".

481. [Tangut] VIII 20 [Tangut] |
W. I.98[5] The dissyllable 謳唱 song

482 [Tangut] VI 56 | [Tangut] 2423
(i) The dissyllable W. I.138[2]
(ii) CCC. 28a | [Tangut]
御史 Censor

483. [Tangut] V 94 [Tangut] | 0577
?

484 [Tangut] V A 96 | [Tangut] "to make"
?

485 [Tangut] VI 10 | [Tangut] 4326
(a) VI 103 | [Tangut] X of [Tangut] 0810
(i) The dissyllable CCC. 33a 樂人

0486 1140 chain

0487 0464 chain

0488 – 5156

0486 – 5168

0490 independent

0491 4148 chain

0492 ~~4515 2 chain~~
5152 – 4660 – 1503

0493 5017 chain

0494 0157 chain

0495 2285 chain

0496 4550 chain

0497 – 3740

0498 3226 chain

0499 0148 chain

0500 1369 chain

485

music

樂

486

?

487

W.I. 11

B.187[2]

488

(a

(i) CCC. 216[3]

B.215[3]

489

(a)

?

490

name

491

?

492

(a)

?

music |

39

485 (cont)

musician? : (ii) by itself. CCC. 32a

樂 "music" W.II 26³ I 98⁵ ditto

486. [Tangut] III 166 | [Tangut] 1140

(a) III A 18 ditto See 1140

?

487 [Tangut] VIII 89 | [Tangut] "wheel" 464

W.I. 112¹⁹ II 6⁵ 78⁶ 乘 vehicle yāna

B.187²

488 [Tangut] IX A 152 | [Tangut] [? error for]

(a) VIII 28 | [Tangut] 5156

(i) CCC. 22b [Tangut] | 和 [Tangut] Nevskii I 289 "to mix"

216³

B.215³ 治 govern etc (possibly causative)

489. [Tangut] VII 83 [Tangut] |

(a) VII A 63. ditto (reversed)

?

490 [Tangut] V A 78 Family or clan name B.163⁴

491 [Tangut] III 166 [Tangut] | foot 4148

?

4148 chain foot

492 [Tangut] IX A. 90 [Tangut] | 5440 (? error)

(a) VII 55 | [Tangut] 5152

?

493 [Tangut] I A 72 [Tangut] |

?

494 [Tangut] VI A 11 | [Tangut] 4443

?

495 [Tangut] V.18 V18 [Tangut] | 2285

?

496. [Tangut] III 19 [Tangut] | 4550

?

497 [Tangut] III 22 | [Tangut] 3740

(a) I 95 ditto

?

498 [Tangut] III 46 [Tangut] [Tangut]

(a) V 23 [Tangut] | 3850

CCC. 30a [Tangut] | 大人

An enclitic or particle

W.II 130^5,9 ?

499 [Tangut] VII 19 [Tangut] | 0134

(a) V 2 [Tangut] | x of [Tangut] 0134

(b) VII 20 [Tangut] | 0502

(c) VIII 64 | [Tangut] x 2251

?

500 [Tangut] V 102 [Tangut] |

?

39

0501 1884 pair

0509 4889 chain

0502 0148 chain

0510 - 1979

0503 4011 chain

0511 0287 pair

0504 0444 chain

0512 independent

0505 2482 chain

0513 ? 4529 chain

0506 5623 chain

0514 - 0753

0507 - 0241

0515 0306 pair

0508 independent

0516 independent probably

minus 1

* 40

501. [Tangut] V A 94 [Tangut] | "Name of country". Presumably a double name. N.B. No distinguishable diff[ce] from 500. (v. 1884)

502. [Tangut] VII 20 | [Tangut] 0499

?

503. [Tangut] IX 82 [Tangut] | "head" (4011)

(a) IX 131 | [Tangut] "throat" "neck" See 1318

C.C.C. 18[b] 項 (nape of) neck: W. I. 136[6,18]

鑠 : W. I. 216[18] mgrin

"throat": I 170[5] 咽 "throat" ? (4011 chain)

504 [Tangut] II A 28 [Tangut] [Tangut]

Phonetic character?

505 [Tangut] V. 151 [Tangut] | black 2482

?

506. [Tangut] II 15 | [Tangut] See 1144

?

507 [Tangut] VII 21 | [Tangut]

(a) IX 17 ditto

? ~~See~~ See 241

508 [Tangut] VI 26 "Name of family or clan". B 175[3]

~~508 A [Tangut] I. 80 × of [Tangut] | 2994~~

~~Doubtful form, obviously incorrect to some degree.~~ Error for 5477 [Tangut]

509. [Tangut] I. A 101 | [Tangut] 4274 × 5532

(a) I. 86 [Tangut] | |

W. I 212[12] rbod. gtoṅ "utterly renouncing".

510. [Tangut] I. 11 | [Tangut]?

(a) IX 5 ditto v. 1979

? [Tangut] [Var] v. 0187A

511. [Tangut] V 111 [Tangut] | 0287

(a) IX 20 ditto

?

512. [Tangut] IX 6 "Family or clan name". [Tangut] + [Tangut]

513. [Tangut] · VII A 24 [Tangut] | 4529

?

514 [Tangut] III 135 | [Tangut] 07530

(a) III A 75 ditto

(i) The disyllable zum. pa "fear"?

515 [Tangut] V 19 [Tangut] | 0336

(a) V 81 ditto

? Distinguish from 514. See 306

516 [Tangut] (VII 59-60)

C.C.C. 35[a] 七. W. I 220[10] bdun. pa "seven"

0517 4878 pair [0524] – [1098]

0525
0528
0530

0518
0290
0403

| 𗁬 passim 世尊 lokajyestha

'world honoured' 0526 – 1370

518 (ii) | 𗁬 hjig-rten-gyi k'ams

"the external world" B. 249² 0527 – 1066

(iii) | 𗁬 世尊 Lokajyestha

Lokanātha Epithet of Buddha W II 76⁴

[0519] interpolated 0528 0525 chain

0520 – 1502

0521 – 2902

0522 – 3979

0529 0586 chain

0523 [5116] chain

0530 0525 chain

517.
518
519
520
521
522
523

minus 1

41

517. [Tangut] V 54 [Tangut] | cf. VIII 35
[Tangut] "Name of family or clan. Possibly a double name, but the order is curious. CCC 23ᵃ 沙 'sand'. ? See 946 q.v.

518 [Tangut] IX 79 | [Tangut] 0290
(a) V 41 ditto
(b) VI 7 | [Tangut] 0403
(i) By itself, CCC 27ᵃ 31ᵇ 35ᵃ etc. 世 "family, generation (Tib. rus) loka 'world'
(ii) ~~The disyllable~~ [Tangut] 世界 "the finite world" B.249. See 290.

519 [Tangut] IX 107 "Family or clan name.

520 [Tangut] IX 107) 反 |
(a) I. 116 ditto v. 1502
?

521 [Tangut] IX 107 [Tangut] | 2902
(a) I. 121 ditto ?

522 [Tangut] IX 107 [Tangut] |
(a) I. 91 ditto
?

523. [Tangut] VIII A 59 | [Tangut] 4102
?

524. [Tangut] VII 5 | [Tangut]
(a) V 140 ditto See 1098
?

525. [Tangut] I. 19 | [Tangut]
(a) I 16 ditto
(b) IX 72 | [Tangut] 530
B. 99 [Tangut] | cat. under "cattle". 1795

526. [Tangut] I. 19 [Tangut] |
(a) I. 13 ditto See 1370
?

527 [Tangut] IX 52 [Tangut] |
(a) I. 42 ditto reversed See 1066
B. 99 (a) cat. under "cattle".

528 [Tangut] I 16 [Tangut] |
(a) I. 19 ditto cf. 525.
~~ex~~ B. 99 Cat. under "cattle" in several combinations:—
(i) | [Tangut] 581
(ii) | [Tangut] 530
(iii) | [Tangut] 1702 (See 0586)

529 [Tangut] I. 16 [Tangut] [Tangut] 0277
(a) II 36 | [Tangut]
Presumably a vegetable

530 [Tangut] IX 72 [Tangut] | 1838
B. 99 [Tangut] | cat. under "cattle" cf. 528

0531 – [1188] | VII 5 | 524 0539 2812 chain

0540 3086 chain

0532 – 5273 | I.19 | 525

0541 4276 chain

0533 0731 chain

W.I.78' 希 rare, seldom

B.233[5]

0534 – 3064 | IX 52 | 527

528

0535 0479 pair

0542 0159 chain

0536 0478 pair

0537 0424 chain 529 0543 independent

0538 0282 pair

0282

5681 – 1156

1814

0544 4868 chain

530

(4681?)

531.

532

(i) c.c.

(ii) The

533.

534.

535.

536

537.

538

minus |

42

531. [Tangut] I.19 | [Tangut]

(a) VIII 84 ditto See 1188

?

532 [Tangut] mau I 98 [Tangut] |

(a) VIII A 42 ditto

(i) C.C.C. 16^a | [Tangut] 猫兒 "cat"

(ii) The dissyllable B.100 cat. under "wild animals".

533. [Tangut] I.29 [Tangut] | 3729

?

534. [Tangut] IX 79 [Tangut] |

(a) VII 27 ditto

(i) The dissyllable B.99 cat. under 'horse'

535. [Tangut] I.29 [Tangut] | 0479

(a) I.16 ditto

"floss-silk" See 479 cf. 536

536 [Tangut] I.29 [Tangut] | 0478

(a) I.16 ditto

? See 478 cf. 535

537. [Tangut] IX 25 | [Tangut] v 1924 [Tangut]

? (a) I.114 [Tangut] |

? v. 577A

538 [Tangut] IX.25 | [Tangut] "herdsman"

(a) III 27 ditto

? See 282

539 [Tangut] IX 25 [Tangut] | 2812

?

540 [Tangut] IX 179 | [Tangut] 2449

(i) | [Tangut] W.I.192^5 ñe.gnag "intensely black": (ii) The dissyllable W II 44^12 略 summarily (iii) II 50'' (doubtful) Dict 1^a6

541. [Tangut] IX 159 | [Tangut] 4276

(a) VI A 23 ditto

(b) VII 67 | [Tangut] 2238

(i) W.I.94^12 [Tangut]

(ii) C.C.C. 18^a | [Tangut] 小人 "the small man": W.I.136^3 微 "small, minute": I 192^18 cun zad.pa ditto: I 218^9 ñe [dkar] "intensely [white]"

II 12^10, 26'', 46^3

542. [Tangut] VII A 2 [Tangut] | 0160

(a) VII A 134 | [Tangut] x of [Tangut] Phon. 546

?

(a) is no doubt a phonetic group

543. [Tangut] VIII 35 "Name of country": B.185^5 煌 Huang

544 [Tangut] III 117 | [Tangut] 4868

(a) III 37 ditto

(b) VI 31 | [Tangut] 0739

0553 ~~interpretation~~

0554 0545 pair

0545 = 0554

0555 - 1277

0546 0154 chain

0556 - 4767

0547 - [1134]

0557 - 4768

0548 - 1125

0558 ~~0199~~ 0200 chain

0549 ≠ 5413 pair

0550 independent

0559 - 4369

0551 - 1320

0560 0504 chain

0552 independent

544.

545

546.

547.

548

549.

550.

551.

552.

minus 1

43

544. (cont.)

(i) W.I.98² 黄 192¹² ser "yellow".

(ii) I 192⁴, 194⁵, 226³ [Tangut] | ser. skya (1273)

"white + yellow" i.e. Lamas + laymen.

545 [Tangut] VII 31 [Tangut] | 1277

(a) III A 81 ditto

? See 554

546. [Tangut] VII A 134 [Tangut][Tangut]

Phonetic character. B.125⁴

547. [Tangut] IX 25 [Tangut][Tangut] |

(a) IX 12 ditto

? cf. 548

548 [Tangut] IX 25 [Tangut] |

(a) IX 12 ditto

? cf. 547

549. [Tangut] V 121 [Tangut] |

(a) III A 59 ditto

?

550. [Tangut] VI 75 × by itself | |

W.I.134⁴?

551. [Tangut] IX 121 | [Tangut] 1320

(a) IX A 97

?

552. [Tangut] VI A 59 × by itself | |

? B.175⁴ part of P.N.

553. [Tangut] I.8 × by itself | |

?

554 [Tangut] III A 81 | [Tangut]

(a) VII 31 ditto

? See 545

555 [Tangut] III 22 | [Tangut]

(a) II 22 ditto See 1277

?

556 [Tangut] III 17 | [Tangut]

(a) IX 146 ditto

? cf. 557

557 [Tangut] III 17 | [Tangut][Tangut]

(a) IX 146 ditto v. 4768

(i) The disyllable C.C.C.17² 鵪鶉 + "quail" cf. 556

558 [Tangut] III A 134 [Tangut] |

(a) III 170 [Tangut] |

? [Nos. at 0200.] cf. 200

N.B. The base of both characters probably is [Tangut]

559. [Tangut] IX 4 [Tangut] |

(a) IX 17 ditto noticed

?

560 [Tangut] V 18 [Tangut] |

?

0561 1406 chain

0567 2461 chain

0562 2193 chain

0568 interpreter

W.I.134[14] 藿

0565 0685 chain

0569–0643

0563
+5144 – 4284 q.v.
L1980

0570 3918 chain

W.II.128[9] 賣不 "is it real or not?"

0571–1375

0571A 2180 chain

0573 4080 chain

0564–4695

0566 0073 chain

561

?

562

W.I.1

spell

565
~~564~~

W.I.16

423)

grudgi

563
~~564~~

(a)

(b)

B.89

the op

B221[2]

W.I.114[10]

192[8]

"through

B.249[4]

(ii)

"truth"

564

(a) III

~~566~~ ?

566

(a)

minus 1

44

561 [Tangut] V 89 | [Tangut] v.1406
?
562. [Tangut] V A 24 [Tangut] | 2193
W. I 132[12] 134[14] 呪 196[17]? dhāraṇī
spell, curse.
565 ~~564~~ [Tangut] IX 121 [Tangut] | 0685
W. I. 168[9] 慳 II 68[12] 80[9] 惜 (Sovt. p. 423) matsara, lobha, avaricious, grudging.
563 ~~564~~ [Tangut] Xir IX A 76 [Tangut] | ? 5144
(a) IX 90 ditto
(b) VII 82 | [Tangut] truth 1980
B. 89 [Tangut] above [Tangut] below. | is [Tangut], the opposite of [Tangut]? 4284
B 221[2]
W. I, 114[10] 實 real, true, honest, sincere 192[8] rab "excellent" 192[10] rab.tu "thoroughly" 208[16] nges.pa "truly"
B. 131[2]
B. 249[4] yan. dag. pa "truth"
(ii) | [Tangut] (i.e. (b) above) bden.pa "truth" W. I. 208[10]
564. [Tangut] III A 82 [Tangut] | 4695
(a) III. 60 ditto
~~566~~ ?
566 [Tangut] VIII 30 [Tangut] |
(a) VII A 81 ditto
See 73.

567. [Tangut] III 143 [Tangut] | v.1927
?
568 [Tangut] IX 79 × by self | |
Passim eg. CCC. 20[b] 30[a] 32[a] 34[a,b] 諸 "all":
Reduplicated | | [Tangut] (CCC. 34[a]
諸處爲婚 "all . . . marry" See 191.
569. [Tangut] III 63 | [Tangut]
(a) IX. 20 ditto See 643
(i) The disyllable CCC. 26[b] 碡石[Tangut] "green jasper"
570. [Tangut] VIII A 55 [Tangut] |
(a) V 143 | [Tangut] v.1621
?
571. [Tangut] V 133 [Tangut] |
(a) V. 128 ditto See 1375
?
571A [Tangut] VI 4 X of [Tangut] | See (574)
etc X
572. See overleaf
573. [Tangut] VI 54 | [Tangut] 4080
(a) III A 68 ditto
(i) The disyllable CCC. 34[a] 長大 ~~"old~~ "senior & great" (ii) [Tangut] | W. I. 125[13]
盛長 "great senior (iii) W. I. 192[15]
B. 130[1] 197[2]
[Tangut] | hp'ags skyes.po "holy & venerable man 增長 ditto W. II. 90[9] 122[5]
4080 chain

0572 -3115 W.I.134⁴ looks like 'at'

0574 2180 pair

0575 0895 pair

[0577A 0424 chain

0578 2285 chain

0576 3929 chain 578 [Tangut] | 臥具 'bedding'

W.II 96⁷ 132⁵

0577 3226 chain

0579 1283 chain

0582 = {0595 / 0596A}

0679-0355-1292-3105 / 4201 / 0947 — -3692- : 0800, 1566-5594, 1512, 1716, 2305-0842, 2323, 2551, 4866, 5658, 5689-3609

0580 -3559

0581 1650 chain

581 *[Tangut] | v. 2885

n [Tangut] | B 246⁷ 馬老 means simply 'the horse'

0582 [0596A / 0595] 0679-0355-1292-3105 / 4201 / 0947

582(ii) 勤策 ? ditto W.II 142¹²

572.

573

574 [Tangut]

(a)

575 [Tangut]

(a)

576 [Tangut]

577 [Tangut]

"A par

(a) III

(b) III

(c) III

(d) III

(e) III

(f) III

(g) V

(h) V

(i) V

(j) V

(k) V

minus |

572. [Tangut] I.A31 | [Tangut] 2115

(a) I A60 ditto

C.C.C. 1b3 B175' tr. 崇 崇 high, noble

573 See preceding page.

574 [Tangut] V132 [Tangut] | 2180

(a) Probably VI 4 ditto See 571A

?

575 [Tangut] V 132 | [Tangut]

(a) V 12 ditto

?

576 [Tangut] V132 | [Tangut]

?

577 [Tangut] NA III 121 [Tangut] [Tangut]

"A particle" (aa) I 76 5454 (v below)

(a) III 7 | [Tangut] (1780) × (4389) 4760

(b) III.31 | [Tangut] v.1654

(c) III 33 | [Tangut] v.1791

(d) III 75 | [Tangut] (4340) × 108

(e) III 118 [Tangut] × by | [Tangut] 3758 v.1415

(f) III 175 | [Tangut] 4041

(g) V 49 | [Tangut] 4978

(h) V 94 | [Tangut] 0483

(i) V 109 | [Tangut] 0375 ~~0577~~

(j) V 126 | [Tangut] ? × (2111) 1953

(k) V 169 [Tangut] × by | [Tangut] 2061 4340

5454
45

(l) I 76 | [Tangut] (misspelt)

(ll) V A95 | [Tangut] × (0966) 2212

(m) IX 106 | [Tangut] 4293

C.C.C. 7b W I.134[4] II 66[7] 80[9].

Meaning not quite clear

q.v. B.172' tr. 更安 'more established'

577A [Tangut] × of I.114 [Tangut]

Probably inaccurate for 537

578 [Tangut] IX 77 [Tangut] | 3948

(a) IX A 58 [[Tangut]] See 0234

?

579 [Tangut] VIII 17 | [Tangut] See 1283

?

Used as a Phonetic

580 [Tangut] VI A 28 [Tangut] | misspelt 3559 ~~4390~~

(a) III 144 ditto reversed

?

581 [Tangut] II 36 | [Tangut] v.1650

(a) III A11 [[Tangut]] ditto

(i) B.99 [Tangut] | cat. under cattle 528

An affix to names of animals

582 [Tangut] × of VII 110 [Tangut] | v.595 : VII 59-60

(ii) [Tangut] | W. I 120' 140[3] II 6[4] 精進

"Virya valour, fortitude" [Soot. p. 427]

(i) (iii) By itself I 108[8] 168[10] 精 essence, spirit B. 215[3]

0583
- 3780
- 0584 – 0926 – 2982
- 2156

0588 [illegible]

0589 0078 [illegible]

0590 0078 [illegible]

0584 0583 chain

0591 [illegible] chain

0585 3346 chain

[illegible] B.121' 報身 sambhogakāya

0592 0148 chain

592 (ii) The dissyllable W.II.2[9] bya.ba' perform

巳畢 "already completed" B 200'

0586
0529 – 0279

0587 4722 chain

0593 2482 chain

583. [illegible]
(aa)
(a)

Corresp

meaning

(i) W II 10
(ii) II 2
(iii) B.24

yod.pa.

B196' 有

584 [illegible]

(a) VI

(i) C.C.C.19

(ii) W.I.132

W.I.134[16]

585 [illegible]

(i) C 37[a] W.

pense, re

(ii) W.II.60

586 [illegible]

(a) I.

(b) III

Presuma

587 [illegible]

(a) VII

?

minus |

(b) IX 75 [Tangut] | 2156

46

583. [Tangut] dus III 141 | [Tangut] 3780
(aa) IX 24 ditto
(a) VI 117 | [Tangut] see 584

Corresponds to Ch. 有 with double meaning of same word

(i) W II 10⁷ 22⁶ "there is" [ends sentence]

(ii) II 2⁹ 26⁸ "have" or existence

(iii) B. 248 reduplicated || =

yod.pa.de.la "whatever there are.

B.196¹ 有 having

584 [Tangut] VI 117 [Tangut] | see 583.

(a) VI 114 | [Tangut] 0926

(i) C.C.C. 19ᵇ 生 to be born W II 22¹²

(ii) W. I. 132¹¹ 起 to raise, start, begin

W. I. 134¹⁶

585 [Tangut] VI 55 [Tangut] | 3346

(i) C 37ᵃ W. I. 110¹, 134⁴, II 44¹¹, 72³ 報 "recompense, retribution, punishment". B.197³ (verb)

(ii) W. II. 60¹¹ 果 "fruit"

586 [Tangut] II 35 [Tangut] |

(a) I. 16 | [Tangut] × of [Tangut]

(b) III 98 [Tangut] | × of [Tangut]

Presumably a vegetable.

587 [Tangut] ? VII A 143 [Tangut] | to have

(a) VII 40 ditto

?

588 [Tangut] III 97 "Family or clan name."

589 [Tangut] VIII 4 [Tangut] [Tangut] [Tangut]

~~"red net jade"~~ "a garland of red jade."

590 [Tangut] VIII 9 | [Tangut] stone 601

(a) III 58 [Tangut] | crystal 5157

(b) VIII 4 see 589

(i) C.C.C. 4ᵇ 13ᵇ 玉 jade B.168²

(ii) (a) above B.102 cat. under "jewels"

B 181² 瑠璃 ~~"crystals"~~ q.v. 79

591 [Tangut] VII 8 [Tangut] | 2150

(a) IX 32 ditto

?

~~592 [Tangut] IX 17 | [Tangut]~~

592 [Tangut] III 113 [Tangut] | 5159

W. II 44¹² [Tangut] ~~"to transact, carry out"~~ distinguish S-H. 451 discriminate

(a) IX 91 [Tangut] | v. 2145

(b) IX 92 [Tangut] | 4317

593 [Tangut] VII 103 [Tangut] | rock

cf. 594

0594 2482 chain

0598
0358
4601

0599
0633
0600
3722

[0595 = 0582 chain]

0600 0599 chain

[0596 = 0670 3795 chain]

0601 0078 chain

0602 – 0644

[0596A = 0582 chain]

0603 – 0645

0597 3001 chain

594

595

596.

596A.

597

minus 1 minus 3

47

594 䉕 IX 1 [illegible] | mountain 2801
(a) I 24 [illegible] | 4211
(b) III 96 [illegible] | v. 1948
(c) VI 101 | [illegible] v. 1933
(d) VII 6 | [illegible] 2215
(e) VII 103 | [illegible] See 593.
(i) (c) above | 山羊 "mountain sheep"
C.16[b] B.101 cat. under wild animals.
(ii) W.I.218[3] | [illegible] crag "rock."
The general meaning is "rock."

595 [illegible] (VII 59-60)
? Error for 582

596 [illegible] error for 670 B 230[1] sic
(a) V 3 | [illegible] "ocean" v. 2221
(b) IX 66 | [illegible]
(i) (a) above B.102[2] cat. heading "rivers & seas."
(ii) | [illegible] B 102. cat. under "rivers & seas" – "river water"

596A. [illegible] VIII 62 X of [illegible] 0947
?

597 [illegible] III 90 [illegible] | 2983
?

597A [illegible] error for [illegible] 529

598. [illegible] I 11 [illegible] |
(a) VIII 20 ditto See 358
(b) I 4 | [illegible] 4104
?

599. [illegible] VI 80 | [illegible]
(a) VI A 71 ditto
(b) III 164 | [illegible] to swell 3722
(c) III A 16 | [illegible] 0600
W.I.110[17] [illegible] 138[5] II 82[2] to hide
B.230[3] s.v.

600 [illegible] III A 16 [illegible] | See 599
C.C.C. 6[a] | [illegible] 劫殺 "Kalpa slayer."

601 [illegible] IX 48 [illegible] | diamond v. 78
(a) VI 100 [illegible] |
(b) VIII 9 [illegible] | "jade" v. 590
C.C.C. 13[a, b2] 14[a2] 22[a] W.I.134[11] 石 "stone"

602. [illegible] V 32 | [illegible]
(a) VII 113 ditto
?

603 [illegible] V 32 | [illegible]
(a) IX 76 ditto
[(b) V A 14 [illegible] | x of [illegible]]
[(c) VI A 119 [illegible] | x of [illegible]]
? 4605
Used as phonetic in (b) + (c)

0604
- 5596
- 1459 – ? or 2485 chain – 0155
  - [0927] – ~~5019 – 1874~~
  - 1455
  - 5588

0605 – 0646

0606 2130 chain

0607 – 3356

0608 2662 chain

0609
- 4610 – 3030
- 0560
- 4385 – 1321
- 0610

0610 0609 chain

0611 – 2790

0612 0112 pair

0612A – 2790

0613 – 2794

0614 – 3570

0615 2837 chain

0616 0214 chain

0617 – 3324A

0618 3331 chain ~~0214 chain~~

0619 2371 chain

604.

(a) I

(b) I

B. 173[5]

605

(a)

?

606

?

607

(a) I

?

608

?

609

(a) I

(b) I

(c) I

(d)

(i) C.C.C.

(iii) The

B 17

610.

Phonetic

minus 3

48

604. [Tangut] V 32 | [Tangut] [misspelt] 5596
(a) IX 20 [Tangut] ditto
(b) III 118 | [Tangut] "hand" v. 1459
B. 173[5]

605 [Tangut] V 32 | [Tangut]
(a) IX 76 ditto
?
cf. 603

606 [Tangut] IX 10 [Tangut] | 2130
?

607 [Tangut] III 11 | [Tangut] 3356
(a) III 1 ditto
?

608 [Tangut] IX 17 | [Tangut]
?

609 [Tangut] VI 34 | [Tangut] 4610
(a) III 34 ditto
(b) V 18 | [Tangut] 0560
(c) V 176 | [Tangut] 4385
(d) VII A 133 | [Tangut] x cf [Tangut] See 610
(i) C.C.C. 28[a] 城 or 皇 supreme city (wall) B 174[1]
(ii) The dissyllable C.C.C. 33[a] 34[a] 準 to prepare, make ready 備 B 174[5] 164[4] tr. 提舉 B 220[1]

610. [Tangut] VII A 133 [Tangut][Tangut]
Phonetic character

611 [Tangut] I 85 | [Tangut] 2799
(a) VI 99 ditto
?
N.B. See 136A. I 85 has [Tangut] incorrectly.

612 [Tangut] I 85 [Tangut] | 0112
(a) I 14 ditto

X? 612 A v. 136 A

613. [Tangut] I 85 | [Tangut] 2794
(a) VI 99 ditto
(i) The dissyllable B. 99 cat. under 'horse'

614 [Tangut] I 6 | [Tangut]
(a) V 51
?

615. [Tangut] VII 56 | [Tangut] 2837
?

616. [Tangut] III 161 [Tangut] | See 618
?

617. [Tangut] III 161 [Tangut] |
?

618. [Tangut] VI 90 [Tangut] | See 214 pleasure, love
(a) | [Tangut] See 616
B. 160[3] 慕 to desire, admire

619 [Tangut] IX 102 | [Tangut] 1570
?

From here on the pairs are arranged correctly.

0620 – 0621 | 0627
0629
4230 0449 [1107]

B 223[4] 段 ~~...~~ piece. 237[3]

0621 0620 ~~chain~~ pair

0622 ~~3049~~ 3066 chain X? 0628 – 0743

0623 2371 chain

0624 0825 chain | 0629 0627 chain

0625 2407 pair

0626 2351 chain | 0630 4183 chain

626 (i) 險 'dangerous' W. II. 144[6]

0631 0651 pair

0632 0411 pair

620 ...

621 ...

622. ...

623 ...

B. 166[1]

624 ...

(a)

625 ...

(a) II

A diss...

C.C.C. 22[b]

626. ...

(a) ...

(i) C.C.C. 5[b]

...ear. W. ...

(ii) The ...

山僉

minus 3

49

620 [Tangut] IX 135 [Tangut] |

(a) IX 11 ditto See 621

?

621 [Tangut] IX 11 | [Tangut]

(a) IX 135 ditto

?

622. [Tangut] II 35 [Tangut] | 3069

?

623 [Tangut] I A 32 | [Tangut] (miscopied 3886)

B. 166'

624 [Tangut] IX 133 [Tangut] | 0825

(a) IX 161 ditto

?

625 [Tangut] V 79 [Tangut] [Tangut] [Tangut]

(a) III 21 [Tangut] | 2407

A dissyllabic name of a country.

C.C.C. 22b By itself 硃 "vermilion".

626. [Tangut] I. 9 | [Tangut]

(a) II 1 ditto

(i) C.C.C. 5b 危 "dangerous". Name of a star. W. I. 222[6]

(ii) The dissyllable C.C.C. 12b 峗 嶮

627. [Tangut] VII A 36 | [Tangut] (error for ...)

(a) VII A 112 ditto See 629

(b) VII A 16 | [Tangut] 4230

(i) By itself W. II 29 結 ~~knot, tie~~, bond S.-H. 386

(ii) [Tangut] | C.C.C. 15a 蒜 garlic

628 [Tangut] VI 134 [Tangut] |

(a) VII 22 ditto

(i) The dissyllable C.C.C. 24b 紐子 a knot, a button-knot

629. [Tangut] VII A 112 [Tangut] |

(a) VII A 36 ditto See 627

?

629 A [Tangut] VII 47 [Tangut] of | [Tangut]

? Error for 661

Uncertain ? not authentic.

630 [Tangut] VIII 6 [Tangut] | 4183

? a fruit

631 [Tangut] VII A 9 [Tangut] |

(a) II 4 ditto

C.C.C. 27a 磑

632 [Tangut] IX 79 | [Tangut] 0411

(a) III 40 ditto See 411

?

49

0633 0599 chain

0641 independent

0642 5477 chain

0634 0418 pair

0643 0569 pair

0635 - 0958

0636 1891 chain

0644 0602 pair

0637 ~~0078 chain~~ take over

0645 0603 ~~chain~~ pair

0638 ~~-3879- 0721~~
{3879 — 0721
4304A — ?1638

0646 0605 ~~pair~~

0639 2149 chain

0647 3980 chain

0640 5672 pair

0648 4179 pair

633
(a)
?
634
(a
?
635
(a
? In IX
636
?
637
(a) I
?
638
(a) VI
B.253'
639.
?
640
(a) VI
(i) By itself empty void, 220
(ii) The
II 8'

50

633 [illegible] VI A 71 [illegible] | "to hide"
(a) VI 80 ditto See 599
?

634 [illegible] VII 25 [illegible] |
(a) VI 100 ditto See 418
?

635 [illegible] VIII 42 | [illegible]
(a) IX 76 [[illegible]] See 958
? In IX 76 [illegible]

636 [illegible] V A 121 [illegible] | v. 1891 "one, a"
?

637 [illegible] I.6 | [illegible] "crystal"
(a) VIII 6 ditto See 78
?

638 [illegible] I A 30 | [illegible] 3879
(a) VI A 40 ditto
B. 253[1] possibly [illegible] "blazing"

639. [illegible] V 59 [illegible] (|) "to make"
?

640 [illegible] V 98 [illegible] |
(a) VI 10 ditto
(i) By itself W I 132[17] 空 ether (ākāśa) B 180[1] (? Phonetic)
void, empty 220[7] 224[6] nam. mk'a "heaven"
(ii) The dissyllable C.C.C. 4[b] W. I 92[15] 96[8]
II 8[1]

虛空 "void, ether"

641. [illegible] VII 74 "man's name"
Used as phonetic W II 66[11] 110[9]

642. [illegible] V. 49 | [illegible] 5477
?

643. [illegible] IX 20 [illegible] |
(a) III 63 ditto See 569
C.C.C. 26[b] 碡 碌

644. [illegible] VII 113 [illegible] |
(a) V 32 ditto See 602
?

645. [illegible] IX 76 [illegible] |
(a) V 32 ditto See 603
? cf. 646

646 [illegible] IX 76 [illegible] | 0605
(a) V 32 ditto
? cf. 645

647. [illegible] III 26 [illegible] | 0649
?

648. [illegible] III. 161 [illegible] | 4179
(a) V 120 ditto

50

0649 3980 chain "wood"

0650. 1354 pair IX 20

0651 – 0631 pair

0652 4427 chain

0653 4473 chain

0654 4451 chain

0655
4557
4447

0656 4079 chain

0657 4868 chain

0658 0057 pair

0659 4651 chain

0660 5323 pair

0661 4814 chain

0662 – 0182 pair

0663 0322 chain

0664 0322 chain

0665 5237 chain

649.

649.

(a)

CCC.3

cake

650.

(a)

?

651.

(a)

?

652.

(a)

?

653.

?

654.

(i) The

"tea-

655.

(a) VI

(b) VI

(c) IX

?

minus 3

649A 𗏺 See 656

51

649. 𗏺 V.59 | 𗏺 'on' see 25
(a) III 26 | 𗏺 See 647
C.C.C. 33ᵃ | 𗏺 胡餅 ...
cake [Hu means several things; here possibly "pepper"]

650. 𗏺 VI A 124 𗏺 |
(a) VI A 79 ditto See 1354
?

651. 𗏺 II 4 𗏺 | [N.B. error]
(a) VII A 9 | 𗏺 See 631.
?

652. 𗏺 VI 46 𗏺 | ? 4427
(a) III 91 | 𗏺 4403 ?
?

653. 𗏺 III 120 𗏺 | 4473
?

654. 𗏺 VI 1 | 𗏺 4452
(i) The dissyllable C.C.C. 23ᵇ 茶臼 "tea-pot".

655. 𗏺 IX A 16 𗏺 |
(a) VI A 123 ditto reversed
[(b) VII 16 𗏺 | × of 𗏺 v. 1420 1689]
(c) IX 129 | 𗏺 4447
?

656. 𗏺 IX 48 𗏺 | 4079
(a) I 16 ditto [misspelt]
(i) The dissyllable C.C.C. 17ᵃ 蛆蟲 "maggots & worms".

657. 𗏺 VII A 11 𗏺 | 3253
C.C.C. 22ᵇ 赤沙 "red sand"

658. 𗏺 IX A 154 𗏺 |
(a) IX 30 ditto See 57
?

659. 𗏺 VII 15 | 𗏺 [? error for 𗏺 4637]
[𗏺] B. 167³ the 攝 to help 128⁵ [30] 還 return

660. 𗏺 VII 15 𗏺 |
(a) I 49 ditto
?

661. 𗏺 VIII 41 𗏺 | 5076
→ (a) VIII 47 | 𗏺 4299
? v. 629 A

662. 𗏺 III 5 | 𗏺
(a) III 53 ditto See 182
?

663. 𗏺 VIII A 39 𗏺 |
? See 664

664 𗏺 IX 132 | 𗏺 "eye"
(a) VIII A 39 v. 0663
?

665 𗏺 IX 8 𗏺 | 5237
(a) VI 23 ditto
W. I. 190¹⁷ rlan "wet, moist".

57

0666 – 5459 IX 48

0671 – 4533 V 59

0667 0078 chain VII

0672 – 0148 chain

0668 4098 chain IX

0673 – 2630 – 5706 – 5710

0669 – 3048 VII 15

(2184 + 0674)

0670 3795 chain

The Nevsky. B. 220[3] 河 土 seems to translate 0675 0809 chain

0676 4454 chain III 12

0677 2944 chain

0678 2351 chain IX A

0679 0582 chain

666

(a)

?

667

?

668

(a)

?

669

(a)

?

670

B. 98

complete

or

[distant

[wate

[“riv

(i) By itsel

224[5]

(ii)

[The two

indistingu

V. 596

52

666 [Tangut] IX 132 [Tangut] |

(a) IX 119 ditto

?

667 [Tangut] VI 100 [Tangut] | "stone" v. 601(a)

?

668 [Tangut] III 35 [Tangut] | 4098

(a) III A 77 | [Tangut] See 237'

?

669 [Tangut] IX 48 | [Tangut]

(a) V 109

?

670 [Tangut] I 14 | [Tangut]

((a) V 3 ^x 2221 (v0596) (b) IX 66 3630)

B. 98 [Tangut] [water] on top [Tangut] [not] complete. | means "river water" or [Tangut] [also "river"] or [Tangut] [Tangut] [distant ....] or [Tangut] ["sea"]. [Tangut] [Tangut] [water ....] is the word for | o [Tangut] ["river island"].

(i) By itself C.C.C. 7b 河 W.I. 214³ etc. (W.I. 170⁹) 224³ khuï "river".

(ii) | [Tangut] C.C.C. 12a 江 河 "river". (B. 230')

[The two Hsi-hsia words seem to be as indistinguishable as the Chinese ones]

V. 596

671 [Tangut] VIII 40 [Tangut] |

(a) V 166 ditto reversed

?

672 [Tangut] II 10 | [Tangut] See 173

W.I. 226' gcig.pa "single, solitary"

673 [Tangut] VII 70 | [Tangut]

(a) VIII 45 ditto reversed

?

674 [Tangut] VII A 69 [Tangut] |

(a) III. 87 ditto reversed

W. II 94⁴ 補 "to repair, help(?)"

675 [Tangut] VII 88 | [Tangut] See 383

Some kind of vegetable

676 [Tangut] VI 124 [Tangut] | 4454

(a) VI. A 9 ditto

?

677 [Tangut] VII 88 [Tangut] | 2944

?

678 [Tangut] VII 110' | [Tangut]

?

679 [Tangut] ? VII 110 | [Tangut] See 582

(a) VIII 28 | [Tangut] "true, real" See 355 ^x

?

677 A [Tangut]

W. II 2¹¹ Phonetic 若 jo

0680
+0440
-0447
-1037
-2518-0834
-3222
-3270
-3347
-3954-3195
-5073
W. I. 134 相 mutual

0685
+0689
-0565
-0686
-0687

0686 0685 chain

0681 2736 chain

0687 0685 chain

0682 4479 pair

0688 5690 chain

0689 0685 chain

0683 1252 chain

0684 2494 chain

0690 2519 chain

0691 5217 chain

680
(a)
(b)
(c)
(d)
(e)
(f)
(g)
(h)

This wo…
it repres…
II. 42 ?
(ii) The …
681.
?
682.
(a)
W. I. 136
"to rely o…
683.
?
684.
?

(i) IX 19 [Tangut] | 1037 minus 3

53

680 [Tangut] VII 43 [Tangut] | "friend"

(a) II 4 ditto See 0440

[(b) I.10 [Tangut] | ? error See 681]

(c) I.89 [Tangut] | ×(0834) 2518

(d) III 54 | [Tangut] × of [Tangut] 3347

(e) III 67 ditto × of [Tangut] ×(3145) 3924

(f) III 90 | [Tangut] 5073

(g) VI 128 | [Tangut] 3222 — (gg) 0447 | [Tangut] 0447

(h) IX 17 | [Tangut] 3270

This word is most obscure. In W. II 18[5] it represents 共; in II 48[10] 相; in II.42[8] ? I.134[7] ? B.165[3] 188[5] 164[15] 朋友 "friend"

(ii) The Disyllable I 100[5] ? meaning.

681. [Tangut] I.A61 [Tangut] |

(a) I 10 ditto

? See 680 (b).

682 [Tangut] IX 62 [Tangut] |

(a) III 94 ditto

W. [I.136[17,18] 138[9] Not quite clear; ? 恃 "to rely on, trust". I 168[11] ?

683. [Tangut] VII 88 | [Tangut] v. 1252 [Tangut]

?

684 [Tangut] IX A132 | [Tangut] v. 1206

?

685. [Tangut] II 33 | [Tangut] 0689

(a) II A22 ditto.

(b) VI 15 | [Tangut] 0686

(c) VI A42 | [Tangut] 0687

(d) IX 121 | [Tangut] 0565

(i) W. I.136[12] [Tangut] 惜 138[4] ? II 24[4] ? Soot. compassionate, pity, to spare [? sparing]

(ii) Diss. at (d) above W II 80[9] 慳 惜 Soot. a grudging, mean heart.

686. [Tangut] VI 15 [Tangut] |

? See 685 (b)

686A [Tangut] N 331 dbih

Pretty clearly an error

687 [Tangut] VI A42 [Tangut] |

? See 685 (c)

688. [Tangut] VII 34 | [Tangut]

?

689. [Tangut] II A22 [Tangut] |

(a) II 33 ditto See 685 (a)

?

690 [Tangut] VI 94 [Tangut] |

? See 694

691 [Tangut] IX 41 [Tangut] |

?

0692 4183 chain

0699 0040 pair

0694 5106 chain

0693 2519 chain

0700 4183 chain

0701 0781 pair

0695 5110 chain

0702 0798 pair

[0703] 0731 chain

0695 bis 4326 chain

0704 - 2373

[0696] - [0720]

0705 0731 chain

0697 0752 chain

0706 0993 pair

0698 2072 chain
+0723

X 2 6

692.

A kin

694

693.

(a)

(b)

(c)

(d)

(i)

695.

(i) The

animals"

otter"

bis 694

696

(a) VII

697 696

698.

(i) The

X 2 695's
minus 3

54

692. [Tangut] IX 41 [Tangut] |

A kind of fruit?

694 [Tangut] I.97 [Tangut] | 0216 See 296

?

693. [Tangut] IX 4 | [Tangut] pure 2519

(a) I.65 | [Tangut] 5109

(b) VI 94 | [Tangut] 0690

(c) VI A 113 | [Tangut] 4543

(d) VI A 129 | [Tangut] 5189

(i) [Tangut] | C.C.C. 15a 醋 W.I. 136¹ 138¹¹

醬 醋 "(sauce & pickles &) vinegar".

695. [Tangut] VII 33 [Tangut] | "water"

(i) The dissyllable B.100 cat. under "wild animals" & translated 水 獱 "water otter".

bis 695 [Tangut] III 131 | [Tangut] 4326

? Possibly [Tangut]

696 [Tangut] III 47 | [Tangut] [0720]

(a) VIII 12 ditto [[Tangut]]

?

697 ~~696~~ [Tangut] I 112 [Tangut] |

?

698. [Tangut] VII 64 | [Tangut] See 723

(i) The dissyllable ~~noured~~ C.C.C. 22a 枓 栱? See 783A

699 ~~698~~ [Tangut] V 75 [Tangut] | 0040

(a) VII 2 ditto

(i) W.I. 124^9,10 134^12 車 192^15 224^10 śin.rta vehicle, cart "chariot" See 40.

(ii) W I 220^14 me.bʒi Name of Lunar mansion".

700 ~~699~~ [Tangut] II.4 | [Tangut] "fruit".

(i) The dissyllable 梨 "pear".

701 ~~700~~ [Tangut] I.105 [Tangut] |

(a) V 81 ditto See 784

?

702 [Tangut] IX 82 [Tangut] |

(a) II 1 ditto

?

703 [Tangut] II.15 | [Tangut] "tree".

? a sort of tree

704 [Tangut] I.67 [Tangut] | 2373

(a) IX 41 ditto

?

705 ~~704~~ [Tangut] I 146 | [Tangut] "tree"

C.C.C. 4b 桂 "cassia". B 163⁵

706. [Tangut] III 85 [Tangut] | 0993

VII 111 [Tangut] is a name of a family or a clan. Possibly a double name B.92 [Tangut] above the whole of [Tangut] | is a clan or family name, spelt | [Tangut].

0707 0731 chain 0716-1546

0708 1891 chain

0717 0718 pair

0709 1891 chain

0710 0763 pair 0719 0790 pair

[0720] 0696 pair

[0710 A 1436 chain]

0711 5369 chain

0721 0638 chain

0712 0731 chain

0722 2845 chain

0713-0769

0723 ⊢0698 1766

0714 0809 chain

0715 1338 chain

0718-0717

707. ?

708. ?

709. ?

710 (a) (i) "cross-

710 A ? VII 59-6 Probably

711. ?

712 ? probabl

713 (a) VII ?

714 ?

715- CCC 22ª

718 ?

minus 3

55

707. V.A.69 |

?

708. VII 23 | "one, a" v.1891

?

709. V.A.103 | "one, a" v.1891

?

710 II 28 |

(a) III. 87 ditto

(i) The dissyllable C.C.C. 22[a]

"cross-beam in a roof"?

710A X of V 31 | 896

? VII 59-60 error for 1223

Probably ~~genuine, cf. 13.~~ [++++]

711. VI 31 | v. 1500

?

712 III 27 | "tree"

? probably a kind of tree.

713 V 84 | 0769

(a) VIII 64 ditto

?

714 I 11 | 0809

?

715 [cf. V A 5 1524] phon. ko

C.C.C. 22[a] Pretty certainly error for

718 VI 126 |

?

716. VII 10 | 1596

(a) VII A 107 ditto

?

717. [VII 59-60]

(a) VI 126 |

?

719 ~~718~~. III 73 |

(a) V 20 ditto [ ]

?

720 ~~719~~. VIII 12 | cf. 1562 0696

(a) III 47 ditto See 696

?

~~720 III 81~~

721 ~~720~~ I 109 | 3879

?

722 III 81

(a) VIII 13 |

?

723 III 69 |

(a) VII 46 | ditto v.1766

(b) VII 64 | See 698

(i) C.C.C. 5[b], 8[a], 24[b] bushel B.122[2]

(ii) | C.C.C. 22[a]

(iii) | W.L. 222[1] c'u. smad name of a constellation

0724-0786

0731
- 0259-2901
- 0917
- 0964
- 0346
- 0712
- 0755 [1010]
- 0757
- 0765 0787
- 0801
- 0828 0707
- 0845 0891-5511
- 0851
- 0871
- 0882 0884-0772
- 0962 bis 0968
- 0978
- 0989
- 0998
- 0999
- 1002
- 1003
- 1017
- 1019
- 1020 1692
- 1995
- 2282
- 2685
- ~~3729-0533~~

- [0705]
- 3729-0533
- 3135
- [4373]
- 4539
- [0703]

0725 2224 chain

0726 0857 chain

0727 4029 chain

0735 1781 chain

0732 1180 chain

0733 4653 chain

0734 4123 chain

0728 0925 pair

0736 3160 chain

0737 5350 pair

0729 0857 chain

0738-0986

0730 4029 chain

0739 4868 chain

0731 ~~0259 chain~~ see opposite

B.221[4]: 園 garden

0740 0741 chain

724

(a)

C.C.C.

eye

an

725.

?

726

?

727.

(a) II

(b) IX

B.181[3] 垂

728.

(a) I

?

729

(a) V

?

730.

(a) IX

?

731

(a) IX 2

(b) V 15

minus 3

724 [Tangut] II 1 | [Tangut]

(a) I 50 ditto

C.C.C. 14ª | [Tangut] 龍眼 "dragon's eye"; a sort of plant or tree. Possibly an error for [Tangut]

725. [Tangut] VII 7 [Tangut] |

?

726 [Tangut] VIII 1 [Tangut] | 849c/857

?

727. [Tangut] VIII 91 [Tangut] | 2478

(a) III 35 [Tangut] | 0730

(b) IX 65 [Tangut] | 0779

B.181³ 垂 "to droop, drop"

728. [Tangut] IX 61 [Tangut] |

(a) IA 5 ditto See 925

?

729 [Tangut] V 19 [Tangut] | 0857

(a) V 83 ditto

?

730. [Tangut] III 35 | [Tangut] See 727

(a) IX 5. | [Tangut] See 915

?

731 [Tangut] IX 52 | [Tangut] (misspelt)

(a) IX 27 ditto "bamboo" See 259.

(b) V 159 | [Tangut] 0964

735A [Tangut] P.N. B.176³ 175³

56

(c) VI 21 [Tangut] | "tree" 0917

(i) C.C.C. 13ᵇ [Tangut] | 梅 "plum" (flower)

B. 230¹ q.v. ? thicket

732. [Tangut] VIII 91 [Tangut] [Tangut] [Tangut]

C.C.C. 23ᵇ 甑 "pan, boiler"

733 [Tangut] VI A 117 [Tangut] [Tangut] 4653

A phonetic character ts'an?

734. [Tangut] IX 81 [Tangut] | 5220

?

735 [Tangut] IX 66 | [Tangut] 3111

?

736 [Tangut] IX 66 | [Tangut] 5182

?

737. [Tangut] IX 85 [Tangut] | [5404A] 5350

(a) V. 62 ditto

?

738 [Tangut] IX 85 | [Tangut]

(a) V 11 ditto

(i) C.C.C. 22ª The dissyllable 板 棚堂

739 [Tangut] VI 31 [Tangut] | "yellow" 0544

?

740 [Tangut] IX 1 | [Tangut] See 741

?

0741
- 0939
- 0740
- 2181
- 3277–3534
- 3668
- 4071–4603
- 4491
- 5295
- 5542

0746–1882

0747 3467 chain

0748–0962

0749 0745 chain

0742–2118A

0743 0628 pair

0750 4027 chain

0743A 4996 pair

0751–0802

0744 0965 chain

0752
- 2787
- 0118
  - 3839
  - 4132 – 1790
    - 1043
    - 4143
    - –3522–3525–5544
  - 4448
    - 3752–0697
  - 4676
  - 5072

0745
- 0747 – 0771
  - 0902

741
(a)
(b)
(c)
(d)
(e)
(f)
(g)
(i) W.I.19
(ii) (e) ab
B. 165³

742
?

743
(a) VI
(i) The di
"a knot"

743A
?

744
(a) III
?

745
(a) IX 8
(i) The Hsiang
beam (suppor

[Tangut] B.230² q.v. minus 3

741 [Tangut] IX 60 | [Tangut]
(a) IX A 49 ditto — See 939
(b) III 105 [Tangut] | — 4371
(c) V A 51 [Tangut] | — 2181
(d) VI 128 | [Tangut] — 4491
(e) VIII 57 | [Tangut] — 3668
(f) IX 1 [Tangut] | — See 740
(g) IX 48 | [Tangut] — x(3534) 3277
(i) W.I.192¹ bzuir II 46⁴ 持 'to grasp'
(ii) (e) above W.I.206⁷ gzhui. ba "to grasp"
B.165³ (doubled) B 172⁵ tr. 計

742 [Tangut] IX 60 | [Tangut] — 2118 A
?

743 [Tangut] VII 22 | [Tangut] — 0628
(a) VI.134
(i) The dissyllable 紐子 CCC. 24ᵇ "a knot"

743A [Tangut] VIII 89 X of [Tangut] | 4976
? — ? error for 908

744 [Tangut] IX 60 [Tangut] |
(a) III 10 ditto
?

745 [Tangut] IX 84 | [Tangut] beam 749 [Tangut]
(a) IX 80 ditto
(i) The dissyllable CCC 22ᵃ 檐 栿 'beam (supporting the) eaves'

746A [Tangut]
CCC 34ᵇ 襃 error for 1227

57

746 [Tangut] V 57 | [Tangut]
(a) V 34 ditto
?

747 [Tangut] IX 72 [Tangut] | — 3467
?

748 [Tangut] V 154 | [Tangut]
(a) V 52 ditto — See 962
?

749 ~~750~~ [Tangut] IX 80 [Tangut] | eaves
(a) IX 84 ditto — See 745.
(b) V 28 [Tangut] | — 900
(c) VI 32 [Tangut] | tablet — See 771
(i) CCC. 22ᵃ (4 times in all) 栿 beam, side
(ii) The dissyllable See 745
(iii) (b) above 重 栿 "heavy beam"

750 [Tangut] V A 82 [Tangut] |
?

751 ~~752~~ [Tangut] IX 74 | [Tangut]
(a) IX 75 ditto
? — v. 1968

752 [Tangut] VIII 8 [Tangut] | — 2787
(a) VI 73 ditto
(b) I. 5 | [Tangut] — x 0118
(c) I. 50 | [Tangut] — x 3996
[(d) VI A 74 | [Tangut] Error for [Tangut] 774]

0760
3664
[0759]
0781 bis
1759–4379

0753 0514 pair

0761 0809 chain

0762–1177
~~768~~ 762 W.I.168[14] "plough"

0754
3119–4500
[0856]

B.186[4]

0755 0731 chain

0763–0710

0757 0731 chain

[0758] 4183 chain

0764 5553 chain

[0759] 0760 chain

0765 0731 chain

752
~~753~~
c.c.c.
(i) The
(ii)

752A
753
~~754~~.

(a) III

(i) The

"fright

753A
754
~~755~~.

(a) VII
(b) VII

W.II.46[10]
c.c.c. 4[b]

755.

W.I.224

~~756~~ (a

756.

?
757
~~758~~.

758

c.c.c. 14[a3]

759

c.c.c. 27[a]

757A

minus 3

58

752 ~~753~~ (cont) v. 3018 A
C.C.C. 27ª q.v.
(i) The dissyllable W.I.108¹⁶ 民 "people"
(ii) (cf above 凡夫 "all men". B.162⁵
752A 𗀀 See 778. Probably correct
753 ~~754~~. 𗀀 III A75 𗀀 | 0514
(a) III 135 ditto
(i) The dissyllable W.I.190⁷ zum.pa "frightened".
753A 𗀀 See 695.bis
754 ~~755~~. 𗀀 II 24 𗀀 | 3119.
(a) VII A70 ditto
(b) VII 10 𗀀 | W.I.108¹⁴ 肢體 "limbs". W.I.124¹⁰ 支 "branch"; 134¹⁰ 肢 "limbs"
W.II 46¹⁰ C.C.C. 4ᵇ B 180⁵ 枝 "branch";
755. 𗀀 III 77 | 𗀀 "wood" or "tree"
W.I.224¹⁸ rtsibs "spokes"
~~756~~ (a) VII A 30 | 𗀀 [𗀀]
756. 𗀀 III 47 𗀀 | See 4.
?
4011 chain
757 ~~758~~. 𗀀 III 69 | 𗀀 ~~"wood" or~~ "tree"
~~a kind of tree~~ C.C.C. 22ᵇ 桶 "barrel, bucket".
758 𗀀 or 𗀀 III 47 | 𗀀 "fruit"
C.C.C. 14ª³ 桃 "peach"
759 𗀀 VI 6, 𗀀 | See 760
C.C.C. 27ª 硯 "ink-slab"
757A 𗀀 See 𗀀 Possibly correct.

760 𗀀 VII A22 𗀀 | "paper"
(a) V 1 ditto
(b) V.69 𗀀 | "paper" 1759
(c) VI 6, | 𗀀 "ink-slab" 0759
(d) VIII 6 𗀀 | 0781 bis
C.C.C. 27ª 墨 "ink"
761. 𗀀 VII A38 𗀀 | 5271 𗀀
C.C.C. 33ᵇ² 酯 ;
761A 𗀀 See 𗀀 791
762 𗀀 IX.20 𗀀 |
(a) V 48 ditto [𗀀] See 1177
(i) The dissyllable C.C.C. 27ª 犁 鏵 "plough & plough-share"
763 𗀀 III 87 | 𗀀
(a) II 28 ditto See 710
(i) The dissyllable C.C.C. 22ª 檁 "cross-beam in a roof"
(ii) | 𗀀 C.C.C. 22ª 椳木
763A 𗀀 See 758
764. 𗀀 VII 22 | 𗀀 5534
:
765 𗀀 V 3 | 𗀀 "wood" or "tree"
C.C.C. 18ᵇ | [𗀀] 𗀀 海棠 "sea palace" (flower). Sh[oul]d be 𗀀 Nevski I 466

0766 5701 pair

0767-3231

0768-0796

0769 0713 pair chain

[0770] 1128 chain

0772 0582 chain

[0773] 2674

0771 0745 chain

0774 - [0903]

0775 intpendent

0776 4775 chain

[0777 error for 1232]

0778 : 0809 chain

0779 4029 chain

0782 2819 pair

0781 - 0701

0782

0783 2211 + 2214

0781-bis 0760 chain

766

(a) I

W.I.170

767

(a) I

(i) C.C.C. 35b

(ii) The ...

shake to move

768

(a) I

(i) The ...

"dragon

phonetic

also i...

769

(a) V

?

770

?

772

C.C.

773

(a) VII

C.C.C. 26a

771.

? B345

minus 3

766 [Tangut] II 13 [Tangut] |

(a) VII 14 ditto [Tangut]

W.I. 170[9] 擔 "to carry on the shoulders"

767 [Tangut] I. 69 | [Tangut] 3231

(a) IX 95 ditto

(i) C.C.C. 35[b] W.I. 112[6] II 14[6] 24" 動 "to move"

(ii) The dissyllable W.I. 136[2] 搖動 shake (a liquid) ~~to move~~ [Tangut]: 170[4] just 動

768 [Tangut] IX 63 | [Tangut]

(a) I 134 ditto [Tangut]

(i) The dissyllable C.C.C. 13[b] 龍 栢 "dragon cypress" (flower). Possibly a phonetic representation of the Chinese. [Tangut] also in C.C.C., possibly correct.

769 [Tangut] VIII 64 [Tangut] | 0713

(a) V 84 ditto

?

770 [Tangut] VI 59 [Tangut] |

?

— [Tangut] See after [Tangut]

772 [Tangut] VI 28 [Tangut] | [Tangut]

| [Tangut] C.C.C. 14[a] 梯枝 "lichee"

773 [Tangut] V 32 | [Tangut]

(a) VII 113 ditto

C.C.C. 26[a] The dissyllable reversed. [Tangut]

771. [Tangut] VI 32 | [Tangut] See 749

? B 345[2] 簡 "tablet" etc.

779(A) [Tangut] Error for 798 ~~[illegible]~~

C.C.C. 22[b] 鑿 "chisel" 59

"knife? + fork"

774 [Tangut] VI 56 | [Tangut]

(a) VI A 74 ditto [Tangut] B 216[3] [Tangut] ditto

(i) The dissyllable W.II 18[8] 20[12] 澡 "to bathe" 浴

773 A [Tangut] See 754

775 ~~774~~ [Tangut] III 72 "Family or clan name."

776 [Tangut] III 72 [Tangut]

?

777 ~~776~~ [Tangut] VII 9 [Tangut] | 1238

(a) VII 64 ditto [Tangut in both cases]

? [Tangut] ? right.

778 [Tangut] I. 110 [Tangut] | 5271

?

779 ~~778~~ [Tangut] IX 65 | [Tangut] See 727

C.C.C. 27[b] 略 "summary, outline."

780 ~~779~~ [Tangut] V 81 | [Tangut] 2819

(a) IX 142 ditto ?

781 ~~780~~ [Tangut] V 81 | [Tangut]

(a) I. 105 ditto See 701

C.C.C. 13[a] 炭 "slope"?

782 [Tangut] III A 53 | [Tangut]

(a) V 57 ditto See 782

(b) III 15 [Tangut] | 2211

? See 958

0781 bis [Tangut] VIII 6 | [Tangut] 0760

0783 0782 chain

0791

0784 1864 chain

0785 1000 pair

0793 – 0702

0786 0724 pair

0794 5013 chain

0787 0731 chain

[0795] 1396 pair

0788 – 0904

0796 0768 pair

[0789] 2013 chain

0797 0033 pair

0790 – 0719

0798 0799 chain

783

784 A

See 723

784

785

786

787

c.c.c. 14

788

789

789 A

790

minus 3

60

783 [Tangut] V 57 [Tangut] |

(a) III A 53 ditto

W. I. 132[13] q.v. 破 to ~~break~~ split up

784A [Tangut] III 69 X of [Tangut] |

See 723. Probably an error for 698.

784 [Tangut] VI A 57 | [Tangut] 5717

?

785 [Tangut] III 138 [Tangut] |

(a) IX 123 ditto See 1000

?

786 [Tangut] I 50 [Tangut] | 0724

(a) II 1 ditto

?

787 [Tangut] IX 21 | [Tangut] "wood" or "tree"

C.C.C. 14[b] 柏 "cypress" or "cedar"

788 [Tangut] IX 37 | [Tangut] "vine"

(a) I 63 ditto See 904

?

789 [Tangut] VI 21 [Tangut] |

?

789A [Tangut] Error for 761 [1180]

790 [Tangut] V 20 | [Tangut]

(a) III 73 ditto [[Tangut]] See 719

?

788A V. 696

791 [Tangut] VII A 29 | [Tangut] ? 1993

(a) IX 152 ditto

(b) IX A 14 | [Tangut] ? 3723

?

792 [Tangut] II 1 | [Tangut] 5316

?

792A [Tangut] IX 71 X of [Tangut] | 950

Possibly an error for [Tangut] which is X of [Tangut]

793. [Tangut] II 1 | [Tangut]

(a) IX 82 ditto See 702

C.C.C. 14[a] 榴 "pomegranate" ~~persimmon~~

794 [Tangut] IX 146 | [Tangut] 5013

?

795 [Tangut] III 3 [Tangut] |

(a) VIII 94 See 1396

?

796 [Tangut] I 134 [Tangut] |

(a) IX 63 ditto See 768.

For meaning see 768

797 [Tangut] I. 8 | [Tangut]

(a) IX 17 ditto See 33

?

798 [Tangut] VII 21 [Tangut] | See 799

C.C.C. 22[b] 鏨 "a chisel, punch"

0799
┗0798
┗[2740]

0807 0945 pair

0808 4183 chain 8080 ?

0800

0809 ?

- 5271
  - 0761
  - 0778
  - 1689
  - 2802
  - 2803
  - 2810
  - 2835–2855
  - 2836
  - 2866
  - 2895
    - 3131
    - 5649
  - 2898
  - 4523
  - 5388
- 0383
  - 0675 [1189]
  - 1911
  - 1942
    - 1926
    - 1931
    - 4002
    - 4476–0870
    - 5043–4584
  - 2225
- 0714
  - 2843
    - 0361
    - 0442
  - 2852
  - 3487
  - 3704
- 0990
  - 3923
  - 3969
  - 4870
  - 5479
- 3114–3362

0801 0731 chain

0802 0751 pair

0803 important !

0804–2354

0805 2616 pair

0810 0954 pair

[0811] 2279 chain

0806 2581 chain

799
(a)
(b)
W.I.168
800
?
800A
801
ccc.14
801A
802
(a) IX
Nevski
803
name
804
(a) VI
ccc.
"shor
805
(a) VIII
(i) ccc.14b
"sound".
806
(a) VI
?

minus 3

61

799 [Tangut] [VII 59-60
(a) VII 21 | [Tangut] "chisel" See 798
(b) VII 23 | [Tangut]
W.I.168[9] 持 B.166[1] "to arrive" ?B.177[1] ?.N.
800 [Tangut] VI 29 [Tangut] | 3692
?
800 A [Tangut] I 31 X of [Tangut] | Error for 810
801 [Tangut] III 74 | [Tangut] "tree"
C.C.C. 14[a] 櫻 "cherry"
801 A [Tangut] See 790
802 [Tangut] IX 75 [Tangut] | ? 07510
(a) IX 74 ditto
Nevski I 498 "to call, summon" v.1968
803 [Tangut] VI A 66[b] Family or clan name
804 [Tangut] VI 123 | [Tangut] (misspelt) 2357
(a) VI 79 ditto
~~C.C.C. 25[a] [Tangut] "leg of a boot"~~ C.C.C. 25[a]
短 "short" [opposed to "long"
805 [Tangut] IX 41 [Tangut] |
(a) VIII 19 ditto
(i) (C.C.C. 14[b]) | [Tangut] ["long"]) 瓠子 "gourd". B.102 ditto. cat. with vegetables
806 [Tangut] III A 60 | [Tangut] "patrio"
(a) VI A 101 ditto v.2581
?

807 [Tangut] IX 7 [Tangut] | [Tangut]
(a) VIII 7 ditto. See 945
?
808 [Tangut] III 29 | [Tangut] "fruit"
(i) The dissyllable C.C.C.14[a] 李子 "plum".
809 [Tangut] VI/VIII 30 | [Tangut] x (many) 5271
(a) VII A 12 ditto
(b) I.11 | [Tangut] 0714
(c) I.34 | [Tangut] x 3114
(d) III 134 | [Tangut] x 0383
(e) VIII 25 | [Tangut] 0990
(i) The dissyllable W.I.134[18] 樵薪 ~~(not strictly translated)~~ fuel & firewood
(ii) (d) above C.C.C.14[b] 菜蔬 "vegetable food".
810 [Tangut] V 30 [Tangut] | 1954 see 0800A
?
811 [Tangut] VIII 27 [Tangut] | 4833
(i) I.45 [Tangut] | [3258]
(ii) V.147 [Tangut] | [3487]
(i) By itself C.C.C.33[b] [Tangut] | 被馬 ? covered horse
(ii) The dissyllable C.C.C.33[b] 馬鞍 "horse's saddle".

[0812] [0813] pair IX

0819 0233 chain

0820 integument ?

[0813] - [0812] III 29

0821 integument

0814 1778 chain

0822 0014 chain

0815 0850 pair

0823 3202 chain

0816 0140 chain

0824 1781 chain

0825

0817 0886 pair V

0826 - 0397 pair

0818 0897 pair

0827 1338 chain

(i) B.164[3] 柱 脚 pillar base?

B.168[1] 柱

812.

813.

814.

815.

816.

817.

818.

C.C.C. 23[b]

minus 3

62

812. [Tangut] III 156 [Tangut] |
(a) V.16 ditto — See 813
?

813. [Tangut] V.16 | [Tangut]
(a) III 156 ditto — See 812
(i) [Tangut] | C.C.C. 33[a] 月土 帯 韃

814. [Tangut] VIII 13 [Tangut] |
(a) IX A98 ditto — V.177[8/2]
?

815. [Tangut] V.29 [Tangut] |
(a) V 173 ditto
?

816. [Tangut] IX A45 [Tangut] | 0140
(a) IX.72 | [Tangut] 3168
?

817. [Tangut] VI.125 [Tangut] | S.E. 886
(a) VII 52 ditto
(i) The dissyllable 廁 廊 "verandah"

818. [Tangut] I.111 | [Tangut]
(a) VI.14 ditto
C.C.C. 23[b] 籠 "basket"

819. [Tangut] III 26 [Tangut] | "self" See 233.
B. 234[1] tr. 可

820. [Tangut] Probably VII 61
C.C.C. 14[a] 葫 15[a] "gourd"

821. [Tangut] VII 61 character incomplete, probably to be so reconstructed
?

822. [Tangut] VII 61 [Tangut] | See 14
B. 252[2] | [Tangut] zii. zes byed. pa "to tremble in fear"

823. [Tangut] VI.62 [Tangut] | sin 3202
C.C.C. 28[b]

3202 chain

824. [Tangut] VI A61 [Tangut] | 2622
?

825. [Tangut] IX 161 | [Tangut] 0624
(a) IX 133 ditto
(b) IX 116 [Tangut] | 2258
?

826. [Tangut] IX 161 | [Tangut] 0392
(a) IX 107
?

827. [Tangut] VI 4 | [Tangut] 1524
(a) V 64 [Tangut] | 0909
(ii) | [Tangut] C.C.C. 22[a] 柱 木却
"pillar . . . "

0828 0731 chain

0829 2217 chain

829 |[Tangut] 流傳 to hand down by tradition. B.341^2 W.I 270^{18}

B.188^3 漂 rifting 232^3

0830–0853

0831 4027 chain

0832 4027 chain

832 W.II 104^{11} 已 "already". I 266^8

0833 1080 chain

B.188^4 q.v. 206^5 q.v. 220^1 q.v.

0834 0680 chain

828 [Tangut character]

(a)

(b)

C.C.C. 13^a

829 [Tangut character]

(a) III

(i) W.I. 21

(ii) |[Tangut]

830. [Tangut character]

(a) I

(i) The ...

almo...

831. [Tangut character]

?

832 [Tangut character]

(a) I. 23

(b) I. 60

(c) II 5

(d) III 8

(e) III 3

(f) III 50

(g) III 59

(h) III 71

(i) III 111

(j) III 14

minus 3

63

828 [Tangut] IX 39 | [Tangut]
(a) V 36 | [Tangut] × 0891
(b) V A 69 | [Tangut] 0707
CCC. 13ª 松 "pine tree"

829 [Tangut] IX 81 [Tangut] | ?
(a) III A 83 ditto See 2217
(i) W.I. 214⁵ 218² _k-dab_ ? "intimate"
(ii) | [Tangut] B. 102 cat. under "rivers + seas" 'flowing long'

830. [Tangut] VIII 72 | [Tangut]
(a) I 73 [[Tangut] twice]
(i) The dissyllable (reversed) 栗杏 "chesnut + almond (or apricot)".

831. [Tangut] IX 53 | [Tangut] 1152
? See 832 (f)

832 [Tangut] III A 10 | [Tangut]
(a) I. 23 | [Tangut] "to lose one's way" × 3095
(b) I. 60 | [Tangut] – 1836
(c) II 5 | [Tangut] – See 1027
(d) III 8 | [Tangut] – 5006
(e) III 31 | [Tangut] – v. 1794
(f) III 50 | [Tangut] – × 1152
(g) III 59 | [Tangut] – × 2117 2898 3456 4494
(h) III 71 | [Tangut] – 5163
(i) III 111 | [Tangut] 5510
(j) III 145 | [Tangut] – 2011

832 bis [Tangut] see 872

(k) V 48 | [Tangut] – 5886
(l) V 62 | [Tangut] – × 4265
(m) V 112 | [Tangut] – 1799
(n) V 153 | [Tangut] – 0933
(o) V 172 | [Tangut] – 4386
(p) V A 2 | [Tangut] – 4300
(q) V A 23 | [Tangut] ? – v. 1976
(r) V A 32 | [Tangut] – 4487
(s) V A 56 | [Tangut] 5535
(t) V A 82 | [Tangut] – 0780
(u) VI 77 | [Tangut] – 1525
(v) IX 61 | [Tangut] – [0992]
(w) IX 66 | [Tangut] – v. 1739
CCC 30ᵇ W.I. 168¹ Dicc. 1ª 3
W.I. 166¹⁸ 進 "to offer" [respects]
B 163³ + often: ? thereafter 告 to inform, plead.

833. [Tangut] IX 52 [Tangut] | "path" 1080
(b) IX 40 [Tangut] | 5002
(a) VII 22 ditto See 1081
(i) B.179¹ W.I. 108¹, 138⁷ [Tangut] | 經典 sūtra
(ii) By itself B. 180¹ 181¹ [translates 道 'path' mārga] W.I. 172³ 266¹⁹

834 [Tangut] VI 10 | [Tangut] 2518
?

834A [Tangut] Form of 833 in B 180¹ 181¹

0835 1449 chain

0836 2906 chain

0837 2279 chain

0838 2485 chain

0839 2851 chain

0840 5301 chain

0841 2928 chain

0842 0582 chain

0843
0914
0848

0844 0982 pair

0845 0731 chain

0846 1343 chain

0847 2928 chain

0848 0843 chain

0849 4544 chain

835.

836.

837

838

(i) CCC.32

839

(a) IX

840

841

(a) IX

842

843.

(a) I.

(b) VIII

(i)

minus 3

64

835. [Tangut] III 71 [Tangut] | ribs v. 2002
? 1449 chain 2002

836. [Tangut] III 70 [Tangut] | "arrow" 2123
?

837 [Tangut] VI 49 [Tangut] | 4833
?

838 [Tangut] IX 38 [Tangut] | "hand" v. 1459
(i) C.C.C. 32[b] | [Tangut] 箏 "harpsichord"

839 [Tangut] IX 38 [Tangut] | 2851
(a) IX 79 ditto reversed
?

840 [Tangut] III 70 [Tangut] | (misspelt) 5301
?

841 [Tangut] IX A 158 [Tangut] | 0915
(a) IX A 52 [Tangut] | ×0847
?

842 [Tangut] III 70 [Tangut] | 2305
?

843. [Tangut] IX 38 | [Tangut]
(a) I. 107 ditto See 914
(b) VIII 87 | [Tangut]
(i) [Tangut] | C.C.C. 24[a] 棹子 "table"?

844 [Tangut] III A 48 [Tangut] |
(a) V 9 ditto
?

844 A [Tangut] Error for [Tangut], see 629.

845. [Tangut] III 70 | [Tangut] "tree"
W.I. 216[14] sein. ldan "Acacia catechu."

846 [Tangut] III 70 [Tangut] | "hair" v. 1343
?

847 [Tangut] IX A 52 | [Tangut] v. 841
(a) VII 58 [Tangut] | 2752
(b) IX 172 [Tangut] | ×4532
?

848 [Tangut] VIII 87 [Tangut] | v. 843 (b)
?

848 A [Tangut] Error for [Tangut]

~~848B [Tangut] [VII 37, 60 ?]~~
~~C.C.C. 22[a] [Tangut] Er~~

848 B. [Tangut] Error for [Tangut] See 886

849 [Tangut] IX A. 43 | [Tangut]
?

849 A [Tangut] Error for [Tangut] 1240

849 B [Tangut] Error for [Tangut] 1242

849 C [Tangut] VIII. 1 × of [Tangut]

Doubtful. Possibly error for 857

64

0850 - 0815

0858 . 5465 chain

0859 2027 chain

0851 0731 chain

0860 5733 chain

0852 3393 chain

0853 0830 pair

0854 3896 chain

0861 2193 chain

0855 - 0938

0862
0916 1346 - 1978
3414

0863
0864
1473
[3237]

[0856] 0754

B 224³ φ v. 0956

0857
0729
0726

0864 0863 chain

850

(a) V

?

851.

?

852.

?

853.

(a) V

N.B. 854.

854

~~(a) IX~~

855

(a) IX 3

C.C.C. 22a

~~856~~

856

?C.C.C. 1²5

857

(a) V 19

(b) VIII

?

65

850 [Tangut] V.173 | [Tangut]

(a) V.29 ditto See 815

?

851 [Tangut] V.76 | [Tangut] "tree or wood"

?

852. [Tangut] IX 17 [Tangut] | "to laugh" 3393

?

853. [Tangut] I 73 [Tangut] |

(a) VIII 72 ditto See 830.

The dissyllable means 栗 杏 "chestnut & almond (or apricot)".

854 [Tangut] VII 52 | [Tangut] 3252

~~(a) IX 34 | [Tangut]~~ ?

N.B. 854 seems to have [Tangut] & 855 [Tangut]

855 [Tangut] IX 77 | [Tangut]

(a) IX 34 ditto See 938

(C.C.C. 22a. The dissyllable) 欄 楯

~~856 [Tangut]~~ "railing + ...

856 [Tangut] VII 10 | [Tangut] See 754

? C.C.C. 1a 5 末 summit, twig B.165[4]

857 [Tangut] V 83 | [Tangut] (0726)

(a) V 19 ditto

(b) VIII. 1 0726

?

858 [Tangut] III A 92 [Tangut] | 0972

?

859 [Tangut] VIII 28 | [Tangut] misspelt 3530

?

860 [Tangut] III A 122 [Tangut] | 5733

(a) IX 59 ditto

(b) III 42 [Tangut] | 4095

(i) The dissyllable C.C.C. 23b 瓶盞 "jar or bowl."

(ii) [Tangut] | C.C.C. 23b 燈盞 "lamp bowl."

(iii) [Tangut] | C.C.C. 33b 盞 鑼

861 [Tangut] VI 21 [Tangut] | 3474

?

862 [Tangut] I.17 | [Tangut]

(a) V 6 ditto

?

863 [Tangut] II 27 | [Tangut]

(a) III 18 ditto. See 864

(b) II A 8 | [Tangut] See 1473

(c) VI 86 | [Tangut] [3237]

N.I 168[14] 債 "debt, obligation"

864 [Tangut] III 18 [Tangut] |

(a) II 27 ditto See 863

?

0865–0918

0866 [3058] pair

0867 0906 chain

0868 1891 chain

0869 3465 chain

0870 0809 chain

0871–0940

0872 independent

0873–3954

0874–1009

0875–2827

0876–2847

0877 0731 chain

0878–5223

[0879] 5017 chain

0880 2130 chain

0881 3024 chain

0882 0731 chain

870A

865

(a)

?

866

(a)

?

867

?

868

?

869

(i) C.C.C. 25

(ii)

"a sort of

870

?

871

(a) VI

?

872

Nevski I 489

873

(a) IX

?

870A [Tangut] W. I. 134[16]

865 [Tangut] IX 9 | [Tangut]

(a) I 5 [[Tangut]] See 918

?

866 [Tangut] IX 9 [Tangut] |

(a) VI 33 ditto

?

867 [Tangut] I. 99 [Tangut] |

?

868 [Tangut] V 28 [Tangut] | "one, a" v. 1891

?

869 [Tangut] III A 49 | [Tangut] 3412

(i) C.C.C. 25b [Chinese] "bag, pocket."

(ii) | [Tangut] W. I. 212[16] 218[15] gruel, bun "a sort of broil." (See 2797)

870 [Tangut] VI 26 [Tangut] | 4476

?

871 [Tangut] VIII 26 | [Tangut]

(a) VI 23 ditto See 940

?

872 [Tangut] [VII 59-60]

Nevski I 429 [Tangut] Doubtful? v. 735A

873 [Tangut] V 76 | [Tangut]

(a) IX 27 ditto

?

877A [Tangut] Transln of [Tangut] 2542 66
Error for 941

874 [Tangut] VI 26 | [Tangut]

(a) V 78 ditto See 1009

?

875 [Tangut] V 81 [Tangut] |

(a) IX 142 ditto

?

cf. 876

876 [Tangut] V 81 | [Tangut]

(a) IX 142 ditto

?

cf. 875

877 [Tangut] V 4 | [Tangut] "wood" "a tree"

?

878 [Tangut] III 3 | [Tangut] 5223

(a) I 50 ditto

?

879 [Tangut] VIII. 81 [Tangut] | 3634

?

880 [Tangut] I. 72 | [Tangut]

?

881 [Tangut] I A 94 [Tangut] | 3640

(a) I A 90 [Tangut] | ×(1382) 3986

?

882 [Tangut] IX 34 [Tangut] "wood" "a tree"

?

0883 3795 chain

883 Le Handbook p.20 | 𗼇 西藏

hsi̯ ts'ang Tibet [? translit.]

B.163[4] part of P.N 錫. 錫 hsi

0884 0731 ~~0682~~ chain V

0885 4544 chain

0886 – 0817

0887 4011 ~~chain~~ IX

B.196[3] 陰 yin shade etc. Skandha S.H.

0888 1438 chain

0889 0293 pair

0890 · 0907 pair

0891 0731 chain

0892 – 3117

892 | 𗼇 三藏 Tripiṭaka W.I 269[15]

B.192[3]

883. (a)

(i) The ...

"rivers ...

Often ...

214[4] sin...

883A

?

884

(a) VI

?

885

(a) I 1

(i) The ...

"jungle ...

886

(a) VI 1

(i) The ...

887

(a) VIII 3

(b) IX 1

(i) (a) above ...

minus 3

67

883. [illegible] SI & VI 24 | [illegible] "sea" 2221

(a) VI 130 | [illegible] 5047

(i) The dissyllable B 102ª cat. under "rivers & seas" [tr. 西海]

Often used as a Phonetic W.I. 190[17] 錫 214[4] sin.

883A [illegible] X V 30 [illegible] | See 810

?

Error for 954

884 [illegible] VI 11 | [illegible] ~~4207~~

(a) VI 28 | [illegible] "lichee" v. 772

?

885 [illegible] VIII 17 [illegible] | 4544

(a) I 11 [illegible] | 0922

(i) The dissyllable at (a) 蕪 荑 C.C.C. 15ª "jungle & thick grass"

~~886~~

886 [illegible] VII 52 | [illegible]

(a) VI 125 ditto See 817

(i) The dissyllable C.C.C. 22ª 廊 廊

887 [illegible] V. 59 [illegible] | 4011 "head"

(a) VIII 3 [illegible] | table? 2479

(b) IX 13 [illegible] | tong? 1059

(i) (a) above C.C.C. 28ª q.v.

(ii) (b) above C.C.C. 33ᵇ 饅頭

(iii) | [illegible] C.C.C. 32ᵇ 笠 bamboo sun-hat [? wrong, a musical instrument] The word obviously corresponds to Ch. 頭 "head" in various normal & idiomatic uses. 4011 chain

888 [illegible] V. 59 [illegible] | toe 3555

?

889 [illegible] IX 81 [illegible] |

(a) V 98 ditto See 293

?

889A [illegible] N. 317 ? T. ko

Obviously an error ? for 891

890 [illegible] III. 62 [illegible] |

(a) III 30 ditto

?

891 [illegible] V 36 [illegible] | ? fiction v. 828

(a) V A 86 | [illegible] 5511

? v. 889A

892 [illegible] VII 54 | [illegible] 3117

(a) VII 25 ditto

[(b) V 44 | [illegible] error for 893.]

?

B. 179² ? Phonetic 三 san or 'tree' (not usual word)

0893–1578

0902 2149 chain

[0894 2485 chain

[0903] 0774 pair

0895–0575

0896 – 1436 chain

0904 0788 pair

0897 0818 pair

0905 0997 pair

0898 3014 chain

0899 chain
1624
3908 – 4185 – 0079 bis – 0082
4493 – 1395
5847 – 3702
3728

0906
0952
0867

0900 0745 chain

0907–0890

0901–0977B

[0908] 1252A, B.188 q.v. fasten, connect
4976–0743A – 4538 B191 lit. 貫 to string, thread
B 192² ? 含 ? hence B.206⁴ 力口

893
(b)
?
894.
?
895
(a)
C.C.C. 32ᵇ
893 A
896
?
897
(a) I 11
?
898
?
899
(a) V
(b) II
B.187⁵ 朽
900
? v.749
901
?

minus 3

68

893 [Tangut] IX 52 | [Tangut]

(b) V 44 ditto v.1578

?

894. [Tangut] VII 23 [Tangut] | "foot"

?

895 [Tangut] V 12 [Tangut] | 0575

(a) V 132 ditto

C.C.C. 32^b | [Tangut] 琵琶 "guitar"

893A [Tangut] Error for [Tangut] 946

896 [Tangut] V 31 | [Tangut] 710 A ?v. 1223

?

897 [Tangut] VI 14 [Tangut] | "basket" v.818

(a) I 111 ditto

?

898 [Tangut] VI 4 [Tangut] |

?

899 [Tangut] II 8 | [Tangut] [[Tangut]

(a) V 113 ditto v.1624

(b) II A 32 | [Tangut] [[Tangut]] 3908

B.187^5 朽 rotten, decayed

900 [Tangut] V 28 | [Tangut] beam v.749(b)

?v.749 'heavy beam'

901 [Tangut] I.54 | [Tangut]

?

902 [Tangut] IX 66 | [Tangut] s.o.g. 3955

?

~~903 [Tangut] II 6~~ 902A [Tangut] misspelt v.921

902B [Tangut] Error for [Tangut] 1252

903. [Tangut] VI A 74 [Tangut] | "to bathe"

(a) VI 56 ditto [[Tangut]] See 774

(ii) The dissyllable W II 18^3, 20^12 澡浴 "to bathe"

(i) By itself B 346^3 滌 to cleanse

904 [Tangut] I.63 [Tangut]

(a) IX 57 ditto [[Tangut]] See 788

| [Tangut] C.C.C. 14^a 蒲桃 "wild grape"

905 [Tangut] V 20 [Tangut] |

(a) I 49 ditto See 997

?

906 [Tangut] III 6 | [Tangut] [? error, see (a)]

(a) I.99 | [Tangut] 0867

(a) IX 49 | [Tangut] i.e. ditto 1595

?

907 [Tangut] III 30 | [Tangut]

(a) III 62 ditto See 890

?

908 [Tangut] V 87 | [Tangut] B.130^5

(a) II 9 ditto [[Tangut]] W I.266^7

C.C.C. 32^a 入 "to enter" See 1252A

V.743A B.132^4

68

0731

0909 1338 chein

0910 3088 chein

0911 1966 chin

0912 4157 chein

0913 4029 chein

0914 0845 chein

0915 2928 chein

0916 0862 chein

909

?

910

?

911

(a)

W.I. 148

912

?

913

?

914

(a) IX

ccc. 23

915

(a) VI

(b) IX

(i) The

"short

916

(a) I 17

(b) III 17

(c) IX A

(i)

minus 3

69

909 [Tangut] V 64 | [Tangut] 0827
?

910 [Tangut] V.102 [Tangut] | 4604
?

911 [Tangut] II A 24 [Tangut] | ? 1966
(a) I 29 ditto
W.I.148[4] 屈 "to bend, oppression".

912 [Tangut] IX 79 | [Tangut] 4157
?

913 [Tangut] IX 5 [Tangut] | See 730
?

914 [Tangut] I 107 [Tangut] | [Tangut]
(a) IX 38 ditto See 843
CCC. 23[a] 盤 "vessel, tub, tray"

915 [Tangut] IX 179 [Tangut] | 5320
(a) VIII 83 [Tangut] | 2199
(b) IX A 158 | [Tangut] ×0841
(i) The disyllable W.I.114[2] 崖際 "shore limits"

916 [Tangut] V 6 [Tangut] |
(a) I 17 ditto
(b) III 172 | [Tangut] 3414
(c) IX A 44 [Tangut] "west, ~~south~~" ×(1978) v.1346
(i) | [Tangut] CCC 15[a] 瓜 "gourd". B.102
cat. under "vegetables".

917 [Tangut] VI 21 [Tangut] | v.731(c)
(a) I 9 [Tangut] | 2585
(aa) I 47
(b) I 89 | [Tangut] 1692
1995
(c) I 104 [Tangut] | 1002
(d) I 146 [Tangut] | [0705]
(e) I.A.1 [Tangut] | ×(0533) 3729
(f) II 15 [Tangut] | 1003
(g) II 15 [Tangut] | (to take) [0703]
(h) II A 26 [Tangut] | 0968
(i) III 27 [Tangut] | 0712
(j) III 69 | [Tangut] 0757
(k) III 70 [Tangut] | 0845
(l) III 74 [Tangut] | 0801
(m) III 76 [Tangut] | 0755
(n) V 3 [Tangut] | 0765
(o) V 4 [Tangut] | 0877
(p) V 16 [Tangut] | 0962
(q) V 62 [Tangut] | 0998
(r) V 76 [Tangut] | 0851
(s) V 169 | [Tangut] 0978
(t) VI 4 | [Tangut] 3135
~~(u) VI 11 [Tangut]~~ (u) VI 11 [Tangut] ×0772 0884
(v) VI 19 [Tangut] | 0999
(w) VI 36 | [Tangut] 0346
(x) VI 75 | [Tangut] [4373]

0921 0015 chain

0922 4544 chain

0923 1864 chain

0918 0865 pair

0924 1891 chain

0925–0728

0919 0959 chain

229³ S.H. 399

B.227³ tr. 惹 to irritate; provoke.

B.230⁴ s.v. [looks like 染]

0926 0583 chain

W.I.132¹² 煞 murder by wilful infliction

| [Tangut] W.I.136² 燒殺 to burn + destroy

[0927] 0604 chain

0920 5591 pair chain

917 con

(4) V

(3) VI

(aa) VI

(bb) VI

(bbb)

(cc) IX

(dd) IX

(ee) IX

(ff) IX

CCC. 8ª 13⁶

N.B. word

918. [Tangut]

(a) IX

?

919 [Tangut]

(b) II 14

(a) V 3

(c) VII

(i) cc (c) abo

'impure, d

919A [Tangut]

919B [Tangut]

920 [Tangut]

(a) IX 6

minus 3

70

917 cont.

(y) VI A 114 | [Tangut] 4539

(z) VII 24 [Tangut] | 2382

(aa) VIII 25 | [Tangut] 0989

(bb) VIII 87 | [Tangut] 1017

(bbb) — IX 21 0781

(cc) IX 34 | [Tangut] 0882

(dd) IX 39 [Tangut] | 0828

(ee) IX 69 [Tangut] | 1020

(ff) IX 72 [Tangut] | 1019

CCC. 8a 13b 22b2 etc. W. I 138" etc. 木 wood, tree

N.B. wood; tree is [Tangut]

918. [Tangut] I 5 [Tangut] |

(a) IX 9 ditto [Tangut] See 865

?

919 [Tangut] IX 56 [Tangut] | ? 0959

(b) II 14 | [Tangut] 1207 W. I. 220[10]

(a) V 38 ditto [Tangut]

(c) VII 51 [Tangut] | v.1595

(i) (c) above W I 96[12] 汙 ? II 26[8] 垢穢 "impure, defiled" See 3202

919A [Tangut] Error for [Tangut] 959

919B [Tangut] Error for [Tangut] 952

920 [Tangut] IX 5 [Tangut] | 5591 and

(a) IX 6 ditto

921 [Tangut] II 6 [Tangut] | 0015

(a) V 66 ditto See 15

?

922 [Tangut] I. 11 | [Tangut] See 885.

(i) The disyllable CCC. 15a 蕪 荑 "jungle + thick grass"

922A [Tangut] [VII 59-60]

923 [Tangut] VII A 27 [Tangut] | 1571

?

924 [Tangut] VI A 102 [Tangut] | 2965

?

925 [Tangut] I. A. 5 | [Tangut]

(a) IX 61 ditto See 728

926. [Tangut] VI 114 [Tangut] | 0584

(a) III 122 [Tangut] | 2982

CCC. 6a6 W. I. 132" 196 殺 murder 196[7] gsod. pa "to kill"; 196[17] g-sed "executioner"; 176[7] [Tangut] "destroy"

927. [Tangut] IX. 64 [Tangut] | "hand" v.1459

error for 1248

~~(a) VII 15 [Tangut] |~~

CCC. 5b | [Tangut] 心 宿 name of constellation "Heart-star".

W. I. 222[1] (constellation)

70

0928 3109 chain

0929 1805 pair

0930 0951 pair

0931 4428 chain

0932 4425 chain

0933 4027 chain

0934 3230

0935 0985 chain

0936 H1006 pair

0937 independent

0938 0855 pair

0939 0741 chain

0940 0871 pair

0941 3086 chain

0942 4355 chain

0943 3226 chain

0944 4208 chain

928

?

929.

(a) II

?

930.

(a) II

(i) The

931.

(a)

(i) C.C.C. 2

C.C.C. 23a

932

?

933.

?

934

(a) IX

Neoshi I

935

(i) The diss

minus 3

71

928 [Tangut] III 78 [Tangut] [Tangut] [Tangut] 3109

?

929. [Tangut] II.6 [Tangut] | v.1806

(a) III 101 ditto

?

930. [Tangut] VI 73 [Tangut] |

(a) III 96 ditto See 951

(i) The dissyllable C.C.C. 26b 芭罷

931. [Tangut] III 80 [Tangut] |

(a) VI 11 ditto

(i) C.C.C. 24a 筋 & (ii) The dissyllable C.C.C. 23a 筋

932 [Tangut] II 15 [Tangut] | 4425

?

933. [Tangut] V.153 [Tangut] |

?

934 [Tangut] IX 149 | [Tangut]

(a) IX 17 ditto [[Tangut]]

Nevski I 495 "to beat"

935 [Tangut] VIII A 106 [Tangut] |

(i) The dissyllable C.C.C. 23a [illegible]

936. [Tangut] I 67 [Tangut] |

(a) I 54 ditto See 1006

?

937 [Tangut] II A 25: Name of a country

Nevski I 495 fên or fêng

938 [Tangut] IX 34 [Tangut] |

(a) IX 77 ditto See 858

The dissyllable C.C.C. 22a 欄楯 "railing"

939 [Tangut] IX A 49 [Tangut] | "to grasp"

(a) IX 60 ditto See 741

?

940 [Tangut] VI 23 [Tangut] |

(a) VIII 26 ditto See 871

?

941 [Tangut] III 3 [Tangut] | 4604

(a) VIII 84 | [Tangut] [[Tangut]] 2542

?

942 [Tangut] V 79 | [Tangut] 4355

?

943. [Tangut] VIII 9 [Tangut] | 3600

(a) IX 42 [Tangut] | 3571

?

944 [Tangut] V 79 [Tangut] | tone 4208

71

0945 - 0807 I 67

(a) I 54 ditto

0946 2027 chain

0947 0582 chain

0948 1781 chain

0949 0953 chain

0950
┴ 2652 – 0295 – 2064
[3564

0951 - 0930 (a) VIII 84

0952 0906 chain

pair
0953
┬ 4696
└ 0949

[0883A] [0800A]
0954 } – 0810

0955 3587 chain

0956 3149 chain

B.224³ ϕ | 芰 樓 至 Rucika

0957 0474 pair

0958 0635 pair

945

(a) I

?

946

(a) I

CCC. 23ᵃ

947

?

948

?

949

?

950

(a) IX

Nevski I

951

(a) VI 7

(i) The Hsi-...

952

(a) III 6

?

72

945 [Tangut] VIII 7 | [Tangut]

(a) IX 7 ditto See 807

?

946 [Tangut] I 57 [Tangut] | 4463

(a) VI A 87 [Tangut] | 4404

C.C.C. 23ᵃ [Tangut] | 沙 [Tangut] "sand"

947 [Tangut] VIII 62 [Tangut] | [0582]

?

948 [Tangut] V A 77 [Tangut] | 4665

?

949 [Tangut] V. 136 [Tangut] | See 953 (b)

?

950 [Tangut] IX 71 | [Tangut]

(a) IX 3 | [Tangut]

Nevski I 482

951 [Tangut] III 96 | [Tangut]

(a) VI 73 ditto See 930

(i) The dissyllable C.C.C. 26ᵇ 芭 [Tangut]

952 [Tangut] IX 49 [Tangut] |

(a) III 6 ditto ?

?

953. [Tangut] III 86 [Tangut] |

(a) IX 92 ditto

(b) V 136 | [Tangut] 0949

(i) The dissyllable ~~C.C.C.~~ W. I. 194¹⁴ lo. tog "harvest" (ii) The same reversed C.C.C. 9ᵇ 甲 乙 "1st & 2nd stems". B 176⁴ 甲

954 [Tangut] I 31 | [Tangut] [Tangut]

(a) V 3 | [Tangut] i.e. ditto

?

955 [Tangut] VI 11 | [Tangut] 5606

(a) VI 64 | [Tangut] 1377

(b) VI 127 | [Tangut] See 1216

(c) VIII 84 | [Tangut] 5191

(d) IX 180 | [Tangut] See 1276

(i) (b) above C.C.C. 23ᵇ 茶 [Tangut] "tea"

956 [Tangut] IX 148 [Tangut] | 3149

Nevski I 489

W II 4¹ Used as Phonetic

957 [Tangut] VI 21 [Tangut] |

(a) VIII 31 ditto See 474

?

958 [Tangut] | IX 76 [Tangut] |

(a) VIII 42 ditto

B. 96 [Tangut] on top (?) [Tangut] follows.

(0958)

(0782)

W.I 270[20]

958. B260[2] Name of a mountain; [illegible]
phonetic 蘭 Lan mountain.

0959
└0919 ┬1207
└1595–1637┬1627
├1630
├2503
├2735–2604┬2572
├2737 ├1631 └5715
└4254 └2867

0960–2951

0961

0962 0748 pair

0963–0994

0731
0964 0259 chain

0965
┼0744
└4956 ┬1211
└4995–5021–1522

0966 3226 chain

[0977A]
0967–0976

0968 0731 chain

0969 5066 pair

0970
┼5092–3321
┼4629–3057
├5422
└5341

W.I.134[3] 炣 to fry?

962 b…

958 (c…

As for…

The t…

indicat…

the nam…

is tran…

959.
(a) IX
?

960.
(a) III
?

961.
?

962.
(a) V
?

963.
(a) VI
?

964
?

962 bis 1016 [illegible]

73

958 (cont.)

"As for | , [illegible] | [translated 蘭 蕙, two kinds of orchids] are names of ('both' orchids) mountains."

The text seems to be clear & to indicate that the disyllable is the name of two mountains, but is translated as above.

959. [illegible] V 38 | [illegible] in pure 0919

(a) IX 56 ditto See 919

?

960. [illegible] I.108 | [illegible]

(a) III 76 ditto

?

961. [illegible] I A87 translated by itself.

?

962. [illegible] V 52 [illegible] |

(a) V 154 ditto See 748

?

963. [illegible] V 32 | [illegible]

(a) VI 42 ditto

?

964. [illegible] V.159 [illegible] | See 731

?

965. [illegible] III 10 | [illegible]

(a) IX 60 ditto See 744

(b) VII A 91 | [illegible] 'faith, truth 4952

?

966 [illegible] VII A 23 [illegible] | 2212

?

967. [illegible] I.145 | [illegible]

(a) VIII 35 [[illegible]] ditto

?

968 [illegible] II A 26 | [illegible] "tree"

C.C.C. 14b 榆 "elm"

969 [illegible] III 93 [illegible] |

(a) V 156 ditto

(i) The disyllable W.I. 98[5] apparently = 絃 管 "stringed & wind instruments"

970 [illegible] I.106 | [illegible] X(3321) 5092

(a) I 120 ditto

(b) VII A 94 | [illegible] [5541]

(c) VIII 6 | [illegible] X 3057 [4629]

(d) VIII 97 | [illegible] [illegible] 5422

(i) C.C.C. 33a W.I. 134[b.17] 燒 "to burn, bake"

(ii) W.I. 216[5] | [illegible] [illegible] "[illegible], burnt offering."

73

0971 [1015] pair

0976 0967 pair [=0977A]

0972 5465 chain

0977 – 5146

0977B 0901 pair

0978 0731 chain

0973-1007

0979 1105 chain

0974-3243

0975 5396 pair

0980 4205 pair

971.

972

973.

974

975

minus 3

74

971. [Tangut] IX 43. [Tangut] |
(a) ~~diti~~ I 11 ditto
?

972 [Tangut] mih mo ?'o I.47 [Tangut] | 5465
(a) III 178 | [Tangut] fuel 5494
(b) III A 92 | [Tangut] 0858 ~~0992~~
(c) VIII 5 | [Tangut] xxx 4800
(d) IX 41 | [Tangut] burn 0012
(e) IX 119 | [Tangut] 0187
(f) IX 140 | [Tangut] fire 5463
C.C.C. 8a 23b 24a3 W.I 11.2[10] 火 224[11] B.253
me "fire" B.127[5] ... 火巨

973. [Tangut] III 75 | [Tangut]
(a) IX 49 ditto See 1007
(i) The dissyllable C.C.C. 21b 沉香 "ice water incense"?

974 [Tangut] V 7 | [Tangut]
(a) VII 105 ditto
(i) The dissyllable C.C.C. 16b 犲狼 B.100 cat. under "wild animals" "wolf, fox". v. 977
(ii) See 977 (ii)

975 [Tangut] VII A 26 [Tangut] |
(a) II 16 ditto [?]
?

976 [Tangut] VIII 35 [Tangut], | (misspelt)
(a) I 145 ditto See 967
?

977 [Tangut] VI 58 | [Tangut]
(a) VI 38 ditto
(ii) W.I.194[3] bziis "wolf" (? error for 974)
[Tangut] (i) W.II 48[12] The dissyllable 舟船 "boat, ship?".

977 A. [Tangut] Error for 967 Right form of 967?
977 B. [Tangut] VII 59-60 X in I 54 [Tangut] | See 901 Nevski I 468

978 [Tangut] V 169 [Tangut] | "wood, tree"
(i) The dissyllable 匣子 C.C.C. 24a "small box, étui".

979 [Tangut] VII 14 [Tangut] |
(a) III 147 | [Tangut] 1142
(b) VIII 20 [Tangut] | x 5831
(i) By itself W.I. 114[4], 136[1] B.180, 181
現 224[17] snan.pa "to appear".
(ii) B.179 耀 "glorious". B.346[1] ... W.I 265[18]
(iii) [illegible] (b) above W.II.12[12] 稱揚 v. 5431 "to publish & display". See also 1289

980 [Tangut] VII 14 [Tangut] |
(a) V 20 ditto
B.101 cat. under "wild animals"

74

0981 1891 chain

0982-0844

0983 1992 chain

0984 3587 chain

0985

0986 0738 pair

0987 2596 chain

0988 0291 pair

0989 0731 chain

0990 0809 chain

0991 4639 chain

[0992] 4027 chain

0993-0706

0994 0963 pair

0995-4084

0996 1018 pair

minus 3

75

981 [Tangut] IX 9 [Tangut] | [sic, 2 characters]
B 171[4] B 223 币 circuit

982 [Tangut] V 8 | [Tangut]
(a) III A 48 ditto
?

983 [Tangut] V 147 [Tangut] [Tangut] not to go (or behave) 1992
C.C.C. 14[b] 鑵

984 [Tangut] V 7 [Tangut] | 5606
W. I. 135[7] (might be one of several verbs 'fish, cage, bind' etc.)

985 [Tangut] V 185 | [Tangut] 4475
(a) II 7 ditto
(b) VIII A 106 | [Tangut] 0935
(c) IX A 47 | [Tangut] [1023]
(i) C.C.C. 23[a] (b) above 椗 匙

986 [Tangut] V 11 [Tangut] | 0738
(a) IX 85 ditto
(i) The dissyllable C.C.C. 22[a] 杈 栅 堂

987 [Tangut] IX 9 [Tangut] | See 55
(i) The dissyllable C.C.C. 24[b] 禮 心
0

988 [Tangut] VI 23 [Tangut] |
(a) V 100 ditto
?

989 [Tangut] VIII 25 [Tangut] "root of tree"
?

990 [Tangut] VIII 25 [Tangut] | v. 809(e)
C.C.C. 14[a] | [Tangut] 檎
Nevski I 470 (Chinese) apple?

991 [Tangut] III 71 [Tangut] [Tangut]
?

992 [Tangut] IX 61 [Tangut] |

993 [Tangut] VII 111 Name of family or clan
(a) III 85 | [Tangut] See 705
The dissyl. B. 176[2]
A dissyllabic family name (See 706).

994 [Tangut] VI 42 [Tangut] | [Tangut]
(a) V 32 ditto See 963
C.C.C. 14[a] [Tangut] | 棗 棗 "jujube ~~date~~ tree"

995 [Tangut] IX 68 | [Tangut]
(a) IX 53 ditto
?

996 [Tangut] IX 68 [Tangut] |
(a) VI 10 ditto
* 刺 "thorn (tree?)" W. I 156[12]

minus 3

76

997 [Tangut] I 49 | [Tangut]

(a) V 20 ditto See 905

?

998 [Tangut] V 62 | [Tangut] "wood or tree"

?

999 [Tangut] VI.19 | [Tangut] "wood or tree"

B 200[5]: phon.

1000 [Tangut] IX 123 | [Tangut]

(a) III 138 ditto See 785

?

1001 [Tangut] VI 19 | [Tangut] |

(a) VI A 104 ditto See 312

?

1002 [Tangut] I 104 | [Tangut] "wood or tree"

Nevski I 488 [Tangut]

1003 [Tangut] II 15 | [Tangut] "wood or tree"

?

1004 [Tangut] VI 19 | [Tangut] 4518

?

1005 [Tangut] VI 53 [Tangut] | See 301

(i) The dissyllable C.C.C. 23[a] 檠子 "a stand for bending a bow"

1006 [Tangut] I.54 | [Tangut]

(a) I 67 ditto See 936

?

1007. [Tangut] IX 49 [Tangut] |

(a) III 75 See 973

(i) The dissyllable 沉香 "ice-water incense(?!)" C.C.C. 21[b]

(ii) C.C.C. 13[b] 棠 (?) 海棠 "pear tree" [q.v.]

1008 [Tangut] IX A 17 | [Tangut] 4274 × 2126

(a) I A 102 | [Tangut]

(i) The dissyllable C.C.C. 32[b] 吹笛 "blowing flute" W.I.98[5] q.v.

(ii) | [Tangut] C.C.C. 32[b] 管 "reed pipe"

(iii) | [Tangut] C.C.C. 32[b] 笛 "flute"

(iv) [Tangut] | C.C.C. 32[b] 簫 "bamboo flute"

(v) [Tangut] | C.C.C. 32[b] 笙

(vi) | [Tangut] C.C.C. 32[b] 篳篥

(vii) [Tangut] | C.C.C. 32[b] [[illegible] pipe] 七星 "seven stars"

1009 [Tangut] V 78 [Tangut] |

(a) VI 26 ditto See 874

?

1009A [Tangut] X 9 V 47 | [Tangut]

?

1010 [Tangut] VII A 30 [Tangut] | 0755 See 754(b)

(i) C.C.C. 22[a] | [Tangut] 椽 準 (?)

1011 1340 chain

1012 1713 chain

1013 2906 chain

1014 1992 chain

[1015] -0971

1016 5632 chain

1017 0731 chain

1018 -0996

1019 0731 chain

1020 0737 chain

1021 5477 chain

1022 - 2894

[1023] 0985 chain

1024 0476 chain

minus 3

77

1011 [Tangut] VI A 118 [Tangut] [Tangut] 4402

?

Possibly a phonetic group.

1012 [Tangut] VII 26 [Tangut] | "sand" 4867

(a) III A 1 [Tangut] | 5667

(b) VII 93 [Tangut] | 5588

?

1013 [Tangut] Kan V 82 [Tangut] | "arrow" 2123

(a) V A 131 [Tangut] × by [Tangut] | Phon. nan 2666

(b) VI A 117 [Tangut] × by [Tangut] | Phon. 733

(c) VII A 133 [Tangut] × by [Tangut] | Phon. 610

?

(a) (b) + (c) are all Phonetic characters not to go (?) together

1014 [Tangut] V 185 [Tangut] [Tangut] 1992

?

1015 [Tangut] I. 11 | [Tangut]

(a) IX 43 ditto See 971

?

1016 [Tangut] V 15 [Tangut] | "long"

B. 219[5] 桅 'mast'

1017. [Tangut] VIII 87 [Tangut] | "tree"

CCC. 13[a] W.I. 134[15] B 223[2] 園 "garden"

B. 187[1] tr. 苑 'park'

1018 [Tangut] VI 10 | [Tangut]

(a) IX 68 ditto

?

1019. [Tangut] IX 72 | [Tangut]

CCC. 14[a] | [Tangut] 甘 [Tangut] sugar?

1020. [Tangut] IX 69 | [Tangut]

?

1021 [Tangut] VII 14 [Tangut] [Tangut] (same goat)

(a) VIII 58 [Tangut] | [Tangut] ? 5421

Very common. = 香 in all its senses "fragrance, incense, the sense of smell." CCC. 21[a,b4] W.I. 98[7], 142[10], 146[6] 216[4] [bdug.pa 'incense'] 216[14] [spos 'incense'] II 10[3] 14[10] 20[12]

(ii) | [Tangut] ["white incense"] CCC. 21[a] 乳香

(iii) | [Tangut] CCC. 21[b] 安息香

1022 [Tangut] III 7 | [Tangut]

(a) III 13 ditto

?

1023 [Tangut] IX A 47 [Tangut] | v. 985

CCC. 23[a] 盔 "helmet"

1024. [Tangut] VI 24 [Tangut] |

(a) IX 151 ditto See 476

?

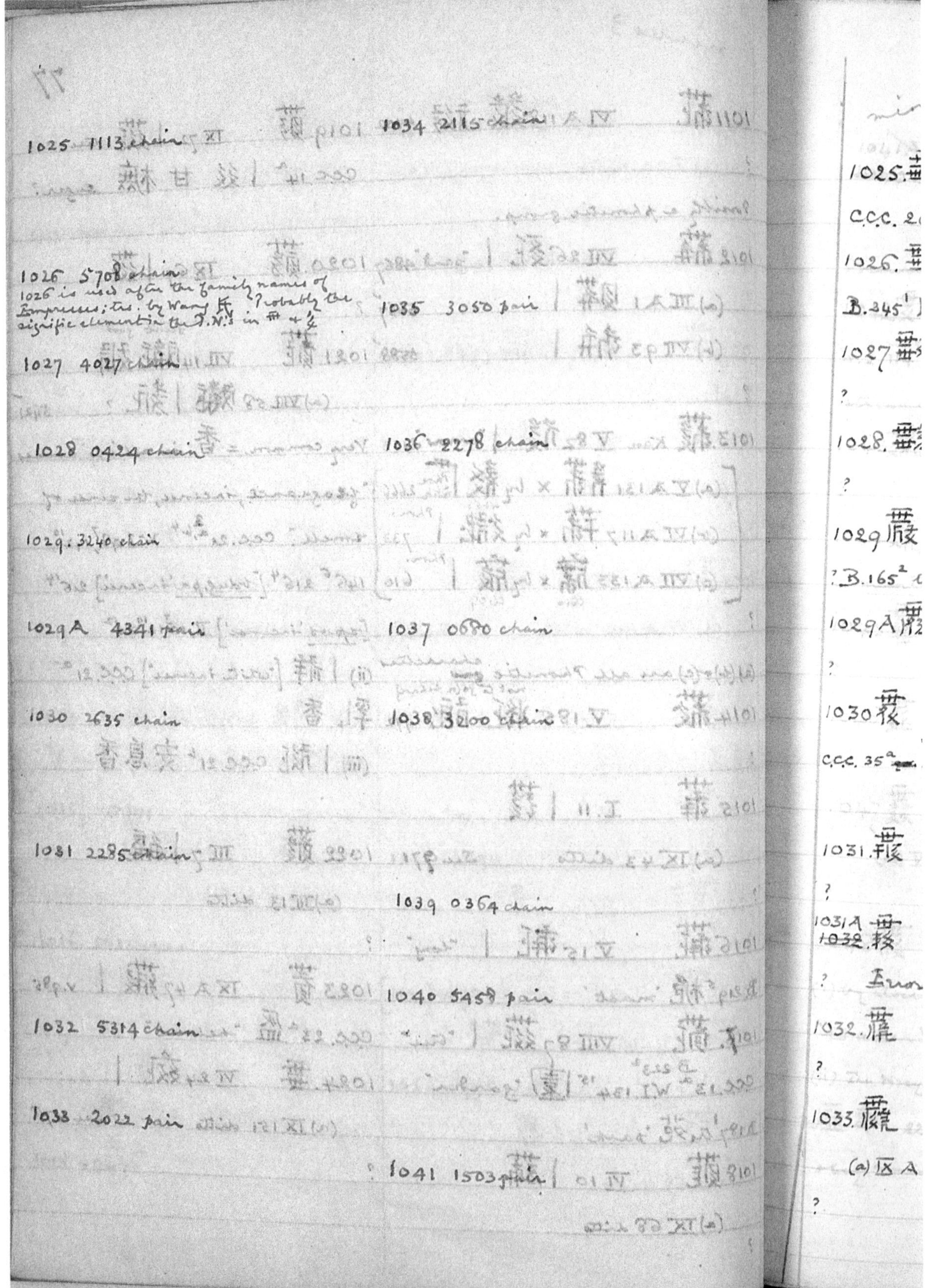

minus 3

78

1025. [Tangut] IX 5 [Tangut] | see 1113

C.C.C. 20[b] 姨 "mother's sister"

1026. [Tangut] IX 115 [Tangut] | 5068

B. 345[1] 氏 'family' (after proper name) ~~possibly plural~~ W.I. 265[14] 266[5]

1027 [Tangut] II 5 [Tangut] | v. 832

?

1028. [Tangut] I. 81 [Tangut] | 3379

?

1029 [Tangut] I 103 [Tangut] | back teeth 3240

? B. 165[2] tr. 備 to prepare

1029A [Tangut] X of III 76 | [Tangut]

?

1030 [Tangut] III 169 [Tangut] | 2635

C.C.C. 35[a] 累 'to join'?

1031. [Tangut] IX 19 [Tangut] | 3948

?

1031A ~~1032~~ [Tangut] X of I. 76 | [Tangut] 5454

? Error for 577

1032. [Tangut] VI 26 | [Tangut] to assemble v. 1962

?

1033. [Tangut] I 139 [Tangut] | to retire, return,

(a) IX A 103 ditto v. 2022

?

1034 [Tangut] III 123 [Tangut] | 2115

(a) VIII A 68 [Tangut] | 3715

?

1035 [Tangut] III 15 [Tangut] |

(a) I. 48 ditto

?

1036. [Tangut] I 43 [Tangut] | 2308

(a) IX 29 [Tangut] |

(i) (a) about B. 101 cat. under "wild animals."

1037. [Tangut] IX 19 | [Tangut] v. 680

?

1038 [Tangut] IX 171 [Tangut] [Tangut] lofty majesty 3200 1900

(a) VII 7 | [Tangut] 'flag' 1042

W.I. 138[11] 140[9] 幡 'Patākā' "flag, banner" 3200 chain

1039 [Tangut] III 36 | [Tangut] v. 364

(?) Simpl. B. 192[1] 幽 深 dark + deep, wild + remote 5458

1040 [Tangut] VII 96 [Tangut] | drink

(a) VI 37 ditto

CCC. 36[a]

1041 ~~1040A~~ [Tangut] <IX 171> cf. 1038 present T.S.P. II 19 X of | [Tangut] v. 1513

W.I. 112[1] 幡 "patākā" flag, banner"

B. 168[5]

1042 3200 chain

1043 0752 chain

1044 3226 chain

1045 1781 chain

1046 1438 chain

1047 3907 chain

1048 3468 chain

1049 4276 chain

1050 5314 chain

1051 2167 chain

1052 2601 chain

[1053] indigenous

1054 1876 chain

[1054A] 4352 pair?

1055
⊥2107 ⊤2106 ⊥4746

1056 2309 chain

. . .

1057 2309 chain

~~1041A~~
~~1040~~

?

Obscure

1042

W.I. 114

streame

1043

?

1044

a mantr

1045

?

1046

?

1047

(a) V

?

1048

(i) by itsel

"to attend

(ii) The Hsia

歷事 22

obey

minus 3

79

~~1040 B.~~ 1041A is 2355 [illegible] X of III 136 | [illegible]

?

Obscure or doubtful form.

1042 [illegible] VII 7 [illegible] | banner v. 1038

W.I. 114[8] 幢 "dhvaja, ketu pennant streamer, flag" II 6[12]

3200 chain

1043 [illegible] I 103 | [illegible] v. 1791

?

1044 [illegible] IX A 141 [illegible] v. 355

a mantra or mystical sound.

1045 [illegible] IX 117 | [illegible] 1364

?

1046 [illegible] III 169 | [illegible] 2487

?

1047 [illegible] III 123 [illegible] | 3907

(a) VI 14 ditto

?

1048 [illegible] VI 12 | [illegible] 3029

II 38[7] B 239[2]

(i) by itself W.I. 142[3] 侍 196[2] miaq. pa "to attend, wait on." B. 189[2]

(ii) The Hsyllable W.I 108[10] 歷侍 II 6[3] 歷事 22[8] 承事 "to serve, to obey & minister to."

1049 [illegible] I 95 [illegible] | 4229

?

1050 [illegible] IX 19 | [illegible] to assemble v. 1962

?

1051 [illegible] III A 78 | [illegible]

?

cf. 1139

1052 [illegible] I A 33 [illegible] | 5191

?

1053 [illegible] VII 8 Name of family or clan

~~W II 78" 夜 5416 night~~? II 14" Phonetic

1054 [illegible] IX 38 [illegible] | goats v. 1881

B. 180[1] 場 area, place W.I 172[3] do. 266[19]

B. 170[1]

1054A [illegible] X of IX 51 | [illegible] 4552

?

1055 [illegible] VII 8 | [illegible] v. 2107

(a) I 135 ditto

?

1056 [illegible] I 119 [illegible] | 1057

B. 165[4]?

1057 [illegible] V 139 | [illegible] ~~horse~~ 2279

(a) I 119 | [illegible] 1055

(b) III 61 | [illegible] 5617

(c) VII 114 | [illegible] 1058

C.C.C. 28[2,4] W.I 92[6] 118[9] 134[7] II 4" 軍 "army" II 130[4]

1058 2309 chain

1059 4011 chain

1060 independent

1060. 頂 "summit (of a mountain W.II2[5]

(iii) |鋑頂禮 "to bow in adoration W.II4[4] et passim

1061 – 1485

1062 1064 pair

1063 0022 chain

1064 – 1062

1065 2754 chain

1066 0527 pair

1067 4011 chain

1068 4722 chain

1069 – 3120

1070 – 1092

1071 0345 chain

1072 3269 chain

minus 3

80

1058 [Tangut] VII 114 [Tangut] | See 1057

?

1059 [Tangut] IX 13 | [Tangut] "head" v. 887

(i) The dissyllable C.C.C. 33b 饅頭 steamed bread loaf.

4011 chain

1060 [Tangut] [VII 59.60]

(i) C.C.C. 18a 頂 II/4 4 do. I 200 2 B. 216 gtong "forehead"

(ii) | [Tangut] I 202 2 gtong.tor ušnīṣa top-knot.

1061 [Tangut] VI 2 | [Tangut] family 1485

(a) VI 79 ditto

?

1062 [Tangut] IX 80 [Tangut] |

(a) IX.50. ditto See 1064

?

1063 [Tangut] II 1 [Tangut] | "snake" v. 22

(a) V 177 [Tangut] | v. 2056

(b) IX 120 | [Tangut] [? misspelt] v. 1168

(i) C.C.C. 6b 16a W.I. 132 3 142 16 龍 "dragon"

(ii) C.C.C. 10a 辰 "5th branch."

(iii) (b) above B. 100 cat. under "wild animals" (or lit. 'long dragon')

v. 724

1064 [Tangut] IX 50 | [Tangut]

(a) IX 80 ditto See 1062

?

1065 [Tangut] IX 19 [Tangut] | v. 1775

(a) VII 99 [Tangut] | 2677

?

1066 [Tangut] I 42 [Tangut] |

(a) IX 52 ditto inverted See 527

(i) The dissyllable B. 99 cat. under "cattle"

1067 [Tangut] VI. 111 [Tangut] | "head" 4011

?

1068 [Tangut] IX A. 39 [Tangut] | 4722

(a) V 175 | [Tangut] See 1164

C.C.C. 32a 35b W II 70b 富 "wealth, wealthy"

1069 [Tangut] I. 42 | [Tangut]

(a) V 11 ditto

?

1070 [Tangut] IX 72 | [Tangut]

(a) IX 72 ditto See 1092

?

1071 [Tangut] II 15 [Tangut] | See 345(c)

?

1072 [Tangut] V 128 [Tangut] |

?

1073 5344

1074 1650 chain

1075 4396 chain

1076 chain
- 4857-3538
- 0094
- 1135

1077 3654 sub-chain
tr.
B. 123[1] 妻 wife (sic!) 205[2] 委 throw down to depute,

1078 – 1079

1079 1078 pair

1080 chain
- 0833 – 5002
- 0075 – 4068 – 5665 – 2316 – 1806 / 4342 – 3562 / 3558
- 1081
- 3648

1080 (iii) | B. 249[4] (half-way)
ci. bar mdor | ? VI

1081 1080 chain

1082 4439 chain

1083 2710 chain

[1084] 2972 chain

1073.
(a)
?
1074.
(a) V
W.I.226[6]
1074 A
1075
(i) The
1076.
(ii) |
"star"
1076
(a) V 14
(b) III.13
(c) III 8
(i) C.C.C. 4[6] 8[a]
"gold" (ii)
1077.
(a) VII
依 (verb)
1078
(a) III 4
?

element in 3611, 3744

minus 3

81

1073. IX 52 |

(a) IX 29 ditto

?

1074. VIII 84 | v.1650

(a) V 104 | See 0456

W.I.226[6] B.193[2]

1074A See after

1075 V 7 | "pearl" 5224

(i) The dissyllable C.C.C. 12[b] 碧 珃 珠

~~1076~~ "green jade . . . . pearl" B.102 cat under "jewels"

(ii) | C.C.C. 8[a] 羅 猴 星 "Rāhula star"

1076 Ke V A 54 | silver

(a) V 143 ditto

(b) III 13 x by | 1135

(c) III 85 | 0094

Common & certain

(i) C.C.C. 4[b] 8[a] 25[b] W.I.92[6] 金 192[3] gser "gold" (ii) | B 180[2] W.I.92[6] 金剛 "vajra, diamond"

1077. V 142 | 3654

(a) VII 24 | 3797

依 (verb) to conform to, comply with W.II 88[8]

1078 IX 34 |

(a) III 49 ditto See 1079

?

1079 III 49 |

(a) IX 34 ditto See 1078

?

1080 Ca VII 22 |

(a) IX 52 ditto See 833

(b) I 62 | q.v. 3648

(c) VI 13 | See 1081

(d) VII A 83 | See 1075

(i) C.C.C. 27[a] 29[b] 37[a] W.I.112[10] B.179, 249.

道 "marga path." B.246[5] road

(ii) | I 192[14] mu. stegs II 4[12]

~~道~~ 外道 "tirtha, ascetic, one of another cult."

1081 VI 13 | See 1080

?

1082 I 16 | 4439, 2657

(a) I 23

?

1083 I 20 | foot

(i) The dissyllable C.C.C. 33[a] 粥 "gruel, ~~cg~~ congee."

1084 V 104 |

?

1085 - 0374

1086 - 1918

| W.II.128" 如是 "it is thus".

1087 2130 chain

1088 1130 chain

[1089] 3032 pair

1090 5677 chain

I.144³ 光耀 'glorious'

1091 4734 chain

1092 1070 pair

1093 independent

B.175² Part of P.N.

[1094] 4939 pair

[1095] - 4140

[1096] 2149 chain

?

1085

(a) I

W.I.92⁴

·cuming

lta.ba

X "to appe

1086

~~1087~~

(a) III

C.C.C. 35ª =

B.256 yin

~~1085~~

?

1087

(a) I 4

?

1088

?

1089

(a) VII 3

?

1090

(a) I 5

W.I 124⁶ II 26³

1090A

1090B

? 𗀀 W.II.156[8] 頂 summit (See 1060)

82

1085 [Tangut] IX 109 [Tangut] | 0374

(a) IX 49 ditto

W.I. 92[4] 96[13] 見 "to see, seeing, discerning darśana" 190[8] 194[10] 216[17]

lta.ba "to see" B.253[1] ston.pa "to appear".

1086 [Tangut] ngu V. 1 | [Tangut]

(a) III 171 [Tangut] ditto

CCC. 35[a] = "is" W.I.96[6] II 22[11] 52[1] 是 "is"

B.256 yin "to exist". B.160[4]

~~1086 [Tangut] IX 174 | [Tangut]~~

?

1087 [Tangut] I.86 [Tangut] | v. 2130

(a) I 42 [Tangut] | v. 2128

?

1088 [Tangut] IX 174 | [Tangut] "star" v. 1130

?

1089 [Tangut] III 97 [Tangut] |

(a) VII 39 ditto

?

1090 [Tangut] IX 174 [Tangut] | 5677

(a) I 51 [Tangut] | x (5222) 0223

W.I 124[6] II 26[3] 光耀 "glorious" 172[6]

1090A [Tangut] W.I.100[5] might be 0601

1090B [Tangut] Error for 1095

1091 [Tangut] XI VIII 38 [Tangut] | 4734 [Tangut]

CCC. 10[b] 11[a] 日 "day" [after numerals]

W.I.138[10] ? B.162[5] 167[1]

1092 [Tangut] IX 72 [Tangut] |

(a) IX 72 ditto See 1090

1093 [Tangut] [VII 59-60]

(i) By itself W.I. 108[10] II 24[8] 104[11] [?] 150[5] 成 194[15]

sgrub.pa complete, perfect.

(ii) | [Tangut] W.I 110[6] 118[2] II 36[12] 成就

I 218[16] hgrub.pa "completion perfection, siddhi; to attain perfection"; "to fulfil completely" W.II 88[11]

1094 [Tangut] I.1 [Tangut] |

(a) VII 9 ditto

B.103 [Tangut] | cat. "sick".

1095 [Tangut] III 85 | [Tangut]

[(a) I 68 ditto

(a) III A 114 [Tangut] | x of [Tangut]]

? 70[6] B 92 [Tangut]

(a) is a ? ... group.

1096 [Tangut] I.101 | [Tangut]

?

1097 4027 chain

[1098] [0524] pair

5708 chain

1099 chain (cut chain) 3693 (0238) 0100, 5482, 5393

1100 3210 chain

1101 4027 chain

1102 5293 chain

1103 4011 chain

1104 5477 chain

1105
1122
1108 – 0979 1142 / 5431 – 5059 2498 / 3377

take over

1106 0151 chain

[1107] 0627 chain

1108 1105 chain

1097
?
1098
(a) VI
?
Used as a
1099
(a) I.
(b) III
(c) III
(d) IX
?
1100
(a) VI
(b) III.
(i) C.C.C. 6a 鞍
(ii) B.185, 186
(iii) 隱
1101
(a) I. A.
C.C.C. 32a W.
B.161 ... 安
1102
?

minus 3

83

1097 V.A.119 | 3035

?

1098 V 140 |

(a) VII 5 ditto See 524

?

Used as a phonetic W.I.96[12] 丘 B.186[1]

1099 VII 24 | a final particle q.v. 2153

(a) I.A.27 | ? 3693

(b) III 38 | x of See 5694 5100

(c) III 57 | 5482

(d) IX 172 | 5393

?

1100 III.139 |

(a) VI 87 ditto

(b) III.66 | 4362

(i) C.C.C.6[a] 鞍 "saddle" (q.v.)

(ii) B.185, 186[1] 安 in [Ch'ang-]an. B.168[2]

(iii) 隱 tranquillity W.II 144[1]

1101 IX 52 | 4027

(a) I.A.108 ditto

C.C.C.32[a] W.I.110[7] 136[14] II 18[2] 樂 "joy."

B.161[3] tr. 安

1102 IV 4 | ? 5293

?

1103 IX.12 | "head" 4011

(b) I.23 | ? 2655

(c) V 94 | ? 5074

(d) VII 20 | 5275

(a) VIII 1 ditto.

W.I.224[11, 15] ? mgo, bu "first born" bu "young (of an animal)". chain 4011

1104 VIII 80 | 5477

?

1105 IX 40 |

(a) III 31 ditto See 1122

(b) III.66 |

?

1106 VII 96 | 0151

(a) IX 115 ditto See 151

W.II 2[3] Hsia (Kingdom)

C.C.C.9[a] 25[a2] 夏 "summer" B 261 tr.

1107 VIII 80 | 4230

?

1108 III 66 | See 1105

(a) VII 14 | 0977

~~(i) C.C.C.13[a] 瑙 "agate, cornelian"~~

(i) C.C.C.16[a] 腦 "brain" B 215[4]

(ii) C.C.C.13[a] | 瑪瑙 B.103. cat. under "jewels" jade horse ornament, agate or cornelian.

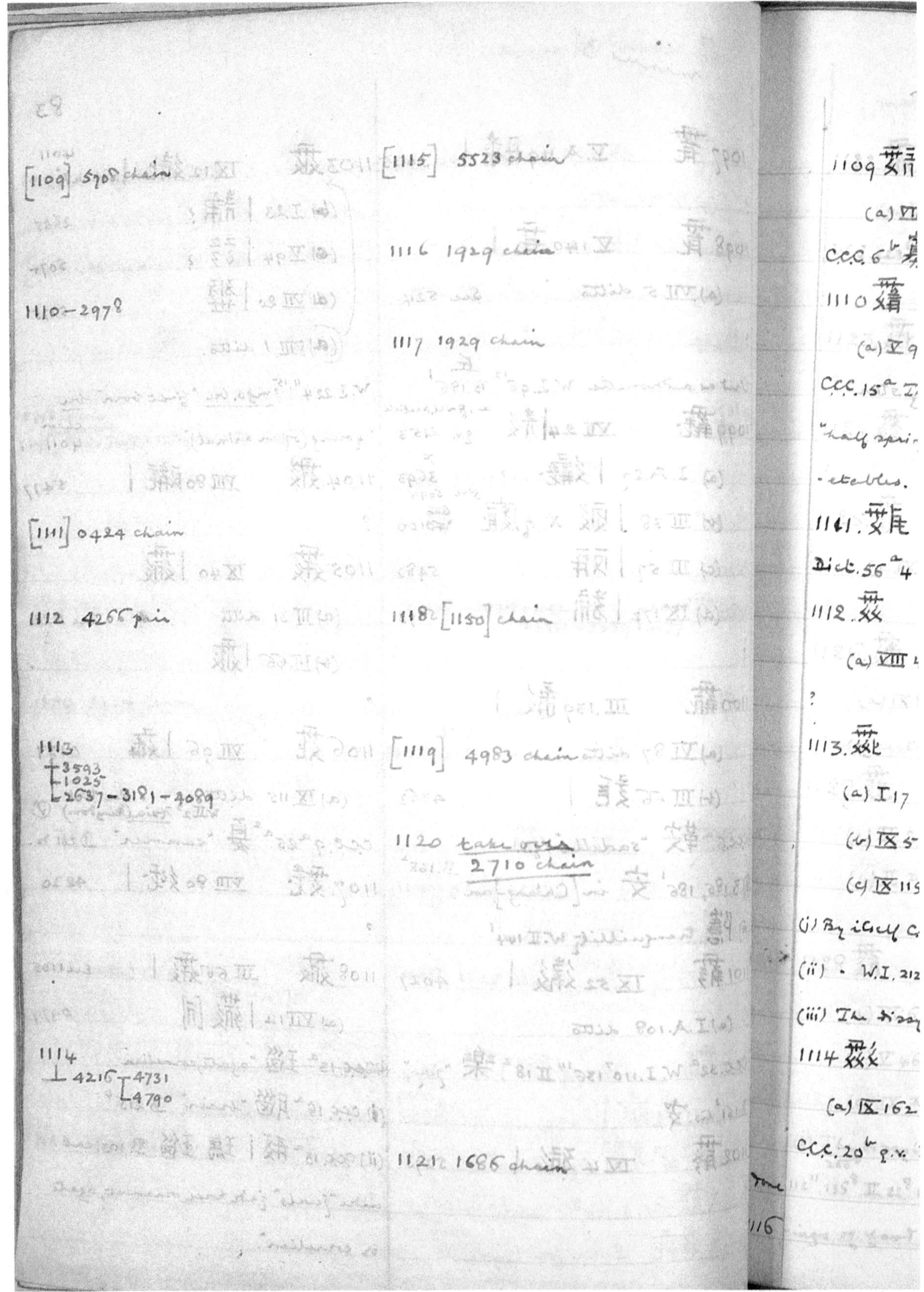

minus 3

84

1109 [Tangut] II A5 [Tangut] | 1956

(a) VII 115 [Tangut] | 3998

C.C.C. 6b 寡 "solitary, widow (ster)".

1110 [Tangut] VII 96 | [Tangut]

(a) V 95 | [Tangut] x of [Tangut] v. 2978

C.C.C. 15a The dissyllable + [Tangut] 半春菜 "half spring vegetable" B.102 cat. under "veg-etables.

1111. [Tangut] III 148 [Tangut] | "father" v. 424

Dict. 56a 4

1112. [Tangut] III. 66 [Tangut] |

(a) VIII 4 ditto

?

1113. [Tangut] I 14 | [Tangut] 3593

(a) I 17 ditto

(b) IX 5 | [Tangut] "aunt" see 1025

(c) IX 115 | [Tangut] 1637

(i) By itself C.C.C. 20a 31a 母 "mother"

(ii) " W.I. 212[12] -mo female affix. C.C.C. 20a

(iii) The dissyllable 娘娘 "mother".

1114 [Tangut] VIII 62 [Tangut] | 4218

(a) IX 162 ditto

C.C.C. 20b q.v. ? term of relationship

1115 [Tangut] III 148 [Tangut] |

?

1116 [Tangut] I 98 [Tangut] |

?

1117 [Tangut] mo I 126 [Tangut] | "cattle" v. 1934

(a) I 98 | [Tangut] See 1116

(i) C.C.C. 5b 牛 W. I. 190[16] 214[9] ba glan "ox" B.215[1]

(ii) C.C.C. 9b 丑 "2nd branch"

(iii) The dissyllable B. 99 cat. under "cattle".

1118 [Tangut] IX A 142 [Tangut] |

(a) IX 137 ditto See 1150

?

1119 [Tangut] IX 72 [Tangut] | 3121

W. II 80[4] 秉 "to grasp"

1120 [Tangut] VII 5 | [Tangut] grain 2710

(a) VII 9 ditto

(b) III 60 [Tangut] | foot 5440

(i) The dissyllable C.C.C. 15b 斛斗 B.169[4] bushel .... B.221[3] 稼穡 crop harvest

(ii) (b) above C.C.C. 33a 食 饌

1121. [Tangut] VIII 33 [Tangut] | 5339

(a) VII 33 | [Tangut] v. 1610

?(ii) The dissyllable 守護 "to protect, guard" W. II 128[8]

1122 1105 chain

1129 1128 chain

1123 1891 chain

1130 (ii) skar.mda "shooting star"

B.252[4]

1124 4651 chain

1130 chain
- 0076
- 2173
- 2515 - 2678 - 0129
- 2863
- 3861
- 4618
- 4909

1125 0548 pair

1126 4203 pair

1127 0457 chain

1128
- 0441
- 4309 - 5646 – 0376, 2134, [0770], 2739
- 5302 – 1129

| 綏 W.II.78[6] 求 願 to pray for

B.204[1] 求

1131 – 5328

1122.

(a) IX

W.I.222[6]

1123.

?

1124.

?

1125.

(a) IX 25

?

1126.

(a) IX 8

Pretty certain

1127.

(a) V. 26

(b) II A 11

?

1128

(a) VI 67

(b) V 46 |

(c) IX A 127

(i) The disyllab

2568

112[11] 138[8] II 22[8] 46[4]

"ings of food"

minus 3

85

1122. [Tangut] III.31 [Tangut] |

(a) IX 40 ditto [[Tangut]] See 1105

W.I.222[6] mon. gru "name of lunar mansion"

1123. [Tangut] III.67 [Tangut] | "a" v. 1891

?

1124. [Tangut] III 106. [Tangut] | "spirit" v. 473.

?

1125. [Tangut] IX 12 | [Tangut]

(a) IX 25 ditto cf. 1134

?

1126. [Tangut] IX 12 family or clan name [Tangut]

(a) IX 8 [Tangut] |

Pretty certainly a double name

1127. [Tangut] II 23 | [Tangut] "to receive"

(a) V. 26 ditto See 457 x(4989)

(b) II A 11 | [Tangut] 4987

?

1128 [Tangut] V 5 | [Tangut] 0441 ~~4~~

(a) VI 67 ditto See 441

(b) V 46 | [Tangut] x(1129) 5302

(c) IX A 127 | [Tangut] x 4309

(i) The disyllable C.C.C. 21[a] W.I. 96[1] 108[6] 266[8] 112[11] 138[8] II 22[8] 46[4] 供養 "to make offerings of food" B, 122[3]

(ii) By itself C.C.C. 21[b] W.I. 168[2] B. 219[1] 132[2] 求 prayer "to seek" II 86[9,11] doubled B. 131[3]. B. 169[1] 173[2] 供 offerings

1129. [Tangut] III 60 | [Tangut] 5302

W.II 44[4] 請 "to ask"

1130. [Tangut] ye V 141 [Tangut] |

A (a) V 108 ditto See 76

F (b) I.5 [Tangut] | 3861

H (c) I.18 [Tangut] | 4909

B (d) I.28 [Tangut] | 2173

G (e) VII 17 | [Tangut] 4618

C x (f) VII 26 | [Tangut] xx 2515

I (g) IX 140 [Tangut] | 2863

D (h) IX 174 [Tangut] | See 1088

(i) C.C.C. 5[a,b] passim 宿[(a)] C.C.C. 6[a] 星[(b)]

I 226[1] 53a "star" [sometimes specifically "planet"].

(ii) The disyllable C.C.C. 4[b] W.I 220[7] 222[11] 星宿 rgyu.skar "a lunar mansion or fixed star."

1131. [Tangut] VII 18 | [Tangut]

(a) V. 83 ditto

?

1132 5094 chain

1133 5094 chain

[1134] +0547 pair

1135 1076 chain

1136
┼3753
└3751

1137 0233 chain

1137 | 以 [| doubtful] 以為

"to consider as" W. I. 168³

1138 1317 chain

1139 5314 chain

1140
┼0486
└5425–5724

1141 0159 chain

1142 ~~independent~~ 1105 chain

1143 5188 chain

1144 5623 chain

1145 3931 chain

1146 3269 chain

1131A

1132

(a) VI

(b) I.

(c) IX

W. I. 192⁸ d

1133

?

1134

(a) IX 25

?

1135

?

1136

(a) VII A

(b) VII 4

?

1137

also q

W. II 26¹ [indis

迴 "to turn,

1138

?

1139

B. 91 above

| is the word

"altogether com

minced 3

86

1131 A [Tangut] Error for [Tangut] 1143

1132 [Tangut] IX 43 [Tangut] | 5094 heat

(a) VI 48 ditto

(b) I. 57 | [Tangut] See 1133

(c) IX 137 | [Tangut] warm v. 2040 ?

W. I. 192[8] dros.pa "warm"

1133 [Tangut] I 57 [Tangut] | "warm" See 1132 ?

?

1134 [Tangut] IX 12 | [Tangut]

(a) IX 25 ditto cf. 1125

?

1135 [Tangut] III. 13 [Tangut] [Tangut] "gold + silver"

?

1136 [Tangut] VII 48 | [Tangut] 3753

(a) VII A 101 ditto

(b) VII 48 [Tangut] 3751

?

1137 [Tangut] VIII. 1 | [Tangut]

also 92[3] B 212[1] (title) 213[3] (do.)

W. II 26[1] [indistinct, looks more like [Tangut]]

迴 "to turn, bend".

1138 [Tangut] VIII 1 [Tangut] | v. 1327

?

1139. [Tangut] ts'yuan VI A 75 [Tangut] | to assemble v. 1962

B. 91 [Tangut] above or the whole of [Tangut].

| is the word for [Tangut] [Tangut] [Tangut] [Tangut]

"altogether completely collected".

cf. 1051

1140 [Tangut] III A 18 [Tangut] |

(a) III 166 ditto See 486

(b) III 7 [Tangut] | $ 5425

1141 [Tangut] IX A 172 [Tangut] | 5164

?

1142. [Tangut] III 147 [Tangut] | ~~x by itself~~ 0979

?

1143. [Tangut] IX 43 | [Tangut]

(i) The Disyllable C.C.C. 24[b] [but [Tangut]]

襖子 "lined jacket, robe".

1144 [Tangut] IX 43 | [Tangut] 2713

(a) II 15 [Tangut] | See 506

(b) IX 147 | [Tangut] v. 2041

?

1145 [Tangut] VI A 67 [Tangut] | 3931

(a) (ditto) (I 57)

[(b) ([Tangut]) (VI A 103) x by [Tangut] |]

?

(b) is a Phonetic group

1146 [Tangut] VIII 8 [Tangut] | quarter q.v. 3269

(a) I 9 [Tangut] | ? v. 2028

B. 165[4] 166[3]

1147 — 3884 A

[1148] 0390 pair

1149 5468 chain

[1150]
+1118
[3399
[5101

1151 0271 chain

1152 4027 chain

[1153] 3784 pair

(2536 — 1154) pair

1155 4027 chain

1156 0538 chain

1157 5677 chain

1158 1199 chain

1159 4868 chain

1160 0148 chain

[1161] 1869 chain

1162 1340 chain

1163 1361 chain

1147 䕟

?

1148. 帀

(a) V

?

1149 䕉

(a) II

?

1150 ○ 莇

(a) IX

(b) II

(c) III. 16

W.I. 98" 細

1151 ○ 氈

?

1152 䕸

(a) VIII A

(b) IX 60

? (c) IX 53

1153 蒿

(a) VIII

?

1154 𦨴 VI

(a) VII 8

? country.

minus 3

87

1147 [illegible] II 15 | [illegible] ~~"wool velvet"~~

?

1148. [illegible] V 162 | [illegible] 0390

(a) V 107 ditto

?

1149 [illegible] I 20 [illegible] | 5468

(a) II A 20

?

1150 [illegible] IX 137 [illegible] |

(a) IX A 142 ditto 1118

(b) II 18 [illegible] | 3339

(c) III 167 | [illegible] 'first turn' 5181

W.I. 98" 細 224^8 ndrob "fine, subtle"

1151 [illegible] IX 70 [illegible] | 'nose' 2583

?

1152 [illegible] III 50 [illegible] | x5355

(a) VIII A 61 [illegible] | 05386

(b) IX 60 | [illegible] See 1155

? (c) IX 53 [illegible] | 0831

1153 [illegible] IX 53 [illegible] |

(a) VIII 1 ditto

?

1154 [illegible] VI 35 [illegible] | 2536

(a) VII 8 ditto

?

1155 [illegible] IX 60 [illegible] | See 1152

?

1156 [illegible] IX 67 [illegible]

?

~~1157 [illegible] VI [illegible]~~

1157 [illegible] VIII A 50 [illegible] |

B. 168^5 dissyl. + doubled.

1158 [illegible] III 132 [illegible] |

(a) III A 13 ditto See 1199

?

1159. [illegible] IX 86 | [illegible] 4868

(a) V 59 | [illegible] [illegible] See 1178

(i) By itself C.C.C. 21^a 銅 W.I. 214^8 zans "copper"

cat. under 'jewels' B.102

(ii) (b) above C.C.C. 12^b 銅鍮 "copper"

1160 [illegible] V 90 [illegible] | 4501

?

1161 [illegible] VI 109 | [illegible] "iron" [illegible] See 1194

B.102 the dissyllable cat. under 'jewels'

C.C.C. 12^b 錫 "pewter or tin",

1162 [illegible] V 175 [illegible] |

(a) I. 114 ditto See 1340

?

1163 [illegible] VII 62 [illegible] | 'brave' v. 1373

(i) By itself W.I. 100^4 利 "sharp" 128^17 164^6 快 "keen"

(ii) [illegible] | W.I. 92^6 96^5 114^16 etc. 金剛 vajra "diamond"

1164 4722 chain

1165 4083 chain

1166 2027 chain

1167 0126 chain

1168 0022 chain

1169 · 1699 pair

1170 1361 chain

1171 3438 chain

1172
└1197 - 4009

1173 ~~...~~ important

1174 1862 chain

1175 4783 chain

1176 2906 chain

1177 0762 pair

1178 4868 chain

1179 1894 chain

1180
┼1210
├0732
└1181

1181 1180 chain

1164A
also B.34

1164

?

1165

?

1166

?

1167

?

1168

(i) The disy...

animals" (

1169

(a) IX 129

?

1170

?

1171

(i) By itself

(ii) The disy...

"scissors, ...

1172

(a) VI 33.

?

1173

country.

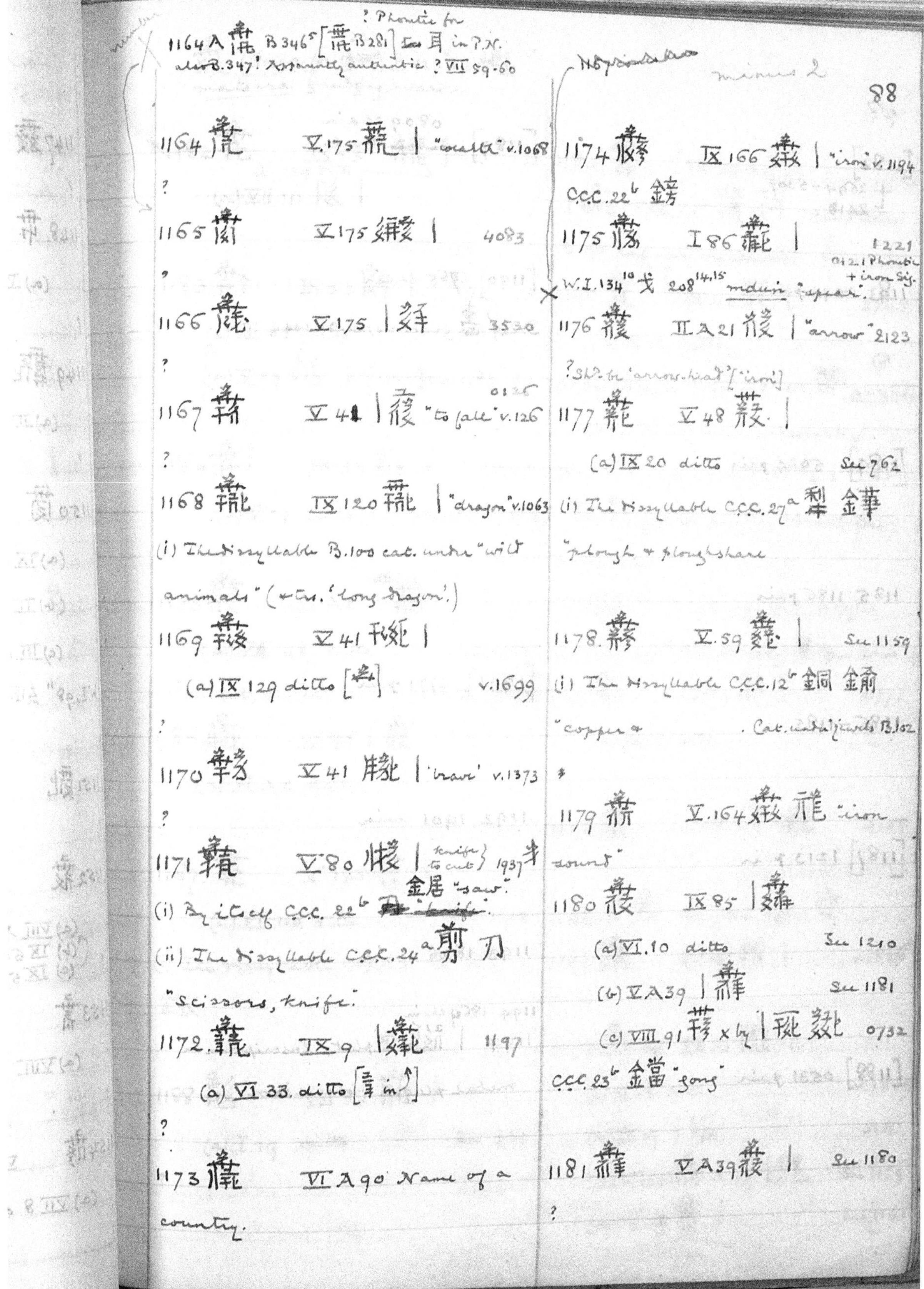

[1182]
+2694-5307
2418

1183 0093 pair

[1184] 5024 pair

1185 1186 pair

1186-1185

[1187] 1213 pair

[1188] 0531 pair

0809 chain
[1189] ~~independent~~

[1190] 2765 chain
3.229 惠 gracious, kindness

[1991] 2771 pair

1192 1901 chain

1193 1826 chain

1194 1869 chain
1194 | B. plate. Inscription on metal plaque of black iron

1182
(a) I
1183.
(a) III
(b) V;
1184
(a) V
1185
(a) VI
? chisel,
1186
(a) VI A
1187.
(a) VI
(i) The disyll
鈸
1188
(a) I.19

[Tangut] (Error for ~~1223~~ 1222) B.123[5] tr. 慳
matsara grudging, avarice

89

1182 [Tangut] IX 53 [Tangut] |
I 134 ditto reversed
(a) VII 111 [Tangut] |

?

1183. [Tangut] IX 53 [Tangut] |
(a) III 85 ditto
[(b) V 79 [Tangut] | [error] See 1184]

?

1184 [Tangut] IX 53 [Tangut] | 5024
(a) V 79 ditto (but misspelt See 1183(b))

?

1185 [Tangut] VI A2 [Tangut] |
(a) VI 98 ditto See 1186
? "chisel, punch" See ~~779~~ 798 [Tangut]

1186 [Tangut] VI 98 | [Tangut]
(a) VI A2 ditto.

?

1187. [Tangut] V 145 [Tangut] |
(a) VI 110 ditto See 1213
(i) The dissyllable C.C.C. 23[b] 火 炉
鏉

1188 [Tangut] VIII 84 [Tangut] |
(a) I. 19 ditto See 531

?

1189. [Tangut] [VII 59-60]
| [Tangut] C.C.C. 14[b] 薄荷 "thin lotus"
B.101 cat. under 'vegetables'.

1190 [Tangut] IX 113 [Tangut] | 2765
(a) VI 43 ditto
(i) By itself W. I. 90[9] 270[20] II 2[8] etc. 慧 prajñā
"wisdom, discernment, understanding.
(ii) The dissyllable W. I. 108[19] II 2[10] etc. [Tangut]
智慧 jñāna prajñā "knowledge and wisdom.
(iii) [Tangut] | B. 248[1] B. 172[1] śes-rab prajñā
(iv) W. I. 92[10] (exceptionally) 惠 "gracious"

1191 [Tangut] VI. 62 [Tangut] | 4771
(a) VI 16 ditto

?

1192 [Tangut] I. 118 [Tangut] [Tangut] 4168

1192A [Tangut] etc. see after [Tangut]

1193 [Tangut] III 145 [Tangut] | v. 1825

?

1194 [Tangut] VII 33 [Tangut] |
(a) III 58 ditto v. 1869
(b) III 99 | [Tangut] 5136
(c) V 164 [Tangut] x by | [Tangut] 1158 See 1179
(d) VI 109 [Tangut] | See [1161]

(over)

1195 1218 chain

(b) B.192[4]

1196 2278 chain

1197 1172 chain

1198 1199 chain

1199 ⊥1158 ⊥1198

1200 3526 chain

1201 4479 chain

1202 1538 chain

1203 5030 chain

1204 1332 pair

1205 independent

1206 2494 chain

1206 鎧 "armour" W. I 102[3]

1207 0959 chain

1208 1862 chain

1194 (cont.)

(c) VI 128

(b) IX 16

(i) C.C.C. 12[b]

(d) above

cat. inter

(ii) W.I. 136[6]

1195 [Tangut character]

(a) I A 4

(b) IX 4

C.C.C. 7[a] W.I.

military;

1196 [Tangut character]

(a) VI 6

(i) C.C.C. 22[b] (a)

1197 [Tangut character]

(a) IX 9

(b) I. 14

W.I. 132[16] 鉤

1198 [Tangut character] V

?

1199 [Tangut character]

(a) III 132 d

(b) VI A 9

minus 2

1194 (cont)

(c) VI 128 | [Tangut] See 1208

(d) IX 166 | [Tangut] See 1174

(i) C.C.C. 12^{b} 鐵 "iron" [in the disyllable (d) above) The same disyllable B 102 cat. under "jewels".

(ii) W.I. 136^{6}? [鑁 or] 械

1195 [Tangut] VIII 23 [Tangut] |

(a) I A 42 ditto See 1218

(b) IX 4 | [Tangut]

C.C.C. 7^{a} W.I. 134^{10} 136^{16} 武 "soldier, military" B.346^{1}

1196 [Tangut] II 4 | [Tangut] 2918

(a) VI 65 | [Tangut] See 1323

(i) C.C.C. 22^{b} (a) above 斤斧 "axe, hatchet"

1197 [Tangut] VI 33 [Tangut] | 1172

(a) IX 9 ditto

(b) I.14 | [Tangut] 4009

W.I. 132^{16} 鈎 "fish-hook"

1198 [Tangut] VI A 91 [Tangut] |

?

1199 [Tangut] III A 13 | [Tangut]

(a) III 132 ditto [[Tangut]] See 1158

(b) VI A 91 | [Tangut] See 1198

minus 3

90

1200 [Tangut] VI 119 [Tangut] | v.1748

?

1201 [Tangut] IX 62 [Tangut] | 4479

(a) IX A 163 [Tangut] | 4904

?

1202 [Tangut] I.16 | [Tangut] v.1538

?

1203 [Tangut] VII 33 [Tangut] | 5030

(a) III 96 ditto

(i) The disyllable W.I. 132^{11} 慈愍 "compassionate & sympathetic" Possibly an error for 2297A ??

1204 [Tangut] V 16 [Tangut] |

(a) V 4 See 1332

?

1205 [Tangut] [VII 59-60]

?

1206 [Tangut] IX 11 [Tangut] | [3654]

(a) IX A 132 [Tangut] | See 684

? 甲 "armour, (tortoise) shell W.I. 168^{17}

1207. [Tangut] II 14 [Tangut] | "defile" v.919.

?

1208 [Tangut] VI 128 [Tangut] | "iron" v.1194

C.C.C. 22^{b} 鑷子 "pincers"

1209 2760 pair

1210 1180 chain

1211 is a compound ideogram 'metal verification'

1211 0965 chain

1212 - 4811

1213 - 1187

1214 0443 pair

1215 2150 chain VI

1216 3587 chain

1217 - 4892

[1218]
1195
3638

1219 3026 chain

[1220] - [1825]

1221 4783 chain

1222
4521 — ?4519
1886 - 0432 — 5324
5329

B.123^5 ... stingy not break

1209.
(a) VIII
(b) V
?
(b) is ?

1210.
(a) IX
ccc. 23b
1210A

1211
Dict. 54a

1212
(a) III 171
Dict 1b 4

1213.
(a) V 145
The disylla

1214
(a) V 7.
[Zach "bell,

1215.
The disyllable
'needle & thre

91

1209. [Tangut] IX A 169 [Tangut] | 2760

(a) VIII A 94 ditto

[(b) V A 129 [Tangut] x by [Tangut] | [Tangut]]

?

(b) is ? a Phonetic group.

1210. [Tangut] VI 10 [Tangut] |

(a) IX 85 ditto See 1180

C.C.C. 23b 鼎 "a tripod".

1210A [Tangut] Error for 1159.

1211 [Tangut] III.61 [Tangut] | Truth 4952

Dict. 54a 5 B 272 343 2,4 1,3,4 } 印 "seal", to print W I 271 8

1212 [Tangut] III 27 | [Tangut]

(a) III 171 ditto

Dict 1b 4

1213. [Tangut] VI 110 | [Tangut]

(a) V 145 ditto See 1187

The dissyllable C.C.C. 23b 火炉 鏉

1214 [Tangut] IX 68 | [Tangut]

(a) V 7 ditto See 4463

[Zach "bell, gong"] which is 1159

1215. [Tangut] VIII 12 [Tangut] | 3618

The dissyllable C.C.C. 25b 針 線 "needle & thread".

1216 [Tangut] VI 127 (VIII 12) [Tangut] | v. 955

(i) The dissyllable C.C.C. 23b 茶 [Tangut] 銚

1217 [Tangut] V 77 [Tangut] |

(a) V 80 ditto

C.C.C. 22b 鈴 "small bell".

1218 [Tangut] I A 42 [Tangut] | "military"

(a) VIII 23 ditto See 1195

(b) VII 81 | [Tangut] ~~sickle~~ 3638

(i) C.C.C. 22b 刀 "knife".

(ii) The dissyllable W.I. 136 16 apparently 刀 "knife, sword".

1219 [Tangut] III 146 [Tangut] | 4380

?

1220 [Tangut] V 20 [Tangut] |

(a) V 29 ditto v. 1825

?

1221 [Tangut] V 91 [Tangut] | ...

(a) I 86 | [Tangut] "spear" See 1175

?

1222 [Tangut] VII 32 | [Tangut] garland 4521

(a) IX 34 ditto

(b) III 119 [Tangut] x by | [Tangut] x (8432) 1886

W.II. 25 12 仰 "to look up to, respect"

v. 1181A

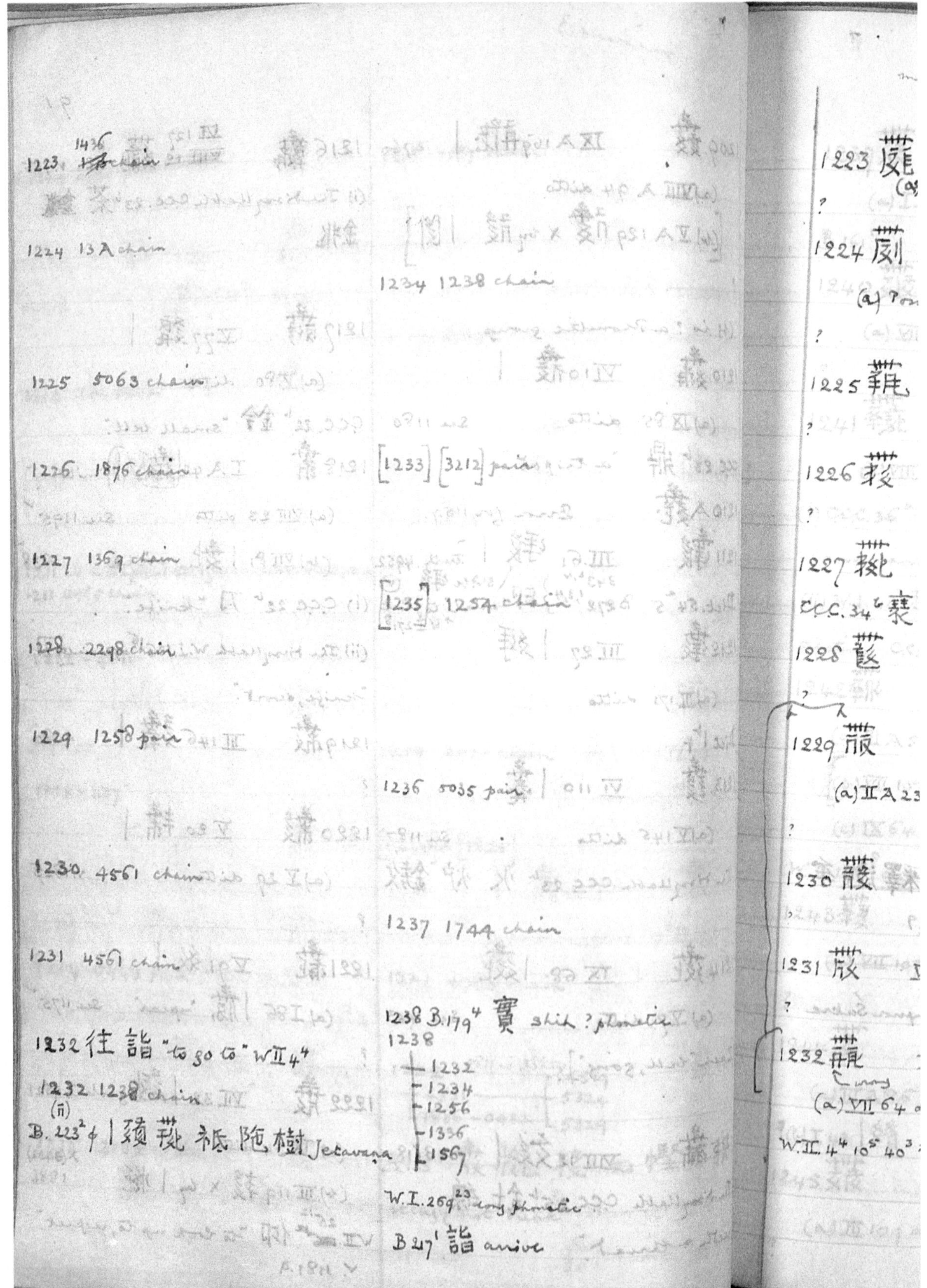

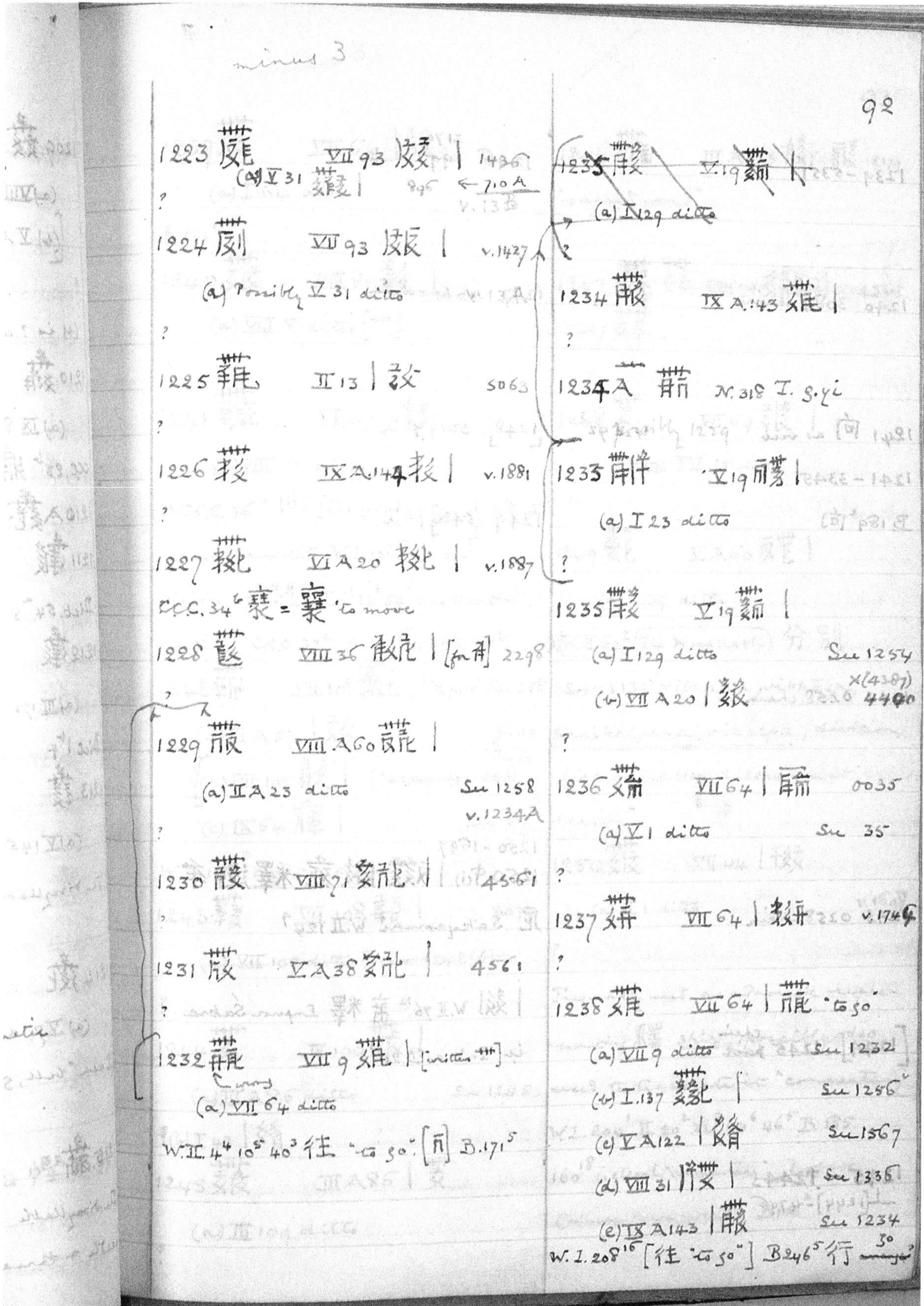

1239 - 5351

1240 3084 ~~chain~~ IX

1241 向 as verb W.II 92[3]

1241 - 33451

B. 189[2] 向

1242 0258 chain

1243 0258 ~~chain~~

[1244] 1245 ~~pair~~ chain

1245 — ~~1244~~ [1244] - 4796

1246 2179 ~~1992~~ ~~chain~~ IV

1247 ~~4561 chain~~

[1248] 5019 pair

1249 [5430] pair

1250 - 1597

1250 (i) | 釋迦牟尼 Śakyamuni W.II 124[9]

| W.II 76[12] 帝釋 Emperor Śakra i.e. Indra B. 211[3]

1239

(a) I

B. 161[1]

1240

(a) V

?

1241

(a) VI

(i) C.C.C. 36

-yana-sa

(ii) W.I. 110[7]

disting. C

1242

(a) III A

(b) VII

(c) IX 6

W.I. 196[8]

1243

(a) ~~VII~~

?

1244

(a) III A 8

?(b) I 43 |

1245

(a) III 109

?

1239 [Tangut] VII 64 | [Tangut]

(a) I.64 ditto

B.161^{1}

1240. [Tangut] VIII 81 [Tangut] |

(a) VIII 8 ditto [‡]

?

1241 [Tangut] VI.67 | [Tangut]

(a) VIII.16 ditto

(i) C.C.C. 36^{a} 向 [The four] stages of Hīnayana sanctity. W.I.108^{17} B.212^{1}

(ii) W.I.110^{7} 趣 II 6^{1} 22^{3} 54^{10} "destination, destiny." C.C.C. 37^{a} B.123^{5} v. S.-K. 138^{b}.

1242 [Tangut] VII 108 [Tangut] | "to fight" See 258

(a) III A 57 | [Tangut] 3429 / 3070

(b) VII 107 [Tangut] | [? error, see 1243]

(c) IX 64 [Tangut] | See 317

W.I.196^{8} dgra "enemy".

1243 [Tangut] VII 108 [Tangut] | 3070

(a) ~~VII 107 ditto? See 1242(b)~~

?

1244 [Tangut] III 109 [Tangut] |

(a) III A 86 ditto See 1245

?(b) I 43 | [Tangut] ?

1245 [Tangut] III A 86 | [Tangut]

(a) III 109 ditto

?

93

1246 [Tangut] III A 103 [Tangut] [Tangut] 2179

"sacred word".

1247. [Tangut] ~~[Tangut] VIII 71 [Tangut] | 4564~~

1247 [Tangut]

1248 [Tangut] VII 69 [Tangut] |

(a) ~~I 45~~ VII 15 ditto

?

1249 [Tangut] V A 60 [Tangut] |

(a) I.39 ditto

(i) W.II 62^{2} (The disyllable) 分別 (Soot. p139) "vibhajya, vibhāga, parikalpana, vikalpa, division, discrimination, discernment, reason"

1250. [Tangut] VII 44 | [Tangut]

(a) II 1 ditto v.1697

?

Frequently used as a phonetic representing 釋 shih, possibly also used to translate it "commentary" W.I. 204^{1} II 20^{2} 22^{9} 44^{6} 46^{5} B.185 160^{18} is clearly "commentary". Probably Chinese loan-word? B.1.26^{2}

93

1251 3829 chain

1252
3975
0683 3190-1676

B.123[4] 含 to cherish

1253 0084

1254
[1235]-4400-4387
1820

1255 2343 pair Ⅶ 6

1256 1238 chain Ⅷ 8

(a) Ⅷ 8 ditto

1257 3226 chain

1258-1229

1259-1261

1260 1744 chain

1261 1259 pair Ⅶ 108

1262 2579 chain Ⅲ

(a) Ⅲ 109 ditto

1251

?

1252

1252 A

This chain

908

1253

(a) Ⅱ 12

1254

(a) Ⅴ. 19

(b) Ⅸ 84

W. I. 196[3]

minus 4

94

1251 [Tangut] VII 3 [Tangut] |

?

1252 [Tangut] ? VII A 88 | [Tangut] 3975

(a) VII A 14 ditto.

(b) VII 88 [Tangut] | See 683

W. II 20[7] 40[1] 隨 "to follow; after, according to." 92[2] 118[9] B. 126[2]

I 206[5] njeu-sui "after".

1252 A [Tangut]

This character is identical with 908 q.v. & may well be the correct form. B. 123[4]

It is the form found at III 36[1] where [Tangut] | translates 舍

1253 [Tangut] I. 18 | [Tangut]

(a) II 12 ditto See 84

(i) The disyllable C.C.C. 34[a] 奉送 "to receive & escort."

1254 [Tangut] I. 129 | [Tangut] 1235

(a) V. 19 ditto See 1235

(b) IX 84 [Tangut] | v. 1820

W. I. 196[3]: g.yog "servant" B 160[2] 策

(ii) The disyl. B 94 v. 4444

1255 [Tangut] I. 137 [Tangut] | 2343

(a) I A 111 ditto

?

1256 [Tangut] I. 137 | [Tangut] v. 1238

? possibly B 176[1]

1257 [Tangut]. VI. 67 [Tangut] | [4167]

?

1258 [Tangut] II A. 23 | [Tangut]

(a) VIII A 60 ditto See 1229

?

1259 [Tangut] II 35 | [Tangut]

(a) II A 6 ditto See 1261

?

1260 [Tangut] I. 26 [Tangut] |

(a) I 49 ditto v. 1744

?

~~1261 [Tangut] III 109~~

1261 [Tangut] II A 6 [Tangut] |

(a) II 35 ditto See 1259

?

1262 [Tangut] IV A 2 [Tangut] | see 2519

(a) III 118 | [Tangut] See 1331.

(b) IV A 5 [Tangut] | 1263

C.C.C. 11[b] W. I 96[13] II 32[5] 濁 "turbidity, impurity, decay."

1263 2519 chain

1264–0124

[1265]
⊥1831–1832

1266 1269 pair

1267 2193 chain

[1268] 5543 pair

1269–1266

[1270] 4435 chain

1271 5188 chain

1272
┬[4547]
└2311

1272(i) W. II. 2⁹ 逮 得 "attained"
獲 "to obtain W. II 94⁴ + passim
By itself B. 171¹ 報 recompense

1273 3906 chain

1274 5340 chain

1275 4435 chain

[1276] 3587 chain

1263.

1264

(a) III

1265

(a) III A

1266

(a) VII

1267.

1268

(a) I. 46

(b)

(i) The diss...

"father, da...

1269.

(a) V 93. d

1270

minus 本

95

1263. [Tangut] IV A 5 | [Tangut] impure v. 1262

?

1264 [Tangut] IV A 3 | [Tangut]

(a) III 112 ditto See 124

?

1265 [Tangut] VI. 89 | [Tangut] 1831

(a) III A 91 ditto

?

1266 [Tangut] V 93 [Tangut] |

(a) VII. 10 ditto See 1269

?

1267. [Tangut] III 57 | [Tangut] v. 359

?

1268 [Tangut] I 92 [Tangut] | [5543]

(a) I. 46 ditto

(b) I

(i) The dissyllable C.C.C. 20[a] [Tangut][Tangut]

"father, daddy".

1269. [Tangut] VII 10 | [Tangut]

(a) V 93 ditto See 1266

?

1270 [Tangut] V A. 140 [Tangut] | v. 1275

?

1271 [Tangut] VIII 50 | [Tangut] 5188

(a) III 173 [Tangut] | See 61

?

1272. [Tangut] IX 180 | [Tangut]

(a) IX A 138 ditto

(b) IX A 84 | [Tangut] 2311

(i) | [Tangut] C.C.C. 36[b] (? q.v.) 37[a] 得達

~~W. II 2[9] (ditto wrong)~~ II 130[3] W. I. 108[11] (? q.v.)

"to reach, attain, obtain."

(ii) By itself I 136[12] 達 ditto.

易及 "to reach" W. I. 162[7]

1273. [Tangut] I. 33 [Tangut] | 3906

?

1274 [Tangut] VIII 39 [Tangut] | 5540

?

1275 [Tangut] VIII 39 [Tangut] | 4435

(a) V A 140 | [Tangut] See 1270

(i) C.C.C. 6[a] 23[b] 盖 [a] "cover, sheathe"

(ii) W. I. 110[17] II 84[6] 覆 cover

(iii) C.C.C. 23[b] 篁 veil (?), basket

(iv) C.C.C. 23[b] 床 frame of a basket?

1276 [Tangut] IX. 180 [Tangut] | "tie" v. 955

?

1277 0535 pair

1278 5314 chain

1279 4435 chain

1280 4983 chain
1280A 𘄦 W.I 172[4] 厭 "to dislike, hate."

1281 1313 chain

[1282] indépendant

1283 ~~434~~
† 4548
L 0579

1284 2412 chain
1284 | 𘄦 B.245 'Forest of categories' (name of book)

1285 2412 chain IV

1286 1889 chain

1287 independent

1288 0154 chain

1289 3526 chain

1290 independent

1291 3226 chain
1291. Alternatively begins sentence & means 則 "then" W.II 88[11,12]

1277 𘄦
(a) III
?
1278 𘄦
1279 𘄦
(a) IX 7
?
1280 𘄦
(i) The dissy
"The cap (or balcony?)
(ii) By itself
1281. 𘄦
?
1282 𘄦
"A name". N
1283. 𘄦
(a) V 104
(b) VIII. 17
?
1284 𘄦
(i) C.C.C. 36[a] W.I.
196[2] 218[6] sde
II 134[4] 部[3] sec

minus A

96

1277 [Tangut] II 22 [Tangut] |

(a) III 22 ditto See 555

?

1278 [Tangut] II 39 [Tangut] | 5314

?

1279 [Tangut] IX 72 [Tangut] | 4435

(a) IX 78 ditto

?

1280 [Tangut] VIII 39 | [Tangut]

(i) The dissyllable C.C.C. 21^{a} 軒冕

"The cap (or hood?) of a carriage (or balcony?)

(ii) By itself II 48^{11} 138^{6} 蓋 "cover, lid"

1281 [Tangut] VII 4 [Tangut] | "silk" v. 1313

?

1282 [Tangut] VIII 15 [Tangut] |

"A name". Nevski I 402

1283 [Tangut] V 116 [Tangut] | 4548

(a) V 104 ditto

(b) VIII. 17 [Tangut] | See 579

?

1284 [Tangut] III 42 [Tangut] |

(i) C.C.C. 36^{a} W.I. 132^{16} 類 W.I. 118^{6} 部 196^{2} 218^{6} side "class, species". B. 126^{2} II 134^{4} 部[3] section (of a book)

1285 [Tangut] VI 124 [Tangut] | 2412

(a) IX 144 ditto

(c) III 80 | [Tangut] See 0204

W. I. 108^{6} 138^{7} 142^{18} 像 "statue, image"

B. 241^{2} 形 Nevski I 245

1286 [Tangut] I A 63 | [Tangut]

?

1287 [Tangut] I A 71 [Tangut] [Tangut]

"man's name

W. II 52^{4} Phonetic.

1288 [Tangut] VII 27 [Tangut] |

(a) V 2 ditto See 154

?

1289 [Tangut] II. 4 | [Tangut] 3526

(i) By itself W. II. 14^{6} 現 "to appear, display". (Doubted) B. 162^{5}

(ii) | [Tangut] W. II 32^{4} 52^{7} 112^{10} 示現 "to appear"

1290. [Tangut] IX A 77 × by itself (1.5)

?

1291 [Tangut] KU V A 116 [Tangut] [Tangut]

(a) VI 46 [Tangut] | 3916

(ii) X by "Auxiliary word".

(i) C.C.C. 36^{b} 是則 W. II 22^{1} 32^{12} 52^{6} I 108^{7} B 254^{4}

~~Does not generally represent any fixed Chinese word. Ends the sentence & means "because"~~ 故 (or begins it)

B. 195^{5} B. 228^{2} (twice) begins sentence

Left margin: 1263, 1264, III (a), 1265, (a) III A, 1266, (a) VII, 1267, 1268, (a) I, the dissyl., begins sentence I $88^{11,12}$, 1269

1293 2204 chain Ⅱ 22

1292 0582 chain

1294 1313 chain

VIII 59

1295 4703 chain VII

VIII 15

1296 – 3294 [2189A]

VIII 17

1297

3762

3162

B.167 震 to quake

1291 (con

1292

(a) VII

(b) IX

This is no

(i) C.C.C. 6

name of co

(ii) C.C.C. 23

make thin

(iii) C.C.C. 30

(iv) C.C.C. 30

speech.

(v) W. I. 96 |

future]: W. II

(vi) W. II 2 | 憒

B. 191

(vii) W. II 18 |

B. 250 mi[…]on

(viii) B. 272 343

B. 122 […]

Nevski I 2

minus 4

1291 (cont)

1292 [Tangut] I A 98 | [Tangut] "true" v. 355

(a) VII 46 | [Tangut] 3105✓

(b) IX 56 | [Tangut] ˣ4201

This is rather a puzzling word.

(i) C.C.C. 6ᵃ | [Tangut] 攀 鞍

name of constellation?

(ii) C.C.C. 23ᵃ [Tangut] | 作物 "to make things" (?)

(iii) C.C.C. 30ᵃ | [Tangut] 見有[在]

(iv) C.C.C. 30ᵇ [Tangut] | 實話 "true speech".

(v) W.I. 96⁷ | [Tangut] 現 "[past] present [& future]": W.II 140⁹ (270⁶) 現在 ditto. B 347²

(vi) W.II 2⁵ | [Tangut] 如來 Tathāgata

B. 191³

(vii) W.II 18⁴ | [Tangut] 現前

B. 250² mṅon.pa manifest

(viii) B 272 (343²) [Tangut] | tr. 令 ~~[illegible]~~ 上

B. 122³ tr. 現令

Nevski I 244

97

1293 [Tangut] VI 122 [Tangut] | [2204]

(a) I. 20 | [Tangut] 0245

(b) II 7 | [Tangut] 3973✓

(c) IX A 29 | [Tangut] 2196✓

(i) (c) above B. 100 cat. under "horse"

The correct form is perhaps [Tangut].

1294 [Tangut] V 45 [Tangut] |

(a) VIII A 15 ditto See 1313

(i) By itself C.C.C. 8ᵇ 絲 "silk thread" W.I 134¹⁵ (q.v.)

(ii) The dissyllable C.C.C. 25ᵇ 絹絲 "silk gauze, & silk thread".

1295 [Tangut] V 83 [Tangut] |

(a) V 27 ditto

(b) V 58 [Tangut] |

(i) (b) above 嵒谷 "cliff & valley"

1296 [Tangut] IX 75 | [Tangut] 2189A

(a) VII 88 | [Tangut] [possibly the same!] 3244

?

1297 [Tangut] VI 45 [Tangut] | 3762

(a) VI A 27 ditto [illegible]

(b) IX A 136 | [Tangut] 3162

C.C.C. 12ᵇ 動 W.I. 196⁹ sa.yo.ba "(earth)quake"

[1298] 4083 chain

1299 3606 pair

1300 4027 chain

1301 4276 chain

1302 1406 chain

1303 1313 chain

1304 – 4502B

1305
1314 – 1308
1315 – 1310
0342

1306 3036 pair

1307 4775 chain

1308 1305 chain

1309 1313 chain

1310 1305 chain

1311 0148 chain

1312 1313 chain

1313
1294
1281
1303
1309
1312
1316
1867 – 0299, 1606
5379 – 5612

1298

1299

(a) VIII

1300

W. I. 208[15] 21

Morph. 'earth

1301

1302

1303

"silk strip."

B. 103

1304

1305

(a) IX 9 ditto

(b) V A 70

(i) The disyllable

B. 103 cat. under 'silk'

(ii) (b) above B. 103

minus A

98

1298 [Tangut] VI 99 [Tangut] | 4083

?

1299 [Tangut] V 83 [Tangut] | 3606

(a) VIII 7 ditto

?

1300 [Tangut] ? VA2 [Tangut] |

W. I. 208[15] 218[11,15] skem "dry, drought."

Morph. 'earth' over 'fire'.

1301 [Tangut] VI 99 | [Tangut] 5316

?

1302 [Tangut] IX A 40 [Tangut] | v. 1406

?

1303 [Tangut] VI 18 [Tangut]

"silk strip."

B. 103 | [Tangut] cat. under "silk"

1304 [Tangut] IX 9 [Tangut]

?

1305 [Tangut] III 26 | [Tangut] 'silk gauze'. v. 1314

(a) IX 9 ditto

(b) VA 70 | [Tangut] 1315

(i) The disyllable C.C.C. 25[b] 綾羅

B. 103 cat. under 'silk'.

(ii) (b) above B. 103 cat. under 'silk'.

1306 [Tangut] I. 143 [Tangut] |

(a) VIII 82 ditto

(i) The disyllable

B. 103 cat. under 'silk'

1307 [Tangut] VIII A 82 [Tangut] | 4775

(i) The disyllable

B. 103 cat. under 'silk'.

1308 [Tangut] IX 1 [Tangut] | 'silk gauze' See 1314

(i) C.C.C. 23[b] 紗 "gauze, net"

(ii) [Tangut] | B. 103 cat. under 'silk'. 1606

1309. [Tangut] III 58 [Tangut] | See 1313

?

1310 [Tangut] III 132 [Tangut] | 'silk gauze' See 1314

B. 103 cat. under 'silk'

1311 [Tangut] IX 13 | [Tangut] v. 1441

(i) The disyllable, B. 103 cat. under 'silk'.

C.C.C. 25[b] 緊絲

1312. [Tangut] III 29 [Tangut] | v. 1313

(i) By itself W. I. 138[11] 綵

(ii) The disyllable B. 103 cat. under 'silk'.

1313 [Tangut] VIII A 15 | [Tangut]

(a) V. 45 ditto See 1294

(b) III 29 | [Tangut] See 1312

(c) III. 58 | [Tangut] See 1309

(d) III. 66 | [Tangut] See 1867

1314 1305 pair

1314 (d) | 設 B.180⁴ 羅綢 silken net

Dissyl. woven B.169³ tr. 羅錦

1315 1305 chain

1316 1313 chain

1317 ⊥ 1327 – 1138
1910
1990 – 2315

1318 4011 chain

1319 1992 chain

1320 0551 pair

1321 0609 chain

1322 5063 chain

1323 2278 chain

1313 con…

(e) VI

(f) VI 9

(g) VII

(h) VII

(i) B. 103 cat. …

(ii) W. I. 98³

(iii) W. I. 98″

(iv) The dissy…

gauze + silk

1314

(a) III 26

(b) III 132

(c) IX 1

(i) C.C.C. 9ᵃ 羅

(ii) B. 103 cat. un…

1315

(a) I. 135

(i) The dissyllab…

(ii) C.C.C. 25ᵇ W.

B. 169³ tr. 巾

1316

B. 103 The dissyll…

minus 4

99

1313 cont.

(e) VI 18 | [Tangut] x of [Tangut] See 1303

(f) VI 97 | [Tangut] 5379

(g) VII 4 | [Tangut] See 1281

(h) VII 20 | [Tangut] See 1316

(i) B. 103 cat. heading 'silk'. W.I. 138" 帛 'silk'.

(ii) W. I. 98³ 綠 "green" B. 169 羅 gauze

(iii) W. I. 98" 綵 "coloured (silk)".

(iv) The dissyllable C.C.C. 25ᵇ 絹 絲 "silk gauze & silk thread".

1314 [Tangut] IX 9. [Tangut] |

(a) III 26 ditto See 1305

(b) III 132 | [Tangut] See 1310

(c) IX 1 | [Tangut] See 1308

(i) C.C.C. 9ª 羅 'silk gauze'.

(ii) B. 103 cat. under 'silk' C.C.C. 25ᵇ 綾 羅

1315 [Tangut] V A 70 [Tangut] | See 1305

(a) I. 135 [Tangut] | See 342

(i) The dissyllable B. 103 cat. under 'silk'

(ii) C.C.C. 25ᵇ W. I. 98" 錦 "brocade".

B. 169³ tr. 巾

1316 [Tangut] VII 20 [Tangut] 'silk' See 1313

(B. 103 The dissyllable) cat. under 'silk'.

1317. [Tangut] VIII A 54 | [Tangut] 1327

(a) VIII 30 ditto

?

1318 [Tangut] IX 131 [Tangut] | neck 0303

B. 94. [Tangut] ideogram & the whole of [Tangut].

| is [Tangut]; the word for [Tangut] ('throat').

[Tangut] [Tangut] [Tangut] [Tangut] ["– "wild animal bone throw"]

The last 4 words are most obscure, possibly tan. ts'ie phonetics?

W. I. 190⁶ mgrin "throat". 4611 chain

1319 [Tangut] IX 147 [Tangut] | ? 3554

?

1320 [Tangut] IX A 97 [Tangut] | 0551

(a) IX 121 ditto

?

1321 [Tangut] V. 18 [Tangut] | [4393]

?

1322 [Tangut] V 98 [Tangut] | 5063

? to empty Nevski I 207

1323 [Tangut] [Tangut] VI 65 [Tangut] | v. 1196

(i) The dissyllable C.C.C. 22ᵇ 斤斧 "axe hatchet".

99

1324 1325 pair

1325–1324

1326–2191

1327 1317 chain

[1328] 2906 chain

1329 4455 chain

[1330] 4544 chain

1331 2519 chain

1332–1204

1333 1552 chain

1334 1572 chain

1335 1338 chain

1336 1238 chain

1337 1929 chain

1338 1335 / 3619 1344 / 2293–1524+0827–0909

1339–2821

1324

(a) VI.

1325

(a) VI

B.251 苦

1325A

1326

(a) III

1327

(a) VIII

(b) I.89

(c) VIII

(d) IX 13

1328

1329

1330

1331

minus 4

100

1324 [Tangut] VI 121 [Tangut] |

(a) VI A 68 ditto See 1325

?

1325 [Tangut] VI A 68 | [Tangut]

(a) VI 121

B.251 苦 zug. rnie "bitter (pain)"

1325A [Tangut] Insert at 82

1326 [Tangut] V 40 | [Tangut] 2191

(a) III 119 ditto

?

1327 [Tangut] VIII 30 [Tangut] |

(a) VIII A 54 ditto See 1317

(b) I.89 [Tangut] | ? v.1910

(c) VIII 1 | [Tangut] See 1138

(d) IX 136 [Tangut] | 'scholar' v.1990 (2315)

? hard Nevski I 212

1328 [Tangut] VII 16 [Tangut] | "arrow" 2123

?

1329 [Tangut] V A 141 [Tangut] | 4455

?

1330 [Tangut] VII.16 | [Tangut] 4563

?

1331 [Tangut] III.118 [Tangut] | 'impurity' v.1262

?

1332 [Tangut] V.4 | [Tangut]

(a) V.16 ditto See 1204

? mow, cut? Nevski I.207

1333 [Tangut] VI A 83 | [Tangut] 1552

?

1334 [Tangut] III A 72 [Tangut] |

(a) III 84 ditto v.1572

?

1335 [Tangut] VIII 32 [Tangut] |

(a) IX 74 ditto See 1338

(b) VI 4 | [Tangut] 2293

(c) VI 89 | [Tangut] See 1344

?

1336 [Tangut] VIII 31 | [Tangut] "to go" v.1238

?

1337 [Tangut] VIII.29 [Tangut] | "horn" v.1925

?

1338 [Tangut] IX 74 | [Tangut] 1335

(a) VIII.32 ditto See 1335

(b) VIII.12 [Tangut] 3610

?

1339 [Tangut] VIII 71 | [Tangut]

(a) VII 83 ditto [[Tangut]]

?

1340
1162
4402 1011
3409-5039)

1341 ~~3443~~ chain

1342 1929 chain

1348
1598-2927
0846
1600-1601
1771
2300
3869
4451

1344 1338 ~~chain~~

1345 - 2722

B.216[4] []

1345A 3515 pair

1346 0862 ~~chain~~

1347 3793 pair

1348 4395 pair

1340
(a) VI
(b) VI
? intracta

1341.
(a) VI 37
?

1342.
(a) VI 101
(b) I.14
(c) III 32
(d) V 44
(e) V A 3
(f) VI 26
(g) IX 2
(i) By itself CC
(ii) (e) above B.99
(iii) (b) above B.
(iv) (c) above

1343
(a) IX 17 di
(b) I 40
(c) II 9
(d) III 19

101

1340 [Tangut] I.114 | [Tangut]
(a) V 175 ditto — See 1162
(b) VI 98 [Tangut] | — 4462
? intractable ... Nevski I 209

1341. [Tangut] VIII 71 | [Tangut] — 4310
(a) VI 37 ditto [[Tangut]] | [Tangut] — 5446
?

1342 [Tangut] VIII 71 [Tangut] | — 1929
(a) VI 101 ditto — v. 1929
(b) I.14 | [Tangut] — v. 1551
(c) III 32 | [Tangut] — ×(1429) v. 1585
(d) V 44 | [Tangut] sincere — 1997 ~~1844~~
(e) IX A 30 [Tangut] | cattle — v. 1934
(f) VI 26 [Tangut] × by [Tangut] | ram 1930
(g) IX 2 | [Tangut] — 2508
(i) By itself C.C.C. 7^a 16^b 羊 ? "ewe" "sheep".
(ii) (e) above B.99 牛羊 "ox & sheep".
(iii) (b) above B.99 cat. under "sheep".
(iv) (c) above [written [Tangut]] B.99 cat. under 'sheep'.

1343 [Tangut] I 29 | [Tangut]
(a) IX 17 ditto — v. 1598
(b) I 40 | [Tangut] — 2300
(c) II 9 | [Tangut] — v. 1771
(d) III 19 | [Tangut] — 3869

1343 (cont)
(e) III 70 | [Tangut] — See 846
(f) V.17 | [Tangut] — 4451
(g) IX A 53 | [Tangut] — ×(1641) 1800
(i) W.I. 134^2 II 76^5 毛 B.252^2 spu "hair"
(ii) The disyllable B.99 cat. under 'sheep'

1344 [Tangut] VI 89 [Tangut] | — See 1335
?

1345 [Tangut] VIII 71 | [Tangut] — 2722
(a) V 183 ditto
?

1345A [Tangut] × III 40 [Tangut] × by | [Tangut]
? error for 1343

1346 [Tangut] IX A 44 [Tangut] | "gourd"? — v. 916
(a) III 135 [Tangut] | ? — v. 1978
C.C.C. 11^a B.185 西 W.I. 222^3 ... "West".

1347 [Tangut] I 9 [Tangut] | [Tangut] |
(a) I 27 ~~[Tangut]~~ ditto
? rich man (Nevski)

1348 [Tangut] I 8 [Tangut] |
(a) VIII 29 ditto.
C.C.C. 10^a 兌 gold, metal (Nevski)

1349 1891 chain

1350 2150 chain

1351 0271 chain

1352 1353 chain

1353
├1352
└4370

1354 = 0650

1355 [illegible]

[1356] – [2110]

[1357]
├0378
└[5331]

B.229³ 知

1358 2421 pair

1359 3815 pair

1360 1361 chain

1361 chain
├0071
└1373 ┬1163
├1170
├1360
├1374
└4359

1361 (ii) In B.248³ represents
sems. dpa both in Tib. ctrl.
sems. dpa = Bodhisattva, &
sems. dpa. c'en. po = Mahasattva
∴ = sattva.

1353A

1349

C.C.C. 27

?WII.68

1350.

1351

1352

(a) VI

1353

(a) V

(b) V

(i)

1354

(a) VI

1355

name. B

1356

(a) VIII

1353A [Tangut] B.238[3] 庭 hall
minus [Tangut]

102

1349 [Tangut] I.9 [Tangut] | "a" v. 1891
C.C.C. 27[b] [Tangut] | 加官
? W II.68[12] 憍 "boasting" B.187[4] 迹 traces footprints

1350. [Tangut] VII 69 | [Tangut] 3618
?

1351 [Tangut] I 58 [Tangut] | sister 4308
?

1352 [Tangut] VI 50 [Tangut] |
(a) VII A 49 ditto See 1353
? incl. Nevski I 199

1353 [Tangut] VII A 49 | [Tangut]
(a) VI 50 ditto
(b) VII A 113 | [Tangut] 4370
(i) | [Tangut] C.C.C. 24[b] 尺 "a Chinese foot."

1354 [Tangut] VI A 79 | [Tangut]
(a) VI A. 124 ditto See 650
?

1355 [Tangut] II A. 31 Family or clan name. B 160[2] 忘 B. 191[3] h.

1356 [Tangut] VI 82 | [Tangut]
(a) VIII 17 ditto
?

1357 [Tangut] VI 73 [Tangut] | v. 378
(a) VI 30 ditto
(b) VI 25 | [Tangut] [5331]
(i) W. I. 132[10] 168[7] 識 vijñāna S.-H. 152 'cognition' parijñāna "intelligence, perception"
(ii) W. I. 132[10] 情 "feeling, passion, sensation" B. 248 sems "mind."
(iii) See 1361

1358 [Tangut] I. 13 [Tangut] |
(a) VII 22 ditto
?

1359. [Tangut] I. 13 [Tangut] |
(a) VIII 1 ditto
?

1360. [Tangut] VII 76 [Tangut] | v. 1373
?

1361 [Tangut] Kyi V 128 | [Tangut] "brave".
(a) IX 125 ditto See 71
(b) IX 18 [Tangut] | 1373
(i) W. I. 112[6] 勇 II 10[9] 猛 "brave".
(ii) | [Tangut] 1357 B. 248. sems. dpa "brave mind"; W. I. 198[8] ~~byan. c'ub~~ bodhi, "bodhi, wisdom." [This is rather obscure; it is difficult to say which is right.
See B. 248

1362 v 1891 chain

| W. II 78[6,9] 1306 修行 to mend one's ways. S.-H. 321.

1363 1369 chain

1364 1781 chain

1365 4066 chain

1366 ?

1367 5690 chain

1368–1708

1369
+ 2963
+ 0500
+ 1887 – 1227
+ 3814 – 1363} 3161}
+ 4337

1362
(i) C.C.C. 21[b]
repai
to pract
W. I. 134[15] 8812
(ii) W. II 70[7]

1362A

1363
same
?

1364
(a) I. 2
(b) I 11
(c) V. 66
(d) V 126
(e) V 150
(f) VI 60
(g) VII 57
(h) VIII 11
(i) IX 117
(ii) C.C.C. 21[b] 23[a]
(iii) W. II 24[5] 室
(iii) (c) above W.
(iv) C.C.C. 20[b] ?
(v) (b) above C.C.
B. 235[5] q.v.

103

1362 III 116 | "a" v.1891

(i) C.C.C. 21b 37a 修 II.50 do. B.251 spyod.pa repair "to practise, cultivate." II 78

W.I.134 138 224 ? B.122

(ii) W.II 70 | 修習 "to practise."

1362A see Nevski I 194.3 misspelt. See 3003 ?

1363 VII 87 | 3814 same as 3161

?

1364 VIII.18 | "hollow" v.1689

(a) I.29 | 4763

(b) I 117 | 3855

(c) V.66 | 4021

(d) V 124 | (3834) 3853 ?

(e) V 150 | 3853

(f) VI 60 | 2403

(g) VII 57 | 5033

(h) VIII 11 | 3111

(i) IX 117 | 1045

(i) C.C.C. 21b 23a 帳 curtain B.168 B.172

(ii) W.II.24 室 "house"

(iii) (c) above W.II 48 舍宅

(iv) C.C.C. 20b ?

(v) (b) above C.C.C. 23a 天 窻

B.231 q.v.

1365 IX.18 |

(a) III 41 ditto

?

1366 V 1 - [lost]

?

1367 I.13 | 5690 divine

(a) III 137 | 3848

(b) III 139 | 5409

(c) III 160 | 5212

(d) VIII A 23 | 2931

(e) IX 115 | 3777

(i) C.C.C. 3a + passim 天 "heaven" [as opposed to 'earth' + 'man'] W.I 192 tha 196 ? II 44 "the 33 heavens"

§. This word appears to be specifically "heaven" not "god."

1368 I A 19 |

(a) VII 44 ditto

(i) | [see 73] W.I 212 218 ?.po "a sort of devil."

1369 III 37 |

(a) IX 43 ditto

(b) II 2 | 4337

iii | v.1371

1370 0526 pair

1371 5990 chain

1372
3602
1908
1951

1372

(a) IX 158 ditto 3602

(c) VII 114 | v.1951

(d) I 27 | 1908

損 'to injure, destroy' W I 160

B 246^5 討伐 'to punish'

1373-1361 chain

1374 1361 chain

1375 0571 pair

1376 2327 chain

1377 3587 chain

1378 independent (or 1383?)

1379 1717 chain

1380 1929 chain

1369 (con

(c) V

(d) V

~~(e) VI~~

(f) VI

(i) By ...

W.I.190^5

relation

(ii) The ...

W.II 18^5 ...

-ants."

1370.

(a) I.19

1371

(i) The disyl...

"Good! Good

1372

(a) IX 158

(b) I 27 ~~(a) IX~~

B 212^4

W. I. 94^20 壞

200^15 ...pa

1373

(a) V 42 |

(b) V 117 |

minus 4

104

1369 (cont)

(c) V 88 | [Tangut] × 1227 v. 1887

(d) V 102 | [Tangut] 0500

~~(e) VI 83~~

(f) VI A 34 | [Tangut] × 1363 3814

(i) By itself ~~(f) IX~~ CCC. 20a W. I. 142[5] 親

W. I. 190[5] ñe. ba 192[13] ñe "kindred, relations." B. 237[3]

(ii) The dissyllable CCC. 20b 34b 親 戚 W. II 18[5] 眷 屬 "relations & dependents."

1370. [Tangut] I. 13 | [Tangut]

(a) I. 19 ditto See 526

?

1371 [Tangut] III 83 | [Tangut] 4267

(i) The dissyllable II 40[4,5] 善 哉 "Good! Good!" 130[5] do. passim B. 121[4]

1372 [Tangut] IX 130 | [Tangut]

(a) IX 158 ditto v. 3602

(b) I 27 ~~(a) IX 158 ditto~~ | [Tangut] v. 1908

B 212[4] break CCC. 31a II. 1169

W. I. 94[20] 壞 96[12,14] 破 134[2] 毀

200[15] njig. pa "to destroy, annihilate"

1373. [Tangut] IX 18 | [Tangut] "brave" v. 1361

(a) V 42 | [Tangut] v. 1170

(b) V. 117 | [Tangut] v. 1374

(c) VI A 92 | [Tangut] 4359

(d) VII 62 | [Tangut] "sharp, keen" v. 1163

(e) VII 76 | [Tangut] v. 1360

~~(f) VII 114 [Tangut] |~~

(i) | [Tangut] W. I. 214[8] B. 125[4] spa. ldan "brave" v. 0071

(ii) II 6[7] 性 "nature, self."

B. 173[5]? 125[4]

1374. [Tangut] V. 117 [Tangut] | "brave" v. 1373

?

1375. [Tangut] V. 128 | [Tangut]

(a) V 133 ditto See 571

?

1376 [Tangut] I 97 [Tangut] | 2327

(a) III. 15 [Tangut] | 5450

? to call Nevski I 210

1377. [Tangut] VI 64 [Tangut] "tea" See 955

?

1378 [Tangut] IX 177 × by itself | [Tangut]

?

1379 [Tangut] VI A 53 [Tangut] | "green" v. 1724 purple

v. 1399 A which may be the right form.

1380 [Tangut] VII 19 [Tangut] | "cattle" v. 1934

(i) | [Tangut] W. II 34[7] 產 財 "property + wealth."

1381 0315 pair

1382 3024 chain

1383 3741 chain

1383A ? = 0271

1384 4153 chain

1385 0013 chain

1386 4027 chain

*1387 2231 chain

1388 1891 chain

1389 0249 chain

1390 3269 chain

1391
+1394
3920–2034

1392 = 2728

1393 0020 chain

1394 1391 chain

1395 0899 chain

1381

(a)

?

1382

?

1383.

(a)

B.160^5

1383A

?

1384.

?

1385.

?

1386

?

1387

?

1388

?

1389

(a) I.

(b) I.

(c) I. 2

(d) III 3

minus 4

105

1381. [Tangut] V.4 | [Tangut]
(a) V 99 ditto — See 315
?

1382 [Tangut] VII A122 [Tangut] | 3985
?

1383. [Tangut] III A64 [Tangut] | 3741
(a) III 36 ditto
B.160^5 || Ch. 蕩漾 ? vast waves

1383A [Tangut] XI.38 | [Tangut]
: Possibly error for 271

1384. [Tangut] IA.86 [Tangut] | 4153
?

1385. [Tangut] I.60 | [Tangut] "to hear" v.13.
?

1386 [Tangut] V.172 [Tangut] |
?

1387 [Tangut] V.184 [Tangut] |
?

1388 [Tangut] VA98 [Tangut] | "a" v.1891
?

1389 [Tangut] IX 44 [Tangut] | xx See 249
(a) I.105 ditto
(b) I.1 [Tangut] | ? 3037
(c) I.26 [Tangut] | ? 3787
(d) III 37 | [Tangut] ? 4872
(e) III.168 [Tangut] |
[(f) III A105 [Tangut] × by [Tangut] |]
?
(f) is a Phonetic character.

1390. [Tangut] I 60 [Tangut] | 3040
(a) III 132 | [Tangut] 3423
B 227^4 'other 152^7
W. I.94' II 50^5 別 42^10 叢? "separate, different."

1391 [Tangut] I 56 | [Tangut] 1394
(a) II A1 ditto
?

1392 [Tangut] VII 22 [Tangut] | 2728
(a) I.22 ditto
?

1393 [Tangut] VII 22 [Tangut] | v.20
[Tangut] 交 (C.C.C. 24^9?) to interlock, closet?
W. II 26' 跌 to cross (the legs)

1394 [Tangut] II A1 [Tangut] |
(a) I.56 ditto — X(2034)
(b) III.156 [Tangut] | 3920
?

1395 [Tangut] II 41 [Tangut] | "to sit" 4185
?

N.B. 1391–1395. The initial element may well be 巾 & more properly classified after 自?

1396 – [0795]

1397 – 0174

1398 –
5400 – 2509
2687 – 1769
2074
3792

1399 5285 chain

1400 4550 chain

1401 4933 chain

1402 – 5350

1403 4059 chain

1404 interpolated

1405 2461 chain

1406
4662
0561
1302

1407 2969 chain

1408 0233 chain

1409 2027 chain

1396

(a)

1397

(a)

1398

(a)

(i) C.C.C. 12[b]

(ii) W. II. 36

1399

1399A

(A) C.C.C. 8

1400

1401

(a) I

1402

(a) VII

1403

(a) IX 14

(b) VIII 8

minus 4

106

1396 [Tangut] VIII 94 | [Tangut]

(a) III 3 ditto See 795

?

1397. [Tangut] VIII 94 | [Tangut]

(a) IX 20 ditto See 174

?

1398 [Tangut] V A 139 | [Tangut] × 5400

(a) II A 7 ditto

(i) C.C.C. 12b 漲 "to rise" (of the tide).

(ii) W.II. 36[1] 滿 "complete, full"

1399 [Tangut] IX 94 [Tangut] |

1399A [Tangut]

(A) C.C.C. 8a W.I. 98[3] 紫 "purple, dark red". Error for 1379

1400 [Tangut] IX 154 [Tangut] |

?

1401 [Tangut] II 28 [Tangut] |

(a) I 18 4910

?

1402 [Tangut] I.16 | [Tangut]

(a) VII 21 ditto

?

1403. [Tangut] I 29 [Tangut] [Tangut]

(a) IX 143 [Tangut] × by [Tangut] |

[(b) VIII 84 [Tangut] × by [Tangut] |]

?

1404. [Tangut] IX.7 Family or clan name.

1405 [Tangut] VI 14 [Tangut] |

(a) VII 25 ditto

(i) The dissyllable W.I.100[5] 桎 梏 "fetters".

1406 [Tangut] IX 57 | [Tangut] 4662

(a) V 109 ditto, but 父

(b) V 89 [Tangut] | v. 561

(c) IX A 40 | [Tangut] v. 1302

W.I.134[11] (v. 1826) poss. 坑 a pit

1407. [Tangut] IX 178 [Tangut] | 2530

?

1408 [Tangut] III 118 [Tangut] [Tangut] 4576

(a) III A 116 [Tangut] × by [Tangut] |

?

(a) is a phonetic character.

1409 [Tangut] II 9 [Tangut] | 4462

(a) III 94 [Tangut] | ~~(error)~~ is ditto 4422

W.II 24[7] (a) above 開 飾

1410-2210

1411 independent

1412 1564 chain

1413 2969 chain

1414 —
⊥ 1616-3533

1415 3226 chain

1416 [Tangut] Bhikṣu W III 2[6]

1416-2N6
┼2916
└1417

ɸ ii B. 225[3] Viśākhā~~mitra~~

1418 308 chain

1419 3244 pair

1420 1781 chain

1421 1449 chain

1422 4883 chain

1423-2805

1424-4540

1425-3935

1410 [Tangut]

(a) VI

?

1411 [Tangut]

name. III

1412 [Tangut]

(a) VI

(b) VIII

?

1413 [Tangut]

?

1414 [Tangut]

I 22

? Demon

1415 [Tangut]

?

1416 [Tangut]

(a) VI 22

(i) C.C.C. 5th 箕

constellation

(ii) The

"winnowing

Frequently

1417 [Tangut]

A Phonetic ch

minus 4

107

1410 [Tangut] V 68 | [Tangut]

(a) VI 21 ditto

?

1411 [Tangut] III.118 Family or clan name.

1412 [Tangut] III 150 [Tangut] | 4170

(a) VI A 52 | [Tangut] 4077

(b) VIII 49 | [Tangut] v. 2059

?

1413 [Tangut] I.59 | [Tangut] 2038

?

1414 [Tangut] I 59 | [Tangut]

I 22 ditto [[Tangut]]

? demon Nevski I 207

1415 [Tangut] III 118 [Tangut] v. 577

?

1416 [Tangut] I A 84 | [Tangut]

(a) VI 22 ditto

(i) C.C.C. 5b 箕 "winnowing basket" (name of a constellation) W.I 222' č'ie. stot ditto.

(ii) The dissyllable [Tangut] 箕 (C.C.C. 26b) "winnowing fan & winnowing basket".

Frequently used as a Phonetic.

1417 [Tangut] I A 75 [Tangut]

A Phonetic character

1418 [Tangut] VI 86 [Tangut] | 4604

?

1419 [Tangut] V A 45 [Tangut] |

(a) V 186 ditto

? to bite Nevski I 210

1420 [Tangut] VII.16 [Tangut] v. 655 1689

?

1421 [Tangut] VII 25 [Tangut] | "flesh"

(a) VII 37 ditto reversed v. 1449

(i) I 216² ts'il "fat"

(ii) | [Tangut] I 218'⁴ śa, za "meat eater" Piśāca.

chain 1449

1422 [Tangut] IX 17 [Tangut] | 4883

(a) I.16 ditto

(b) VI 36 | [Tangut] 4955

?

1423 [Tangut] I 51 [Tangut] |

~~(a) IX 4 ditto~~ v. 2805

?

1424 [Tangut] VI 113 | [Tangut] 4540

(a) V.6 ditto

?

1425 [Tangut] VI 113 | [Tangut] 3935

(a) VI 50 ditto

?

1426 - 25 (2597)
├2596
└5651-2535-2053

1427 13A chain
├0013A
└1224

1428 2461 chain

1429 1929 chain

1430 0271 chain

1431
├1706
├2673
└4152

1432 5038 chain

1433 3170 pair

1434 0424 chain

1435 - 3424

1436 -13B chain
├0013B
└1223 - 0896
[0710A]

1437 4326 chain

1438 4157 chain

1438 W.II 144' 有 "to have" (and similar)

B 246⁷ verbal affix tr: 令

W.II 126⁵ tr: 其

1438 bis overleaf

1425

W.I.

mighty

1426

(a)

[(b)

(c)

?penis, v

(b) proba

1427

(a) VI

?

1428

?

1429

?

1430

?

1431

(a) III 4

(b) VI 2

(c) VIII 7

(i) CCC. 11ª

(ii) (a) abov

year."

minus 4

108

1425 A [Tangut]

W. I. 130[17] 光 "brilliant"

might be error for 1429

1426 [Tangut] V 130 | [Tangut]

(a) III 32 ditto

[(b) V A 138 [Tangut] x by [Tangut] |]

(c) VIII 4 [Tangut] x by | [Tangut] [Tangut]

? penis, vulva Nevski I 201

(b) probably a Phonetic?

1427 [Tangut] V 31 | [Tangut] (? misspelt) 13 A

(a) VII 93 | [Tangut] see 1224

?

1428 [Tangut] V 114 | [Tangut] v. 1927

?

1429 [Tangut] V 66 [Tangut] | v. 1585

?

1430 [Tangut] V 31 | [Tangut] listen 4308

?

1431 [Tangut] II 3 x by itself [||]

(a) III 41 [Tangut] | past 4152

(b) VI 2 [Tangut] | 'coming' 2673

(c) VIII 7 [Tangut] | current v. 1706

(i) C.C.C. 11[a] 年 "year"

(ii) (a) above C.C.C. 11[a] 前年 "former year"

(iii) (b) above C.C.C. 11[a] 來年

(iv) (c) above C.C.C. 11[a] 去歲

1432 [Tangut] III A 102 [Tangut] | 5038

?

1433. [Tangut] III 37 [Tangut] | ? 3170

(a) I 78 ditto

B. 160[5] tr. 古 or 古 166[5] tr. 昔

1434 [Tangut] III 52 | [Tangut] 3899

C.C.C. 20[b] 姑 "paternal aunt"

1435. [Tangut] I 79 | [Tangut]

(a) I 41 ditto

?

1436 [Tangut] V 31 | [Tangut] ~~(? misspelt)~~ 0013 B

(a) VII 93 | [Tangut] [[Tangut]]

?

N.B. Either 1435 or 1436 must end in [Tangut], probably, but not certainly, the latter. former

1437 [Tangut] V A 138 [Tangut] [Tangut] 4779 1426

Probably a Phonetic character

1438 [Tangut] W. II 4 [Tangut] |

(a) III 5 ditto.

W. II 24[4] 30[3] 46[3] Very obscure; possibly a verbal affix.

108

1438 bis
+ 3555 — 0888
  2621
— 1443 — 3580
  5309
└ 4419 — 2487 — 1046

1439 5499 pair

1440 0148 chain

1441 0148 chain

1442 2593 chain

1443 1438 bis chain

1444 4455 chain

1445 1992 chain

1446 independent

1447 2482 chain

1448 independent

B161 tr. 阝 φ(i) B201

1449 chain 1421, 2002 (0835), 2605, 4556, 4747
+ 1421
— 2002 — 0835
└ 4556 — 4747

1450 1876 ~~1745~~ chain

1451 independent

1452 2141 chain

1438

(a

(b

(c

C.C.C. 19

1439

(a)

?

1440

(a)

?

In W.I. 19

1441

(a) III

(b) V

(c) VI

(d) IX

(i) (d) above

C.C.C. 25

1442.

?

1443

[(a) III A1

?

(a) is a Phon

minus 3 two 1438's!

109

1438 [Tangut] III.117 | [Tangut] × 3555
(a) III A 127 ditto
(b) III 119 | [Tangut] v. 1443
(c) V 9 | [Tangut] × 4419
C.C.C. 19[a] 指 "finger"

1439 [Tangut] III 154 [Tangut] | 5499
(a) III 158 ditto
?

1440 [Tangut] V 84 | [Tangut] 2255
(a) V 163 | [Tangut] 2557
?
In W.I. 192[16] used as Phonetic for Gau (cana)

1441 [Tangut] VI 85 [Tangut] | "belt" v. 148
(a) III 64 | [Tangut] × 1563
(b) V 183 | [Tangut] × 2726
(c) VI A 15 [Tangut] | × 4937
(d) IX 13 [Tangut] | see 1311
(i) (d) above B. 103 cat. under "silk"
C.C.C. 25[b] 緊絲 tight silk thread.

1442. [Tangut] VII 42 [Tangut] |
?

1443 [Tangut] III 119 [Tangut] | v. 1438
[(a) III A 106 [Tangut] × by [Tangut] |]
?
(a) is a Phonetic character

1444 [Tangut] VII 81 [Tangut] |
? to mow Nevski I 211

1445 [Tangut] I. 147 [Tangut] | "not"
?

1446 [Tangut] I 20 "Family or clan name"
~~(a) I 11 [Tangut] | [Tangut]~~
~~Probably a double name~~

1447 [Tangut] I 97 | [Tangut] "black"
?

1448 [Tangut] III 4 "Family or clan name"
A common Phonetic W.I. 90[11] 92[7], 132[16] II 4[3] W.I 269[15] B.188[3] etc. B 179[4] 唐 Tang 陀 to

1449 [Tangut] VII 37 [Tangut] | "fat" v. 1421
(a) VII 25 ditto reversed.
(b) III 55 | [Tangut] ? (+4747) 4556
(c) III 77 | [Tangut] ribs v. 2002
(d) IX 141 | [Tangut] ? 2605
C.C.C. 19[a] W.I 98[9] 134[2] II 24[3] 肉 "flesh".

1450 [Tangut] III 92 [Tangut] | v. 1745
?

1451 [Tangut] III 20 "Family or clan name"

1452 [Tangut] III 116 [Tangut] |
?

1453-5370

1454 4207 chain

1455 0604 chain

1456

4244-3129

1457

4315-4394

1458 2455 chain

1459 0604 chain

1460-5571

1461 4775 chain

1462 4396 chain

1463 3514 chain

1453

(a) III

?

1454

(a) III

(b) V

(i) W.I 108

(ii) The

"to

1455

C.C.C. 20

1456

(a) IX

Possibly a

1457

(a) VIII

?

1457A

1458

(a) III 90

(b) III 182

(c) V 47

(d) V 180

(e) VIII 25

? Arm

minus 3

110

1453 [Tangut] VI 96 [Tangut] | 5370

(a) III 128 ditto

?

1454 [Tangut] III 92 [Tangut] | 4207

(a) III 124 ditto

(b) VI 83 [Tangut] | [[Tangut]] 4416

(i) W. I 108[16] 休 "to desist" B.164[1] to. 絕

(ii) The dissyllable W II 6[9] 56[3] 休息

"to desist or cease". v. Nevski I 212

1455 [Tangut] V 75 [Tangut] | 1459

C.C.C. 20[a] 哥 "elder brother"

1456 [Tangut] V 75 "Family or clan name"

(a) IX 59 | [Tangut] × 3129 4244

Possibly a double name.

1457 [Tangut] VIII 37 | [Tangut] × 4394 4315

(a) VIII 70 ditto

?

1457A [Tangut] see 92.

1458 [Tangut] ta IX.147 [Tangut] | "leg" 2485

~~(a) III 90 | [Tangut] (a) 4511~~

~~(b) III 182 [Tangut] | (b) ? 3565~~

~~(c) V 47 [Tangut] | (c) ? 4421~~

~~(d) V 180 | [Tangut] (d) ? 5249~~

~~(e) VIII 25 | [Tangut] (e) 0838~~

? Nevski I 262

1459. [Tangut] tou III 118 [Tangut] | v.604

[(a) III 90 | [Tangut] handkerchief 4511]

[(b) III 182 [Tangut] | 3565]

(c) V 47 [Tangut] | 0155 ~~1459~~

(d) V 75 | [Tangut] "elder brother" v.1455

[(e) V 180 | [Tangut] 4421]

[(f) VIII 25 | [Tangut] 5249]

[(g) IX 38 | [Tangut] "harpsichord" ? v. 838]

(h) IX 64 | [Tangut] × v. 927

(i) By itself C.C.C. 19[a] W I 90[9] 136[6] 手

190[12] 218[5] leg "hand"

(ii) (a) above 手帕 C.C.C. 25[b] "hand-kerchief".

1460 [Tangut] IX 67 [Tangut] |

(a) IX 125 ditto

?

1461. [Tangut] V A 89 | [Tangut] 3154

(a) VII A 43 | [Tangut] 5029 ~~1461~~

B.125[5]

1462. [Tangut] VIII 34 [Tangut] | jewel 4396

?

1463 [Tangut] V.126 [Tangut] | 3514

(a) V 97 ditto [[Tangut]] 4196

(b) I 47 right

? ~~W. II 78[3] 左~~ ~~lips~~ (shoulder)

1473 bis
1818
3271
1755-4345-4633

1464-3769

1471 2366 chain

1472 1474 pair

1465 0157 chain

1466 0148 chain

1473 0863 chain

1473 (b) B 104 cat. under "women's clothing"

1467 2027 chain

1474 輔 purohita retinue W.II 86[5]

1468 3086 chain

1474-1472

1469-0288

1469 W.II 78[4] tr. 着 to show, to represent 着 in same sense?

B.125[1] tr. 受 B.227[3]

1475 5310 chain

1476 1833 chain

1477 3603 pair

1470 1833 chain

1478-5700

1464
(a)
W.I.224
"lift
1465.
?
1466
W.I.132[13]
1467.
W.II 94[4]
1468
(a) VII
C.C.C.31[a2]
"strike"
1469
(a) I.
(i) C.C.C.35[a]
(ii) W.I.142[7]
attachment
1470
(a) VI
?

minus 3

1473 bis [Tangut] IX gap Nevski I 205
v. (b) v. 1937 (ii) to see minus 2

111

1464 [Tangut] IX A 34 | [Tangut]

(a) VII 95 ditto

W. I. 224⁶ s.yon p'yogs.pa II 78³ 左

"left (hand)" B. 169⁵ (? 1463)

1465. [Tangut] I 7 [Tangut] | 4443

?

1466 [Tangut] II 34 | [Tangut] 1611 1498

W. I. 132¹³ 決 "(of a river) ~~to burst its banks~~" to beat into new channels

1467. [Tangut] III A 50 [Tangut] | 4463

W. II 94⁴ 處 "place" B. 193¹ 襲 to inherit?

1468 [Tangut] IX 177 [Tangut] | 4604

(a) VII 104 [Tangut] | v. 205

C.C.C. 31a² [Tangut] | 打 拷 "to beat or strike" B. 167¹

1469 [Tangut] IX 89 [Tangut] |

(a) I. 80 ditto reversed v. 288

(i) F.C.C. 35a 滞 "to stop, neglect"

(ii) W. I. 142⁷ 著 "to manifest, display, wear attachment" II 38⁴ ditto 150⁶ B. 230⁴ 232¹

1470 [Tangut] III A 37 [Tangut] |

(a) VI A 35 ditto v. 1833

?

1471 [Tangut] I 68 | [Tangut] 4764

(a) I A 110 | [Tangut] 5504

?

1472 [Tangut] I 5 [Tangut] |

(a) I 1 ditto v. 1474

The disyllable II. 130¹⁰ 臣 B. 174⁵

W. I. 196² blon.po "high officer"

1473 [Tangut] II A 8 [Tangut] | v. 863

(b) IX 17 | [Tangut] [[Tangut]] 1473A 3271

(a) III 18 | [Tangut] [ditto] 1818 v. 1818

(c) II 37 ditto 1755

~~1474~~ ?

1474 [Tangut] I 1 | [Tangut]

(a) I 5 ditto v. 1472

(i) By itself W. II. 18¹² 臣 "minister, official" B 233³ 官吏

(ii) The disyllable W. I. 196² blon.po "high officer" II 130¹⁰ 臣 "minister"

1475 [Tangut] VIII. 15 | [Tangut] 5310

?

1476 [Tangut] I A 85 [Tangut] | v. 1833

? cf. 1470

1477 [Tangut] III 72 [Tangut] | 3603

(a) I. 17 ditto

?

1478 [Tangut] II 10 | [Tangut] 5700

(a) II A 9 ditto

?

1479 2635 chain
| | B.192² tr. 漸漸 gradually I (a)
B.224³ 後 last

1480 3026 chain

1481 0186 chain

1482 1711 pair

1483 2906 chain

1484 – 1489

1485 1061 pair

1486 [illegible]

1487 0752 chain

1488 | [illegible] 舍城 "city" W.II 2⁴
do. B.185³ 廈 'mansion' B341² 宮 do

1488
+3950
2761
4405 – 4647
5075

1489 1484 pair

1490 1492 chain

1479
(a)
(b)
C.C.C.3
"the th
1480
?
1480 A
1481
For X
sheep.
(ii)
1482
(a) V
?
1483
?
1484
(a) VI
?
1485
(a) VI
C.C.C.20⁶
W.I.196¹⁷

minus 2

112

1479 [Tangut] me I 90 | [Tangut] and 2013

(a) VII A 15 [Tangut] | 3369

(b) IX 125 [Tangut] | 2584

C.C.C. 3[a] etc. 下 "lower" in the sense of "the third of three." W.I. 268[5]

1480 [Tangut] VII 57 [Tangut] | 4398

?

1480 A [Tangut] Error for 1607

1481 [Tangut] V A 34 [Tangut] [Tangut]

For X see 104 頑羊 a kind of sheep.

(ii) | [Tangut] B. 101 cat. under "sheep."

1482 [Tangut] III 4 [Tangut] |

(a) VIII 14 ditto v. 1711

?

1483 [Tangut] I. 113 [Tangut] | "arrow" 2123

?

1484 [Tangut] VII 96 [Tangut] |

(a) VII A 48 ditto

?

1485 [Tangut] VI 79 [Tangut] |

(a) VI 2 ditto

C.C.C. 20[b] 姓 W.II 56 ditto "family" W.I. 196[17] ? B. 160[14]

1486 [Tangut] VI 79 "Family or clan name."

1487 [Tangut] II 6 | [Tangut] v. 1790

?

1488. [Tangut] I 58 [Tangut] | house 3950

(a) III 170 ditto

(b) I 21 | [Tangut] 2761

(c) V 50 | [Tangut] 5075

(d) IX 172 | [Tangut] 4405 (4647)

(i) C.C.C. 34[b] 家 "house, home"

(ii) C.C.C. 10[a] [Tangut] | 星宮 "celestial mansion" [zodiacal sign]

(iii) | [Tangut] C.C.C. 21[b] 家宅 "house" W.I. 96[14] 門戶 "gate" C.C.C. 34[a]

(i) W.I. 224[8] gnas "house"

(iv) W.I. 100[13] 位 "place"

(v) W.I. 168[4] 堂 B. 186 院 "palace, hall"

1489 [Tangut] VII A 48 | [Tangut]

(a) VII 96 ditto

?

1490 [Tangut] V 155 [Tangut] |

(a) II. 6 ditto v. 1492

(b) III A 21 | [Tangut] 2907

?

1491 1492 chain

1492
1490–2907
1491
4053

1493 independent

1494 4213 chain

1495 – 2036

1496 4627 chain

1497 – 2325

1498 5264 chain

1499 1891 chain

1500 5369 chain

1501 Family name? corrupt
3268 0366
3999

1502 0520 pair

1503 5152 chain

1504 5545 pair

1505 5556 chain

1506 1903 chain

1491

1492
(a) Ⅴ
(b) Ⅱ
(c) Ⅵ

1493.
name

1494
(a) Ⅲ

1495
(a) Ⅰ

1496

1497
(a) Ⅰ

1498
c.c.c. 27 W.
Ⅱ 6' 24 土
(ii)
W.Ⅱ 118'

minus 2

113

1491 [Tangut] VII A 55 [Tangut] | v. 1492

?

1492 [Tangut] II 6 | [Tangut]

(a) V. 155 ditto v. 1490

(b) II 39 | [Tangut] 4053

(c) VII A 55 | [Tangut] v. 1491

?

1493. [Tangut] II 6 "Family or clan name."

1494 [Tangut] V. 6 [Tangut] |

(a) III 53 ditto

?

1495 [Tangut] V. 155 | [Tangut] ?

(a) I 29 ditto v. 2036

?

1496 [Tangut] I. 140 | [Tangut] 5176

?

1497 [Tangut] IX 47 | [Tangut] 2325

(a) I 19 ditto

?

1498 [Tangut] IX 47 | [Tangut] misspelt 5264 5264

CCC. 27b W. I 94[12] 國 W. I 192[14] yul

II 6[1] 24[7] 土 "country, region."

(ii) | [Tangut] 刹 土 kṣetra "land, universe"

W. II 118[1] S.-H. 250

1499 [Tangut] VII. 31 [Tangut] | 3898

?

1500 [Tangut] VIII 56 | [Tangut] 5369

(a) V. 131 | [Tangut] v. 711

?

1501 [Tangut] I. 42 "Family or clan name."

(a) IX. 17 [Tangut] |

Presumably a double name

1501 A [Tangut] misspelt, see 15

1502. [Tangut] I 116 | [Tangut]

(a) IX 107 ditto v. 520

?

1503 [Tangut] IX. 16 | [Tangut] 4660

? chain 5152

1504 [Tangut] VI 34. [Tangut] |

(a) IX 4 ditto

? cf. 1505

1505 [Tangut] VI. 34 [Tangut] | (misspelt) 5556

(a) IX 4 ditto

? cf. 1504

1506 [Tangut] IX A 15 [Tangut]· |

(a) III A 28 ditto v. 1903

(b) III A 129 | [Tangut] 3597 × 5712

(c) VII 20 | [Tangut] 3604

(d) VII 86 [Tangut] | v. 1904

W.I 134[10] [Tangut] to brandish (a knife).

1507 - 1510
⊥ 1510 - 4720

1508 2179 ~~1992~~ chain

1509 0752 chain

1510 1507 pair

1511 0752 chain

1512 0582 chain

1513 - 1401

1514 4213 chain

1515 2149 chain

1516 3755 chain

1517 - 1544

1518 3078 chain

1519 independent

[1520] - 4173

[1521] - 4664

1522 0965 chain 土

1523. [Tangut]

?

1524 [Tangut]

(a) V

(i) The

under '

Note. S

a lost

1525 [Tangut]

?

1526 [Tangut]

Phonet

1527 [Tangut]

name.

1528 [Tangut]

(a) V

B. 95 " [Tangut]

| is a

It is

characte

Used as

W.I. 190[9] 19

1529 [Tangut]

(a) V 3

?

minus 2

114

1506 cont.

(e) IX A.162 | [Tangut] v.198

(i) W.I.134[2] 脫 "to strip off (feathers)"

(ii) W.I.138[13] 摘 "to pick (flowers)"

(iii) I 134[10] 136[16] ?

1507 [Tangut] III 148 | [Tangut]

(a) VI 9 ditto v.1510

W.I.100[1] [Tangut] "handsome; licentious"?

1508 [Tangut] TWA III A 104 [Tangut] [Tangut]

"mystical word"

1509 [Tangut] nê III A20 [Tangut] [Tangut] 3845

?

Possibly a Phonetic character.

1510 [Tangut] VI 9 [Tangut] |

(a) III 148 ditto v.1507

(b) III 75 | [Tangut] 4720

?

1511 A [Tangut] V 31 ~~[Tangut]~~ =13B

~~See 1436~~. Possibly error for [Tangut]

1511 [Tangut] III 19 [Tangut] [Tangut] 3845

Possibly a Phonetic character

1512 [Tangut] II 19 [Tangut] | 3692

?

1513 [Tangut] II 19 [Tangut] | "flag" v.1401

?

1514 [Tangut] I 123 [Tangut] |

B.126[4] 132[5]

1515 [Tangut] I 133 | [Tangut] "to make"

(a) VI A 8₁ | [Tangut] possibly ... 1919

?

1516 [Tangut] III 53 [Tangut] | 3756

(a) I.16 ditto [[Tangut]]

?

1517 [Tangut] II 4 | [Tangut]

(a) II 20 ditto v.1544

?

1518 [Tangut] VII 102 [Tangut] | "still" v.1898

?

1519 [Tangut] VII 102 "Family or clan name."

1520 [Tangut] I 52 | [Tangut]

(a) IX 56 ditto

?

1521 [Tangut] III 103 | [Tangut]

(a) III 86 ditto

(3) The disyllable B.100 cat. under 'wild animals'.

1522 [Tangut] III A 31 [Tangut] [Tangut]

A phonetic sign?

1523 3906 chain

1524 1338 chain

1525 4027 chain

1526 4052 chain

1527 independent

1528 – 0333

1529 4268 pair

1530 2736 chain
劉 | W.I. 266[21] part of royal title
聖 祐 'sacred protector'

1531 3354 chain

1532 2485 chain

1533 0444 chain

1534 4052 chain
(b) B. 132[3] 安穩施 'to give peace'

1534 (
(i) by ...
broad,
(ii) | ...
...
1535. 皮
1536
(a) IX
(b) V
[(c) V
C.C.C. 26[b]
1537
(a) VI
?
1538
(a) VII
(b) I.
(c) VII
?
In (a) to (c)
& that may

minus 2

115

1523. [Tangut] I 52 [Tangut] |

?

1524 [Tangut] V A 5 [Tangut] | 2293

(a) VI 4 [Tangut] | v. 827

(i) The dissyllable reversed B. 100 cat. under 'camel.'

Note. See 715. (a) perhaps belongs to a lost [Tangut]

1525 [Tangut] VI 77 [Tangut] |

?

1526 [Tangut] III A 133 [Tangut] [Tangut]

A Phonetic character.

1527 [Tangut] III A 3 Family or clan name.

1528 [Tangut] KA V A 127 | [Tangut]

(a) V A 125 ditto v. 333

B. 95 "[Tangut] ideogram [Tangut] follows. | is a sacred word [[Tangut] [Tangut]]. It is used {as a / in the 'mother of characters' [[Tangut] [Tangut]]."

Used as a Phonetic character W.I. 190[9] 194[1] KA 192[7] GĀ B 126[1]

1529 [Tangut] III 31 [Tangut] | 4268

(a) V 38 ditto

?

1530 [Tangut] VIII 67 | [Tangut] 2736

(i) The dissyllable C.C.C. 32[a] 祐助 "to protect & help." B. 216[2]

(ii) | [Tangut] C.C.C. 36[a] 資粮 W.I. 168[7] 資糧 sambhāra "sustenance for body ~~& soul~~"

1531. [Tangut] II A 19 | [Tangut] 2885

(a) III 140 [Tangut] | 5259

(i) The dissyllable B. 100 cat. under 'wild animals' [lit. "old rat"]

(ii) By itself C.C.C. 9[b] 子 "The first branch" [rat in the animal cycle] B. 176[5]

(iii) Often used as a Phonetic, W.II. 66[11] + B. 185[5] 惠 Hui

1532. [Tangut] VI 77 [Tangut] | 2485

?

1533 [Tangut] III 52 | [Tangut] v. 444

?

1534 [Tangut] III 31 [Tangut] |

(a) VI 84 ditto

(b) I. 26 | [Tangut] 2341

(c) III A 133 [Tangut] x by | [Tangut] v. 1526

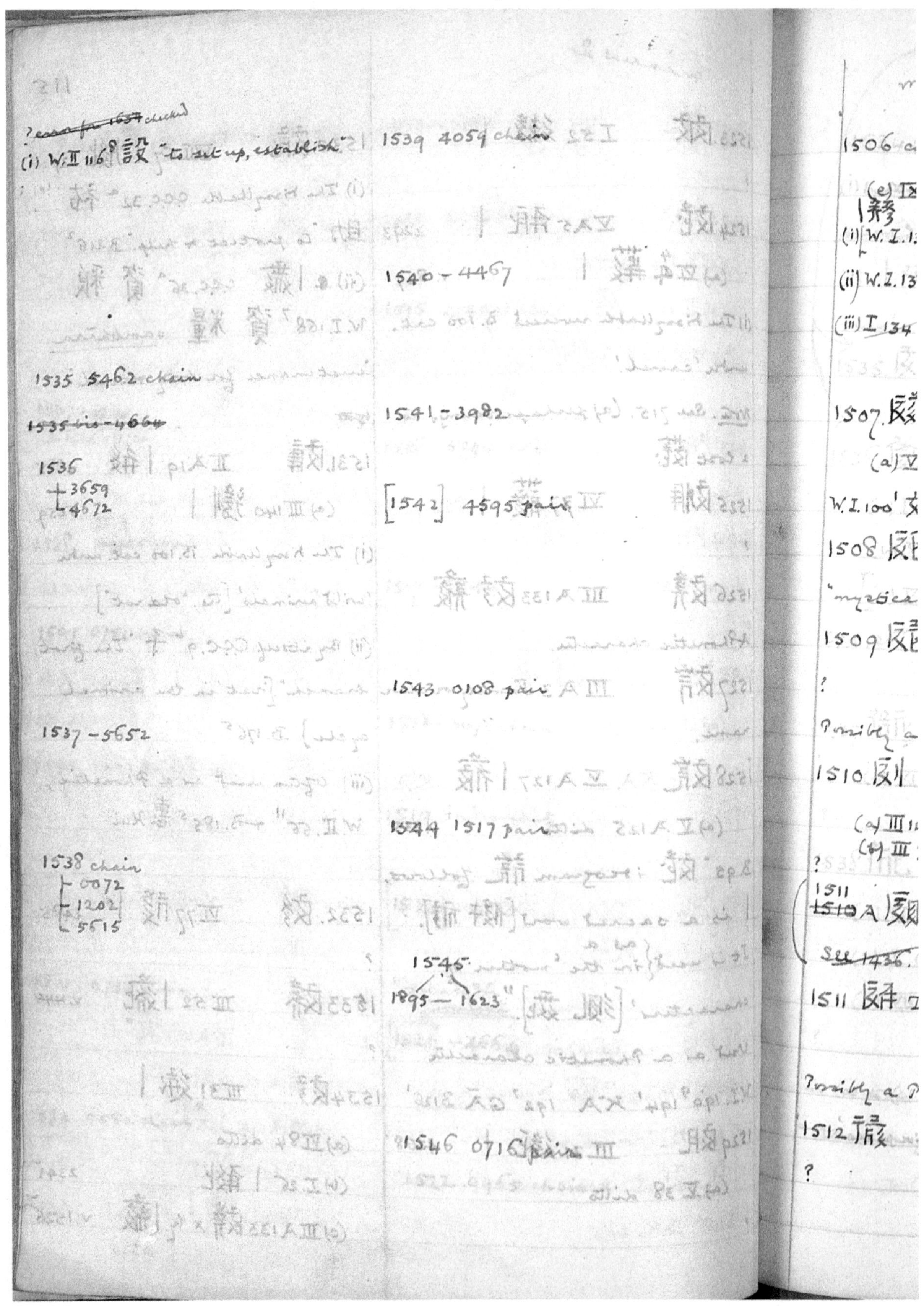

116

1534 (cont)

(i) by itself. W.II 36³ 廣 'vipula broad, extensive'

(ii) | [Tangut] B.102 cat. under 'rivers and seas'.

1535. [Tangut] III 74 [Tangut] | 5403

1536 [Tangut] V.44 | [Tangut] 3659

(a) IX 34 ditto

(b) V 135 [Tangut] | 4672

[(c) VI 103 [Tangut] | x of [Tangut] v.310]

c.c.c. 26ᵇ 器 'instrument'

1537 [Tangut] VII 10 | [Tangut] 5652

(a) VII 6 ditto

?

1538 [Tangut] IX 40 | [Tangut] 0072

(a) VII 10 ditto v.72

(b) I.16 [Tangut] | v.1202

(c) VII 27 | [Tangut] 5615

?

In (a) to (c) the sign is spelt [Tangut] and that may well be the right form.

1539 [Tangut] VIII 84 [Tangut] |

(a) IX 143 [Tangut] x by | [Tangut]

(b) I 29 [Tangut] x by [Tangut] | (misspelt v. 1576 A)

?

1540 [Tangut] V.118 | [Tangut] 4467

(a) V A 72 ditto

?

1541 [Tangut] V.1 | [Tangut]

(a) III 96 ditto.

?

1542 [Tangut] I.82 [Tangut] |

(a) I.13 ditto

?

1543 [Tangut] VII 68 | [Tangut]

(a) V A 75 ditto v.108

?

1544 [Tangut] II 20 [Tangut] |

(a) II 4 ditto v.1517

?

1545 [Tangut] V 119 [Tangut] | [Tangut]

(a) VI 44 [Tangut] x by | [Tangut] v.1895

(b) IX 1 [Tangut] x by | [Tangut]

?

1546 [Tangut] VII A 107 [Tangut] |

(a) VII 10 ditto

?

1546 A pair of 4417

1547 3883 pair

1548 1571 pair

1549 2448 chain

1550 2115 chain

1550 A 5162 pair

1551 1929 chain

1552 ┌ 1332
└ 4348

1553 ⊥ 3673–4545–4204

1554 2395 chain

1556 4775 chain

1557 1781 chain

1558 – 2112

1559 · ┬ 4496
└ 1696–4292

1560 3238 pair

1546 A

?

1547

(a) III

(i) The

日 "

1548

(a) VII

?

1549

(a) VI

?

1550

?

1550 A

?

1551

(i) The

(ii) By itself

character

cycle";

1552

(a) VI

(b) IX 14

?

minus 1

1546A [Tangut] II 32 x of | [Tangut]

?

1547 [Tangut] IX.1 [Tangut] |

(a) III 1 ditto [干]

(i) The dissyllable [with 干] C.C.C. 10^b 明日 "to-morrow".

1548 [Tangut] IX 11 [Tangut] |

(a) VIII.68 ditto v.1571

?

1549 [Tangut] VI 5 [Tangut] | 2448

(a) VI 58 ditto

?

1550 [Tangut] I A 57 [Tangut] | 2115

?

1550A [Tangut] VIII 12 x of [Tangut]

?

1551 [Tangut] I.14 [Tangut] | v.1342

(i) The dissyllable B.99 cit. under "sheep"

(ii) By itself C.10^a 未 "the 8th horary character" ("sheep" in the animal cycle".

1552 [Tangut] ?

(a) VI A 83 [Tangut] | 1333

(b) IX 146 [Tangut] | 'globe' bowl 4348

?

117

1553 [Tangut] IX 39 | [Tangut]

(a) IX 49 ditto

?

1554 [Tangut] V.48 | [Tangut] male 2930

?

1555 [Tangut] VIII A 63 Name of country.

1556 [Tangut] V.48 [Tangut] |

C.C.C. 17^a 鵲 "magpie, jay".

1557 [Tangut] I.82 [Tangut] | "cliff"? [Tangut]

(a) VI.38 ditto v.1782

?

1558 [Tangut] I.82 [Tangut] | 2112 q.v.

(a) I.38 ditto

C.C.C. 1^b 2

1559 [Tangut] [Tangut] III 11 | [Tangut]

(a) II 17 ditto

(b) VI 36 | [Tangut] "ehi"

(i) C.C.C. $31^{a,b}$ 32^a $35^{a,b}$; W.I.$96^{6,15}$ 此 B 2469

II 30^{10} 斯 "this" B.127^3

(ii) The dissyllable "now" v.4496

1560 [Tangut] VII A 58 [Tangut] |

(a) VII.66 ditto

?

1561 3398 pair

1562 - 2791

1563 0148 chain

1564
4170 – 1412 – 2059
4077 – 3563

1565 - 3774

1566 0582 chain

1567 1238 chain

1568 2662 chain

1569 5301 chain

1570 2371 chain

1571 - 1548

1572
1334
2113 – 1574
5371

1573 3026 chain

1574 1572 chain

1575 4277 chain

1561
(a)

1562
(a)

1563
(a)

1564
(a)

1565
(a) VI

1566
(a) VII
(i) (a) above

1567

1568

minus 1

118

1561 [Tangut] II.1 [Tangut] |

(a) VII 14 ditto

?

1562 [Tangut] III 73 [Tangut] |

(a) V 20 ditto

?

cf. 719

1563 [Tangut] III.64 [Tangut] | 1441

(a) VII 46 [Tangut] | 3103

?

1564 [Tangut] IX.1 [Tangut] | 4170

(a) IX 7 ditto

?

1565 [Tangut] VII.67 | [Tangut]

(a) VII 33 ditto cf. 1566

?

1566 [Tangut] IX 5 [Tangut] | 3692

(a) VII 33 | [Tangut] 5594 cf. 1565

(i) (a) above B.100 cat. under 'horse'.

1567 [Tangut] V A 122 [Tangut] | v. 1238

?

1568 [Tangut] IX A 21 [Tangut] |

?

1569 [Tangut] IX.6 [Tangut] | 2445

(a) III 20 | [Tangut] 2137

(i) [Tangut] | W.I.224[17] "rgyags.pa" "powerful"

1570 [Tangut] IX.121 [Tangut] | 2362

(a) I.29 [Tangut] | to set (of sun) 3886

W.I.222[17] (b) IX.102 v. 0619

1571 [Tangut] VIII.68 | [Tangut]

(a) IX 11 ditto v. 1548

?

1572 [Tangut] III.84 | [Tangut] [Tangut]

(a) III A 72 ditto v. 1334

(b) I.38 | [Tangut] ~~? error for 1574~~ 2113

?

1573 [Tangut] VII 53 [Tangut] | 4398

?

1574 [Tangut] I.27 | [Tangut] v. 2113

~~(a) ? See 1572 (b).~~

(i) | [Tangut] [Tangut] B.101 cat. under 'wild animals'.

1575 [Tangut] VIII 84 [Tangut] | 4277

(a) IX 143 ditto

[(b) VI 51 [Tangut] x by [Tangut]]

(i) By itself C.C.C.4[b] 兎 "hare or rabbit"

1576 0065 chain

1577 interpreted

1578 0893 pair

1579 5264 chain

1580 5110 chain

1581 interpreted

1582 – 2133 A

1583 – 4854

1584 ⊥ 3255 – 3394 – 4294 ⊥ 5385

1586 – 0250 friar

1585 1929 chain

1587 1929 chain

1588 1929 chain

1589 – 0202

1575

(ii) The

or rab

anima

1576

1576A

1577

name;

1578

(a) I

?

1579

?

1580

C.C.C. 12a 13

canal:

1581

name;

1582

C.C.C. 33b

a banque

1583

(a) IX 136

(i) The

W.I. 210

minus 1

119

1575 (cont.)

(ii) The dissyllable, C.C.C. 16a 兎 "hare or rabbit". B.101 cat. under "wild animals".

1576 [Tangut] III 95 [Tangut] | "all" 0063 v.72

?

1576A [Tangut] error for [Tangut] 1539

1577 [Tangut] VII 70 "Family or clan name".

1578 [Tangut] V 44 [Tangut] | 弁

(a) IX 52 ditto v. 893

?

1579 [Tangut] V 44 [Tangut] | 5264

?

1580 [Tangut] V 44 | [Tangut] "water"

C.C.C. 12a 13a W.I.134[17] 渠 "irrigation canal".

1581 [Tangut] V 44 "Family or clan name".

1582 [Tangut] VII A140 [Tangut] |

C.C.C. 33b 筵 "a bamboo-mat, hence a banquet" [here probably the latter]

1583 [Tangut] III 11 | [Tangut] misspelt 4854 ?

(a) IX 136 ditto

(i) The dissyllable

W.I.210[3] sdig.pa "a scorpion".

1584 [Tangut] VIII 38 | [Tangut]

(a) VII 36 ditto

?

1586 [Tangut] III 32 | [Tangut]

(a) I 105 ditto [手]

?

1585 [Tangut] III 32 [Tangut] | "sheep" v.1342 Nevski I 424 [Tangut]

(a) V 66 [Tangut] | [Tangut] [手] v.1429

(i) The dissyllable (written [Tangut]) B.99 cat. under "sheep".

Note. 1585 + 1586 must have the same central member, probably 手

1587 [Tangut] V.139 [Tangut] | 5949

(a) III A74 | [Tangut] v.1588

(i) (a) above B.99 cat. under "sheep".

1588 [Tangut] III A74 [Tangut] | v.1587

(i) The dissyllable B.99 cat. under "sheep".

1589 [Tangut] VII 90 [Tangut] |

(a) V 48 ditto [Tangut] v. 202

3293 – 1598A

1590 4889 chain

1596 ~~3913~~
⊥ 3913 – 5193 – 5203

1597
┼ 5027 – 5501 – 4210
└ 2401

1591 2306 chain

1598 1343 chain

1592 2569 chain V

1593 – 2676

1599 independent

1600 1343 chain

1594 2716 chain

1595 0959 chain

1601 1343 chain

1602 independent

1590
(a) I
(b) II
(c) II
(d)

1591
(a) I

There ...
distingui...
characte...
(i)
(ii) By itself

1592.

1593
(a) IX

1594

1595
(a) III A
(i) The Hsi-...
垢 穢 "..."
(ii) By itself

minus!

1590 [Tangut] VI 4 [Tangut] | 5434
(a) I. 27 [Tangut] | v. 297
(b) II 1 [Tangut] | 2651
(c) II 19 | [Tangut] "flower" 3859
(d) VII 36 | [Tangut] v. 344

1591 [Tangut] IX 135 | [Tangut]
(a) VI 93 ditto

There seems to be no means of distinguishing between these two characters.

(i) [Tangut] | B. 100 cat. under 'horse'.
(ii) By itself W. I. 190[18] bkra "beautiful".

1592. [Tangut] I. 119 [Tangut] | 2569
(a) I 36 ditto
?

1593 [Tangut] I. 44 | [Tangut] 2676
(a) IX 104 ditto
?

1594 [Tangut] IX 134 [Tangut] | 2716
?

1595 [Tangut] VII 51 | [Tangut] defiled v. 919
(a) III A 89 [Tangut] | excrement v. 1637
(i) The dissyllable W. I. 96[12] 汙 ? II 26[8], 垢 穢 "impure, defiled".
(ii) By itself W. I. 96[14] 汙 "to defile".

1598 A [Tangut] × of 3293

120

1596 [Tangut] V. 139 | [Tangut] 3913
(a) I. 30 ditto
W. I. 108[9]

1597 [Tangut] V 19 | [Tangut]
(a) III A 40 ditto
(b) VII 25 [Tangut] | 2401
(i) The dissyllable W. I. 224[5] dmod. pa "curse, oath"

1598 [Tangut] IX 17 [Tangut] | 'hair'
(a) I 29 ditto v. 1343
(b) VI 106 [Tangut] | [Tangut] 2927
(i) The dissyllable B. 99 cat. under "sheep"

1599 [Tangut] VIII 92 "Family or clan name." B. 177[1] P. N. 174[5] part of P. N. q. 1602

1600 [Tangut] IX A 53 [Tangut] 'hair' v. 1343
(a) V A 113 | [Tangut] v. 1601
?

1601 [Tangut] V A 113 [Tangut] | v. 1600
?

1602 [Tangut] VIII 92 "Family or clan name." cf. 1599

1604 2353 chain V

1604 2279 chain

1605 3200 chain

1606 1313 chain

1607 4609 pair

1608 0048 pair

1609 3586

1610 1686 chain

1611 0148 chain

1612 2569 chain VI

1613 4630 pair

1614 chain linked to 3420 chain
3420
3870

1615 0201 chain

1616 1414 chain

1617 ? 0271 chain

1618 2777 chain

minus |

良 abb? of 1614 signific of badness

121

1603 [illegible] III 44 [illegible] | 2371

?

1604 [illegible] V.166 [illegible] |

(i) |[illegible] B.100 cat. under 'horse'

1605 [illegible] VII 55 [illegible] [illegible] 3200 1900

?

chain 3200

1606 [illegible] V.89 |[illegible] v.1867

(i) By itself C.C.C. 24^b 巾 "cloth"

(ii) |[illegible] B.103 cat. under 'silk'.

1607 [illegible] II 9 [illegible] | 4609

? (a) I 11 ditto [[illegible]]

?

1608 [illegible] VIII 61 |[illegible]

(a) VII 33 ditto v.48

? The dissyl. B.238^5 tr. 分別

1609 [illegible] kiwa V 89 |[illegible] 3586

(a) V 51 ditto

C.C.C. 1^b 1

1610 [illegible] VII 33 [illegible] | v.1121

?

1611 [illegible] V 140 [illegible] | 5159

(a) II 34 [illegible] | "to burst the banks" v.1466

?

1612 [illegible] I 22 [illegible] | 2569

(i) The dissyllable reversed I.198^4 a kind of ulcer? thog.pa "anthrax".

1613. [illegible] IX A 95 [illegible] | 4630

? a double name

1614 [illegible] IV 3 [illegible] | 3420

(a) V 168 ditto

(b) IX 4 |[illegible] 3870

(i) C.C.C. 19^b 29^b W.I.136^7 惡 224^12 nes.pa "evil, bad"

(ii) W.I. 224^9,15 nan "wickedness".

(iii) C.C.C. 36^a W.I.108^16 塗 'mire'; (the three) evil ways'

1615 [illegible] VI/VII 115 [illegible] | "anger" v.201

?

1616 [illegible] I 22 [illegible] | 1414

(a) I 59 ditto [[illegible]]

(b) IX 9 [illegible] | 3533

?

1617 [illegible] VII A 3 [illegible] | 3284

?

1618 [illegible] VIII 35 [illegible] [illegible]

(a) I.16 [illegible] [illegible] x by [illegible] |

(b) III 81 [illegible] x by [illegible] |

?

1619 2027 chain

1620 2149 chain

1621 3918 chain

1622 4326 chain

1623 1545 chain

1624 0899 chain

1625 2777 chain

1626 – 2636

| B.163³

1627 0959 chain

1628 2569 chain

1629 4651 chain

1630 0959 chain

1631 0959 chain

1632 3188 chain

1633 3079 chain

1619

(a)

W.I.214

1620

(a)

?

1621

(a) V

?

1622

?

1623

(a) VI

?

1624

(a) II

B 167² tr.

1625

(a) I.16

~~(b) I.36~~

(b) VIII 3

?

minus 1

122

1619 [Tangut] V.60 | [Tangut] 3530

(a) VII 101 [Tangut] | 2276

W.I.214[12] "skyon" "doṣa, fault, defect."

1620 [Tangut] III 36 | [Tangut]

(a) VIII 90 | [Tangut] v.2051

?

1621 [Tangut] V 142 [Tangut] | v.570

(a) VI 44 [Tangut] x by [Tangut] [Tangut] error v.1623.

?

1622 [Tangut] VI 28 | [Tangut] ? 1955

?

1623 [Tangut] IX 1 [Tangut] [Tangut]

(a) VI 44 [Tangut] x by [Tangut] [Tangut] misspelt v.1621 (a)

? v.1545

1624 [Tangut] V.113 [Tangut] |

(a) II 8 ditto v.899

B 167[2] the 涼 B 212[3] 毀 destroy

1625 [Tangut] III 81 [Tangut] [Tangut] 2777 1628

(a) I.16 [Tangut] x by | [Tangut]

~~(b) I.36 [Tangut] | error v.1628~~ *

(b) VIII 35 [Tangut] x by [Tangut] | v.1618

?

1626 [Tangut] I.120 | [Tangut]

(a) VI 1 ditto v.2636

(i) The dissyllable W.I.108[5] 誹謗 II 76[8] do. : II 34[2] 謗毀 slander, defamation 90[2] do.

(ii) by itself II 80[8] 誹 slander

1627 [Tangut] VI 52 [Tangut] | "excrement" v.1637

?

1628 [Tangut] VI 29 [Tangut] | 2359

~~(a) [Tangut] I 36 ditto [misspelt as 1625]~~

(W.I 198[3] The dissyllable) mdze leprosy

1629 [Tangut] VI 29 [Tangut] | 4651

?

1630 [Tangut] IX 88 [Tangut] | "excrement" v.1637

?

1631 [Tangut] II 37 [Tangut] | 2735

?

1632 [Tangut] IX 17 [Tangut] | 3188

(a) I 17 ditto

(b) I 26 [Tangut] x by [Tangut] |

?

1633 [Tangut] I.124 [Tangut] | 3079

(a) VII 73 ditto

W.I.206[8] 212[13,14...] "c'ad.pa" "punishment."

1634 3391 chain

1635 3465 chain

1636 3629 chain

1637 0959 chain

1638 0638 chain

1639 0809 chain

1640 1694 chain

1641 0298 pair

1642 4226 chain

1643 3226 chain

1644 3188 chain

1645 3226 chain

1646 independent

1647 2935 chain

1648 3449 chain

1649 5186 pair

1634

W.II 80

1635

(a)

(b)

?

1636

(a)

?

1637

(a) V

(b) V

(c) VI

(d) VI

(e) IX

(f) IX

W.I. 216[6]

ditto

1638

?

1639

?

1640

?

minus 1

123

1634 [Tangut] VI 77 [Tangut] | 3391
W.II 80[9] [Tangut] "jealousy, envy". cf. 1642
1635 [Tangut] V A 50 | [Tangut] misspelt 3465
(a) III 125 | [Tangut] 3516
(b) IX 37 | [Tangut] v 2808
?
1636 [Tangut] VII A 42 [Tangut] | 3629
(a) V 31 ditto
?
1637 [Tangut] III A 89 | [Tangut] 'defile' v. 1595
(a) V. 16 | [Tangut] 2503
(b) VI 52 | [Tangut] v. 1627
(c) VII 51 | [Tangut] 4254
(d) VII A 126 | [Tangut] 2737
(e) IX 50 | [Tangut] x 2735
(f) IX 88 | [Tangut] v. 1630
W.I. 216[6] p'yi. sa "excrement": 170[4] 糞 ditto. B 128[1]
1638 [Tangut] V 85 | [Tangut] {? 3879, 4304A}
?
1639 [Tangut] III 132 [Tangut] | 5271
?
1640 [Tangut] XI 28 | [Tangut] 5294
?

1641 [Tangut] VI A 80 [Tangut] |
(a) VII 75 ditto v. 298
?
1642 [Tangut] IX A 35 | [Tangut] 4226
W.II 80[9] [Tangut] "jealousy, envy". cf. 1634
1643 [Tangut] III 91 [Tangut] | 3600
?
1644 [Tangut] I. 26 [Tangut] [Tangut] 3188
?
1645 [Tangut] I. 112 "true word, mantra mystical sound."
1646 [Tangut] VI. 115 "Family or clan name"
1647 [Tangut] IX 41 [Tangut] | (IX 9!) 2635
?
1648 [Tangut] IX 9 [Tangut] | 3449
(a) V 2 | [Tangut] 4379
1649 [Tangut] IX 41 [Tangut] | 5186
(a) V 9 ditto
(i) [Tangut] | W.I. 208[13] 212[12] zags.pa "leash, noose."

1649 A [Tangut] sic [Tangut] 2331

1650
+0581
-1074-0456
-1652
-1653
-3689-1837

1651 2283 chain

1652 1650 chain

1653 1650 chain

1654 3226 chain

1655 5155 chain

1656 5155 chain

1657-1991

1658 2149 chain

(ii) The dissyllable 功 工巧 Silpa-sthāna "arts + sciences W. I 178"

1659 3526 chain

[1660] 4066 chain

1661
+3585
-4175

1662-~~3738~~
-[3738]-3031

1663 3962 chain

1664 3091 pair

1650
(a) I
(b) I
(c)
(d)
(e) I
(ii)
(i) 老
1651
?
1652
?
1653
?
1654
(a) IX
W. II 20[7] 設
-eish" B.
1655
(a) IX.
?
1656
?

minus 1

124

1650 [Tangut] III A 11 [Tangut] | — [Tangut] an affix after animal names — v. 581

(a) II 36 ditto

(b) III A 69 [Tangut] | ×(1837) 3689

(c) VII 84 | [Tangut] v. 1652

(d) VIII 84 | [Tangut] ×(0456) v. 1074

(e) IX A 118 | [Tangut] v. 1653

(ii) [Tangut] | B. 100 cat. under "camel."

(i) 老 "old", age. W. I. 154[8] B. 128[3]

1651 [Tangut] V. 150 | [Tangut]

?

1652 [Tangut] VII 84 [Tangut] | v. 1650

?

1653 [Tangut] IX A 118 [Tangut] | v. 1650

?

1654 [Tangut] III 31 [Tangut] | v. 577

(a) IX 6 | [Tangut] × 5062

W. II 20[7] 設 80[4] 建 "to set up, establish." B. 163[3] 170[1]

1655 [Tangut] III 31 | [Tangut] 5155

(a) IX A 137 | [Tangut] [Tangut] v. 1656

?

1656 [Tangut] IX A 137 [Tangut] | v. 1655

?

1657 [Tangut] V 170 | [Tangut] — misspelt?

(a) IX 136 ditto thought ?? v. 1991

?

1658 [Tangut] V 170 | [Tangut] 2139

C.C.C. 22[b] 匠 "workman" 28[a] 工 "work, labour" Dict 1[b]3 B. 177[1,2]

1659 [Tangut] V 170 | [Tangut] 1743

(i) The dissyllable B. 100 cat. under "horse"

Nevski I 379 "muscles"

1660 [Tangut] V 170 | [Tangut]

?

1661 [Tangut] I 22 | [Tangut] 3585

(a) VI 26 ditto

(b) V A 68 | [Tangut] 4175

(i) The dissyllable C.C.C. 26[b] 鍬 "hoe, spade, shovel."

1662 [Tangut] II 1 [Tangut] | [3738]

(a) VI 18 ditto

?

1663 [Tangut] III 173 [Tangut] | ? chain 3962

?

1664 [Tangut] VIII A 46 [Tangut] | 3091

(a) IX 79 ditto

(i) By itself W. I. 112[16] 伏 "(to lay) under control"

(b) IX 128 [Tangut] | (misspelt) v. 1995 A

1665 3889 chain

1668 4277 chain

1666 3889 chain

1669 5229 pair

1670 3775 chain

1667
- 3917 bis
- 1863 — 1865, 3536–2828
- 3531
- 4033
- 4656
- 4709

1671 4023 chain

B. 215^4 麝 musk deer

1672 3226 chain

132^{13} 獵 wild animal

1673 3226 chain

1664 (c

(ii) II 12

unde

Verb

(iii) II 4

(iv) The

Discipl

(v)

1665

?

1666

(a) III

(b) VII

(i) c.c.c. 9^6

(ii)

1667

(a) II 6

(b) I 8

(c) I. 13

(d) V 8

(e) VI 1

(f) IX 9

(i) W. II 132 wrong refs

190^{16} ri.

98^7 $218^{4,8}$

minus |

125

1664 (cont.)

(ii) I 120⁸ 140¹⁵ 調 "to discipline, bring under control." I 178³ B. 199⁵ q.v.

(iii) Verb II 4¹² 降 "to subjugate"

(iv) The disyllable II 2⁷ 調 伏 "to discipline, bring under control".

(v) 䏞 | B. 99 cat. under "horse".

1665 [Tangut] VII 5 [Tangut] | v. 1666

?

1666 [Tangut] II 1 [Tangut] | 3889

(a) III 1 ditto

(b) VII 5 | [Tangut] v. 1665

(i) C.C.C. 9ᵇ 戊 "the 5th stem". B. 176⁵

1590

(ii) | [Tangut] B. 100 cat. under "horse".

1667 [Tangut] III 173 [Tangut] | 4708 ~~3917 misc~~

(a) II 6 ditto

(b) I 81 | [Tangut] 1863

(c) I. 139 | [Tangut] 4709

(d) V 89 | [Tangut] 4656

(e) VI 17 | [Tangut] 4633

(f) IX 9 | [Tangut] "bear" 3531

(i) W. ~~I 132~~⁷ (wrong refs) 野 132¹³ 獸 "wild animal" 190¹⁶ ri. dvags "game animal." 98⁷ 218⁴,⁸ ?

(ii) The disyllable C.C.C. 16ᵃ 野 獸 "wild animal" B. 100 chapter heading.

1021

(iii) [Tangut] | [Tangut] B. 101 cat. under "wild animals"

(iv) (c) above B. 101 cat. under "wild animals".

1575

1668 [Tangut] VI 51 [Tangut] [Tangut] "hare or rabbit". 4217

C.C.C. 10ᵃ 夘 "4th horary character" (hare in the animal cycle)

1669 [Tangut] II 1 [Tangut] | 5229

(a) IX 159 ditto

?

1670 [Tangut] VIII 1 [Tangut] | 3775

(a) III 11 ditto

B. 131¹

1671 [Tangut] V. 158 [Tangut] | 2748

[Tangut] | C.C.C. 28ᵃ 磨 堪

1846

1672 [Tangut] V A 81 "mantra mystical sound" v. 355

1673 [Tangut] V A 80 "mantra mystical sound" v. 355

1674–4700 chain

1675 0322 chain

1676 1252 chain

1677 3202 chain

1678 – 5507

1679 – 2792

1680 0424 chain

1681 ┬ 3297 └ 3053

1682 5645 chain

1682 | [Tangut] (2065) guttural sound Dict 2ª2

Title of Ch. 8.

1683 – 3573

1684 2178

1685 3226 chain

1686 ┴ 5339 – 1121 – 1610

1687 2461 chain

1688 – 2012

1689 1781 chain

minus 1

1674 [Tangut] V 158 | [Tangut] 4700

(a) IX 152 ditto

?

1675 [Tangut] V 33 [Tangut] | "eye" v. 322

? Nevski I 375 eyelid

1676 [Tangut] IX 103 [Tangut] | 3190

?

1677 [Tangut] VIII 21 [Tangut] | 3202 'rin

(a) VII 82 ditto

C.C.C. 6^b 28^a 刑 "punishment" 3202 chain

1678 [Tangut] V 73 | [Tangut] 5501

(a) IX 20 ditto

?

1679 [Tangut] V 70 | [Tangut] 2792

(a) IX 4 ditto

?

1680 [Tangut] VIII A 96 | [Tangut] 5476

?

1681 [Tangut] III 133 | [Tangut] 3297

(a) IX 2 ditto

(b) IX 87 | [Tangut] 3053

?

1682 [Tangut] III 143 [Tangut] | 5645

(a) V A 11 ditto

(i) The trisyllable C.C.C. 18^b 咽喉

1686 A [Tangut] VII 59-60(?)

126

"throat, throat"

1683 [Tangut] III 37 | [Tangut] 3573

(a) VIII 26 ditto

?

1684 [Tangut] III 37 [Tangut] | 2178

(a) I 28 ditto

(i) W II 2^4 22^6 26^1 城 city [written [Tangut]]

24^9 ?

(ii) I 224^7 mk'ar (ant-) hill.

1685 [Tangut] III 35 [Tangut] [Tangut] auxiliary word 2342(?)

(a) V 92 | [Tangut] ? v. 2024

Dict 1^b 1 B. 163^5 165^2 與

1686 [Tangut] III 35 ~~[Tangut]~~ | [Tangut]

(a) VIII 8 [Tangut] ditto

?

1687 [Tangut] IX 50 [Tangut] | 2461

1688 [Tangut] I 46 | [Tangut] ? v. 2012

(a) ~~[illegible]~~ I. 33. ditto [[Tangut]]

?

1689 [Tangut] see II 1 [Tangut] | v. 1781

(a) I 22 [Tangut] | v. 1701

(b) I 98 | [Tangut] 3649

(c) III A 42 [Tangut] | 3434 ?Phon. T'in 45

1694
5293–1640

1695 5310 chain

1696 1559 chain

1697 1250 pair

1698 4499 pair

1698 Φ.1. |巖 須 彌 Sumeru

W.I, 178[9] | 0387

Φii B.223[3] |[illegible] 須 達 Sudatta 4269

[1690]
2544
2756–0285

1691 [illegible]

1699 –1169 pair

1692 0731 chain

1693 –1870

minus | see 1660
~~1689 ~~ ~~V 170 |~~

127

1689 (cont)
(d) V 110 | v.323
(e) VIII 16 x by | v.1420
(f) VIII 18 | "house" v.1364
(g) IX 150 | 4665
(i) (c) above C.C.C. 21b 舍屋 "house dwelling"
(ii) (d) above C.C.C. 7b 陽 "the sun's rays"
(iii) C.C.C. 22a 墻 "a wall"
(iv) C.C.C. 28b | 3760 州主 B 233[3] "the ruler of a district". (v) W. I 271[1] B. 164[4] 188[1] 城
II. A curiously varied collection, apparently 'dwelling place' is the central meaning. See 5474

1690 I 46 | 2644
(a) III 82 ditto
(b) VIII A 79 | x (0285) 2756
?
sh? lc

1691 V 33 Family or clan name
B. 227[5] 供 ? phon.

1692 I 47 "wood, tree"
?

1693 VI 36 |
(a) IX 157 | v.1870
?

1694 I 46 | 5294
(a) I. 106 ditto
[(b) III 82 2043 x by 0133 |] v. 133
(i) The dissyllable C.C.C. 17a 蝴蝶 "butterfly"

1695 VIII 3 | 5310
?

1696 SU VI 36 | "this"
(a) I 28 | 4292
Passim 如 lta, ltar "like"

1697 II |
(a) VII 44 ditto v.1250
?

1698 VI 36 |
(a) VII 31 ditto ~~v.1250~~
?
Frequently used as a Phonetic.

1699 IX 129 |
(a) V 42 ditto v.1169
(i) | W. I. 96[8,9] 132[15] 2nd gin 3202 2669 懺悔
(Hotrus) (Soot) p.478) "to ask pardon & repent"
(ii) By itself W II 18[1] 懺 "to ask pardon"
(iii) | W. II 78[7] same as (i) 84[10] do.
4316

1700 5569 chain

1701 1781 chain

1702 2285 chain

1703 1704 chain

1704 1705 1703 3517

1705 1704 chain

1706 1431 chain

1707 1929 chain

1708 1368 pair

1709 important

1709 Φ(i) | 夜摩 Yama name of a heaven W.II 86[3]

Φii B.226' yakṣa

1710 ~~1712~~

1712 3511–1795

1711–1482

1700

(i) II

(ii)

1701

W.I.216

1701 A

1702

(i)

(ii)

1703

?

1704

(a) V

1705

(a) IX

(b) IX

?

1706

(i) The

current

128

1700 [Tangut] VII 96 | [Tangut] 5514
(i) II 14[6] 呑 "to swallow".
(ii) [Tangut] | [Tangut] I 226[2] k'yun. mid "to swallow".

1701 [Tangut] I 22 | [Tangut] 1689
W.I. 216[15].

1701A [Tangut] Error for 24

1702 [Tangut] I. 48 | [Tangut] [misspelt] v. 2265
(i) [Tangut] | B. 99 cat. under "cattle" 0528
(ii) [Tangut] | B. 99 cat. under "sheep".

1703 [Tangut] IX 88 | [Tangut] v. 1705
?

1704 [Tangut] V 39 × by [Tangut] [1] |
(a) V. 143 | [Tangut] v. 1705

1705 [Tangut] V. 143 [Tangut] | v. 1704
(a) IX 60 [Tangut] | 3577
(b) IX 88 [Tangut] | v. 1703
?

1706 [Tangut] VIII 7 | [Tangut] chain v. 1431
(i) The dissyllable C.C.C. 11[a] 去歳 "current year" B. 167[1] ...

1707 [Tangut] IV. 1 [Tangut] | cattle 1934
(i) [Tangut] | B. 99 cat. under "cattle". 1710

1708 [Tangut] VII 44 [Tangut] | 1368
(a) I A 19 ditto
?

1709 [Tangut] VIII. 14 "Family or clan name". A very common Phonetic.
(a) III A 113 [Tangut] × by [Tangut] | 2318 (DE) 2317
(b) III A 117 [Tangut] × by [Tangut] | 2277 RE 2299
(c) III A 132 [Tangut] × by [Tangut] | 5436 (T'I) 5488
(d) V A 132 [Tangut] × by [Tangut] | 3491 [HE] 2389 2395
(e) V A 134 [Tangut] × by [Tangut] |
(f) VI A 128 [Tangut] × by [Tangut] | 5230 5237
(g) VIII A 103 [Tangut] × by [Tangut] | 4406
(h) VIII A 111 [Tangut] × by [Tangut] | 4750 4823
All these are phonetic characters

1710 [Tangut] IX 28 [Tangut] |
(a) I. 125 ditto v. 1712
(i) | [Tangut] B. 99 cat. under "cattle" 1707

1711 [Tangut] VIII 14 | [Tangut]
(a) III 4 ditto v. 1482
?

1712 1710 chain

1713
‡ 4774 – 4642 ┬ 4867 – 1012 ┬ 5388
└ 5243 └ [5667]

1714 | 4454 chain

1715 – 5513

1716 0582 chain

1717
┬ 1724 ┬ 1379
└ 1868 ├ 1721
├ 1722
├ 1733
├ 2809
└ 2824

[1718] – [1851] pair

[1719] [2617] pair

1720 – 4862

1721 1717 chain

1722 1717 chain

1723 1736 chain

1724 1717 chain

1712

1713

1714

1715

1716

1717

1718

"rainbo

minus 1

129

1712 [Tangut] I.125 | [Tangut]
(a) IX 28 ditto v.1710
~~(i) | [Tangut] B.99 cat. under "cattle"~~
(b) II 44 | [Tangut] ×1795 3511
(i) (b) above B.99 cat. under "cattle"

1713 [Tangut] II 1 | [Tangut]
(a) VI 51 ditto
?

1714 [Tangut] II 1 [Tangut] | 4454
?

1715 [Tangut] II 1 | [Tangut] 5513
(a) VIII 29 ditto

1716 [Tangut] VI 104 [Tangut] | 3692
?

1717 [Tangut] VI 104 [Tangut] 1724
(a) V.13 ditto (misspelt)
(b) III 66 [Tangut] | v.1868
?

1718 [Tangut] VI 104 [Tangut] |
(a) VI 133 ditto
(i) The dissyllable C.C.C. 9[a] 虹 蜺 "rainbow" [in both cases]

1719 [Tangut] V.12 [Tangut] |
(a) VIII 19 ditto
?

1720 [Tangut] V.13 | [Tangut] 4562
(a) III 37 ditto
(i) The dissyllable B.103 cat. under 'silk'.

1721 [Tangut] VI A 127 [Tangut] | 'green' v.1724
?

1722 [Tangut] I.17 [Tangut] | 'green' v.1724
?

1723 [Tangut] V.17 [Tangut] |
(a) V 12 ditto v.1736
?

1724 [Tangut] V.13 [Tangut] | v.1717
(a) VI 104 ditto
(b) I.17 | [Tangut] v.1722
(c) VI A 53 | [Tangut] purple 1379
(d) VI A 127 | [Tangut] v.1721
(e) VII 118 | [Tangut] 2824
(f) VIII 45 [Tangut] | 2809
(g) VIII 98 | [Tangut] v.1733
C.C.C. 6[b] 青 "blue, green" B185[5] ditto W.II.10[2]
W. I. 224[12] tjoi "green"

1725 -1726

1726 1725 pair

1727 2485 chain

1728 4079 ~~0043~~ chain

1729 4396 chain

1730 -5246

1731 0384 pair

1732 2485 chain

1733 1717 chain

1734 2485 chain

1735 5085 chain

1736 1723 2920

1737 3893 chain

B.166[1] 絕 cut off, end

1738 #2933 pair

1732 4027 chain

1740 5630 chain

minus |

130

1725 [illegible] VII A 47 [illegible] |
(a) VII A 45 ditto reversed
?

1726 [illegible] VII A 45 [illegible] |
(a) VII A 47 ditto reversed
B.166² (doubled)

1727 [illegible] V 132 [illegible] | eg 2485
(a) V.15 | [illegible]
~~W.I.132¹⁷~~ (b) VIII 26 [illegible] | v.1732
W.I.132¹⁷

1728 [illegible] V.132 [illegible] [illegible] 4079 ~~4082~~
(a) IX 151 [illegible] | 4835
?

1729 ~~1730~~ [illegible] V 3 | [illegible]
?

1730 [illegible] V 3 | [illegible] 5246
(a) VI 23 ditto [[illegible]]
?

1731 ~~1732~~ [illegible] VI 104 | [illegible]
(a) III 134 ditto v.384

1732 ~~1733~~ [illegible] VIII 26 | [illegible] v.1728
?

1733 [illegible] VIII 98 [illegible] | "great" v.1724
?

1734 [illegible] V 15 [illegible] | v.1727
?

1735 [illegible] V.136 [illegible] | 5096
(a) I A 36 ditto
B.252⁴ 失 "to err."

1736 [illegible] V 12 | [illegible]
(a) V 17 ditto v.1723
(b) IX 164 | [illegible] 2920
B.167³ 168² Nevski I 431 "seven"

1737 [illegible] I 45 [illegible] | 2
(a) I.48 ditto reversed
W.I.134⁵ II 8⁵ 斷 to cut off, end II 126¹⁰ end (noun)
II 46⁵ 終 "to end." I 168¹¹ B.231⁴ q.v.

1738 [illegible] III 144 [illegible] | 2933
(a) VI 65 ditto
?

1739 [illegible] IX 66 [illegible] | 0832
?

1739A ~~1740~~ [illegible] ~~VI 30 | [illegible]~~ ~~v.246~~
....
~~(a) I A 26 | [illegible]~~
? Error for 1873

1740 [illegible] V 99 [illegible] | 3071
?

1741 3898 chain [illegible] VIII 98

1742 2143 chain

[illegible] B.193[4] 幾 ? how many? V

1743 3526 chain

1743 B 245[7] 化 'to alter, change'.

1744 [illegible] 1260 1237

1745 1876 chain

1746 2754 chain

1747 4027 chain

1748 important [illegible] VII 47

1749 4276 chain

1750 4046 pair 3675

1750 Φi | [illegible] 鳩槃荼

Kumbhāṇḍa W.I.170[10] [illegible]

Φii W.I 271[16] Kumāra[jīva]

1751 3503 pair

1752 0036 chain [illegible]

1753 3680 pair [illegible]

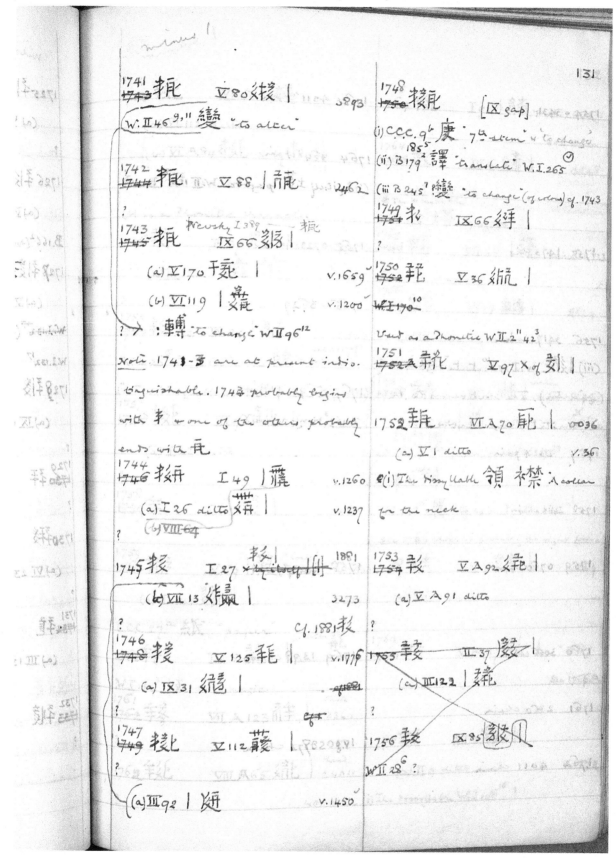

minus 1

131

1741 ~~1743~~ [Tangut] V 80 [Tangut] | 3893

(W. II 46 9, 11 變 "to alter"

1742 ~~1744~~ [Tangut] V 88 | [Tangut] 2462

?

1743 ~~1745~~ [Tangut] Nevsky I 389 — [Tangut] IX 66 [Tangut] |

(a) V 170 [Tangut] | v. 1659

(b) VI 119 | [Tangut] v. 1200

? → : 轉 "to change" W II 96[12]

Note 1743-5 are at present indistinguishable. 1743 probably begins with [Tangut] & one of the others probably ends with [Tangut]

1744 ~~1746~~ [Tangut] I 49 | [Tangut] v. 1260

(a) I 26 ditto [Tangut] | v. 1237

~~(b) VIII 64~~

?

1745 [Tangut] I 27 [Tangut] | ~~[illegible]~~ 1881

(b) VII 13 [Tangut] | 3273

?

Cf. 1881 [Tangut]

1746 ~~1748~~ [Tangut] V 125 [Tangut] | v. 1776

(a) IX 31 [Tangut] | ~~cf 1881~~

? ~~cf~~

1747 ~~1749~~ [Tangut] V 112 [Tangut] |

?

(a) III 92 | [Tangut] v. 1450

1748 ~~1750~~ [Tangut] [IX gap]

(i) C.C.C. 9[b] 庚 "7th stem" & "to change"

(ii) B 179[2] 185[5] 譯 "translate" W. I. 265

(iii) B 245[7] 變 "to change (of colour)" cf. 1743

1749 ~~1751~~ [Tangut] IX 66 [Tangut] |

?

1750 ~~1752~~ [Tangut] V 36 [Tangut] |

~~W I 170~~[10]

Used as a phonetic W II 2[11] 42[3]

1751 ~~1752A~~ [Tangut] V 97 × of 刻 |

1752 [Tangut] VI A 70 [Tangut] | 0036

(a) V 1 ditto v. 36

(i) The dissyllable 領 襟 "a collar for the neck"

1753 ~~1754~~ [Tangut] V A 92 [Tangut] |

(a) V A 91 ditto

?

~~1755 [Tangut] II 37 [Tangut] |~~

~~(a) III 122 | [Tangut]~~

?

1756 [Tangut] IX 85 [Tangut] |

W II 28[6] ?

1754 – 3431

1755 1473 bis

1756 3417 chain

(iii) W. I 172[10] 上上 "highest (quarter)". The word seems to be a (limited?) superlative.

1757 2324 pair

1758 2485 chain

1759 0760 chain

1760 3066 chain

1761 2360 chain

1762 4011 chain

1763 4011 chain

1764 4648 pair

(i) By itself 土塔 "pagoda" W. II 114[8] B.168[3]

1765 0723 chain

1766 – 5629

1767 5690 chain

B 167[3] ~~tiozpb wound~~

1768 ~~4569 pair~~

1769 1398 chain

1770 1772 chain

1754

~~1755~~

B.216

1755

~~1756~~ 手

1756

~~1757~~ 手

W. II 28

1757

~~1758~~ 手

1758

~~1759~~ 手

1759

~~1760~~ 手

C.C.C. 27

1760

W. I 152[3]

1761

~~1762~~ 手

1762

132

1754 ~~1755~~ VI.61 |

(a) VI 112 ditto

[(b) VI A84 × ty 赤 |]

B.216[3] 研 to rub

(b) is a Phonetic character.

1755 ~~1756~~ II 37 | 1413 bis

(a) III 122 | ×4345

?

1756 ~~1757~~ re IX 85 | 5369

W.II 28[6] ? B.186[5] q.v. tr. 除 to get rid of

(ii) The Disyllable W.I 172[10] 下 lowest (quarter)

1757 ~~1758~~ III 98 | 2324

(a) I 22 ditto

?

1758 ~~1759~~ I.117 | 2485

?

1759 ~~1760~~ V 69 | "ink" v.760

(a) I.144 | 4379

C.C.C. 27[a] 紙 "paper"

1760 IV 5 | false 3066

W.II 152[3] 技 to do magic

1761 ~~1762~~ VII A 123 | white 2360

?

1762 VIII A 65 | thread 4011

?

4011 chain

1763 ~~1764~~ I 92 | peak 2646

?

1764 ~~1765~~ III 6 | 4011 chain 4648

(a) I 16 ditto

(ii) The Disyllable W.I.138[7] 塔 "pagoda" × on seal in ...

1765 ~~1766~~ VII 46 | "bushel" v.723

B.169[4] (a measure?)

1766 ~~1767~~ VI 17 | 5629

(a) IX A 134 ditto reversed

B.169[3] 緡 a string (of cash)

1767 ~~1768~~ IX 2 | virtue useful 5675

(a) IX 17 | soot (?) ×4267

341[3] B 260[2] 恩 "favour, grace" W 270[19]

1766A

W.I.142[5] 展 "to extend, stretch"

See 1769, which is probably the right form.

1769 IX 2 | 4569

(a) VIII 7 ditto

?

1769 ~~1770~~ V A 117 | 2687

See 1766A

1770 VII 3 |

v.1772

(a) II 9 ditto

(i) The Disyllable W.I.108[15] ?

1771 1343 chain

1772
- 1770
- 1773
- 2334

1773 1772 chain

1774 5578 chain

1775 0304 chain

1776 2754 chain

1777 2149 chain

1778
- 0814
- 5119
- 5232

1779 2707 chain

1780 4080 chain

28 entries
1781
- 1557
- 1689 — 0323
  - 1364 — 1045
    - 2403
    - 3111 — 0735
      - 2465
      - 3113
      - 3264
      - 5303
    - 3853
    - 3853 bis
    - 3855
    - 4021 — 2321
      - 3864 — 3852
    - 4763
    - 5033
  - 1420
  - 1701
  - 3434
  - 3649
  - 4665
- 2387

1782 3514 chain

1783
- 2057 — 2090

v.3107 minus

133

1771 ~~1772~~ II 9 | "hair" v.1343

?

1772 ~~1773~~ II 9 |

(a) VII 3 ditto v.1770

(b) I 3 | 2334

(c) II A 18 | × of 1773

(i) By itself I 222[12] ?

(ii) The Hsyllable W. I. 108[16] ?

(c) is a phonetic character?

1773 ~~1774~~ II A 18

? a phonetic character

1774 ~~1775~~ VI 94 | "Family or clan name."

Possibly a double name.

B.176[5] P.N. tr. 康 [? wrong]

1775 ~~1776~~ VIII 63 | v.304

(a) VIII 10 | 2684

(b) IX 43 | 3383

?

1776 ~~1777~~ V 97 | 2754

(a) V 125 | v.1746

(b) VII 97 | 4381

(c) IX 19 | v.1065

C.C.C. 33[a] 折 to pluck, break off.

W.I.134[3] 碎 break ~~broken~~

1777 ~~1778~~ VIII 84 |

?

1778 ~~1779~~ IX A 98 | v.814

(a) VIII 13 ditto

(b) IX 106 | flood 5119

(c) IX 153 | 5232

B.232[5] ? 沈 'to sink'

1779 ~~1780~~ III 156 | 2707

??

1780 III 102 | perfection 4145

? 4080 chain

1781 ~~1782~~ VI 38 |

(a) I 82 ditto v.1557

(b) II 1 | trailing v.1689

(c) III 53 | 2387

C.C.C. 56 壁 W.I 222[6] "~~cliff~~ k'rums, small "cliff, name of a lunar mansion".

1782 ~~1783~~ VI 21 | 3514

?

1783 ~~1784~~ VI 38 |

(a) VIII 60 ditto v.2057

?

1784 2335 chain

1785
3535
3882
4088

B.215[3] phon.

1786 3263 chain

1787 3532 pair

1788 3226 chain

1789 4326 chain

1790 0752 chain

1791 3226 chain

1792 3296 pair

1793 2149 chain

1794 4027 chain

1795 1716 chain

1796 independent

1797 0073 chain

1798 2703 chain

Phon. B.199[4]

minus 1

134

~~1785~~ 1784 [Tangut] IX A 151 [Tangut] | 4988

(i) W.I. 224[10] mjigə "fear".

(ii) [Tangut] | [sic] W.I. 136[17] 逼迫 "to oppress or persecute".

~~1786~~ 1785 [Tangut] IX 118 [Tangut] | "leopard" 3535

(a) IX 134 ditto reversed

(b) I 64 [Tangut] |

(c) V 71 [Tangut] | 4088

(i) C.C.C. 7ª 16ª 虎 "tiger" B.221[3]

(ii) C.C.C. 10ª 寅 "3rd horary character" ("tiger" in the animal cycle)

1786 [Tangut] III 12 [Tangut] |

(i) [Tangut] | B.100 cat. under "wild animals"

~~1788~~ 1787 [Tangut] IX 118 [Tangut] | 3532

(a) IX 134 ditto

?

~~1789~~ 1788 [Tangut] [Tangut] IX 88 | [Tangut] 4389

? W.I. 266[6] 孫 grand-son B.206[3]

~~1790~~ 1789 [Tangut] IX 96 [Tangut] | 4959

?

1790 [Tangut] VIII 84 [Tangut] | ? 4132

(a) I 103 [Tangut] | ? v.1043

(b) I A 70 [Tangut] × by [Tangut] | Phonetic 4022

(c) II 3 [Tangut] | ? 4143

1790 cont.

(d) II 6 [Tangut] | ? v.1487

(e) IX 83 [Tangut] | "abuse" × 3522

?

~~1792~~ 1791 [Tangut] [Tangut] III 33 [Tangut] | v.577

?

~~1793~~ 1792 [Tangut] III 156 [Tangut] |

(a) V 27 ditto

?

~~1794~~ 1793 [Tangut] III 12 [Tangut] |

(a) V A 135 [Tangut] | × 2338 3228

~~1795~~ 1794 [Tangut] III 31 [Tangut] | v.832

?

~~1796~~ 1795 [Tangut] V 102 | [Tangut] calf 3511

(i) | [Tangut] B.99 cat. under "cattle" 0525

(ii) [Tangut] | ditto

?

~~1797~~ 1796 [Tangut] VII A 59 "Family or clan name".

~~1798~~ 1797 [Tangut] ši VII 18 | [Tangut] "to eat" v.13

(i) disyl. W.II 130[1] 俱共 "all together".

~~1799~~ 1799 [Tangut] Čiu VII A 57 [Tangut] v.1804

(a) IX A 112 [Tangut] |

?

1798 overleaf

1800 4104 chain

1798 insipidness

1802 2353 chain

1801 3812 chain

1801 Φ1 | [illegible] 旃檀 candana

W.I. 178^6

1803 4104 chain

1804 2703 chain

1805 – 0929

1806 1080 chain

1807 – 1808

1808 ~~1807~~ pain

1809 3274 pain

1810 1949 chain

1811 – 3343

1812 0184 chain

1813 – 5630

1814 0538 chain

1815 – 5653

1800
1799
~~1800~~

W.I

B.23

1798
1800

name

1802
~~1802~~

?

1801
~~1802~~

?

1803
~~1804~~

(a) I

(b) I

(c) I

(d)

W.II 18

1804
~~1805~~

(a) VI

B.186^5 降

1805
~~1806~~

(a) II

?

1806
~~1807~~

(i)

minus 1

1800 1799 ~~1800~~ [Tangut] T'A III 100 [Tangut] 's

[Tangut] W II 24^{9} 42^{2} 其 he, his B.181^{1} 方

B.239^{2}

1798 ~~1800~~ [Tangut] VII A 60 "Family or clan name".

1802 ~~1803~~ [Tangut] IX 70 | [Tangut] 2353

?

1801 ~~1802~~ [Tangut] VII 22 [Tangut] | 3812

?

1803 ~~1804~~ [Tangut] D'A III 101 [Tangut] | "that"

(a) III 39 ditto

(b) VII 24 | [Tangut] 3659

(c) VIII 4 | [Tangut] 2219

(d) VIII A 51 | [Tangut] 5412

W.II 18^{5} 此 "this"

1804 ~~1805~~ [Tangut] V 85 [Tangut] | "hall" v.1945

(a) VII A 57 [Tangut] | × v.1799

B.186^{5} 降 "to descend, ~~degrade, subtract, submit~~" q.v.

1805 ~~1806~~ [Tangut] III 101 | [Tangut] v.929

(a) II 6 ditto

?

1806 ~~1807~~ [Tangut] VI A 4 [Tangut] | 2316

(i) | [Tangut] B.100 cat. under 'horse'.

135

1807 ~~1808~~ [Tangut] II 6 | [Tangut] 'ring'

(a) I 91 ditto v.1809

?

1808 ~~1809~~ [Tangut] I 91 [Tangut] |

(a) II 6 ditto

ccc.13^{a} W I.134^{17} 糞 "dung, manure".

1809 ~~1810~~ [Tangut] III 163 [Tangut] | 3274

(a) IX 44 ditto

?

1810 [Tangut] VII 40 [Tangut] |

?

1811 ~~1812~~ [Tangut] VII A 52 [Tangut] | 3343

(a) VI 107 ditto & reversed

?

1812 ~~1813~~ [Tangut] VI 68 [Tangut] |

(a) V 65 ditto v.184

(i) The dissyllable B.100 cat. under 'wild animals'

1813 ~~1814~~ [Tangut] III 110 | [Tangut] misspelt? 5650

(a) III 107 ditto

? cf.1817

1814 ~~1816~~ [Tangut] IX 84 [Tangut] [Tangut] 4681

?

1815 ~~1816~~ [Tangut] III 110 | [Tangut]

(a) III 107 ditto

?

1816 0015 chain

1817 3980 chain

1823 4414 pair

[1824] 2217 chain | IX 90

B160⁵ tr.

1818 1473 bis chain

[1825] [1220] pair

1819 4531 chain

1826 +4520 / 1193

1820 1254 chain

W.I.134″ | ? perhaps not a doublet; by violence

1821 - 2468 | VI 68

1827 3149 chain

1822 4531 chain

1828 2383 chain III 101

minus |

136

1816 ~~1817~~ [Tangut] IX 84 [Tangut] v.15

?
1817 ~~1818~~ [Tangut] IX 84 [Tangut] | 0025

(i) The dissyllable B.103 translated ~~outer~~ 上著 "outer clothing".

(ii) [Tangut] | B.103 translated 下著 "underclothes".

1818 ~~1819~~ [Tangut] III 18 [Tangut] | v.1473

?
1819 ~~1820~~ [Tangut] III 18 [Tangut] | v.1822 ?

W.I.134[12] 壓 "to crush, press down".

1820 [Tangut] IX 84 | [Tangut] v.1254

Dict 163 B.164[5] tr 命 167[5] 169[5]

1821 ~~1822~~ [Tangut] III 18 | [Tangut] 2468

(a) VIII 63 ditto

(i) The dissyllable CCC.27[a] 碾 場 "threshing floor".

1822 ~~1823~~ [Tangut] IX 84 [Tangut] | 4531

(a) V.166 ditto

(b) III 18 | [Tangut] v.1819

(c) IV 2 | [Tangut] 2281

W.I.102[3] 134[10] II 4[8] 62[3] 忍 kṣānti "patience, endurance". I 224[14] bzod.pa S:H.237

kṣānti: I 218[9] mjed "suffering"; I 212[18] gnon.po "oppression".

1823 ~~1824~~ [Tangut] III A22 [Tangut] |

(a) III A56 ditto

?
1824 ~~1825~~ [Tangut] I 126 [Tangut] |

W.I.100[8] 動 "to move, stir, mutable". B.160[5]

1825 ~~1826~~ [Tangut] V 29 [Tangut] |

(a) V 20 ditto

1826 ~~1827~~ [Tangut] NA III 121 | [Tangut]

(a) III 111 ditto 4520 v.1220

(b) III 145 | [Tangut] v.1193

W.I.134[11]: :168[14] 屠 "to butcher".

Used as a phonetic in W.I.192[7] -ndhu

1827 ~~1828~~ [Tangut] IX 9 [Tangut] | 3149

(a) III 5 ditto

(i) The dissyllable CCC.21[b] 樓 閣 WII 48[1] 樓 觀 a tower, or pavilion, monastery

1828 ~~1829~~ [Tangut] I.14 [Tangut] |

(a) III 16 ditto [Tangut]

?

1829 4506 chain

1830 1891 chain

1831 [1265] ~~pair~~ check

1832 [1265] chain

1833 ‡1470 1476

1834 ~~4446~~

1835 5310 chain

φi B.225[4] Bhadrapāla

1836 4327 chain

1837 1650 chain

1838 4276 chain

1839 -4000 chain

1840 - 3958

1841 2494 chain

W.I.268[8] 本 'original'

1829
~~1830~~

W.I.

B.199

1830

W.II.78

1831
~~1832~~

(a) V

(b) I

?

1832
~~1833~~

A Phon

1833
~~1834~~

(a) III

(b) I

?

1834
~~1835~~

(a) VI

?

1835
~~1836~~

?

1836
~~1837~~

(ii) B.166[3]

137

1829 ~~1830~~ [Tangut] I 147 [Tangut] | 4586

(a) III 78 ditto

W. I. 214[7] ca II 66[7] (I 154[4] II 96[8]) 分 "division, part"

B. 199[2] 分 223[3] ditto q.v.

1830 [Tangut] I. 60 [Tangut] | v. 1891

W. II. 78[3] 偏 "on one side"

1831 ~~1832~~ [Tangut] III A 91 [Tangut] | [1265]

(a) VI 89 ditto

(b) III A 106 [Tangut] × by [Tangut] [Tangut] v. 1832

?

1832 ~~1833~~ [Tangut] III A 106 [Tangut] [Tangut]

A Phonetic character

1833 ~~1834~~ [Tangut] VI A 35 | [Tangut]

(a) III A 37 ditto v. 1470

(b) I A 85 | [Tangut] v. 1476

?

1834 ~~1835~~ [Tangut] VI A 62 | [Tangut]

(a) VI 73 ditto

?

1835 ~~1836~~ [Tangut] I. 60 | [Tangut]

?

1836 ~~1837~~ [Tangut] I. 60 [Tangut] | 1832 q.v.

(i) B. 166[3]

1837 ~~1838~~ [Tangut] I 77 [Tangut] | 3689

?

1838 ~~1839~~ [Tangut] VI 48 | [Tangut] 5570 and

(a) II 31 v. 0454

B. 97 [Tangut] centre followed by [Tangut].

As for |, a younger man or a younger sister calls an elder sister [Tangut] [Tangut]"

(ii) [Tangut] | c.c.c. 20[a] 阿姐 "elder sister"

1839 ~~1840~~ [Tangut] IX A 82 | [Tangut] 4000

(a) V. 20 ditto

?

1840 [Tangut] V 42 | [Tangut]

(a) V 30 ditto

?

1841 ~~1842~~ [Tangut] VII 38 [Tangut] | v. 2494

(a) I 11 ditto

(b) V 16 | [Tangut] [Tangut] 2936

[(c) V 113 | [Tangut] error for 1842]

(d) VII 25 | [Tangut] 3322

(i) W. I. 134[4] II 22[3] 根 I 194[2] "root" B 187[2]

(iii) [Tangut] | c.c.c. 14[b] B. 101 cat. under "vegetables" 蔓菁

(iv) [Tangut] | c.c.c. 15[b] 乾薑 "dried ginger"

(ii) The disyllable II 18[2] cont.

本根 "origin source"

1850 - 1858

[1851] - [1718]

1842 - 5171

1843 ~~2975~~ 5465 chain

1852 3226 chain

1844 - 4154

1853 3354 chain

1845 3662 chain

1846 上 4412 ⌈0209 ⌊4106

1854 4728 pair

1847 independent

1848 足 "foot" W II 4[5]

1848 上 2236 - 2454

1855 5623 chain

1856 5055 pair

1849 - 5627

minus!

1841
~~1842~~ cont.

(iv) [Tangut] | C.C.C. 28ª Name of a Temple; translated by 大恒曆 corrected to 典禮 B.191²

1842
~~1843~~ [Tangut] VII 38 | [Tangut] 5171
(a) V 113 ditto

?
1843
~~1844~~ [Tangut] V 57 [Tangut] | 103 2915

?
1844
~~1845~~ [Tangut] VII A120 | [Tangut] 4154
(a) VII 103 ditto

?
1845
~~1846~~ [Tangut] V 57 [Tangut] | woven 5062

?
1846
~~1847~~ [Tangut] VII A114 | [Tangut] × 4412

(a) III 12 ditto

?
1847
~~1848~~ [Tangut] VIII A66 × by itself [!] |

C.C.C. 25ª [Tangut]
1848
~~1849~~ [Tangut] IX 129 | [Tangut]

(a) IX 17 ditto

W. I 112¹⁸ 128⁹ II 4⁴ 40² 足 I 142¹⁵ 步 "foot, leg": I 168¹⁴ 足 ditto
1849
~~1850~~ [Tangut] VII 99 | [Tangut] 5627

? (a) VIII 71 ditto (misspelt)

?

138

1850 [Tangut] III 137 [Tangut] |

?
1851
~~1852~~ [Tangut] VI 133 [Tangut] | [Tangut]

(a) VI 104 ditto V. 1718

(i) The disyllable C.C.C. 9ª 虹蜺 "rainbow" [in both cases]

1852
~~1853~~ [Tangut] III 51 [Tangut] |

W.I. 96¹⁰,¹⁵ + passim 等 sign of plural I 214¹ at end of a long list.
1853
~~1854~~ [Tangut] II 11 [Tangut] | wolf 3366

(i) The disyllable B 100 cat. under "wild animals".

1854
~~1855~~ [Tangut] IX 109 [Tangut] |

(a) IX 39 ditto

(ii) The disyllable C.C.C. 9ᵇ 卓午 "morning + midday".

(i) by itself B.166²
1855
~~1856~~ [Tangut] IX 109 | [Tangut] v. 2041

?
1856
~~1857~~ [Tangut] IX 109 [Tangut] |

(a) VII 64 ditto

?

1857 2494 chain

1858? 1850 pair

1859 3123 chain

1860 3685 chain

1861 2482 chain

1862 3838 pair

1863 1667 chain

1864
5715 — 0784, 0923, 3501, 5659

1865 1667 chain

1866 — 4062 ~~pair~~

minus 1 minus 2

139

1857
~~1858~~ [Tangut] VIII A 74 [Tangut] |

(a) IX 176 | [Tangut] ×2307

(i) | [Tangut] B.102 cat. under 'rivers + seas' cf. 1887

(ii) The dissyllable B.185[3] 本致 "origin + source"

1858 [Tangut] III 137 × of | [Tangut]

? v.1850

1859 [Tangut] IX 114 | [Tangut] 3427

(i) [Tangut] | W.I. 112[13] ~~144~~[9] 奮迅 "sudden ~~1860~~ + quick."

1860 [Tangut] VI 133 [Tangut] | 3904

(a) I 62 | [Tangut] 2659

(b) III 47 [Tangut] |

(i) By itself C.C.C. 28[b] 誦 "to recite" B.230[5]

(ii) (b) above W.I. 108[5] 266[8] II 16[3] 18[10] 34[1] 讀誦 "to read + recite"

(iii) | [Tangut] C.C.C. 32[b] 簫 "bamboo pipe" v.1008

(iv) [Tangut] | C.C.C. 28[b] Name of a temple, translated 閻門, which means "side door"! B 176[1]

(v) C.C.C. 21[a] ?

1861 [Tangut] VI 101 | [Tangut]

?

1862 [Tangut] IX 48 [Tangut] |

(a) VI 18 ditto

?

1863 [Tangut] I 81 [Tangut] | "wild animal" v.1667

(a) I A 35 [Tangut] × by [Tangut] v.1865 ×(2828)

(b) II 4 [Tangut] | 3536

(i) | [Tangut] (sic!) B.100 cat. under "wild animals"

1864 [Tangut] VI A 63 | [Tangut] 5717

(a) VII A 92 ditto

(i) The dissyllable C.C.C. 37[a] 輪迴 "the return of the wheel (cakra)." W.II 156[1]

1865 [Tangut] I A 35 [Tangut] v.1863

~~(a) IX 103~~ ?

Possibly a phonetic character 1864 A [Tangut] in IX 103 + C.C.C. 31[b] is apparently an error for [Tangut] 2342

1866 [Tangut] V 2 | [Tangut] 0062

(a) VII 21 ditto v.62

(i) The dissyllable C.C.C. 7[a] 16[a] W.I. 94[16] 101[3] 獅子 W.I. 194[11] sen.ge "lion"

1867 1313 chain

1868 1717 chain

1869
1194 — [1161], 1174, 1179, 1208, 5136

[1870] 1693 ~~chain~~ pair

1871 1892 ~~chain~~ pair

1872 4561 chain

1873
0246, 1877, 2937, 4884 — ? 2032

1874 5019 ~~0604~~ chain

1875 2363 pair

1876
1881, 1885 — 1054, 1226, 1745 — 1450, 3273; 1878, 1883 — 2249 — 1879, 3798, 5288

1877 1873 chain

1878 1876 chain

1879 1876 chain

1880-3460

1882 minus 2

140

1867 [Tangut] III 66 [Tangut] | "silk" v.1313
(a) V 89 [Tangut] | "cloth" v.1606
(b) VII 42 | [Tangut] (misspelt) v.299
(i) (b) above B.103 cat. under "men's clothing"
B.169[2] tr. 段 'piece' (of silk)

1868 [Tangut] III 66 | [Tangut] v.1717
?

1869 [Tangut] III 58 | [Tangut] "iron" [Tangut]
(a) VII 33 ditto v.1194
?

1870 [Tangut] IX 157 [Tangut] |
(a) VI 36 ditto v.1693
?

1871 [Tangut] VIII A 91 [Tangut] |
(a) VIII A 92 ditto
?

1872 [Tangut] IX 75 [Tangut] | to come 1968
?

1873 [Tangut] si VI 30 ~~? VII 59-60~~ [Tangut]
(a) I 20 [Tangut] ditto v.246
(c) III A 2 | [Tangut] 2937
(d) VIII A 69 | [Tangut] "dead" v.1877
B.128[1]
ccc. 19[b] 死 W I 194[8] hsi "to die"
(b) I A 26 | [Tangut] 4884

for variant see 02216

1874 [Tangut] VII 50 | [Tangut] 5019
?

1875 [Tangut] IX 82 [Tangut] |
(a) V 2 ditto
?

1876 [Tangut] IX A 26 | [Tangut] "goods"
(a) IX 157 ditto v.1881
(b) VI 51 | [Tangut] 商 v.1885
ccc. 26[b] 賣 "to sell"

1877 [Tangut] VIII A 69 [Tangut] | v.1873
ccc. 6[b] 亡 W. I. 196[9] 214[10] hsi
"dead"

1877A [Tangut] see 1742

1878 [Tangut] IX 54 [Tangut] | "goods" v.1881
(a) IX 44 | [Tangut] 2249 ~~cf. 1879~~
?

1879 [Tangut] IX 54 [Tangut] | 2249 ~~cf. 1878~~
W. I. 134[8] ?

1880 [Tangut] VII 66 | [Tangut] 3460
(a) VII A 108 ditto
?

1885 1876 chain

1881 1876 chain

1886 1222 chain

1887 1369 chain

(ii) |𗴂 商 "merchant" W.II 132⁹

B.219⁴ 商

1882 0746 pair

1888 0433 pair

1883 1876 chain

1889
5317 1286
5559 2359

1884 -0501

1884

1881

(a)

(b)

(c)

(d)

(e)

(f)

(i) W.I.

(ii) |

There

this

Proba

above

possibly

There i

, In

as shin

1882

(a) V

?

1883

?

1884

(a) V

Possibly a

minus 2 minus 1

number separately 1884A 𗴂 VII 57 (?) v. (ii)

141

1881 𗴂 IX 157 [Tangut] [Tangut] | "to sell"

(a) IX A 26 ditto v. 1876 ?

(b) I 27 | 𗴂 ×

(c) V 6 | [Tangut] ~~(d) VI 51 | [Tangut]~~ v. 1745 ~~v. 1885~~ v. 1883

(d) IX ~~144~~ 38 | [Tangut] "area, place" v. 1054

(e) IX 54 | [Tangut] v. 1878 ?

(f) IX A 144 | [Tangut] v. 1226

(i) W. I. 134[1] 貨 化 "property, goods"

(ii) | [Tangut] CCC 34[b] 嫁 "to marry".

There is some confusion between this character & 𗴂 1745; (b) above is probably & other entries ~~probably this is~~ 𗴂 possibly an error for this character. There is also perhaps another separate 𗴂. In CCC 34[b] the sound is given as shih.

1882 [Tangut] V 34 [Tangut] | 0746

(a) V 57 ditto

?

1883 [Tangut] V 6 𗴂 | "good" v. 1881 ?

?

1884 [Tangut] VII 57 "Name of country"

(a) V A 94 | [Tangut] v. 501

Possibly a dissyllabic name.

×

1885 [Tangut] VI 51 [Tangut] | "to sell" v. 1876

1886 𗴂 III 119 [Tangut] [Tangut] 1992 v. 1222

(a) IX 173 [Tangut] | v. 432

× means "not to respect".

1887 [Tangut] V 88 [Tangut] | "near, kindred" v. 1369

(a) VI A 20 | [Tangut] to move v. 1227

~~1888 [Tangut] V 117 | [Tangut]~~

~~(a) IX 4 ditto v. 433~~

B. 90 "[Tangut], [Tangut] & [Tangut] in succession. | means not near ([Tangut])".

(i) CCC 36[a] W. II 22[3] 遠 "distant"

(ii) W II 4[11] 久 "a long time".

(iii) [Tangut] | ~~cat.~~ B. 102 cat. under "rivers & seas" cf. 1857

B. 188[2] q.v.

1888 [Tangut] V 117 | [Tangut]

(a) IX 4 ditto v. 433.

1889 [Tangut] VI 70 | [Tangut] × 5317

(a) I 57 ditto

(b) VIII 3 [Tangut] [|] 5559

(i) | [Tangut] CCC 28[a] Name of a temple,

1890 0106 pair

1891
- 5001
- 0065 – 4949
- 0207
- 0636
- 0708
- 0709
- 0868
- 0901
- 1123
- 1349
- 1362
- 1388
- 1830
- 1971
- 2161
- 2200
- 2250
- 2378 – 5635 – 5641
- 2869
- 2892
- 2930 – 3157 – 5574
- 2974
- 3422
- 3520
- 3599
- 3876 – 0450
- 3898 – 1499 – 5377
- 4017
- 4527 – 2768 – 4528
- 5064 – 5028
- 5098
- 5478
- 5548
- 5577
- 5699
- 5611 – 4445
- 5705 – 4452

Verbal prefix B. 171^5, 186^3

B. 192^3 (looks like a causative) 193^3 v. 193^4

1891 W II 4^4 | [Tangut] either = 而起 "and arise" or simply participial "arising"

| [Tangut] 一面 "on one side" ~~"facing"~~ W. II 4^5

W. II 128^9 [Tangut] [Tangut] | [Tangut] 是事 [Tangut] 實不 "Is this business correct or not?"

v. B 271. meaningless prefix.

Verbal prefix W. I. 132^9 II v. 2155

minus!

142

1889 cont.
translated 巡撿 "to inspect & check or to inspect patrols."

1890 [illegible] IX 72 [illegible] | 0106
(a) VII 112 ditto

?

1891 [illegible] A VIII 66 | [illegible] 5801
(a) V 27 ditto
(b) I 9 | [illegible] v. 1349
(c) I 60 | [illegible] "on one side" v. 1830
(d) IA 51 | [illegible] + 5577
(e) II 7 | [illegible] + 5699
(f) III 18 | [illegible] + x(0450) 3876
(g) III 20 | [illegible] + {1497 {5377 3898
(h) III 29 | [illegible] 2869
(i) III 49 | [illegible] xx(5641) x(5635) 2378
(j) III 67 | [illegible] v. 1123
(k) III 83 | [illegible] chapter + 3422
(l) III 108 | [illegible] + x{2768 {4528 4527
(m) III 114 | [illegible] v. 207
(n) III 116 | [illegible] "to practice" v. 1362
(o) III 129 | [illegible] + 2974
(p) III 154 | [illegible] 2250
(q) V 28 | [illegible] v. 868
(r) V 95 | [illegible] [illegible] 吹 + xx 2930 x(3157) xx(5574)

(s) V 104 [illegible] x by | [illegible] 1971
(t) V 113 | [illegible] perfume + 5478
(u) V 138 | [illegible] + 5548
(v) V 144 | [illegible] a drop. + x(4452) 5705
(w) V 182. | [illegible] + 3599
(x) VA 16 | [illegible] scroll + x(4445) 5611
(y) VA 98 | [illegible] v. 1388
(z) VA 103 | [illegible] v. 709
(aa) VA 118 | [illegible] + 4017
(bb) VA 121 | [illegible] v. 636
(cc) VI 88 | [illegible] + 3520
(dd) VI 102 | [illegible] + 2892 ~~4017~~
(ee) VI 117 | [illegible] 2200
(ff) VII 18 | [illegible] + 5098
(gg) VII 23 | [illegible] v. 708
(hh) VII 25 | [illegible] 2161 x 0066
(ii) VII 35 | [illegible] to [illegible] v. 68
(jj) IX 59 | [illegible] + 5064
(iii) IX 9 | [illegible] 0981

This word, although it is translated by Wang & others as 'one, a', seems in fact to be a meaningless prefix like Ch. 阿 (also a).
(ii) ~~[illegible]~~ at W.I. 136[9] translates 所生. | [illegible] ccc 33[b] 已畢 + W.I. 114[17] means "completely". (ii) ccc. 28[b] v. 5679

1892-1871

1899 2193 chain

1893 · 4470 chain

1894 3226 chain

1900 儀 "rule, etiquette" B.272[2]

~~1900 cha~~

1895 1545 chain

1900 3200 chain

| W.I.271[10] part of royal title 天儀

1896-0083 pair

1901 | W.I.265[14] part of royal title translated 禮集 "personifying (?) good manners" or "assembling rites" (?)

1897 3078 chain

| 餓鬼 preta hungry ghost W.II 76[9]

1901 4243 4168 — 1192; 4168 — 1192; 4220 — 3622; 3623; 5058

B.176' tr. 閤 123' tr. 同 same, mutual

1898 2183 chain

B.188' 軌 rule

(ii) W.II 140[10] 如 "like"?

1891

1892

(a)

1893

(a)

1894

(a)

1896

(a) VI

1897 ~~1896~~

(a) VII

(i) ~~W.II.7~~

地

hell"

(ii) |

of the

1898

VIII

(a) ~~VII A~~

(b) VII

~~Disordered~~ minus!

143

1891 cont.
seems to translate 都 "all".

1892 VIII A92 |
(a) VIII A91 ditto ... v. 1871

?
1893 V.165 | 4470
(a) V A114 ditto

?
1894 VI 44
(a) V 119 | v. 1545

?
1896 I 20 |
(a) VII 71 ditto v. 83

?
1897 III 75 | 2976
(a) VII 102 | 1518
(i) The dissyllable W II 76[9] 82[7] 地獄 "earth prison naraka hell".
(ii) | W.I. 214[5] 224[11] gśin-rje "lord of the dead".

1898 VII A39 | v. 2193
(a) VIII 79 ditto
(b) VII A115 | 3283

(i) The dissyllable W.I. 218[14] yi-dvags II 76[9] 82[3] 餓鬼 "hungry ghost, preta". W.I. 170[2]

1899 VIII A77 | 4828

?
1894 VIII A32 mystic sound mantra v. 353

1900 II 9 | brightness majesty 3200
(a) I 128 ditto 1605
(b) VII 55 × by | 1605
(c) IX 171 × by ditto flag, banner (1042) 1038
(i) the dissyllable W.I. 110[1] "lofty" 136[3] 威儀 "dignity, respect-inspiring deportment" I 224[16] c'a-byan

1901 III 61 | chain 3206 1243
(a) VI 47 ditto
(b) II 42 | 'righteousness' 4168
(c) VIII 20 | 4220
A most intangible character
(i) | c.c.c. 29[6] 有禮 "(the gentleman) has good manners"
(ii) | W.I. 110[1] ? II 34[10] ? 50[9] 亦爾 II 140[10] 如是

| [Tangut] B. 203² (part of royal title) tr. 恭肅 reverent + respectful

1902 4651 chain

1903 [Tangut] 1506 — 0198 ~~0198~~ 0228 4981 1904 3567 3604 – 5712

1904 1903 chain

1905 2658 chain

1906 4516 chain

1907 – 2052

1908 1372 chain

[1909] [5116] chain

1910 1317 chain

1911 0809 chain

1912 4156 chain

1913 4156 ~~chain~~

Th. Dingl. B 224⁴

minus |

144

1901 (cont.)

(iii) | [Tangut] C.C.C. 28a Name of a temple translated 大恒曆 corrected to 典禮 B.166' ro.

(iv) | [Tangut] C.C.C. 28b 閤門 Name of a temple "side door."

(v) C.C.C. 27b | [Tangut] 取則

1902 [Tangut] III 61 [Tangut] 'land'

?

1903 [Tangut] III A 28 | [Tangut] "to strip off"

(a) IX A 15 ditto v.1506

(b) VII 80 | [Tangut] v.228

(c) IX 131 [Tangut] | 4981

?

1904 [Tangut] VII 86 | [Tangut] 'to strip off'

? v.1506

1905 [Tangut] I 61 [Tangut] | ? 2658

(a) II 1 ditto

? early morning Nevski I.231

1906 [Tangut] VIII 13 [Tangut] | ? 4516

?

1907 [Tangut] V 19 | [Tangut]

(a) VI A 56 ditto v.2052

C.C.C. 24a 矮 "a cow (bed)" Y0571A

1908 [Tangut] I 27 | [Tangut] "to destroy" v.1372

? not || to fig... 0688 ... of 0685

1909 [Tangut] I 27 | [Tangut] ? 5116

(a) III 75 ditto

? 1908 A16 ...

1910 [Tangut] I 89 | [Tangut] ? v.1327

?

1911 [Tangut] I 89 | [Tangut] 'vegetable' v.383

(i) The dissyllable C.C.C. 14b 菠薐 "spinach & water chestnut."

1912 [Tangut] III 124 [Tangut] |

(a) III 5 ditto

(b) VII A 100 [Tangut] | v.1913

C.C.C. 21b 34b W.I.94[10] II 4[4] 8[3] 10[5] 20[8] (q.v.)

定 samādhi abstract contemplation. v.4156

1913 [Tangut] VII A 100 | [Tangut] v.1912

B.96 "The whole of [Tangut] plus [Tangut] an ideogram. | is | [Tangut] or [Tangut] ("pure silence", apparently another term for contemplation). It means

0270, 0014, 3783, 5380, 4272, 4647

1914
⊥ 3933 – 4786 – 2546 – 2088#

1915 0014 chain

1916 4960 pair

1917 0092 chain

1918 1086 pair

1919 2149 chain

1920 3263 chain

1921 4326 chain

1922 independent

B.207[3]

1923
⊥ 4853
⊥ 4383 – 4849

1924 0424 chain

1913
of mi
without
[tran
east
.ebic.
W.I.102

1914
(a)
C.C.C. 2

1915
?

1916
(a)
W.I. 110'5
(b)
N.B. Also
written

1917
~~(a) V~~
"to appr

145

1913 (cont)
[Tangut] "a state of mind in which one can remain without distraction" 卅 [Tangut]
[translated 杓 迦 shao ka] (These last two words appear to be phon-etic.)
W.I.102[1] 144[2] 禪 dhyāna meditation

1914 [Tangut] III 141 | [Tangut]
(a) IX 17 ditto
C.C.C. 28[a] 30[a] 告 "to inform, plead"

1915 [Tangut] I A 91 | [Tangut] confused v.14
?

1916 [Tangut] VI A 58 [Tangut] |
(a) VI A 49 ditto
W.I.110[15] 142[2] 散 "to dispel (doubt)" B 220[2]
(b) | [Tangut] 分散 to scatter (rain)
N.B. Also, or perhaps more correctly written [Tangut], certainly right v. B 180[5]

1917 [Tangut] ~~III 171~~ IX A 104 | [Tangut] "to go" v 92
~~(a) V 1~~ W.I.134[17] | [Tangut] 枉害
"to oppress & injure."

1918 [Tangut] ? III 171 [Tangut] |
(a) VI 1 ditto
B.256 否 ma.yin W.I.218[1] min 187[3]
"not to be". B245[5] 非 "not to be".
Note compound of [Tangut] [Tangut].

1919 [Tangut] VI A 81 [Tangut] |
?

1920 [Tangut] VII 85 [Tangut] |
(a) I 14 ditto
?

1921 [Tangut] V 151 [Tangut] |
(a) VIII A 37 [Tangut] |
?

1922 [Tangut] I 30 Family or clan name. Dict. 1[a] 6 B 345[2] 番名 B 195[3]

1923 [Tangut] I 128 | [Tangut] "like, as" 4853
(a) VI A 17 ditto
(b) V 176 | [Tangut]
C.C.C. 37[a] W.I. 94[9,15] 96[15] II 4[8] 18[2] [Tangut] |
無量 "immeasurable".
"value" Koshi I 214
Presumably the corresponding character is 量. ~~[struck through]~~

1924 [Tangut] VI 8 | [Tangut] "later" v.424
(a) VI 53 | [Tangut]
(b) IX 25 [Tangut] | v.1537
?

1925 1929 chain

B.192³ q.v.

1926 0809 chain

1927 2461 chain

1928 2461 chain

1929
- 1342 — 1551
  - 1585 — 1429
  - 1931
  - 1934 — 1117 — 1116
    - 1380
    - 1707
    - 1925 — 1337
      - 3155
      - 3874
    - 3338 — 5392
  - 1997 — 2633
  - 2509 — 2502
- 1587 — 1588
- 1930 1932
- 3204
- 5584 — 5586

1930 1929 chain

1931 0809 chain

1932 1929 chain

1933 2482 chain

1934 1929 chain

minus 1

146

1925 [Tangut] V 118 [Tangut] | "cattle" ~~"ox"~~ v. 1934
(a) I 47 | [Tangut] horn (skin) 3874
[(b) VI A 78 [Tangut] × by [Tangut] | ...]
(c) VIII 28 | [Tangut] 3155
(d) VIII 29 | [Tangut] v. 1337
W. I 226[1] rwa II 48[4] 角 "horn"

1926 [Tangut] V 118 [Tangut] [Tangut]
B 102 [Tangut] [Tangut] | cat. under ~~The disyllable, plus 1926 repeat~~ vegetables. To be distinguished from 1931 ~~a second time cat. under vegetables~~.

1927 [Tangut] IX 48 | [Tangut] v. 1928
(a) III 143 | [Tangut] v. 567
(b) V 114 [Tangut] | v. 1428
B. 188[3] 滯 "to obstruct"

1928 [Tangut] III 21 [Tangut] |
(a) IX 48 [Tangut] × v. 1927
?

1928A [Tangut] × of VII 76 [Tangut] | v. 1932
Error for 1929

1929 [Tangut] ts'i VI 101 [Tangut] | "sheep"
(a) VIII 71 ditto × v. 1342
(b) I 7 | [Tangut] 5584
(c) III 130 [Tangut] | 3204
(d) V 139 | [Tangut] × 1588 1587
(e) VI 26 [Tangut] × by [Tangut] | v. 1930
(i) By itself CCC 16[b] 羖 羊歷

~~B. 99 cat. heading "sheep"~~
(ii) [Tangut] | B. 99 cat. under "sheep"
(iii) | [Tangut] B. 99 cat. under "sheep"

1930 [Tangut] VI 26 [Tangut] [Tangut] "sheep & rams" 1342
B. 99 cat. heading for "sheep."

1931 [Tangut] VI 101 [Tangut] [Tangut] Phonetic + [Tangut] vegetables
B. 102 [Tangut] | [Tangut] cat. under "vegetables". To be distinguished from 1926

1932 [Tangut] VII 76 | [Tangut] error for 1929
| [Tangut] B. 99 cat. under sheep

1933 [Tangut] VI 101 [Tangut] | "rock" v. 594
(i) The disyllable CCC 16[b] 山羊 B 101 cat. under "wild animals" "mountain sheep." [Tangut] phonetic + wild animal

1934 [Tangut] rue V A 30 | [Tangut] "sheep" v. 1342
(a) I 126 [Tangut] "ox" × (1116) v. 1117
(b) IV 1 | [[Tangut] for 判 [Tangut]] 1707
(c) V 118 | [Tangut] "horn" v. 1925 × 5392
(d) V 137 [Tangut] | yak 3338
(e) VII 19 | [Tangut] "property" v. 1380
(i) CCC 7[a] 16[a] 牛 "cattle" B. 99 chapter heading.
(ii) The disyllable W. I 132[18] 牛羊

1940 0148 chain

1935
⊥3539 ⊤3540
5598

1941 4651 chain
239'

1936 ~~2103A~~ 5486 chain (i) By itself B.124⁴ as 田

1937 3438 chain

1942 0809 chain

1938 – 4610A

1939 2278 chain

1943 3783 chain

minus 1

147

1934 (cont).
"cattle & sheep".
(iii) (a) above B.99 cat. under "cattle"
(iv) (d) above C.C.C. 16b 犂牛

1935 [Tangut] ya VIII.14 |[Tangut] 3539
(a) II 20 ditto
?

1936 [Tangut] V 9 |[Tangut] {2433 2103A
W.I.120[13] II 8[9] 10[11] 吼 "to roar, bellow"
[Tangut] cattle + [Tangut] mouth

1937 [Tangut] V 34 |[Tangut] to write 3438
(a) V 80 |[Tangut] saw v.1171
(i) ~~The dissyllable~~ C.C.C. 24a (a) above 剪刀
"scissors & knife"
(ii) |[Tangut] C.C.C. 24b 裁縫
"to cut out & sew".

1938 [Tangut] I 20 [Tangut] | ? 4610A
?

1939 [Tangut] RA IX 75 [Tangut] "in" 1972
(a) V 72 [Tangut] | ? 4644
C.C.C. ~~28~~ 27-30 passim 司 "temple".
B 227[4] a verb apparently 書 ? misspelt
Nevski I 215

1940 [Tangut] I 87 |[Tangut] belt v.148
(a) I.119 |[Tangut] ? 2921
(b) VII 17 |[Tangut] v.135
(i) By itself C.C.C. 30b 枷ロ "to bind"
(ii) (b) above C.C.C. 35b 纏縛 "to bind, entangle" W.I.138[1] q.v.

1941 [Tangut] RA IX 75 [Tangut] | "earth"
(a) III 94 [Tangut] | 4632
(i) The dissyllable C.C.C. 13a 田疇
C.C.C. 26b 田地 "cultivated land"
1939 Phonetic + 青 grain

1942 [Tangut] RÂ IX 151 |[Tangut] vegetable v.383
(a) I 27 [Tangut] × by |[Tangut] ×0870 4475
(b) III 165 |[Tangut] 4002
(c) V 118 [Tangut] × by |[Tangut] v.1926
(d) V 160 [Tangut] × by |[Tangut] ×4504 5043
(e) VI 101 [Tangut] × by |[Tangut] v.1951
(i) The dissyllable C.C.C. 14b 蔓菁菜
青 vegetable 青 significant
(ii) |[Tangut] C.C.C. 14b 蔓菁.
(iii) |[Tangut] [Tangut] C.C.C. 15a 吃兜芽

1943 [Tangut] MBE I.61 |[Tangut] not 3783
B.170[3] q.v.

1944 4083 chain

1945 2703 chain

1946 2703 chain

1947 5030 chain

1948 2482 chain

1949

⊥ 4413 ⊤ 1810
3961 – 2733
4314
4888

1950 3891 chain

1951 1372 chain

1952 4716 pair

1953 3226 chain

1954 3812 chain

1955 4326 chain

1956 5708 chain (a)

1957 – 2026 A

1958 0271 chain

1958 | 知識 to know W.III 4[7]

148

1944 [Tangut] ABE I 61 | [Tangut] straight 4083
(i) The dissyllable C.C.C. 22b 体 工
1943 Phonetic

1945 [Tangut] the IX 80 | [Tangut]
(a) V 85 | [Tangut] "to descend" × v.1804
(b) V 172 | [Tangut] v.1946
W.I.110' (doubled) 堂 "hall, court"
I 166 魏 "lofty"

1946 [Tangut] V.172 [Tangut] "hall" v.1945
? Nevski I 239 wrinkles

1947 [Tangut] VIII 57 [Tangut] | [illegible] v.242
?

1948 [Tangut] III 96 | [Tangut] "rock" v.594
? Nevski I 223

1949 [Tangut] I 11 | [Tangut] creature 4413
(a) II 27 ditto
B.345' W.I.266 [Tangut] | part of royal title

1950 [Tangut] gai VI 59 | [Tangut] to think 4749
(a) I A 38 | [Tangut] ? 2129
(b) II 11 | [Tangut] 3830
W.II 50 思 "to think of" B.188 惟 "to consider"

1951 [Tangut] VII 114 | [Tangut] "destroy" v.1372
?

1952 [Tangut] VII 1 [Tangut] | ? name of planet 4716
(a) V 52 ditto
?

1953 [Tangut] V 126 [Tangut] | (a particle) 0577
(a) IX A 96 [Tangut] | ? 2111
?

1954 [Tangut] IU III 72 [Tangut] | to strike 3812
(a) III A 76 ditto
(b) V 66 [Tangut] | ? 3778
?

1955 [Tangut] V 139 | [Tangut] man 4964
(a) VI 28 [Tangut] | ? 1622
?

1956 [Tangut] VIII 45 [Tangut] | solitary single 5708
(a) II A 5 | [Tangut] solitary × 3998 1109
(b) IX 76 | [Tangut] ? 4328
? 1 not 2412 "the same"

1957 [Tangut] IX 114 [Tangut] | (doubtful)
? cf. 2429

1958 [Tangut] nê III A 27 | [Tangut] to hear 3057
(a) IX 62 | [Tangut] ? 5031
"ix" 1972 3779 ?
B.92. [Tangut] ideogram, [Tangut] follows.
| is the same as | [Tangut], as [Tangut] hear & as [Tangut]. 3699 to hear
C.C.C. 30a,b 36b W.I.92' 知 224" sees "to know" B 197

1959 3240 chain

1960 – 1916

1961 4653 chain

1962 5314 chain

B 201⁴

1963 3918 chain

1964 4076 / 3794

1965 2989 chain

1966 – 0911

1967 – 5327

1967A [illegible] B W.I 176² [illegible] 'truth'
Error for 1980

1968 4561 chain

1958

1959

1960

1961

1962

(a)

(b)

(c)

(d)

(e)

B 344⁴

(i) CCC 34

(ii)

1963

1964

(a) I.

(b)

149

1958 (cont.)
"to know"

1959 [Tangut] VII 39 [Tangut] | front tooth 5722
(a) IX A 57 | [Tangut] ? v. 2025
W.I. 208[18] mé'e "eye-tooth" 3240 chin v. 1998A

1960 [Tangut] VI A 49 | [Tangut] 1916
(a) VI A 58 ditto
?

1961 [Tangut] I 20 [Tangut] | earth, soil 4653
(a) VI A 26 ditto
?

1962 [Tangut] ndzê VI 103 [Tangut] | to assemble, collect 5314
(a) VII 116 ditto
(b) V 52 [Tangut] | (particle) 4859
(c) VI 26 [Tangut] | ? v. 1032
(d) VI A 75 [Tangut] | all together v. 1139
(e) IX 19 [Tangut] | ? v. 1050
(i) C.C.C. 34[b] B 344[4] W.I. 94[5] 108[1] 集 "assemble, accumulation" W.I. 165[13]
(ii) | [Tangut] W.II 2[6] translates 皆 "all"

1963 [Tangut] V 13 [Tangut] | disease 3918
?

1964 [Tangut] VI 66 | [Tangut] (misspelt form)
(a) I. 51 | [Tangut] ? 4076
(b) VI 8 [Tangut] | ? 3794

1964 (cont.)
W.I. 168[3] : B. 188[4] q.v.

1965 [Tangut] I A 18 [Tangut] | ? 2989

1966 [Tangut] I 29 | [Tangut] to bend, oppression 0911
(a) II A 24 ditto
?

1967 [Tangut] I 29 | [Tangut] 5327
(a) V 83 ditto
? 1966 phonetic + [Tangut]

1968 [Tangut] IX A 100 | [Tangut] 0074 v. 74
(a) III 45 [Tangut] | ought 2317
(b) IX 75 | [Tangut] 1872
B 90 [Tangut] 0751 on one side [Tangut] 0802 on the other side. | is the same as [Tangut] 2795 + as [Tangut] 4056 [transl. 至 + 到 "up to"] 4561 + "to reach"] + means [Tangut] |
[a postposition]"
Generally speaking the word means "to come to, to reach" in various connections.
(i) C.C.C. 10[b] 下 "to fall" (of snow)
W.I. 194[14] ditto (of rain)
(ii) B. 253 hoi 來 W.I. 208[9] tr. "to come"
B. 254[2] mé'i. ba. "to come."
B. 173[3]

1973 - 3166 pair

B.187[5] 田各 to refine; outline, sketch S.H. p.360.

1974 - 3927

1969 ~~1966~~ 4561 chain
(a) is an error for 1982

1975 5375 chain

?This. B. 200[5]

1970 0464 chain

1976 4027 chain

1971 1891 chain

1977 4661 chain

1972 2278 chain

1978 0862 chain

1979 0510 pair

150

1968 (cont)

(iii) (a) above W.I 226[11] ... "to reach (an age of 100 years)."

(iv) W.I.126[1] 屈 "to oppress" (? a mis-translation.

(v) CCC.34[a] | 緕 賔客 "guests, visitors" (? arrived guests).

(vi) W.I.168[7] ? 204[13,14]

1969 [Tangut] IX 99 [Tangut] | "to reach" 4056
(a) I 47 [Tangut] B 245[2] 3980
(i) By itself W.I.96[7] etc 來 to come (I 47 error for 1982)

(ii) The disyllable C.C.C.30[b] 到來 "to come & arrive"

(iii) [Tangut] | W II 2[5] & passim 如來 Tathāgata.

1970 (1969) [Tangut] IX A 101 | [Tangut] give, offer 4432
(a) IX 155 | [Tangut] 4460 ?

?
1971 (1970) [Tangut] V 104 [Tangut] Imperative 1891 5679

?
1972 [Tangut] VIII 82 | [Tangut] centre 2308
(a) VIII 76 | [Tangut] ? v. 2030
(b) IX 75 [Tangut] | temple 1939

A preposition "in, within" CCC.30[b] 在. B 180[1] 中

內 W I 100[7] as an attribute

1972 (cont)

中 W I.108[8] II 46[4]

To complete since W.II 22[6] 76[5]

1973 [Tangut] V 18 [Tangut] | ? 3166 卡
(a) VII 40 ditto
B.168[2] 187[2] tr.s. 殊 to kill, exterminate

1974 [Tangut] VIII 82 | [Tangut] ? 3927
(a) I 8 ditto
? B 246[3] 吾 Wu (part of name)

A common Phonetic 1972 Phonetic?

1975 [Tangut] VIII 82 [Tangut] | 5375
(a) VI 101 ditto
(b) VII 39 [Tangut] x by [Tangut] | "lake" v0296
(i) The disyllable C.C.C.15[a] 盐 W.I 138[11] 鹽 "salt".

1972 Phonetic?

1976 [Tangut] V A 23 [Tangut] | to offer v.832

?
1977 (1976) [Tangut] III 135 | [Tangut] ? 2260

?
1978 [Tangut] III 135 | [Tangut] "west" v.1346

Nevsky I 228
1979 (1978) [Tangut] IX 5 [Tangut] | [Tangut]
(a) I 11 ditto v. 510

1980 0563 chain

1981 3066 chain

1982 3980 chain

1983 3980 chain

1984 ⊢ 2585

1985
└ 4675

1986 4710 pair

1987 3269 chain

1988 3317 chain

1989 3317 chain

1990 1317 chain

1991 1657 pair

1992
- 3025
- 1445
- 2179
- 2776
- 4222
- ×
- 0121
- 1014
- 0983
- 2174
- 2595
- 2773
- 2953
- 3396
- 3433
- 3554 – 1319
- 3681
- 4006
- 4560
- 4757
- 5616

1980
(ii) Th
"tru
(i) W.I
1981
?
1982
?
1983
?
1984
(a)
?
1985
(a) I
(b)
B.90
| is a
name
(b) is a
1986
(a) II
?
1987
?

minus 1

151

1980 [Tangut] VII 82 [Tangut] | v.563

(ii) The disyllable W. I. 208[10] bden.pa "truth"

II 154[6] B 200[5]

(i) W. I. 118[5] 150[6] 諦 satya "truth"

1981 [Tangut] IX 5 [Tangut] | false 3066

?

1982 [Tangut] VIII 8 [Tangut] | [illegible] 3980

(a) I 47 ditto (misspelt)

? v.3084

1983 [Tangut] V A1 | [Tangut] "on" v.25

?

1984 [Tangut] I 27 | [Tangut] ? 2585

(a) VI A96 ditto

?

1985 [Tangut] ša(n) VII 87 [Tangut] | "name"

4675

(a) III A65 [Tangut] x by | [Tangut]

[(b) VII A130 [Tangut] x by [Tangut] | v.465

1992 'not' 'low' 4116

B.90 [Tangut] ideogram [Tangut] follows. "| is a mountain. It means the name of a country." B.175[5] Part of P.N.

(b) is a Phonetic character.

1986 [Tangut] IX 103 [Tangut] | ? 4710

(a) II 6 ditto

?

1987 [Tangut] I.2 [Tangut] | ? 3748

?

1988 [Tangut] IX A24 [Tangut] | ? 3317

(a) IX A131 ditto [[Tangut]]

(b) IX 166 [Tangut] | ? 1989

?

~~1989 [Tangut] I 164~~

1989 [Tangut] IX 166 | [Tangut] ? 1988

?

1990 [Tangut] IX 136 | [Tangut] ? v.1327

(a) I 11 [Tangut] | q.v. 2315

W. II 52[10] 士 "scholar" n. "official"

1991 [Tangut] IX 136 [Tangut] |

(a) V 170 ditto ? v.1657

(i) | [Tangut] W II 22[9] 思惟 28[5] 思忖 "thought, reflection".

1990 Phonetic +?

1992 [Tangut] VII I 30 | [Tangut] 'not yet' 3025

(a) I 20 ditto 1445

(aa) I 147

(b) III 7 | [Tangut] ? 4222

1886

[(c) III 119 [Tangut] x by [Tangut] | to inspect 1222]

(d) VII 39 | [Tangut] ? 2776

(e) VIII A62 | [Tangut] exact 2179

(f) | [Tangut] is x of:- to go, behave 2462

(i) [Tangut] I.16 2595

(ii) [Tangut] I 28 ? 2174

(iii) [Tangut] I 86 v.121

1980 VII 82 | 1995 0731 chain

(ii) The Transliteration W.I. 208

(i) W.I. 118 150

1981 IX 5 | 1996 – 3432

1982 VIII 83

1997 ~~chain 2633~~ 1929 chain

1983 V.A1

1998 B.246[4] 'new' 130[2] do.

1998 4141 chain

B. 206[3] 215[3] do.

1995 A ? 3091 chain

1993 0791 chain

1994 4972 chain

1999 3825

minus 1

152

1992 cont.
(iv) [Tangut] I.90 ? 3681
(v) [Tangut] I102 ? 4006
(vi) [Tangut] II 2 ? 5616
(vii) [Tangut] II 43 ? 4560
(viii) [Tangut] III 106 yin (opp. to yang) 3396
(ix) [Tangut] III 172 ? 3433
(x) [Tangut] III 178 ? 2953
(xi) [Tangut] III 182 ? x(1319) 3554
(xii) [Tangut] V 147 q.v. 983
(xiii) [Tangut] V 185 ? v.1014
(xiv) [Tangut] VI 18 yang (opp. to yin) 2773
(xv) [Tangut] VI 132 ? 4757

The usual word for "not" 不 ma; precedes the word to which it relates.

1993 [Tangut] IX 152 [Tangut] | ? 0791
(a) VII A 29 ditto
?

1994 [Tangut] IX 16 | [Tangut] a give 4972
(1) The disyllable ~~W.I.108~~ W.I.108[9] 布施 II 50[10] 施
"dāna almsgiving" II 140[7] B.166[1] B 211[3]

1995 [Tangut] I 89 [Tangut] | "wood" ~~"tree"~~
W.I.192[4] ndab 194[4] to.ma B.181[1]
葉 "leaf" (of a tree etc.) B 221[4]

1995 Phonetic + 艹 wood

1996 [Tangut] I 40 [Tangut] | ? 3432
(a) I A 59 ditto
?

1997 [Tangut] V 44 [Tangut] | "sheep" 1342
(a) IX 71 | [Tangut] ? 2633
C.C.C. 19[a] 筋 "sinews"

1998 [Tangut] VI A 43 [Tangut] | ? 4141
(a) V 90 ditto
(b) I 24 [Tangut] | ? 4146
new Nevski I 225
Dict. 1[a] 3 C.C.C. 7[b]

1995A [Tangut] x of IX 128 [Tangut] |
? Error for [Tangut] 1664

1998A [Tangut] Error for [Tangut] 1959 ~~possibly error for [Tangut]~~
B.103 [Tangut] | "elephant's tooth
象牙 "cat. under 'precious things"

1999 [Tangut] I 20 [Tangut] | ? 3825
(a) IX 73 ditto
?

2000 3546 pair

2001 4097 pair

2002 1449 chain

2002 |[Tangut] 那 提 Nadi WII4² [2010] - 2476

φii II 142"

2003 - 5435

2004 2710 chain

2005 2158 chain

2006 2873 pair

2007 3226 chain

2008 2519 chain

2009 2027 chain

2011 4027 chain

2012 1688 pair

2013 2635 chain

28/12/38 2000

(a

2001

(a

Note.

2001

. foreign

2002

(a)

C.C.C. 18

2003

(a) I

W.I. 216²

2004

2005

2006

(a) VII

(1) The Di

"precio

. . . . " c

153

2000 IIIA29 | ? 3546
(a) VII 63 ditto
?
2001 V15 | ? 4097
(a) V 112 ditto

Note. There is no discoverable difference between 2000 & 2001. 2001 is checked by 2003

2002 III 77 | "flesh" v.1449
(a) III 71 | ? v.835
C.C.C. 18b 月力 "ribs" chain 1449

2003 V 15 | 5435
(a) IX 27 ditto
W.I. 216[2] 218[14] apparently 3a.ba "to eat"

2004 III 67 | 5452
? chain 5440

2005 III 61 | 2158 (chain)
?

2006 V 118 | 2873
(a) VII 90 ditto
(i) The dissyllable B.102 cat. under "precious things C.C.C. 12b 珊瑚 . . . . " "coral" (in both cases)

2007 I 123 | warm 5062
(a) IX 59 | 3621
(i) | B.103 cat. under 'silk'. B.168[5]
Nevski I 233 chain 5062

2008 VIA14 | pure 2519
?

2009 VIA55 | 4061
?

2010 IX 59 | ? 2476
(a) IX 90 ditto [misspelt 枇]
? 朩 is right B.169[2] 兩 'ounce'.

2011 III 145 | to offer? 0832
W.I. 98[13]?

2012 I 33 | ? v.1688
(a) I 46 ditto
?

2013 III 145 | 2635
(a) V 9 ditto
(b) I 90 | (misspelt?) lower 1479
(c) I 94 | ? 3320
(d) V 67 | after 3278
(e) IX 14 | ? 4343
The commonest conjunction in the language :– "and, also"

2013 (ii) See 1080 (iv)

2018 2120 pair

2019 5623 chain

2020 independent

2014 0752 chain

2021 4276 chain

2015 4837 pair

2022-1033

2022 (i) W I 168[6] 還 'to return' II 86[9]

2016-2345

(iii) v. 4316.

B. 227[4] 歸 return

2017 5305 chain

2023 2285 chain

2024 3226 chain

2013

更 c

并 c

To com

又復

又 W.

復 W I

2014

?

2015

(a)(

?

2016

(b) V

?

Note.

distingu

2015 i

2017

(a) IX

(i) The

not ag

minus |

154

2013 (cont.)
更 C.C.C. 26[b]
并 C.C.C. 34[b]
To complete meaning C.C.C. 35[b] W.I. 138[3]
又復 W.I. 98[1] 134[7]
又 W.I. 108[1]
復 W II 4[6] B 245[7] 2[7] 'again'?
2014 [illegible] I 9 [illegible] | q.v. 3996
?
2015 [illegible] IX 107 [illegible] | ? 4837
(a) (ditto III 99)
~~(b) VII 38 | [illegible]~~
?
2016 [illegible] VII 41 | [illegible] 2345
(b) VII 38 ditto
?
Note. In so far as they can be distinguished 2014 [illegible] ends in [illegible], 2015 in [illegible] & 2016 in [illegible]
2017 [illegible] V 6 [illegible] | 5305
(a) IX 39 [illegible] | 2152
(i) The disyllable C.C.C. 30[b] 參差
not agreeing Nevski I. 219 chain 5305

2018 [illegible] V 140 [illegible] | ? 2120
(a) IX 91 ditto
?
~~[illegible]~~ 2019 [illegible] V 142 [illegible] | 2713
? chain 2713
2020 [illegible] V A 3 'Family or clan name'
(a) V A 15 [illegible] [illegible] x by [illegible] (2085) | 2094
(a) is presumably a Phonetic group
2021 [illegible] IX 122 | [illegible] passion 4236
(a) I 6 [illegible] | ? 3316
CCC 35[b] W.I. 132[11] II 68[12] 貪 "greed".
chain
2022 [illegible] IX A 103 | [illegible]
(a) I. 139 ditto V. 1033
W. I 208[9] p'yir ɣoi.ba "to return": II 4[5] 退 "to recede, retire". I 168[5]; II 46[4];
(ii) [illegible] | (5159 'already?') C.C.C. 34[a] 迴歸 "to return"
2023 [illegible] VI 97 [illegible] | 'animal' q.v. 2026
?
2024 [illegible] V 92 [illegible] | auxiliary word q.v. 1685
? to bring Nevski I 219

2025 3240 chain

2026 2285 chain

2026A 1957 pair

2027
4463 – 0946 – 4404
2569 – 1467
5187 – 4462 – 1409 – 4422
2914
4061 – 2009
3530 – 0859
1166
2799 – 1619 – 2276
3698 – 3530
3679
4788

2028 3259 chain

2029 indépendant

2030 2278 chain

2031 4537 pair

2032 1873 chain

2033
4552
5079

B. 201[4] 懈 lazy 233[1] tr. 悠悠 distant, remote
| 謪 ? = (b) B. 201[4] 239[1] 懈怠 lazy & remiss

2034 1391 chains

2035 4454 chain

2036 1495 pair

2037 4881 pair

2038 3930 chain
2038 (i) 疑 'doubt' W.I.158[18] B.233[5]

2039 3891 chain

2025
2026
(a)
2026A
Very
2027
(a)
(b)
(c)
2028
2029
name
2030
2031
(a) VI
Note, 203

minus 1

155

2025 [Tangut] IX A 57 [Tangut] | eye-tooth v. 1959
?

2026 [Tangut] V 141 [Tangut] [Tangut] 'animal' cf. 3240 chain 2285
(a) VI 97 | [Tangut] v. 2023
?

2026A [Tangut]. X of IX 114 | [Tangut] v. 1957
Very probably misspelt, in a part of the KS. which may well be injured.
Nevski I 229 [Tangut] 千 54 ...

2027 [Tangut] VI 17 | [Tangut] q.v. 4463
(a) VIII 13 ditto
(b) III A 44 | [Tangut] ? 5187
(c) VI 30 [Tangut] | ? 2560
?

2028 [Tangut] I 9 | [Tangut] ? v. 1146
?

2029 [Tangut] I 29 "Family or clan name"

2030 [Tangut] VIII 76 [Tangut] | "in" v. 1972
? ~~(a) VI 2~~

2031 [Tangut] IX 79 [Tangut] | ? 4537
(a) VI 2 ditto
?

Note. 2030 + 2031 are barely distinguishable. 2030 seems to begin 𠂉

2032 [Tangut] Ye VIII 57 [Tangut] | ?4894 nyin [ru 4894]
?

2033 [Tangut] IX 43 | [Tangut] 4552 q.v.
(a) IX A 128 ditto
(b) IX 99 | [Tangut] q. 5079
Dict 1b4. ? W. II 84[10]

2034 [Tangut] VIII 57 [Tangut] | ? chain 3920
?

2035 [Tangut] VIII 57 [Tangut] | complete; ample 4454
?

2036 [Tangut] I 29 [Tangut] | ?
(a) V 155 ditto v. 1495
?

2037 [Tangut] IX 79 [Tangut] | 4881
(a) III 83 ditto
? Nevski I 239

2038 [Tangut] VIII 90 [Tangut] | because of 3930
(i) By itself W. I 210[3] doṅs.pa "apprehension" B 249[3] tʻe.tsʻom.za.ba "doubt".
(ii) | [Tangut] W. I 110[12] II 6[7] 28[2] 疑惑 vicikitsā mohā "doubt & delusion"

2039 [Tangut] to IX A 92 [Tangut] | 4749. "to think"
(i) By itself W. II 22[1,10] 思 B 249[1] rnal 'byor/ bsgom.pa "to think, meditation" du
B. 231[3]

B. 233[5]

2040 5094 chain

2041 5623 chain

2042 2115 chain

2043 3026 chain

2044 3276 chain

2045 3500 chain

2046 3430 chain

2047 4276 chain

2048 4276 chain

2049 3226 chain

2050 4276 chain

2051 2149 chain

2052 1907 pair

2053 1426 chain

2054 2179 chain

[2055] 2085 chain

[2056] 0022 chain

minus 1

156

2039 (cont)

(ii) The dissyllable C.C.C. 31b2 思惟 "to think & reflect".

(iii) [Tangut] | C.C.C. 34b 思念 "to think & meditate"

(iv) C.C.C. 21a ?

2040 [Tangut] IX 137 [Tangut] | "warm" v.1132

CCC 8b 和 "a favourable (wind)"

W.I. 214[7] dron "warm (water)"

2041. [Tangut] IX 147 [Tangut] | v.1144

(a) III 62 | [Tangut] 3828

(b) IX 109 [Tangut] | v.1855

? thick Nevski I 225

2042 [Tangut] IX 147 [Tangut] | 2115

B.161[4] 稠 crowded, dense

2043 [Tangut] I 86 [Tangut] | stay v.3026

(a) VII 28 [Tangut] | × 4398

?

2044 [Tangut] I 57 | [Tangut] 3981

(a) VIII 55 [Tangut] | × 4264

?

2045 [Tangut] I 57 [Tangut] | 3500

(a) V 136 ditto

?

2046 [Tangut] VIII A 109 [Tangut] | 2364

(i) [Tangut] | C.C.C. 32b 笛 "flute" (v.1008)

B.176[4] part of P.N.

2047 [Tangut] III 118 [Tangut] | 4229

(a) IX A 105 [Tangut] | v.2048

?

2048 [Tangut] IX A 105 | [Tangut] v.2047

W.I. 136[4] 暗 "dark"

2049 [Tangut] V 47 [Tangut] [Tangut] 3500

?

2050 [Tangut] I 36 [Tangut] | 2275

?

2051 [Tangut] VIII 90 [Tangut] | v.1620

?

2052 [Tangut] VI A 56 [Tangut] | "low"

(a) V 19 ditto v.1907

?

2053 [Tangut] IX A 102 [Tangut] | 2585

?

2054 [Tangut] ? VII A 31 [Tangut] [Tangut] "sacred word" v.2065

2055 [Tangut] VII 61 [Tangut] | "a sound"

?

2056 [Tangut] V 177 | [Tangut] "Rayon" v.1063

?

2057 1783 chain

2058 — {2096 A, 2420}

2059 1564 chain

2060 2085 chain

2061 3226 chain

2062 0180 chain

2063 2085 chain

2064 2652 chain

2066 2127 pair

2065 2085 chain

2067 3226 chain

2067 中類 W.I.178[5] lei But the word is nyagrodha v. 2303

157

2057 [illegible] VIII 60 [illegible] |
(a) VI 38 ditto v. 1783
(b) III 133 | [illegible] v. 2090
!
2058 [illegible] III A 126 | [illegible]
(a) III 42 ditto
?
2059 [illegible] VIII 49 [illegible] | v. 1412
?
2060 [illegible] I 100 [illegible] | "a sound" v. 2065
?
2061 [illegible] V 169 [illegible] v. 577
?
2062 [illegible] V 177 [illegible] | 5025
evil sound
2063 [illegible] VIII 61 [illegible] | "a sound" v. 2065
B 246[3,7] 桓 Huan (Proper name)
2064 [illegible] VIII 53 | [illegible] v. 295
C.C.C. 19[a] 氣 "breath"
W.I. 168[6] 息 "breath" II. 148[5] 止
2065 [illegible] VIII 53 [illegible] |
(a) I 11 ditto v. 2085
(b) | [illegible] as follows:—
(i) I 100 [illegible] v. 2060
(ii) VI A 126 [illegible] 5580
(iii) VII 61 [illegible] v. 2055
(iv) VII A 54 [illegible] v. 2086 [illegible]
(v) VII A 96 [illegible] 2955
(vi) VIII 61 [illegible] v. 2063
(vii) IX 139 [illegible] 5663
(c) II A 14 [illegible] x by [illegible] | 2089
[(d) V 164 [illegible] x by [illegible] |]
(e) V A 13 [illegible] x by | [illegible] 2097
(f) V A 14 [illegible] x by | [illegible] 2077
(g) V A 15 [illegible] x by | [illegible] 2094
[(h) IX A 156 [illegible] x by [illegible] |]
(i) By itself II 8[12] 音 W.I. 192[1] ghosa "sound".
(ii) The disyllable W.I. 90[6] 意 [error for 音] I 114[11] 音 聲 "sound, voice svara, ghosa
(iii) | [illegible] B. 249[4] ñan, t'os W. II 4[3] 聲 聞 śravaka.
(b)–(h) are probably all Phonetic characters.
2066 [illegible] III A 97 [illegible] |
(a) III A 96 ditto
?
2067 [illegible] IX A 133 [illegible] v. 355
mystical sound, mantra

2068 3225 chain

2069 3795 chain

2076 2710 chain

2070 3226 chain

2071
├2290
└0217-4941

2077 2085 chain

2078 is ? 𘘚 + means 'gai'; 5530 is a ... of food.

2078 2710 chain

2072 4615 chain

2073 3226 chain

2079 – 3553

2074 1398 chain

2080 – 3099B

2075 2519 chain

2075 (ii) The disyllable 恬惔 peaceful

+ .... W.I.164'[18] II 144'

| 𘟙 W.I.4[8] 靜慮 dhyāna quiet contemplation

2081 3226 chain

206
my...
2069
(i) By i...
conc...
(ii) Th...
"sia...
2070
~~2069~~
sound,
2071
~~2070~~
(a)
(b)
?
2072
(a)
2073
...ical so...
2074
?
2075
(i) By its
calm, tr...
靜 ditto
(ii) |
017

158

2068 [Tangut] VII A1 [Tangut] "mystical sound, mantra"

2069 [Tangut] V9 [Tangut] | 2221

(i) By itself W.I 132[17] 螺 I 192[4] dui "conch-shell" II 94[9] passim

(ii) The disyllable C.C.C. 21[a] 海螺 "sea conch-shell".

2070 [Tangut] I A55 [Tangut] "mystical sound, mantra" = 2083 bis

2071 [Tangut] I 22 [Tangut] | 2290

(a) VI 18 ditto

(b) III A88 | [Tangut] 0217

?

2072 [Tangut] V 24 | [Tangut] 4615

(a) III A121 ditto

?

2073 [Tangut] IX 103 [Tangut] "mystical sound, mantra."

2074 [Tangut] I A83 | [Tangut] 2687

?

2075 [Tangut] ME I 20 | [Tangut] "pure" 0311

(i) By itself C.C.C. 36[b] W.I. 94[3] 寂 "silence calm, tranquillity, nirvāṇa" W II 4[8] 靜 ditto [Tangut] sound not-being

(ii) | [Tangut] W.I 90[4] 寂滅 "silence extinction"

0175

(iii) | [Tangut] W.I 202[4] t'ub "muni sage"

Note. No doubt derived from [Tangut] "no sound"

2076 [Tangut] na III 71 [Tangut] | v. 2077

(ii) The disyllable C.C.C. 21[a] 磬鍾

(i) By itself 罄 "jar, vessel" W.I. 158[5]

2077 [Tangut] V A14 [Tangut] v. 2065.

Presumably a Phonetic character

2078 [Tangut] VIII 53 [Tangut] | 5530

(a) III 71 | [Tangut] v. 2076

(i) By itself 鈴 small bell

(ii) (a) above C.C.C. 21[a] 磬鍾

2079 [Tangut] VIII A97 | [Tangut] 3553

(a) VIII A98 ditto

?

2080 [Tangut] V 32 | [Tangut] 3093

(a) V 2 ditto

?

2081 [Tangut] Li IX A116 [Tangut]

(a) I A9 [Tangut] x by [Tangut] |

A mystical sound, mantra

(a) is ? a Phonetic character

2082 3226 chain

2083 3226 chain

2084 – 5092

2085
⊥ 2065 – 2058
2060
2063
2077
2086
2089
2094
2097
2955
5580
5663

2086 2085 chain

2087 – 5493

2088 1914 chain

2089 2085 chain

2090 1783 chain

2091
⊥ 3647 – 3082
3911
3956 – 3217
5255

2092 2969 chain

2093 2506 chain

2094 2080 chain

2095 2167 chain ?

2095 (ii) The Hsiyü. C.C.C. 19[b] 和合
'union + concord: W II 130" 親穆
'mutually attached.'

2096 independent

2097 2085 chain

2098 3226 chain

2099 – 0065 Asia
W.I. 269[23] 于闐 Yü-t'ien Khotan

2100 3226 chain

159

minus
2083 bis [Tangut] I A 33 [Tangut] = 2070

2082 [Tangut] II 19 [Tangut] | 3226

2083 [Tangut] I A 44 [Tangut] mystical? sound, mantra

2084 [Tangut] VI 85 [Tangut] |
(a) VII 93 ditto

2085 [Tangut] I 11 | [Tangut] :
(a) VIII 53 ditto v. 2065
(i) The dissyllable W I 90[5] 意 [error for 音] 98[6] 150[1] 聲 音 114[11] 音聲 sound, voice.

2086 [Tangut] VII A 54 [Tangut] | 'a sound' v. 2065 ?
?

2087 [Tangut] V 81 | [Tangut] misspelt 5493
(a) V 119 ditto

2088 [Tangut] VIII A 72 [Tangut] | 2148
[(a) IX 42 | [Tangut] misspelt error for 2436, 2484

2089 [Tangut] II A 14 [Tangut] [Tangut] sound v. 2065
B. 175[1] P.N.

2090 [Tangut] III. 133 [Tangut] | v. 2057

2091 [Tangut] V A 100 [Tangut] | 3647
(a) IX 10 ditto

2092 [Tangut] VIII A 4 [Tangut] | 2988
?

2093 [Tangut] VIII A 1 [Tangut] |
?

2094 [Tangut] V A 15 [Tangut] [Tangut] 2065 2099
? The sound of 2020 (V. A. 3)

2095 [Tangut] VI 33 | [Tangut] 5069
[(a) VI. A 118 [Tangut] × by [Tangut] |] 1011 4402
?

2096 [Tangut] VI. 77 × by self [|] |
?

2096 A [Tangut] error for [Tangut] 2430

2097 [Tangut] V A 13 [Tangut] [Tangut] v. 2065

2098 [Tangut] VIII A 3 [Tangut] "mystical sound" mantra

2099 [Tangut] V 157 | [Tangut] 0065
(a) IX 15 ditto
B. 179[2] 于 yü ? phonetic.

2100 [Tangut] V 39 [Tangut] "mystical sound" mantra

2101 | 5026

2102 4972 chain

2103 4148 chain

2103 A 1936 pair

2104 5506 pair

2105 3226 chain

2106 1035 chain

2107 1035 chain

2108 4510 chain

[2109] 2149 chain

[2110] 1356 pair

2111 3226 chain

2112 - 1558

2113 1572 chain A

minus 1

160

2101 ~~2100~~ VIII 73 | 5026

(a) VII A110 ditto

B91 " plus the whole of . | is | [translated 惡聲 evil sound]. It means [translated 罵詈語 to say a curse or swear-word].

2102 I 56 | to give 4972

C.C.C. 28[a] | 宣 ~~[sic sound fei or hui, so not chêng] "to summon . . .~~ 徽 (To proclaim excellent)

2103 VIII A 2 | sound 4148

?

2103A X of V 9 'to bellow' 4148 chain v. 1936

Error for , but ? not an error.

2104 VII A 97 | 5536

(a) VII A 98 ditto

?

2105 IX A117 'mystical sound' mantra v. 355

2106 VI A 46 | v. 2107

?

2107 I.135 | v. 1055

(a) VII 8 ditto

(b) VI 101 | 4746

(c) VI A 46 | v. 2106

(i) By itself C.C.C. 13[a] B221[4] W.II.14[12] 林 "forest" II 132[7] B245 metaph. 'collection' v. 1284

(ii) (b) above C.C.C. 8[a] The group (?) of Pleiades. ~~v. 1284~~

2108 IX 42 | 4570

(a) V 6 | 5313

B227[5] [] 盧 rice vessel? phon. lu string

2109 V A 65 | 2149

?

2110 VIII 17 |

(a) VI 82 ditto

?

2111 IX A 96 | ? 1953

2112 I 38 | 1558 f. v.

(a) I 82 ditto

Dict. 1[4] 5

2113 I 38 | ~~[misspelt?]~~ v. 1574

(a) I 27 |

(b) IX A5 | 5371

(i) By itself C.C.C. 16[b] 黄羊 "yellow sheep"

(ii) (b) above B101 cat. under "wild animals"

2114 5034 chain

2115
┬ 3786
├ 1034 – 3715
├ 1550
├ 2042
├ 2153
├ [3754]
└ 5673

W.II 148' [Tangut] [Tangut] 過 於

2116 2167 chain

2117 4027 chain

2118 2906 chain

2118 A 0742 pair

2119 4600 pair

2120 – 2018

2121 ⊥ 4920 – 2266
└ 5680

2122 5034 chain

2123 2906 chain

2123 A 0360 pair

minus 11

161

2114 [Tangut] I 17 | [Tangut] 5034

2115 [Tangut] IX 52 | [Tangut] 3786

(a) IX 33 ditto ← (b) I 36 [Tangut] | 2163

(c) ~~III 123~~ IA 57 | [Tangut] 1550

(d) III ~~...~~ 123 | [Tangut] x (3715) 1034

(e) III 168 | [Tangut] 5673

(f) VII A 102 | [Tangut] [3754]

(g) IX 147 | [Tangut] 2042

W. I 98[12] II 34[7] 84[6] 多 "many" I 134[5] 永 "everlasting" (kalpas) I. 192[15] rnam "greatly"

2116 [Tangut] V 40 [Tangut] | 2167 number

~~(a) I 36 (b) IX 147 2042~~

2117 [Tangut] I 70 | [Tangut] 4494

2118 [Tangut] VI A 78 [Tangut] [Tangut] arrow horn 2123 1925

[Tangut] + [Tangut] differentiated from 2117

2118A [Tangut] x IX 60 [Tangut] | v. 742

? Possibly an error for 2526 on IX 168

2119 [Tangut] IX 168 [Tangut] | 4600

(a) IX 122 ditto

?

2120 [Tangut] IX 91 | [Tangut] ? 2018

(a) V 140 ditto

2121 [Tangut] IV 2 | [Tangut] 4920

(i) The disyllable C.C.C. 9[a] 霜雪 "frost, snow".

(a) II 32 ditto [Tangut]

~~2122~~

2122 [Tangut] III 106 | [Tangut] 5034

(a) III 70 ditto

q. 1950

2123 [Tangut] IX 2 [Tangut] | 2906

(a) IX A 67 ditto

(b) I 113 | [Tangut] 1483

(c) II A 21 | [Tangut] ? I trans. omit. 1176

(d) III 70 | [Tangut] ? Trans. omit. 0836

(e) V 82 | [Tangut] ? 1013

(f) VI A 78 [Tangut] x by | [Tangut] arrow horn 2118

(g) VII 1 | [Tangut] ? 2769

(h) VII 16 | [Tangut] ? 61328

W. I 214[5] 224[17] mdah arrow

2123A [Tangut] x of VII 30 | [Tangut] v. 360

?

Possibly IX 168

2123B 4206 pair

2124 ~~2125 pair~~
2125
3936

2125 – 2124.

2126 4889 chain

2127 – 2066

2128 2130 chain

2129 3891 chain

2130
4269 bis
0606
0880
1087 – 2128

2131 · 5677 chain

2131 | 䶊 B.250[2] ḫts'an.ba

rgya.ba "Buddhahood"

~~(ii) The dissyllable B.259 translates~~

光明 ~~in Sutra titles~~

2132 5677 chain

2132 (iii) The dissyllable reversed.

照明 "to illuminate" W.II 100[1]

2133 2482 ~~pa~~ chain

2133 A 1582 pair

minus 1

162

2123B 𗀀 (X of 𗀀 | VI 12) 4206
?

2124 𗀀 (IX gap)
(a) IX A 36 𗀀 |
C.C.C. 29[a]: Nevski I 439 "to wait"

2125 𗀀 IX A 36 | 𗀀
?

2126 𗀀 I A 102 𗀀 | "flute" v. 1008
(a) IX 39 𗀀 | 3667
C.C.C. 7[b] 21[a] 32[b2] W II 4[12] 鼓 W.I. 192[13]
rna "drum" passim

2127 𗀀 III A 96 | 𗀀 2066
(a) III A 97 ditto
?

2128 𗀀 I 42 | 𗀀 cf. 2130(c) v. 1087

2129 𗀀 I A 38 𗀀 | "to think of" v. 950 1950

2130 𗀀 I 42 | 𗀀
(a) VII 57 ditto 4269 bis
(b) I 72 𗀀 | 0880
(c) I 86 𗀀 | X (2128) v. 1087 ?
(d) IX 10 | 𗀀 0606
(i) W.I. 218[6] rig B. 181 明 "knowledge" B. 196[1]
(ii) W.I. 100[4] 𗀀 𗀀 | 明 "knowledge"

2131 𗀀 swi VI 71 𗀀 | 5677
(a) I 3 ditto noun
(b) III 83 𗀀 | camp 5095
(c) VI 71 | 𗀀 bright 2132
(d) VIII A 50 | 𗀀 1157
C.C.C. 10[b] W.I. 90[2], 92[4] & passim 明 "bright" & also in Buddhist terminology "enlightenment, knowledge" prabhāsa & vidyā
(ii) | 𗀀 W.I. 190[9] skya.rens "(bright streak) morning twilight"
(iii) (c) above W.I. 142[4] 明 照 220[7] snan.ba "to shine, illuminate."

2132 𗀀 VI 71 | 𗀀 v. 2131 767
(i) By itself W II 26[3] 照 to illuminate W.I. 192[3] gsal "bright." B. 128[5]
(ii) The disyllable. See 2131 (iii).

2133 𗀀 I. 31 | 𗀀
?

2133A 𗀀 X of VII A 140 | 𗀀 v. 1582

2134 1128 chain

2135 0181 pair

2136 = 5099

2137 5301 chain

2138 – 0438

2139 2149 chain

B.189³ 述 'to publish

2140 5315 pair

2141
⊢0166
└1452

2142 independent

2143
├2146
├2462 – 1742
├4444
└2157

213

?

2135

(a

?

2136

(a

?

2137

?

2138

?

2139

(a

(i) W.I.138

doing

WII 76⁸

(ii) The

make,

(iii) (a)

2140

(a

The

168⁶ II

[very obscu

163

2134 [Tangut] III 33 | [Tangut] 5646

?

2135 [Tangut] VI 37 [Tangut] | 0181

(a) VI A 65 ditto

?

2136 [Tangut] III 12 | [Tangut]

(a) V 66 ditto

?

2137 [Tangut] III 20 [Tangut] | 1569

?

2138 [Tangut] IX 39 | [Tangut] 0438

?

2139 [Tangut] xi VIII 6 [Tangut] | 2149

(a) V 170 [Tangut] | 1658

(i) W.I.138[17] 作 218[6] byed, making doing [used participially]

W II 76[8] ditto

(ii) The dissyllable C.C.C. 23a 做造 "to make, or do".

(iii) (a) v.1658

2140 [Tangut] IX 151 [Tangut] | 5315

(a) VII 111 ditto

The dissyllable C.C.C. 30b 立便 W.I. 168[6] II 46[7] 64[1]

[very obscure] B 246[7] 疾速 'rapidly'

2141 [Tangut] VI 56 | [Tangut]

(a) III 76 ditto v.166

(b) III 116 | [Tangut] 1452

(i) The dissyllable C.C.C. 20b 21b 脩蓋, 脩造 "to repair & build. B 212[4]

2142 [Tangut] II 3 "Family or clan name." B.163[4]

2143 [Tangut] II A 29 | [Tangut]

(a) II 43 ditto v.2146

(b) VII 18 [Tangut] | 4444 x(1742)

(c) VII 47 | [Tangut] 2462

~~(d) VIII 111~~

(d) VIII A 104 [Tangut] · xly | [Tangut] 2157

(i) W.I 138[9,10,5,12,13] | [Tangut] B.94

(obscure)

(ii) (c) above C.C.C. 29a 行遣

~~(iii)~~

(iii) | [Tangut] C.C.C. 36a (twice) 受用 "received for use, property(?)"

W.I.194[18] tsis spyod "riches"

2144 2147 chain

2145 0148 chain

2146 2143 chain

2147
- 0330 bis (=0368)
- 2144

2147 (ii) W.I 168[10] 積 "to collect, hoard".

(iii) | 㛏 W.II 94[12] 積 集 "to collect ~~+ assem~~ gather together".

2148 4489 pair

2149

2149
- 3938
- 0021
- 0047
- 0256
- 0316
- 0484
- 0639
- 1096
- 1515 - 1919
- 1620 - 2051 - 1777
- 1793 - 3228 - 2338
- 2109
- 2139 - 1658
- 2160
- 2222 - 3017 - 3371 - 3285
- 3483 - 3497 - 3674 - 3550 - 0413
- 3925
- 3890
- 4004
- 4135
- 4228
- 4338
- 3955 - 0197
  - 0481
  - 0902
  - 5160 - 3104
    - 5166
- 4386
- 4490
- 5169
- 2370 ? -

minus!

164

2144 [Tangut] III 121 [Tangut] | v. 2147

?

2145 [Tangut] IX 91 | [Tangut] to transact v. 592

Dict 56^b 1

2146 [Tangut] II 43 [Tangut] |

(a) II A 29 ditto v. 2143

B 94 v. 4444

2147 [Tangut] rue III 56 [Tangut] | v. 330 bis

(a) IX 42 ditto

(b) III 120 | [Tangut] v. 2144

(i) C.C.C. 9^b [Tangut] "10th stem" B. 167^5 do.

(ii) ~~CCC~~ W.I. 208^18 ?

2148 [Tangut] VA 106 [Tangut] | 4489

(a) V 167 ditto [[Tangut] for |]

?

2149 [Tangut] WI II 3 | [Tangut] two 3938

(a) II 43 ditto

(b) I 101 [Tangut] | 1096

(c) I 133 [Tangut] | x(1919) 1515

(d) III 2 [Tangut] | x 0256

(dd) III 6 — 3017 xx(2338)

(e) III 12 [Tangut] | x(3228) 1793

(f) III 13 [Tangut] | 0047

(g) III 36 [Tangut] | x(2051) 1620

(h) III 43 [Tangut] | 4135

(i) III 84 [Tangut] | x 3497 3483

(j) III A 90 [Tangut] | ?x 2370

(k) III A 120 [Tangut] | 5169

[(l) V 47 [Tangut] x by [Tangut] |]

(m) V 50 [Tangut] | 4386

(n) V 59 [Tangut] | 0639

(o) V 74 [Tangut] | 4228

(p) V 82 [Tangut] | 4338

(q) V 167 [Tangut] | 4490

(r) V 181 [Tangut] | 3925

(s) VA 35 [Tangut] | : sing x 3955

(t) VA 65 [Tangut] | 2109

(u) VA 96 [Tangut] | 0484

~~(v) VA 109 [Tangut]~~

(w) VI 81 [Tangut] | 4004

(x) VI A 31 [Tangut] | ditto 3570

(y) VII 12 [Tangut] | 0021

(z) VII 38 [Tangut] x by | [Tangut] 2162

(aa) VIII 4 [Tangut] | to approach 2222

(bb) VIII 6 [Tangut] | x (1658) 2139

(cc) VIII 10 [Tangut] | 0316

(dd) VIII 84 [Tangut] | 1777

(ee) IX 32 [Tangut] | 3674

The ordinary auxiliary verb for "to make, do" corresponding to Tibetan byed-pa.

2150
+0591
-2151
-3471 -3615?
-3518 -1215
-1350

2151 2150 chain

2152 5305 chain

2153 5708 chain

2153A ? = 2154

2154
4194
2159

2155 4613 pair

Final particle W.I.166[18] 已

竟 "utmost, extreme (adj.)" W.II 86[8]

B.200[1] (q.v.) 224[3] ends sentence

W.I.132[9] "are finished"

214

(i) ccc.

(ii)

(iii)

ccc.

(iv)

B.229[2]

2150.

(a)

(b)

(c)

(d)

2151

2152

2153

(a)

(b)

minus 1

165

2149 (cont.)

(i) CCC. 20b 做 to do (the Buddha-law) 21b ditto: 21b | 修造 "to make & repair: 23a | 做造 to make & do: 32a 爲 be done

(ii) (i) above CCC. 29a 休做

(iii) | CCC. 30a 行遣

CCC. 33b 34a

(iv) | CCC. 34b 嫁

B. 229[2] q.v.

2150. IX 32 | 0591

(a) VII 8 ditto

(b) V 96 | 3471

(c) VII 18 | × {1215, 1350} 3618

(d) VIII 84 | v. 2151

?

2151 VIII 84 | v. 2150

?

2152 IX 39 | 2017

?

chain 5305

2153 gli IX 39 | "one" v 44

(a) VI 81 | × 5068

(b) VII 24 | ×? 1699

(aa) 0292

(c) VII 52 | 3725

(d) IX A1 | 3937

A rather nebulous particle. Usually a final particle like 也 eg. B. 255. CCC 1a 7

But sometimes means rather "one, a" eg. | W.II. 2[4] B. 199[3] 223[2] B. 180[1] 一時 "once"

B. W.I. 138[3,4] |

This seems wrong, ends the previous sentence.

2153A. × of VII 29 | 2159

?

2154 V 152 | 4194

(a) III 170 ditto

(i) The disyllable W.II 2[10] 50[5] 善巧 "skillful, clever."

2155 VII 42 |

(a) III 18 ditto

A common final particle. Original meaning 'to finish' possibly retained. CCC. 36b 已 CCC. 27a | 了 畢: CCC. 33b | 已畢 W. I 114[17] ditto, to complete sense: | B. 250[2]

2156 0583 chain

2157 2143 pair

2158
┬ 4638
└ 2005

2159 2154 pair

2160 3226 chain

2161 1891 chain

2162 2149 chain

2163 2115 chain

2164
┬ 2743
└ 3832 – 3107 – 2813

2165 4454 chain

2166 3226 chain

2167
┬ 4147
├ 2116
├ 3759 – 5069 ┬ 0451
│ ├ 1051
├ 3763 – 3118 ┐ ├ 2095
├ 3912 │ ├ 5016
├ 3963 – 5205 │ ├ 5367
├ 3844 – 2170 └ 0389
├ 4047
├ 4189
├ 4845
└ 5664 – 3300

166

2155 cont.

rdzogs.pa "complete, perfect
II 126
W.I 198[12] ditto: | W.II 220[9] snar.ma
"a lunar mansion".

2156 IX 75 |
(i) C.C.C. 29[a] 許 grant, allow, permit to approve(?) W II 84[5]
得 to attain
(ii) C.C.C. 20[b] 氣 spirit ?
B.126[1] ? phon.

2157 VIII A 104
Phonetic character

2158 V 71 | 4628
(a) VI 86 ditto
(b) III 61 | ? 2005
?

2159 VII 29 | 2154
?

2160 V 76 | v. 2169
?

2161 VII 25 | 1891
?

2162 VII 38
?

2163 I 36 | 2115
?

2164 RI IX 4 | 2743
(a) IX 4 ditto
(b) VIII 52 | 3832
(i) C.C.C. 19[b] 34[b] 37[a] W.I 108[12] 136[10] 得
B. 255[2] rñed "to obtain, attain
'Dark words' with two shades of meaning
(ii) C.C.C. 36[b]:
B.126[2] ? phon.

2165 III 57 | 4454
?

2166 VII 76 | v. 2169
?

2167 V.34 | 4147
(a) III 7 ditto
(b) III 31 | 3912 x 5205
(c) V 24 | nine 3963
(d) V 40 | 2116
(e) VII 7 | circuit? 4047 x 2170
(f) VII A 119 | six 3844
(g) VIII 17 | all x 3719 x 3300
(h) VIII 32 | "eight" 5664
(i) VIII 37 | '100' 4845

add 'seven'

2168 5110 chain

2169 3226 chain

(ii) | W.I.170^13 ? how does he dare?"

2170 2167 chain

2171 4574 chain

2172 screen W.II 144^7

2173 3163 pair

2173 1130 chain

2174 1992 chain

2175 4505 pair

2176 5656 pair

2177 4701 chain

2178
⊥ 1684
3137 — 2296
— 3127
— 3140
— 5634

167

2167 cont.

(j) IX 4 | 𗏁 myriad 4189 ××0359

(k) IX 127 | 𗏁 "four" ×3118 3763

C.C.C. 26b 數 "number"

W.I. 198[10] 222[18] ?

The usual word for "number".

2168 𗏁 I 96 𗏁 | "water"

W.II. 12[10] 波 "wave" I 156[11] ~~B.160[5]~~

† B.160[5] | 𗏁 'wave'

2169 𗏁 V 129 𗏁 | 3600

(a) V 76 | 𗏁 v 2160

(b) VII 76 | 𗏁 v 2166

Not so far found except in the dissyllable C.C.C. 29a 31a W.II 82[2] 不敢 "not to dare" B.165[4]

2170 𗏁 V 146 | 𗏁 "six"

(i) C.C.C. 15b 20a W I 224[5] 五 "five"

(ii) | 𗏁 W.I. 192[16] Pañcāla lina len

2171 𗏁 V 146 | 𗏁 2997

?

2172 𗏁 VIII 68 | 𗏁 misspelt

(a) IX 76 ditto [𗏁] v. 3163

C.C.C. 24a 欄 (fire) screen, railing.

W II 48[5] 障 "screen".

2173 𗏁 I 28 | 𗏁 "s(ai)" 1130

C.C.C. 8a 孛 "comet"

2174 𗏁 I 28 𗏁 𗏁 not C.50, behav 1992

?

2175 𗏁 I 22 𗏁 | 4505

(a) VI 77 ditto [𗏁]

B 100 The dissyllable [𗏁] cat. under 'horse'

Note: 𗏁 is probably right.

2176 𗏁 VIII A 18 𗏁 | 5856

(a) VI 72 ditto

?

2177 𗏁 I 28 𗏁 | misspelt 4701

The dissyllable [𗏁] C.C.C. 13a 塵土 dust & earth

2178 𗏁 I 28 | 𗏁 cig 1684

(a) III 37 ditto

(b) IX 39 𗏁 | wind 3137

C.C.C. 10a 巽 "mild, gentle" ? civilised

(chain linked to)
2179/1992 chain
0335
1246
1508
2054
2574
3216
4430-3880

2179 A 0271 chain

[2180]
571 574

2181 0741 chain

2182 4651 chain

2183 4789 chain

2183 Regnal period on coin

B. Coin plate; translated 聖福

2184 5190 chain

2185 0674 pair

2186 2989 chain

2187 - 5414

2188 x 0214 chain

2189 5293 chain

2189 A 1296 pair

168

2179 VIII A 62 | not 1992
(a) | × of :–
(i) III A 103 1246
(ii) III A 104
(iii) V A 124
(iv) V A 128 × 3880
(v) VII A 31
(vi) VII A 129 v. 2574
(vii) VIII A 95
(i) W.I. 92[4] etc. 梵 Brahma. Apparently simply a phonetic reproduction of Ch. "fan".
(ii) W.I. 190[4] 204[8] translates T. ts'ans. pa "pure".
(a) means "A sacred word".

2179 A × of V 57
Probably an error for 3766

2180 VI 4 |
(a) V 132 |
C.C.C. 6[b] 丘 "mount"

2181 V A 51 | 0741

2182 IX 98 | "earth"
(a) I 122 | 4682
(b) III 13 | × 0659 4687
C.C.C. 6[b] 墓 "grave"

wrong lines; should be 3664 A.

2183 (VII 59-60)
(a) I 24 | × 4789
C.C.C. 17[b] 27[a] W.I. 92[9] 96[6] etc. 聖 "holy", ārya, sadhu
cf. 3832A

2184 I A 88 | 5190
(a) VI A 47 | 3280
W.I. 108[11] 窮 "poor, exhausted"
? Also used as a Phonetic.

2185 III 87 | 0674
(a) VII A 69 ditto, reversed
W.I. 224[11] rgyun II 12[7] 紹 "stream"

2186 IX A 46 | 2989
?

2187 VIII 79 | 5414
(a) IX 23 ditto
?

2188 VI 129 VI 129 | 4864
?

2189 V 61 | 5290

2189 A × of IX 75 | v. 1296
? error for 3294

2190 2206 pair

2191 1326 pair

2192 5428 chain

2193
- 1898 - 3283 - 3474 { 0861 / 2253 - 0359 - 1267 / 4495
- 0562
- 2833
- 4828 - 1899
- 5200

2194 - 2993

2195 0185 pair

2196 ~~2204 chain~~

2197 5637 chain
+ 5637
~~0244~~

2198 5671 chain

2199 2928 chain

2200 1891 chain

2201 4060 chain

2202 4060 chain

2202 (iii) | bad, sdig 'evil devils' B.249²

2190
(a)
2191
(a
2192
2193
(a)
(b).
(c).
(d)
(e)
(i) By il
(ii) The
II 76⁹ 82
preta
(iii) By i
a luna
2194
2195
(a) V
(I) The his

169

2190 [Tangut] VI 24 [Tangut] | v. 2206

(a) VIII 49 ditto

?

2191 [Tangut] III 119 | [Tangut] | 1326

(a) V 40 ditto [[Tangut]]

?

2192 [Tangut] VI A 54 [Tangut] |

2193 [Tangut] VIII 79 [Tangut] | misspelt v. 1898

(a) VII A 39 [Tangut] [[Tangut]] ditto

(b) III 120 | [Tangut] 4828

(c) V 110 [Tangut] | 5200

(d) V A 24 | [Tangut] 0562

(e) VIII A 78 [Tangut] | calamity 2833

(i) By itself W II 28[9] 鬼 "ghost" B 128[1]

(ii) The dissyllable W.I. 218[14] yi. dvags II 76[9] 82[3] 餓 鬼 "hungry ghost, preta. W.I. 170[2]

(iii) By itself I 220[9] nam. so name of a lunar mansion.

2194 [Tangut] III A 124 | [Tangut]

2195 [Tangut] VI 99 [Tangut] | 0185

(a) V 65 ditto

(i) The dissyllable. B. 100 cat. under "horse".

2196 [Tangut] IX A 29 [Tangut] | 1293

(i) The dissyllable B. 100 cat. under "horse"

2197 [Tangut] IX 4 [Tangut] | 5637

(aa) IX 74 ditto

(a) I 24 [Tangut] | ×3261 4496

(b) II 40 | [Tangut] 0244

(i) (b) above W.I. 212[12] ṅc'i. bdag "Lord of Death.

2198 [Tangut] I A 96 [Tangut] | 5671

(a) I A 21 [Tangut] | 5443

?

2199 [Tangut] VIII 83 [Tangut] | 0915 [Tangut]

2200 [Tangut] VI 117 [Tangut] | 1891

2201 [Tangut] VII A 28 [Tangut] | v. 2202

2202 [Tangut] IX 130 | [Tangut] 4060

(a) V A 62 ditto

(b) VII A 28 | [Tangut]

(i) By itself W. I 122[14] 魔 ~~B 649~~ I 192[17] ~~bdud~~ "devil" B. 162[3]

(ii) The dissyllable W. I 136[12] ?

2203 bis – 2774

2203 take over 0126 chain

2204
- 4994
- 0725
- 1293 – 0245
- 2205 – 2196, 3543

2205 02204 chain

2206 – 2190

2207 – 4407

[2208]
- 3528 – 4979
- 4799

2209 3269 chain

W. II 126^5

2210 1410 pair

2211 0782 chain

2212 3226 chain

2213 2351 chain

2214 0782 chain

2215 2482 chain

2216 2710 chain

2203 bis [Tangut] I 53 | [Tangut] 2774
(a) I 53 ditto

170

2203 [Tangut] IX A 66 | [Tangut] 0126
(a) IX A 8 ditto
(b) V 29 | [Tangut] 0336
?

2204 [Tangut] IX 8 | [Tangut] ? 4994
(a) VIII 8 ditto
~~(b) I 53 | [Tangut]~~
(c) II 14 | [Tangut] v. 2205 ?
(d) VI 122 | [Tangut] 1493
(e) VII 7 | [Tangut] 0725
W.I. 100[14] 126[17] 142[17] 死 "to die"

2205 [Tangut] II 14 [Tangut] | "to die" v. 2204

2206 [Tangut] VIII 49 | [Tangut]
(a) VI 24 ditto v. 2190

2207 [Tangut] III 15 | [Tangut] 4407
(a) V 29 ditto

2208 [Tangut] IX 75 | [Tangut] x 4979 3528
(a) III 96 ditto [[Tangut]]
(b) II 4 [Tangut] | 4799
?

<u>Note</u>. It is perhaps wrong to distinguish between [Tangut] + [Tangut]

2209 [Tangut] III 25 | [Tangut] quarter 3269
(i) [W.I. 94" II 18[6] 失 "to err"] v. 4478
(ii) | [Tangut] ~~B. 248~~ B. 172[5] 232[1] ~~p'a. rol~~ W II 2[10] 彼岸 "the further shore pāramitā"
(iii) | [Tangut] [Tangut] B. 248[1] p'a. rol. du ditto "to attain the" p'yin. pa

2210 [Tangut] VI 21 [Tangut] | 1410
(a) V 68 ditto

2211 [Tangut] III 15 | [Tangut] 0782
(a) III A 115 [Tangut] x by | [Tangut] v. 2214
[(b) VI 93 [Tangut] x by [Tangut] |]
?

2212 [Tangut] V A 95 [Tangut] | 0577
(a) VII A 23 | [Tangut] 0966
ccc. 12[b] 摧 "to break"

2213 [Tangut] V 58 [Tangut] |
?

2214 [Tangut] III A 115 [Tangut] [Tangut] 2211
A phonetic character

2215 [Tangut] VII 6 [Tangut] | 0594
?

2216 [Tangut] IX 61 | [Tangut] foot 5440
ccc. 33[a] 細 | [Tangut] 細麪 "fine flour"
chain

2217.
0829
[1824]
3046
5277

2218 2692 pair

2219 4104 chain

W.II.78⁴ [Tangut] | [Tangut] [Tangut] '(he) said to Buddha.'

2220 4541 chain

2221 3795 chain

2222 2149 chain

2222. B 245² ? 谷欠 'wish' [doubtful]

2223 2845 chain

2224 2581 chain

2225 0809

2226 2703 chain

2226. Lo's Handbook p.16 says 忄龍 means 平聲 'level tone'

2227 0159 chain (take over)

171

2217 [Tangut] III A83 | [Tangut] "to flow"

(a) IX 81 ditto — See 829

(b) I 126 | [Tangut] — [1824]

(c) VII 65 | [Tangut] — 3046

(d) VIII 22 | [Tangut] — 5277

?

2218 [Tangut] VIII 57 [Tangut] |

(a) VIII 16 ditto

?

2219 [Tangut] YE VIII 4 [Tangut] | "he" 1803

(a) III 100 [Tangut] | "he" 1800

(b) VI 81 [Tangut] | 5049

(c) VII/VIII 111 [Tangut] | 5297

Passim. One of the commonest post-positions, equivalent to I-kye Ch. 之 "of", but sometimes "to"

2220 [Tangut] V 3 [Tangut] | 4542

?

2221 [Tangut] ria V 3 [Tangut] | river (0670) 596

(a) I 37 | [Tangut] 2399

(b) V 9 | [Tangut] "conch" v. 2069

(c) VI 13 [Tangut] | 4674

(d) VI 24 [Tangut] | × (5047) 0883

(e) VIII 75 | [Tangut] 4903

2221 cont.

(f) IX 86 [Tangut] | ? 2404

(i) C.C.C. 12[a] a frequently 海 "ocean"

(ii) (b) above C.C.C. 21[a] 海螺 "sea conch"

(iii) | [Tangut] W.I.190[5] rgya.mtsʻo "ocean".

2222 [Tangut] VIII 4 [Tangut] | "to make"

臨 "to approach" W.II 126[10] B 125[5]

2223 [Tangut] IX 95 [Tangut] |

(a) I 15 ditto

(i) The dissyllable B.102 cat. under "vegetables".

2224 [Tangut] IX 95 [Tangut] | 2541

2225 [Tangut] VIII 57 | [Tangut] 0383

2226 [Tangut] YE VIII 57 [Tangut] | 2703

(a) VIII 16 ditto

(b) V 18 | [Tangut] 4300 (b) V 18 4325

(c) IX 80 [Tangut] | 1945 q.v.

B 207[3] q.v.

2227 [Tangut] IX 95 | [Tangut] 0159

(a) II 4 ditto

(b) III A 70 [Tangut] | × 5164

2232 2231 chain

2233 2231 chain

2234 – [5417]

2235 3417 chain

2228 2351 chain

2236 1848 chain

2229 – 4999

2237 – 5655

2231
- 0452
- 0338 — 2232
- 1337 — 2233
- 5282

2238 4276 chain

2239 – 3842

B.176[5] 匠 mason B.163[5] ? the same
mine B.169[4]

172

2227 (cont.)
This word means "sweet" in various connections. B161[4] 酸 'sweet'
(i) (b) above W.I 98[9] appears to translate 甘 "sweet" B.221[5] 甘
(ii) | C.C.C. 7[b] W.I. 90[2] etc 甘露 "sweet dew" i.e. Amrta ambrosia.
(iii) | C.C.C. 33[b] 酸 酪

2228 IX 175 | 3944
(a) VIII 110 | 0678
?
2229 IX 95 | 4999
(a) VIII 84 ditto
?
2230 IX 175 x by itself ||
?
2231 VIII A16 |
(a) IX 4 ditto v. 452
(b) I 24 | 5282
(c) I 130 | 0338
(d) V 184 | 1387
(i) (c) above W II 18[7] 睡 眠 W I 196[6] "to sleep"

2232 V A7 | "sleep" 0338
?
2233 III 59 | "sleep" 0338
?
2234 VI 7 | [5417
(a) I 53 ditto
?
2235 VII 67 | 5369
2236 IX 17 | 1848
(a) IX 129 ditto
(b) III 50 | 2454
?
2237 VIII 68 | 5655
(a) VIII 4 ditto
(i) The dissyllable II 26[12] 相 lakṣana "distinctive sign, phenomenon".
v. 2626A
2238 VII 67 | 0541
?
2239 IX 123 |
(a) I 4 ditto
?

172

2240 5311 pair

2241 5285 pair

2242 2245 chain

2243 4965 chain

2244 0460 chain

2245
- 2727
- 2243
- 3524
- 5889 – 2332

2245[6] – 2513

2247 5623 chain

2248 +812 pair

2249 1876 chain

2250 1891 chain

2251 0148 chain

2252 2254 pair

2253 2193 chain

2240

2241

2242

B. 171[3]

2243

2244

(a) II

(i) (a)

2245

(a)

(b)

(c)

(d)

Passim

N.B. Cf.

2246

(a) III

W.I. 190[3]

173

2240 [Tangut] IX 41 [Tangut] | 5311

(a) VII 16 ditto

cf. 2241

2241 [Tangut] IX 41 [Tangut] | 5285

(a) VII 16 ditto

2242 [Tangut] IX 115 | [Tangut] "two" v. 2245

B. 171³ [Tangut] to combine, unite Newski I 369

2243 [Tangut] I A 23 [Tangut] | 4965

2244 [Tangut] III 107 [Tangut] | 0460

(a) III A 63 | [Tangut] 0439

(i) (a) above B. 99 cat. under "sheep"

2245 [Tangut] gni III A 45 [Tangut] "three" 2727

(a) VI A 38 ditto

(b) IX 115 [Tangut] | v. 2242

(c) IX 138 [Tangut] | pair x (2332) 5589

(d) IX A 81 | [Tangut] 3524

Passim "two".

N.B. Cf. T. gñis

2246 [Tangut] NI III 46 | [Tangut]

(a) III 38 ditto v 2513

W.I. 190³ k'yod "thou" B 197¹ do. 汝

2247 [Tangut] IX 63 | [Tangut] 5623

2248 [Tangut] VI 27 [Tangut] |

(a) VI 77 ditto

2249 [Tangut] IX 44 [Tangut] | 1878

(a) IX 54 ~~ditto~~ [Tangut] 1879

(b) I 87 [Tangut] | 5288

(c) IX 10 | [Tangut] 3798

x ?

2250 [Tangut] III 154 [Tangut] | 1891

?

2251 [Tangut] VIII 64 [Tangut] | 0499

(a) V 84 [Tangut] | [Tangut] x 1440

(b) VIII A 80 2255

2251A ~~2252~~ [Tangut] V 44 [Tangut] |

This is an error for [Tangut] v. 3073

2252 [Tangut] VIII 11 [Tangut] |

(a) III 38 ditto [Tangut]

W.I. 96¹⁵ II 18¹ [Tangut in both] 罪 "sin"

2253 ~~2254~~ [Tangut] V 37 | [Tangut] 3474

(a) VII 30 [Tangut] | x 0359

B 172⁴

x 2249A [Tangut] see || 2010

2254 - 2253

2255 0148 chain

2256 4192 pair

2257 4829 pair

2258 0825 chain

2259 4508 pair

2260 4661 chain

2261 + 2573 pair

2262 - 2924

2263 2377 chain

2264 2285 chain

2265 2306 chain

2266 2121 chain

2267 ⊥ 2287-2291

2268 2279 4833 chain

2269 0340 pair

174

2254 [illegible] III 38 | [illegible] "silk"

(a) VIII 11 ditto v. 2252

?

2254A [illegible] Error for [illegible] 3079

2255 [illegible] VIII A 80 | [illegible] [misspelt]

2256 [illegible] VII 5 Family or clan name

(a) VI 55 [illegible] |

Possibly a double name

2257 [illegible] VII 5 [illegible] | 4829

(a) VIII 82 ditto

?

2258 [illegible] IX 116 | [illegible] 0825

? B. 187[2] q.v. tr. 分

2259 [illegible] I 55 [illegible] | 4508

(a) I 34 ditto

2260 [illegible] III 15 [illegible] | 4661

(a) III A 23 ditto

(b) III 135 [illegible] | ? 1977

?

2261 [illegible] III 44 [illegible] | 2573

(a) I 44 ditto

?

2262 [illegible] VII 73 | [illegible] 2924

(a) VII 69 ditto [illegible]

(i) [illegible] | B. 100 cat. under "camel".

(i) By itself W. I. 168[13]: 負 "to carry on back".

2263 [illegible] I 26 [illegible] | 0263

2264 [illegible] VIII 67 [illegible] | 2285

(a) I 48 [illegible] | [misspelt] 1702 v. 2265

(i) | [illegible] B. 99 cat. under "horse"

2265 [illegible] IX 176 [illegible] | 2306

?

2266 [illegible] IX 61 | [illegible] 4920

?

2267 [illegible] VIII 67 | [illegible] ×2291 2287

(a) IX 125 ditto [illegible]

?

2268 [illegible] V 180 [illegible] | 4833

(a) IX 24 | [illegible] 2455

| [illegible] + | [illegible] B. 99 + 100 cat. under "horse" 0340

2269 [illegible] VI 132 | [illegible] "fat"

(a) III 1 ditto

?

2270 +4163 pair

5283 2271 pair

2272 2279 chain

2273 ✓
2292 - 3342

2274 2283 chain

2275
4276 chain

2276 2027 chain

2277 2283 chain

2278
- 4271
- 2308 - 1036 - 5343
  - 1972 - 1939 - 4644
    - 2030
  - 2642 - 2641
    - 5275
  - 4304 - 2918 - 1196 - 1323

2279 2309 chain

2281 4531 chain

2280 2485 chain

2282 0731 chain

2283
- 4733
- 2274
- 2277
- 2304

175

2270 ~~2271~~ V 180 | 4163

(a) III 28 ditto

?

2271 ~~2272~~ VI 69 | 5283

(a) VII 111 ditto

B. 166[2] tr. 陣 to arrange etc.

2272 ~~2273~~ tsyu VI 100 | 4833

(a) V 103 | 4382

(b) IX 134 |

C.C.C. 33[b] 繮 "reins, bridle."

2273 ~~2274~~ I 82 | "garden peas"

(a) V 20 ditto v. 2292

(i) | B. 101 cat. under "wild animals"

(ii) | W.I. 192[4] 194[6] 226[3] ser. skya

a. 白黄 "Laymen & Lamas".

2274 ~~2275~~ III A 111

Phonetic character

2275 ~~2276~~ VIII 43 | 2400

~~(a) I 36 ditto~~ I 36. 2050

(a) VI 27 | 5316

(b) VI 135 | 2288

?

2276 ~~2277~~ VII 101 | 1620

?

2277 ~~2278~~ III A 117 1709

A Phonetic character

2278 ~~2279~~ V 2 | 4271

(a) V 27 ditto

(b) V 28 | v. 2308

?

2279 ~~2280~~ Re IX 18 | 2309 "horse"

(a) V 58 ditto

~~(b) I A 23~~

(b) V 139 | 1057

(c) VI 120 | 2286

(d) IX 151 | 4833

C.C.C. 6[a] 16[a] 33[b] B. 99 "catalogue heading"

馬 "horse".

2281 ~~2282~~ IV 2 | 1822

?

2280 VII 101 | 2775

?

2282 ~~2283~~ VII 24 | "wood" 0717

?

2283 ~~2284~~ III 84 | 4733

(a) III A 24 ditto

(b) III A 111 x by | 2274

(c) III A 117 x by | 2277

(d) III A 118 x by | 2304

2288 4276 chain

2286 2309 chain

2287 2267 chain

2289 4127 chain

2284 0199 pair

2285
- 2626
- 0495
- 1651
- 2026 – 2023
- 2264 – 1702
- 2299
- 2312 – 0578 – 0234
- 3948 – 1031
- 2748

2290 2071 chain

2291 2267 chain

2292 2273 chain

176

2283
~~2284~~ cont.
? B.163[1] tr. 命 187[2]

This is a common Phonetic. (b)-(d) are all Phonetic characters

2284 A [Tangut] Error for 2289.
W.II 2[7]
Both forms are frequent, but the other seems to be correct.

2284 [Tangut] VI 93 [Tangut] | 0199
(a) I 14 ditto

2285
~~2286~~ [Tangut] VI 36 | [Tangut] 2626
(a) VI 6 ditto
(b) III 95 | [Tangut] 2312
(c) V 18 | [Tangut] 0495
(d) V 141 [Tangut] × by dissyllable ×2023 2026
(e) V 150 [Tangut] | 1651
(f) VII 5 | [Tangut] 2299
(g) VII 50 | [Tangut] 2971
(h) VIII 67 | [Tangut] VIII 56 2748 ×(1702) (i) IX 20 | [Tangut] 2264 ×(1031) 3948

(i) By itself [?in error] W II 76[9] 傍 "side, on one side, dependent".
(ii) The dissyllable W.II 82[3] 傍生 "born on one side" i.e. as an animal Tiryagyoni. I.168[12] 畜生 ~~ditto?~~ "born as animals".

2288 [Tangut] VI 135 [Tangut] |
?

2286
~~2287~~ [Tangut] VI 120 [Tangut] horse 2279

2287
~~2288~~ [Tangut] IX 125 [Tangut] | 2267
(a) VIII 67 ditto
(b) VIII 101 | [Tangut] [misspelt] v.2291
?

2289 [Tangut] I 19 [Tangut] | 4127 ~~2264~~
(a) I 6 ditto [[Tangut]]
(i) By itself C 16[b] W.I.152[12] 象 W.I.190[16] 192[3] "~~stag~~ glan. po "elephant".
(ii) [Tangut] | B.100 cat. under "wild animals".
(iii) | [Tangut] B.103[3] "ivory" cat. under "precious things"

2290 [Tangut] VI 18 | [Tangut]
(a) I 22 ditto
?

2291 [Tangut] VII 101 [Tangut] | v.2288
?

2292 [Tangut] V 20 [Tangut] | 2273
(a) I 82 ditto
(b) VIII 36 | [Tangut] 3342
(i) CCC.15[b] 豌 "garden peas"
(ii) [Tangut] | B.100 cat. under "horse"
(iii) [Tangut] | B.101 cat. under "grain"

2293 1338 chain

2294 -3242

2295 2309 chain

2296 2178 chain

2297 ? 3091 chain

2298 +4478 L1228

2299 2285 chain

2300 1343 chain

2301 2309 chain

2302 3942 pair

2303 - 3570

2303 中(i) | [Tangut] 尼拘類

Nyagrodha the banyan tree

W. I 178[5]

2304 2283 chain

2305 0582 chain

2293

(a

B 16

2294

(a

The

ccc.

veget

2295

(i)

2296

?

2297

(i) |

2298

(a)

(b)

(i) with

road)"

(ii)

a disobe

177

2293 [Tangut] VI 4 [Tangut] | 1335
(a) V A 5 | [Tangut] 1524
B 160[3] [161[4] [Tangut] tr. 代 generation?]

2294 [Tangut] IX 18 [Tangut] [Tangut]
(a) VII 105 [Tangut] x by | [Tangut]
The trisyllable B 102 cat. under "vegetables"
C.C.C. 15[a] 馬齒菜 "horses' teeth vegetable".

2295 [Tangut] IX 125 [Tangut] | 2309 2264
(i) [Tangut] | B. 99 cat. under "horse"

2296 [Tangut] VII 101 [Tangut] | 3137
?

2297 [Tangut] VI 5 [Tangut] | q.v. 2942
(i) | [Tangut] B. 99 cat. under "horse" 3241

2298 [Tangut] IX 54 [Tangut] | 4478
(a) I 84 ditto
(b) VIII 36 | [Tangut] 1228
(i) With [Tangut] C.C.C. 29[b] 失 "to miss (the road)" W.I. 98[13]: Dict 1[a]4?
(ii) [Tangut] | W II 18[5] 乖違 "to quarrel & disobey"

2299 [Tangut] VII 5 [Tangut] | 2285
?

2300 [Tangut] I 40 [Tangut] | 1343
C.C.C. 21[b] 末 powdered (incense)
W.I. 218[18] [wrongly ref.] p'ye.ma "powder

2301. [Tangut] III 99 [Tangut] |
(i) The disyllable B. 99 cat. under 'horse' [& translated 鞍馬 saddle horse]

~~2302~~ N.B. The difference between 2300 & 2301 is slight & obscure.

2302 [Tangut] V 127 [Tangut] | 3942
(a) VI 16 ditto
(i) The disyllable B. 99 cat. under 'horse'

2303. [Tangut] IX 5 | [Tangut] 3510
(a) VII A 121 ditto
?
Frequently used as a Phonetic.

2304 [Tangut] III A 118 [Tangut] [Tangut]
A Phonetic character

2305 [Tangut] I 63 [Tangut] | 3682
(a) III 70 | [Tangut] 0842
(i) [Tangut] | B. 100 cat. under 'horse'

2306 – 2309

2307 2494 chain

2308 2278 chain

2309

2310 – 3313

2311 1272 chain

2312 2285 chain

2313 2309 chain

2314 2279 chain

178

2306 敄 VI 93 敀 | 1591

(b) IX 176 | 𘟙 2265 2307

(a) IX 135 ditto

v. 3402

W. I. 98[3] II 2[10], 8[2] etc. "alaṁkāra adorned glorious

(ii) 㪉 | 莊嚴 ~~stately, austere~~ W. I 152[2]

2307 𘟙 IX 176 ~~𘟙~~ | 𘟙 | 1857

(a) VI 82 𘟙 | "rug" ~~felt~~ v. 2544

(b) IX 77 𘟙 | 416

C.C.C. 24[a] 33[b] 毡 "carpet, rug" + v. 2896

2308 𘟙 V 28 | 𘟙 v. 2278

(a) I 43 | 𘟙 1036

(b) III 9 𘟙 | 2642

[(c) III A35 𘟙 × by 𘟙 𘟙]

(d) VIII 82 𘟙 | "in" 1972

(e) IX 29 | 𘟙 4304

(i) C.C.C. 3[a] etc. 中 B. 2305 W. I 198[6] gun

"The centre, middle (of tree)"

(ii) Also, like 中, used as a postposition for "in" W. I 220[7] -la etc.

2309 𘟙 ne V 58 | 𘟙

(a) IX 18 ditto

(b) IX 34 𘟙 | 𘟙 2714

(c) IX 125 | 𘟙 2295

This word seems to mean both

2309 cont.

'horse' & 'a horse-shaped ornament'. W. I 190[16] 224[15] rta "horse".

(i) C.C.C. 10[a] 午 7th horary character ("horse" in the animal cycle)

(ii) The disyllable B. 99 cat. under "horse".

(iii) | 𘟙 1108 C.C.C. 13[a] 瑪瑙 B. 103 cat. under "jewels", 'jade horse ornament, agate or cornelian'.

2310 𘟙 VI 92 | 𘟙

(a) I 6 ditto

(i) 𘟙 | 2268 B. 99 cat. under 'horse'.

2311 𘟙 IX A 84 𘟙 | 1272

W. II. 76[7] 及 "to reach" 96[8] etc.

2312 𘟙 Ta III 95 𘟙 | 2285

C.C.C. 16[b] 騾 "mule"

2313 𘟙 IX 137 𘟙 | 2309 horses

?

Note. There is no obvious difference between 2312 + 2313.

2314 𘟙 IX 134 𘟙 | 2272

C.C.C. 33[b] 嚼鐵 "iron bit".

2315 1317 chain

2316 1080 chain

2317 4561 chain

2318 4561 chain

2319 0599 chain

2320 3587 chain

2321 1781 chain

2322 4561 chain

2323 0582 chain

2324—1757

2325 1497 pair

2326 5301 chain

2327
4785—3132
1376—5450
5401

~~B 217 啓 to inform~~

The Tiny L. B 217 啓 請 217 召 請

B. 227 q.v.

2328 3628 pair

179

2315 I 11 | "officer" 1990
(i) | 0003 ? B.100 cat. under "horse"

2316 IA34 | [?=] 5665
(a) VIA4 | 1806
?

2317 DE III 45 | come 1968
(a) III A 112 x by 2317
(b) III A 113 x by | 1779 } Phonetic characters
W.I.100[4] + passim 當 "ought, must".
Used as an Imperative prefix
B.124[4] 125[1,2]
(a) + (b) are Phonetic characters.

2318 III A 113 2317 1779
A Phonetic character

2319 IX 133 | swell 4272
W.I.108[15]? 132[17]? possibly 藏 "treasury" which is
218[2] gnas "place"
B.124[5] 住 to dwell

2320 V 91 | 5606
?

2321 V 3 | 4021
C.C.C. 29[a]

2322 III A 112 2317
A Phonetic character.

2323 I 19 | 3692
(i) | B.99 cat. under horse [tr. 白純 "pure white"]

2324 I 22 | 1757
(a) III 98 ditto
?

2325 I 19 | 1497
(a) IX 47 ditto
?

2326 V 74 | 2445
(a) I 11 | 5299
(b) VII 10 | 4249
?

2327 I 19 | x(3132) 4785
(a) VIII 5 ditto
(b) I 97 | x(5450) 1376
(c) IX 123 | 5401
C.C.C. 30[6 2] 追 "to pursue, follow after"
B.216[5] 召 to summon

2328 I 27 | 3628
(i) The disyllable C.C.C. 24[b] (i)

2329 2517 pair

2330 2353 chain

2331 – 2365

2332 2245 chain

2333 0462 pair

2334 1772 chain

2335
⊥ 4988 [1784
3584 – 4237

2336 – 0253 [illegible]

2337 0042 chain

2338 2149 chain

2339 independent

2340 independent

2342 3226 chain

2342. B 245[2] | [illegible] . . . . . . [illegible] 'to say'
(words said between two elements)
apparently [illegible] before + [illegible] after
B. 195[5] + foll. change a verb.
B 224[3] | [illegible] tr. 語 説

180

2329 [Tangut] I 37 "Family or clan name."
(a) I 52 [Tangut] |
Possibly a double name

2330 [Tangut] V 54 [Tangut] | 2371

2331 [Tangut] I 37 | [Tangut] 2365
(a) I 115 ditto
[(b) IX 9 [Tangut] × by [Tangut] []]
?

2332 [Tangut] I A 103 [Tangut] | 5589
?
Note 2331 & 2332 are barely distinguishable

2333 [Tangut] I 37 [Tangut] | 0462
(a) II 31 ditto

2334 [Tangut] I 3 | [Tangut] 1772
?

2335 [Tangut] V 34 | [Tangut] ×4988
(a) IX 118 ditto
?

2336 [Tangut] I 3 | [Tangut] 0253
(a) V 4 ditto
B.168[4]

2337 [Tangut] IX 132 | [Tangut] ? 5373

2338 [Tangut] III 122 [Tangut] | 3228
?

2339 [Tangut] III 40 × by itself [|] |
W.II 42[6] The doublet character 實 "solid, real."

2340 [Tangut] III 121 × by itself | [|]
?

2341 see next page ← [Tangut]

2342 [Tangut] n.a. III 70 [Tangut] | gen. word 3226
(a) III 155 | [Tangut] 5083 (aa) 2630 Preface
(b) V 51 [Tangut] | ×3677
(c) VII 28 | [Tangut] 5020
(d) VII 68 | [Tangut] 5003
(e) VII 79 | [Tangut] 5720
(f) [Tangut] [Tangut] × of (2736)
(i) I 17 [Tangut] ×3600
(ii) I 59 [Tangut] 5082
(iii) III 28 × [Tangut] 3701
(iv) III 35 [Tangut] × (2024) 1685
(v) III 46 [Tangut] × (3850) 0498
(vi) III 121 [Tangut] × (many) 0577
(vii) III 121 [Tangut] 5679
(viii) V 1 [Tangut] 5364
(ix) V A 116 [Tangut] × (3416) 1291 × 5643
(x) VI 24 [Tangut] × (3327) 5346
(xi) VII 29 [Tangut] 4570

2342. B.253⁴ a verb gsol.pa "to say".

2343-1255

2344 4030 chain
B.237⁴ 教化
(ii) The dissyllable W.II 94¹⁰ 勸化 "to exhort to conversion, convert."
ro. | [illegible] B. plate. Last 2 characters on 2 metal plaques; transl. 命令

~~2344 2680~~

2345 2076 pair

2346 & 2347 pair

2341 4052 chain
B.170¹ tśi 施 to give

2347-2346

181

2342 cont.

(xii) VIII 54 [Tangut] (1852) × 2474

(s) [Tangut] [Tangut] × of (0335)

(i) I 112 [Tangut] 1645

(ii) I A 44 [Tangut] 2083

(iii) I A 55 [Tangut] 2070 2083 bis

(iv) V 39 [Tangut] 2100

(v) V A 80 [Tangut] 1673

(vi) V A 81 [Tangut] 1672

(vii) VII A 1 [Tangut] 2068

(viii) VIII A 3 [Tangut] 2098

(ix) VIII A 17 [Tangut] 4224

(x) VIII A 32 [Tangut] 1894

(xi) VIII A 36 [Tangut] 5497

(xii) IX 103 [Tangut] 2073

(xiii) IX A 116 [Tangut] 2081

(xiv) IX A 117 [Tangut] 2105

(xv) IX A 133 [Tangut] 2067

(xvi) IX A 141 [Tangut] [Tangut] 1044

This word appears to be specifically a noun, meaning "word".

C. 30b W.I. 96[13] 98[6] 206[5] II 16[8] 言 word

C. 31a 承 "orders".

(f) means "auxiliary word".

(s) means "true word, i.e. mystic word mantra."

7/1/39

2343 [Tangut] I A 111 | [Tangut] 1255

(a) I 137 ditto

?

2344 [Tangut] VI 7 | [Tangut] × 2680

(a) I 1 | [Tangut] 5489

(b) III 91 | [Tangut] 5005

(i) (a) above C.C.C. 30a 31a 指揮

(ii) (b) above W.I. 146[12] 147[1] 教授 "to instruct."

(iii) | [Tangut] C.C.C. B 160[2] 28b 承旨 "to receive purport" S.H. 213

2345 [Tangut] VII 38 [Tangut] | 2016

(a) VII 41 ditto

?

2346 [Tangut] VI A 98 [Tangut] |

(a) VI A 97 ditto

2346 [Tangut] I 26 [Tangut] | 1534

[Tangut] W.II 36[3]

(i) The dissyllable W.II 36[6] 廣設 "to spread widely"

2347 [Tangut] VI A 97 | [Tangut]

(a) VI A 98 ditto

?

181

2348 — 3151

2350 — 2849

2351
- 0626
- 2213
- 3944 – 2228 – 0678

2349 2353 chain

2352 — 4133

2353
- 2371 – 1603
- 1802
  - 2330
  - 2349 – 2361
  - 2362 – 1570 – 0619
    - 3886 – 0623
  - 2453 – 2358
  - 4640 – 2368

2354 0804 pair

2355 — 3858

2356 5690 chain x

2357 — 4777

2358 2353 chain

2359 1889 chain

2360 chain link to 2482 chain
- 2482 – chain
- 1761
- 2414 – 2640
- ~~2482~~
- 3167
- 5228

2361 2353 chain

2362 2353 chain

2348–56 'compare 2208–2215.

182

2348 [Tangut] III 172 | [Tangut] 3151

(a) V 14 ditto

?

2350 [Tangut] VI A 50 | [Tangut] 2849

(a) VI 106 ditto

?

2351 [Tangut] II 1 [Tangut] | Sangwas 0626

(a) I 9 ditto

(b) V 39 [Tangut] | 3944

(c) V 58 | [Tangut] 2213

(i) The disyllable C.C.C. 12b 峗 嶮

2349 [Tangut] I 101 [Tangut] | slope 2371

(a) VII 79 | [Tangut] ? 2361

? B.1684 [[Tangut]]

2352 [Tangut] IX 75 [Tangut] | 4133

(a) VI A 41 ditto

?

2353 [Tangut] VI 35 [Tangut] 2371

(a) IX 53 ditto

(b) IX 70 [Tangut] | 1802

?

2354 [Tangut] VI 79 [Tangut] |

(a) VI 123 ditto

W.I 132[15] 扠 192[5] sog.ma "stalk".

?a fork or hunting spear

2355 [Tangut] I A 68 | [Tangut] 3858

(a) III 136 ditto

?

2356 [Tangut] V 66 [Tangut] | 2527

× C.C.C. 4b 霄 "sky, mist" 2356A v.2372

2357 [Tangut] VII 87 | [Tangut] 4777

(a) VIII 11 ditto

2358 [Tangut] IX 82 [Tangut] | ? 2362

C.C.C. 12a 嶺 "mountain range"

2359 [Tangut] III 49 | [Tangut] 5317

?

2360 [Tangut] I 115 | [Tangut] "black"

(a) III 138 ditto v2482

(b) I 26 | [Tangut] ? 3197

(c) VII A 123 | [Tangut] ? 1761

(d) IX 101 | [Tangut] ? 5228

(e) IX 144 | [Tangut] conch-shell 2414

C.C.C. 7a 12b 15b 21a & passim 白 W.I 190[3]

dkar "white"

2361 [Tangut] VII 79 [Tangut] | ?

2362 [Tangut] V 2 [Tangut] | slope 2371

(a) VI 119 | [Tangut] v.2368

(b) IX 82 | [Tangut] mountain range 2358

(c) IX 121 | [Tangut] ? 1570

2363
+ 1875
4118

2364 3430 chain

| 彨 W.I.265[19] 邪去 "driving out heterodoxy". Part of royal title[F].

B.175' part of P.N. 125[4] 朋

2365 2331 pair

2366 3130 chain

2367 2144 chain

2368 2353 chain

2369 3430 chain

2370 2149 chain

2371 2553 chain

2372 | [Tangut] 法[Tangut]師 "teacher"

2372 3897 chain

2373-0704

2363

2364

2365

2366

2367

W.I. 94

183

2363 [Tangut] V 2 | [Tangut] 1875
(a) IX 82 ditto
(b) VII 19 | [Tangut] 4118
?

2364 [Tangut] III 49 | [Tangut] 3430
(a) III 34 [Tangut] | 3735
(b) VIII A 109 | [Tangut] 2046
(i) By itself W. I. 96[13] 100[7] etc. 邪 "heteros-
-ous to prevent. B 179[3] depravity
(ii) | [Tangut] C.C.C. 7[a] 巨蟹 "great crab"
name of constellation.

2365 [Tangut] I 115 [Tangut] |
(a) I 37 ditto
?

2366 [Tangut] V A 88 [Tangut] | 3130
(a) VIII 86 ditto
(b) III 19 [Tangut] | 5292
(c) VII 3/19 [Tangut] | ×4764
?

2367 [Tangut] VI 18 [Tangut] |
(a) I 8 ditto
(b) VI 4 | [Tangut] 4738
W. I 94[15] II 6[11] 高 "high, lofty" I 190[12]
rab superior.

2368 [Tangut] V 119 [Tangut] | v. 2362
?

2369 [Tangut] IX A 145 | [Tangut]
W. I. 138[1] ;
?

2370 [Tangut] III A 90 | [Tangut] 2149
?

2371 [Tangut] IX 53 [Tangut] | 2353
(a) VI 35 ditto
(b) I 101 | [Tangut] ×2361 2349
(c) III 44 | [Tangut] 1604
(d) III 92 | [Tangut] 2443
(e) V 2 | [Tangut] 2362
(f) V 54 | [Tangut] 2330
(g) V 59 | [Tangut] 4640
C.C.C. 12[a] 坡 "slope"
Note. It is difficult to distinguish
between 2370 + 2371.

2372 [Tangut] VI 78 [Tangut] "Buddhist"
C.C.C. 20[b] 21[a] 27[b] etc. + passim 法
"law"
B 344[1] sic;
Note. Also ? more correctly written [Tangut]

2373 [Tangut] IX 41 | [Tangut] 0704
(a) I 67 ditto
?

2374 2377 chain

2375–4766

2376 2506 chain

2377 | B.160' name of temple
- 0263–2263
- 3967 – 2374, 4323
- 4125

| W. I 266[21] part of royal title

國 正 'maintaining the country'

| ditto[23] 民正 " – – people'.

2378 1891 chain

2379 2381 chain

2380 3066 chain

The Tangut B.205' tr. 矯詐 feigned & deceptive

2380A 2383 pair

2381
- 0421
- 2379

2382 – 2380A

2383 – 1828

2384 – 4861

2385 – 5284

B.173' 徵 proof, evidence etc.

~~2378 1891 chain~~ B.193[5] 少 few

2386 4425 chain

2387 1781 chain

184

2374 [Tangut] III 126 [Tangut] | 3967
C.C.C. 20[a] 忠 sincerity W.I. 118[5] 直 upright B 207[3]

2375 [Tangut] VIII 2 | [Tangut] 4768
(a) V 41 ditto
?

2376 [Tangut] I A 39 [Tangut] | 2506
C.C.C. 27[b] 中 middle B. 169[5]

2377 [Tangut] [VII 59-60]
(a) III 126 | [Tangut] ×2263, 0263
(b) VII 1 | [Tangut] 4323 ×2374 3967
(c) IX 33 | [Tangut] 4125
C.C.C. 27[b] 28[b] 正 orthodox, correct B. 344[2]
W.I. 108[9] ?

2378 [Tangut] III 49 [Tangut] | 1891
(a) IX 34 | [Tangut] × 5641 5635

2379 [Tangut] VI 16 | [Tangut]

2380 [Tangut] check! 月 VI A 22 [Tangut] | false v. 3066
(i) W.I. 214[5] | [Tangut] gya. gyu intrigue I 170[8] 詐 false, deceptive.

2380A [Tangut] × of VI 102 [Tangut] |

2381 [Tangut] ?
(a) III 42 | [Tangut] 0421
(b) VI 16 | [Tangut] 2379
(i) W.I. 122[12] 離 to divi, depart
(ii) W.I. 138[10] 混 confusion, chaos. B 346 4 169[3]
Dict. 1[a] 7 B p. 387 雜 various, mixed

2382 [Tangut] VI 102 | [Tangut] cf. 3435
?

2383 [Tangut] III 16 | [Tangut] 1828
?

2384 [Tangut] VI A 36 | [Tangut] 4869 ?
(a) VI 107 ditto
C.C.C. 1[b] 3 B. 194[1] 略 outline

2385 [Tangut] III 52 | [Tangut] 5284
~~(a) I 119 ditto misspelt~~
(b) III 40 ditto
~~(c) VI A 23 | [Tangut]~~
? C.C.C. 35[a] 稀 rare B 162[1] to 熟 ripe

2386 [Tangut] VI 32 [Tangut] |
(a) I 119 ditto
(a) IX 20 | [Tangut] 3287
(b) IX 164 [Tangut] | ×2922 2919
(i) (a) above [?] B. 100 cat. under camel.

2387 [Tangut] III 53 [Tangut] | 1781
?

2389 2395 chain

2390 0214 chain

2391 2395 chain

2392 independent? or 4326 chain

2393 4326 chain

2394 0457 chain

2395
- 3782
- 2389
- 2505 – 3991
- 2530 – 0110
  - 0227
  - 1534
  - 2732
  - 3607
  - 4562
  - 2391
- 4908

B.125[3] 資 ? phon. (tzŭ)

B.188[5] 塵 dust, this world

2397 independent

2396 2968 chain

2397A v. 1203

2398 – 2408

2399 3795 chain

2400 4276 chain

2401 1597 pair

2402 5690 chain

2403 1781 chain

2404 3795 chain

2389

2390

2391

2392

2393

2394

2395

2397

2396

N.B. No. 2388.

185

2389 [Tangut] VA 134 [Tangut] [Tangut] 2395 1709
Phonetic character.

2390 [Tangut] VIII 97 [Tangut] | 0214
?

2391 [Tangut] III A 137 [Tangut] | 2530
?

2392 [Tangut] I 140 | [Tangut]
?

2393 [Tangut] IX 22 [Tangut] | 4753
?

Note. Presumably 2392 3? sh'd ent in [Tangut]

2394 [Tangut] IX 72 | [Tangut] 0457

2395 [Tangut] V 43 [Tangut] | 3782
(a) III 113 ditto
(b) I 18 [Tangut] | 4908
[(c) I 119 [Tangut] | error for 2386]
(d) V A 134 [Tangut] × by | [Tangut] v. 2389
(e) IX 16 [Tangut] | × 2530
(f) IX 29 | [Tangut] × 2505
CCC. 18a 29b 35a + passim 子 W.I. 190[5] bu 'son, child;'

2397 [Tangut] VII 91 "Family or clan name"

2396 [Tangut] VI 28 | [Tangut] 2968
?

2397 A ~~2396~~ [Tangut] Disyllable v. [Tangut] ~~not~~ Probably an error?
W. II 78[10] 愍 "to grieve" II 94[10]
~~2397 [Tangut] VI 28~~ Possibly the correct form of 1203

2398 [Tangut] See VII 25 | [Tangut]
(a) VII A 95 ditto
W. II. 10[3] 涼 "cool" 144[1]

2399 [Tangut] I 37 | [Tangut] ocean 2221
(i) The disyllable B. 102 cat. under "rivers & seas"

2400 [Tangut] I 36 [Tangut] | 4765
(a) VIII 43 [Tangut] | × 2275

2401 [Tangut] VII 25 | [Tangut] 1597
?

2402 [Tangut] VI 33 [Tangut] | 5690 divine
(W. II. 16[1]) (i) The disyllable 后 "empress"
B 279[3,4]

2403 [Tangut] VI 60 | [Tangut] 1364
?

2404 [Tangut] IX 86 | [Tangut] ocean 2221
(i) The disyllable B. 102 cat. under 'rivers & seas.'

2405 – 5242

2406
4839
4848

~~2406 4839 pair~~

2406 | [Tangut] [Tangut] ~~sems. dpa.~~

c'en.po Mahāsattva B.248[4] etc.

no.' | [Tangut] Reign period on coin. B. I

Complete; translate 大安

2407 – 0625 ~~pair~~

2408 2398 pair

2409 4276 chain

2410 ~~independent~~

2411
4842 – 2759
4843 3373

2412
1285 – 0204
1284

2413 2710 chain

2414 2360 chain

2415 – 4840

2416 – 4217

2417 independent

2418 [1182] chain

186

2405 [Tangut] III 21 | [Tangut] 5242

(a) VIII 93 ditto

2406 [Tangut] IX 58 [Tangut] |

(a) V 157 ditto but [Tangut] 4839

W.I. 92^{13} + passim 大 190^{15} 194^{2} c'en "great" mahā B.187^{5} 宏 vast, spacious

Note There is no discoverable difference between 2405 + 2406; sh^d 2406 be [Tangut]?

2407 [Tangut] III 21 | [Tangut] 0625

(a) V 79 [Tangut] x by [Tangut] [Tangut] |

A double name of a country. B.177^{1} P.N.(1)

2408 [Tangut] VII A 95 [Tangut] |

(a) VII 25 ditto

B 195^{5} 殊 Phon.

N.B. A common Phonetic.

2409 [Tangut] VII A 118 | [Tangut] 4970

2410 [Tangut] [Tangut] V 148 "Man's name"

W.I. 98^{7} ditto

2411 [Tangut] III 17 | [Tangut] 4842

(a) V 52 ditto

(b) V 47 [Tangut] | ant 4843

?

2412 [Tangut] IX 144 | [Tangut] 1285

(a) VI 124 ditto

[(b) I 118 [Tangut] x by [Tangut] |]

(c) III 42 | [Tangut] 1284

[(d) V 49 [Tangut] x by [Tangut] |]

C.C.C. 20^{b} 30^{b} W.II.52^{3} 同 "the same as, like" (takes [Tangut]). v.1956

2413 [Tangut] IX 144 | [Tangut] 3122

chala 5440

2414 [Tangut] IX 144 [Tangut] | white 2360

(a) III 9 | [Tangut] v.2640

(a) above B.102 cat. under "precious things" + translated 螺鈿 "conch shell + ..."

2415 [Tangut] I 142 | [Tangut]

(a) V 157 ditto

?

2416 [Tangut] I 142 | [Tangut] 4217

(a) VII 7 ditto

?

2417 [Tangut] IX 144 Family or clan name

2418 [Tangut] VII 111 | [Tangut] [1182]

?

2419. B246[3] [illegible] Ing. Name of country (independent)

2420 independent

2421 – 1358

2422 0463 chain

2423 3893 chain

2424 2309 chain

2425 4262 chain

2426 4064 chain 2334 q.v.

(d). B.121[1] '[illegible] 敬禮 ([illegible]) worship'

2427 – 4686 ? Double family name

187

2419 [Tangut] II 4 Family or clan name

2420 [Tangut] IX 4 Family or clan name

2421 [Tangut] VII 22 | [Tangut]

(a) I 13 ditto

?

2422 [Tangut] VII 62 [Tangut] | 0460

(a) V 109 ditto

(i) The dissyllable B.99 cat. under "sheep"

2423 [Tangut] VI 9 [Tangut] | 3893

(a) VI 56 [Tangut] | 0482

(i) C.C.C. 28b 29a 30a 判 "to cleave, separate, half". B.195[2] divide, v.S.-H.

(ii) (a) above W.I.138[2]

(iii) W.I.194[16] 214[1]?

B.179[3] 制 regulation B.346[1] W.I 265[18].

2424 [Tangut] VI 65 [Tangut] |

(a) I 71 | [Tangut] 5576

(i) The dissyllable C.C.C. 33b 馬鞭 "horse-whip"

(ii) By itself W.I.136[6] ?鞭 whip

2425 [Tangut] II 4 [Tangut] | 3445

2426 [Tangut] VII 22 [Tangut] | 4064

(a) VIII 7 ditto

(b) II 15 | [Tangut] 5533

(c) V 70 [Tangut] | ×3436 3965

(d) VI 67 | [Tangut] 4574

(e) VI 104 | [Tangut] 2431

(i) (d) above W.I.108[7] 136[15] etc. 作禮 B.128[4] to worship, reverence 198[10] p'ying hts'al "respectful greetings". Wang translates 敬 "to worship"

(ii) (e) above W.I.108[15] 禮 "to worship"

Note. 2426 appears to have 攵 as against 夂 in 2425. (a)-(e) all have 攵

2427 [Tangut] VII 22 Family or clan (name)

(a) VI 96 | [Tangut] 4686

B.p.92 [Tangut] ideogram [Tangut] ideogram. | is the name of the | family.

(a) is rather mysterious. The name may be dissyllabic.

B.169[5] tr. 折

2428 4028 pair

2436-2484

2437-3043

2428A 3303 pair

2429 3663 chain

2438 3685 chain

2430 2058 pair

2431 4064 chain

2439 4396 chain

| [Tangut] B.176^{3} 絡 燈 everlasting lamp

2432 2741 pair

2433 5486 chain

2440-3042

2434 0398 pair

2441-0359A

2435 4933 chain

188

2428 [Tangut] IX A 22 [Tangut] | ency/. 4028
(a) IX A 38 ditto

?
2428 A [Tangut] x of I 87 | [Tangut] ? 3503 ~~[illegible] 2427~~

2428 B [Tangut] error for [Tangut] 2095

2429 [Tangut] VI.9 [Tangut] | 4535
B.123[2]

2430 [Tangut] III 42 [Tangut] | 2058
(a) III A 126 ditto

2431 [Tangut] VI.104 [Tangut] | 2426
(i) The dissyllable W.I.108[15] 禮 "to worship, revere".

?
2432 [Tangut] VII A 37 [Tangut] | 2741
(a) I 78 ditto

?
2433 [Tangut] IX 64 | [Tangut] 5449
(a) V 9 [Tangut] | 1936
W.I.134[1] 哀 "to wail" (cuar) ~~[illegible]~~ ~~2103A~~

2434 [Tangut] IX 1 | [Tangut] 0398
?(a) III 134 ditto

2435 [Tangut] IX 11 [Tangut] | 4933
(a) II 32 ditto
(i) The dissyllable C.C.C.18[6] 脊 背 "spine, back".

2436 [Tangut] c VII A 67 | [Tangut] 2484
(a) IX.42 ditto (misspelt v.2058)

2437 [Tangut] V 32 | [Tangut] 3043
(a) IX 1 ditto

2438 [Tangut] IX 1 [Tangut] | "name" 3685
(a) II 1 | [Tangut] ("name"?) 4748
(b) VII 21 [Tangut] | ? 300 0300
(c) VIII 6 [Tangut] | ? 3764 bis
Dict 1[b]1
W.I.198[10] used as a phonetic B 215[1]

2439 [Tangut] IX 34 [Tangut] | 3348
(a) III 127 [Tangut] 2890
[(b) VIII 4 [Tangut] x by [Tangut] | W.II 112[4]]
(i) By itself C.C.C. 網 net W.I 192[12] 218[7] [illegible] "cord, garland".
(ii) The dissyllable C.C.C. 21[a] 瓔珞

2440 [Tangut] V 32 | [Tangut] 3042
(a) IX 1 ditto

?
2441 [Tangut] I 1 | [Tangut]
W.I.110[3] 步 pada "step, pace" passim.

2442 2485 chain

2443 5440 chain

2444 ~~0022 chain~~

take over 0022 chain

W.I.132[17] 龍 turtle

2445 5301 chain

2447 # 2485 chain

2446 2493 pair

2448. See 5376 hdao "consummated".

v. B.185[4] 倉余 (after a number) odd, + more

2448 chain
1549
3971 0222 — 0026
3977

2449 3086 chain

2449 許 to grant, permit W.II.108[3]

幾 "how many?" ~~"chance" (& other meanings W.II 138[7]~~

189

2442 [Tangut] V A 29 [Tangut]

A Phonetic character

~~2443 [Tangut] I A 93~~

2443 [Tangut] I 74 [Tangut] | 5540

(a) VI 118 ditto

(b) IX 29 [Tangut] | suddenly 4253

?

2444 [Tangut] I A 93 | [Tangut] 0022

(a) I 116 ditto

(b) IX 34 | [Tangut] 3661

(i) C.C.C. 17a 蛙 "frog" W.I. 210[1] sbal

"frog" W.I 132[17]?

(ii) ~~W.I.~~ | [Tangut] W.I. 214[7] rus. sbal

tortoise & frog? W.I. 132[16]?

2445 [Tangut] VIII 82 [Tangut] | 5301

(a) V 105 ditto

(b) I 69 | [Tangut] 3827

(c) V 40 | [Tangut] 5306

(d) V 74 | [Tangut] 2326

(e) VI 76 | [Tangut] 3633

(f) VII A 84 | [Tangut] 0429

(g) IX 6 | [Tangut] 2137 1569

(i) The dissyllable W.I. 110[18] 遊戲

vikrīḍita "play, sport."

(ii) (e) above C.C.C. 33a 打諢

"to strike..."

2447 ~~2446~~ [Tangut] V 57 [Tangut] |

(a) V 87 ditto

(i) The dissyllable C.C.C. 19a 脚脛

"leg, shin"

2446 [Tangut] ? VII 59 [Tangut] — in text

(a) VII 99 [Tangut] | 2493

?

2448 [Tangut] VI 58 | [Tangut] 1549

(a) VI 5 ditto

(b) IX 1 [Tangut] | 3971

~~(i) C.C.C. 5a 亢 "protecting (star)"~~

~~(ii)~~ (i) C.C.C. 5a 亢 W.I. 220[14]?

"powerful? (star)"

(ii) I 146[11] 度 to save, carry over B.164[2]

seems to mean 'retain'

(iii) W.I. 134[4] ~~II 4[9]~~ 脱 ~~"to escape, avoid"~~

(iv) 超 "to ~~retain~~ save" W.II 4[9]

2449 [Tangut] IX 89 [Tangut] | 3086

(a) VII 44 [Tangut] | 3267

(b) IX 179 [Tangut] | 0540

Dict 1a6

Very obscure W.I 134[4]? B.252?

(iii) (b) above 略 "sketch, summary?"

189

2450 4810 pair

2451 -0028

2452 3578 pair

2453 2353 chain

2454 ~~1848 chain~~

2455 2279 chain

2456 2492 chain

2457 4023 chain

2458 - 2480

2459 2972 chain

2460 0073 chain

2461
+1405
1687
1928 — 1927 — 0567
1428

2462 2143

2462 | as very with 朘 ~~both~~ meaning 行 W.II 92[5]

W.I.132[13] 畋 to hunt (wild animals)

W.I.134[10] ? 揮 to wield (a spear)

190

2450 [Tangut] IX 66 [Tangut] | 4810
(a) III 75 ditto
(i) Bz itself. C.C.C. 24^a 跆 "to tread on" W II 48^4 ?
階 to ascend, step up W II 142^12 stairs ?
(ii) The dissyllable W. I 134^12 踐 蹁 蹁
"to trample . . . .

2451 [Tangut] VII 112 | [Tangut] 0028
(a) I 110 ditto
(i) | [Tangut] B. p. 100 cat. under 'horse'.

2452 [Tangut] V 2 [Tangut] | 3578
(a) IX 103 ditto [[Tangut]]

2453 [Tangut] III 92 [Tangut] | 2371

2454 [Tangut] III 50 | [Tangut] 2236

2455 [Tangut] IX 24 [Tangut] | 2268

2456 [Tangut] I A 40 [Tangut] | 2492
(a) I 128 ditto
(b) IX 105 | [Tangut] ×4832 3480
?

2457 [Tangut] VII 98 [Tangut] | 2478

2458 [Tangut] VI 30 | [Tangut]
(a) V 57 ditto
?

2459 [Tangut] I 2 [Tangut] | 2972
(a) I 44 ditto
?

2460 [Tangut] VI A 112 [Tangut] | 0093
?

2461 [Tangut] VII 25 | [Tangut] 1405
(a) VI 14 ditto
(b) III 21 | [Tangut] 1928
(c) IX 50 | [Tangut] 1687
(i) The dissyllable W. I. 100^5 桎 梏
"fetters"

2462 [Tangut] VII 47 [Tangut] |
(a) V 88 [Tangut] | 1742
(b) [Tangut] | v. 1992 (4006). See I. 16, 28, 86, 90, 102 II 2, 43 III 106, 172, 178, 182 V 147, 185 VI 18, 132.
(i) Bz itself C.C.C. 21^b 27^a 行 to walk (along a road): 27^b 行 to behave? & passim. B. 193^2
(ii) The dissyllable C.C.C. 29^a 30^a 行 遣

2463 indeterminate

2464 chain
0090
2525

0090 chain

2465 1787 chain

2466
3189
3248

2467 3795 chain

2468 1821 pair

2469 2306 chain

2470 – 4044 Double family name

2471 2485 chain

2472 3417 chain

2473 – 3418

2474 3226 chain

B193 to wander

2475 2489 pair

2476 2010 pair

191

2463 [Tangut] V 15 Name of country

2464 [Tangut] VIII A 5 [Tangut] | 90
(a) VII 10 ditto
(b) VIII A 44 | [Tangut] v. 2625
C.C.C. 24ª 枕 "pillow".

2465 [Tangut] V 87 [Tangut] | 3111
?

2466 [Tangut] ?
~~(a) III 75 [Tangut]~~
(b) IX 20 | [Tangut] 3248
(c) IX 129 | [Tangut] v. 3189
?

2467 [Tangut] V A 83 [Tangut] | 5684
? B. 4. 98

2468 [Tangut] VIII 63 [Tangut] | ~~2468~~
(a) III 18 ditto v. 1821
(i) The dissyllable C.C.C. 27ª 石展 場 "threshing floor"

2469 [Tangut] V 88 [Tangut] | floor 3859

2470 [Tangut] VIII 3 Family or clan name
(a) III 42 | [Tangut] 4044
Possibly a double name. Diary. B. 174[4]

2471 [Tangut] III 3 [Tangut] | 3486
(i) C.C.C. 25ª (The dissyllable) 靴底 ? "The sole(?) of a boot"

2472 [Tangut] (Stone) VII 88 [Tangut] | 3417
(i) [Tangut] | C.C.C. 22ª 提木 "wooden pillar, or support" (?) v. 763
(ii) [Tangut] | C.C.C. 22ª 石頂 ~~stone~~ "cap stone" (?)

2473 [Tangut] III A 33 | [Tangut] 3418
(a) III A 107 ditto

2474 [Tangut] VIII 54 [Tangut] [Tangut] 2342
(a) III 51 | [Tangut] 1852
W I. 100[7] 乃 "then" 100[4] 108[17] to complete the sense. 170[16]

~~2475 [Tangut]~~
~~C.C.C. 25ª 鞋 "shoe, slipper"~~

2475 [Tangut] VIII 28 [Tangut] |
(a) I A 105 ~~[Tangut]~~ ditto
C.C.C. 25ª 鞋 "shoe, slipper"

~~2476 [Tangut] I A~~

2476 [Tangut] IX 90 [Tangut] |? owner 2010
(a) IX 59 ditto [[Tangut]]

2477 4071 chain

2482 chain linked to 2360 chain
- 2360 q.v.
- 0128 - 3606
- 0505
- 2520 - 1861, 2133, 2483
- 2660
- 2709 - 2699
- 2801 - 0594 - 0593, 1933, 1948, 2215, 4211
- 3245
- 3441
- 3475
- 4852
- 4997
- 5285

2478 4029 chain

W.I.268[8] 集 to collect B.167[1] 125[2]
W.I 270[20]

2478 B 341[3] 輯 'to compose, compile

B.189[1] 綜 total

2479 4011 chain

2479φ. 1蘶祇龐 優樓頻羅 Uruvilva W.II.4[1]

φ ii B.215[2]

φ iii B.225[3] upāsaka φ iv B.225[3] upāsikā

2483 2482 chain

2484 2436 pair

2480 2458 pair

2485 see over

2481 2521 pairs

192

2477 [Tangut] lo IX 87 | [Tangut]
A very obscure particle C.C.C. 35a
豈 how? W II 24[4] 46[3] 76[10] 84[6] I 108[10]
B.187[3] 189[2] tr. 莫 not yet, do not

2478 [Tangut] VII 63 | [Tangut] 4029
(a) V 158 | [Tangut] 1671
(b) VII 98 | [Tangut] 2457
(c) VII A 142 | [Tangut] 2679
(d) VIII 91 | [Tangut] 0730 × 0779 0727
(i) By itself B.185[3] 蘊 "to collect"
(ii) | [Tangut] W.I.194[9] ndus.pa "united."
B 167[5]

2479 [Tangut] yu VIII 3 | [Tangut] head 0887
(i) The dissyllable C.C.C. 28b 案頭
table?

2480 [Tangut] V 57 [Tangut] |
(a) VI 30 ditto
?

2481 [Tangut] IX 5 [Tangut] |
(a) I 124 ditto
?

2482 [Tangut] NYA III 138 [Tangut] | "white"
(a) I.115 ditto
(b) I 50 | [Tangut] × v. 2520
(c) I 71 [Tangut] | 4852
(d) I 97 | [Tangut] | 1447
(e) I 145 [Tangut] | 4947
(f) III 18 | [Tangut] 3245
(g) III 50 [Tangut] | 5286
(h) III 80 [Tangut] | × 2699 2709
(i) III 146 [Tangut] | 2660
(j) V 145 [Tangut] | . × 2801
(k) V 151 | [Tangut] 0505
(l) V A 40 [Tangut] | 3441
(m) VI 109 [Tangut] | 3475 × 0128 (n) IX 86 [Tangut] |
C.C.C. 8b 15a,b 17a 21b W.I. 98[3] 黑 I. 192[5]
nag.po "black"

2483 [Tangut] IX A 7 [Tangut] | 2520

2484 [Tangut] IX 42 [Tangut] | misspelt 2485

(a) VII A 67 ditto

2485 [Tangut] V 87 | [Tangut] v. shin 2447
(a) V 57 ditto
(b) I 117 | [Tangut] 1758
(c) I A 41 | [Tangut] 5319

2485
- 2447
- 0041
- 1458 – ? or 0604 chain – 0838
  - 3565
  - 4421
  - 4511
  - 5219
- 1532
- 1727 – 1732
  - 1734
- 0894
- 1758
- 2486
- 2488
- (2442)
- 2775 – 2280 n
- 2980 – 3234 – 5139 – 5138
- 3426
- 3461
- 3486 – 2471
  - 5208
- 4361
- 5319

2486 2485 chain

2487 1438 bis chain

2488 2485 chain

2489 – 2475

2490 3697A chain

2491 3697A chain

2492
└ 2456 – 3480 – 4832

2493 – 2446

2494
- 1841 – 2936
  - 3322
- 1857 – 2307 – 0116
  - 2544 – 2547
    - 2552
    - 4193
- 2962
- 3654 – q.v.
- 3821

24

c.c.c.

(ii)

2486

c.c.c.

2487

(b)

193

2485 (cont)

(d) III 54 [Tangut] x by | [Tangut] 4631 4361
(e) III 97 | [Tangut] thigh 3461
(f) V 19 | [Tangut] 0041
(g) V 21 | [Tangut] 3426
(h) V 132 | [Tangut] × 1727
(i) V A 129 [Tangut] x by | [Tangut] 2442
(j) VI 77 | [Tangut] 1532
(k) VI 105 | [Tangut] 2486 sole of foot 2486
(l) VI A 5 | [Tangut] × 2480
(m) VII 23 | [Tangut] 0894
(n) VII 39 | [Tangut] × 2775
(o) IX 111 | [Tangut] 3486
(p) IX 147 | [Tangut] ?× 1458
(q) IX A 153 | [Tangut] "hoof" v. 2488

ccc. 19a[2] W.I.136[6] 脚 "leg": W II 48[1] 足 foot or leg?

(ii) (o) above 靴 "boot"

2486 [Tangut] VI 105 [Tangut] "leg" v. 2485

ccc. 19a 根 sole of foot?

2487 [Tangut] VII A 109 [Tangut] | 4419

(b) III 169 [Tangut] | 1046

2488 [Tangut] IX A 153 [Tangut] | v. 2485

B.100 [Tangut] | cat. under "horse" & translated 白蹄 "white hoof" (2451)

2489 [Tangut] I A 105 | [Tangut] "shoe"

(a) VIII 28 ditto tr. 靴 v. 2475

(j) The disyllable B.104 cat. under "women's clothing"

2490 [Tangut] ya VIII 24 [Tangut] |

(a) VII 13 | [Tangut] ša 0243

C.35a I 132[7] etc. "ten"

2491 [Tangut] IX 38 [Tangut] | 10 0243

B.194[1]

2492 [Tangut] I 128 | [Tangut] × 2456

(a) I A 40 ditto

2493 ~~2494~~ [Tangut] VII 99 | [Tangut]

(a) VII 59 | ? (? ditto)

2494 ~~2495~~ [Tangut] I 11 | [Tangut] "root"

(a) VII 38 ditto × v. 1841
(b) III 175 | [Tangut] [3290A] × 3654
(c) VI 92 | [Tangut] 3821
(d) VIII A 74 | [Tangut] × 1857
(e) IX 43 | [Tangut]

B.187⁴ 源 source, origin

2495 5632 chain

2496 - 4190

2497 - 0191

2498 1105 chain

W.I.268[22] long phonetic string q.v.

(ii) φ.B.199[1] φ(iii) B 231[2]

2499 independent

2500 - 5354

2501 2954 chain

2502 1929 chain

2503 0959 chain

2504 4651 chain

194

2494 ~~2495~~ cont.

Corresponds to Ch. 本 in all its ("original, meanings i.e.) "this" (C.C.C. 34[a] + ? 35[b]) "root, origin" (W. I 98[10]) "tranquil"? (W. II 26[7]) W. II 38[7] 46[4]

(iii) (d) v. 1857 B. 161[1] 131[3] q.v.

(ii) The dissyllable II 18[2] 本 根 "origin, source".

2495 [Tangut] VI A III [Tangut] |

?

Note. There is no discoverable difference between 2494 + 2495. -4 is [Tangut] or even [Tangut]

2496 [Tangut] IX 9 | [Tangut] 4190

(a) I 5 | ditto [[Tangut]]

?

2497 ~~2498~~ [Tangut] VIII 62 | [Tangut] 0191

(a) IX 162 ditto

(i) The dissyllable C.C.C. 34[a] v. obscure; possibly 娶婚 "to marry a wife."

2498 [Tangut] I A 11 | [Tangut] 5059

?

Used as a Phonetic W. II 34[3] B. 215[2]

2499 ~~2500~~ [Tangut] VII 27 "Family or clan name"

B. 246[5] 竹 chuh (part of name) 126[4]

2500 [Tangut] IX 5 | [Tangut] 5354

(a) III 35 ditto

(i) The dissyllable 駱駝 C.C.C. 16[a] "camel" [both words mean 'camel']

B. 100 Chapter heading.

?

cf. 2511

2501 [Tangut] IX 21 | [Tangut] 2954

(a) VI 55 [Tangut] | 5573 ~~2954~~

(i) The dissyllable C.C.C. 29[b] ? 强 凌

W. I. 96[12] 侵 陵 "to seize + outrage" W. I. 138[1] B. 205[2]

~~(ii) By itself B. 205[2] 侵~~

2502 [Tangut] III 23 | [Tangut] 2508

(i) The dissyllable B. 99 cat. under 'sheep'.

2503 [Tangut] V 16 [Tangut] | 1637

~~2504 [Tangut] I 38 | [Tangut]~~

2503A [Tangut] Error for 2504

2504 [Tangut] [I 38 | [Tangut]]

(a) IX 143 ditto

W. I. 132[17] 204[14] ? B 171[3]

2505 2395 chain

2506
+2526
2093
2376

2507 5170 pair

2508 1929 chain

2509 1398 chain

2510 3993 chain

2511 -5362

2512 3012 pair

2513 2246 pair

2514 3354 chain

2515 1130 chain

2516 2681 pair

195

2505 [Tangut] IX 29 [Tangut] | 2395
(a) IX 36 | [Tangut] 3991
W.I.196[2] 224[13] ts'a. bo "grand-child, nephew".

2506 [Tangut] I 32 [Tangut] | 2526
(a) I A 10 ditto
(b) I A 39 | [Tangut] with 2376
(c) VIII A 1 | [Tangut] 2093
B.232[1] W.II 16[10] 境 "region, sphere".
(ii) | [Tangut] ditto W.II 2[5]

2507 [Tangut] VIII 84 [Tangut] | 5770
(a) IX 159 ditto
?

2508 [Tangut] IX 2 [Tangut] | "sheep" 1342
(a) III 23 [Tangut] | 2502
(i) (a) above B. 99 cat. under "sheep"

2509 [Tangut] IX 178 | [Tangut] 5400
B 125[5] [[Tangut]] 195[5]
Frequently used as Phonetic.

2510 [Tangut] V 25 [Tangut] |
(a) VII 52 ditto
(b) VII 84 [Tangut] | 4477
W.I.222[17]
B.125[3] as 機 ? phonetic K1. 126[1]

2511 [Tangut] IX 5 | [Tangut]
(a) III 35 ditto

2512 [Tangut] IX 8 [Tangut] 3012 | q. 2510 [Tangut]
(a) IX 126 ditto

2513 [Tangut] Ne III 38 [Tangut] | "thou"
(a) III 46 ditto v. 2246
C.C.C. 32[a] W.I.134[13] 204[13,14] 208[7] II 206[8]
II 82[5] B.125[2]
Obscure. Possibly "thou" in imperat. verbs. (thou)
W.I.170[13]?

2514 [Tangut] VI A 125 | [Tangut] 2885
(i) The disyllable C.C.C.16[b] 老鼠 "old rat"

2515 [Tangut] VII 26 [Tangut] | "star" 1130
(a) V 72 [Tangut] | 2678
C.C.C.8[a] 參 name of star 'Orion'
W.I.220[9] lag. ditto | [Tangut] 5207

2516 [Tangut] V 141 [Tangut] | 2081
(a) IX 104 ditto

2517–2329 double family name

2518 0680 chain

2519
- 0311
  - 0321
  - 2075
- 0693
  - 0690
  - 4543
  - 5109
  - 5189
- 1262
  - 1263
  - 1331
- 2008
- 3644

2520 2482 chain

2521–2481

2

2522–4420 double family name

2523 5678 chain

2524
- 2893
- 5614

2525 0031 pair

196

2517 [Tangut] I 52 | [Tangut] 2329

?

2518 [Tangut] I 89 | [Tangut] 0680

(a) VI 10 [Tangut] | 0834

Dict. 1a 3 0366

2519 [Tangut] ~~VI~~ V 42 | [Tangut]

(a) VI 66 ditto x0311

(b) IV A 2 | [Tangut] impure x1262

(c) V A 133 [Tangut] x by | [Tangut] NYIN 3644

(d) VI A 14 [Tangut] | 2008

(e) IX 4 [Tangut] | vinegar (?) x0693

(i) By itself C.C.C. 4b 清 "pure" B. 228

(ii) The dissyllable W. I 100 116 II 2 5,9

清 淨 "pure"

2520 [Tangut] I 50 [Tangut] | "black" 2482

(a) I 31 [Tangut] | 2135

(b) VI 101 [Tangut] | 1861 ?

(c) IX A [Tangut] 2483

?

2521 [Tangut] I 124 | [Tangut] 2481

(a) IX 5 ditto

Dissyl. B. 188 宛 然 as if, same as, as it were.

2522 [Tangut] yin VIII A 25 Family or clan name

(a) III A 108 [Tangut] x by [Tangut] | NYIN 4894

(b) V 116 | [Tangut] Yinki 4420

(c) V A 133 [Tangut] x by [Tangut] | NYIN 3644

(i) | [Tangut] B. 186 天 竺 "India"

(ii) ? corrupt W. I 174 進 (iii) B 177 part of ? P.N.

2523 [Tangut] NA III 121 | [Tangut] "the" "that"

(a) III 48 | [Tangut] "place" 3574

(b) V 35 | [Tangut] "I" x3983

(c) VI 20 | [Tangut] 2932

(d) VIII 11 | [Tangut] "in" ?x5624

~~(e) IX 7 | [Tangut]~~

(e) IX 74 | [Tangut] "although" 5642

(i) (b) above 是 我 "I myself" W. I. 158 8 so translates 'you', 'thou'

Note. Used as a Phonetic W. I 190 17 210 1

2524 [Tangut] I 34 | [Tangut] v. 2893

(a) IX 7 ditto

(b) VII 111 | [Tangut] 5614

See also 2533.

~~2525 [Tangut] I A 10~~

~~(a) I 32~~

2525 [Tangut] I 72 [Tangut] | 31 (to where)

(a) I A 28 ditto

?

2525A [Tangut] x of V 66 [Tangut] "sky" error for 2527

2526 2506 chain

2527 | 𗀀 Regnal period on coin, (+ seal.)

B. Coin plate; translated 天祐

CCC1.6. (Date of preface 21st year) trans.

2527 5690 chain

2528 4079 chain

2529 independent

2530 2395 chain

B.176[5], 177[1] (part of P.N.

2531 chain
0069
0367

2532 0254 pair

2533 -2647

2534 4775 chain

2535 1426 chain

2536 -11514

2537 4775 chain

2538 W II 144' (doubtful) 消 to melt

2538 - 4860

2539 - 4218

2529A [Tangut] W.I.132[16] 綱網 net

197

2526 [Tangut] I A 10 [Tangut] | region

(a) I 32 ditto

W.I.192[1] sgrog to call out, make a noise.

2527 [Tangut] ts'yu VI 104 | [Tangut] 5690

(a) V 12 ditto

(b) VI 66 而部 v. 2525A sky 2356

(c) IX 104 | [Tangut] 0370

C.C.C. 4[a] 10[a] 乾 "celestial"

C.C.C. 7[b] 天 "heavenly"

2528 [Tangut] VI 104 | [Tangut]

2529 [Tangut] I 35 Family or clan name.

2530 [Tangut] IX 16 | [Tangut] "son" v. 2395

(a) I 59 [Tangut] | 3607

(b) II 33 | [Tangut] 4562

(bb) III A 137 2391

(c) V 48 [Tangut] | 1534

(f) V 98 [Tangut] | 0110

(g) V 182 [Tangut] | 0227

(h) VIII 88 [Tangut] | 2732

C.C.C. 20[b] 34[a] 男 "male". B.174[5]

2531 [Tangut] VII 109 | [Tangut] "to meet".

(a) I A 107 ditto v. 69

(b) III 97 | [Tangut] 367 to meet

?

2532 [Tangut] I 34 [Tangut] | 0254

(a) V 4 ditto

C.C.C. 10[a] 11[b] 坤 'earth' (as opposed to 'heaven')

2533 [Tangut] IX 21 | [Tangut]

(a) II 1 ditto v. 2647

?

N.B. misspelt in IX 21 with [Tangut]

2534 [Tangut] IX 21 | [Tangut] 2657

2535 [Tangut] VI 51 [Tangut] | 5657

(a) IX A 102 | [Tangut]

(i) | [Tangut] B.101 eat. and? wild animals.

2536 [Tangut] VII 8 | [Tangut]

(a) VI 35 ditto

?

2537 [Tangut] I 35 × by [Tangut] | 4775

?

2538 [Tangut] V 104 | [Tangut] 4860 ~~477~~

(a) V 33 ditto (both [Tangut])

~~B.221[2] 蝗 'locust'~~

2539 [Tangut] VI 51 | [Tangut] 4218

(a) VIII 17 ditto

cont.

2540 3761 chain

2541 2581 chain

2542 3086 chain
B 227[4]
W.II 144[1] (takes 俳中) B.200[3] s.v.
B.187[5] 入 'entry' B207[3,4] 納 'receive'

2543 0148 chain

2544 ~~2306~~ 2494 chain

~~2555 0036 chain~~

2545 -2762

2546 1914 chain

2547 ~~2306~~ 2494 chain

2548 3783 chain

2549 3086

2550 2969 chain

2551 0582 chain

2552 ~~2306~~ 2494 chain

2553 4868 chain

2554 -2745 A

2555 0036 chain

2556 3783 chain

198

2539 (cont.)

(i) The Nasyllable W.I.134[16]?

B 221[2] 蝗蟲 locust

Note. The difference between 2538 + 2539 is obscure.

2540 IX 57 | 2581

2541 IX 57 | 2581

(a) IX 95. |

?

2542 VIII 84 | 9941

W.I.100[14] 150[17] etc 入 208[10] ʒugo.pa 208[12] njug. "to enter". [takes II 86[10]]

2543 V A 120 | 5159

(a) I A 66 | 3072

?

2544 VI 82 | "rug" v. 2307

(a) I 55 | 4193

(b) VIII 84 | 2547

(c) IX 88 | 2552

C.C.C. 23[a] 25[a] 毛氈 (house) rug; felt (hat).

2545 VI 82 |

(a) VI 43 ditto

?

2546 V 140 | 2786

(a) VIII A 72 | ? 2088

?

2547 VIII 84 | v. 2544

?

2548 VII 50 | 3783

2549 V 163 | 4604

2550 VIII 88 | 3038

(a) IX 178 | 1407

2551 I 17 | 3692

2552 IX 88 | v. 2544

2553 III A 79 |

2554 VI 30 |

2555 VII A 105 | 0039

2556 I A 74

A Phonetic character.

198

2557 0148 chain

2558–5348 Double family name :
B.125³ tr. 惺 ?prom.

2559 2989 chain

2560 2027 chain

2561 5792 pair

2562
⊥ 2602 – 2592
– 3871
– 5549

2563 2577 pair

2564 4208 chain

2565
⊥ 2590–2610

2566 (ii) The disyllable 醜陋 "hideous, ugly" W I 170 16 10

2566 3282 chain

2567 3596 chain

2568 2601 chain

2569
– 1592
– 1612
– 1628
– [5461]

2570 – 2579

2571 – 3274 A

φi B.226¹ ganthava

199

2557 [Tangut] V.163 [Tangut] | 1440

2558 [Tangut] VI 30 Family or clan name
(a) I 64 | [Tangut]
Presumably a double name B.176[5] part of P.N.

2559 [Tangut] VIII A 41 | [Tangut] 5157
(a) III 177 | [Tangut] 4969

2560 [Tangut] VI 30 | [Tangut]? 2027

2561 [Tangut] VI 61 [Tangut] |
(a) VI 32 ditto

2562 [Tangut] VI 11 | [Tangut] "liver"
(a) VI 24 ditto
C.C.C. 18[b] 肺 "lungs"

2563 [Tangut] VIII 1 [Tangut] |
(a) V 70 ditto v. 2577

2564 [Tangut] IX 17 | [Tangut] bone 4208

2565 [Tangut] III A 38 | [Tangut]
(a) I 8 ditto v. 2590

2566 [Tangut] V A 26 [Tangut] |
(a) VII 69 ditto
(b) I 67 | [Tangut] 4001

2567 [Tangut] II 4 | [Tangut] 3439
(i) The dissyllable C.C.C. 30[a] [Tangut] 蹤迹 "foot-print" [both words]

2568 [Tangut] VI 20 [Tangut] | v. 2601

2569 [Tangut] I 36 | [Tangut] misspelt
(a) I 22 | [Tangut] 1612
(b) I 119 | [Tangut] ditto 1592
(c) III 129 [Tangut] |
(d) VI 29 | [Tangut] 1628
C.C.C. 19[b] 瘡 "ulcer" W.I.198[3,4]
(ii) (d) above W.I.198[3]

2570 [Tangut] VII 111 | [Tangut] [misspelt]
(a) IX 78 ditto v. 2579
(i) The dissyllable [Tangut] C.C.C. 19[b]

2571 [Tangut] V 39 [Tangut] |
[Tangut]?
Used as Phonetic W.II 4[2]

2572 0959 chain

2573 -2261

2574 2179 chain

2575 0127 pair

2576 interpretant

2577 -2563

2578 4227 chain

2579 2570 pair

2580 2594 pair

2581
- 0806
- 2541 - 2224
- 2582
- 2587

2582 2581 chain

2583 0271 chain

2584 2635 chain

2585 1984 pair

2586 2596 chain

200

2572 [Tangut] VI 25 [Tangut] | "urine" v. 2604

?

2573 [Tangut] I 44 | [Tangut]

(a) III 44 ditto

W.I. 218' hgram.pa "cheek"

2574 [Tangut] ŠWA VII A 129 Sacred word ~~sound~~

v. 2179

2575 [Tangut] IX 125 [Tangut] | 0127

(a) IX 93 ditto (variant form see 0127)

?

2576 [Tangut] IX A 91 × by self | [|]

?

2577 [Tangut] V 70 | [Tangut]

(a) VIII 1 ditto v. 2563

?

2578 [Tangut] IX 124 | [Tangut]

?

2579 [Tangut] IX 78 [Tangut] |

(a) VII 11 ditto v. 2570

(i) The dissyllable C.C.C. 19b [Tangut]

2580 [Tangut] V 29 [Tangut] |

(a) I 17 ditto v. 2594

?

2581 [Tangut] VI A 101 [Tangut] |

(a) III A 60 ditto reversed

(b) II A 27 | [Tangut] v. 2582

(c) VI A 94 [Tangut] | v. 2587

(d) IX 57 | [Tangut] × 2224 2591

W.I. 100[14] 臭 "to stink 212[17] 218[15]"

srul.po "putrid"

2582 [Tangut] II A 27 [Tangut] "putrid" v. 2581

?

2583 [Tangut] III 16 [Tangut] | "ear" 0271

(a) III 98 ditto v. 271

(b) IX 70 | [Tangut] 1151

(c) IX A 37 | [Tangut] q.v. 2911

C.C.C. 18a W.I. 98[7] 鼻 "nose"

2584 [Tangut] IX 125 | [Tangut] 1477

(i) | [Tangut] C.C.C. 33b 攀胃鞦 "stomach encircling girth"?

2585 [Tangut] VI A 96 [Tangut] |? 1984

(a) I 27 ditto (misspelt)

Nevski I 450 [Tangut]

2586 [Tangut] IX 125 [Tangut] | 3308

(i) | [Tangut] B.100 cat. under "horse"

2587 2581 chain

2588 4005 chain

2589 2603 chain

2590 2565 chain

2591 5356 chain

2592 2562 chain

2593
┬ 5590
└ 1442

2594 - 2580

2595 1992 chain

2596 chain
└ 4159 - 3308 ┬ 0055 - 0987
├ 2586 ┐ 4482
└ 4586

2597 1426 chain

2598 - ~~2599~~ 2608

2599 - 2609 ~~2598 ...~~

2600 - 3163
~~└ 3165 - 4666~~

2601
┬ 5197 ┬ 1052
├ 2568 └ 4606 ~~...~~
└ 5177 └ 3451

201

2587 [Tangut] VIA94 | [Tangut] "putrid" v. 2581

?

2588 [Tangut] III 29 [Tangut] |

(a) III 165 ditto but [Tangut]

?

Note. The final element must be [Tangut]

2589 [Tangut] VII 10 [Tangut] [Tangut]

?

2590 [Tangut] I 8 [Tangut] | 2565

(a) III A 38 ditto

(b) IX A164 [Tangut] | 2610

Nevski I 448 "penis"

2591 [Tangut] I.141 [Tangut] |

~~C.C.C. 18[6] 肋 W.I. 216[15] "logs" "ribs"~~

?

2592 [Tangut] I A53 | [Tangut] "liver" v. 2603

C.C.C. 18[6] 脾 "spleen, stomach"

2593 [Tangut] I 17 | [Tangut] 5590

(a) VII 33 ditto

(b) VII 42 | [Tangut] 1442

?

2594 [Tangut] I 17 | [Tangut]

(a) V 29 ditto v. 2580

?

2595 [Tangut] I 16 [Tangut] [Tangut] not to go. below 1992

?

2596 [Tangut] [VII 59.60]

(a) I 70 [Tangut] | 4159

C.C.C. 18[6] 肋 W.I. 216[15] "logs" "ribs"

2597 [Tangut] III 32 [Tangut] | 1426

(a) V 130 ditto

Nevski I 449 penis

2598 [Tangut] IX 91 | [Tangut] 2608

(a) I 41 ditto

? cf. 2599

~~2599 [Tangut] V~~

2599 [Tangut] IX 91 ~~I 41~~ | [Tangut] 2609

(a) I 41 ~~IX 91~~ ditto

? cf. 2598

2600 [Tangut] V 109 | [Tangut] 3165

(a) V A17 ditto

?

2601 [Tangut] I 80 | [Tangut] 5197

(a) VI 2 ditto

(b) III 74 | [Tangut] 5177

(c) VI 20 | [Tangut] v. 2568

~~(d) VII 6~~ ~~25~~

W.I. 216[6] nay "pus" 170[3] 膿 ditto

2603 4026 2589

2608 2598 pair

2609 2599 pair

2602 2562 chain

2610 2565 chain

2611 5468 chain

2612 4059 chain

2604 0959 chain

2613 4278 pair

2605 1449 chain

2606 2710 chain

2614 chain 2607 0095

2607 2614 chain

202

2603 [Tangut] VI 74 | [Tangut] 4026

(a) IX 44 ditto

(b) VII 10 [Tangut] × by | [Tangut] 2589 ?

?

~~2603 [Tangut] I 102~~

2602 [Tangut] VI 24 [Tangut] | "lungs"

(a) VI 11 ditto v. 2562

(b) I A 53 [Tangut] | "spleen, stomach" v. 2592 ?

(c) V 122 | [Tangut] 5549

(d) V A 22 [Tangut] × by | [Tangut] ← 5623 3871 ?

C.C.C. 18[b] 肝 "liver"

2604 [Tangut] I 102 [Tangut] | 2135

(a) V 78 [Tangut] 5715 ?

(b) VI 25 | [Tangut] v. 2572

W.I. 216[6] gcin "urine" II 68[2] ?

B. 128[1]

2605 [Tangut] IX 141 [Tangut] | flesh 1449

chain 1449

2606 [Tangut] VII 116 [Tangut] | foot 5440

2607 [Tangut] IX 141 | [Tangut] [misspelt]

(a) IX A 89 | [Tangut]

?

2608 [Tangut] I 41 [Tangut] |

(a) IX 91 ditto v. 2598

cf. 2608

2609 [Tangut] I 41 [Tangut] |

(a) IX 91 ditto v. 2599

cf. 2608

2610 [Tangut] IX A 164 [Tangut] | 2590

2611 [Tangut] V 16 [Tangut] | 5468

2612 [Tangut] VII 74 [Tangut] |

~~(a) VII 11~~

2613 [Tangut] VII 74 [Tangut] | 4278

(a) VII 11 ditto

(i) By itself W.I. 134[16] [Tangut] "locust"

(ii) The disyllable C.C.C. 17[b] [Tangut] [Tangut] "locust" (in both cases)

2614 [Tangut] IX A 89 [Tangut] | 2607

(a) IX 141 ditto

(b) III 85 [Tangut] | 6095

(i) | [Tangut] W.I. 198[3] g.ya.ba "infectious ulcer"

[2615] 4011 chain

[2616] -0805

[2617]-[1719]

2618 - 5178

2619 3918 chain

2620 3226 chain Properly [Tangut character] W.I 266[19]

2621 1438 bis chain

2622 1781 chain

2623 5336 chain

2624 2464 chain

2625 3918 chain

[2625] (ii) The dissyllable, see [Tangut character]

2626 2285 chain

2627 3597 chain

2628 5623 chain

2629 - 4099

2615 IX 104 |

?

2616 VIII 19 | 0805

(a) IX 41 ditto

2617 VIII 19 | 1719

(a) V 12 ditto

?

2618 V 106 | 5178

(a) V A 97 ditto

?

2619 IX 104 |

?

2620 I 29 | 2342

W. II 2³ 序 "preface"

2621 VI 5 | 3555

B.90 " minus , | is the word for nails of the feet & hands".

(i) By itself W. I. 194⁷ sen.mo "nail"

(ii) | c.c.c. 19ª 指爪 "finger nails"

2622. VI 34 | 5691

(a) VI A 61 | 0824

?

2626A B. 227⁵ 231⁵ 形 error for 2237

203

2623 IX 109 | 2645

(i) The dissyllable C.C.C. 25ᵇ 木梳 "wooden comb".

2624 VIII A 44 | "pillow" 2464

?

Error 2625 IX 75 | 3915 Right form 2791 A

(a) V 181 ditto []

C.C.C. 19ª 病 "disease" [] N.B. probably right

2626 VI 6 | 2285

(a) VI 36 ditto

[(b) V 141 x by the dissyllable]

?

2627 IX 115 | 3597

(a) I 17 ditto

(b) IX 49 | 4897

(i) (b) above W. I. 226⁴ tyis.pa "child"

W. II 10⁷ 42¹² etc. 童子 "youth" kumāra

2628 IX 112 | 4034

?

2629 IX 115 | 4099

(a) I 36 ditto

?

2630 0673 chain

2631 3226 chain

2632 independent

2633 chain 1929 ~~1997~~

2634 -3617

2635
- 2013 – 1479 – 2584
- 1030 – 3278 – 3369
- 1647 – 3320 – 3523 – 0144, 0789, 3281
- 4780 – 4343 – 3994 – 3152, 4015

2636 1626 chain

2637 1113 chain

2638 4011 chain

2639 5356 chain

2640 2360 chain

2641 2278 chain

2642 2278 chain

204

2630 [Tangut] VIII 45 | [Tangut] 0673
(a) VII 70 ditto [illegible]
(b) III 157 [Tangut] | 5706
?

2631 [Tangut] VII A 86 [Tangut] | word 3226
?

2632 [Tangut] III 48 x by itself | [Tangut]
W.I 94[1] 差 "different" II 42[10] 50[8] 偏
"biassed, partial" II 52[5] 異 "different"
104[8] do. C.C.C. 1a5 殊 "different"

2633 [Tangut] IX 71 [Tangut] | sinews 1997
?

2634 [Tangut] VII 31 | [Tangut]
(a) VII 19 ditto
C.C.C. 5b 7a 女 "woman" name of a constellation W.I 222[2] byi. bžin ditto.

2635 [Tangut] V 9 [Tangut] [Tangut] "and"
(a) III 145 ditto v. 2013
(b) II 12 | [Tangut] 4780
(c) III 169 | [Tangut] 1030
(d) IX 41 | [Tangut] 1647 ~~2636~~
?

2636 [Tangut] VI 1 [Tangut] |
(a) I 120 ditto v. 1626
(i) The dissyllable W.I. 108[5] 誹 謗
II. 76[8] do.: II 34[2] 謗 毀 "slander, defamation"

2637 ~~2638~~ [Tangut] IX 115 | [Tangut] mother 1113
(a) IX 112 [Tangut] | 3181
B. 124[4] B. 193[1] tr. 國

2638 [Tangut] III 161 [Tangut] | head 4011
?
4011 chain

2638A [Tangut] Probably error for [Tangut] 1586

2639 ~~2640~~ [Tangut] III 82 [Tangut] | 5356
C.C.C. 19a 臍 "navel"

2640 [Tangut] III 9 [Tangut] | v. 2414
The dissyllable B. 102 cat. under "precious things" & translated 螺 珊 "conch shell & ...."

2641 ~~2642~~ [Tangut] V 17 [Tangut] | 2642
B. 181[2] 幹 "to manage, ability"

2642 [Tangut] III 9 | [Tangut] 2308
(a) V 17 | [Tangut] 2641
(b) V 155 | [Tangut] 5275
(i) | [Tangut] W.I. 190[10] snin. po "quintessence"
(ii) By itself B. 215[1] 蕊 bud

2643 0133 chain

2644 1690 chain II 76[8] etc.: II 54[2]

2645 5336 chain

2645 | [Tangut] B.104 cat. under 'woman's clothing'

B.193[4] 梓 to print?

2646 4011 chain

2646 v. 3945

2647 2533 pair

2648 3328 pair

2649 上 3837-3914

2650 3905 chain

2651 4889 chain

2652 2652 0950

2653 4775 chain

2654 4439 chain

2655 4011 chain

2656 4775 chain

2657 4775 chain

205

0133 · 1694

2643 [Tangut] III 82 [Tangut] [Tangut] 0133

~~(a) I 46 [Tangut] | [[Tangut]] ? error for 2644~~

?

2644 [Tangut] III 82 [Tangut] | [misspell] 1690

(a) I 46 [Tangut] | [[Tangut]] i.e. ditto ? ~~See 2643 (a)~~ ?

2645 [Tangut] VIII 19 | [Tangut] 5340

(a) IX 104 | [Tangut] v. 2623

(i) (a) above C.C.C. 25[b] 木 梳 "wooden comb"

B. 104 cat. under "woman's clothing."

2646 [Tangut] VII 42 [Tangut] | 4011

(a) I 92 [Tangut] | ? 1763

W.I. 208[14] 214[10] 216[14] 218[5] "rtse" peak, summit. B. 186 終 "end, whole" 4011 chain

2646 A [Tangut] X of VIII 24 [Tangut] |

? Error for 2665 ~~or 2718~~

2647 [Tangut] II 1 [Tangut] |

(a) IX 21 ditto v. 2533

2648 [Tangut] II 9 [Tangut] |

(a) V 10 ditto

2649 [Tangut] V 43 | [Tangut]

(a) III 113 ditto

(W II 35?) (i) The disyllable 時 乃 "then"

2650 [Tangut] IX 44 | [Tangut] 3405

B. 181[3] 特 "special" ? 192[4]

2651 [Tangut] II 1 | [Tangut] 1590

?

2652 [Tangut] IX 3 [Tangut] | 950

(a) ? IX 71 ditto × (2064) etc. 0295

(a) VII 41 [Tangut] |

(b) VIII 19 [Tangut] | 3564

(i) (a) above W.I. 96[11] 138[5]

By itself B. 193[1] tr. 含 ?

See 792 A

2653 [Tangut] VII A 79 [Tangut] | 5174 B

2654 [Tangut] I 23 | [Tangut] 1082

2655 [Tangut] I 23 [Tangut] | first born 1103

4011 chain

2655 A [Tangut] ~~[IX gap?]~~

Error for 2652 C.C.C. 33[b]

2656 [Tangut] VIII A 57 [Tangut] | 2857

2657 [Tangut] II 1 [Tangut] | 4775 3581 ~~3405~~

(a) I 65 [Tangut] | ×× 5429 × 3067

(b) III 44 [Tangut] | [Tangut] 3068 × 3435

(c) IV 1 | [Tangut] 2661

2661 4775 chain

2662
- 3612-0220
- 0608
- 1568
- 3224
- 3669

W.I.132[14] specifically 鷹 a hunting hawk

2663
3226 chain

2664 5465 chain

2658
- 1905
- 0393

2665 3785 chain

2659 ≠ 2770 chain

2666 2771 chain

2660 2482 chain

2657

2657 (cont)

(d) VI 18 | [Tangut] 4784

(e) VI 35 [Tangut] | 3826

(f) VII 18 [Tangut] | 'wren' 3614

(g) VIII A 57 | [Tangut] 2656

(h) IX 21 [Tangut] | 2534

(i) IX 57 | [Tangut] 0419

(j) IX 77 [Tangut] | 3405

(i) The ordinary word for "bird".

CCC. 6b 雀 W.II 46 8 鳥

(ii) The disyllable CCC. 16b 飛 禽 "flying bird"

(iii) | [Tangut] CCC. 16b 鷹 鵰 'eagle' (in both cases)

(iv) (d) above CCC. 17a 雀子 "sparrow" ?

2658 [Tangut] II 1 | [Tangut] 1905

(a) I. 61 ditto

(b) V 108 [Tangut] | 0393

?

2659 [Tangut] II 1 [Tangut] | 2770

(a) III 99 ditto

?

2660 [Tangut] III 146 | [Tangut] 2482

?

206

2661 [Tangut] IV 1 | [Tangut] "bird" 2657

(a) VI 10 | [Tangut] 2435

Phonetic ... 2669

2662 [Tangut] V A 66 [Tangut] | 3612

(a) IX 75 ditto q.v. for disyl.

(b) I 122 [Tangut] | to surpass victory 3224

(c) IX 17 [Tangut] | 0608

(d) IX 31 [Tangut] | 3669

(e) IX A 21 | [Tangut] 1568 2662

(i) W. I. 98 10 更 "more"

(ii) (b) above II 16 7 26 12 44 10 殊 [or 最] 勝 "very rare, extraordinary"

B. 168 3

2663 [Tangut] III 25 [Tangut] | 5040

2664 [Tangut] II 1 [Tangut] | 5465

(a) I. 6 ditto

?

2665 [Tangut] II 14 [Tangut] |

(a) VII 52 ditto

(b) VIII 24 [Tangut] |

?

2666 [Tangut] V A 131 [Tangut]

A Phonetic character Nan

2667 4027 chain

2668 3761 chain

2669 4027 chain

2670 – 5695

2671 – 2666 <u>not</u> a pair

2672 0092 chain

2673 1431 chain

2674 [0773] pair

2675 4029 chain

2676 1593 pair

2677 2754 chain

2678 1130 chain

2679 4023 chain

Reverse to 4030

2680 chain
- 4030 ~~[illegible]~~
- 2344
  - 5005 – 3178
  - 5489
- 3100 – 3311 – 4126
- 5512

2681 – 2516

207

2667 [Tangut] IX 98 [Tangut] | 4027

?

2668 [Tangut] nyu V 99 | [Tangut] 3843 ?

?

2669 [Tangut] K'e V 21 [Tangut] | 4027

?

2670 [Tangut] K'e V 21 | [Tangut]

(a) VIII 6 ditto

?

2671 [Tangut] nyu V 99 "Family or clan name"

(a) V A 131 [Tangut] × by | [Tangut]

2672 [Tangut] nyu V 99 | [Tangut] 92 to 90

?

2673 [Tangut] VI 2 | [Tangut] year 1431

(i) The dissyllable C.C.C. 11[a] 來年 "the coming year".

1431 chain

2674 [Tangut] VII 113 [Tangut] |

(a) V 32 ditto

C.C.C. 26[a] The dissyllable reversed 刻 义 "knife? & fork"

2675 [Tangut] I A 65 | [Tangut]

?

2676 [Tangut] IX 104 [Tangut] | 1593

(a) I 44 ditto

2677 [Tangut] VII 99 | [Tangut] 1065

2678 [Tangut] V 72 | [Tangut] "Orion" 2515

(a) IX 93 | [Tangut] "north"

2679 [Tangut] VII A 142 [Tangut] | 2478

2680 [Tangut] VI 91 [Tangut] | learn 4030

(a) VIII A 19 ditto

(b) VI 7 [Tangut] | 2344 q.v.

(c) VI 107 [Tangut] | ? 5512

(d) VI A 10 [Tangut] | 3100 cf. 2682

(i) By itself W.I 184[8] II 6[6] 教 "to teach" W.I 110[4] 化 "to change, improve". B.187[1] B 193[2]

(ii) The dissyllable C.C.C. 19[6] 教習 "to teach the practice of"

(common) 266[4] B 231[2]

(iii) [Tangut] W.I. 96[10] 弟子 "disciple"

2681 [Tangut] IX 104 [Tangut]

(a) V 141 ditto v. 2516

The name of a constellation.

C.C.C. 5[6] 房 8[a] 人 W.I. 222[1] tha nts'ams

2682 4164 ~~4030~~ chain

2691 intelligent(?)

2692 - 2218 ?

2683 - 4035

2693 3335 chain

2684 0304 chain

2685 0731 chain

2694 1182 chain

2686 4651 chain

2687 1398 chain

2687 (ii) The Hsia-yü 强盛 "powerful" cf. 4397

W.II 130^8.

W.II 130^3 益 'to increase'

2688 interpolated(?)

2695 2716 chain

2689 3685 chain

2690 3443 chain

2690 逝 "to pass away W.II 124^{10}

2696 2716 chain

208

| 𗀀

2682 [Tangut] VI 91 [Tangut] | 4313 4030

W.I. 94² 師 II 6⁶ 40³ do. I 224⁷ bšes

"teacher". B 344¹

cf. 2680

2683 [Tangut] V 2 | [Tangut] 4305

(a) VIII 84 ditto

?

2684 [Tangut] VIII 10 [Tangut] | 1775

2685 [Tangut] I 9 | [Tangut] "wood, tree"

C.C.C. 21ᵃ 檀 sandal-wood.

2686 [Tangut] II 44 [Tangut] "country"

?

2687 [Tangut] IX 92 [Tangut] | 5400 ~~2687~~

(a) I A 83 [Tangut] | 2014

(b) V A 117 | [Tangut] 1769

~~(i) | [Tangut]~~ W.I. 98¹⁰ 增 190¹⁰ 194⁷ 224¹⁷ np'el "to increase".

2688 [Tangut] II 2 Family or clan name

2689 [Tangut] I 62 [Tangut] | 1868

?

2690 [Tangut] I 61 [Tangut] | 3443

(a) II 3 [Tangut] | 4043

| [Tangut] C.C.C. 6ᵃ 驛馬 "postal horse"

Name of a constellation.

B. 174³ do. 官

2691 [Tangut] I 61. Family or clan name.

2692 [Tangut] VIII 16 | [Tangut] 2218

(a) VIII 57 ditto

cf 2703

2693 [Tangut] VI 11 [Tangut] | 3335 "tree"

(a) VII 33 [Tangut] × by disyllable

C.C.C. 9ᵃ 秋 W.I. 196⁴ 226¹¹ ston "autumn" B 172³

2694 [Tangut] I. 134 [Tangut] | [1182]

(a) IX 53 ditto

(b) V A 101 [Tangut] | 5307

(i) [Tangut] | C.C.C. 15ᵃ 韭 "leek"

(ii) [Tangut] | C.C.C. 15ᵇ 蓽豆 . . . "beans" B. 101. cat. under grain

(iii) [Tangut] | C.C.C. 32ᵇ 箄 策

2695 [Tangut] V 78 [Tangut] |

(a) ditto V 137

(b) VI 18 [Tangut] | 2715

C.C.C. 15ᵇ 床 'B 101 The first, cat. under "grain"

2696 [Tangut] IX A 113 [Tangut] |

C.C.C. 15ᵇ 朮 glutinous grain

(ii) | [Tangut] cat. under "grain"

2697 2710 chain

2704 (4215)
L 2841 – 3767

2698 3587 chain

2699 2482 chain

2706 5623 chain

2705 2716 chain

2700 2710 chain

2701 3416 pair

2707
[2708, 1799, 4469]

2702 2710 chain

[Tangut] B.177³ cn. 廣

2703 | [Tangut] [Tangut] 瑜繕那 yojana

2708 2707 chain

W II 114⁸

2703
⊥ 2226 [1945 [1804 – 1799 – 3250; 1946]; 4300; ~~4325~~]

2709 2482 chain

209

2697 [Tangut] IX 34 [Tangut] | 2710
(a) III 103 | [Tangut] 2717
?

2698 [Tangut] V 134 [Tangut] | 5131
?

2699 [Tangut] V 2 [Tangut] | 2709
(i) | [Tangut] B.101 cat. under "grain"

2700 [Tangut] VIII 74 [Tangut] | 2710
(i) C.C.C. 15b 蕎麥 "buck wheat"
(ii) [Tangut] | B.101 cat. under "grain."

2701 [Tangut] VIII 74 [Tangut] |
(a) III 159 ditto
?

2702 [Tangut] IX A 114 [Tangut] | 2710
(a) IX 75 | [Tangut] 4375
(i) ~~The Dissyllable~~ (a) above C.C.C. 26b 子樓

2703 [Tangut] YU VIII 16 | [Tangut] 2226
(a) VIII 57 ditto
cf. 2692

Note. Used as a Phonetic W.II 22[7]
(iii) | [Tangut] C.C.C. 15b 豌豆 "beans"
(i) ~~(iii) The~~ Dissyllable C.C.C. 15b 黑豆 "black beans"

2704 [Tangut] (IX gap)
(a) VII 3 [Tangut] |
(i) C.C.C. 15b 麥 "wheat"
(ii) (a) above. B.101 cat. under "grain".

2706 [Tangut] IX 57 | [Tangut] 2713

2705 [Tangut] VII A 87 [Tangut] | "rice" 5235
C.C.C. 15b 麥麵 (a) flour W.I 134[18] (?) 138[11]
穀 "grain"
~~Note. There seems to be no doubt of the existence of this character~~

2706A [Tangut] Error for [Tangut] 2713 q.v.

2707 [Tangut] I A 24 | [Tangut]
(a) I A 73 ditto
(b) III 156 [Tangut] | 1779
(c) VII 40 | [Tangut] 4469
(Written [Tangut]) B.179[3] 惇 "honest, staunch" W.I.265[18]
W.II 24[6] 博 "well-read".
[These may belong to [Tangut]?] 2713

2708 [Tangut] . I A 73 [Tangut] |
(a) I A 24 ditto
?

2709 [Tangut] III 80 [Tangut] | black
(b) V 2 | [Tangut] 2699
(iii) [Tangut] C.C.C. 15b 蓽豆 ... "beans"
B.101 cat. under "grains".

209
(30 entries)

transfer to 1120

2710
- 1120 – 5440
- 2697 – 2717
- 2700
- 2702 – 4375
- 2844 – 2831
- [5113]
- 5613
- 5618

- 0373 – 4036
- 1083
- 2216
- 2606
- 3122 – 2413
- 4990
- 5452 – 2004
- 5457
- 5474
- 3932
- ~~5452~~
- 5921
- 5530 – 2078 – 2076

2714 2309 chain

2715 2716 chain

2716
- 2695 – 2715 – 2696
  - 4626
- 1594
- 2705 – 5235
- 3415
- 5185

2711 5623 chain

2712 4544 chain

2713 5623 chain

2717 2710 chain

210

2710 [Tangut] VII 9 [Tangut] | q.v. 1220

(a) VII 5 ditto

(b) II 2 | [Tangut] 5618

(c) II 2 | [Tangut] 5613

(d) VI 84 | [Tangut] 2844

(e) VIII 65 | [Tangut] [5113]

(f) VIII 74 | [Tangut] 2700

(g) IX 34 | [Tangut] 2697

(h) IX A 114 | [Tangut] 2702

(ii) The disyllable C.C.C. 15b 斛斟

(i) C.C.C. 8b 15b 穀 "grain" W. I 136 ditto. B. 101. Chapter heading. The ordinary word for 'grain', presumably the origin of the 'ideogram' [Tangut].

2711 [Tangut] V 47 [Tangut] | 2713

2712 [Tangut] V A 137 [Tangut] |

2713 [Tangut] V 84 | [Tangut] 0372

(a) V 47 | [Tangut] [Tangut] 2711

(b) V 61 | [Tangut] [Tangut] 4034

(c) V ~~67~~ 142 | [Tangut] 2019

(d) ~~V 142~~ IX 43 [Tangut] | [Tangut] 1144

(e) IX 57 [Tangut] | [Tangut] 2706

B. 195² [Tangut] 目逵 friendship cf. 2707

2714 [Tangut] IX 34 [Tangut] | 2309

2715 [Tangut] VI 18 | [Tangut] 2695

(a) IX 152 | [Tangut] [Tangut] 4626

(b) IX A 113 | [Tangut] [Tangut] 2696

(i) C.C.C. 15b 粟 "millet", maize

(ii) The disyllable B. 101 cat. under "grain".

2716 [Tangut] V 137 | [Tangut] 2695

(a) V 78 ditto

(b) VI 123 | [Tangut] pestle 3415

(c) VII 72 [Tangut] | 5185

(d) VII A 87 [Tangut] | 2705

(e) IX 134 | [Tangut] 1594

The common word for 米 "rice"

(i) By itself C.C.C. 15b twice.

(ii) (c) above C.C.C. 15b 糯米 "glutinous rice"

(iii) [Tangut] | C.C.C. 15b 粳米

(iv) [Tangut] | C.C.C. 15b 炒米 "roasted rice"

(v) [Tangut] | C.C.C. 15b 蒸米 "steamed rice".

2717 [Tangut] III 103 [Tangut] | 2697

?

2718 4983 chain

2719 4037 chain

2720 - 2721

2721 2720 pair

2722 1345 pair

2723 - 0130 ~~pair~~

2724 - 4735

2725 - 4453

2726 0148 ~~[illegible]~~

2727 2245 chain

2728 1392 pair

2729 - 3350

2730 ~~interpretant~~

2731 4396 chain

2732 2395 chain

2733 1949 chain

2734 3575 chain

211

2718 [Tangut] VIII 88 [Tangut] |

2719 [Tangut] Tsi VI A 119 [Tangut]

A Phonetic compound. B.186[1] 2469 (子)

2720 [Tangut] III 125 | [Tangut]

(a) III 91 ditto

?

2721 [Tangut] III 91 [Tangut] |

(a) III 125 ditto

?

2722 [Tangut] V 183 [Tangut] | 1345

(a) VIII 71 ditto

?

2723 [Tangut] IX 131 | [Tangut] 0130

(a) III 44 ditto

?

2724 [Tangut] IX A 110 | [Tangut]

(a) II 13 ditto

?

2725 [Tangut] II 12 | [Tangut]

(a) II 25 ditto.

B 246[7] 方文 to let go

2726 [Tangut] V 183 [Tangut] | 1441

(a) V 67 | [Tangut] × 4042

?

2727 [Tangut] VI A 38 [Tangut] | "two" 2245.

(a) III A 45 ditto

C.C.C. 32[a] 35[b] 三 "three"

2728 [Tangut] I 22 | [Tangut] 1392

(a) VII 22 ditto

?

2729 [Tangut] III 84 | [Tangut] 3350

(a) III 109 ditto

The Tiny L. B.172[5]

2730 [Tangut] III 43 "Family or clan name"

? 2736

2731 [Tangut] III 66 | [Tangut] 4396

?

2732 [Tangut] VIII 88 | [Tangut] 2530

?

2733 [Tangut] VII 30 | [Tangut] 3961

2734 [Tangut] III 66 [Tangut] | 3575

(a) VI 100 ditto ×× 4158

(b) VI 12 [Tangut] | × 3470 3481

?

~~2735 [Tangut] I 10 | [Tangut]~~

~~(a) I A 61 [[Tangut], correctly]~~

~~(b) III 46 [Tangut] | "auxiliary word"~~

~~(c) III 124~~ see 2842.

2735 0959 chain

2736
0681
1530
3386

B 175[3] 副 assistant

2737 0959 chain

2738 3446 chain

2739 1128 chain
B.191[5] 宗 sect

[2740] 0799 chain

2741–2432
2741 φ(i) | mantra 曼陀羅
W II 120[12]
φ(ii) B.195[5] φ(iii) B.225[5] Mañjuśrī

2742 5428 chain

2743 2164 chain

2745 4512 chain

2745 A 2554 pair

2744 3123 chain

2746 2751 chain

212

2735 [illegible] IX 50 [illegible] | "excrement" v.1637
(a) I 102 | [illegible] "urine" 2604
(b) II 37 | [illegible] 1631
(c) VI A 12 | [illegible] 2867
?

2736 [illegible] I.10 | [illegible] 0681
(a) I A 61 ditto [[illegible] correctly]
[(b) [illegible] | "auxiliary word" See 2342]
(c) VIII 67 [illegible] | 1530
(d) IX 77 [illegible] × by | [illegible] 3386
(i) (c) above C.C.C. 32[a] 祐 助 "to help" (in both cases)
(ii) | [illegible] W.II 16[1] 妃 "wife, imperial concubine"

2737 [illegible] VII A 126 [illegible] | "excrement" v.1637
?

2738 [illegible] I 10 | [illegible] to say 4515
Dict. 1[b]2

2739 [illegible] III 174 | [illegible] 3646
(i) By itself W.I. 138[9] 貨 "property"
(ii) The dissyllable W.I. 138[9] 借 "to borrow"
(iii) W.II 50[10] ?

2740 [illegible] VII 23 [illegible] | 0799
?

2741 [illegible] I 78 | [illegible] 2432
(a) VII A 37 ditto
B.195[5] 曼 Phon. ~~wide~~

2741A [illegible] Error for [illegible] 2924

2742 [illegible] V 43 [illegible] | 5428
(a) VII 85 ditto
(a) VI A 54 | [illegible] 2192
?

2743 [illegible] IX 4 [illegible] | 2164 ditto
(a) IX 4 ditto
W.II 2[9] 得 "to attain" B 246[9] to'o'i fia?

2745 [illegible] VII 21 [illegible] | 4457 aboriginal
?

2745A [illegible] × of VI 30 [illegible] |
Probably an error for [illegible] 2554

2744 [illegible] V 114 [illegible] | 3123
(a) V 56 ditto 3123
?

2746 [illegible] W.II 42 [illegible] | v.2731
(i) C.C.C. 31[b] 可 "to be able"
(ii) W II 40[8] 54[9] 應 "ought" I. 134[9]
(iii) Meaning obscure W.I. 96[13] 138[2] 134[3] II 82[4] B. 170[2]
(iv) 宜 ought to, proper to W.I 154[5]
(v) ~~[illegible]~~ 理 "doctrine, principle" W.II 88[10] 90[2] B. 188[1] (clear)

2747 [illegible]

2748 2285 chain

2749
⊥4316 - 4311

2750 - 4327

2751
├ 4456
└ 2746

2752 2928 chain

2753 4202 pair

2754 (iii) | [Tangut] 除滅 "[illegible]" (get rid of)
or destroy W.II 84[10] 78[7] etc.

2754
├ 4464
└ 1776 ┬ 1065 - 2677
├ 1746 - 3988
└ 4381

2755 - 3288

2756 1690 chain

2757 2758 chain
└ 2758

2758 "[illegible]"
├ 2757
└ 4823 ┬ 4742
├ 4750
├ 4822
└ 5622

213

2747 [Tangut] VIII A49 "Family or clan name." B.177' part of P.N.

2748 [Tangut] VII 56 [Tangut] | 2285

?

2749 [Tangut] IX 91 | [Tangut]

(a) IX A30 ditto

?

2750 [Tangut] IX 167 | [Tangut]

(a) IX A139 ditto [[Tangut]]

This word seems to mean "to take" but it represents various words in translation:– C.C.C, 27[b] W.I 136[17] 取 "to take" C.C.C. 27[b] 接 "to take" I 192[16] 214[11] len "to obtain" I 216[3] hp'rog "to take" I 96[11]? 138[4]? II 58[5] II 108[5] B 193[2]

2751 [Tangut] IX 82 | [Tangut]

(a) IX 128 ditto

(b) II 42 | [Tangut] v.2746

? ~~(c) IX A 50~~

2752 [Tangut] VII 58 | [Tangut] 0847

?

2753 [Tangut] V 43 [Tangut] |

(a) VII 53 [Tangut] | i.e. ditto

?

2754 [Tangut] III 25 | [Tangut]

(a) III 60 ditto

(b) V 97 [Tangut] | 1776

(i) by itself W.I 112[13] 除 "to ~~remove~~ get rid of" 176[3] 218[11] nbre byed.pa "to strike out"? 226[1] sel.ba "to remove, cleanse"

(ii) | [Tangut] W.I 200[2] sel.ba "to remove cleanse" II 38[11] 除去 "to remove & get rid of".

2755 [Tangut] VI 54 [Tangut] | 3288

(a) I A67 ditto

2756 [Tangut] VIII A79 [Tangut] | 1690

(a) VIII A76 | [Tangut] 0285

?

2757 [Tangut] VII A46 [Tangut] | 2758

?

~~2758 [Tangut] VI 63 [Tangut]~~

2758 [Tangut] ?

(a) VII A46 | [Tangut]

(b) VIII 98 [Tangut] |

2759 2411 chain

2760 −1209 ~~−1209~~ ~~1209~~

2761 1488 chain

2762 2545 pair

2763–2764

2764 2763 pair

2765
- [1190]
- 2766
- 4051
- 4186–3816–5140–5215

2766 ~~2765 chain~~

2767 3579 pair

2768 1891 chain

2769 2906 chain

2770 − 2659

2771 − [1191]

214

2759 [Tangut] VI 63 [Tangut] | 4842
(i) ~~(a)~~ C.C.C. 17^a 蜘蛛 "spider"
(ii) | [Tangut] [Tangut] W.I.198³ "spider's web (?) abscess"

2760 [Tangut] VIII A 94 | [Tangut] 1909
(a) IX A 69 ditto
[(b) III A 110 [Tangut] × by [Tangut] | 2274 2283
(c) III A 111 [Tangut] × by [Tangut] |
(d) VIII A 101 [Tangut] × by [Tangut] |]
?
Note. (b)–(d) are Phonetic characters

2761 [Tangut] I 21 | [Tangut] 1488

2762 [Tangut] VI 43 [Tangut] |
(a) VI 82 ditto

2763 [Tangut] I 21 | [Tangut]
(a) V A 4 ditto v. 2764
C.C.C. 24^b 襯 "underclothing"

2764 [Tangut] V A 4 [Tangut] |
(a) I 21 ditto v. 2763
W.I 134³ 剝 "to peel, flay"?

2765 [Tangut] VI 43 | [Tangut]
(a) IX 113 ditto v. [1190]
(b) III A 136 | [Tangut]
(c) V 7 | [Tangut]
(d) VII 9 | [Tangut]
(i) C.C.C. 17^b 智 (+ passim) "wise, wisdom, jñāna B 246¹ wisdom (noun) B 179³"
(ii) The dissyllable W.I 108¹⁹ II 2¹⁰ etc. 智慧 jñāna prajñā "wisdom & knowledge" B. 231²

2766 [Tangut] V 7 [Tangut] | "wisdom" v. 2765

2767 [Tangut] I. 131 [Tangut] |
(a) VI 101 [Tangut] | i.e. ditto
?

2768 [Tangut] V 113 [Tangut] | 4527
?

2769 [Tangut] VII 1 [Tangut] | "arrow" 2123
?

2770 [Tangut] III 99 | [Tangut] 2659
(a) II 1 ditto
?

2771 [Tangut] VI 16 | [Tangut] [1191]
(a) VI 62 ditto
?

2772 3086 chain

2773 1992 chain

2774 2203 bis pair

2775 2485 chain

2776 1992 chain

2777
1618 — 1625

2778
├ 3309 – 0146
└ 0247

2779 5017 chain

2780
└ 3298 – 2959[8]
(a) W. I. 266[8] tr. 永嘗
B 205[2] 232[1] ('forever')

2781 2784 pair

2782 — 4253 Double Family name?

2783
┬ 3995
└ 3840

2783 (iii) 国貝壽 ayuşman W III 2" etc.
S.-H. p. 250

2784 — 2781

2785 3542 chain

215

2772 [Tangut] yau VIII A108 [Tangut] | 3086

(a) II A16 ditto

B.250[2] 何 "what?" B.170[4]

2773 [Tangut] VI 18 [Tangut] [Tangut] 1992 (not to go on before)

C.C.C. 8[b] 9[a] 陽 "brightness etc. yang, as opposed to [Tangut] = 陰 yin

2774 [Tangut] I 53 [Tangut] |

(a) I 11 ditto

?

2775 [Tangut] VII 39 [Tangut] | 2485

(a) VII 101 | [Tangut] 2280

?

2776 [Tangut] VII 39 [Tangut] | "not" 1992

2777 [Tangut] I 16 [Tangut] [Tangut]

(a) III 81 [Tangut] x by | [Tangut] 1625

(b) VIII 35 [Tangut] x by | [Tangut] 1618

?

2778 [Tangut] I 16 | [Tangut] 3309

(a) I 8 ditto

(b) II 19 | [Tangut] 0247

?

2779 [Tangut] VII A 128 [Tangut] [Tangut]

2780 [Tangut] ~~VII ger.~~ [Tangut]

(a) VIII 8 | [Tangut] 3298

(i) W. I 100[8] 136[11] II 60[3] 永 eternal

(ii) W II 36[11] 久 long (time)

(iii) B.185 長 "long-lasting (in Ch'ang-an) B.174[1] 172[5]

2781 [Tangut] VII A13 [Tangut] |

(a) IX 96 ditto

?

2782 [Tangut] IX 96 | [Tangut] 4255

?

2783 [Tangut] IX 97 | [Tangut] ? 3995

(a) VI 42 ditto

(b) VII 3 | [Tangut] "family" 3840

(i) C.C.C. 35[a] W. I 108[18] 壽 194[16] ts'e "(long) life B272[3]

(ii) W. I 96[2] 136[10] 世 "generation" etc.

(iii) | [Tangut] B.248 ts'e. dar. ldan. pa ayuṣman "long-lived"

2784 [Tangut] IX 96 | [Tangut]

(a) VII A13 ditto

?

2785 [Tangut] VII A68 [Tangut] | 3542

(a) I 99 ditto

(b) IX 49 | [Tangut] 2786

?

2786 3542 chain

2787 0752 chain

B. 203³ 庶

2788 0445 chain

2789 5678 chain

2790 – 0611 pair

2791 – 1562

2791 A. "Tiny-Tsing"

W.II.130² 疾

2792 1679 chain

2793
⊥ 4121 – 3985

2794 0612 pair A VIII

2795 4561 chain

2796 South family name??
⊥ 3301
⊥ 3413

2797 4572 chain

2798 4276 chain

2799 2027 chain

216

2786 [Tangut] IX 49 [Tangut] | v. 2785

?

2787 [Tangut] VI 73 | [Tangut] 0752

(a) VIII 8 ditto

(i) The dissyllable W.I 108[16] 民 (II 130[7]) "the people" C.C.C. 29[a] 民庶 B 161[5] 173[3]

v. 3018 A

2788 [Tangut] III 74 [Tangut] | 0445

2789 [Tangut] V 92 | [Tangut] I 3383

2790 [Tangut] VI 99 [Tangut] | 0611 [Tangut]

(a) I 85 ditto

2791 [Tangut] V 20 | [Tangut] 1592

(a) III 73 ditto

2791 A [Tangut]

Probably the right form of [Tangut] 2625 "disease" Yes v. W.II 130[2]

2792 [Tangut] IX 4 [Tangut] | 1679

(a) V 70 ditto

?

2793 [Tangut] I 133 | [Tangut]

(a) V 184 ditto

?

2794 [Tangut] VI 99 [Tangut] |

(a) I 85 ditto

(i) The dissyllable B. 99 cat. under "horse"

2794 A [Tangut] x of III A 25 [Tangut] |

error for 3084

2795 [Tangut] V 21 [Tangut] | 4056 1968 "to reach"

v. 1968

2796 [Tangut] IX 107 "Family or clan name"

(a) II 26 [Tangut] | 3301

(b) III 159 [Tangut] | 3413

?

2797 [Tangut] IX 107 [Tangut] | 4574

(a) V 104 ditto

(b) V 146 [Tangut] | 217[?]

C.C.C. 7[a] [Tangut] W.I. 218[15] bum (see 0869) "bottle"

2798 [Tangut] hwa V A 126 | [Tangut] ? affix

(i) [Tangut] | C.C.C. 23[b] 急隨鉢子 beggar's alms bowl

2799 [Tangut] MU I A 46 | [Tangut] 4061

?

A common Phonetic

2800 5199 pair

2801 2482 chain

2802 0809 chain

2804 4183 chain

2805 1423 pair

2806 -2889

2807 2812 chain

2808 3465 chain

2809 1717 chain

2810 0809 chain

2811

2812
- 2825 - 2846
- 0539
- 2807

2813 2164 chain

2814 -2859

2815 2853 pair

2803 0809 chain

217

2800 [Tangut] IX 51 [Tangut] | 5199
(a) III 105 ditto
W.I.94[4] II 22[1] 坵 I 214[11] dri.ma
"dirt". B.228[5]

2801 [Tangut] rie V 145 | [Tangut] 2482
(a) IX 1 | [Tangut] × 0594
~~C8~~ C.C.C. 8[b] + passim 山 W.I.190[12] ri
"mountain" B.186[5] q.v.

2802 [Tangut] VII A 32 [Tangut] | 5271
(i) [Tangut] | C.C.C. 22[a] 椽 準
?

2804 [Tangut] III 2 | [Tangut] "fruit" 4183
?

2805 [Tangut] IX 4 [Tangut] | (misspelt)
(a) I 51 ~~ditto~~ ditto v. 1423
?

2806 [Tangut] VI 64 | [Tangut]
(a) VIII 17 ditto
?

2807 ~~2806~~ [Tangut] VI 100 [Tangut] [Tangut]
?

2808 [Tangut] IX 37 [Tangut] | 1635
C.C.C. 34[a] 毯 "(horse) blanket"
?

2809 ~~2808~~ [Tangut] VIII 45 | [Tangut]
?

2810 ~~2809~~ [Tangut] IX 61 | [Tangut] 5271
?

2811 ~~2810~~ [Tangut] III 93 [Tangut] | 2888
(a) V 156 ditto
?

2812 [Tangut] II 1 [Tangut] |
(a) IX 151 ditto v. 2825
(b) VI 100 [Tangut] × by | [Tangut]
(c) IX 25 | [Tangut] 0529
?

2813 [Tangut] VII 118 [Tangut] | 3107
?

2814 [Tangut] VI 113 | [Tangut]
(a) VIII 1 ditto
?

2815 ~~2814~~ [Tangut] III 62 [Tangut] |
(a) III 30 ditto
(b) VIII 42 [Tangut] | [Tangut] × by
?

2803 [Tangut] IX 124 | [Tangut] 5271
?

2816 2861 chain VIII

2817 – 2883 III

2818 chain

+ 2823
+ 0030
+ 2820

2819 0780 pair

2820 2818 chain

2821 1339 pair III

2822 2861 chain

2823 2818 chain

2824 1717 chain

2825 2812 chain

2826 2870 pair VII

2827 0875 pair III

2828 1665 chain

2829 – 2884

2830 – 3640

2831 ? 2710 chain

218

2816 [Tangut] V/VI 36 [Tangut] |

(a) VII 14 ditto

(b) III 37 | [Tangut] ×2822 4873

? cf. 2819

2817 [Tangut] III 32 | [Tangut]

(a) IX 49 ditto (misspell)

?

2818 [Tangut] DO III 48 [Tangut] | 2823

(a) IX 53 ditto

(b) III 47 [Tangut] | "poison" 0030

(c) III A7 | [Tangut]

Tassim 毒 dug "poison"

2819 [Tangut] IX 142 [Tangut] | 0780

(a) V 81 ditto

? cf. 2827/2847 cf. 2817

2820 [Tangut] III A7 [Tangut] "poison" v. 2818

?

2821 [Tangut] VII 83 [Tangut] | 1339

(a) VIII 71 ditto

?

2822 [Tangut] V 89 | [Tangut] 4873 ~~2816~~

?

2823 [Tangut] IX 53 | [Tangut] "poison"

(a) III 48 ditto v. 2818

?

2824 [Tangut] VII 118 [Tangut] |

?

2825 [Tangut] IX 151 | [Tangut]

(a) II 1 ditto v. 2812

(b) I 121 | [Tangut] 2846 reversed

(c) VI 100 [Tangut] × by dissyllable

(i) [Tangut] | [[Tangut]] B. 100 cat. under "wild animals"

2826 [Tangut] I 115 [Tangut] |

(a) VIII 48 ditto

?

2827 [Tangut] IX 142 [Tangut] | 0875

(a) V 81 ditto

? 2847 cf. 2819

2828 [Tangut] I 88 [Tangut] 3536 curing

?

2829 [Tangut] VIII 3 | [Tangut] 2884

(a) I 35 ditto

?

2830 [Tangut] III 93 | [Tangut] 3640 high v. 2930

2831 [Tangut] IX 41 | [Tangut] [2844?]

? ~~v. 2930~~

2832 5579 pair

2833 2193 chain

2834
⊥ 2879-2882

2835 0809 chain

2836 0809 chain

2837
┼ 3110
└ 0615

2838-2872

2839 2806 pairs

2840 2877 pair

2841 2704 chain

2842 interpreted

2843 0809 chain

2844 2710 chain

219

2832 [Tangut] IX 32 [Tangut] |

(a) VI 55 ditto

?

2833 [Tangut] VIII A 78 | [Tangut] 2193

1285

W.II 18[10] 災 'calamity' W.I.136[12] ?

B 193[5] 患

2834 [Tangut] I 55 | [Tangut]

(a) VI 100 ditto.

2835 [Tangut] IX 7 | [Tangut] 5271

(a) IX A 126 | [Tangut] 2855

2835 A [Tangut] | ? error for 2844

2836 [Tangut] I A 14 | [Tangut] 5271

(i) [Tangut] | C.C.C. 16[a] 麻 稗

(ii) | [Tangut] B.101 cat. under 'grain'

2837 [Tangut] II 29 [Tangut] |

(a) II 29 ditto

(b) VII 56 [Tangut] | 615 ?

?

2838 [Tangut] VIII 42 [Tangut]

(a) IX 76 [Tangut] x by | [Tangut]

2815

?

[Tangut]

2839 [Tangut] VIII 17 [Tangut] |

(a) VI 64 ditto

?

2840 [Tangut] VI 19 [Tangut] |

(a) III 17 ditto.

(i) The dissyllable B.101 cat. under 'grain'

2841 [Tangut] VII 3 | [Tangut] 2704

(a) VI 35 [Tangut] 3767

(i) C.C.C. 15[b] 大麥 'big wheat'

(ii) The dissyllable B.101 cat. under 'grain'

2842 [Tangut] I 22 "Family or clan name"

(a) VII 27 | [Tangut] 0442

? a double name.

2843 [Tangut] VII 7 | [Tangut] "vegetable" possibly an error 0383

(a) VIII 6 | [Tangut] 0361

?

+ 4.442

2844 [Tangut] VI 84 [Tangut] | 2710

(a) IX 41 possibly misspelt see 2831 ?

(i) | [Tangut] C.C.C. 16[a] 麻 稗

(ii) [Tangut] | B.101 cat. under 'grain'.

219

2845
- 2223
- 0722
- 2887

2846 2822 0148 chain

2848 0148 chain

2847 0876 pair

2849 2349 pair

2850 – 2854

2851
- 0839
- 2878

2852 0809 chain

2853 – 2815

2854 2850 pair

2855 0809 chain

2856 – 2886

2857 2865 chain

220

2845 [illegible] I 16 | [illegible] 2223
(aa) IX 95 ditto
(a) III 81 [illegible] x by | [illegible] 0722
(b) VIII 13 [illegible] x by | [illegible] 2887
(i) The disyllable B.102 cat. under "vegetables"

2846 [illegible] I 121 [illegible] | 2825 ~~0148~~
?

2848 [illegible] VIII 3 [illegible] | 0148
?

2847 [illegible] IX 142 [illegible] | [illegible]
(a) V 81 ditto 0876
?
cf. 2819, 2827

2849 [illegible] VI 106 [illegible] |
(a) VI A 50 ditto
?

2850 [illegible] I A 13 | [illegible]
(a) VIII 47 ditto v. 2854
?

2851 [illegible] IX 79 [illegible] |
(aa) IX 38 ditto reversed
(a) IX 140 | [illegible] 2878
(i) (a) reversed C.C.C. 26b 掃帚
"a broom for sweeping"

2852 [illegible] V 4 | [illegible] "vegetable" 0383
(i) [illegible] | C.C.C. 15a 常葱 "ordinary

2852 (cont.)
onion".
(ii) | [illegible] C.C.C. 15a 蒜 garlic
B 101 cat. under "vegetables".
(iii) | [illegible] C.C.C. 15a 韮 "spring onion" 2694

2853 [illegible] III 30 [illegible] | [illegible] 2815
(a) III 62 ditto
?

2854 [illegible] VIII 47 [illegible] |
(a) I A 13 ditto v. 2850
?

2855 [illegible] IX A 126 [illegible] | 2835
?

2856 [illegible] VI 60 | [illegible]
(a) VIII 20 ditto
?

2857 [illegible] VII 7 [illegible] | 2565
(a) V 44 ditto
(i) The disyllable B.102 cat. under "vegetables"

2858 [illegible] IX 112 | [illegible]
?

2859 2814 pair

2860 0809 chain

2861
⊥ 2816–4873–2822

2862 0016 chain

2863 1130 chain

2864
⊥ 2866
5470

2865
⊥ 2857
3133–5202 bis

2866 2864 chain

2867 0959 chain

2868–2881

2869 1891 chain

2870–2826

2871 3835 chain

2872 2838 pair

2873–2006

50% finished

221

2859 [Tangut] VIII 1 [Tangut] | 2814

(a) VI 113 ditto

?

2860 [Tangut] VII 58 [Tangut] | 5271

B. 132[3]

2861 [Tangut] VII 14 | [Tangut] × 2816

(a) V 36 ditto

?

50% finished

2862 [Tangut] VI 57 [Tangut] | 0018

2863 [Tangut] IX 140 | [Tangut] "star" 1130

Name of a ?planet star C.C.C. 7[b] 掃

"the broom star" W. I. 222[14]

2864 [Tangut] I 6 | [Tangut] 2866

(a) II 25 ditto

~~(b) I 115~~

(b) II 6 | [Tangut] 5470

?

Note. To be distinguished from 2869

2865 [Tangut] V 44 | [Tangut] 2857

(a) VII 7 ditto

(b) IX 39 [Tangut] |

(1) The disyllable B. 102 cat. under "vegetables"

2866 [Tangut] II 25 [Tangut] |

(a) I 6 ditto

?

2867 [Tangut] VI A 12 [Tangut] | 2735

?

2868 [Tangut] I 63 | [Tangut]

(a) VIII 12 ditto

?

2869 [Tangut] III 29 [Tangut] | 1891

?

Note. There is no obvious means of distinguishing 2868 + 2869.

2870 [Tangut] VIII 48 | [Tangut]

(a) I. 115 ditto

?

2871 [Tangut] V 111 [Tangut] | 3835

(a) VII A 116 ditto

?

2872 [Tangut] IX 76 [Tangut] [Tangut]

(a) VIII 42 [Tangut] (1) | [Tangut]

?

2873 [Tangut] VII 90 | [Tangut] 2006

V 118 ditto

(1) The disyllable C.C.C. 12[b] 珊 瑚

"coral" (in both cases) B 102 cat. under "precious things".

2874 2889 pair

2875 – 2888 A

2876 - 2880

2877 - 2840

2878 2851 chain

2879 2834 chain

2880 2876 pair

2881 2868 pair

2882 2834 chain

2883 2817 pair

2884 2829 pair

2885 | [illegible] (581) B 245^5 tr. 老鼠 'rat'

SCHOOL OF ORIENTAL & AFRICAN STUDIES

SCHOOL OF ORIENTAL & AFRICAN STUDIES LONDON

222

2874 [Tangut] IX 4 [Tangut] |

(a) V 117 ditto

?

2875 [Tangut] VII 25 [Tangut] |

?

2876 [Tangut] VI 55 | [Tangut]

(a) II 25 ditto

(B.102) (The dissyllable) cat. under "vegetables"

2877 [Tangut] III 17 | [Tangut] 2840

(a) VI 19 ditto

(i) The dissyllable B.101 cat. under "grains"

2878 [Tangut] IX 140 [Tangut] |

(i) The dissyllable reversed C.C.C. 26b 掃帚 "a broom for sweeping"

2879 [Tangut] VI 100 [Tangut] | 2834

(a) I 55 ditto

(b) VII 113 [Tangut] |

?

2880 [Tangut] II 25 [Tangut] |

(a) VI 55 ditto

(i) The dissyllable, B.102 cat. under "vegetables"

2881 [Tangut] VIII 12 [Tangut] |

(a) I 63 ditto

?

2882 [Tangut] VII 113 | [Tangut]

?

2883 [Tangut] IX 49 [Tangut] |

(a) III 32 ditto

?

2884 [Tangut] I 35 [Tangut] |

(a) VIII 3 ditto

?

2885 [Tangut] VII 90 | [Tangut] wrg 3366 — 3354 chaly — šwi

(a) II A 19 [Tangut] | 1531

(b) VI A 125 [Tangut] | 2514

~~(ii) (b) C.C.C. 16b 老鼠~~ also

B.221² 鼠

(i) By itself W.I. 210¹ tyi. ba "rat"

(ii) (b) above C.C.C. 16b 老鼠 "old rat"

(iii) (a) above B.100 cat. under "wild animals"

2886 2856 pair

2893 2524 chain

2887 2845 chain

2894 1022 pair

2888 – 2811

2895 0809 chain

2888A 2875 pair

2889 – 2874

2896 – 5201

2890 4396 chain

2897 independent

2898 0809 chain

2891 4396 chain

2899 – 2900

2892 1891 chain

223

2886 [Tangut] VIII 20 [Tangut] |
(a) VI 60 ditto
?

2887 [Tangut] VIII 13 [Tangut] [Tangut]
(a) III 81 [Tangut] × of [Tangut] | (0722, 2845)
?

2888 [Tangut] V 156 | [Tangut]
(a) III 93 ditto
?

2888A [Tangut] × of VII 25 | [Tangut]
?

2889 [Tangut] V 117 [Tangut] | [Tangut] 2874
(a) IX 4 ditto
C.C.C. 21ᵇ 草 "grass" (incense)"
W.I. 98⁷ ?

2890 [Tangut] III 127 | [Tangut] 2439
(a) II 24 | [Tangut] 2891
(b) III 149 [Tangut] |
C.C.C. 6ᵇ 羅 "net" W.I. 132¹⁵ 檻 a stockade, game trap

2891 [Tangut] II 24 [Tangut] | 2890
?

2892 [Tangut] VI 102 [Tangut] | 1891
?

2893 [Tangut] IX 7 [Tangut] |
(a) I 34 ditto V. 2524
?

2894 [Tangut] III 13 [Tangut] |
(a) III 7 ditto
?

2895 [Tangut] I A 52 | [Tangut] 5271
(a) VII 87 | [Tangut] 3131
(b) VIII 87 [Tangut] × by | [Tangut] [Tangut] 5649
(c) IX 141 error for 2614
?
~~C.C.C. 16ᵃ 蒲 rushes~~ [? error for 2896]

2896 [Tangut] I 29 | [Tangut]
(a) IX A6 ditto
(ii) | [Tangut] C.C.C. 24ᵃ 苫
[presumably means "rush mat"]
(i) The dissyllable C.C.C. 16ᵃ 蒲葦 "rushes & reeds."

2897 [Tangut] I 88 Family or clan name

2898 [Tangut] IX 139 [Tangut] | 5271
?

2899 [Tangut] VII 64 | [Tangut]
(a) IX 49 ditto
~~B.10~~ The dissyllable B. 102 cat. under "vegetables"

2900 2889 pair

2906
- 2123

W. I 132[15] 弩 cross-bow

21/1/39

2901 ~~0259~~ 0731 chain

2907 1492 chain

2908 – 2912

2902 0521 pair

2909 – 4411

2903 0381 pair

2910 independent

2904 5477 chain

2911 0271 chain

2912 2908 pair

2905 5515 pair

2906
- 2123
  - 0836
  - 1013
  - 1176
  - 1328
  - 1483
  - 2118
  - 2769
- 4297
- 4504
- 4553

2913 0273 chain

224

2900 [Tangut] IX 49 [Tangut] |
(a) VII 64 ditto
(i) The dissyllable B.102 cat. under "vegetables".

21/1/39
2901 [Tangut] III 86 | [Tangut]
B.172[5]

~~2902 [Tangut] I 6~~

2902 [Tangut] I 121 | [Tangut]
(a) IX 107 ditto

?
2903 [Tangut] II 37 [Tangut] |
(a) IX 74 ditto

2904 [Tangut] III 66 [Tangut] |
(a) IX 49 ditto
(b) I 24 [Tangut] × by dissyllable

?
2905 [Tangut] na III A 14 [Tangut] | "spittle"
(a) III 149 ditto
C.C.C. 19[a] 涕 W. I. 216[7] snabs "mucus". ×2123

2906 [Tangut] IX A 67 | [Tangut] "arrow"
(a) IX 2 ditto
(b) III 31 | [Tangut] 4297

2906 cont.
(c) VII 112 | [Tangut] 4504
(d) IX 35 | [Tangut] 4533
W. I 132[15^2] 弓 bow

2907 [Tangut] III A 21 [Tangut] |

2908 [Tangut] VII A 8 | [Tangut] [misspelt]
(a) VII 98 ditto v. 2912
? W. II 130[3]: 遂 B 126[2]

2909 [Tangut] V 30 | [Tangut]
(a) I 115 ditto

2910 [Tangut] V 30 Family or clan name

2911 [Tangut] IX A 37 [Tangut] | nose 2583
~~(a) I 87~~ W. I. 174[4] [Tangut]

2912 [Tangut] VII 98 [Tangut] |
(a) VII A 8 ditto [[Tangut]] v. 2908

2913 [Tangut] IX 48 [Tangut] [Tangut]
(b) III 96 [Tangut] × by [Tangut] | v. 273
(a) I 84 [Tangut] × by [Tangut] |

2914 2027 chain

2915 4846 pair

2916 1416 pair

2917 – 5498

2918 2278 chain

2919 4425 chain

2920 1736 chain

2921 0148 chain

2922 4425 chain

2923 independent

2924 2262 pair

2925 – 4201 A

2926 0271 chain

2927 1343 chain

2928

5320 – 0915 – 0841 – 0847 – 2752; 4532 – 4438
0915 – 2199
5320 – 4177
5320 – 4182
5320 – 5318
0446 – 4591 – 4492
0446 – 4907

2929 3393 chain

2930 1891 chain

*2929 A [Tangut] Trs. of [Tangut] 4337
Error for 1369

225

2914 [Tangut] VI 15 [Tangut] | 4462

2915 [Tangut] V 30 [Tangut] |

(a) VII 59 ditto

?

2916 [Tangut] VI 22 [Tangut] | 1416

(a) I A 84 ditto

(i) The dissyllable C.C.C. 26[b] [Tangut] 箕 winnowing fan + v. basket

2917 [Tangut] VI 22 | [Tangut]

(a) I A 104 ditto

?

2918 [Tangut] I 47 [Tangut] | 4304

(a) II 4 [Tangut] | ×(1323?) 1196

2919 [Tangut] IX 164 | [Tangut] 2386

(a) III 115 | [Tangut]

2920 [Tangut] IX 164 ~~III 116~~ [Tangut] | 1736

2921 [Tangut] I 119 [Tangut] misspelt | to tied 1940 *

2922 [Tangut] III 115 ~~IX 164~~ [Tangut] | 2919

2923 [Tangut] I 21 Family or clan name

2924 [Tangut] VII 69 [Tangut] | 2262

(a) VII 73 ditto

?

2925 [Tangut] V 149 | [Tangut]

2926 [Tangut] VI 106 [Tangut] "ear"

(i) The dissyllable C.C.C. 25[a] 耳 墜 隊 土

2927 [Tangut] VI 106 ([Tangut] |) v. 1598

?2927 A [Tangut] error for 3176

2928 [Tangut] VII A 117 [Tangut] | ×5320

(a) ditto

(b) IX 173 [Tangut] | ×0446

II 150[12] 近 near

2929 [Tangut] III A 8 | [Tangut] "to laugh"

(i) Passim 喜 dgah "joy"

(ii) | [Tangut] W. II 90[7] 94[9] dgah.bo "joyful"

(iii) [Tangut] | W. I 90[3] etc kun.dgah.bo = Ānanda.

2930 [Tangut] V 95 [Tangut] | 1891 ×5574

(a) VIII A 28 | [Tangut] 3157

B. 91 [Tangut] at the top [Tangut] follows. | is (the same as) [Tangut]. 2830 The word for [Tangut] [beneath the shore?]

2931 5690 chain

2932 5678 chain

2933 - 1738

2934
├ 5639
└ 2938

2935 0271 chain

2936 2492 chain

2937 1873 chain

2938 2934 chain

2939 5248 chain

[2940] 2998 pair

2941 3626 chain

2942 ? 3091 chain

2943 - 3177

2944
├ 2677
└ 2945

226

2930 cont.
not complete, not perfect".
B.249 半 "half"
?

2931 [Tangut] VIII A23 [Tangut] | 1367

2932 [Tangut] VI 20 [Tangut] | 2523
W.I.108[9] II 80[8] C.C.C. 37[a] B.188[4] 過

2933 [Tangut] VI 65 | [Tangut] 1738
(a) III 144 ditto

2934 [Tangut] VI 89 [Tangut] | 5639
(a) VII 58 ditto
(b) I 62 | [Tangut] 2938
W.I 126[14] 種 vija, bija (S.-K. p.426) "seed, sort, species" 190[18] 218[1] ris "figure, design?"

2935 [Tangut] VI 89 [Tangut] | "ear"
?

2936 [Tangut] V 16 [Tangut] | "root" 1841
C.C.C. 29[b] 35[b] W.I + II passim 利 patu tīkṣṇa "profit, benefit"

2937 (2936) [Tangut] III A2 [Tangut] | 1573
?

2938 [Tangut] I 62 [Tangut] | "seed" v. 2933
?

2939 [Tangut] VIII A6 | [Tangut] 5248
(i) [Tangut] (2268) | B.100 cat. under "horse"

2940 (2939) [Tangut] ?
(a) I 80 [Tangut] | 2998
W.I.134[14] [Tangut] | 墮胎 to cause a child to abort

2941 (2940) [Tangut] III 83 [Tangut] | 3626
(a) V A27 ditto
?

2942 [Tangut] IX 128 | [Tangut] 1664 (1995 A)
(a) VI 5 | [Tangut] ? 2297
(i) (1664) | [Tangut] B.99 cat. under "horse" + translated 調御 "a horse broken in to harness?"

2943 [Tangut] I 14 | [Tangut]
(a) IX 45 ditto
?

2944 [Tangut] ?
(a) VI 97 [Tangut] | 2945
(b) VIII 88 | [Tangut] 0677

2945 2944 chain

2946 4073 chain

2947 5310 chain

2948 4661 chain

2949 independent

2950 independent

2951 0960 pair

2952 4073 chain

2953 1992 chain

2954
- 0138
- 2501 – 5573
- 3949

2955 2085 chain

2956 –3148

2957
- 2966
- 2967

2958 0262 chain (takeover)

227

2945 [Tangut] VI 97 [Tangut] | [2944]
(i) | [Tangut] (i.e. "white |") C.C.C. 15a 胡椒 "sour pepper"
(ii) | [Tangut] (i.e. "head |") C.C.C. 15b 椒 "pepper"
(iii) | [Tangut] (i.e. root |) C.C.C. 15b 乾薑 "dried ginger" (1841)
This word seems to be a generic one for 'spice'

2946 [Tangut] VI 118 [Tangut] |
(a) VI 10 ditto [[Tangut]]
?

2947 [Tangut] V A 18 | [Tangut]
C.C.C. 30a.2.b 證 + 驗 "evidence, proof"

2948 [Tangut] III 57 | [Tangut]
?

2949 [Tangut] V 148 "Family or clan name"
v. 5404 phon. 金

2950 [Tangut] II A 17 "Family or clan name"
B. 347³, 王 P.N. Wang

2951 [Tangut] III 76 [Tangut] |
(a) I 108 ditto
?

2952 [Tangut] VI A 100 [Tangut] |
?

2953 [Tangut] III 179 [Tangut] not to go as above 1992
?

2954 [Tangut] III 179 | [Tangut] v. 138
(a) III A 54 ditto
(b) IX 20 [Tangut] | v. 2501
(c) IX A 33 [Tangut] |
(i) (b) above. C.C.C. 29b ? 强凌 ?
W I 96¹² 侵陵 "to attack or disparage"
W. I. 138¹
By itself B. 171³ trs. 凌 insult, maltreat

2955 [Tangut] VII A 96 [Tangut] "sound"
Presumably a Phonetic.

2956 [Tangut] VII 39 | [Tangut]
(a) III 34 ditto
?

2957 [Tangut] III 86 [Tangut] | 2966
(a) V 95 ditto
(b) VIII 74 | [Tangut] 2967
?

2958 [Tangut] III 42 | [Tangut]
(a) III 174 ditto
?

2959 2780 chain

2960 3700A chain

2960 (iii) | 蒞 勤 精 virya

"energy, zeal" W II 4[8]

2961 4886 pair

2963 1369 chain

2962 2494 chain

2964 –2973

2965 1891 chain

2966 2957 chain

2967 2957 chain

2968 4773 chain

B, 203[4]

2969

3038 – 1413

3290 – 2550 – 1407

2998 – 2092

2970 3783 chain

2971 2285 chain

228

2959 [Tangut] VI 39 [Tangut] | 3298

2960 [Tangut] VIII 2 [Tangut] | v. 329

(a) III 70 | [Tangut] 3448

(i) W.II 62^5, 4^8 勤 virya "energy, zeal"

(ii) (a) above W.I. 138^1 ?

(ii) W.I 176^4 强 strong, powerful

(iii) [Tangut] | C.C.C. 27^a 教習 "to teach the practice of"

2961 [Tangut] IX 43 [Tangut] | 4386?

(a) VI 2 ditto

(i) The disyllable B.102 cat. under "rivers & seas".

2962 [Tangut] IX 43 [Tangut] | 1369 "kinties"

(a) III 37 ditto

(i) The disyllable C.C.C. 20^b 34^b 親戚 W.II 18^5 眷屬 "relatives & dependents".

2962 [Tangut] IX 43 [Tangut] | 2494 host origin

2964 [Tangut] V 19 | [Tangut]

(a) V 19 ditto

?

2965 [Tangut] IX A 111 [Tangut] |

(a) VI A 102 | [Tangut] 0924

?

2966 [Tangut] V 95 | [Tangut] 2957

(a) III 86 ditto

~~(b) VII 85 [Tangut] | [Tangut]~~

?

2967 [Tangut] VIII 74 [Tangut] | 2957

2968 [Tangut] VIII 3 | [Tangut] 4273

(a) II 1 [Tangut] |

(b) V 12 [Tangut] | [Tangut] | 0428

(c) V 12 [Tangut] | 4312

(d) VI 28 [Tangut] | 2396

(f) IX 9 [Tangut] | 4636

(g) IX 43 [Tangut] |

(e) VIII 33 [Tangut] | 4334

(i) [Tangut] | W.I. 224^9 ngan.po "old"

By itself B. 201^4 猛 "fierce, violent".

2969 [Tangut] III 114 | [Tangut] "lazy"

(a) VIII 31 ditto v. 3038 3290

(b) II 1

?

2970 [Tangut] VIII A 9 | [Tangut] 3783

?

2971 [Tangut] VII 50 [Tangut] |

2972 ⊥ 2459 [1084]

2973 ≠ 2964 pair

2974 1891 chain

2975 5465 chain

2976 3078 chain

2977 4577 chain

2978 1110 pair

2979 4734 chain

2980 2485 chain

2981 3026 chain

2982 0583 chain

2983 3001 chain

2984 0148 chain

229

2972 I 44 | 2459

(a) I 2 ditto

(b) V 104 | [1084]

?

2973 V 19 |

(a) V 19 ditto

?

2974 III 129 | 1891

CCC.1a5

2975 IX A 140 | 5213

(a) V 57 | 1843

CCC.9a 霧 "fog, mist" B.168[4]

2976 VIII 18 | 3078

(a) ~~III 75~~ V 97 ditto x(1518)

(b) III 75 | 1897 ~~1518~~

(i) The 2 syllable CCC.30[6] 獄 裏 "prison" (in both cases)

(ii) (b) above W.I.168[1] II.76[9] 82[3]

地獄 naraka hell.

2977 VIII 83 |

? ~~(a) V 97~~

~~2978~~ Note. In 2976 the first element is 扉 & the second has a ʼ; 2977 & no ʼ

2978 V 95

(a) VII 96 | v.1110

CCC.15a The 2 syllable +

半春菜 "half spring vegetable"

B.102 cat. under "vegetables"

2979 I 14 | 4734

?

— is indexed as if it was

2980 VI A 5 | 2485

(a) VI 63 | 3234

W.I.136[6] ? 蹴 to kick, tread on

2981 VII A 4 | 3304

?

2982 III 122 | 0926

W.I.134[16] v.3239

2983 III 57 | 3001

(a) III 90 0597

?

2984 III A 98 4827

Verb W.II 4[12] 制 to ~~restrain,~~ convert, govern

W.II 48[11] 遮 to ~~hinder~~ cover, screen

W.I.214[5] sel. bm to cleanse remove

W.I.202[12] ? 護 guard, preserve

B.179[3] 195[2] 去 drive out to exclude W.I.265[18]

B.129[4] tr. 免 avoid

2985 5106 chain

2986 independent

(4450) (2987) pair

2988 2959 chain

2989
+0139–5175–2559
1965
2186

2990 – 5292

2991
+2996–4554
3016

2992 4775 chain

2993 2194 pair v. 3636

2994 5477 chain

2995 4775 chain

2996 2991 chain

2997 4804 chain

2998 – [2940]

2999 4208 chain

230

2985 [Tangut] V 114 [Tangut] | 5106

?

2986 [Tangut] V 138 "Family or clan name"

Note. 2983-6 are all much alike

2987 [Tangut] II 9 [Tangut] |

(a) III 94 ditto [[Tangut]]

(i) The dissyllable C.C.C. 25b 鋪帛 broad (?) silk.

2988 [Tangut] VIII A 58 [Tangut] | 3038

(a) VIII A 4 [Tangut] | 2092

?

2989 [Tangut] I A 54 | [Tangut] 0139

(a) IX A 88 [[Tangut]] ditto

(b) I A 18 | [Tangut] ? 1965

(c) IX A 46 [Tangut] | 2186

?

2990 [Tangut] VII A 93 | [Tangut]

(a) VII A 61 ditto

The dissyl. B.196[2] 顛倒 S.-H. 475 viparyaya error

2991 [Tangut] III A 34 | [Tangut]

[(a) II 9 ([Tangut] × by [Tangut] |) ditto

(b) III A 20 (1509) 3845

(c) VII 76 [Tangut] |

2992 [Tangut] V 8 [Tangut] | misspelt 4775

W. II 48[9] 鵂鶹 "owl"

2993 [Tangut] ?

(a) III A 124 [Tangut] |

(i) [Tangut] | W. I 110[12] II 6[7] 28[2] 疑惑 vicikitsā mohā "doubt and illusion" 2038

2994 [Tangut] I 80 | [Tangut] misspelt fragment 5477

?

2995 [Tangut] IX 160 [Tangut] | 4821

?

2996 [Tangut] II 9 [Tangut] |

(a) III A 34 ditto

(b) III 118 [Tangut] | 4554

?

2997 [Tangut] V 19 [Tangut] |

(a) V 83 ditto [[Tangut]]

(i) The dissyllable C.C.C. 16b 鳳凰 male + female phoenix

2998 [Tangut] I 80 | [Tangut]

?

2999 [Tangut] IX 160 [Tangut] | bone 4208

?

3000 3156 pair

3001 5281 chain

3002 3756 chain

3003 4775 chain

3004 4275 pair

3005 3583 chain

3006 3014 chain

B.188[5] 扣 to tie 194[2] tr. 化

W.I.134[4]

3007 #4441 chain

3008 4775 chain

3009 4775 chain

3010 4856 pair

231

3000 [Tangut] VII 82 [Tangut] |

(a) I 12 ditto

(i) The dissyllable W.I.190[6] c'u. srin "sea-monster" 192[6], 218[14] srin.po "worm"

3001 [Tangut] III 131 [Tangut] | 5281

(a) IX A 135 ditto

(b) III 6 [Tangut] | 5070

x(0597)

(c) III 57 [Tangut] | 2983

(i) The dissyllable 煩 惱 "the troubles (of rebirth)." (common)

3002 ~~3002~~ [Tangut] VII 82 [Tangut] | 3756

?

3003 [Tangut] VI 125 [Tangut] |

W.I.134[2] 168[17] 羽 "feathers" 218[2] ditto? 206[4]? See also 92

3004 [Tangut] IX 8 [Tangut] | 赤

(a) V 1 ditto

? [illegible]

3005 ~~3004~~ [Tangut] IX 177 [Tangut] | "[illegible]" 5692

C.C.C.16[b] 鵰 "eagle, hawk"

3006 [Tangut] VII 89 [Tangut] |

(i) I 111 ditto

W.I 96[2] 應 "proper, worthy".

W.I.128[10] 調 "harmonious"

W.I.194[10] mdzes "beautiful"

B.161[2] 168[3] (doubles) 187[3] 被 (?)

3007 [Tangut] IX 8 [Tangut] |

(a) III 180 ditto

?

3008 [Tangut] VII 109 [Tangut] | to fly

(a) V 47 [Tangut] | 4741

(i) By itself C.C.C.8[b] 鶴 "crane"

(ii) (a) above C.C.C.16[b] 鷥 鷺 鶴

(iii) | [Tangut] C.C.C.32[b] 箜 篌 "lute, guitar"

3009 [Tangut] - I 129 [Tangut] | to fly

W.I 220[14] dbo "Name of a lunar mansion."

3010 [Tangut] VI 23 [Tangut] |

(a) I 11 ditto

~~[illegible]~~ (i) The dissyllable ~~W.I.134~~[16] C.C.C.17[a] 蜫 "fly". ~~[illegible]~~ W.I.134[16]?

3011
4513 — 4215

3012 - 2512

3013 independent

3014
3006
0898

B.169³ 對 pair (numerator of flags)

3015 - 4187

3016 2991 chain

3017 2149 chain

3018 4083 chain

3019 3054 chain

3020 3654 sub. chain

3021 4427 chain

3022 0148 chain

3023 5640 chain

3024
3640 - 0881 - 3986 - 1382

3025 1992 chain

3026
2043 - 4398 — 1480
3791 — 1573
4091 - 3304 - 2981 — 4365
4380 - 1219

II 140'' 壯 string

B.193¹ q.v. to 朱 193⁴⁵₃₀

3011 [Tangut] IX 8 [Tangut] [Tangut]
(a) I 84 [Tangut] × by [Tangut] |
(b) IX 31 [Tangut] |

?

3012 [Tangut] IX 126 | [Tangut] 2512
(a) IX 8 ditto

?

3013 [Tangut] I 54 Family or clan name

3014 [Tangut] I. 111 | [Tangut]
(a) VII 89 ditto v. 3009
(b) VI 4 | [Tangut] 0898
(i) By itself W. II 16[6] 合 "to fold (the hands)" B.161[3]
(ii) | [Tangut] C.C.C. 20[a] 和 合 "harmonious & in concord"

3015 [Tangut] IX 23 | [Tangut] 4187
(a) VII 20 ditto
C.C.C. 1[b] 1 B.192[4] tr. 尊

3016 [Tangut] VII 76 [Tangut] | 2991

?

3017 [Tangut] III 6 | [Tangut]
(a) VI 31 [Tangut] | "number" 3371
(i) (a) above W.I. 136[6] [Tangut] "limit" 身

3018A [Tangut] W. I. 265[14] + [16] in 2 phrases, parts of royal titles
(i) [Tangut] | translated 定民 ordering the people
(2) [Tangut] | " 民益 benefitting the people

232

3018 [Tangut] III 57 [Tangut] | 4083

?

3019 [Tangut] VII 45 | [Tangut]
W. II 18[2] 消 "to disperse, dissipate"
W. I. 208[7] [ditto]

3020 [Tangut] IX A 20 [Tangut] | 3290 A, 3654
(i) By itself W. I. 192[8] urban "strong"?
(ii) The dissyllable I 96[5] 112[2] 150[4] etc. 堅固 "solid & strong".

3021 [Tangut] VII 91 [Tangut] | 4403

?

3022 [Tangut] IX 150 [Tangut] | 5159

?

3023 [Tangut] IX 59 | [Tangut] 4376

?

3024 [Tangut] V 9 | [Tangut] 3640
(a) IX A 50 ditto

?

3025 [Tangut] I 20 [Tangut] | "not" 1992
(a) I 30 ditto
W. I. 96[7] 未 "not yet" & passim

3026 [Tangut] V 101 | [Tangut]
(a) V 86 | [Tangut] 2043
(b) V 2 | [Tangut] 3791
(i) The dissyllable C.C.C. 29[b]: ~~恃 "to trust, rely on"~~ strong, 淩 [?= 浚] 弱 [deep] & weak

3027 4577 chain

3028 0258 chain

3029 3468 chain

3030 0609 chain

3031 1662 chain

3032 – [1080]

3033 5483 pair

3034 5473 pair

3035 4027 chain

3036 0022 chain

3037 0249 chain

3038 2969 chain

3039 4087 pair

233

3027 [Tangut] IIA4 [Tangut] |

(a) II 4 ditto

?

3028 [Tangut] III 130 [Tangut] | 3872

(a) VIII 21 [Tangut] | 3627 [4581 bis]

W. I 134[8] q.v. II 130[2] v. 3522

3029 [Tangut] IX 99 [Tangut] | 3468

(a) VII 27 ditto

(b) III 37 | [Tangut]

(c) VI 12 [Tangut] | 1048

(i) By itself. W II 80[2] 轉 "to turn (a wheel)"

(ii) The disyllable C.C.C. 28[b] 30[a] 扃 分

(iii) (c) above W. I 108[10] 歴 侍 II 6[3] 歴事 22[8] 承事 "to serve, obey & minister to".

3030 [Tangut] VIIA73 | [Tangut] 4610

?

3031 [Tangut] VIIA41 [Tangut] |

?

3032 [Tangut] VII 39 | [Tangut]

(a) III 97 ditto

?

3033 [Tangut] V120 | [Tangut] 5483

(a) VA8 ditto

?

3034 [Tangut] II 1 [Tangut] | "3rd stem"

(a) I 3 ditto

C.C.C. 9[b] 丁 "4th stem"

3035 [Tangut] V138 [Tangut] |

(a) VA119 | [Tangut] 1097

?

3036 [Tangut] III 57 [Tangut] | "snake" v. 22

?

Used as a Phonetic. (nu)

3037 [Tangut] I.1 | [Tangut] 1389

W. I 138[5]

3038 [Tangut] VIII 31 [Tangut] | 2969

(a) III 114 ditto

(b) I 59 [Tangut] | 1413

(c) VIII 88 [Tangut] | x(1407) 2550

(d) VIIIA58 | [Tangut] x 2092 2988

W II 14[7] 懈 "lazy" 3330A v. ~~3038~~

3039 [Tangut] III 68 [Tangut] | "elder brother" ~~family~~

C.C.C. 20[a] 弟 "younger brother"

W. I. 196[2]

3040 3269 chain

3041
4286 - 5628
5703

B.223[2] | 皷 頻 蕊 蘤 孤獨善
樹園 Jetavana garden.

3042 2440 pair

3043 2437 pair

3044 0271 chain

3045 0322 chain

3046 2217 chain

3047 5310 chain

3048 0669 pair

3049 4109 chain

3050 - 1035

3051 5455 chain

3040

3041

3042

234

3040 [Tangut] VI 88 | [Tangut] quarter size 3269

(a) I 60 | [Tangut] 1390

W.II 14[11] 餘 "in addition" I 214[1] 218[13]

? ṣ̌an "other, additional"

B.186[4] trs. 別 other, extra

3041 [Tangut] I 77 | [Tangut] ? [Tangut]

(a) I.11 ditto

(b) I 5 | [Tangut]

B.172[2] q.v.

(i) By itself translated by 人 "man" in C.C.C. 7[a] | [Tangut] "man-horse; Centaurus" & C.C.C. 27[b] [Tangut] | 万人 "all mankind"

(ii) The dissyllable. In W.II 42[3] translates [Tangut] 姓 "family name" [actually in the passage in question "(Brahman) caste"] Used as the explanation of a large number of characters representing family or clan names. For full list see App[x].

3042 [Tangut] IX 1 [Tangut] | 2440

(a) V 32 ditto

? cf. 3043

3043 [Tangut] IX 1 [Tangut] | 2437

(a) V 32 ditto

?

3044 [Tangut] III 122 [Tangut] | "ear" 0271

?

3045 [Tangut] III 65 [Tangut] | [Tangut] 3645

?

3046 [Tangut] VII 65 [Tangut] | 2217

?

3047 [Tangut] V 82 | [Tangut]

?

3048 [Tangut] V 109 [Tangut] | 0667

(a) IX 48 ditto

?

3049 [Tangut] IX 16 [Tangut] | [misspelt]

(a) VII 76 [Tangut] | (?ditto)

(b) IX 60 [Tangut] |

?

3050 [Tangut] I 48 | [Tangut]

(a) III 15 ditto [[Tangut]...[Tangut]]

?

Note 3047–50 are barely distinguishable.

3051 [Tangut] V 95 [Tangut] | 5213 [illegible]

C.C.C. 7[a] 玄 "dark".

3052 3084 chain

3053 1681 chain

3054 — 3055 / 3019

3055 3054 chain

1306 3056 pair

3057 0271 chain

W.I.136[4] 覺 apprehend / to understand

[3058] 0866

[3059] 0970 chain

3060 [4985] pair

3061 independent

φ i B.201'

3062 3066 chain

3063 4183 chain

3064 0534 pair

3065 3066 chain

B.201[5] q.v.

235

3052 [Tangut] I 48 | [Tangut]

?

3053 [Tangut] IX 87 [Tangut] | 1681

?

3054 [Tangut] VII 8 | [Tangut]

(a) VII 45 [Tangut] | 3019

W II 82[5] 消 "to melt, disperse"

W I 134[13]? 170[13]

B.130[1] 破 to break

3055 [Tangut] ? VII 59-60

(a) VII 8 [Tangut] |

W.I. 208[8 f6.] bcom.pa "to disperse, overcome (poison)".

3056 [Tangut] VIII 82 [Tangut] |

(a) I 143 ditto

(i) The dissyllable B.103 cat. under 'sick'.

3057 [Tangut] III 65 [Tangut] | "to hear"

(a) III 122 | [Tangut] 4322

(b) III 162 [Tangut] | 4905

(c) III A27 [Tangut] | to know 1958

W I 100[14]: 聞 "to hear" (a precise?)

3058 [Tangut] VI 33 | [Tangut]

(a) IX 9 ditto

?

3059 [Tangut] VI 33 [Tangut] | (ii) 4629

?

3060 [Tangut] VI 33 [Tangut] |

(a) III 162 ditto

?

3061 [Tangut] VI A 51 [Tangut] | name

B.91 The centre of [Tangut] + the ideogram [Tangut]. | is the word for |, the name of a family (+) a country. B.177[1] part of P.N. 160[4] 125[5]

Used as Phonetic W II 52[4] B 216[3] 三

3062 [Tangut] IX 54 | [Tangut] v.3069

3063 [Tangut] III 44 | [Tangut] "fruit"

(i) The dissyllable C.C.f. 14[a] 菓子 "fruit".

3064 [Tangut] VII 27 | [Tangut]

(a) IX 79 ditto

(i) The dissyllable B.99 cat. under "horse"

3065 [Tangut] IX 102 [Tangut] | 3066.

(i) By itself W.I. 128[18] 諂 "to flatter"

(ii) [Tangut] | W.I. 214[5] g.ya.g.yu "intrigue".

(iii) The dissyllable v.3066 (ii)

3066 (ii) (H above 諭諂 "flattering orders" W.I.170^8

3066
- 3069 ⌐ 0622
- 1760 └ 3062
- 1981
- 2380
- 3065
- 5669

3067 4775 chain

3068 4775 chain

3069 3066 chain

3070 0258 chain

3071 5630 chain

3072 0148 chain

3073 5630 chain

3074 0322 chain

3075 independent

3066 [Tangut]

(a)

(b)

(c)

(d)

(e)

(f)

W II 6

B. 201^5

3067 [Tangut]

(a) V

?

3068 [Tangut]

(a) V

?

3069 [Tangut]

(a) I

(b) I

(c) I

B. 205^1

3070 [Tangut]

(a)

?

236

3066 [Tangut] IX 177 [Tangut] |

(a) VII 58 ditto

(b) I 83 | [Tangut] 5669

(c) IX 5 | [Tangut] 1760

(d) VII A 22 [Tangut] | v.2380

(e) IX 5 | [Tangut] ? 1981

(f) IX 102 | [Tangut] "flatter" v.3065

W II 60[4] 妄 "false"

B. 201[5] q.v.

3067 [Tangut] VII 107 [Tangut] | 3068

(a) VII 85 | [Tangut] 5429

?

3068 [Tangut] III 44 [Tangut] | 2657

(a) VII 107 [Tangut] | × 3067

?

3069 [Tangut] VII 58 [Tangut] |

(a) IX 177 ditto

(b) II 35 | [Tangut] 0622

(c) IX 54 [Tangut] | v.3062

B. 205[1] 欺 cheat, ~~insult~~

3070 [Tangut] VII 107 | [Tangut] (~~[illegible]~~) 1242

(a) VII 108 | [Tangut] 1243

?

3071 [Tangut] IX 17 [Tangut] |

(a) IX 74 ditto tʻé-RE

(b) V 44 | [Tangut] 3073 × 3077 (3071)

(c) V 99 | [Tangut] 1740

(d) IX 48 [Tangut] | 0177

(i) (b) above W. II. 36[3] 策勤 ? "stimulation of energy".

(ii) The dissyllable W. I. 168[11] 苦 pain, distress

3072 [Tangut] I A 66 | [Tangut] 2543

3073 [Tangut] V 44 [Tangut] | v.3071

(a) V 63 [Tangut] | 3077

(i) The dissyllable W II 36[3] 策勤

3074 [Tangut] VI 134 [Tangut] | "eye"

W. I. 100[4] 根 208[17] rtsa. ba

"indriya, sense-organ".

3075 [Tangut] IX 107 [Tangut] | "name"

Used as a Phonetic II 4[3] 20[1]

Note. 3074-5 are indistinguishable

3074 perhaps has [Tangut]

3076 0165 pair

3077 5630 chain

3078
2976–1518

3079
1633
3080

3080 3079 chain

3081 5640 pair

3082 2091 chain

3083 4262 chain
3083. mnon. sum, dic by S. pa.
"to declare (?) personally" B.250[1]

3084
1240
0269
3052
3341 – 3336

B.232[5] 覓 seek

3085 0092 chain

3086 chain
2772
2449 – 0540
3086
3267
4604 – 0059
0910
0941 – 2542
1416
1468 – 0205
2549
3112
3211
3768 – 4399
3885 – 4031
4246 – 0189
4567
4597
4602
4756
5085 – 5561
5304 – 3239 – 5723 – 4481

3076
(a)
Passi

3077
?

3078
(a) V
(1) The
"priso

3079
(a) I
(b) I
W.I.98
pain"
3080
?
3081
(a)
?
3082
?

237

3076 [Tangut] VI A 93 [Tangut] | 0165

(a) VI 33 ditto

Passim 罪 sdig. pa "sin".

3077 [Tangut] V 63. | [Tangut] 3073

?

3078 [Tangut] V 97 | [Tangut] ×(1518) 2976

(a) VIII 18 ditto

(i) The disyllable C.C.C. 30[6] 獄 裹 "prison" (in both cases)

3079 [Tangut] VII 73 | [Tangut] 1633

(a) I 124 ditto

(b) I 132 | [Tangut] [Tangut] 3080

W. I. 98[10] 108[16] II 18[2] 32[12] 苦 "bitterness pain" I 134[3]? B 124[4] salt (sea)

3080 [Tangut] I 132 [Tangut] | v. 3079

?

3081 [Tangut] VIII A 70 [Tangut] |

(a) V 86 ditto

?

3082 [Tangut] VI 70 [Tangut] | 3647

?

3083 [Tangut] IX 93 [Tangut] | 3490

C.C.C. 36[6] W. II 2[10] 56[4] 94[8] 80[5] 140[6] 證 "to prove, experience, conviction" B. 216[5]

W. I. 120[17] ~~138 140[6]~~ 証 "to testify, prove" |

3083A [Tangut] Error for [Tangut] 1844

3084 [Tangut] VIII 8 | [Tangut] 1240 ×3336 3341

(a) VIII 81 ditto

(b) I 48 [Tangut] | (c) [Tangut] | III A 25[7] 3352

(d) V 144 [Tangut] | 0269

B 128[2] B. 171[3] 1882 q.v.

(i) W. I. 132[12] II 36[3] 便 "convenient"

(ii) W. II 64[1] 追 "to ~~follow~~ search"?

(iii) [Tangut] | C.C.C. 27[a] 搜 尋 "to investigate & examine"

B. 121[4]

3085 [Tangut] III A 123 [Tangut] | 92

3086 [Tangut] II A 16 | [Tangut] "what"

(a) VIII A 108 ditto v. 2772

(b) V 104 | [Tangut] ×4604

(c) IX 89 | [Tangut] ×2449

W. II 22[9] B. 254[1] 何 what? ci

3087 [Tangut] V 155 | [Tangut]

(a) IX 152 ditto

(i) The disyllable C.C.C. 15[a] 苦 蕖

B. 101 cat. under "vegetables"

3088 3087 pair

{3093} 2080 pair

3094 interpendent

3095 4027 chain

3095. The Tangl. B 246[5] 相失 "to lose oneself"

3089
├ 4093
├ 0034
├ 4946
└ 5391

3096 3492 chain

3097 4027 chain

3090 0019 pair + ...

3098 4027 chain

3099 4027 chain

3091 – 2180
└ 1664
?? [1995A – 2942 – 2299

3100 2680 chain

[Tangut] | W.I.265[16] part of royal title 德化 "transforming virtue"

3092 3262 pair

3101 + 4680 pair

3088 [Tangut]

(a)

(i) The

(ii) | [Tangut]

3089 [Tangut]

(a)

(c)

(d)

?

3090 [Tangut]

(a)

?

3091 [Tangut]

(a)

(i) The

discip

3092 [Tangut]

(a) VI

~~ditto~~

238

3088 [Tangut] IX 152 [Tangut] |

(a) V 155 ditto v. 3087

(i) The dissyllable 苦蕖 C.C.C. 15[a]

(ii) | [Tangut] C.C.C. 14[b] 百茉 [yeh]

3089 [Tangut] V 171 | [Tangut] 4093

(b) II 14 | [Tangut] 4946

(a) III 170 ditto

(c) VII 92 | [Tangut] 5391

(d) IX 34 | [Tangut] 34 0034

?

3090 [Tangut] IX 79 [Tangut] | 19

(a) V 77 ditto

?

3091 [Tangut] IX 79 | [Tangut] 1664

(a) VIII A 46 ditto

(i) The dissyllable W.II 2[7] [124''] [B. 237[3]] 調伏 "to discipline, bring under control".

3092 [Tangut] I 1 [Tangut] |

(a) VIII 50 ditto

~~ditto~~ surprised v. 3262

3093 [Tangut] V 2 [Tangut] |

(a) V 32 ditto

?

3094 [Tangut] IX 67 × by itself | [|]

?

3095 [Tangut] I 23 [Tangut] |

[(a) VIII 12 (?) [Tangut] [Tangut] 4578 4578]

(b)–(d) 3097-9

? See 3097-3099

3096 [Tangut] III 36 [Tangut] |

(a) V 115 ditto

?

3097 [Tangut] I A 80 [Tangut]

A Phonetic character

3098 [Tangut] I A 77 [Tangut]

A Phonetic character

3099 [Tangut] I A 76 [Tangut]

A Phonetic character

3100 [Tangut] VI A 10 | [Tangut] 2680

(a) V 121 [Tangut] | [illegible] 3311

W.II 66[12] 70[7] ~~B. 249~~ 習[1] "to practise" ~~[illegible]~~] B 249[1] sgom-pa "to meditate on" chain 2680

3101 [Tangut] IX 65 [Tangut] |

(a) VII 112 ditto

?

3102 5349 pair

3103 0148 chain

3104 2149 chain

3105 0582 chain

3105B 3199 pair (authentic?)

3106 4882 chain

3107 (ii) 饒益 "abundant" W.II 142^{6}

3107 2164 chain

B.193^{1+3} [[illegible]] 福, 治

Dict 56^{b} [illegible] | regnal period 正德 德

[3108]-[3917]

(i) The Hsing ... [illegible] 苗葉 [c.c.c.15^{a}]

3109 +5270 0928

(ii) | [illegible] c.c.c.14^{b} 百葉

3110 2837 chain

3111 1787 chain

[illegible] ?w

3102 [illegible]

(a) V

?

3103 [illegible]

?

3104 [illegible]

?

3105 [illegible]

B173^{2} [illegible]

3105A

~~3106~~ [illegible]

× Erro[illegible]

3105B [illegible]

?

3106 [illegible]

?

3107 [illegible]

(a) VII

A very [illegible]

(i) By i[illegible]

(ii) The [illegible]

increas[illegible]

(iii) | [illegible]

W.I. 206^{7}

[Tangut] ? error for [Tangut]

3102 [Tangut] VII 46 [Tangut] |

(a) V 62 ditto

?

3103 [Tangut] VII 46 | [Tangut] 1563

?

3104 [Tangut] VI 128 [Tangut] | 5160

?

3105 [Tangut] VII 46 [Tangut] | 1292

B 173[2] twice ×5 [Tangut]. 日 or 曰?

3105A

~~3106~~ [Tangut] VI 135

× Error for [Tangut] 2288

3105B [Tangut] × of III A 95 [Tangut] |

?

3106 [Tangut] II A 15 | [Tangut]

?

3107 [Tangut] I A 64 | [Tangut] 3832

(a) VII 118 | [Tangut]

A very puzzling word

(i) By itself W.I.198[11] B.162[3] B.203[2,3]

(ii) The disyllable W.I 138[4] 益 "to increase" II 40[5] 42[7] 利益

(iii) | [Tangut] C.C.C. 29[a] 卹治

W.I. 206[7] 220[11] yons. su-skyarinba

239

3108 [Tangut] VIII 11 | [Tangut]

(a) V 28 ditto

?

3109 [Tangut] V 37 [Tangut] | [Tangut]

(a) I 23 ditto

(b) III 78 [Tangut] (0928) × by | [Tangut] [Tangut] 0928 5575 5193

?

3110 [Tangut] II 29 | [Tangut]

(a) II 29 ditto

W.I.134[11]

B 245[5] possibly 巢 "nest"

3111 [Tangut] VIII 11 [Tangut] | "house" 1364

(a) I 14 | [Tangut] 3264

(b) V 87 | [Tangut] 2465

(c) VI 135 | [Tangut] 5303

(d) IX 48 | [Tangut] 3113

(e) IX 66 [Tangut] | 0735

(i) C.C.C. 36[b] W.I. 96[13] II 4[9] 門 "gate, door" B 346[3] II 144[1] B.169[4])[b]

(ii) The disyllable C.C.C. 23[a] 門 簾 "door screen"

(iii) [Tangut] | C.C.C. 21[b] 家宅 "house, home" W.I. 96[14] 門戶 "gate"

C.C.C. 34[a] ?

3112 3086 chain

3113 1781 chain

3114 0809 chain

3115 0572 pair

3116 2790 pair

3117 0892 pair

3118 2167 chain

3119 0754 chain

3120 1069 pair

3121 4983 chain

3122 2710 chain

3123.

W I.172[8] 賊 thief

3123
- 2744
- 3124–4100
- 3125
- 3427–1859

3124 3123 chain

3125 3123 chain

3112

?

3113

?

3114

(a) V

C.C.C. 23

tree" I

3115

(a) I

?

3116

3117

(a) V

3118

(a) V

(i) By i.C.

cardin

(ii) |

cake."

3119

(a) II

(b) I

3112 [Tangut] III 10 [Tangut] | 4604

?

3113 [Tangut] IX 48 [Tangut] | "zati" 3111

?

3114 [Tangut] P'U I 34 [Tangut] |

(a) VIII 2 [Tangut] 3362

C.C.C. 23b W.I 92 7 118 12 etc 樹 "vṛkṣa tree" B 180 5

3115 [Tangut] I A 60 [Tangut] |

(a) I A 31 ditto

?

3116 [Tangut] V 11 [Tangut] |

3117 [Tangut] VII 25 [Tangut] | 892

(a) VII 54 ditto

3118 [Tangut] VI 86 [Tangut] | "four" 3763

(a) V 107 | [Tangut] 0389

(i) By itself C.C.C. 11a 隅 "angle, cardinal point"

(ii) | [Tangut] C.C.C. 33b 角子 "a pointed cake."

3119 [Tangut] VII A 70 | [Tangut]

(a) II 24 ditto [L]

(b) I 84 [Tangut] | 4500

240

3119 (cont.)

B.181 條 "branch"

3120 [Tangut] V 11 [Tangut] |

(a) I 42 ditto

?

3121 [Tangut] I 47 | [Tangut] 4303

(a) VIII 88 | [Tangut] 2718

(b) IX 72 | [Tangut] to grasp [1119]

?

3122 [Tangut] IX A 32 [Tangut] | fool 5440

(a) IX 144 [Tangut] | ? 2413

3123 [Tangut] V 56 | [Tangut] 2744

(a) V 114 ditto

(b) V 37 | [Tangut] ~~to steal~~

(c) V A 48 | [Tangut] [Tangut] 3427

(d) VII 77 | [Tangut] to steal

W.I 196 7 com. rkun 214 1 rkun "robber"

3124 [Tangut] VII 77 [Tangut] |

(a) VII 115 | [Tangut] 4100

W.I 138 8 [Tangut] 盜 "to steal, rob."

3125 [Tangut] V 37 [Tangut] |

?

3126 5433 chain

3127 2178 chain

3128 4123 chain

3129 1456 chain

3130
⊥2366–3292
 └4764–1471–5534

3131 0809 chain

3132 2327 chain

3133 2865 chain

3134 – [4726]

3135 0731 chain

3136 5690 chain

3137 | labial semivowels

Dict 2a 3. Title of Ch. IX

3137 2178 chain

B. 192[3] ?Phon.

3138
3721 — 3818

3139 – 5716

3140 2178 chain

3126

?

3127

?

3128

?

3129
~~3130~~

?

3130

(a) V

(i)

? temple

3131
~~3132~~

?

3132

?

3133
~~3134~~

(a) I

?

3134

(i)

cat. und

"amber

Note.

241

3126 [Tangut] V 122 [Tangut] |

?

3127 [Tangut] V 77 [Tangut] | "wind"

?

3128 [Tangut] VIII A 75 [Tangut] |

?

3129 ~~3130~~ [Tangut] IX 39 | [Tangut] 4244

?

3130 [Tangut] VIII 86 | [Tangut] 2366

(a) V A 88 ditto

(i) [Tangut] | C.C.C. 28ª 御史

? temple secretary

3131 ~~3132~~ [Tangut] VII 87 [Tangut] | 2895

?

3132 [Tangut] V 77 [Tangut] | 4785

?

3133 ~~3134~~ [Tangut] IX 39 | [Tangut] 2865

(a) I 68 | [Tangut] {5115 / 5202bis?

~~(b) VI 14 | [Tangut]~~

?

3134 [Tangut] IX 39 ~~[IX 50a]~~ | [Tangut]

(i) | [Tangut] C.C.C. 12ᵇ W.I. 92¹⁰ B. 102

cat. under "precious things": 琥珀

"amber".

Note. Misspelt [Tangut]

3135 ~~3136~~ [Tangut] VI 4 [Tangut] "wood, tree"

3136 ~~3137~~ [Tangut] VI 4 [Tangut] | 3203

3137 ~~3138~~ [Tangut] IX 39 | [Tangut] 2178

(a) V 77 | [Tangut] 3127

(b) V A 107 | [Tangut] "north" 3140

(c) VII 101 | [Tangut] 2295

(d) VIII 71 | [Tangut] 5634

C.C.C. 8ᵇ 10ᵇ & passim 風 W.I. 228³ etc.

rlun "wind"

3137A [Tangut] Error for 3135.

3138 ~~3139~~ [Tangut] IX 39 [Tangut] [Tangut]

(a) I 16 [Tangut] × by | [Tangut]

(b) IX 156 [Tangut] × by [Tangut] |

3139 ~~3140~~ [Tangut] IX 39 | [Tangut]

(a) V 78 ditto

3140 [Tangut] V A 107 [Tangut] | "wind"

(C.C.C. 8ᵇ The disyllable) 朔風

"north wind".

N.B. Not the usual word for "north"; composed of [Tangut] "wind" + [Tangut] "cold"

3141 – 4058 VI

[3147] independent V

3142 – 5718 VI

3148 2956 pair

3143 – 4991

3149
1827
0956

3144
2367–4738
4117
5051
5490

3151 2348 pair

3150 0036 chain

3152 2635 chain

{3145} 0680 chain

3153 3160 chain

3146 4350 pair

3141

3142

3143

3144

3145

3146

242

3141 [Tangut] IX 39 | [Tangut]
(a) VI ditto (14)

3142 [Tangut] VI 89 | [Tangut]
(a) V 57 ditto
(i) The dissyllable C.C.C. 7b 旋風 "whirlwind".

3143 [Tangut] IX 52 ~~29~~ | [Tangut]
(a) IX 4 ditto
(i) The dissyllable C.C.C. 29a

3144 [Tangut] BE I 8 [Tangut] | 2367 high ×(4738)
(a) VI 18 ditto. 2367
(b) I 3 [Tangut] | 4117
(c) I 44 [Tangut] |
[(d) V 132 [Tangut] × by [Tangut] [Tangut] |]
(e) VI 35 | [Tangut] 5051
C.C.C. 12b 29a 高 "high"

3145 [Tangut] IX 72 [Tangut] | 3924
?

3146 [Tangut] VIII 28 [Tangut] |
(a) III A 101 ditto
?

3147 ~~3148~~ [Tangut] III A 130 Family or clan name.

3147A [Tangut] N. 329 blank
Probably corrupt.

3148 [Tangut] III 34 [Tangut] |
(a) VII 39 [Tangut] ditto

3149 ~~3150~~ [Tangut] III 5 | [Tangut]
(a) IX 9 ditto
(a) IX 148 | [Tangut] 0956
(i) The dissyllable C.C.C. 21b 樓閣 W.II 48 (142.12) 樓觀 "lofty hall" W II 140.12

3151 ~~3152~~ [Tangut] V 14 [Tangut] | 2348
(a) III 172 ditto
(b)
?

3150 [Tangut] I 45 | [Tangut] 0036
?

3152 [Tangut] I 26 | [Tangut]
?

3153 ~~3154~~ [Tangut] VII A 124 [Tangut] | 3160
(a) VII 36 | [Tangut] 5437
?

3154, 4775 chain

3155 1929 chain

3156 - 3000

3157 1891 chain

3158 3324 pair

3159 independent

3160
- 3153 - 5437
- 3658 - 4107
- 5182 - 0736

B.123³ trs. 繞 to encircle, enwrap

3161 same as 1363 1369 chain
error

3162 1297 chain

3163 - 2172

3164 4541 chain

3164 W.II 110⁹ 木罢 ? Phonetic

3165 2600 ~~chain~~ pair

3166 - 1973

3154
(a) II
(b) V
(i) (a) al
"hanging

3155

3156
(a) VI
(i) The
"sea-mo
"worm".

3157
(a) VI

3158
(a) VI

3159
name.

3160
(a)
(b)

243

3154 [Tangut] II 15 [Tangut] | 4775
(a) II A 12 [Tangut] | 4391 × 5029
(b) V A 89 [Tangut] | 1461
(i) (a) above W.I. 192² hp'yai.ba "hanging down".

3155 [Tangut] VIII 28 [Tangut] | 1925

3156 [Tangut] I 12 | [Tangut] 2000
(a) VII 82 ditto
(i) The disyllable W.I. 190⁶ c'u.srin "sea-monster" 192⁶ 218¹⁴ srin.po "worm".

3157 [Tangut] VIII A 28 [Tangut] | 2930
(a) VI A 86 | [Tangut] to Kmin 5574

3158 [Tangut] VIII 72 [Tangut] |
(a) VIII 47 ditto

3159 [Tangut] VIII 72 "Family or clan name. B.176³ part of P.N.

3160 [Tangut]
(a) VII A 124 | [Tangut] × 5437 3153
(b) VIII 78 | [Tangut]
(c) VIII 86 | [Tangut] × (0735) 5182
(i) (c) reversed W.I. 218¹⁷ hk'or "retinue".
By ideog B.165² 圍 surround B.131⁵
Note. There is some confusion between this character & 3163.

3161 [Tangut] VII 87 | [Tangut]
?

3162 [Tangut] IX A 136 [Tangut] |

3163 [Tangut] IX 76 | [Tangut]
(a) VIII 68 ditto [[Tangut]]
B.95 [Tangut] ideogram [Tangut] ideogram.
| means "to make a barrier [[Tangut]]"

3164 [Tangut] IX A 124 | [Tangut] 4542
B.227⁵ 壁 partition W.I. 134¹⁷

3165 [Tangut] V A 17 [Tangut] | 2600
(a) V 109 ditto
~~(b) VIII A 33 | [Tangut] 4666~~
B.164⁴ 168¹ W.I. 134¹⁷ 開 to divide up

3166 [Tangut] VII 40 | [Tangut] ? 1973
(a) V 18 ditto
?

3167 2360 chain

3168 0140 chain

3169 4484 chain

3170 (−1433) ~~4033 pair~~

3171 3930 chain

3171 (ii) |彨 業 障 karmāvaraṇa W.II.128[7] ? q.v. v.5717

"the hindrance of (past) karma B.185[1], 186[4] tr. 傳 version (of a sūtra)

W.II 84[12] 86[1] etc. 232[4]

3172 3962 chain

3173 4729 chain

3174 −4666

3175 5217 chain

3176 0313 pair

3177 2943 pair

3178 4030 chain

[3179 v. 829 ?]

3179 5045 chain

3180 3699 chain

3181 1113 chain

3182 − 0365 Double name

3167

?

3168

?

3169

?

3170

(a) III

?

3171

C.C.C. 35

"action

3172

(a) I

?

3173

(a) IX

?

3174

W.I. 134

3175

?

3176

(a) VI

?

244

3167 [Tangut] I 26 [Tangut] | -which 2360

?

3168 [Tangut] IX 72 [Tangut] | 0816

?

3169 [Tangut] IX 108 [Tangut] | q.v. 4484

?

3170 [Tangut] I 78 | [Tangut] ? 1433

(a) III 37 ditto

?

3171 [Tangut] VI 105 [Tangut] | because 3930

C.C.C. 35[b] W. II 18[2] 70[4] 業 karma

"action, work, deed" I. 168[14]

3172 [Tangut] II 40 [Tangut] | ? 3962

(a) I 94 ditto

?

3173 [Tangut] III 141 [Tangut] |

(a) IX 115 ditto

?

3174 [Tangut] VI A 89 | [Tangut]

(a) VIII A 33 ditto

W. I. 134[11] [[Tangut]] app. 坑塹 a pit or ditch [Tangut] ? correct

3175 [Tangut] I A 58 | [Tangut]

?

3176 [Tangut] III 46 [Tangut] |

(a) VI 122 ditto 1189

?

3177 [Tangut] IX 45 [Tangut] |

(a) I 14 ditto

?

3178 [Tangut] III A 87 | [Tangut] q.v. 5005

(i) C.C.C. 36[b] The Dissyllable 指示

"to point out & indicate".

By itself B. 188[2] 指 2680 chain

3179 [Tangut] III A 58 [Tangut] |

(a) III 94 ditto

(b) III 63 [Tangut] | 4086

(c) VII 64 [Tangut] | messenger 5053

C.C.C. 35[b] W. II. 6[1] 轉 Verb vartana, pravartana, vrtti "to turn, transform, change, birth & rebirth

3180 [Tangut] IX 99 [Tangut] |

(a) VI 1 ditto

(i) The Dissyllable Dict 56[a] 7

3181 [Tangut] IX 112 | [Tangut] 2637

(a) IX 63 [Tangut] | 4089

3182 [Tangut] VI 33 Family or clan name

(a) IX 9 [Tangut] | 0365

Presumably a double name.

3183 3685 chain

3191 – 0437A

3192 5728 chain

3184 0157 chain

3185 4619 chain

3186 4083 chain

3193 – 4157

3194 4651 chain

3187 3226 chain

3195 – 4938

3188
1632
1644

3189 2465 chain

3195A 5128 chain

3190 3775 ~~1252~~ chain

3183

(a) II

B.211[2]

3184

?

3185

3186

(a) VI

G.C.C. 27[6]

W II 16[3] ?

3186A

See

3187

B 173[1] 希

3188

(a) IX

(b) I 2

?

3189

W II 48[4]

3190

(a) IX

W. II 84[7]

245

3183 [Tangut] II A34 [Tangut] | "name"
(a) III 22 | [Tangut] "Buddha" × 3897
B. 211² tr. 佛

3184 [Tangut] II A33 [Tangut] |
?

3185 [Tangut] I 58 [Tangut] | 4619

3186 [Tangut] VI 78 [Tangut] | 4502
(a) VI 103 |[Tangut] [Tangut] 0080
C.C.C. 27^b | [Tangut] 加官 (1349)
W.II 16³ ?

3186 A See 3174
[Tangut] See 1391–1395.

3187 [Tangut] II 38 [Tangut] | 3677
B. 173¹ 希 rare, few etc.

3188 [Tangut] I. 17 | [Tangut] 1632
(a) IX 17 ditto
(b) I 26 [Tangut] × by [Tangut] disyllable 1644
?

3189 [Tangut] IX 129 [Tangut] | 2466
W.II 48⁴ 蹬 "step"

3190 [Tangut] IX 103 [Tangut] | 3975
(a) IX 103 | [Tangut] 1676
W. II 84⁷ 愧 "ashamed"

3191 [Tangut] I 22 | [Tangut]

3192 [Tangut] ? VII 26 [VII 59–60] v. 3195A [Tangut]
(i) | [Tangut] C.C.C. 20⁶ 36^a etc. 菩薩 Bodhisattva
(ii) | [Tangut] W.I. 98⁹ 134¹² 衆生 "all creatures" B. 131³

3193 [Tangut] I 11 | [Tangut]
(a) VIII 3 ditto
(i) The disyllable B. 102 cat. under "vegetables"

3194 [Tangut] IX 129 [Tangut] | "earth"
B. 248 W.II 2¹¹ 岸 "shore"

3195 [Tangut] I 11 [Tangut] |
(a) III 172 ditto
W.I. 96¹⁴ 108¹³ etc. 種 "sort, kind".
214¹⁰ *kun. gyi* "universal"
198¹¹ 200¹³ *rnam. par* "entirely"
218⁴ *sna. tshogs* "various sorts".
154⁷ 雜 "variegated"

3195A [Tangut] VII 26 | [Tangut]
Misspelling of 3192

3196 – 4367

3197 0233 chain

3198 0229 pair

3199 – 3105B

3200 chain – 1900 < 1605; 1038 – 1042

3200 ┼ 1900; 1605; 1038 – 1042

| [Tangut] B. 201[4] tr. 威肅 'majestic'.

3201, 0038 pair

3202 | [illegible] 'accumulated defilement' W. II 4[11]

3202 ┼ 1677; 0142; 0823

3203 5690 chain VI

3204 1929 chain

3205 5057 chain

3206 – 4612

246

3196 [Tangut] I 128 | [Tangut]
(a) IX 30 ditto
?
3197 [Tangut] VI 13 [Tangut] "self" 干 cf. 3198
?
3198 [Tangut] I 128 | [Tangut]
(a) IX 30 ditto cf. 3196
?
3199 [Tangut] III A 95 [Tangut] |
?
3200 [Tangut] I 128 | [Tangut] 1900
(a) II 9 ditto
(b) VIII 55 [Tangut] × by dissyllable 1605 (1048) banner
(c) IX 171 [Tangut] × by dissyllable 1048
(i) W. I. 110[7] 威 "majesty" 194[5] 331 "brightness"
(ii) The dissyllable W. I. 110[1] 巍 "lofty"
136[3] 威儀 "dignity, respect-inspiring deportment" I 224[16] c'a. byan
3201 [Tangut] IX 131 | [Tangut] 0038
(a) V 1 ditto [Tangut]
?
3202 [Tangut] VIII 82 | [Tangut] punishment 1677
(a) VIII 21 ditto
(b) VI 62 | [Tangut] q.v. 0823
(c) IX 59 | [Tangut] urn 0142

(i) C.C.C. 31[b] 32[a] 罪 "sin, transgression"
(ii) W. I. 90[12] 過 "transgression"
(iii) | [Tangut] 1699 repent W. I. 96[8,9] 132[14] etc. 266[19] 懺悔 "to repent" B 259 B. 170[1]
(iv) | [Tangut] W. II 4[11] 累 染 infuse 0919

3203 [Tangut] V 64 [Tangut] |
(a) VI 4 | [Tangut] 3136
(b) VI 57 | [Tangut] × 5274
(c) VII A 66 | [Tangut] × 3809
?
3204 [Tangut] III 130 | [Tangut]
3205 [Tangut] III 38 [Tangut] | 5057
(a) III 94 ditto
(b) III 150 [Tangut] | 3272
(i) (b) above W. I 96[13] 逼迫 II 18[7] 逼 to constrain, compel, harass
W. II 118[7] 逼切 to harass & remove
3206 [Tangut] I 1 | [Tangut]
(a) III 34 ditto [[Tangut] for [Tangut]]
(i) The dissyllable C.C.C. 26[b] 財産 "wealth, property"

3207 3783 chain

3208 4396 chain

W.II 132² 財

3209 4396 chain

3210 ~~1100~~
└1100-4362

3211 3086 chain

[3212]-[1233]

3213
┬5211
├3945-3227-5456
└5719

3214 - 4024

3215 3226 chain

3216 2179 chain

3217 2091 chain

3218 -5441

3218 Also used with (dagter) verbs to form a causative

= 起 "to come forth"

| = 令起 "to bring forth, create"

W.II 4¹²

W.I 134^{1,39} a clear causative

3207

C.C.C. 35⁶

W.II 54¹²

Note.

3208

(a) IX

(b) VI

(i) C.C.C. 35

W.I. 138

(ii)

W.I. 136

3209

C.C.C. 13

3210

(a) III

?

3211

?

3212

(a) V

?

3213

(a) V

(b) VI

28/1/39

247

3207 IX A 28 | 3783

C.C.C. 35[b] 貧 "poor"

W.I. 54[12] 窮 "poor"

Note. "money" "not"

3208 VIII A 38 |

(a) IX A 86 ditto

(b) VI 87 |

(i) C.C.C. 35[a, b] 物 "things, property"

W.I. 138[7,8] etc. do. I 190[8] 192[10] not "wealth"

(ii) This disyllable C.C.C. 12[b] 貨物

W.I. 136[17] 財寶 "property or jewels."

3209 VI 87 |

C.C.C. 13[b] W.I. 138[11] 金錢 "cash money" B. 169[3]

3210 VI 87 |

(a) III 139 ditto v. 1100

?

3211 VII 27 | 4604

?

3212 I 23 |

(a) V 19 ditto

?

3213 V A 64 | 5211

(a) V 11 ditto

(b) VI 131 | 5718

28/1/39

3213 cont.

(c) IX A 13 | 3945 tongue

?

3214 I 93 |

(a) VI 2 ditto

C.C.C. 11[a] W.I. 96[10] 今 "this (day, year etc.)"

3215 III 96 | want

(a) V 49 ditto v. 3226

C.C.C. 1[a] 7 to talk (language)

3216 VIII A 95 "sacred word"

B. 95 ideogram follows.

| is a sacred word, used in the Saddharmapuṇḍarīkā."

3217 V 2 | 3956

3218 I 23 | 5441

(a) I 38 ditto reversed

This auxiliary verb appears to correspond to T. byed.pa. It is used with nouns to convert them into verbs, either simply or with a causative C.C.C. 30[b] 36[b] = 令 35[b2] = 爲 33[b] B. 252 W.I. 132[18] 134, 136[1], 190[14] Note esp. 194[14-15]

3219 4439 chain

3220 - 5052

3221 4127 chain

3222 0680 chain

3223 3223 W.I.265 (?right)

3224 2662 chain

3224 B.248 śes.rab prajñā "wisdom"

B.187 增 add(itional), more

3225 4485 chain

B.192 言語 language

3226 3215 2082 2342 2631

3227 3213 chain

3228 2149 chain

3229 5523 chain

3230 0934 chain

[3231] 0767 chain

[Tangut] V 49 | [Tangut]

3215 III 96 ditto

2082 II 19 | [Tangut]

2631 VII A 86 | [Tangut]

2342 III 70 | [Tangut] [Tangut]

3677 V 51 [Tangut] |

3187 II 38 | [Tangut]

5015 V 41 | [Tangut]

5003 VII 68 | [Tangut] [Tangut]

5020 VII 28 | [Tangut]

5083 III 155 | [Tangut]

5720 VII 79 | [Tangut]

2342-0355 [Tangut] [Tangut] defines:—

1044 IX A 141 [Tangut]

1645 I 112 [Tangut]

1672 V A 81 [Tangut]

1673 V A 80 [Tangut]

1894 VIII A 32 [Tangut]

2067 IX A 133 [Tangut]

2068 VII A.1 [Tangut]

2073 IX 103 [Tangut]

2081 IX A 116 [Tangut]

2083 I A 44 [Tangut]

2083 bis I A 55 [Tangut]

2098 VIII A 3 [Tangut]

3226 C.C.C. 18a 言 ~~'word'~~ 'to speak'.

3215 C.C.C. 1a7 'to talk (a language)'

2082. — 2631 —

2342 C.C.C. 30b + many text references 言 'a word'. This word is specifically a noun. C.C.C. 34a 承 'orders'.

3677 C.C.C. 7b 句 'a sentence'.

3187 — 5015 —

5003 — 5020 —

5083 — 5720 —

2342-0355 means strictly 'a true, or real, word, + is used technically for the Sanskrit term <u>mantra</u>, or mystical word.

1044	—	1645	—
1672	<u>K'in</u>	1673	—
1894	<u>u</u>	2067	<u>lei</u> (or <u>ro</u>?)
2068	<u>NČA</u>	2073	—
2081	<u>Lin</u>	2083	<u>p'in</u>
2083 bis	<u>PIN</u>	2098	<u>OM</u>
2100	<u>K'en</u>	2105	<u>Lun</u>
4244	<u>HUM</u>	5497	Â

3219

3220

(a) III

(1) Disyll. W

3221

3222

3223

C.C.C. 6

W. I. 224

3224

W. I. 90

勝 ji

uttam

infini

B. 347 Ph

3225

?B 246 本

3226

(a) III

(b) II

(c) II

(d)

248

3219 [Tangut] III 135 | [Tangut] 4439

?

3220 [Tangut] I 93 | [Tangut] 5052 former

(a) III 91 ditto

(?) Disyll. W.II 122[6] 往昔 "past"

3221 [Tangut] I A 48 [Tangut] |

3222 [Tangut] VI 128 [Tangut] | 0680

3223 [Tangut] yi VIII A 53 [Tangut] | "good luck" 3810

(b) VI 121 [Tangut] 0427 (a) ditto (c) 4289

C.C.C. 6[a] 福祿 prosperity B 345[1] W.I 165

W.I. 224[10] ~~skal~~ ~~du Gnyi?~~ mbu

3224 [Tangut] I.122 | [Tangut] 2662

W.I. 90[10] 108[9] 112[2] etc. II 2[1] 16[7] 80[8] etc.

勝 jina victory, to surpass

uttama W.I. 194[17] gzan.med

infinitely W.I.265[14] [Tangut] | "of surpassing wisdom"

B.347[1] Phon. in name ト B.124[2]

3225 [Tangut] I A 62 | [Tangut]

?~~B 246[3] 桓 Huan P.N.~~

3226 [Tangut] gên V 49 | [Tangut] 3215 to talk

(a) III 96 ditto v.3215

(b) II 19 | [Tangut] 2082

(c) III 70 | [Tangut] na' word 2342 ×2342

(d) VII A 86 | [Tangut] ? 2631

3226 cont.

[(e) [Tangut] | See 2179]

C.C.C. 29[b] 言 "word": (e) means "sacred word". This is definitely a noun meaning "word".

W.II 42[11] B.93 B 231[5]

3227 [Tangut] IX 35 [Tangut] | 3945

(a) III 147 | [Tangut]

?

3228 [Tangut] V A 135 | [Tangut] 1793

(a) III 122 | [Tangut] 2338

?

3229 [Tangut] V 2 [Tangut] | 4273

3230 [Tangut] RE IX 17 [Tangut] | 0934

(a) IX 149 ditto

C.C.C. 32[b] 丈 eibu 10 Chinese feet or an old man ("1 drum")

3231 [Tangut] IX 95 [Tangut] |

(a) I 69 ditto

W.I 136[2] 搖 "to shake, wave" C

248

3232 - 3943

[3237] 0863 chain III

3238 — 1560 I 93 | [Tangut]

3239 3086 chain

|[Tangut] W.I.134[16] 拍 捏 to slap + ...

3233 - 3240 chain

~~3240 chain 0193 - 1029 - 3233 - 5608 - 5722~~ 1959 - 2025

3233A (0089 pair)

3240 |[Tangut] [Tangut] "teeth-tip sounds"

i.e. sibilants Dict 2ª | Title of Ch. VI

3234 2485 chain

|[Tangut] [Tangut] "true dental sounds"

i.e. palatal sibilants Dict 2ª | Title of Ch. VII

3240
- 5722 - 1959 II - 2025
- 0193 - 5608
- 1029
- 3233

3235 - 3799

B 204³ 犯 to transgress

3241 0423 pair

3236 independent

3242 2294 pair

3232 [Tangut]

(a) V

(i) The ...

253³

B. 252¹

injure"

to discu...

3233 [Tangut]

3233A

form of

3234 [Tangut]

(a) V

?

3235 [Tangut]

(a) I

Verb.

(i) C.C.C. 3

a drum...

(ii) [Tangut]

crimina...

3236

(Lo. p. 23

249

3232 [Tangut] VI 63 | [Tangut]

(a) V 120 ditto

(i) The dissyllable W.I.132[17] 3 ... B.252[1] [253[3]] htsʻe. bar byed. pa = 害 "to injure" 255[2] (T. the same) 嬈亂 to disturb or confuse.

.....

3233 [Tangut] V 54 [Tangut] | back teeth 3240

3233A [Tangut] Possibly the correct form of 83 [Tangut]

3234 [Tangut] VI 63 [Tangut] | 2980

(a) V 44 [Tangut] | [[Tangut]] 5139

?

3235 [Tangut] VI 63 | [Tangut] 3799

(a) I 26 ditto

Verb.

(i) C.C.C.32[a,b] W II 4[12] 80[3] 擊 to beat a drum. 鼓 ditto W.II 122[1]

(ii) [Tangut] | W II 84[7] 惡犯 "wicked criminal".

3236 [Tangut] VI 63 x by self [|] |

(Lo. p.23 || = 丁丁 "man by man"

3237 [Tangut] V 186 [Tangut] |

?

3238 [Tangut] VII 66 | [Tangut]

(a) VII A 58 ditto

?

3239 [Tangut] V A 73 | [Tangut] - 53 [illegible]

(a) VIII A 64 | [Tangut] 5723 ~~3240~~

W.I. 134[16] ?

3240 [Tangut] VII 105 | [Tangut] 5722 front teeth

(a) V 106 ditto

(b) I 27 | [Tangut] ? 0193

(c) I 103 | [Tangut] 1029

(d) V 54 | [Tangut] [Tangut] ? 3233

(ii) The dissyllable C.C.C.18[a] 齒牙 "back teeth & front teeth"

(i) By itself W.II 48[3] 齒 back teeth 'all' 1962

(iii) | [Tangut] B.100. cat. under "camel"

0423 cf. 2025

3241 [Tangut] IX 48 [Tangut] | back teeth 0423

(i) [Tangut] | B.99 cat. under "horse"

3242 [Tangut] VII 105 [Tangut][Tangut]

(a) IX 18 [Tangut] 2294 x by [Tangut] 0363 v. 2294

The trisyllable B. 102 cat. under vegetables. C.C.C.15[a] 馬齒菜 "horse's teeth vegetable".

3243 0974 pair

3244 - 1419

3245 2482 chain

3246 in hypentent

3247 4123 chain

3248 2466 chain

3249 0271 chain

3248A } - 4408
3291 }

3250 2703 chain

3251 0394

3252 3896 chain

3253 4868 chain

3254 0159 chain

3255 1584 chain

3256 5305 chain

3257 take over 0168 chain

[3258] 2279 chain

3243

(a) V

(i) The

"wolf,

3244

(a) V

to bite

3245

Nevski

3246

3247

(b) V

(a) V

?

3248

?

3249

?

3248A

?

3250

?

250

3243 [illegible] VII 105 [illegible] |

(a) V 7 ditto

(i) The disyllable C.C.C. 16[b] 狐 狼

"wolf, fox" B.100 cat. under "wild animals"

3244 [illegible] V 186 | [illegible] to bite 1419

(a) V A 45 ditto

to bite Nevski II 516

3245 [illegible] III 18 [illegible] | 2482

Nevski I 459 "black"

3246 [illegible] III 18 Family or clan name

3247 [illegible] I 8 [illegible] | 4123

(b) V A 76 [illegible] × by | | 4885

(a) V 34 ditto

?

3248 [illegible] IX 20 [illegible] | 2466

?

3249 [illegible] V 1 | [illegible] listen 3700

?

3248A [illegible] × of III 42 | [illegible] to end destroy 4408

?

3250 [illegible] IX A 112 | [illegible] 1799

?

3251 [illegible] VII 89 [illegible] |

3252 [illegible] V 143 [illegible] |

(a) III 27 ditto

(b) VII 52 [illegible] | 0854

(i) The disyllable [illegible] (W. I 92[1])

"rhetoric"

3253 [illegible] VII 89 | [illegible]

(a) VII A 11 | [illegible] red sand 0657

?

3254 [illegible] VII 89 [illegible] | "flavour" v. 159

C.C.C. 14[a] 柿 "persimmon"

3255 [illegible] VII 36 [illegible] | 1584

(a) VIII 38 ditto

(b) VII 32 [illegible] | × 3394

?

3256 [illegible] VII 36 [illegible] | 5305

(a) V 107 ditto

? chain 5305

3257 [illegible] IX 37 | [illegible]

(a) IX A 130 ditto

?

3258 [illegible] I 45 | [illegible] 0811 ~~mountain~~

?

3265 4011 chain
B.215 鬚 'beard, awn'

3259
4705
0412

3266 3417 chain

3267 3086 chain

3260 – [3730]

3268 1501 chain

3261 5637 chain

3269 W.I.168? B.165
II 678 向 facing, opposite to, toward

3262 – 3092

3269 chain
3745 – 3748 – 1072
1146 – 2028 – 1987
2209 – 3712 – 0029
3040 – 1390 – 3423

3263
1920
1786

3270 0680 chain

3264 1781 chain

3271 4561 chain

3271 bis 1473 bis chain

3259
(a) VII
3259
3260
(a) V 5
(b) I 7
?
3260
(a) V
?
3261
?
3261A
3262
(a) I
The
3263
(a) VII
(b) III
B 172 (q.v.)
Note A
3264
?

251

3259 Ⅲ 19 | v. 矛

(a) Ⅶ 33

3259 Ⅱ 1 | 4705

(a) Ⅴ 51 ditto

(b) Ⅰ 77 | 0412

? cf 3260

3260 Ⅱ 1 |

(a) Ⅴ 51 ditto

? cf 3259

3261 Ⅸ 4 | 4446

?

3261A B.128[1] Error for 2193

3262 Ⅷ 50 |

(a) Ⅰ 1 ditto

The dissyl. B.229[2] 驚訝 startled & surprised

3263 Ⅰ 14 | ? 1920

(a) Ⅶ 85 ditto

(b) Ⅲ 12 | ? 1786

B 172[3] (q.v.) tr. 幕 'curtain'

Note. A common Phonetic.

3264 Ⅰ.14 | 3111

?

3265 ⅠA 99 | head 4011

(i) By itself C.C.C. 18[b] 毛 "hair"

(ii) The dissyllable C.C.C. 18[b] 頭髮 "the hair of the head". 4011 chain

3266 Ⅰ 14 |

?

3267 Ⅶ 44 | 2449

?

3268 Ⅸ 17 | 1501

(b) Ⅵ 82 | 3999 3268

(a) Ⅰ 89 | 0366

?

3269 Ⅸ 17 | 3745

(a) ⅤA 37 ditto

(b) Ⅲ 25 | to err' q.v. 2209

(c) Ⅵ 88 | additional 3040

(d) Ⅷ 8 | ? (2028) 1146

(i) C.C.C. 11[a] etc. 方 "(the 4 or 10) quarters" (北方)

W.I. 204[13] B.252 p'yogo. Ditto. B246[5] B246[9] q.v.

(ii) C.C.C. 35[a] 邊 "side, edge"

3270 Ⅸ 17 | 0680

?

3271 Ⅸ 17 | 4561

(a) Ⅸ 22 ditto

B.189[2] tr. 仰 to look up, respectful

3271 bis Ⅸ 17 1473

3272 5057 chain

3278 2635 chain

3273 1876 chain

3274–1809

3279 0148 chain

3280 5190 chain

3274A 2571 pair

3275 3587 chain

3276. By itself B 346[1] 纐 'clear'

3276
⊥ 3981–2044–4264

B.195[2]
3276 W.I.265[18] 纐 'to display, make plain'

B.121[3] 'clearly' 171[5]

3281 2635 chain

3282
⊥ 2565–4001

3277 0741 chain

3283 2193 chain

3272
(i) The disyll...
"to constr...

3273
?

3274
(a) III 1...
B.162[4] 16...
Lo p.25 ...

~~3275~~

~~3275~~

3274A
? Nevski I...

3275
?

3276
(a) VI...

(i) By itself...
B.196...
(i) The ...

W.I.100[4] ...
(ii) ...
appear...

3277
(a) VI...

C.C.C. 22...

252

3272 III 150 | 3205
(i) The disyllable W I.96[13] 逼迫 II 18[7] 逼 "to constrain, compel, harass". v.3205

3273 VII 13 |
?

3274 IX 44 |
(a) III 163 ditto
B.162[4] 164[1]
{Lo p.25 瑞 "auspicious"}

~~3275~~
~~3275~~

3274A × of V 39 |
? Nevski I 393 "Veler"

3275 VII A 90 | 3587
?

3276 VII 58 | ×× 3981
(a) VI 112 ditto
~~(i) By itself W II 24[10]~~
{B.196[10] 示現 to proclaim, demonstrate}
(i) The disyllable C.C.C. 30[a] 分白
W.I.100[4] 分明 "clear, plain" ~~distinguish~~ B.180[3]
(ii) | W.II 24[10] 26[10] 顯現 "to appear clearly".

3277 IX 48 | 0741
(a) VI A 45 | 3534
C.C.C. 22[b] 植 "to plant (trees)"

3278 V 67 | 2013
(a) I 53 | × 3523
(b) VII 4 | × 3994 formerly
C.C.C. 32[a] W.II 44[6] & passim
後 "after". A post-position

3279 V A 111 | 5159

3280 VI A 47 | 2184
(a) VI 24 | 5190
(i) By itself W.I 134[2] 斷 "to break off"
II 12[7] 絕 "to (be) cut off".
(ii) The disyllable (but in the negative)
W.I.108[11] 窮 "empty, exhausted"

3281 V A 10 | 3523

3282 VII 69 | × 4001 2565 [2566]
(a) V A 26 ditto
(i) C.C.C. 35[b] 醜 ugly, hateful.
(ii) (W.I.170[10] The disyllable) 醜陋 "ugly"

3283 VII A 115 | 1898
(b) V 127 | × 3474
?

3284 ?0271 chain

3285 2149 chain

3286 4079 chain

3287 4425 chain

3288 2755 pair

3289 5356 chain

3289A 䗗 See 3654

3290 2969 chain

3291 See 3248 A

3293 -1598 A

3292 3130 chain

3294 1296 pair

3295 4208 chain

3296 -1792

3297 1681 chain

3298 2780 chain

B.188[1] | 䗗常往 eternal

B.189[3] ?? 永 228[4] 常

3299 -5364

3289

3299

3284

(a) VII

?3301

3285

?3302

3286

?3303

3287

?3304

3288

(a) VI

?3305

3289

(a) III

(b) IX

(i) The

月土 "b

3290

3291

C.C.C. 37

? same

3298A

N.776

Nevski I

3289B [Tangut] – – – 3652
3299A [Tangut] Correct form of 3654 q.v.

3284 [Tangut] I 38 [Tangut] | (1383A)
(a) VII A3 | [Tangut] [[Tangut]] 1617
?

3285 [Tangut] VIII 78 [Tangut] | 3371
?

3286 [Tangut] I 8 [Tangut] |
?

3287 [Tangut] IX 20 [Tangut] | 2386
?

3288 [Tangut] I A 67 [Tangut] | 2755
(a) VI 54 ditto
?

3289 [Tangut] I 45 | [Tangut] 5356
(a) III 69 | [Tangut] 3333
(b) IX A 107 [Tangut] | 4668
(i) The disyllable C.C.C. 19a 腹 肚 "belly" (in both cases) W.I. 170[5]

3290 [Tangut] II 1 | [Tangut] 2969
?

3291 [Tangut] [VII 59-60]
C.C.C. 37a
? same as 3248A

3298A [Tangut] × of V A 63 | [Tangut]
N. 176 dbhih ? error for ~~3299~~ 3658
Nevski I 398

[Tangut] 253

3293 [Tangut] I 71 [Tangut] | 1598A
C.C.C. 31a 鬆 "hair"
W.I. 190[18] tcan, to. can "matted hair"

3292 [Tangut] III 19 | [Tangut] 3130
?

3294 [Tangut] VII 88 [Tangut] |
(a) IX 75 ditto (misspelt)
? v2189A

3295 [Tangut] VIII 78 [Tangut] | bone 4208
B. 132[1] 屍 corpse

3296 [Tangut] V 27 | [Tangut]
(a) III 156 ditto
?

3297 [Tangut] IX 2 [Tangut] | 1681
(a) III 133 ditto
(i) W.I. 212[18] | [Tangut] ro. lais a sort of devil.

3298 [Tangut] VIII 8 [Tangut] |
(a) VI 39 | [Tangut]
C.C.C. 15a 20a W.I. 100[1] etc 常 constant(ly)
C.C.C. 22a | [Tangut] 平 五 秋
B. 182[1] 恒 constant B. 160[3] 172[4] q.v.

3299 [Tangut] I 16 | [Tangut]
(a) III 6 ditto
(i) The disyllable C.C.C. 24b 裤 肚

3300 2167 chain

3301 2796 chain

3302 independent

3303 – 2428 A

3304 3026 chain

3305 – 4172

3306 – 3307

3307 3306 pair

3308 2596 chain

3309 2778 chain

3310 4844 pair

3311 2680 chain

3312 3829 chain ditto

3313 2318 pair

3314 independent

3315 5300 pair

3316 4276 chain

3316A 4588 pair

3300

?

3301

?

3302

name.

3303

?

3304

(a) VII

?

3305

(a) I

?

3306

(a) III

?

3307

(a) III

3308

(a) V

(b) IX

(c) IX

C.C.C. 18

254

3300 [Tangut] VI 93 [Tangut] | 5664

?

3301 [Tangut] II 26 | [Tangut] 2796

?

3302 [Tangut] IX 77 Family or clan name.

3303 [Tangut] I 87 [Tangut] |

?

3304 [Tangut] III A 128 [Tangut] | 4091

(a) VII A 4 | [Tangut] | 2981

?

3305 [Tangut] I 71 | [Tangut]

(a) I 52 ditto

?

3306 [Tangut] III 23 | [Tangut]

(a) III 59 ditto

?

3307 [Tangut] III 59 [Tangut] |

(a) III 23 ditto

3308 [Tangut] VIII 50 [Tangut] | 4159

(a) V 124 | [Tangut] 0055

(b) IX 36 | [Tangut] 4586

(c) IX 125 | [Tangut] 2586

C.C.C. 18b 胷 "breast"

3309 [Tangut] I 8 [Tangut] | 2778

(a) I 16 ditto

(b) V 18 | [Tangut] 0146

C.C.C. 17b 鱉 "turtle"

3310 [Tangut] IV 5 [Tangut] |

(a) IX 33 ditto

3311 [Tangut] V 121 | [Tangut] to practice 3100

(a) VI 8 | [Tangut] law 4126

W. I 116[8] II 2[10] 4[7] 戒 śīla "precept, morality, commandment

C.C.C. 29a 條 "law, order". 2680 chain 3326

3312 [Tangut] III A 110 [Tangut] [Tangut]

A Phonetic character

3313 [Tangut] I 6 | [Tangut]

(a) VI 92 ditto

?

3314 [Tangut] VII 72 Family or clan name

3315 [Tangut] V 130 [Tangut] |

(a) VII 111

Y. 4779

3316 [Tangut] I 6 | [Tangut] seed 2021

chain 2021

3316A [Tangut] × of I 75 [Tangut] |

?

3317
I 1988-1989

3318 0459 pair

3319 5188 chain

3320 2535 chain
3320 | B. plaq; Inscription in metal plaque; trs. 防守

3321 0970 chain

3322 2494 chain

3323 0148 chain

3324 - 3158

3325 - 3729

3324 A ~~0617 pair~~ error for 3331

3326 3829 chain

3327 3426 chain

3328 - 2648

3329 interpunct

3330 4128 chain

3330 A 3331 chain

3317
(a) IX
?

3318
(a) V 3
~~(a)~~

3319
(a) V
W. I. 100[7]

3320
?

3321
?

3322
B. 164[2]

3323
?

3324
(a) VII
?

3325
(a) V
?

3324 A

255

3317 [Tangut] IX A 131 | [Tangut] ? 1988
(a) IX A 24 ditto
?

3318 [Tangut] III 8₁ [Tangut] | 0459
(a) V 3 ditto

3319 [Tangut] III 8₁ [Tangut] | 5188
(a) V 11 ditto
W.I.100[7] 外 outside

3320 [Tangut] I.94 | [Tangut] ant 2013
?

3321 [Tangut] II 36 [Tangut] | 5092
?

3322 [Tangut] VII 25 [Tangut] | 2494
B.164[2] the 木艮 [illegible] root 171[3]

3323 [Tangut] III 4 [Tangut] | 5154
? [Tangut]

3324 [Tangut] VIII 47 | [Tangut]
(a) VIII 72 ditto
?

3325 [Tangut] IX 117 | [Tangut]
(a) V 54 ditto [[Tangut]]
?

3324A [Tangut] III 161 X of 0617

3326 [Tangut] III 44 [Tangut] |
(a) III A 110 [Tangut] x by | [Tangut] 3312
(b) VI 74 [Tangut] | 4740
(c) VIII 19 [Tangut] | 4012
(i) (b) above C.C.C.10[6] 後日 "to-morrow"
(ii) (c) above C.C.C.10[6] 外後日 "the day after to-morrow"

3327 [Tangut] III 45 | [Tangut] 5346
(a) III 136 | [Tangut] 5693
A particle meaning "in addition, furthermore", sometimes used simply to complete the sense.
W.II 22[4] 況 II 26[9] 52[5] 曾
W.I.108[10] II 22[8]

3328 [Tangut] V 10 | [Tangut]
(a) II 9 ditto
?

3329 [Tangut] IX A 57 x by itself | [Tangut]

3330 [Tangut] IX 125 [Tangut] |
C.C.C.28[a] ? 審 to investigate

3330A [Tangut] x of III 129 [Tangut] |
? Possibly an error for 3038 [Tangut] see 3331 (ii)

3340–0196 pair

3331
-- 3330 A
0617

3339 [1150] chain
3339 (i) W.I.176 柔 gentle

3332–0517 chain

33341 3084 chain

3333 5356 chain

[3334] chain ? 3653 A
0283–4120
0060
3653

3342 2273 chain

3335
3337
2693
4351

3343 1811 pair

3336 3084 chain

3337 3335 chain

3344
3367
3355

3338 1929 chain

3331

(a) III 16

(i) By itself

(ii)

lazy?

3332

3333

3334

(a) IX

(c) IX

3335

(a) III VII

(b) VI

(c) VII

C.C.C. 9

3336

3337

spring

3338

(a) VI

(i) The

& ox B.

3331 [Tangut] III 129 | [Tangut]
(a) III 161 | [Tangut] 148[12]
(i) By itself W.II 66[1] 厭 weary
(ii) | [Tangut] W.II 14[7] 疲 懈 "tired & lazy."

3332 [Tangut] V 8 | [Tangut] 0717
?

3333 [Tangut] III 69 [Tangut] | 3289
?

3334 [Tangut] III A 125 | [Tangut] "south"
(a) IX 108 ditto (b) VII A 64 | [Tangut] [Tangut] 0060
(c) IX 110 | [Tangut] [Tangut] 3653 umbrella
?

3335 [Tangut] (nê) III 19 | [Tangut]
(a) III 97 ~~VII 33~~ | [Tangut] 4351
(b) VI 11 | [Tangut] "autumn" 2693
(c) VII 33 [Tangut] × by | [Tangut]
C.C.C. 9[a] 春 "spring season"

3336 [Tangut] I 5 [Tangut] | v. 3340
?

3337 [Tangut] VII 33 [Tangut] [Tangut]
"Spring & autumn"

3338 [Tangut] V 137 | [Tangut] 1934
(a) VI 97 [Tangut] | 5392
(i) The dissyllable C.C.C. 16[b] 犛 牛 "yak & ox B. 99

3340 [Tangut] Tu III 127 (128?) | [Tangut] —0196 256
(a) V 86 ditto
1,000 B. 177[1] part of P.N.

3338 cont.
(ii) | [Tangut] B. 99 cat. under "oxen."

3339 [Tangut] II 18 | [Tangut]
(ii) | [Tangut] W.I. 198[9] Zi. syur "to give tranquillity." B 220[1]
B 272[2] 2 意恣
(i) By itself W.I 194[6] Zi. ba "tranquillity."

3341 ~~3340~~ [Tangut] III A 25 | [Tangut] (misspelt) 3054
(a) I 5 | [Tangut]
(i) By itself C.C.C. 29[a]
(ii) The dissyllable [[Tangut]] C.C.C. 27[a] 搜 尋 "to investigate & examine"

3342 [Tangut] VIII 36 [Tangut] | 2292
?

3343 [Tangut] VI 107 [Tangut] | 1811
(a) VII A 52 ditto reversed
Dict 1[6]1

3343A ~~3342A~~ [Tangut] IX 5. This is a wrong reference & probably a complete mistake

3344 [Tangut] V 44 | [Tangut] 3367
(a) II 22 ditto
(b) III 1 [Tangut] | 3357
B. 233[1] tr. 念

3345 1241 pair

3346
0400
0585

3347 0680

3348 4396 chain

3349 3354 ~~chain~~

3350 ~~Probably~~
3350 2729 pair

3351
3375 – 3353

3352 3509 ~~pair~~

3353 3351 ~~chain~~

3354 chain
3366 – 1853
2885 – 1531 – 5259
2514
0011
3349
3374 – 3359

3355 3344 ~~chain~~

3356 0607 pair

3357 – 0248 ~~pair~~

3358 4707 pair

3345

(a) VI 6

?

3346

(a) IX

(b) VI

?

3347

?

3348

~~cc. cf~~

(i) (a) abov

3349

(i) The

'small

3350

(a) III

?

3351

(a) VII

(i) The

"Sand fox

Note 3350

257

3345 VIII 16 |
(a) VI 67 ditto

?

3346 III A46 | 0400
(a) IX A4 ditto
(b) VI 55 | ~~incomplete~~ 0585

?

3347 III 54 0680

?

3348 VIII 2 | "pearl" 5224
~~C.C.C. 21~~ (a) IX 34 | 2439
(i) (a) above C.C.C. 21^a 瓔 珞

3349 VII 21 | 3354
(i) The dissyllable C.C.C. 16^b 細 狗
"small dog"

3350 III 109 | 2729
(a) III 84 ditto

?

3351 III A84 | 3375
(a) VII 60 ditto
(i) The dissyllable C.C.C. 16^a 沙狐 野狐
"sand fox, wild fox" B.100 cat. under "wild animals"
Note 3350 + 3351 are indistinguishable

3352 V A102 |
(a) III 20

3353 III 1 | "wild fox"

3354 V 97 | wolf 3366
(a) IX 90 ditto
(b) VII 21 | 3349
(c) IX 57 | 0011
(i) By itself C.C.C. 16^a W.I.134^14 + ?^18 狗
"dog" B.169^5
(ii) (b) above C.C.C. 16^b 細 狗 "small
dog"

3355 III 1 | v. 3344
C.C.C. 16. 戌 The 11th branch (dog) do. B.176^4

3356 III 1 |
(a) III 11 ditto

?

3357 V 97 |
(a) II 19 ditto

?

3358 III 16 |
(a) VI 81 |

?

3359 3354 chain

3360 5050 pair

3361 independent

3362 0809

3363 0214 chain

part of royal title

| W.I.266[21] 福盛

3364 4899 pair

3365 5644 chain III

3366 3354 chain III

3367 3344 chain

3368 5110 chain

3369 2635 chain

3370 4901 pair

3371 2149 chain

B.227[4] 228[1] etc. 祖 (the five) patriarchs

3372 -4181

3373 2411 chain

3359

3360

(a) III A

3361

3362

3363

3364

(a) V

3365

3366

(a) V 97

(b) II 11

(c) VII

(i) C.C.C. 16[b]

(ii) (b) abov

3367

(a) V 4

C.C.C. 16[a]

258

3359 [Tangut] VI A 99 [Tangut] |

?

3360 [Tangut] I 36 [Tangut] |

(a) III A 52 ditto

?

3361 [Tangut] V 173 "Family or clan name"

?

3362 [Tangut] VIII 2 | [Tangut] "tree"

?

3363 [Tangut] IX 126 | [Tangut]

~~Possibly right form of~~ ~~Error for~~ 4864 Yes v. W.I 266[21]

3364 [Tangut] III 109 [Tangut] |

(a) V 32 ditto (misspelt)

cf. 3370

3365 [Tangut] VI 42 | [Tangut]

3354

3366 [Tangut] IX 90 [Tangut] | "dog"

(a) V 97 ditto

(b) II 11 | [Tangut] 1853

(c) VII 90 [Tangut] | "rat" 2885

(i) C.C.C. 16b 狼 "wolf". B.221[3]

(ii) (b) above B.100 cat. under wild animals

3367 [Tangut] II 22 [Tangut] |

(a) V 44 ditto

C.C.C. 16a W.I. 132[18] 猪 "pig" B.128[1]

3368 [Tangut] II 22 [Tangut] | "water"

(i) The dissyllable B.102 cat. under "rivers & seas."

3369 [Tangut] VII A 15 | [Tangut] 1479

(i) | [Tangut] C.C.C. 33b 肚 带 [illegible]

0813

3370 [Tangut] III 109 [Tangut] |

(a) V 32 ditto

? B.176[5] part of P.N.[6] cf. 3364

3371 [Tangut] VI 31 | [Tangut] 3017

(a) VIII 78 | [Tangut] 3285

II 287 ~~3227[4] 228[1]~~

(i) C.C.C. 9b 限 "limit, to fix" W.I. 119[1.5]

(ii) The dissyllable W.I. 136[10]?

(iii) W II 2, 22[5] etc. passim after numerals 第 number....

(iv) W.I. 194[10] apparently merely an enclitic.

3372 [Tangut] V 97 | [Tangut] [misspelt]

(a) I 130 ditto [[Tangut]]

?

3373 [Tangut] V.173 ~~III 109~~ [Tangut] | 4842

3374 3354 chain

3380 3390 pair

3375 3351 chain

3381 interpunct

3382 — 5279

3383 0402 pair

3376 3397 pair

3377 1105 chain

3384 3411 pair

3378 0214 chain

B.219 q.v.

3379 0424 chain

~~3385 interpunct~~

3385 3406A pair

3374

(a) VI

3375

(a) III A

(b) III

(i) The

3376

(a) V 6

3377

3378

B.168[5]

3379

(a) I 8

(i) By

opposed

(ii)

woman"

259

3374 [Tangut] IX 35 [Tangut] |

(a) VI A 99 | [Tangut] 3359

3375 [Tangut] VII 60 [Tangut] |

(a) III A 84 ditto v. 3351

(b) III 1 [Tangut] |

(i) The dissyllable C.C.C. 16[a] 沙狐 野狐 "sand fox, wild fox" B.100 cat. under "wild animals".

3376 [Tangut] IX 66 [Tangut] |

(a) V 65 ditto

?

3377 [Tangut] IV 3 [Tangut] | 5059

3378 [Tangut] V 106 [Tangut] |

B.168[5]

3379 [Tangut] VI 24 | [Tangut]

(a) I 81 | [Tangut] 1028

I 98"

(i) By itself W.II.16[1] 女 "female" as opposed to "male"

(ii) | [Tangut] C.C.C. 34[b] 訟房 ..... woman"

3380 [Tangut] III 37 [Tangut] |

(a) I 28 ditto

3381 [Tangut] IX 100 Family or clan name.

3382 [Tangut] I 32 | [Tangut] 文

(a) VII 27 ditto

(i) The dissyllable B.100 cat. under "camel".

3383 [Tangut] VII A 71 | [Tangut] 0402

(a) VIII 33 ditto

(i) The dissyllable W.II 14[1] 擁護 W.I 214[2] 220[11] srun "to protect". W.II 128[12] 擁獲 B.123[3] do.

Note. 3382 apparently has 文 + 3383 支

3384 [Tangut] III 106 [Tangut] |

(a) VIII 34 ditto

(i) C.C.C. 8[a] 19[b] 陰 yin "female, dark etc".

(ii) I. 198[12] (269[5]) mo "female suffix" of e.g. [Tangut] | rgyal.mo "queen"

3385 [Tangut]

An artificial character W.III 64[7] glossed [Tangut] [Tangut]

3386 2736 chain III

3392 3391 chain

3394 1584 chain

3387 0322 chain

3393
- 4752
- 0852
- 2929
- 2485

3388-0137 pair

3389 0424 chain III

3395-5621

3390-3380

3396 1992 chain

3391
- 3392-3592
- 1634

3397-3376

3386

"auxiliar

(i)

concubine

3386A

?

3387

(a) V.1

(i) C.C.C.18

(ii) W.I.98

3388

(a) VIII

?

3389

3390

(a) III

3391

(a) VII

(b) VI

?

× 3392A [Tangut] v. 3453
3393 [Tangut]

260

3386 [Tangut] IX 77 [Tangut]
"auxiliary (subsidiary) woman"
(i) [Tangut] | W.II 16[1] 妃 "wife, imperial concubine".

3386A [Tangut] x of V 47 [Tangut] |
? might be 3430

3387 [Tangut] I 73 [Tangut] | "eye" 0322
(a) V 161 | [Tangut] 5207
(i) C.C.C. 18[b] 眉 "eye-brow"
(ii) W.I. 98[4] 姿 "beauty"

3388 [Tangut] I 73 [Tangut] | 0137
(a) VIII 35 ditto
?

3389 [Tangut] VI 53 [Tangut] | 1924

3390 [Tangut] I 28 [Tangut] |
(a) III 37 ditto

3391 [Tangut] VIII 46 | [Tangut]
(a) VII 43 ditto
(b) VI 77 | [Tangut] 1634
?

3392 [Tangut] VII 43 [Tangut] |
(a) VIII 46 ditto
(b) I A112 [Tangut] | 3592

3394 [Tangut] VII 32 | [Tangut] 3255
(a) I A100 [Tangut] | 5385
(b) V 40 | [Tangut] 4294
W II 18[6] 怪 "strange"

3394A [Tangut] I 73 | [Tangut] misspelt?
(a) I 14 | [Tangut] in ditto 4752
~~(b) III 104 [Tangut] | [[Tangut]]?~~ — Error for [Tangut]
(c) III A8 [Tangut] | [[Tangut]] "joy" 2929
(d) IX 17 [Tangut] | [[Tangut]]? 0852
W. I 98[6] 笑 "to laugh"
Note. I 73 has [Tangut] but [Tangut] is no doubt right.

3395 [Tangut] IX 108 | [Tangut] 5621
(a) VI 32 ditto
?

3396 [Tangut] III 106 [Tangut] [Tangut] (not to 30 in Ishiwa) 1992
C.C.C. 8[b] 陰 yin as opposed to yang.

3397 [Tangut] V 65 | [Tangut]
(a) IX 66 ditto
?

3398 – 1567

3399 0213 pair

3400 – 5365

3401

3402
- 3401
- 0215
- 0404
- 3823
- 4291
- 5374
- 5389

W.II 76" 端正 proper, upright

3403 5110 chain

3404 – 3408

3405 4775 chain

3406 0396 pair

3398

(a) II 1

Note. 3397

3399

(a) IX

(i) The

"rice-

3399A

3400

(a) III 6

(i) The

CCC. 24b

3401

3402

(a) I 10

(b) II 1

(c) III 1

(d) III

(e) IV

(f) V 6

(i) (d) a

牛土 丹

261

3398 [Tangut] VII 14 | [Tangut]

(a) II 1 ditto [[Tangut]]

?

Note. 3397 + 3398 are indistinguishable

3399 [Tangut] I 40 [Tangut] |

(a) IX 14 ditto

(i) The dissyllable C.C.C. 25b 米分 "rice-flour, powder".

3399A [Tangut] = [Tangut] 3466

3400 [Tangut] I 79 | [Tangut]

(a) III 6 ditto

(i) The dissyllable 衵 C.C.C. 24b B.104 cat. under "woman's clothing".

3401 [Tangut] VI A 35 × by itself [|] |

3402 [Tangut] IX 77 × by itself | [|]

(a) I 104 [Tangut] | ? 5389

(b) II 1 [Tangut] | ? 0215

(c) III 19 | [Tangut] sort of flower? 3823

(d) III A 66 [Tangut] | beautiful 4291

(e) IV 5 | [Tangut] [[Tangut]] 0404

(f) V 69 | [Tangut] ? 5374

(i) (d) above + [Tangut] C.C.C. 13a 牡丹花 red flower

(ii) | [Tangut] W I 98³ II 2¹⁰ 8² (267") etc. (B 181¹) 莊嚴 alamkāra adornment, adorned. glorious.

(iii) By itself W II 24¹⁰ 嚴 garland. glorious. v. 3859.

Note. It is very difficult to distinguish between 3401 which perhaps has [Tangut] + 3402 which has [Tangut]. (d) certainly belongs to 3402, (e) perhaps to 3401. (ii) seems to belong to 3402.

3403 [Tangut] VII 30 | [Tangut] 5110 "water" C.C.C. 12a W I. 132¹³ 河 I 214¹⁴ "river".

3404 [Tangut] I 79 | [Tangut]

(a) VI 23 ditto

e (i) The dissyllable C.C.C. 25a 綿帽 "silk hat"

3405 [Tangut] IX 77 | [Tangut]

3406 [Tangut] VIII 59 | [Tangut] 0396

(a) VII 10 ditto

[(b) VI A 116 [Tangut] (5194) × by [Tangut] (5190) |]

(i) The dissyllable C.C.C. 25b 火囬 火旨

3406A - 3385

3407 5337 pair

3408 3404 pair

3409 1340 chain

3410 5017 chain

B.W.I.132[13] 冓鈍 | 因風 (to spread fire) by means of the wind

3411 - 3384

3412 3465 chain

[3413] 2796 chain

3414 0862 chain

3415 2716 chain

[3416] - 2701

3417 5369 chain

5369 – 1500 – 0711
2472 – 1756
– 2235
– 3266

3406A

3407

(a) VI A

?

3408

(a) I 7

(i) The Hsia

B "sick c

3409

(a) V 16

C.C.C. 30[b]

子 細

Note. 34

3410

(a) I 1

C.C.C. 20[a]

W.I. 100[2]

B. 220[5] (part

"Obey" loo

cases th

of a part

262

3406A [Tangut] v. 3385

3407 [Tangut] IX 107 [Tangut] |

(a) VI A122 ditto

?

3408 [Tangut] | VI 23 [Tangut] |

(a) I 79 ditto

(i) The disyllable C.C.C. 25a 綿帽

B "silk cap"

3409 [Tangut] VI 73 [Tangut] | 4402

(a) V 160 | [Tangut] 5039

C.C.C. 30b2 || [i.e. character doubled]

子細 ? "in detail"

Note. 3408 seems to have 攵 & 3409 攴

3410 [Tangut] [Tangut] VII 3 [Tangut] | 5017 q.v.

(a) I 18 ditto

C.C.C. 20a W.II 48[10] 順 "to obey"

W.I. 100[2] 132[13] II 24[10] 70[8] B 165[1] 204[1]

B.220[5] (particle tr. 常)

"Obey" looks clear enough; in other cases the world looks more like of a particle.

3411 [Tangut] VIII 34 | [Tangut]

(a) III 106 ditto

?

3412 [Tangut] VIII 11 [Tangut] |

(a) III 125 ditto

(b) III A49 [Tangut] | 0869

C.C.C. 26b 囊 "sack, bag, purse"

3413 [Tangut] III 159 | [Tangut]

3414 [Tangut] III 172 [Tangut] | 0916

3415 [Tangut] VI 123 [Tangut] |

C.C.C. 27a 碓 "pestle" B.229[2]

3416 [Tangut] III 159 | [Tangut]

(a) VIII 74 ditto [[Tangut] in both cases]

?

3417 [Tangut] II 3 | [Tangut] 5369

(a) V 131 ditto

(b) VII 88 | [Tangut] 2472

Name of a constellation C.C.C. 5b

底 "bottom, basis" W.I. 220[15] sa. ga

Probably "bottom" in any connection.

3418 2473 pair

3419 3500 chain

3420 嘉 good W.I 132[2]

3420 chain linked to 1614 chain

II 132[2] 嘉

3421 4276 chain

3422 1891 chain

3423 3269 chain

3424 1435 pair

3425 4734 chain

As postpos. after a noun of time

於 "at [evening time] W II 4[3]

B.248[3]–249[1] ... |

yan.gan.gi.ts'e ... dei.ts'e

'if ... then'

3426 2485 chain

3427 3123 chain

3428 – 5676

3429 0258 chain

3386A
3430

- 0152
- 2364 – 2045
- 2369 – 3735
- 3506

3418

(a) III A

3419

3420

(a) IV 3

[(b) VII 1

W.I.98[3] 100

222[12] legs

3421

(a) IX

(i) By

(ii) The

B.171[1] W

normally

W.I.178[2]

3422

W.II 2[3] 22

B.174[2] ?

3423

Dict. 56[a] 7

3424

(a) I

CCC. 1[a] 5

3420 A

263

3418 [Tangut] III A107 [Tangut] | 2473

(a) III A 33 ditto

?

3419 [Tangut] VI 98 [Tangut] |

Noso ka

3420 [Tangut] ka V 168 | [Tangut] "bad".

(a) IV 3 ditto

[(b) VII 14 [Tangut] x [Tangut] |] fragment 5471(?) fragment 1021

W.I.98³ 100³ 好 "lovely" 120³ 善 "good"

222¹² legs.pa "good"

3421 [Tangut] IX 95 [Tangut] | "heart"

(a) IX 55 | [Tangut] 3478

(i) By itself 歡 "joyful" W.I 140¹⁵

(ii) The disyllable ['joyful heart'] B.171¹ W.I.134⁹ normally translates 歡喜 "joyful".

W.I.178² 娛樂 ditto.

3422 [Tangut] III 83 [Tangut] 1891

W.II 2³ 22⁵ etc. 品 "Chapter".

B.174²?

3423 [Tangut] III 132 [Tangut] | 1390

Dict. 56²7

3424 [Tangut] I.41 [Tangut] |

(a) I 79 ditto

C.C.C. 1²5 [[Tangut]] B.164² [70] tr. 時 "at the time of" 188⁵ 223³

3420A [Tangut] See 3460

3425 [Tangut] IX 89 [Tangut] | 4730

~~(a) I 119~~ ?

A conjunction meaning "when" & coming at the end of the sentence but apparently sometimes meaning "then" & coming at the beginning?

Also after nouns. B.232¹ q.v.

W.I.136² 194¹⁵ B.204⁴ 227⁴

II 4⁴ 24⁵ 36² 38¹ 126² v. 3634

3426 [Tangut] V 21 [Tangut] | 2485

3427 [Tangut] V A 48 [Tangut] | "robber" v. 3123

(a) IX 114 [Tangut] | 1859

(i) [Tangut] | [Tangut] W.I.198³ "spider's web(?) abscess".

3427A [Tangut] Error for [Tangut] 5021

3428 [Tangut] I 74 | [Tangut] 5676

(a) I 59 ditto

?

3429 [Tangut] III A 57 [Tangut] |

3430 [Tangut] [IX gap]

(a) III 49 [Tangut] | × 2364

(b) VI 2 | [Tangut] 3506

(aa) V 47 v. 3386A 0152

3431 1754 pair

3432 1996 pair

3433 1992 chain

3434 1781 chain

3434 B.179[4] 闐 t'ien phonetic V.2099

B.163[4] 天 ? part of P.N.

3435 4775 chain

3436 4064 chain

3437 5444 pair

3438

(i) By itself W.I.172[13] 寫 to ...

3438

3947-4787

1937-1171

3439 3596 chain

3440 0353 pair

3441 2482 chain

3442

3432A

3430

(c) IX

C.C.C. 8[a]

"oblique

B.167[2]

3431

(a) VI

?

3432

(a) I 4

3433

3434

(i) The dis...

"dwelling

(ii)

house"

3435

?

3436

?

3437

(a) V

?

264

3432A [Tangut] × of VI 76 | [Tangut]
Error for 3446

3430 cont.
(c) IX A 145 [Tangut] | 2369
C.C.C. 8ª Name of a star 斜 "oblique"?
B. 167²

3431 [Tangut] VI 112 [Tangut] |
(a) VI 61 ditto
?

3432 [Tangut] I A 59 [Tangut] | 1996
(a) I 40 ditto
?

3433 [Tangut] III 172 [Tangut] [Tangut] 1992 (not as 50.a. but as ...)

3434 [Tangut] III A 42 | [Tangut] 1689
(i) The dissyllable C.C.C. 21ᵇ 舍屋 "dwelling house"
(ii) | [Tangut] 5245 C.C.C. 22ᵇ 涅舍 "mud house"?

3435 [Tangut] VI 10 [Tangut] | 2661
? cf. 2381

3436 [Tangut] V 4 [Tangut] | 3965
?

3437 [Tangut] IX 1 [Tangut] |
(a) V 65 ditto
?

3438 [Tangut] IX 151 | [Tangut]
(a) VI 43 ditto (misspelt)
(b) V 34 [Tangut] | a cut × (1171) 1937
(i) The dissyllable W. 2. 108⁵ II 16³ 書寫 "to write, record".
(ii) [Tangut] | C.C.C. 29ª 30ª 判憑 ? "to their proof".
By itself B. 176¹ 書 to write

3439 [Tangut] IX 151 [Tangut] | 3596
(a) I 17 ditto
(b) II 4 [Tangut] | 2567
(i) (b) above C.C.C. 30ª 蹤迹 "foot-print" (both words) C.C.C. 1ª 3

3440 [Tangut] V 168 [Tangut]
(a) VIII 28 ditto [[Tangut]]

3441 [Tangut] V A 40 | [Tangut] "black"
(i) The dissyllable B. 100 cat. under "camel"

3442 [Tangut] VIII 48 Family or clan name.

3443
4310-1341-5446
2690-4043

3444 5553 chain

3445 4262 chain

3446
4515-2738
0264 3485-3482
0455 4260
4150

B.188[2] 陳 to arrange

3447 3795 chain

3448 3700 A chain

3449
4559
1648-4379
3770
4331

3450 3468 chain

3451 2601 chain

3452 3526 chain

B.121[2] nirmāṇakāya 化身

3453 5485 chain

B.121[3] 化 'image' (clear) conversion, magic powers S.20.p.140

3443
(a) IX
(b) I 61
3444
B.163[3] 軌
3445
(a) II
(b) IX
C.C.C.18[6]
3446
(a) VI
(b) III
(c) III
(d) VII
(ii) The
40[10] 宣
to publ
(i) By
"to prea
3447
(a) V

265

3443 [Tangut] IX 34 | [Tangut]

(a) IX 110 ditto

(b) I 61 | [Tangut]

?

3444 [Tangut] V 90 | [Tangut]

B. 163[3] 軌 ? a rule (or P.N.?)

3445 [Tangut] IX 93 [Tangut] | "face" 3476

(a) II 4 | [Tangut] 2425

(b) IX 4 | [Tangut] 5334

C.C.C. 18[b] 額 "forehead"

3446 [Tangut] III A 30 | [Tangut]

(a) VI 76 ditto

(b) III 66 | [Tangut]

(c) III 126 [Tangut] | 0264

(d) VII A 72 | [Tangut] 0455

(ii) The Disyllable W. II 20[6] 38[12] 演說 40[10] 宣揚 "to preach publicly, to publish" 138[10] 言說

(i) By itself W. I. 208[10] smra. ba "to preach" 170[9] 稱 ditto B 187[1] 告

3447 [Tangut] III 12 | [Tangut]

(a) V A 84 ditto

3448 [Tangut] III 70 [Tangut] | 2960

(a) V A 43 [Tangut] | 4242

(i) C.C.C. 4[a] 30[b] 31[b] W. I. 112[9] 事 "business affairs"

(ii) W. I. 206[4] ? rnam "kind of"

(iii) The Disyllable W. I. 138[1] ?

3449 [Tangut] VII 15 | [Tangut] 4559

(a) I 2 ditto

(b) I 51 | [Tangut] [支] 4331

(c) I 107 | [Tangut] [支] 3770

(d) IX 9 | [Tangut] ×(4379) 1648

W. I. 136[6,18] 桁 "a row (of trees etc.)"

3450 [Tangut] VI 114 [Tangut] |

?

3451 [Tangut] IX 60 [Tangut] | vein 0 4608

?

3451A [Tangut] Error for [Tangut] 3473

3452 [Tangut] III 79 [Tangut] |

(a) II 21 ditto

3453 [Tangut] IX A 43 [Tangut] | 5485

(a) III 104 ditto

~~3452 + 3453 are indistinguishable~~

~~it is not clear which is:—~~

B. 161[2]

W. I. 100[2] II 50[10] 化 "change"

3453 is [Tangut]

3454 3757 pair

3455 4127 chain

3456 4027 chain

3457 0809 chain

3458 3993 chain

3459 3984 chain ~~independent~~

3460 1880 pair

3461 2485 chain

3462 – 4574

3463 2309 chain

3464 3467 chain

3465
┬ 3412 – 0869
└ ?1635 ─ 2808
　　　　└ 3616

3466 5141 pair

B. 173[4] tis. 勿 (error for 3483)

3467
┬ 3464 – 4366
└ 0747

3454 (a) I.16 ?

3455 ?

3456 ?

3457 (i) The ... "egg-plan..."

3458

3459 (a) V 5 ?

3460 (a) V ?

3461 c.c.c. 19[a]

3462 (a) V ?

266

3454 [illegible] VI 34 [illegible] |

(a) I.16 ditto

?

3455 [illegible] VIII 9 [illegible] |

?

3456 [illegible] VI 12 | [illegible] 4498

?

3457 [illegible] VI 136 | [illegible] "vegetable"

(i) The dissyllable C.C.C. 14b 茄子 "egg-plant". B.102 cat. under "vegetables"

3458 [illegible] IX 6 [illegible] | 4477

3459 [illegible] VIII 22 Family or clan name

(a) V 52 [illegible] |

Presumably a double name

3460 [illegible] VII A.108 [illegible] | [illegible]

(a) VIII 66 ditto

?

3461 [illegible] III 97 [illegible] | "leg"

C.C.C. 19a 腿 "thigh"

3462 [illegible] I 34 | [illegible]

(a) V 2 ditto

?

3463 [illegible] III A 41 [illegible] |

(a) V 32 | [illegible] 4366

(i) The dissyllable B.99 cat. under "horse"

~~3464 [illegible] IX 109~~

~~(a) I A 97~~

3464 [illegible] IX 109 [illegible] |

(a) I A 97 ditto

(i) | [[illegible]] [illegible] C.C.C. 23a 毛栅 "hair palisade"? "felt curtain"

3465 [illegible] III 125 | [illegible] 3412

(a) VIII 11 ditto

C.C.C. 26b 連袋 ~~[illegible]~~ "connected bag"? "saddle-bag"

v. 4672 A

3466 [illegible] VII 10 [illegible] |

(a) III A 36 ditto

? B.176 part of P.N. [illegible] [[illegible]]

3467 [illegible] I A 97 | [illegible]

(a) IX 109 ditto

(b) IX 72 | [illegible] 0747

?

3468 3029 1048 3450 4214

3469 - 3495

3470 3575 chain

3471 2150 chain

3472 - 4865

3473 - 5418

3474 2193 chain

3475 2482 chain

3476 4262 chain

3477 - 4816

3478 4276 chain

3468

(a) IX 99

(b) VI 14

(i) C.C.C. 34a

Dict 54a 6

(ii) The

3469

(a) VIII 8

3470

(a) III 6

stet

?

Note. I.

3471

? v. 4676

3472

(a) III 37

?

3473

(a) III

?

3474

(a) III 4

(b) V 37

267

3468 [Tangut] VII 27 | [Tangut] ×3029

(a) IX 99 ditto

(b) VI 144 | [Tangut] 3450

(i) C.C.C. 34[a] :

Dict 54[a] 6 B.167[5] (168[1]) tr. 事

(ii) The dissyllable C 28[b] 30[a] 局分

3469 [Tangut] VIII A 26 | [Tangut]

(a) VIII 84 ditto

3470 [Tangut] IX 94 | [Tangut]

(a) III 66 [Tangut] | 4158

~~(i) | [Tangut] W.I.152[2] 莊嚴 stately, austere~~ stet

crossfr [Tangut]

?

Note. To be distinguished from 3402

3471 [Tangut] V 96 [Tangut] | 2150

? v. 4676A

3472 [Tangut] III 172 | [Tangut]

(a) III 37 ditto

?

3473 [Tangut] VI 12 | [Tangut]

(a) III 3 ditto.

?

3474 [Tangut] V 127 [Tangut] |

(a) III 43 | [Tangut] 4495

(b) V 37 [Tangut] | ×2253

3474 cont.

(c) VI 21 | [Tangut] 0861

W.I.108[8] II 18[6] 24[10] 34[7] 珍 "precious, pearl".

3475 [Tangut] VI 108 | [Tangut] that 2482

?

3476 [Tangut] III 172 [Tangut] | 4262

(a) IX 23 ditto

(b) III 52 [Tangut] | 5335

(c) III 61 | [Tangut] mirror 3713

(d) V A 112 [Tangut] | 4263

(e) VI 3 [Tangut] | ×3083 3490

(f) IX 93 [Tangut] | ×3445

(i) C.C.C. 7[b] 18[b] 29[a] W.I.94[7] 面 "face, page" 192[15] begin 194[11] gdoin "face" B.164[4] W.I 4[5] [Tangut] | ditto

(ii) (b) above C.C.C. 29[b] ?

3477 [Tangut] VI 108 | [Tangut]

(a) I 108 ditto.

?

3478 [Tangut] IX 55 [Tangut] | 3421

? Possibly W.I. 266[6] [[Tangut]] tr. 慶 felicity

B 176[5] 174[1] 206[3]

3479 4183 chain

3480 2492 chain

3481 3575 chain ~~2734 chain~~

B.189² 玄 dark, deep

3482 3445 chain

3483 2249 chain

3484 0322 chain

3485 3446 chain

3486 2485 chain

[3487] 2279 chain

3488 - 3489

3489 3488 pair

3490 4262 chain

3491 3492 chain

3492 [Tangut] 伽 | 耶 伽耶

Gaya W.II 4¹

3492
- 3096
- 3491
- 5206

B.227⁵ 繪 sketch

3479 [Tangut]

?

3480 [Tangut]

(a) IV

C.C.C. 24⁴

3481 [Tangut]

(a) IX 94

W II 38¹²

B 246³ 齊

3482 [Tangut]

Phonetic

3483 [Tangut]

(a) III A

C.C.C. 29

不 "not"

3484 [Tangut]

?

Note 3483

3485 [Tangut]

(a) VI

W.II 44¹²

268

3479 [Tangut] IX 22 [Tangut] |

?

3480 [Tangut] IX 105 [Tangut] | 2456

(a) IV A 1 [Tangut] | "skirt" 4832 ~~3480~~

C.C.C. 24b 袴 "trousers"

3481 [Tangut] VI 12 | [Tangut] 2734

(a) IX 94 [Tangut] | 3470

W II 38[12] 要 "important, essential"

B 246[3] 齊 (Ch'i) Tsi[2] (place name).

3482 [Tangut] VI A 120 [Tangut] [Tangut]

Phonetic group.

3483 [Tangut] VIII 84 | [Tangut] 2249

(a) III A 99 [Tangut] x by | [Tangut]

C.C.C. 29a 休 "do not W I 100[3,8] 不 "not" B. 221[5] 調 sic B. 233 莫

3484 [Tangut] V 132 [Tangut] [Tangut] [Tangut] 0322
eye low high

?

Note 3483 + 3484 are indistinguishable.

3485 [Tangut] VI A 95 [Tangut]

(a) VI A 120 [Tangut] x by | [Tangut]

W. II 44[12] 說 "to say"

3486 [Tangut] IX 111 [Tangut] | 2485

(a) III 3 | [Tangut] 2471

(b) V 161 | [Tangut] boot 5208

(i) The disyllable C.C.C. 25a 靴 "boot"

(ii) (a) above C.C.C. 25a 靴 底 "boot-sole"?

3487 [Tangut] V 147 [Tangut] | [0811]

3488 [Tangut] I A 43 | [Tangut]

C.C.C. 19a 股 "leg"

3489 [Tangut] IX 165 –

(a) I A 43 [Tangut] "leg" v. 3488

?

3490 [Tangut] VI 3 | [Tangut] 3476

(a) IX 93 | [Tangut] 3083

?

3491 [Tangut] V A 132 [Tangut] [Tangut] 1709 simplest

Phonetic character

3492 [Tangut] V 115 | [Tangut] 3096

(a) III 36 ditto

(b) V 115 | [Tangut] 5206

(c) V A 132 [Tangut] x by | [Tangut] 1709 3491

~~(d) IX 94~~

B. 129[5] phon. tr. 恒 hêng Ganges

A common phonetic.

3493 - 5081

3501 1864 chain

3494 5287 pair

3502 5531 chain

3495 3459 pair

3503 - 1751

3496 - 5405

3504 - 4732

3505 5599 pair

3497 2149 chain

3506 3430 chain

3498 - 5552

3507 5142 pair

3499 4529 chain

3508 5007 pair

3500
+ 2045
L 3419

3509 - 3352

3493

(a) IX 99

?

3494

(a) IX A 15

?

3495

(a) VIII A

?

3496

(a) V 123

(ii) The

(i) By

3497

3498

(a) II 4

?

3499

?

3500

(b) VI 9

4/2/39

(a) I 5

?

269

3493 [Tangut] V 115 | [Tangut]

(a) IX 99 ditto

?

3494 [Tangut] IX A 149 [Tangut] |

(a) IX A 150 ditto

?

3495 [Tangut] VIII 84 [Tangut] |

(a) VIII A 26 ditto

?

3496 [Tangut] I 14 | [Tangut] 5405

(a) V 123 ditto

(ii) The dissyllable C.C.C. 33[b] 革登

2406

(i) By itself W. I 132[15] | [Tangut] 弩 cross-bow

3497 [Tangut] III A 99 [Tangut] [Tangut]

3498 [Tangut] IX 115 [Tangut] |

(a) II 4 ditto

?

3499 [Tangut] III 172 | [Tangut]

?

3500 [Tangut] V 136 | [Tangut] 2045

(b) VI 98 | [Tangut] 3419

(a) I 57 ditto

4/2/39 ?

?

3501 [Tangut] VI 136 | [Tangut] 5717

~~(a) I 57~~ (looks more like 3500)

C.C.C. 19[a] W. II 78[4] 膝 "knee"

3502 [Tangut] IX 165 [Tangut] |

(a) V 2 ditto

(b) VI 48 [Tangut] | 5097

?

3503 [Tangut] V 97 | [Tangut]

?

3504 [Tangut] VII 44 | [Tangut]

(a) I 43 ditto

?

3505 [Tangut] IV A 4 [Tangut] |

?

3506 [Tangut] VI 2 [Tangut] | 3430

?

3507 [Tangut] I 20 [Tangut] |

(a) IX 73 ditto

?

3508 [Tangut] VIII A 90 [Tangut] |

(a) VIII A 89 ditto

?

3509 [Tangut] III 20 | [Tangut]

(a) V A 102 ditto

?

3510 2303 pair

3517 1704 chain

3518 4295 chain ?

3511 1710 chain

3519 independent

3519 A v. 3628

3512 4454 chain

3520 1891 chain

3513 independent

3521 0345 chain

3514
- 1463–4196
- 1782
- 3805

3522 0752 chain

W. II 130² 怨 敵 'enemy'

3523 2635 chain

3515 1345 A

3516 –4871

3510

(a) IV 5

3511

(a) V 102

(i) W.I.192^13

3512

3513

3514

(a) V 12

(b) III 5

(c) VI

ccc.25ª

bracelet

3515

3516

(a) III 3

270

3510 [Tangut] VII A/21 [Tangut] |

(a) IV 5 ditto

?

3511 [Tangut] II 44 [Tangut] | 1712

(a) V 102 [Tangut] | 1795

(i) W.I.192[13] be'u "calf"

(ii) The disyllable B. 99 cat. under "cattle".

3512 [Tangut] III 40 [Tangut] |

3513 [Tangut] II 44 "Family or clan name"

3514 [Tangut] V 97 | [Tangut] 1463

(a) V 126 ditto [Tangut]

(b) III 58 | [Tangut] 3805

(c) VI 21 | [Tangut] 1782

CCC. 25[a] | [Tangut] [Tangut] [Tangut] "bracelet"

3515 [Tangut] III 40 [Tangut] [Tangut] sic.

?

3516 [Tangut] I 17 | [Tangut]

(a) III 37 ditto

?

3517 [Tangut] IX 60 | [Tangut] 1705

(i) | [Tangut] B. 99 cat. under "cattle".

3518 [Tangut] III 40 [Tangut] |

3519 [Tangut] VI 2 "Family or clan name"

?

3519A [Tangut] × of IX 111 [Tangut] |

?

3520 [Tangut] VI 88 [Tangut] | 1891

3521 [Tangut] II 2 [Tangut] | 0345

3522 [Tangut] IX 83 | [Tangut] 1790

(a) III 91 | [Tangut] 3525

W.I.144 (II 128) 怨 "grumble" 196[8] p'yir. rgol "abuse" [noun] 220[14] ?

3523 [Tangut] I 53 [Tangut] |

~~B.180[4]~~ (a) V 44 | [Tangut] 0144

(b) V A 10 | [Tangut]

~~3524~~ (c) VI 21 | [Tangut] 0789

B.180[4] 垂 to drop, droop

v. 6?

270

3524 2245 chain

3525 0752 chain

3526 (iii) The Nisyllable 變化 "change transformation"

(iii)(a) Sunirmita name of a heaven W II 86⁴

3526
- 3452
- 1289
- 1743 — 1200, 1659

3527 3632 chain

3528 2208 chain

3529 0109 pair

3530 2027 chain

3531 1667 chain

3532–1787

3533 1414 chain

3524

(a) IX 44

3525

B. 164¹

3526

(a) III 79

(b) II 4

(c) IX 6

(i) C.C.C. 3ᵃ

(ii) W.I. 100⁵

(iii) (c) abo

pariṇāma

3527

W.I. 208⁵

I 98⁵

3528

(a) IX

(b) III 3

Dict. 1ᵃ 5

3529

(a) I 1

C.C.C. 5ᵇ

- bom: W.

3528 plant

271

3524 [illegible] IX A81 [illegible] | 2245

(a) IX 44 | [illegible] 5344

3525 [illegible] III 91 [illegible] | 3522

B.164[1] 怨望 to look complainingly

3526 [illegible] II 21 | [illegible] 3456

(a) III 79 ditto

(b) II 4 [illegible] | 1289

(c) IX 66 | [illegible] 1743

(i) C.C.C. 3[a] 變 W.II 18[6] B.180[4] "change, transformation"

(ii) W.I. 100[5] 幻 "magic, illusion";

(iii) (c) above W.II 46[11] 轉變

pariṇāma "change transformation"

3527 [illegible] II 21 [illegible] |

W.I. 208[5] sszu "illusion, artifice"

I 98[5] ?

3528 [illegible] III 96 [illegible] | [2208] ditto

(a) IX 75

(b) III 34 [illegible] | 4979

Dict. 1[a] 5

3529 [illegible] III 96 [illegible] | 0109

(a) I 14 ditto

C.C.C. 5[b] 尾 "tail" name of constellation: W.I. 222[1] shrub ditto

3528 phonetic + 0109 significs B.191[2]

3530 [illegible] VIII 85 [illegible] | 4061

(a) II 2 | [illegible] 3530

(b) V 60 [illegible] | 1619

(c) V 175 [illegible] | 1166

(d) VIII 28 [illegible] | 0859

(e) IX 98 [illegible] | 3679

(f) IX A106 [illegible] | 4788

(i) A most obscure character. In C.C.C. 30[a] II 24[9] & ? C.C.C. 31[b] seems to represent 有 "to have".

(ii) I 98[9] : 2064 ?

B.180[4] 懸 to suspend B.219[4] to.

(iii) [illegible] | C.C.C. 32[a2] 絃 "string" (of an instrument), but here too ? = "having"

3531 [illegible] IX 9 [illegible] |

(i) C.C.C. 16[a] 熊 "a bear"

(ii) | [illegible] B.100 cat. under wild animals 1786

3532 [illegible] IX 134 | [illegible]

(a) IX 118 ditto

cf. 3535

3533 [illegible] IX 9 | [illegible] 1616

271

3534 0741 chain

3535 1785 chain

3536 1667 chain

3537 0194 pair

3538 1076 chain

3539 1935 chain

3540 1935 chain

3541 3918 chain

3542 ⊥ 2785 – 2786

3543 2204

3544 5690 chain

3545 independent

3545 (i) | 龍 目乾連

Maudgalyāyana W.II 4[2] B.224[5]

3546 – 5000

3547 2027 chain

3548 2335 chain

3549 4564

3550 2149 chain

By itself B.175[1] tr. 衣

3534

3535

(a) IX 11

C.C.C. 16[a]

3536

(a) I 88

(i) W.II 4[3] 10[4]

(ii) W.I 19[6]

3537

3538

B.168[5]

3539

(a) VIII

(b) V 1

(c) IX

C.C.C. 11[a]

3540

?

272

3534 [Tangut] VI A 45 [Tangut] | 3277

3535 [Tangut] . IX 134 | [Tangut] "tiger"
(a) IX 118 ditto
C.C.C. 16a 豹 "leopard"

3536 [Tangut] II 4 | [Tangut]
(a) I 88 | [Tangut] 2828
(i) W.II 4³ 10⁴ 晡 "evening" 3-5 p.m.
(ii) W.I 196⁹ :

3537 [Tangut] IX 145 [Tangut] |

3538 [Tangut] VI 90 [Tangut] | 4857
B.168⁵

3539 [Tangut] bwa II 20 [Tangut] |
(a) VIII 14 ditto
(b) V 18 | [Tangut] 3540
(c) IX 104 | [Tangut] Chinese 5398
C.C.C. 11a 東 W.I. 220" sar "East"

3540 [Tangut] V 18 [Tangut] |
?

3541 [Tangut] VII 10 [Tangut] |

3542 [Tangut] I 99 | [Tangut]
(a) VII A 68 ditto
?

3543 [Tangut] II 7 [Tangut] | 1293

3544 [Tangut] III 70 | [Tangut] 436

3545 [Tangut] I 99 Family or clan name
B.174⁵

3546 [Tangut] VII 63 | [Tangut] ? 2000
(a) III A 29 ditto

3547 [Tangut] II 2 [Tangut] | 3530

3548 [Tangut] V 53 [Tangut] | fear 4988
(a) III 154 | [Tangut] 4237

3549 [Tangut] V 65 | [Tangut]
(a) VI 19 ditto

3550 [Tangut] V 51 | [Tangut] 3674
(a) V 51 | [Tangut] "to put on" 0413
(i) C.C.C. 24a The disyllable 衣服

3556 3557 pair

3557-3556

3551 independent

3558 1080 chain

3552 independent

3553 2079 pair

3554 1992 chain

3559 0580 pair

3560 4512 chain

3555 1438 chain

3561 3865 pair

3562 1080 chain

3550 con

"clothing

(ii)

26^{8} 衣 月

'clothing'

3551

B. 188^{3} 漢

3552

name.

3553

(a) VIII

3554

(a) IX

3555

(a) III

(b) V 5

(c) VI

(d) VI

(e) VII

W. I 190^{9}

273

3550 cont.
"clothing" B.103 cat. under 'clothing'.
(ii) [Tangut] | W.II 18⁸ 衣 "clothing"
26⁸ 衣服 ditto. B.103 cat. under 'clothing'. 96⁷ do.

3551 [Tangut] VIII A 99 "Name of country"?
B.188³ tr. 漢 Han [[Tangut]]

3552 [Tangut] VIII A 83 Family or clan name.

3553 [Tangut] VIII A 98 [Tangut] |
(a) VIII A 97 ditto
?

3554 [Tangut] III 182 [Tangut] [Tangut] (not to be confused with) 1992
(a) IX 147 | [Tangut] ? 1319
?

3555 [Tangut] III A 127 [Tangut] | 1438 bis
(a) III 117 ditto
(b) V 59 | [Tangut] 0888
(c) VI 5 | [Tangut] toe nail 2621
(d) VI 15 | [Tangut] 3580
(e) VII 30 [Tangut] | 5309
W.I 190⁹ sor. mo "toe".

3556 [Tangut] VII A 85 [Tangut] |
(a) VII 2. ditto
?

3557 [Tangut] VII 2 | [Tangut]
(a) VII A 85 ditto
1389

3558 [Tangut] III A 105 [Tangut] [Tangut]
(i) [Tangut] | W.I 208¹¹ me. dbal a kind of disease.
Note. Also used as a phonetic, ~~or perhaps merely a phonetic character.~~

3559 [Tangut] III 144 [Tangut] | 0580
(a) VI A 28 ditto reverse
?

3560 [Tangut] VIII 18 [Tangut] | 4512
(a) I.136 ditto
?

3561 [Tangut] I 40 [Tangut] |
(a) IX 21 ditto
B 162³

3562 [Tangut] VIII 32 [Tangut] | 4342 3558
(a) III A 105 [Tangut] × by | [Tangut]
(b) III A 112 [Tangut] (2322) × by [Tangut] (2317) | 2283
(c) III A 118 [Tangut] (2304) × by [Tangut] |
(d) VIII A 105 [Tangut] × by [Tangut] |
(a)–(d) are Phonetic characters P.T.O.

3562 (i) W.I.168⁶ 臨 to stand over, on the brink of?

3563 1564 chain

3564 0950 chain

3565 ?2485 chain

3566 – 4912

3567 1903 chain

3568 – 4388

3569 – 4430A

3570 0614 pair

3571 3226 chain

3572 0409 pair

3573 1683 pair

3574 5678 chain

3574 W.II 2⁶ 所 "place" practically "in (a dwelling place)"

W.II 4⁴ | [Tangut] to a place 處 B.238⁵

W.II 90³ 於 "to"

B.196³ 入 entry āyatana S.K.

3575 ~~2734 chain~~

⊥2734 – 3481 – 3470 – 4158

3562 con

(i) W.I.108⁶

(ii) [Tangut] |

3563 [Tangut]

3564 [Tangut]

(a) III 55

(i) W.II 46⁴ 函

(ii) W.I.134¹

3565 [Tangut]

?

3566 [Tangut]

(a) IX A

B.233¹ tr. 力

3567 [Tangut]

3568 [Tangut]

(a) V 17

C.C.C. Title

of the ha

Also use

3569 [Tangut]

?

274

3562 cont.
(i) W. I. 108⁶ II 38⁵ 立 "to stand".
(ii) [Tangut] | B.100 cat. under "camel".

3563 [Tangut] VI A72 [Tangut] | 4077

3564 [Tangut] VIII 18 [Tangut] |
[(a) III 55 [Tangut] × by [Tangut] |]
(i) W. II 46⁴ 函 "to enfold"
(ii) W. I. 134¹⁵ 繭 "a cocoon" [Tangut]

3565 [Tangut] III.182 | [Tangut] 1458
?

3566 [Tangut] IX A108 [Tangut] |
(a) IX A170 ditto reversed
B.233¹ tr. 力

3567 [Tangut] III A129 [Tangut] |

3568 [Tangut] I 65 [Tangut] |
(a) V 17 ditto reversed
C.C.C. Title + 19ᵃ W. II 16⁶ 掌 "palm of the hand".
Also used as a Phonetic

3569 [Tangut] IX A185 [Tangut] (?) |
?

3570 [Tangut] V 51 [Tangut] |
(a) I 6 ditto

3571 [Tangut] IX 42 | [Tangut] 0943

3572 [Tangut] IX A109 [Tangut] | 0409
(a) IX 105 ditto [[Tangut] in ninth]

3573 [Tangut] VIII 26 [Tangut] | 1683
(a) III 37 ditto

3574 [Tangut] III 48 [Tangut] 2523
This word appears to exist as a noun 處 or 所 "place", but is normally used as a Postpos "in, at". C.C.C. 35ᵉ² W. I. 96⁸ II 4⁴ 6⁴ 10⁵ 22⁸ 32².
druin. du near to B.253²

3574A [Tangut] N. 232 hdzwa.

3575 [Tangut] VI 101 | [Tangut] 2734
(a) III.66 ditto
?

3576. B246[5] 君 'kiun'

3576 5690 chain

3577 0407 pair

3578 – 2452

3579 – 2767 ~~pair~~

3580 1438 bis chain

3581 4775 chain

3582 5687 pair

3583
⊥5692 – 3005

3584 – 4898

3585 1661 chain

3586 1609 pair

3587
- 4162
- 3275
- 3588
- 3589
- 5606 – 0955 – 1216
  - 0984 – 1276
  - 2320 – 1377
    - ~~5606~~
    - 5131 – 0114
      - 0466
      - 0469
      - 2698
      - 5126
      - 5465
    - 5606 – 0955
      - 0984
      - 2320

3588 3587 chain

3589 3587 chain

3590 0362 pair

3575A
B.346[3]

3576

(a) III 96

W.I.132[6] II

I 212[12] 214

3577

(a) I 74

?

3578

(a) V 2

?

Note: Thr…

3577, 3578

3579

(a) I 131

?

3580

?

3581

?

3582

(a) VIII 6

?

3583

(a) VIII 6

?

3575A 入 'to enter' ? error for 3580
B.346[3]

275

3576 ndzu VI 56 | divine 5690
(a) III 96 | 0081
B.179[4]
W.I.132[6] II 24[6] etc. 帝 "emperor"
I 212[12] 214[5] rje "master, lord".

3577 I 43 | 0407
(a) I 74 ditto
?

3578 IX 103 | 2452
(a) V 2 ditto [ ]
?

Note. There is confusion between 3577, 3578 & 3583

3579 VI 101 |
(a) I 131 ditto [misspelt]
?

3580 VI 15 | 'toe' 3555
?

3581 I 65 | 2657
?

3582 I 43 |
(a) VIII 6 ditto
? cf. 3583

3583 I 43 | × 3005 5692
(a) VIII 6 ditto
? cf. 3582

3584 III 44 |
(a) IX 49 ditto

3585 VI 26 | 1661
(a) I 22 ditto
(i) The disyllable C.C.C. 26[b] "hoe"

3586 V 51 | 1609 q.v.
(a) V 89 ditto
?

3587 III A12 | 4162
(a) III 1 ditto
(b) III A109 × | 3589
(c) III A116 × | (1408) 3588
(d) VII A90 | 3275
(e) IX 110 | 5606
?

Note. A common Phonetic. (1408)

3588 III A116

A Phonetic character.

3589 III A109

A Phonetic character

3590 V 4 | misspelt
(a) V 99 ditto [in]

3591 4775 chain

3592 3391 chain

3593 1113 chain

3594 5636 chain

3595 5631 pair

3596
⊥ 3439-2567

3597
⊥ 2627-4897

3598 - 4171

3599 1891 chain

3600 3226 chain

B.194[2] 胡

3601 independent

3602 1372 chain

3603 - 1477

3604 1903 chain

3604 W.I.168[14] 牽 "to drag" (a plough)

3591

?

3592

3593

(a) I 14

(i) ...

"mother"

3594

3595

(a) II 37

W.I.98[4] 矢

3596

(a) IX 15

?

3597

(a) IX 115

?

3598

(a) VIII 17

?

3599

?

276

3591 [illegible] V 4 [illegible] |

?

3592 [illegible] I A112 | [illegible] 3392

3593 [illegible] I 17 [illegible] |

(a) I 14 ditto

(i) Transliterable C.C.C. 20[a] 娘 娘 "mother"

3594 [illegible] VII A104 [illegible] |

3595 [illegible] II 12 [illegible] | "long"

(a) II 37 ditto

W.I. 98[4] 短 208[15] B.131[1] t'uan "short".

3596 [illegible] I 17 | [illegible] × 2567 3439

(a) IX 151 ditto

?

3597 [illegible] I 17 | [illegible]

(a) IX 115 ditto

?

3598 [illegible] I 17 | [illegible]

(a) VIII 17 ditto

?

3599 [illegible] V 182 [illegible] | 1891

?

3600 [illegible] I 17 [illegible] [illegible] 2342

"auxiliary word"

(a) I 128 | [illegible] ×(2563) 5040

(b) III 91 | [illegible] 1643

(c) V 47 [illegible] × by | [illegible] 2049

(d) V 66 | [illegible] 5124

(e) V 129 | [illegible] ×{2160 2166} 2169

(f) VIII 9 | [illegible] ×(3571) 0943

Passim. A negative word preceding the word which it qualifies. Normally 無 "not having", sometimes 不 "not".

3601 [illegible] VI A85 × by self [illegible] |

3602 [illegible] IX 158 [illegible] | "destiny"

(a) IX 130 ditto v.1372

?

3603 [illegible] I 17 | [illegible]

(a) III 72 ditto

?

3604 [illegible] VII 20 [illegible] |

(a) VII A18 | [illegible] 5712

(i) C.C.C. 32[a] 伏 "to control"

W.I. 136[13] : B.188[3]

3603A [illegible] × of V 16 | [illegible]

error for [illegible] 4524

3605 1130 chain

3606 -1299

3607 2395 chain

3608 0424 chain

3609 0582 chain

3610 1338 chain

3611 independent

3612 2662 chain

3613 0424 chain

3614 4775 chain

3614A 3864 chain

3615 2150 chain

3616 3468 chain

3617 2634 pair

3618 2150 chain

3619 0271 chain

277

3605 [Tangut] VI A 60 [Tangut] | 0128
(i) | [Tangut] 2292 B.100 cat. under "horse"

3606 [Tangut] VIII 7 | [Tangut]
(a) V 83 ditto
?

3607 [Tangut] I 59 | [Tangut] 2530
C.C.C. 6b 孤 "solitary"

3608 [Tangut] II 4 [Tangut] | father 0424
(a) II 30 ditto
C.C.C. 20b 叔 "(junior) uncle"

3609 [Tangut] III 125 [Tangut] | 5689
C.C.C. 21a ? 幡 "banner" B.169[3] [[Tangut]] do.

3610 [Tangut] VIII 12 [Tangut] | 1338 ?

3611 [Tangut] [VII 59-60]
C.C.C. 25b W.I.98" 繡 "embroidered"

3612 [Tangut] IX 75 | [Tangut] 2662
(a) V A 66 ditto
(b) III 12 [Tangut] | 0220
(i) the disyllable. II 76" [Tangut] [Tangut] lovely & good B.172[4] 192[5]

3613 [Tangut] IV 5 [Tangut] | "woman"

3614 [Tangut] VII 18 | [Tangut] "bird" 2657
W.II.50' 鷦 鷯 "small bird, wren, tit."

3614A [Tangut] x of | [Tangut] VII A 33

3615 [Tangut] II 34 [Tangut] | {3471, 4676A}
(i) [Tangut] 2216 | C.C.C. 33a 細 麪 "fine flour"

3616 [Tangut] III 125 [Tangut] | 1635
?

3617 [Tangut] VII 19 [Tangut] |
(a) VII 31 ditto

3618 [Tangut] VII 18 | [Tangut] 2150
(a) VII 69 [Tangut] | 1350
(b) VIII 12 | [Tangut] needle 1215
(i) ~~The disyllable~~ (b) above C.C.C. 25b 針 線 "needle & thread". B104 cat. under "women's clothing".

3619 [Tangut] V 57 | [Tangut] (misspelt) 3766
?

3620 0424 chain

3621 3226 chain

3622 1901 chain

3623 1901 chain

3624 4596 pair

3625 4607 chain

3625. It is not clear whether the following belongs here or under

| B.24[8] bkah atsolba "to speak" [honorific]

3626 2941 / 4551

3627 0258 chain VIII

3627 A 4078 pair

3628 ?0410 / 2328

3629 1636 chain

3630 3795 chain VIII

3631 4454 chain IV

3632 3714 / 3527 / 3960

3620

(a) I 61

C.C.C. 20[b]

3621

3622

B.179[4] 186[3]

W.I. 265[19]

B.186[3]

3623

?

3624

(a) IX 16

?

3625

(a) VIII

[C.C.C. 31[a]

B 24

at end of

3626

(a) III 83

(b) VI 119

(i) By itself

equal |

incompara

B 172' s.v.

278

3620 [Tangut] I A 29 [Tangut] | 0424

(a) I 61 | [Tangut] "woman" 0190

C.C.C. 20[b] 舅 "maternal uncle"

3621 [Tangut] IX 59 [Tangut] | 2007

3622 [Tangut] III 119 [Tangut] |

B.179[4] 186[3] 260 ~~? to translate~~

W.I.265[19] etc. B.195[3] 校 "to collate, correct"

B.186[3] tr. 䇿 [or 沓?] to connect, join

3623 [Tangut] VI A 21 [Tangut] |

?

3624 [Tangut] IX 109 [Tangut] |

(a) IX 16 ditto

?

3625 [Tangut] Li VIII 7 [Tangut] | 4607

(a) VIII 7 ditto (b) II 30 | [Tangut] 4599

[C.C.C. 31[a] Apparently a final particle 也了 B.245[2] [Tangut] | 'to say' with [Tangut] at end of quotation'

3626 [Tangut] V A 27 [Tangut] | 2941

(a) III 83 ditto

(b) VI 119 [Tangut] | 4337

(i) By itself W.I.90[8] 92[6] 等 "parallel, equal | [Tangut] asama 無等 W.II.92[12] incomparable B.121[1]

B.172[1] q.v.

3626 cont.

(ii) | [Tangut] W.II.42[8] 50[8] the same.

3627 [Tangut] VIII 21 | [Tangut] 3028

? error for ~~4851~~ 4581 bis

clair 5062 3628 A [Tangut] × of IX 57 [Tangut] |

?

3628 [Tangut] [VII 59-60]

(a) I 27 [Tangut] | 2328

(i) (a) above 旋 [Tangut]

(b) ? IX 111 [Tangut] 0410

3629 [Tangut] V.31 | [Tangut] 1636

(a) VII A 42 ditto

?

3630 [Tangut] IX 66 [Tangut] | 0470

3631 [Tangut] VI A 18 [Tangut] |

3632 [Tangut] VII 20 | [Tangut]

(a) II 3 ditto

(b) II 21 | [Tangut] 3527

(c) VII 16 | [Tangut]

This exceedingly common word normally means 行 "conduct,

278

3632 | as noun = 行 with [illegible] as verb = 行 W.II 92^5 B.193^2

3637 - 3635

3638 1218 chain

3633 5301 chain

take over
3639 0157 chain

3634 5017 chain
3634. W.I.168^9 used as a postpos: after a verb [illegible] | "when born"; just before + exactly parallel to [illegible] [illegible] "when dying" v. 3425 (?ie)

3640
3024 chain

3635 3637 pair

3640A 2830 pair

3641 1781 chain

3636 ? 2993 chain

3642 0322 chain

3632 con[illegible]
behaviou[illegible]
It also [illegible]
業 ccc.
藝 ccc.
For 行 see
W.I 270^{20}

B.230^2 [illegible]

3633 [illegible]
(i) The [illegible]
"to strike [illegible]

3634 [illegible]
(a) VIII [illegible]
W.I.168^9 II
particula[illegible]
B.163^3 [illegible] B

3635 [illegible]
(a) IX [illegible]
?

3636 [illegible]
?

279

3632 cont.

behaviour saṃskāra, ācāra.

It also means:–

業 CCC. 29^b "profession" B.192^4

藝 CCC. 20^a "profession"

For 行 see CCC. 27^b 36^{a,b} 37^a

W.I 270^20 行 ? row, line

B.230^2 clearly 'conduct' (noun)

3633 VI 76 |

(i) The disyllable CCC. 33^a 打諢 "to strike an instrument?"

3634 to IX 97 | 5147

(a) VIII 81 | [0879]

W.I.168^9 II 16^7 時 "time", in particular "(at that) time"

B.163^3 B 234^4 when (after a verb)

3635 IX A161 |

(a) IX A75. ditto

?

3636 IX 49 | (? corrupt)

?

3637 IX A75 |

(a) IX A161 ditto

(i) CCC. 9^a [天] 河 "(heavenly) river"

[Not the usual word]

3638 VII 81 | [1418]

CCC. 26^b 鐮 "sickle"

3639 VII 7 |

(a) V 2 ditto v. 157

(b) VIII 13 | 4931

(i) The disyllable 分離 "to separate, tear asunder".

3640 IX A 50 | 3024

(a) V 9 ditto

(b) I A 94 | 0881

?

3640A × of III 93 |

?

3641 I 98 | 1689

3642 V A6 |

3643 0322 chain

3644 2579 chain

3645 0322 chain

3646 0322 chain

3647 2091 chain

3648 1080 chain

3649 4393 chain

3650 5063 chain

3651 5677 chain

3652 3655 chain
W. I. 132[16] 龍 great sea turtle

3653 3334 chain

3654 2494 chain
(2494)-3654 ┬ 1077-3797-0354
├ 1206-0684
└ 3020

3655
├ 0417
└ ?4546-3652

1/2/39

3643
ccc. 37[a]
83 igo. pa
W II 26[12] 36

3644
A phonetic

3645
(a) III 65
(i) 2075

3646

3647
(a) V A
(b) V 1
(c) VI 4
(d) VI 7
?

3648
ccc. 29[a]

3649
(a) V 38
?

280

3643 [Tangut] I 98 [Tangut] | 0322
CCC. 37a W.I. 148[13] 藿見 to meditate 198[13] B.216[1]
ssigs.pa "to look at, examine"?
W II 26[12] 36[1] : B. 223[1] 'to meditate'

3644 [Tangut] V A 133 [Tangut]
A phonetic character NYIN

3645 [Tangut] I 17 [Tangut] | 0322
(a) III 65 | [Tangut] 3045
(i) [Tangut] | W.I. 202[4] thub "sage, muni"
2075

3646 [Tangut] III 122 [Tangut] |

3647 [Tangut] IX 10 [Tangut] | 2091
(a) V A 100 ditto
(b) V 1 [Tangut] | × {3217 5255} 3956
(c) VI 4 | [Tangut] 3911
(d) VI 70 | [Tangut] 3092
?

3648 [Tangut] I 62 [Tangut] | 1080
CCC. 29a

3649 [Tangut] V A 25 [Tangut] |
(a) V 38 ditto
1/2/39 ?

3650 [Tangut] IX 46 [Tangut] |
(a) IX 59 ditto

3651 [Tangut] I A 79 [Tangut] (5677)
A phonetic character

3652 [Tangut] IX 34 [Tangut] | cf. 3654(b) 4546
(i) [Tangut] | W.I. 214[7] rus-sbal
"tortoise & frog" 132[16]? v.2444

3653 [Tangut] IX 110 [Tangut] | 3334
W.II 48[11] 傘 "umbrella"

3209A
~~3654~~ [Tangut] gno III 175 [Tangut] |
(a) V 142 | [Tangut] to conform to ×1077
(b) VI 73 | [Tangut] cf. 3652 4546 ×(0684)
(c) IX 11 | [Tangut] [illegible] 1206
(d) IX A 20 | [Tangut] 3020
(ii) (d) above W.I. 96[5] B 180[2] 堅固 "firm & strong"
(i) By itself 堅 "firm" W.I. 178[5] [×]

3655 [Tangut] V 125 | [Tangut] "secret" 0417
(a) III A 47 ditto
?

In B 180[2] 3654 is definitely ×
Note 3654 + 3655 are indistinguishable & the division between them is unknown
3654 probably begins with ×

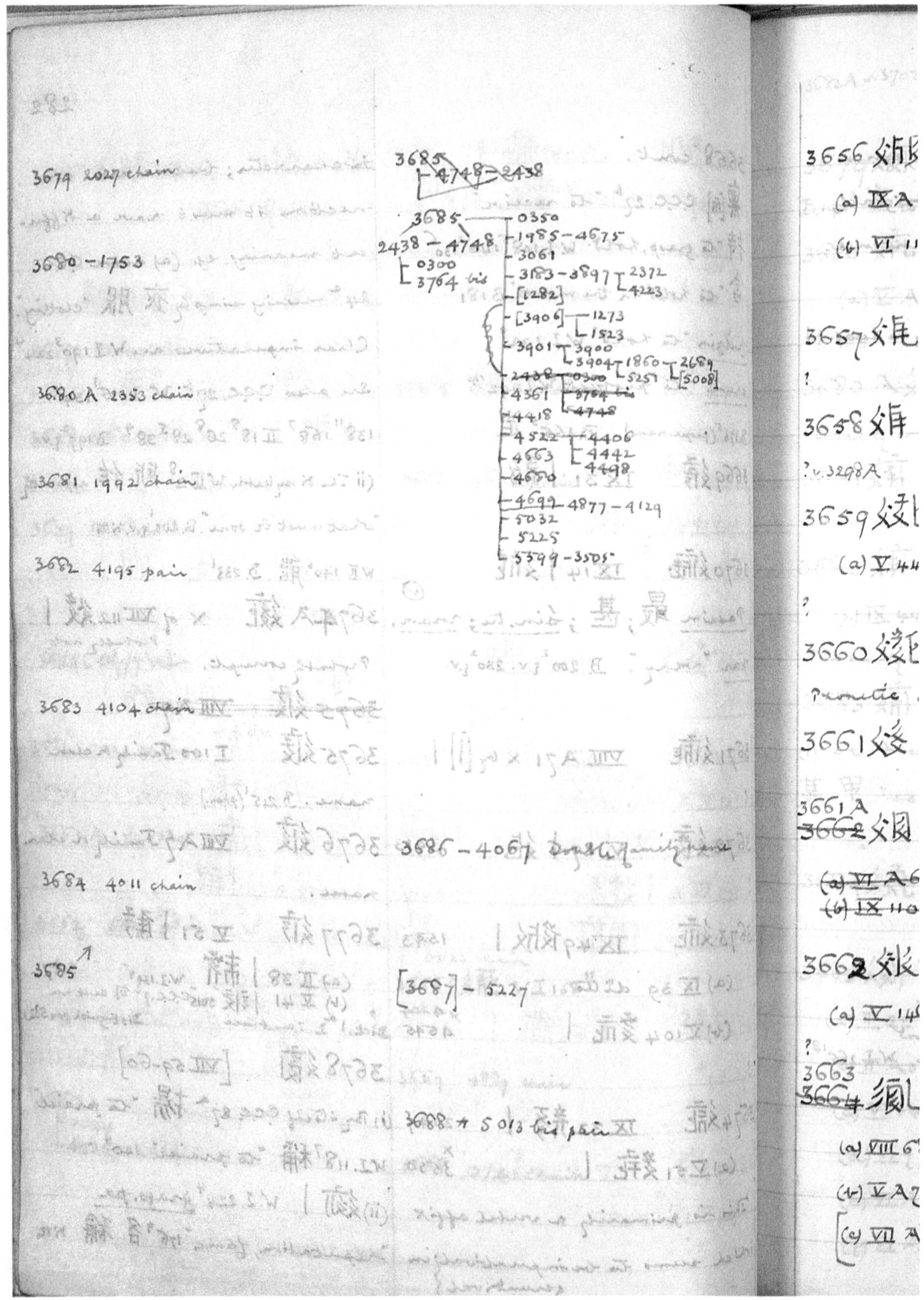

281

3656 [Tangut] I 9 [Tangut] | 4355
(a) IX A 147 ditto
(b) VI 110 [Tangut] | 5093

3657 [Tangut] VII 24 [Tangut] |
?

3658 [Tangut] VIII 78 [Tangut] | 3160
? v. 3298A v. 3298A

3659 [Tangut] IX 34 [Tangut] | 1536
(a) V 44 ditto
?

3660 [Tangut] I A 82 [Tangut] [Tangut] (5677)
Phonetic character.

3661 [Tangut] IX 34 [Tangut] | "frog" 2444

3661A
~~3662~~ [Tangut] ~~IX 110 [Tangut] | frog~~
~~(a) VI A 64~~ | [Tangut] | Probably a
~~(b) IX 110~~ mistake for 3334 q.v.

3662 [Tangut] III 44 [Tangut] |
(a) V 146 ditto
?

3663
~~3664~~ [Tangut] III 136 [Tangut] | 0294
(a) VIII 68 ditto
(b) V A 71 | [Tangut] 4535
[(c) VII A 128 [Tangut] × by [Tangut] |]
~~5017~~ 2779 5017

3664A [Tangut] Probably the correct form of 2183
3664B [Tangut] do. of 3768

(i) By itself C.C.C. 30[b] 字 "a (written) character"
(ii) The disyllable C.C.C. 27[a] 文字 "literature?, writing"

3664 [Tangut] V 1 | [Tangut] "ink"
(a) VII A 22 ditto
C.C.C. 27[a] 筆 "pen"

3665 [Tangut] ndzu VI 95 [Tangut] |
(a) VII 4 ditto
(i) The disyllable W.I. 224[3,4], apparently drai. shon. rhii. pa "old rishi". As [Tangut] by itself is rishi, | may be "old", but may be an ordinary ~~?~~ unit of disyllable | is the only other word with the same sound as [Tangut] "man".

3666 [Tangut] IX 1 [Tangut] [Tangut] 22

3667 [Tangut] IX 39 | [Tangut] 2126

3668 [Tangut] VIII 57 [Tangut] |
A common word meaning "to receive, hold". Represents :—

3656 4355 chain?

3657 4104 chain

3658 3160 chain

3659 1536 chain

3660 5677 chain

3661 0022 chain

3661 A v. 3334

3662 5697 pair

3663
0294
4535 - 2429

3664 0760 chain

3665 4620 chain

0022 chain

3666 ? WI 168" ?

3667 4889 chain

3668 0741 chain V

3668 c...

持 "to gra...

含 "to hol...

tdzin "to...

srun "to...

B.176[5] (proper n...

3669

3670

Passim

par "...

3671

?

3672

?

3673

(a) IX 3...

(b) V 10...

?

3674

(a) V 51

This is pri...

which seems...

282

3668 cont.
稟[示] C.C.C. 27b "to receive"
持 "to grasp, hold" W.I.108[5] 140[12] 130[6]
含 "to hold in the mouth" B.181
hdzin "to hold" W.I.192[9]
srun "to protect" W.I.192[14]
B.176[5] (proper name) B.165[5] 定

3669 [Tangut] IX 31 | [Tangut]

3670 [Tangut] IX 14 | [Tangut]
Passim 最; 甚; sin. tu; rnam. par "very". B. 200[2] q.v. 230[2] q.v.

3671 [Tangut] VIII A 71 × by [Tangut] |
?

3672 [Tangut] V 27 | [Tangut] 3913
?

3673 [Tangut] IX 49 [Tangut] | 1543
(a) IX 39 ditto
(b) V 104 [Tangut] | ×4204 4545
?

3674 [Tangut] IX 32 [Tangut] | 2149
(a) V 51 [Tangut] | × 3530
This is primarily a verbal affix which seems to be imperatival (in gerundival)

... character; but in some connection it must have a different meaning e.g. (a) above C.C.C. 24a meaning simply 衣服 "clothing". Clear imperatives are W. I 190[3] 224[4]
See also C.C.C. 27b W. I.116[1] 134[4] 138[11] 168[7] II 18[8] 26[8] 28[5] 38[9] B 197[2] q.v.
(ii The disyllable W II 2[8] 所作 apparently "what must be done". B. 200[1] q.v. ditto
W II 140[6] 能 B. 233[1]

3674A [Tangut] × of VII 112 [Tangut] |
Probably corrupt. Probably not Error for 3721?

~~3675 [Tangut] VIII A 7~~

3675 [Tangut] I 100 Family or clan name. B. 215[1] (phon.)

3676 [Tangut] VIII A 7 Family or clan name.

3677 [Tangut] V 51 | [Tangut]
(a) II 38 | [Tangut] W.I.134[4] 3187
(b) V 41 | [Tangut] 5015 C.C.C. 7b 句 sentence
? Dict. 1a 2 ? sentence
Distinguish from 5823

3678 [Tangut] [VII 59-60]
(i) By itself C.C.C. 27a 揚 "to praise" W.I. 118[7] 稱 "to praise" 140[4] ?
(ii) [Tangut] | W. I. 224[4] grags. pa "reputation, fame" 176[9] 名稱 ditto

B.216³ 執 to grasp

3669 2662 chain

3670 3980 chain

3670 | [Tangut] Kun.dga.ba "Very joyful" = "Ānanda" B.248² W.I.190³ & passim

| [Tangut] W.I.270¹⁸ 最勝 uttama

3671 interpretant

[3672] 1596 chain

3673 1553 chain

3674 2149 chain

W.I.266⁸ q.v.

3674 W.II 84¹¹ verbal affix, corresponding to 應 "must" in original, but in a different place in sentence.

W104¹ | [Tangut] 無所

cf. 5679 & see W II 130⁶ where they are associated

B.206⁵

B.233² 當

3674A 4673 pair

3675 interpretant

3676 interpretant

3677 3226 chain

B.187² tr. 顧 to take heed of

B.188² tr. 詞 phrase, statement

3678 interpretant

3678 B.346¹ 宣 to proclaim spread abroad W.I.265¹⁸

3682A v. 3702

3679 [Tangut]

B.195² 宣 to

3680 [Tangut]

(a) V A

B.168²

3680 A [Tangut]

Probably con

3681 [Tangut]

?

3682 [Tangut]

(a) IX 44

Probably

3683 [Tangut]

(i) The

某甲 "

3684 [Tangut]

3685 [Tangut]

(a) II 22

(b) II A3

(c) V 54

(d) VI 7

(e) VI A

(f) VI A

3682A v. 3702

283

3679 [Tangut] IX 98 | [Tangut] 3530

B.195[2] 宣 to spread abroad

3680 [Tangut] V A 91 | [Tangut]

(a) V A 92 ditto

B. 168[2]

3680 A [Tangut] X of I A 32 [Tangut] | 3886?

Probably corrupt [illegible]

3681 [Tangut] I 90 [Tangut] [Tangut] (not 630 (as above)) 1992

?

3682 [Tangut] III 56 Family or clan name

(a) IX 44 [Tangut] | 4195

Probably a double name

3683 [Tangut] III 16 [Tangut] | 5049

(i) The disyllable W.I 212[11] tr. by 某甲 "so & so".

3684 [Tangut] IX 31 [Tangut] | [illegible] 4011

4011 [illegible]

3685 [Tangut] I 90 | [Tangut][Tangut] 4748

(a) II 22 | [Tangut] 4418

(b) II A 34 | [Tangut] ×× 3183 ?

(c) V 54 | [Tangut] enumerate × 3901

(d) VI 77 | [Tangut] 4699

(e) VI A 51 | [Tangut] i.s. 3061 ?

(f) VI A 73 | [Tangut] 5225 ? B.172[3] q.v.

3685 (cont.)

(g) VII 9 | [Tangut] 4686

(h) VII 57 | [Tangut] younger, second 5032

(i) VII 87 | [Tangut] (i.d.) × 4675 1985 — VII 100 | [Tangut] 4877

(j) VII A 75 | [Tangut] (i.d.) 0350

(k) VIII 10 | [Tangut] 4669

(l) VIII 15 | [Tangut] (i.d.) [1282]

(m) VIII 38 | [Tangut] × 4522

(n) VIII 41 | [Tangut]

(o) VIII 66 | [Tangut] [3906] — (p) IX. 1 | [Tangut] × 2438

(q) IX A 121 | [Tangut] 4361

(i) Passim 名 "name"

(ii) | [Tangut] W.I. 224[4] grags. pa "reputation" II 4[7] 名稱 ditto?

II 126[2] 名號 'title'

3686 [Tangut] V 65 Family or clan name

(a) I 82 | [Tangut]

Probably a double name

3687 [Tangut] I 31 | [Tangut]

(a) VIII 25 ditto

3688 [Tangut] VII 24 [Tangut] |

(a) VII 71 ditto

3697 A 10 10
L 2490-0243-2491

3689 1650 chain

3691 0424 chain

3692 0582 chain

| 色相 external appearance S.-H. 220

3693 5708 chain

3694 - 4714

3695 - independent

3695 B. plate. Inscription on metal plaque.

3696 5366 pair

3697

3698 2027 chain

3699

3180
3708

(ii) B. 192

B 219 | translates 明; cf.
除闇 abolish ignorance q.v.

3689

(a) I 77

3690

3691

3692

(a) I. 17

(b) I 19

(c) I 63

(d) II 19

(e) V 12

(f) VI 29

(g) VI 10

(h) VIII 4

(i) VIII

(j) IX 5

The prima

is 'colour'

also has

"form,

W. I. 98 142

(ii) |

things."

284A

3689 [Tangut] III A 69 |[Tangut] 1650
(a) I 77 |[Tangut] 1637

3690 [Tangut] II A 2 "Kan's name"

3691 [Tangut] I 31 [Tangut] | "woman"

3692 [Tangut] VI 11 | [Tangut] 4201
(a) I.17 |[Tangut] 2551
(b) I 19 |[Tangut] 2323
(c) I 63 |[Tangut] × 0842 2305
(d) II 19 |[Tangut] 1512 (3609)
(e) V 12 |[Tangut] green vegetable × 5689 ~~3692~~
(f) VI 29 |[Tangut] 0800
(g) VI 104 |[Tangut] 1716
(h) VIII 4 [Tangut] × [Tangut] | [Tangut] [Tangut] 5858
(i) VIII A 107 |[Tangut] 4866
(j) IX 5 |[Tangut] × 5594 1566

The primary meaning of this word is 'colour' 色 mdog; but it also has the extended meanings "form, rupa" of the Chinese word ~~.......~~
W.I.98[2] 142[18] 190[12] 192[10] 214[8] II 28[9] 48[8]
(ii) |[Tangut] c.c.c. 23[a] 作物 "to make things." (1292)

3697A [Tangut] × of VIII 24 [Tangut] |
? ~~.......~~ [Tangut] See 0243

3693 [Tangut] I A 27 [Tangut] | 1099
(a) VII 44 [Tangut] | ? 0238

3694 [Tangut] V 23 |[Tangut]
?B.176[5] part of P.N.

3695 [Tangut] VI A 121 Family or clan name
W.I.98[8]

3696 [Tangut] VI A 29 [Tangut] |
W.I.138[2] 益 "increase, benefit, advantage"

3697 [Tangut] VII 54 |[Tangut] "body" 0210
(a) VI 96 ditto 4208 chain

B 227[4] 神 'spirit' ? phon.

3698 [Tangut] V 43 [Tangut] | 4061

3699 [Tangut] VI 1 |[Tangut]
(a) IX 99 ditto
(b) VI 23 [Tangut] |
(i) By itself W.I.114[8] 決 "to decide" B.195[5] q.v. B 228[2] q.v.
W.II.6[7] [Tangut] 44[10] [Tangut] | 知 "to know" II 140[7] 了知
W II 32[9] 解 "to ~~......~~, explain" 44[10] 110[10] B.229[4] 232[1]
W.II.110[13] ? B.179[3] ? B 161[2,4] ?

(ii) [Tangut] | c.c.c. 20[b] 36[a] W.I 100[9] 菩薩 "Bodhisattva" [translation?, not Phonetic]
(iii) V.96 v.1958

3700 0271 chain

3703 3765 chain

3703 (ii) The disyllable 醫藥 medicinal drugs W II 96^7, 132^5

3704 0809 chain

3700 A
L 0329-2950-3448-4242 I 5071

3705 4119 pair

3701 3226 chain

3706 4128 pair

3707 independent

3708 3699 chain

3709 4326 chain

3710 independent

3702 0899 chain

3711 independent

3700

(a) III 75

(b) VI 1

c.c.c. 29^a 31^a

listen to

(ii) The dis

"to listen

3700A

Probably co

3701

"auxilia

B. 89"

This | i

An excell

used like

& drew att

a sentence

II 28^9 22" B.

Note. Also

3702

136^3 [I]
W. I. 168^3 臣

down"

(ii)

284B

3700 [Tangut] III 163 [Tangut] | 4308
(a) III 75 [Tangut] | × 3766
(b) V 1 [Tangut] | 3249
C.C.C. 29a 31a W.I.136[15] II 22[1] 44[9] 聽 'to listen to' B.128[5] tr. 聞
(ii) The disyllable W.I.128[14] 聽聞 "to listen & hear"

3700A [Tangut] × of IX 114 | [Tangut]
Probably corrupt

3701 [Tangut] TA III 28 [Tangut] [Tangut] 2342
"auxiliary word"
B.89 [Tangut], [Tangut], [Tangut] in succession.
This | is an auxiliary word"
An exceedingly common particle, used like Chinese 者 to follow, & draw attention to, the subject of a sentence. C.C.C. 31b 35a,b W.I.198[7] II 28[9] 22[11] B.205[5]
Note. Also used as Phonetic.

3702 [Tangut] V A 52 [Tangut] | 4185
W.I.136[3] [?] 168[3] 臣人 196[6] Kal.ba 'to lie down'
(ii) | [Tangut] 臥具 "bedding" W.II 96[7] 132[5] 578

3703 [Tangut] VI 52 | [Tangut]
~~(a) VI 11 ditto [misspelt]~~
(a) VI 15 | [Tangut] 4565
?

3704 [Tangut] VI 84 | [Tangut] 0883
(i) The disyllable C.C.C. 14b 芥菜 "mustard" B.101 cat. with "vegetables."

3705 [Tangut] VIII 6 [Tangut] |
(a) I 8 ditto [[Tangut]]
? C.C.C. 18b [[Tangut]] [Tangut]

3706 [Tangut] V 55 [Tangut] |

3707 [Tangut] II 4 "Family or clan name"

3708 [Tangut] VI 23 | [Tangut] q.v. v. 3699
?

3709 [Tangut] III 19 | [Tangut] 0328
?

3710 [Tangut] VIII A 20 "Family or clan name."

3711 [Tangut] VI 56 Family or clan name
~~? [?]~~

3712 視 'to see' W.I.166[4]
3712 – 3269 chain
(a) ?? B.160[1] tr. 提 舉 'to raise'
B.227[2] 鏡 'mirror'

3713 4262 chain

3714 3632 chain

3715 2115 chain

3716 3918 chain

3717 5623 chain

3718 5367 pair
| W.II 78[6] 攝受 'to gather up, receive' B 220[4]

2167 chain
3719 衆 with the specific meaning of "assembly, company". W.II 86[3,5]
kāyika B. 206[4] tr. 禪 ? Buddhist

3720 3325 pair

3721 3138 chain

3722 0599 chain

3723 0791 chain

3724 4083 chain

3725 5708 chain

[3726] independent

3727 0464 pair

3728 0899 chain

3712
(a) IX 10
C.C.C. 30[a] W.I
skye. ba
3713
W.I. 194[11]
3714
(a) VII 20
?
3715
W.I. 92[9,10]
power, an
3715A
3716
(a) VI 17
?
3717
?
3718
(a) VIII A 3
W.I. 112[16] II 7
3719
(a) V 94
W.I. 90[15] 94[2]

285

3712 [Tangut] VIII 16 [Tangut] | 3745
(a) IX 103 | [Tangut] 0029
C.C.C. 30a W. I. 136² 看 to look, see B 256¹
skye. ba "to appear" Dict 1a6 B 173⁵ 174³
3713 [Tangut] III 61 [Tangut] |
W. I. 194" me. loṅ "mirror"
3714 [Tangut] II 3 [Tangut] |
(a) VII 20 ditto
?
3715 [Tangut] VIII A 68 | [Tangut] 1034
W. I. 92 9,10 勢 ~~bala, sthama~~ sthāman
power, authority.
~~3715 A [Tangut] = [Tangut] 4668~~
3716 [Tangut] IX A 9 [Tangut] |
~~(a) VI 17 | [Tangut] error for [Tangut] × 5176~~
?
3717 [Tangut] I 16 | [Tangut] 5623
? 5623 chain
3718 [Tangut] VIII A 31 [Tangut] |
(a) VIII A 34 ditto
W. I. 112¹⁶ II 70⁸ 96¹⁰ 攝 to ~~assist, ...~~ gather up, receive
3719 [Tangut] VIII 17 [Tangut] | 2167 number
(a) V 94 [Tangut] × 5069
W. I. 90¹⁵ 94² 136⁸ 138⁸ 衆 "all, universal"

3720 [Tangut] V 55 [Tangut] | [misspelt]
(a) IX 117 ditto
?
3721 [Tangut] I 16 [Tangut] [Tangut]
(a) IX 39 [Tangut] × by | [Tangut]
(b) IX 156 [Tangut] × by | [Tangut]
3722 [Tangut] III 164 [Tangut] |
?
3723 [Tangut] IX A 14 [Tangut] | ? 0791
?
3724 [Tangut] VII 52 [Tangut] |
?
3725 [Tangut] VII 52 [Tangut] | 2153
?
3726 [Tangut] III 47 Family or clan name
[Tangut]
?
3727 [Tangut] VII 52 | [Tangut] 0464
(a) VIII A 30 ditto
?
3727 A [Tangut] See [Tangut]
3728 [Tangut] VI A 109 [Tangut] | 4186
?

3729 0731 chain

[3730] 3260 pair

3731 independent

3732 independent

3733 4733 chain

[3734] independent

[3735] 3430 chain

3736 4031 pair

3737 independent

[3738] 1662 chain

3739 independent

3740 0497 pair

3741
⊥ 1383
 5404

3742 4011 chain

[3743] –
⊥ [3746] – [5884]

3744 4473 chain

3745 3269 chain

3729
(a) I 29
C.C.C. 14b

3730
(a) II 1

3731

3732

3733
(a) V A 2
B. 175² part

3734
B. 168²

3735

3736
(a) IX 48

3737

3738
(aa) II 1
(a) VII A 4

3724,5,7 { 3739 bis VII 52 | 4083 chain
3738 ter VII 52 |
3738 quater VII 52 | 286

3729 I A1 | 0917
(a) I 29 | 0533
C.C.C. 14^b 楊 "willow"

3730 V 51 |
(a) II 1 ditto
?

3731 VI 49 Family or clan name
?

3732 IX 38 Family or clan name
?

3733 V 19 | 4773
(a) V A 20 ditto
B. 175^2 part of P.N.

3734 I 66 Family or clan name
B. 168^2

3735 III 34 | 2364
?

3736 VI 21 (|)
(a) IX 48 ditto
?

3737 II 26 Name of man.

3738 VI 18 |
(aa) II 1 ditto
(a) VII A 41 | 3031
?

3739 VI 24 Family or clan name

3740 I 95 | 0497
(a) III 22 ditto
?

Distinguish from 3753
3741 III 36 |
(a) ditto
(b) VIII 40 | [misspelt] 5404
?

3742 VIII A 11 | q.v. 4324
4011 chain

3743 V 43 |
(a) I 8 ditto
(i) The dissyllable C.C.C. 20^b 34^a 妻眷
W.I. 96^11 (sic) 妻妾 + 婦女
all meaning "wife"

3744 VII 94 |
W.I. 94^13 制 "restraint, regulation"

3745 V A 37 (|) quater 3269
(a) IX 17 ditto
(b) IX 23 | 3748
C.C.C. 28^b
B 122^4 to 監 superintend, examine

3744 A = 4032

[3746] [3743] chain

[3747] 5690 chain

[3748] 3269 chain

3749 independent

3750 independent

3751 1136 chain

3752 0752 chain

3753 1136 chain

[3754] 2115 chain

3755 0140 chain

3756

3757 – 3454

3758 4561 chain

3746

(a) V 43

(b) VIII

(i) The Dicti

W. I. 96" (tr

all meani

3747

v. 5690

3748

(a) I 20

(b) V 12

(c) VIII

?

3749

3750

3751

(i) By ...

(ii)

clothing

287

3746 [Tangut] I 8 [Tangut] | 3743

(a) V 43 ditto

(b) VIII 99 | [Tangut] [5084]

(i) The dissyllable C.C.C. 20b 妻眷

W.I.96" (twice) 妻妾 + 婦女 :

all meaning "wife"

3747 [Tangut] IX 58 | [Tangut] 2402

v. 5690

3748 [Tangut] IX 23 [Tangut] | 3745

(a) I 20 | [Tangut] ? 1987

(b) V 128 | [Tangut] 1072

(c) VIII 16 | [Tangut] 3712

?

3749 [Tangut] VII 96 Family or clan name

3750 [Tangut] V A 55 X by itself | [|]

3751 [Tangut] VII 48 | [Tangut]

(i) By itself C.C.C. 25a 帽 "cap"

(ii) [Tangut] | B.103 cat. under "men's clothing"

written [Tangut] at 0176

3752 [Tangut] II 2 | [Tangut] 4132

(a) I 112 | [Tangut] 0697

A very common verb meaning "to make" 爲 C.C.C. 27b (or "to be")

Often used to complete the sense.

W.I.96[6] II 10[12] 26[8,9] B.248[7] I 266[8]

II 124[5] 作 to possess (a female body)

B.124[4] 200[4] 206[5] tr. 造

[Variant: 3727A]

3753 [Tangut] VII A 101 [Tangut] |

(a) VII 48 ditto

? Distinguish from 3740

3754 [Tangut] VII A 102 [Tangut] |

?

3755 [Tangut] VII A 125 | [Tangut] 0140

?

3756 [Tangut] I 16 | [Tangut] 1576

(a) ditto [[Tangut]]

(b) VII 82 | [Tangut] 3002

[Var. [Tangut]]

?

3757 [Tangut] I 16 | [Tangut]

(a) VI 34 ditto

?

3758 [Tangut] III 46 [Tangut] | 4561

?

3764 bis 3685 chain

3759 -4791

3761 -3843 -2540
-2668
-5591-2632-0824

3762 1297 chain

3760 4011 chain

3763 2167 chain

3764 3857 pair

3765
-4717-3703-4565

3766 0271 chain

[3767] 2704 chain

3758A

3759

(a) III 96

(1) The Tibetan W.I.

3760

(c) V 1

(d) VIII A

(e) II 31

There is

this chara

shows the

監 "inspe

主 "lord

It is clear

not 𘓐 me

word mean

ngal. po

seems to b

followed b

"prince".

B.180 the

3762 A v. 3832A

3764bis [Tangut] VIII 6 | [Tangut] 2438

288

3758 A [Tangut] ? N. 308 ni

3759 [Tangut] VI 6 | [Tangut]

(a) III 96 ditto

(i) The disyllable W.I. 206^{8} 224^{5} mt[illegible]'on. c'a "weapon"

3760 [Tangut] (ndzu) VI 6 [Tangut] | 'head' 4001

(c) VI 1 [Tangut] | (0756) 0004

(d) VIII A 35 | [Tangut] (receive) 0303 (a) I 56 [Tangut] | (sound, sonorous?) 4290

(e) II 31 | [Tangut] ruler (wang) 4302 (4011 chain)

There is much confusion between this character + [Tangut], but C.C.C. 28^{b} shows that this character means 監 "inspector (of an army)" + 主 "lord, master" (of a district). It is clear therefore that, whether or not [Tangut] means the same thing, this word means "ruler". In 214^{3} + foll. rgyal. po "king" In 216^{16} it seems to be a verbal form being followed by [Tangut] + translated dban "prince".

B. 180^{5} tr. 在 (? wrong)

3761 [Tangut] VI 6 | [Tangut] × 3843]

(a) III 136 ditto [ ]

~~(b) I 56~~ ?

~~(c) II 1~~

3762 [Tangut] VI A 27 [Tangut] |

(a) VI 45 ditto reversed

3763 [Tangut] ka IX 127 [Tangut] | "number" 2167

(a) VI 86 | [Tangut] × (0389) 3118 ~~0389~~

C.C.C. 36^{a} WI 98^{9} + passim 四 "four"

3764 [Tangut] IX 32 [Tangut] |

(a) VI 55 ditto [ ] in both]

3765 [Tangut] VI 36 | [Tangut] × 4717

(a) VI 11 ditto

3766 [Tangut] III 75 | [Tangut] (bis lin) 3700]]

(a) V 57 [[Tangut]] [Tangut] | 3619

3767 [Tangut] VI 35 | [Tangut]

(i) C.C.C. 15^{b} 粳 "upland rice".

(ii) | [Tangut] 2716 [which is the actual reading in C.C.C. 15^{b}] cat. under "grain".

3778 3812 chain

3768 3086 chain
3768. B.255[2] slags 'opportunity'
3768. W.I.132[12] 紖 probably correct form.

3773 -5011

3774 1565 pair

3769 1464 pair

3775
1670
3190-1676

3770 3449 chain

3776
4755
4094

3771
4718-0425

3771
4721
4718-0425

3777 5690 chain

3779 4209 pair

3772
4160-5555

3780 0583 chain (poor?)

3769A 紖 ...
tsang Tibe...

3768 紖

(a) VI A

(i) By itself

(ii) 丨 ...

方便 ...

place; ...

3769 紖

(a) IX A ...

W.II 4[4] ...

3770 紖

3771 紖

(a) I 6 ...

(b) VIII 7

(i) (a) above ...

"relation ...

(ii) ... 丨

uncles"?

3772 紖

(a) IX 52

[(b) V ...

(i) By itself 苟

(ii) The ...

恭 敬 ...

3769A [Tangut] Lo Handbook p. 20. 藏 tsang Tibet v. 883

3768 [Tangut] VII 95 [Tangut] | 4604
(a) VI A 82 | [Tangut] 4399
B. 173[2] 188[2]
(i) By itself W.I. 94[11] 方 "place"
(ii) | [Tangut] W.I. 132[12] 136[7] II 2[10] 4[9] etc.
方便 upāya "convenient to the place; hence "device" See S.-H. Sort. p. 154

3769 [Tangut] VII 95 [Tangut] |
(a) IX A 34 ditto [[Tangut]]
W. II 4[4] 右 "to the right" see 3966

3770 [Tangut] I 107 [Tangut] | 3449

3771 [Tangut] I 22 [Tangut] | ~~x(0425) 4718~~ 4721
(a) I 6 ditto
(b) VIII 7 [Tangut] | x(0425) 4718
(i) (b) above 親家 C.C.C. 34[b] "relatives"
(ii) [Tangut] | C.C.C. 20[b] 阿舅 "maternal uncles"?

3772 [Tangut] VI 38 | [Tangut]
(a) IX 52 ditto
[(b) V ~~38~~ 100 [Tangut] x by [Tangut] |]
(i) By itself 敬 "respectful."
B 233[2] B. ~~139~~ 191[2]
(ii) The dissyllable W.I. 112[12] 140[8] II 16[6]
恭敬 "respectful & reverent."
~~B. 191[2] tr. 恭~~

3778 [Tangut] V 66 | [Tangut] ? 1954
?
(iii) [Tangut] | C.C.C. 27[a] W.I. 140[9] 敬愛 "respectful & loving."

3773 [Tangut] VI 20 [Tangut] |
(a) IX 59 ditto reversed
?

3774 [Tangut] VII 33 [Tangut] |
(a) VII 67 ditto
?

3775 [Tangut] III 11 | [Tangut] 1670
(a) VIII 1 ditto
(b) IX 103 | [Tangut] 3974 & 3975

3776 [Tangut] VI 77 | [Tangut] 4755
(a) VII 37 ditto
(b) VIII 56 [Tangut] | 4094
?

Note. 3775 & 3776 are indistinguishable

3777 [Tangut] IX 115 [Tangut] | 1369
? B. 127[4] transl. tr. 天子

3779 [Tangut] VIII 1 [Tangut] |
(a) III 11 ditto
? v. 1958

3780 ~~3779~~ [Tangut] IX 24 [Tangut] |
(a) III 141 ditto

Passim. An extremely common possessive affix, corresponding to

3872 bis 5128 chain

3784-[1153]

3785
⊥ 2665-3781

3781 3785 chain

3786 2115 chain

3782 2395 chain

3787 0249 chain

3788 independent

3789 3829 chain

3783
+0135
1943
2548
2970
3207
2556

3790-3116

3791 3026 chain

3792 1398 chain

3872 bis
(a) VI

3780 cont
the Tibet
having:

Note 3779
tinguishab

3781

3782

(a) V 43
[(b) V 43

(i) (b) above
"and then"

3783

(a) I 125
(b) I 61
(c) VII 50
(d) VIII A
(e) IX A

Passim.
affix "no
無

3872 bis [Tangut] VII 24 [Tangut] |
(a) VII 71 ditto

290

3780 cont.

the Tibetan ldan, can "possessing, having".

Note 3779 & 3780 are almost indistinguishable.

3781 [Tangut] VIII 24 | [Tangut] 2665

3782 [Tangut] III 113 | [Tangut] 2395
(a) V 43 ditto
[(b) V 43 [Tangut] | error for 3837]
(i) (b) above W II 36[7] apparently 時乃 "and then", or words to that effect.

×

3783 [Tangut] I 21 | [Tangut] 0136
(a) I 125 ditto
(b) I 61 [Tangut] | ? 1943
(bb) I A 74 2556
(c) VII 50 | [Tangut] 2548
(d) VIII A 9 [Tangut] | 2970
(e) IX A 28 | [Tangut] 3207

Passim. A very common negative affix "not" 不 or "not having" 無

3784 [Tangut] VIII 1 | [Tangut]
?

3785 [Tangut] VII 52 | [Tangut] 2665
(a) II 13 ditto
B. 227[5] 廊 verandah

3786 [Tangut] IX 33 [Tangut] | 2115
(a) IX 52 ditto
B. 166[4] tr. 多

3787 [Tangut] I 26 | [Tangut] 1389
B. 125[5]

3788 [Tangut] VIII A 12 "Family or clan name"

3789 [Tangut] I 70 [Tangut] |
CCC. 11[a] [Tangut] + disyllable 一个月 "one month". Apparently a kind of affix?
?

3790 [Tangut] IX 164 [gap]
(a) V 11 | [Tangut]
?

3791 [Tangut] V 2 [Tangut] | 3026
?

3792 [Tangut] II 23 | [Tangut] 5400
?

3793-1347 237^{1}_{3}
The disyl. B.225[3] tr. 長者 S.K.284
gṛhapati 'householder'

3794 1964 chain

3795
┬3447 [0596z]
└5654 ┬0670 ┬2221 ┬0883-5047
 └2467 └3630 ├2069
 ├2399
 ├2403
 ├4674
 └4903

3796 independent

3797 v.3654 subchain v.3797A

3798 1876 chain

3799 3235 pair

3800 3806 chain

3801-~~5551~~
⊥5551-4488

3802 0003 pair

3803 0020 "chain 不"

3793
(a) I 9
B.96
have") It
property
B237[1]
II 18[5] [rather
3794
B 203[1]
3795
(a) III 12
(b) VIII 8
3796
(i) The double
W.I.138[13] ?
3797
(a) VIII 28
See also

291

3793 [Tangut] P'A I 27 | [Tangut] P'A 1347

(a) I 9 ditto

B. 96. [Tangut] ideogram plus the centre of [Tangut], | is | [Tangut]. It is [Tangut] ("to have") It is the word for [Tangut] [Tangut] [?having much jewels or property?] [Lo translates 長]

B 237[1]

II 18[5] [rather cryptic] 130[11] trs. 共 "all"

3794 [Tangut] VI 8 | [Tangut] q.v. 1964

B 203[1]

3795 [Tangut] V A 84 [Tangut] | 3447

(a) III 12 ditto

(b) VIII 87 | [Tangut] 5654

?

3796 [Tangut] III 46 x by itself | [Tangut]

(i) The double character W.I. 138[1] 香納

W.I. 138[13] ?

3797 [Tangut] VII 24 | [Tangut] to confront 1077

(a) VIII 28 | [Tangut] 0354

?

3797A [Tangut]

W.I. 120[1] 蓋 skanda cover

Doubtful form Probably 3797

3798 [Tangut] IX 10 [Tangut] |

3799 [Tangut] I 26 [Tangut] |

(a) VI 63 ditto

?

3800 [Tangut] I 30 [Tangut] |

[Lo p. 25 "foreign"] Dict. 56[a] 4

W.I. 266[5] 番 "foreign" B. 232[1]

3801 [Tangut] V 7 [Tangut] |

(a) VII A 6 ditto reversed

(i) | [Tangut] W.I 120[1], 140[3] II 6[9] 8[4] etc. 精進 B 201[4]

virya "vigour, zeal, pure progress"

II 142[12] 勤 策 virya-plan?

3802 [Tangut] III 58 [Tangut] | 0003

(a) V 155 ditto

?

Note. Apparently this is the correct form; to be distinguished from [Tangut] "six"

3803 [Tangut] V 2 [Tangut] | 0020

(a) I 138 ditto

?

3804 5623 chain

3805 3514 chain

3806
┬ 4798
└ 3800

3807 4083 chain

3808 4902 chain

3809 5690 Thaking

3810 3223 chain

3811 independent

3812
┬ 1954-3778
├ 1801
├ 4711
└ 5550

(b) W.I.136[6] ? 掠 打 plunder + beat

∩ 打 擲 beat + throw down

3804 [Tangut]

(a) VI A

ccc 9b 11a 3.

"year".

Note. 380

-tinguishal

3805 [Tangut]

3806 [Tangut]

(a) III 171

(b) I 30

? II 150[12] 親見

3806A [Tangut]

3807 [Tangut]

?

3808 [Tangut]

(a) V 14

(b) V 22

[(c) VII 3

(i) | [Tangut] B.c

Note. This

distinguish

+ (b) + (c) m

See also 4

292

3804 [Tangut] V 36 [Tangut] | year 4016

(a) VI A 8 | [Tangut] ? 3831

C.C.C. 9b 11a 35a 年 W.I. 214² 226¹¹ lo "year".

Note. 3803 + 3804 are barely dis-tinguishable + cf. 3863

3805 [Tangut] III 58 [Tangut] |

3806 [Tangut] I 17 [Tangut]

(a) III 171 ditto

(b) I 30 | [Tangut] 3800

? II 150¹² 親 'intimate'

3806A [Tangut] See [Tangut] 3857

3807 [Tangut] V 2 | [Tangut] 4502

?

3808 [Tangut] VI 44 [Tangut] | 4902

(a) V 149 ditto

(b) V 22 | [Tangut] 3987

[(c) VII 34 [Tangut] | to 3848]

(i) | [Tangut] B.99 cat. under 'sheep'.

Note. This character is barely distinguishable from [Tangut] (3848) "spirit" + (b) + (c) may belong to the latter.

See also 4635

3809 [Tangut] VII A 66 [Tangut] | 3203 ~~3809~~

(a) VII 42 [Tangut] | (5548) x 5562

(b) VIII 5 [Tangut] | 4483

C.C.C. 24a4 床 "bed"

Dict 1a6

3810 [Tangut] IX 156 | [Tangut] 3323

(a) VIII A 53 ditto

(b) IX 4 | [Tangut] 0427

C.C.C. 9b + passim 福 "good fortune, prosperity" etc

3811 [Tangut] V 147 "Name of country"

3811 A [Tangut] See [Tangut] 4637

3812 [Tangut] III A 76 | [Tangut] x (3778) ~~3812~~ 1954

(a) III 72 ditto

(b) I 33 | [Tangut] 5550

(c) I 139 [Tangut] | 4711

(d) VII 22 | [Tangut] 1801

This word means lit. "to strike", but represents various Chinese words

(i) By itself C.C.C. 32a W.I. 136¹⁸ W.I. 138² 侵 "to invade"

(ii) (b) above W.I. 134¹⁶ ~~136~~ 打 撲 "hit, squash (flies)" (1408)

(iii) | [Tangut] C.C.C. 31a2 打 拷 "to beat, strike"

3813
4200 chain

3814 1396 chain
3814 W.II 90[12] has the diss. reversed
meaning 近親 'near relations'?

3815 - 1359

3816 2765 chain

3817 0364 chain

3818 3138 chain

3819 0271 chain

3820 - 5065

3821 2494 chain

3822 independent

B 176' part of F.N.

3823 3402 chain

3824
⊥ 5102 - 4922 - 4914

3825 - 1999

3826 4775 chain

3813 [illegible]
(a) III 27

3814 [illegible]
(a) VII 87
W.II 90[12] [ ]

3815 [illegible]
(a) I 13 di
?
Note 3814

3816 [illegible]
(a) V 44
W.II 34[2] 70[2]
etc. (Soot.

3817 [illegible]
(a) III 1
(b) III A 6
C.C.C. 12[b] W

3818 [illegible]
3 N. 3721 +

3819 [illegible]

293

3813 [Tangut] I 141 | [Tangut] 4200
(a) III 27 [Tangut] | 0281

3814 [Tangut] VI A 34 [Tangut] | 1369
(a) VII 87 [Tangut] | (not |) 3161 1363
W. II 90[12] [|] 近 "near" [v. opp.] B 161[4]

3815 [Tangut] VIII 1 | [Tangut] 1359
(a) I 13 ditto [|]
?

Note 3814 + 3815 are indistinguishable

3816 [Tangut] III A 9 [Tangut] | 4186
(a) V 44 [Tangut] |
W. II 34[2] 70[2] 通 "to permeate, universal" etc. (Soot. p. 365) 152[10] 達

3817 [Tangut] III 164 | [Tangut]
(a) III 1 ditto
(b) III A 6 | [Tangut] [[Tangut]] (i) 5592
C.C.C. 12[b] W. II 46[3] 淺 "shallow"

3818 [Tangut] IX 156 [Tangut] [Tangut]

3819 [Tangut] VIII 51 [Tangut] | deaf 4601

3820 [Tangut] V 97 | [Tangut]
(a) III 170 ditto
?

3821 [Tangut] VI 92 [Tangut] | 2494
?

3822 [Tangut] V. 102 Family or clan name
Dict. 1[a]6 B 345[2] 195[2] [嵬 ? error] W. I. 265[16] Name of Emperor?

3823 [Tangut] III 19 [Tangut] | glorious 3402
~~[(i) C.C.C. 7[b] 句 "a sentence" probably 3677]~~
(ii) W. I. 134[4]: 168[11] II 106[8]
(iii) [Tangut] | C.C.C. 13[b] 苟葵 peony or mallow.
Note. To be distinguished from 3677. One of these meanings probably belongs to that character; but (iii) belongs here.

3824 [Tangut] VI 35 | [Tangut]
(a) II A 30 ditto
C.C.C. 7[b] 10[b] etc 雨 W. I. 190[14] 194[14] "rain" II 94[10] [verb = noun] D. 180[5]

3825 [Tangut] IX 73 | [Tangut] ? 1999
(a) I 20 ditto
?

3826 [Tangut] VI 35 | [Tangut]
?

3827 5301 chain

3828 5623 chain

3829
- 4794
- 1251
- 3326 — 3312, 4012, 4740
- 3789
- 4287
- 4928
- 5332

3830 3891 chain

3831 5625 chain

3832 2164 chain

3832 A independent

B. 203[4]

3834 1781 chain

3835
- 2871
- 5269

3836 – 4188

3837 2649 chain

3838 – 1862

3838 中 (i) | 妓 … 素訶 sahā world W.II 126[4]

3839 0752 chain VIII

3827

W.I.226[2] sa…

3828

?

3829

(a) I 37…

(b) I 70…

(c) III 44…

(d) VII…

(e) VII 6…

(f) IX 14…

(g) IX A…

(i) C.C.C. 4[6]…

3 La. ba…

(ii) (h) above…

3830

?

3831

?

NoCi 3830…

3832

(a) I A6…

(i) By itself W…

"to increase…

3827 [Tangut] I 69 [Tangut] shebe²

W.I. 226² gar II 48⁸ 舞 "to dance"

3828 [Tangut] III 62 [Tangut] 2041

?

3829 [Tangut] IX 88 [Tangut] | 4794

(a) I 37 ditto

(b) I 70 | [Tangut] 3789

(c) III 44 | [Tangut] 3326

(d) VII 3 | [Tangut] 1251

(e) VII 6 [Tangut] | 4287

(f) IX 146 | [Tangut] 5382

(g) IX A123 [Tangut] | 4928

(i) C.C.C. 4ᵇ W.I. 92⁴ etc 月 W.I. 214⁷ 222¹³

3 la. ba "month"

(ii) (4) above C.C.C. 11ᵃ 月 "month"

3830 [Tangut] II 11 [Tangut] | to think 1950

?

3831 [Tangut] VI A8 [Tangut] | 'year' 3804

?

Note 3830 + 3831 are indistinguishable.

3832 [Tangut] VIII 52 | [Tangut]

(a) I A64 [Tangut] |

(i) By itself W.I. 124³ 128⁶ 138³ etc. 益

"to increase, advantage" B 223² q.v.

(ii) The dissyllable v. 3107. 294

(iii) [Tangut] | B.102 cat, untrs 'rivers trees'

3832A [Tangut]

cII p'ei B346¹ ? B179³ [Tangut] 195² ([Tangut]) cf. 2183 auspicacious

3833 [Tangut] VIII 6 | [Tangut]

Blank see 3764 bis

[3834 [Tangut] V 124 [Tangut] |

should be 3853 bis]

3835 [Tangut] VII A116 [[Tangut] |] 2871

(a) V 111 ditto

(b) VII 116 | [Tangut] 5269

?

3836 [Tangut] III 113 | [Tangut]

(a) III 65 [Tangut] × by [Tangut] | 3914

3837 [Tangut] III 113 [Tangut] |

(a) V 43 ditto

3838 [Tangut] VI 18 | [Tangut]

(a) IX 48 ditto misspelt?

C.C.C. 8ᵃ 19ᵇ 陽 yang as opposed to yin

B.215¹ phon. 娑 so

3839 [Tangut] VI 22 | [Tangut] 0118

?

3840 2783 chain

3841 3851 pair

3842 2224

3843 3761 chain

3844 2167 chain

3845 0752 chain

3845 Φ(i) | [Tangut] [Tangut] 覩史多

Tușita ~~name of a heaven~~ W. III 86[4]

3846
⊥ 5686 ⊤ 4982
⌊ 4984

3846 | [Tangut] C.C.C. 28[a] 内宿 "inner star" (name of temple). ~~castles~~

B. plate. Inscription on metal plaque.

3847 independent

3848 5640 ~~chain~~

3850 3226 chain

3851 ⊤ 3841

3840 [Tangut]

B.186[2] 氏

B.192[8] 代

3841 [Tangut]

(a) I 11 …

?

3842 [Tangut]

(a) IX 12…

(i) | [Tangut]

"celestia…

B.174[3] | [Tangut]

3843 [Tangut]

(a) VI 6

(b) V 14

(c) V 99

~~(d) V 146~~

(d) IX 57

38?

3844 [Tangut]

(a) V 146

C.C.C. 6[b] …

drug "…

Note 384…

the centre…

295

3840 [illegible] še VII 3 [illegible] | long-life, generation
B.186[2] 氏 "family" Dict. 56a 4
B.192[5] 代 generation

3841 [illegible] I 4 [illegible] |
(a) I 11 ditto
?

3842 [illegible] I 4 [illegible] |
(a) IX 123 ditto
(i) | [illegible] (1488) C.C.C. 10a 星宫
"celestial mansion"
B.174[3] | [illegible] tr. 行宫

3843 [illegible] III 136 [illegible] | 3761
(a) VI 6 ditto [ ]
(b) V 14 | [illegible] [ ] 5691
(c) V 99 [illegible] | 2668
~~(d) V 146 [illegible]~~
(d) IX 57 [illegible] | [ ] 2540
~~38~~ ?

3844 [illegible] VII A 119 [illegible] | [illegible] 2167
(a) V 146 [illegible] | "[illegible]" 2170
C.C.C. 6b + passim 六 W.I.190[9]
drug "six".

Note 3843 probably has [ ] in the centre not [ ]

3845 [illegible] III 62 | [illegible] 3995
(a) III 145 [illegible] x by [illegible] | 4576 4863
(b) III A 19 [illegible] x by | [illegible] 4646 1511
(c) III A 20 [illegible] x by | [illegible] 3991 1509
(d) III A 31 [illegible] x by [illegible] | 1522 5021
? B.164[1] 125[5]
(b) to (d) are Phonetic characters.

3846 [illegible] V 11 | [illegible]
(a) II 183 ditto
C.C.C. 1[?] "interior, internal"
W.II.16 中 "central".

3847 [illegible] V 31 x by itself [ ] |
?

3848 [illegible] III 137 ~~x by it~~ [illegible] | 1367
(a) VII 34 0688
C.C.C. 20b 神 "(heavenly) spirit"
W.I.190[9] lha "god". B.179[3] 346[1] 122[2]

~~3849~~ [illegible] ? Error for 3891
W.I.90[10] 思 cint- "to think"
W.II.76[4] 慮 "to think, consider"

3850 [illegible] V 23 | [illegible] 0498
?

3851 [illegible] I 11 | [illegible]
(a) I 4 ditto
?

3852 1781 chain

3853 1781 chain

3854 1781 chain

3855 1781 chain

3856 5563 pair

3857 – 3764

3858 2355 chain

3859 2306 chain

| W.I.269[21] 華嚴 avatamsaka 'garland S.-H. p.387

3860 5690 chain

3861 1130 chain

3862 5702 pair

3863 independent

3.206[4] q.v.

3864
-- 3614A
└ 4329

3865 – 3561

3866 independent

3867 independent

3868 0236 chain

3853 bis v.38

3852

?

3853

C.C.C. 22[a]

3854

(a) VI 22

3855

(i) The dissyll

~~3856~~

3856

(a) V 1 di

?

3857

(a) IX 32

3858

(a) I A

3859

(a) V 88

(b) VIII A

C.C.C. 6[a] 13[a]

"flower. W

3853 bis v. 3834

296

3852 [Tangut] VI 22 | [Tangut] 3854

?

3853 [Tangut] V 150 [Tangut] | 1364

C.C.C. 22[a] 圈 "a circular enclosure"

3854 [Tangut] V 105 [Tangut] | 4021

(a) VI 22 [Tangut] | 3852

3855 [Tangut] I 117 [Tangut] | 1364

(i) The disyllable C.C.C. 23[a] 天窓

~~3856~~

3856 [Tangut] I 13 [Tangut] | (misspelt)

(a) V 1 ditto

?

3857 [Tangut] VI 55 | [Tangut]

(a) IX 32 ditto [1 in x]

?

3858 [Tangut] III 136 [Tangut] | 2355

(a) I A 68 ditto

3859 [Tangut] II 19 [Tangut] | 1591

(a) V 88 | [Tangut] 2469

(b) VIII A 8 | [Tangut] 4020

C.C.C. 6[a] 13[a] 33[a2] etc 花, 華

"flower. W.I. 194[6] 216[5] me. tog. ditto

3860 [Tangut] I 13 | [Tangut] 5675 ~~4678~~

3861 [Tangut] I 5 | [Tangut] "star" 1130

C.C.C. 8[b] 辰 [an hour] a heavenly body"

3862 [Tangut] III 140 [Tangut] |

(a) VII 14 ditto

?

3863 [Tangut] q. 3803/5 VII 6 Family or clan name

? W.I. 266[7] tr. 處 'place' 173[4] ?B 174[5]

3863A [Tangut] VI 3 x or | [Tangut]

Error for 3891

3864 [Tangut] VII A 33 [Tangut] | 3614A

(a) VII 78 | [Tangut] 4329

?

3865 [Tangut] IX 21 | [Tangut] 3561

(a) I 40 ditto

?

3866 [Tangut] IX 40 Family or clan name

3867 [Tangut] VII 18 Family or clan name

3868 [Tangut] I 70 | [Tangut]

?

3869 1343 chain

3870 1614 chain

3871 2562 chain

3872 0258 chain

3873 4208 chain B.160[1]

B.176[1] 160[1,2] 172[2] q.v. 191[5] tr. 量 measure

3874 1929 chain

takeover

3875 0258 chain

3876 1891 chain

3877 independent

3878 independent

3879 0638 chain

3880 2179 chain

3881 independent

3882 1785 chain

φ.1 B 211[2] | 辟支 Pratyeka

3883 - 1547

~~3876 1891 chain~~

3869

3870

3871

3872

(a) III 13

3873

Dict 1b 1 5

3874

C.C.C. 5a 角

of a constr

3875

(a) VIII 10

B.93

gram. |

(i) The Hsay

"to fight,

3876

(a) VII 4c

C.C.C. 10b

W. I 170[5] "to

B. 180[4] 出

297

3869 III 19 | 1343
?
3870 IX 4 | 1614
?
3871 V A 22 2604 5623
?
3872 VIII A 21 | 0258 (4581) 3028
(a) III 130 |

3873 IX A 18 | "body" ability
Dict 1b 1 54a 5 C.C.C. 1b 3 W.II.116[10] 能
3874 I 47 | form 1925
C.C.C. 5a 角 W.I. 220[14] nag.pa name of a constellation.
3875 VIII 19 |
(a) VIII 10 ditto
B.93 [the whole?] ideogram. | is (the dissyllable) or . The word for
(i) The dissyllable C.C.C. 29b 鬪爭 "to fight, quarrel".

3876 III 18 |
(a) VII 40 | 0450
C.C.C. 10b ~~B.180~~ W.II 42[9] 出 "to rise" W.I 170[5] "to give forth"? B177[1] part of P.N.
B.180[4] 出, to emit, give forth

(of the sun)
(ii) W.I. 212[16] 216[18] 218[14] byun, byun. gnas, source, place of origin?

3877 VII 55 Family or clan name
3878 VIII 76 Family or clan name

3879 VI A 40 |
(a) I A 30 ditto
(b) I 110 | 0721 1638 misspelt
?(c) V 85
?
3880 VI A 115 | 4430
?
3881 II 26 Family or clan name

3882 P.I. I 64 | tiger

Note. A common Phonetic.
3883 III 1 | 1547
(a) IX 1 ditto
(i) The dissyllable C.C.C. 10b 明日 "to-morrow"?

3884 3891 chain

3885 3086 chain

3884A 1147 pair

3886 2353 chain

3887 - 3902

3888 - 3903

3889 chain
1666 - 1665
0071

3890
2149 chain

3891 慮 "deep thought" W.II 76[4] v. 2075

3891
4749 1950 2039
3884
4967

3892 3893 chain

3893
1741
2423 - 0482
3892

3894 0148 chain

3887A
宮

3884

B. 237[3]

3885

(a) VI 10

3884A

3886
(a) I A

(i) By itself

"to set"

(ii) The

3887

(a) V 56

3888

(a) V 56

3889

(a) II 1

(b) VII A

ccc. 9[6] 夜

W. II 10[3] 闇

B. 171[5] 暗

3887A [Tangut] B 272⁴ (Doubtful form.) 343³ W.I. 271¹²
宮 'mansion'

298

3884 [Tangut] VIII 75 [Tangut] |
B. 237³

3885 [Tangut] III 14 [Tangut] | 4604
(a) VI 100 | [Tangut] 0431
?
3884A [Tangut] II 14 X of [Tangut] |

2075 W II 76⁴

3886 [Tangut] I 29 | [Tangut] 1570
(a) I A 32 v. 3680A 0623
(i) By itself C.C.C. 10⁶ W.I. 116² 沒 "to set" (of the sun) B. 188³
(ii) The disyllable W I 222¹⁷

3887 [Tangut] III 35 | [Tangut]
(a) V 56 ditto

cf. 3888

3888 [Tangut] III 35 | [Tangut]
(a) V 56 ditto

? cf. 3887

3889 [Tangut] III 1 | [Tangut] 1666
(a) II 1 ditto
(b) VII A 141 | [Tangut] 0077
C.C.C. 9⁶ 夜 "night"
W. II 10³ 闇 "darkness" B. 346⁴
B. 171⁵ 暗 dark

3890 [Tangut] VI A 31 | [Tangut]
W II 26⁷ 瘂 "dumb".

3891 [Tangut] syn VI A 25 | [Tangut] 4749
(b) (a) VIII 12 [Tangut] | (a) XII misspelt VI 3 v. 3863A
(c) (b) VIII 75 | [Tangut] 3884
(i) C.C.C. 34⁶ 思 "thought" B 127³ v. 3884
(ii) W.I. 112⁹ 憂 "anxious" 168¹⁰
(iii) The disyllable W.I. 112¹⁷ 思惟 "thought; reflection 176²,¹³ B 237¹
(iv) | [Tangut] W. I. 218⁸ gdud.pa

3892 [Tangut] VIII 46 [Tangut] |

3893 [Tangut] I 48 [Tangut] | 1737
(a) I 45 ditto [illegible]
(b) V 80 | [Tangut] 1741
(c) VI 9 | [Tangut] X (0482) 2423
(d) VIII 46 | [Tangut] [Tangut] 3892
Verb
W.I 110¹² 136⁷ II 4¹¹ 斷 "to cut off, dispel"
W. II 64³ 絶 "to cut off".

3894 [Tangut] IX 22 [Tangut] |
? B 245

3895 4065 pair

3896
3252–0854

3897 3685 chain
佛說 Buddhacarita W.I 265

3898 1891 chain

3899 0424 chain

3900 3685 chain

3901 3685 series

3902 3887 pair

3903 3888 pair

3904 3685 chain

[3905]
2650
5330 4725
5572

3895

(a) IX 5

3896

(a) V 143

3897

(a) III 65

(b) VI 78

C.C.C. 20b 36a

3898

(a) III 181

(b) VII 31

3899

(a) III 52

C.C.C. 20a

3900

299

3895 [Tangut] II 1 [Tangut] |

(a) IX 5 ditto

?

3896 [Tangut] III 27 | [Tangut]

(a) V 143 ditto

(i) By itself W. II 6[10] 辯 "to discuss." B. 193[5] 才

(ii) The disyllable W. I 90[2] II 4[10] 20[1] 辯才 "discourse, rhetoric" B 201[3]

3897 [Tangut] T'a III 22 [Tangut] | 3183

(a) III 65 [Tangut] | 4223

(b) VI 78 | [Tangut] 2372

C.C.C. 20b 36a + passim 佛 "Buddha"

3898 [Tangut] t'ou III 20 [Tangut] |

~~(a) I 92 [Tangut] | [Tangut]~~

(a) III 181 | [Tangut] 5377

(b) VII 31 | [Tangut] 1499 1499

?

3899 [Tangut] V 41 [Tangut] | 0190

(a) III 52 [Tangut] |

C.C.C. 20a 妹 "younger sister"

3900 [Tangut] VIII 35 [Tangut] |

?

3901 [Tangut] V 54 [Tangut] | name 3685

(a) VIII 35 | [Tangut] 3900 (b) I 92 [Tangut] | 3904

B. 180 列 "to divide, enumerate, classify, ~~rank, order~~"

3902 [Tangut] V 56 [Tangut] |

(a) III 35 ditto

? cf. 3903

3903 [Tangut] V 56 [Tangut] |

(a) III 35 ditto

? cf. 3902

3904 [Tangut] I 92 | [Tangut] misspelt 3901

(a) VI 26 [Tangut] |

(b) VI 133 | [Tangut] 1860

(i) B. 181[3,4] 列 "to divide, enumerate, classify."

(ii) (B. 180[5] the disyllable) 行列 ditto

(iii) (a) above C.C.C. 31b 分折 "to divide, separate."

3904A [Tangut] N. 104 l'ho

Possibly = 3905

3905 [Tangut] [IX sap]

(aa) I 20 4725

(a) III 142 [Tangut] | 5330

(b) VI 109 [Tangut] | 5574

(c) IX 44 [Tangut] | 2650

3917 bis 1667 chain

3906 3685 chain

3907
┬ 1047
└ 5674

3908 0899 chain

W.II 78³ [Tangut] | 起 'arose'

3909 5708 chain

3910 independent

3911 2091 chain

3912 2167 chain

3913 1596 chain

3914 2649 chain

3915 independent

3916 3226 chain

[3917] [3108] pair

3918
┬ 2625 [2791A]
├ 0046
├ 0099
├ 0163
├ 0570 – 1621
├ 2619
├ 3541
├ 3716
├ 3919
├ 5114
└ 5154

3905 cont
W.I.116² 出
160⁷ ditto
3906 [Tangut]
CCC20a⁴
before nou
the Chines
Used as Ph
3907 [Tangut]
(a) III 123
(b) III 168
W.I. 218⁴
3908 [Tangut]
(a) III
(b) V 62
(c) VI 4
CCC.10b WI
3909 [Tangut]
Dict 1a 3[
3910 [Tangut]
?
3911 [Tangut]
?

3905 cont.

W.I.116[2] 出 "to go forth, sent forth"

160[7] ditto "to emit." B.187[3]

3906 [illegible] VIII 66 [illegible] | "name"
(a) I 33 1273 (b) I 52 1523

CCC20[a4] 阿 A prefix a-, used before nouns of relationship, like the Chinese 阿 B.177[1] part of P.N.

Used as Phonetic W.I 194[4]

3907 [illegible] VI 14 | [illegible] 1047
(a) III 123 ditto
(b) III 168 [illegible] | 5674

W.I. 218[4] batsego "heap, pile"?

3908 [illegible] II A32 [illegible] |
(a) III 59 | [illegible] 4493
(b) V 62 [illegible] | 5347
(c) VI 41 [illegible] | 4185

CCC.10[b] W II 10[5] 16[8] 起 "to rise" B.224[4]

3909 [illegible] V 69 [illegible] | solitary 5708

Dict 1[a] 3 [doubled]

3910 [illegible] VI 4 "Family or clan name"

?

3911 [illegible] VI 4 [illegible] | 3647

?

~~3917 [illegible] II 6 | [illegible] 1667~~
~~(a) III 173 ditto~~

300

3912 [illegible] III 31 | [illegible] "number" 2167

3913 [illegible] I 30 [illegible] | 1596
(a) V 139 ditto
(b) V 27 [illegible] | [3672]
(c) VII A 23 [illegible] | [[illegible]] ×5203 5193

?

3914 [illegible] III 66 [illegible] [illegible]

?

3915 [illegible] IX 41 "Family or clan name"

?

3916 [illegible] VI 46 | [illegible] 1291

?

3917 [illegible] V 28 [illegible] |
(a) VIII 11 ditto

?

3917A [illegible] error for [illegible]

3918 [illegible] V 181 [illegible] | misspelt 2625 (2791A)
(a) IX 75 ditto
(b) III 13 | [illegible] 0046 (0163)
(c) III 14 | [illegible] 0063
(d) III 75 | [illegible] 5114
(e) V 13 | [illegible] 1963
(f) VI 45 | [illegible] [[illegible]] 3919
(g) VI 66 | [illegible] 5154

(ii) 疾疫 "sickness & plague W II 130²"

3919 3918 chain

3920 1391 chain

3921 independent

3922
┬ 4227A
└ 3922

(a) B.129⁵ tr. 共同

W.I.134⁷ looks like a postp? 'with'

3923 0809 chain

3924 0680 chain

3925 2149 chain

3926 4393 chain

3927 1974 pair

3928 4473 chain

3929
┬ 0576 ┬ 4225
└ 4524 ┼ 4270
└ 5406 – 5267 – 5407

3930
┬ 4820
├ 2038
└ 3171

3918 con

(h) VII 10

(i) VIII

(j) VIII A

~~(k) IX 75~~

(k) IX A

(i) By itself

"disease"

(ii) The

"disease +

3919

?

3919A

C.C.C. 26⁶

3920

(a) VIII 5

3921

3922

(a) III 18

(b) VIII 4

(c) VIII

W.I.108¹⁸

B.125² B.18

301

3918 cont.

(h) VII 10 | [Tangut] 3541

(i) VIII 44 | [Tangut] 0099

(j) VIII A 55 | [Tangut] ×(1621) 0570

~~(k) IX 75~~ (jj) IX 104 2619

(k) IX A 9 | [Tangut] 3716

(i) By itself W.I. 112⁹ 疾 II 8⁶ 40³ 病 "disease" II. 130² 疫 pestilence, epidemic.

(ii) The dissyllable C.C.C. 19ᵃ 病患 "disease & suffering" [Tangut] |

3919 [Tangut] VI 45 [Tangut] "disease" ?

3919A [Tangut] C.C.C. 26ᵇ 頃 "to bow the head"?

3920 [Tangut] III 156 [Tangut] | [Tangut] 1394

(a) VIII 57 | [Tangut] ? 2034

3921 [Tangut] IV 1 × by itself | |

3922 [Tangut] V 28 [Tangut] | [Tangut] ?

(a) III 181 | [Tangut]

(b) VIII 4 [Tangut] × by [Tangut] | (3692) (5658)

(c) VIII 4 [Tangut] × by [Tangut] | (5651) (1426, 0041)

W.I. 108¹⁸ Dict 1ᵃ 3 II. 128⁸ 共 together B. 125² B. 187⁴ 通

3923 [Tangut] VIII 58 | [Tangut] 0383

(i) The dissyllable C.C.C. 14ᵇ 茵蔯

B. 101 cat. under "vegetables".

3924 [Tangut] III 67 [Tangut] 0680

(a) IX 72 | [Tangut]

3925 [Tangut] V 181 | [Tangut] 2149

3926 [Tangut] VI 45 | [Tangut]

3927 [Tangut] I 8 [Tangut] | ? 1974

(a) VIII 82 ditto

3928 [Tangut] V 68 [Tangut] | 4473

3929 [Tangut] ?

(a) V 132 [Tangut] | 0576

(b) VI 78 [Tangut] | × 4524

3930 [Tangut] VIII 58 [Tangut] | because 4830

(a) III 145 ditto

(b) VI 105 | [Tangut] karma etc. 3171

(c) VIII 90 | [Tangut] doubt 2038

3930 (iii) (b) above 業緣 karma cantation W.I 170[15]

3931
1145
4684
5326

3932 2710 chain

3933 1914 chain

3934 4079 chain

3935 1425 pair

3935A 4977

3936 2124 chain

3937 5708 chain

W.I.134[4] 但 'but'

3938 2149 chain

3939 4651 chain

3940 independent

3941 ~~0008~~ ~~chain~~

3942 - 2302

3930 cont.

(ii) The ...

"because of ...

[followed by ...

(i) By itself ...

因 "because ...

3931

(a) VI A 67 ...

(b) III 88 ...

(c) III 89 ...

3932

3933

(a) III 141 ...

(b) V 130 ...

B. 216[5] 應 ...

3934

3935

(a) VI 113 ...

3935A

302

3930 cont.

(ii) The dissyllable W.I.100[8] 因緣 "because of" II 22[9] 138[7] "reason, cause" [followed by [illegible]]

(i) By itself W II 6[4] as a postposition 因 "because of"

3931 [illegible] I 57 | [illegible] 1145

(a) VI A 67 ditto

(b) III 88 [illegible] | 4684

(c) III 89 [illegible] | 5326

3932 [illegible] V A 61 [illegible] "tools" 5440

3933 [illegible] IX 17 [illegible] | to inform 1914

(a) III 141 ditto

(b) V 130 [illegible] |

B. 216[5] 應 to answer

3934 [illegible] IX A 156 [illegible]

3935 [illegible] VI 50 [illegible] |

(a) VI 113 ditto

3935A [illegible] x of | [illegible] II.13

3936 [illegible] IX 55 | [illegible]

C.C.C. 34[6] 聚 "assembly, society"

W.II. 52[3] 會 sangha "assembly"

3937 [illegible] IX A 1 | [illegible] 2153

A particle beginning the sentence W.II. 4[2] 惟 28[1,3] 42[10] 唯 "in fact, only, but". B 200[3] B.176[4] q.v. [[illegible]] 189[1] (80.)

3938 [illegible] II 43 [illegible] | 2149

(a) II 3 ditto particle

[(b) III 118 [illegible] x by 572 [illegible] |] 1415

B 130[2] tr. 若

3939 ~~3938~~ [illegible] IX 50 [illegible] | [?misspelt] 4070

chain 5440 → Dict. 1[a] 4, 56[a] 4

3940 ~~3939~~ [illegible] I 96 Family or clan name

3941 ~~3940~~ [illegible] VIII 1 | [illegible] 0000

(a) V 1 ditto

C.C.C. 27[a] 34[a] B 124[1] tr. 數 to count

3942 [illegible] VI 16 | [illegible]

(a) V 127 ditto

B. 99 (The dissyllable) cat. under 'horse'

3939A [illegible] x of V 43 | [illegible]
error for 4202

?

3943 3232 pair

3944 2351 chain

3945 3211 chain

| tongue tip sounds i.e. dentals Dict 1b 7 Title of Ch. III

| supra-lingual sounds i.e. palatals Dict. 1b 7 Title of Ch. IV

3946 0436 pair

3947 3438 chain

3948 2285 chain

3949 2954 chain

3950 1488 chain

3951 independent

3952 independent

3953 independent

3954 0873 pair

3943

(a) VI 63

(i) By itself

(ii) The diss

B. 252¹

255² (T.

· turb + comp

3944

(a) IX 175

c.c.c. 18ª W.I

?

3945

(a) IX

3946

(a) VII A 6

(i) | c.c.

(ii) |

3947

(a) IX 151

(b) V 130

B. 176²

(i) By itself W.

(ii) The diss

303

3943 [Tangut] V 120 [Tangut] | 3232
(a) VI 63 ditto
(i) By itself W.I.190[17] ḥts'e "enemy"?
(ii) The dissyllable W.I.132[17] ?
B.252[1] ḥts'e. bar byed.pa. 害 "to injure"
255[2] (T. the same) 嬈亂 "to disturb & confuse".

3944 [Tangut] V 39 | [Tangut] 2351
(a) IX 175 | [Tangut] x 0678 2228
C.C.C. 18[a] W.I.98[8] 134[4] 舌 "tongue".
?

3945 [Tangut] IX A 13 [Tangut] | 3211 x 3227
(a) IX 35

3946 [Tangut] VII A 64 [Tangut] | 0436 ~~3946~~
(a) VII A 65 ditto
(i) | [Tangut] (0693) C.C.C. 15[a] 醋 W.I 136[1] 138[11]
醬醋 "(sauce or pickles +) vinegar"
(ii) | [Tangut] C.C.C. 13[b] 梅 "plum (flower)"

3947 [Tangut] VI 43 [Tangut] | [misspelt]
(a) IX 151 ditto [Tangut] v. 3438
(b) V 130 [Tangut] | 4787 v. 3948A
B.176[2]
(i) By itself W.I.108[6] 畫 "to draw, paint"
(ii) The dissyllable W.I.108[5] II 16[3] 書

3947 cont.
寫 "to write, record". B.173[5] W.I.266[6]

3948 [Tangut] IX 20 [Tangut] | 2285
(a) IX 19 [Tangut] 1031
(i) W.I 212[18] 214[8] ?
(ii) | [Tangut] W.I.228[3] skye.rgu "mankind"
This is a most puzzling word; it looks like a nominal prefix.

3948A [Tangut] x of IX 77 | [Tangut]
(Probably an error for 3947??)

3949 ~~3948~~ [Tangut] IX A 33 [Tangut] | 2934

3950 ~~3949~~ [Tangut] III 170 | [Tangut]
(a) I 58 ditto
W.II 36[1] 舍 I 214[5] k'yim "house"
218[10]? B.187[5] 237[2] 宅 residence, ~~[illegible]~~

3951 ~~3950~~ [Tangut] I 97 "Family or clan name"

3952 [Tangut] I A 109 "Family or clan name"
B.174[2]

3953 [Tangut] I A 3 "Family or clan (name)"
B.175[4]

3954 [Tangut] IX 27 [Tangut] |
(a) V 76 ditto

303

3955 (e) x ty | 3991A

3955 2149 chain

3956 2091 chain

3957 0024 pair

3958 1840 pair

3959 independent

3960 3632 chain

3961 1949 chain

3962
+3172
-1663

3963 2169 chain

3964 3980 chain

3965 4064 chain

3966 v. 3769

3967. Dict. p. 576. | Regnal period

(Dict. dated 6th year)

3967 2377 chain

| W. I. 269[21] 方廣 vaipulya

S.-H. p. 155 broad spacious

| 平等 S.-H. 187 sama impartial universal

3955

(a) V 93

(b) VI 47

(c) VIII 2

(d) IX 56

W. II 48[8]: 言

W. I. 98[5] (c)

3956

(a) V 2

(b) VIII 36

W. I. 98[6] 啼

W. II 42[5] 涕

3957

(a) VII 12

(i) The Hsing

?violent" N

3958

(a) V 42

c.c.c. 10[a]

3958A

3959

3960

304

3955 V A 35 | 2149 to do
(a) V 93 | 0197
(b) VI 47 | 5160
(c) VIII 20 | ? sing 0481
(d) IX 56 | 0902
W II 48[8] ? 謌 "to sing"
W.I. 98[5] (c) above 謌唱 "song"

3956 V 1 | 3647
(a) V 2 | 3217
(b) VIII 36 | 5255
W.I. 98[6] 啼 "to cry, scream"
W.II 42[5] 涕 "to weep"

3957 III 20 | 24
(a) VII 12 ditto
(i) The disyllable W.I. 190[13] nar.ba "strong, ? violent" Name of a Nāgarājā

3958 V 3 |
(a) V 42 ditto
C.C.C. 10[a] 艮 "limit"?

3958A See 4119

3959 VII 16 "Family or clan, name"

3960 VII 16 |

B.188[1] tr. 鑿 to bore, excavate

3961 V 25 | 4413
(a) VII 30 | 2733
B.191[3] tr. E. (possibly phon. P.N.)

3962 I 94 | ? 3172
(a) II 40 ditto
(b) III 173 | 1663

3963 V 24 | 2167 "similar"
(a) VIII 5 |
C.C.C. 4[b] 九 W.I. 222[11] dgu "nine"

3964 VII 33 | 3980
?

3965 V 70 | 2426
(a) V 4 | 3436

3966 N.113 dwi or hwi
W.II. 4[4] 右 "right hand" (left struck out)
↕ Error for 3769

3967 VII 1 | 2377
(a) III 126 | 2374
(b) VII 44 | 4323 goodness 4323
(i) C.C.C. 6[a] 27[b] & passim 德 "virtue"
C.C.C. 32[a] 正 "correct, solid" W.I. 269[11] do.
W.I. 218[12] brtsan.pa "staunch"
II 140[6] 太平
(ii) | W.I. 190[4] sańs.rgyas "Buddha"

3968. v. 829 (ii) (B.102)

3968 5632 chain

B.186[2] 壽 (part of title)

By itself 長 W.II.134[6]

B.191 tr. 普 B.216[4] q.v.

B 223[3] q.v. tr. 舉 whole

3969 0809 chain

3970 0304 chain

3971 2448 chain

v. 5159 for phrase

B.233[1] tr. 休 to desist

3972 4207 chain

3973 – 5252

3974 + 4795 └ 0103

3975 1252 chain

3976 5540 chain

3977 2448 g chain

3978 4276 chain

3979 0522 pair

3968

(a) VII A 1

This word

- exact mea

(i) By itself

(ii) The diss

"long

(iii) W.I.170[5] ?

3969

C.C.C. 14[6] 蓄

3970

3971

(a) V 22

(b) VII 3

C.C.C. 35[b] W I

B.160[2]

W.I.138[10] 漏

to leak

niner pain

W II 214[14] 216

v. 5159

B.122[4] tr. 追

Fundamentall

with all the

technical t

305

3968 [Tangut] IX 11 [Tangut] | "long"

(a) VII A 136 ditto

This word seems to have two distinct meanings:-

(i) By itself W. I 110[15] 鎧 134[2] [甲 "doubtful" "scales" "armour"]

(ii) The dissyllable W. II 52[3] 長遠 "long & distant".

(iii) W. I 170[5] ? "altogether" ~~preposition~~ or the like?

3969 [Tangut] IX 1 | [Tangut] 0383

C.C.C. 14[b] 葍 "carrots, turnips".

3970 [Tangut] VIII 6 [Tangut] |

3971 [Tangut] IX 1 | [Tangut] 2448

(a) V 22 | [Tangut] 3977

(b) VII 30 [Tangut] | 0222

C.C.C. 35[b] W II 46[8] 流 "to flow"

B. 160[2]

W. I 138[10] 漏 II. 2[7] zag.pa zin āsrava "flowing" "to leak", transgress sinner "pain, affliction" v. Soot. p. 425

W II 214[14] 216[8] hbab.pa "to flow"

v. 5159

B. 122[4] tis 過 transgression

Fundamentally this word means "to flow" with all the implications in this Buddhist technical term.

3972 [Tangut] III 157 [Tangut] |

3973 [Tangut] IX 1 | [Tangut]

(a) I 11 ditto

(i) The dissyllable C.C.C. 11[a] B. 230[1] 泉原 "a spring of water". B. 102 cat. under "rivers & seas"

3974 [Tangut] IX 31 | [Tangut] 4795

(a) IX 4 ditto

(b) IX 41 | 廈 0103

(i) The dissyllable B. 160[3] ? 同 -

3975 [Tangut] VII A 14 [Tangut] | 1252

(a) VII A 88 ditto

(b) IX 103 ashamed 3190

?

Note 3974, 3975 & 3775 are much alike.

3976 [Tangut] IX 2 [Tangut] |

v. 5540.

3977 [Tangut] V 22 [Tangut] | 3971

3978 [Tangut] VII 10 | [Tangut] 4233

3979 [Tangut] I 91 | [Tangut]

(a) IX 107 ditto

3980 ~~4561 chain~~ chain
├ 1982
├ 0025 ┬ 0649 – 0647
├ 3964 ├ 1817
├ 3670 └ 1983
└ ? 4986

3981 3276 chain
B.187[2] ts. 科 a class!

3982 1541 pair

3983 – 5678 chain

3984 – 3459 double family name

3985 2793 chain

3986 3024 chain

3987 4902 chain

3988 2754 chain

3989 interjection

3990 4023 chain

3991 2395 chain

3991 A 4426 pair

3980
(b) VII 12
(c) VII 33
(a) VIII 8
(d) IX 14
C.C.C. 3[a] 3[b] 4
W.I. 92[3] 110
W.I. 192[4]
W.I. 194[3]
(ii)
respect
phrase]

3981
(a) VII 58
(b) I 57
(i) C.C.C. 29[a]
(ii) The Hsiy
W.I. 100[4] 分
B.174[1] ts.

3982
(a) V 1

3983
(a) V 92
(b) V A

306

3980 [Tangut] p'u I 47 | [Tangut] error 1982 ~~1969~~

(b) VII 12 | [Tangut] 0025

(c) VII 33 | [Tangut] 3964

(a) VIII 8 | [Tangut] Probably ditto 1982

(d) IX 14 [Tangut] | 3670

B.161³ 上 previous

CCC 3ᵃ 3ᵇ 4ᵃ 上 upper (of three)

B180 上 lofty

W.I. 92³ 110⁷ lofty, supreme uttara

W.I. 192⁴ 224¹⁵ bla.ma "high"

W.I. 194³ mc'og "best."

(ii) | [Tangut] CCC 29ᵇ 敬 尊 "to respect & honour" [not the usual phrase]

3981 [Tangut] ~~VII~~ VII 112 [Tangut] | 3216

(a) VII 58 ditto

(b) I 57 [Tangut] | 2044

(i) CCC 29ᵃ 下 "low" (as opposed to "high")

(ii) The disyllable [分 白] (CCC 30ᵃ)

W.I. 100⁴ 分 明 B.166⁵

B 174¹ tr. 仰 respectful 165³ tr. 辨 discriminate

3982 [Tangut] III 96 [Tangut] | 1541

(a) V 1 ditto

3983 [Tangut] na V 35 [Tangut] | your 2523

(a) V 92 [Tangut] | 2788

(b) V A 21 [Tangut] ~~242~~ 0240

3983 cont.

(c) V A 31 [Tangut] | 4503 q.v.

CCC 31ᵇ etc. 我 I B 223²

W I 198⁷ bdag "self"

W.I. 204¹; B.231¹ 自 231² 'my'.

3984 [Tangut] V 52 | [Tangut] 3459 Family name

3985 [Tangut] VIII A 13 [Tangut] | 4121

3986 [Tangut] I A 90 | [Tangut] 0881

(a) VII A 122 | [Tangut] 1382

~~B.232³ 流 to flow~~ Vide from 3971

3987 [Tangut] V 23 [Tangut] | 3808

3988 [Tangut] IX 31 | [Tangut] 1746

3989 [Tangut] VI A 107 "Family or clan name"

B.186 秦 "Ts'in dynasty" B344¹ do. W.I 271¹⁶

3990 [Tangut] IX 2 [Tangut] |

(a) I. 1 ditto

3991 [Tangut] IX 36 [Tangut] | 2505

3991A [Tangut] IX 2. [Tangut] [Tangut] 3955 'dig' 4426

(a) IX 155 [Tangut] |

3992 independent

3993
⊥ 2510–4477 ⊤ 3458
⊥ 5711

3994 2635 chain
II 78[6] 曾 already
B.192[1] 向 hitherto, previously
B.192[5] 先 B 200[3] 預 beforehand
B.230[2] B 234[1] 昔

3995 2783 chain

3996 0752 chain

3997 independent

3998 5708 chain

3999 1501 chain

4000 chain
⊥ 1839
⊥ 0087

4001 3282 chain

4002 0809 chain

4003 0249 chain

4004 2149 chain

4005
⊥ 2588
⊥ 4807

4006 1992 chain
W.II 122[11] 會 to collect.

3992
(a) V 25
3993
18/2/39
3993 A
3994
(a) I 26
(b) VIII 22
W. II 20[12] 前
W. I. 226[6]
W. I 208[10]
W. I. 168[1]
3995
IX 97
3996
(a) I 9
(b) III 62
(c) VII 104
(i) The ...
Sort. p. 81 B
(ii) ...
3997
W. II 26[4]

307

3992 [Tangut] IX 2 "Family or clan name"

3993 [Tangut] VII 52 | [Tangut] 2510
(a) V 25 ditto

18/2/39

3993A [Tangut] see [Tangut] 4775 ~~4757~~ after

3994 [Tangut] VII 4 [Tangut] | [Tangut] 3378
(a) I 26 [Tangut] | 3152
(b) VIII 22 | [Tangut]. 4015

W. II 20[12] 前 "formerly" B. 173[5]

W. I. 226[6] rñin. pa "ancient, formerly"

W. I. 208[10] sngon. du "previously"

W. I. 168[1] 已 "already" cf. II 86[3]

3995 [Tangut] VI 42 [Tangut] | "long life"
IX 97 ditto

3996 [Tangut] I 50 [Tangut] | 0752
(a) I 9 | [Tangut] ? 2014
(b) III 62 [Tangut] | 3845
(c) VII 104 [Tangut] | 0206

(i) The disyllable W. I. 136[4] II 42[1] 凡事夫

Sort. p. 81 Bālapṛthagjana "Everyman, the ordinary man".

(ii) By itself W. II 154[1] 俗 common, ordinary B. 161[2] (i.e. 頑 stupid)

3997 [Tangut] I 34 "Family or clan name"

W. II 26[4] Used as Phonetic.

3998 [Tangut] VII 115 | [Tangut] 4109

3999 [Tangut] VI 82 | [Tangut] 3268

4000 [Tangut] V 20 [Tangut] | 1839
(a) IX A 82 ditto
(b) V 29 [Tangut] | 37

4001 [Tangut] I 67 [Tangut] | 2566

4002 [Tangut] III 165 [Tangut] | 1942
(a) I 27 [Tangut] × by disyllable.

B. 101 The disyllable "eat. with vegetables"

4003 [Tangut] I 67 | [Tangut] 4098

4004 [Tangut] VI 81 | [Tangut] 2149

4005 [Tangut] III 165 | [Tangut]
(a) III 29 ditto [Tangut] 2588
(b) I 113 | [Tangut]. 4807

4006 [Tangut] I 102 [Tangut] (not to 30) 1992

(i) | [Tangut] [Tangut] W. II 28[12] 集會 "to assemble, collect".

N.B. ?/? is probably correct.

4007 4566 pair

4009 1172 chain

4008 0341 pair

4012 3829 chain

4010 4272 chain

4013 0148 chain

4011
1103 0027 0239 0503 0887 1067 1762 2638 2646 3265 3684 3760 4234 4324 4368 4960
2655 5074 5275 1318 1059 2479 2615 0004 0303 4290 4302 3742
0756

4014
0164
4319

4015 2635 chain

4007
(a) III A

4009

4008
(a) IX A 14

4010
(a) VII A
C.C.C. 28

4011
(a) IX 12
(b) I. 131
(c) I A 99
(d) III 59
(e) III 61
(f) III 161
(g) V 2
(h) V 17
(i) V 59
(j) VI 6
(k) VI 111
(l) VII 42

308

4007 [Tangut] IA4 [Tangut] |

(a) III A39 ditto

4009 [Tangut] I 14 [Tangut] |

4008 [Tangut] III 15 | [Tangut] clothing

(a) IX A146 ditto

4010 [Tangut] VI 5 [Tangut] | roll 4274

(a) VII A135 ditto

C.C.C. 28[b] 吏 "official, officers"

4011 [Tangut] ŋu VIII 1 | [Tangut] first born 1103

(a) IX 12 ditto

(b) I. 131 | [Tangut] ? 0239

(c) IA 99 | [Tangut] hair 3265

(d) III 59 | [Tangut] up to 4234

(e) III 61 | [Tangut] ? 0027

(f) III 161 | [Tangut] ? 2638

(g) V 2 | [Tangut] q.v. 4324 (3742)

(h) V 17 | [Tangut] q.v. 4368

(i) V 59 | [Tangut] head 0887 (2479, 1059)

(j) VI 6 | [Tangut] 'lord' 3760 (0004, 0303, 4290, 4304, 0756)

(k) VI 111 | [Tangut] 1067

(l) VII 42 | [Tangut] peak 2646 (1763)

(m) VIII A65 | [Tangut] ? 1762

(n) IX 31 | [Tangut] 3684

(o) IX 79 | [Tangut] ? 4960 (1318)

(p) IX 82 | [Tangut] neck 0503

(q) IX 104 2615

C.C.C. 18[a, b] & passim 頭 W.I. 190[15] mgo "head".

4012 [Tangut] VIII 19 | [Tangut] 3326

(i) The dissyllable C.C.C. 10[b] 外後日 "the day after to-morrow(?)"

4013 [Tangut] V 34 [Tangut] | 5157

W.II 28[7] 算 "to calculate"

4014 [Tangut] VI 54 | [Tangut] 0164

(a) III 76 ditto

(b) VIII 83 | [Tangut] 4319

(i) By itself W.I. 96[4] 鬐; W 192[17] gtsug-phud "dressed hair usniṣa"

(ii) C.C.C. 25[b] | [Tangut] 冠子 "cap".

4015 [Tangut] VIII 22 [Tangut] | 3994 formerly

W.I. 96[10] 98[1] 始 "to begin" II 90[2] W.I 271[10] B 180[1]

II 42[9] 初 "to begin" B 272[3] 元

B 171[1] tr. 先 189[1] 首 200[4] tr.

4016
5623 chain

4017 1891 chain

4018 – 5395

4019 5411 pair

4020 2306 chain

4021 1781 chain

4022 4023 chain

4023
┬ 3991
└ 4022

4024. B.272[1]

4024 3214 pair

| W.I 271[8] 今現 'present' contemporary
193[1]
B.170[5] doubtful. 186[4] (q.v.) tr. 今

4025 interpreted

4026 2603 chain

4016
(a) VI. 2
(b) V 3
C.C.C. 6
Original

4017
?

4018
(a) III 7.4
?

4018A

4019
(a) IX 1
(b)
(i) The

4020

4021
(a) V
(b) V
(i) By
k'ums
(ii) The

309

4016 [Tangut] VII 15 | [Tangut] 5623
(a) VI 24 ditto
(b) V 36 | [Tangut] "year" 3804
C.C.C. 6[3] 歳 "year" B.185[4] ditto.
(regnal year).

4017 [Tangut] V A 118 [Tangut] | 1891
?

4018 [Tangut] I 89 | [Tangut]
(a) III 74 ditto
?

4018A [Tangut] See [Tangut] 3937

4019 [Tangut] VIII 1 [Tangut] |
(a) IX 122 ditto
(b)
(i) The dissyllable C.C.C. 9[6] 晩 [?]
夕 "evening" [in both cases]

4020 [Tangut] VIII A 8 [Tangut] | flower 3859

4021 [Tangut] V 66 | [Tangut] 1364
(a) V 3 | [Tangut] 2321 ~~4021~~ x (3832)
(b) V 105 | [Tangut] 3854
(i) B.227[4] By: Co ey. C.C.C. 5[6] 室 W.I.192[13] 222[6]
K'uns name of a constellation.
(ii) The dissyllable W.II 48[7] 室宅
"house, dwelling"
B 245[2] 居 house

4022 [Tangut] by I A 70 [Tangut] [Tangut]
Phonetic character

4023 [Tangut] I 1 [Tangut] |
(a) IX 2 ditto
(b) I A 70 [Tangut] x by | [Tangut] [[Tangut]] 4022
?

4024 [Tangut] VI 2 [Tangut] |
(a) I 92 ditto
A temporal (?) adverb, often put in to complete the sense, esp. with imperatives
W.I.132[14] 今 "now" II 28[4]
B.160[1]
To complete the sense W.I.190[3] 204[1] 214[3]
(ii) [Tangut] | C.C.C. 29[6] 朝夕

4025 [Tangut] VIII 4 Family or clan name

4026 [Tangut] IX 44 [Tangut] |
(a) VI 74 ditto
(b) VII 10 [Tangut] x by dissyllables
?

4027
-1101 -0750
-0832 -0933
-2667 -1027
-2669 -1152 -0831
-1300 -1158
-1386 -5386-5358
-1525
-1739
-1794
-1836
-1747
-1976
-2011
-3095 -3097
-3098
-4265 -3099
-4487 -4057
-4494 -4900
-5006 -2117
-5035 -2598
-3456
-5163
-[0992]
-5510
4028 -2428 -5535

B. 121¹ tr. 俱 all

B 223¹ φ(i) 兜率 Tuṣita

4029
-4103
-2478 -0727 -0730-0913
-0779
-2675 -1671
-2457
-2679

4030 (i) as a noun W II 4³ 90²

4030 (i) verb slob.pa "to learn"

[also "teach"] B. 248⁴, 193⁵

4030 take over 2680 chain

4031 π 3736 pair

4033 1667 chain

4034 5623 chain

4032 5486 pair

4035 independent

4036 2710 chain

4037
-4169
-2719
-5427

4038 5017 chain

4039 5314 chain

4027
(a) IX
(b) III
(c) V
(d) IX
(i) The ...
happiness ...

4028
(a) IX
(i) By itself
(ii) 賤 |
5691
150⁶ ...

4029
(a) VII
II 4⁵ 繞

4030
(a) VI
(b) VI
(i) By itself
(ii) The ...
習 "to ...

4031
(a) VI

310

4027 [Tangut] IA108 | [Tangut] 1101
(a) IX 52 ditto
(b) III A10 [Tangut] | 0832 832 to offer (respect)
(c) V 2[illegible] | [Tangut] 2669
(d) IX 98 | [Tangut] 2667
(i) The disyllable W.I.168[3] 樂 joy, happiness.

4028 [Tangut] IX A38 [Tangut] |
(a) IX A22 ditto
(i) By itself W.I.168[3] 足 B.131[5] 満 "enough".
(ii) [Tangut] | 5641 C.C.C. 32[a] W.I.92[12] 108[13] 150[6] & passim 具足 "All, complete"

4029 [Tangut] IX 51 | [Tangut] 4103
(a) IX 52 ditto
(a) VII 63 [Tangut] | 2478
II 4[5] 繞 "to circumambulate"

4030 [Tangut] yo VIII A19 | [Tangut] 2680 ~~4030~~
(a) VI 91 ditto
~~(b) VI 91 | [Tangut] 2682~~
(i) By itself W.II 4[3] 學 siks- to learn
(ii) The disyllable C.C.C. 19[b] 27[a] 教習 "to teach & practice". 2680 chain 4030

4031 [Tangut] IX 48 [Tangut] |
(a) VI 21 [Tangut] |

4033 [Tangut] VI 17 [Tangut] [Tangut] |
W.I.132[15] 攞 (not in S. or S.H.? game trap

4034 ~~4033~~ [Tangut] V 61 [Tangut] | 2713
(a) IX 112 [Tangut] | 2628
?

4032 [Tangut] VII 94 [Tangut] |
(a) III 104 ditto
?

4035 [Tangut] IX 34 Family relation (name)
~~(a) I A106~~

4036 [Tangut] I 94 | [Tangut] 0373
chain 5440

4037 [Tangut] VI 39 | [Tangut] 4159
(a) V 51 ditto
(b) III 178 [Tangut] | 5427
(c) VI A119 [Tangut] (2719) x by | [Tangut] (0603) 2719

4038 [Tangut] I A.106 [Tangut] | 5017
?

4039 [Tangut] I 143 [Tangut] |

4040 [illegible]

4041 3226 chain

4042 0148 chain

4043 3443 chain

4044 2470 pair

4045 0286 pair

4046 – 1750 Double family name

4047 2169 chain

4048 4298 pair

4049 4572 pair

4050 0148 chain

4051 2765 chain

4052
1534 – 1526
2341

4053 1492 chain

4040

4041

4042

(a) IX

W. I. 192

4043.

(i) 1968

"guests,

4044

4045

(a) III

4046

(a) V 3

4049

4047

(a) V

W II 4^4 10

I 136^15

311

4040 [Tangut] IX 44 Family or clan (name)

4041 [Tangut] III 175 [Tangut] | 0577

4042 [Tangut] V 67 [Tangut] | 2726
(a) IX 8 [Tangut] | [Tangut] 4580
W. I. 192[1] bzai "good, strong"

4043 [Tangut] II 3 | [Tangut] 2690
(i) [Tangut][1968] | C.C.C. 34[a] 賓客
"guests, visitors."

4044 [Tangut] III 42 [Tangut] | 2470

4045 [Tangut] III 175 [Tangut] |
(a) III 96 ditto

4046 [Tangut] VIII 55 Family or clan (name)
(a) V 36 | [Tangut] 1760
Presumably a double name. B 125[5] 1261 富

4046 A [Tangut] error for [Tangut] 3769

4047 [Tangut] VII 7 [Tangut] | "number" 2167
[(a) VII 38 [Tangut][2162] × by [Tangut][2149] [Tangut] |]
W II 4[4] 10[5] 12[2] 匝 "circuit"
I 136[15]; B. 131[4] 遍 time (fois)

4048 [Tangut] VIII 19 [Tangut] |
(a) VIII 10 ditto [[Tangut]]
B. 94[1] [Tangut] at the bottom & the whole of [Tangut]. | [Ch. 征 "to conquer"] is the word for [Tangut] | [Ch. 征服 "to conquer & subdue"] a family or clan".

~~404~~

4049 [Tangut] V 3 [Tangut] |
(a) V 25 ditto

4050 [Tangut] I 63 | [Tangut] 0172
(i) The disyllable W. I. 90[14] 112[8] & passim 解脫 194[7] tar.pa "release, salvation, mokṣa, mukti, vimokṣa vimukti (H.S.)

4051 [Tangut] VII 9 [Tangut] |

4052 [Tangut] VI 84 | [Tangut] 1534
(a) III 31 ditto

4053 [Tangut] II 39 [Tangut] |

311

4054 independent

4055 independent

4056 4561 chain

B.188³ q.v.

4056A B245⁵ 今 'now'

4057 4027 chain

4058 3141 pair

4059 — 2512

1403 — 1539

4060

⊥ 2202-2201

4061 2027 chain

4062 5477 chain

4063 0169 pair

4054

B.163⁵ 19

4055

4056

(a) V 2

(b) IX 9

This wa

meaning

(i) As a

到

108⁸

(ii) As a

complet

every

遍 W.I.

k'yab

kun.du

kun.n

4056A

4057

4058

(a) IX

B.173⁵

Note. Dia

312

4054 [Tangut] V 25 "Family or clan name"

B.163⁵ 194¹ 犧

4055 [Tangut] IX 31 "Family or clan name"

4056 [Tangut] III 51 [Tangut] | postpos.? 4561

(a) V 21 | [Tangut] 2795

(b) IX 99 | [Tangut] "to come" 1969

This word seems to have two distinct meanings, v. 1968

(i) As a verb, taking [Tangut], it means 到 "to reach" B.198¹ 227⁵ 232¹ W.I.96⁶,¹⁰, 98² 100⁷ 172³ 108⁸ etc. II 2¹¹ p'yin.pa do. B.248¹

(ii) As an adverb it means "universally completely everywhere etc. W.I.112² 普 遍 W.I.114⁴ W.II 126¹ [Tangut] | 於至 up to

k'yab I 218²

kun.du I.204¹³

kun.nas I.218⁵

4056A [Tangut] error for [Tangut] 4024

4057 [Tangut] VI 41 [Tangut] | 4265

4058 [Tangut] VI 14 [Tangut] |

(a) IX 39 ditto

B.173⁵

Note. Distinguish 4058, 4059 + [Tangut]

1539

4059 [Tangut] IX 143 [Tangut] [Tangut]

(a) I 29 [Tangut] x by [Tangut] [Tangut]

(b) VII 74 | [Tangut]

(c) VIII 84 [Tangut] [Tangut] x by | [Tangut]

?

4060 [Tangut] VA 62 [Tangut] |

(a) IX 130 ditto

(i) 灾 C.C.C. 6ª calamity B.125¹

(ii) 禍 "bad fortune" C.C.C. 9ᵇ B.161¹

(iii) 難 (the eight) difficulties W.I 108¹³ II 72² 82⁴

(iv) 横 "perversity" W.II 18¹⁰

(v) The disyllable W.I.136¹² 危難 "dangers + difficulties".

4061 [Tangut] III 16 [Tangut] | 4462

(a) VI A 55 | [Tangut] 2009

(b) VIII 85 | [Tangut] ?misprint 3530 2799

? (c) V 43 | [Tangut] v. 4311 A [illegible] 3698

4062 [Tangut] I 24 [Tangut] [Tangut]

4063 [Tangut] V 20 "Family or clan name"

(a) IX 109 [Tangut] |

Presumably a double name

4064
2426 - 2431
3965 - 3436
4514
5533

4065-3895

[4066]
1365
[1660]

B. 232[4] 頓 sudden, immediately S.H. 419

4067 3686 pair

4068 1080 chain

|| B. 204[2] tr. 馳 走 ? to hasten after

4069 5526 pair

4070 4651 chain V

4071
2477
5638

B. 233[4,5] 234[1,2,3] 間 to act

4072 4096 chain

4073
2945
2952

4074 0113 pair

4075 4326 chain

4076 1964 chain

4064
(a) VII
?
4065
4066
(a) V 17
(i) [] |
hasten
(ii) | |
4067
? Doub
4068
(a) III
(i) By
(ii) (a)
4069
(a) I 4
?
4070
(a) VIII
難 diff
II 16[9] 20[6] 3
(ii) |
see 41

313

4064 [Tangut] VIII 7 | [Tangut] × 2426
(a) VII 22 ditto

?

4065 [Tangut] IX 5 | [Tangut]
(a) II 1 ditto

4066 [Tangut] III 41 | [Tangut] 1365
(aa) IX 18 ditto
(a) V 170 [Tangut] |
(i) [[Tangut]] | C.C.C. 29[6] 35[6] 趨[利] "to hasten after [profit]".
(ii) | | (doubled) B.161[4] to 趨 |

4067 [Tangut] I 82 [Tangut] 3686
? Double name.

4068 [Tangut] IX 28 [Tangut] |
(a) III 121 | [Tangut] (misspelt) 5665
(i) By itself W.I.132[15] creature? B 132[2] 獸 animals

(ii) (a) above B.100 cat. under "horse".

4069 [Tangut] III 6 [Tangut] |
(a) I 45 ditto

?

4070 [Tangut] V A 49 [Tangut] |
(a) VIII 95 | [Tangut] 4579
(b) IX 50 3939
難 difficult, distress W.I.114[14] 148[12]
II 16[9] 20[6] 30[10] 44[10] 52[7]
(ii) | [Tangut] I 214[12] dka. tub "penance"
see 4109 A

4071 [Tangut] VIII 95 × by itself [||] |
(a) IX 74 [Tangut] |
(b) IX 87 [Tangut] | how? 2477
B.187[5] 訓 "to teach" 233[4] 問

4072 [Tangut] IX 53 [Tangut] |
(a) I 16
(i) [Tangut] | C.C.C. 15[2] 苽 by itself "gourd" B.166[4]
B.102 cat. under "vegetables".
(ii) [Tangut] | C.C.C. 18[6] 腎 "testicles"
Note. I tis impossible to distinguish between 4069 to 4072 + [Tangut]

4073 [Tangut] VI 10 | [Tangut] 2946
(a) VI 118 ditto [[Tangut]]
(b) VI A 100 | [Tangut] 2946

?

4074 [Tangut] IX 53 | [Tangut] 0113
(a) IX 66 ditto

?

4075 [Tangut] III 30 [Tangut] | 4964

4076 [Tangut] I 51 [Tangut] | i.e. 1964
(a) VI 66 ditto? [[Tangut]]
B.173[4]

4077 1564 chain

4078 – 3627 A

4079
- 0656
- 1728 – 4835
- 2528
- 3286
- 3934
- 4805

4080 chain < 0573, 4145 – 1780

4081 independent

4082 0043 chain

4083 chain (0161 chain)
- 0161
- 1165
- 1944
- 3018 – 3724
- 4502 – 3807, 3186 – 0080
- 4598
- 5127

4084 0995 pair

4085 0235 pair

314

4077 [Tangut] VI A 52 [Tangut] | 1412
(a) VI A 72 * | [Tangut] 3563
?

4078 [Tangut] IX 57 [Tangut] |

4079 [Tangut] I 16 | [Tangut] 0656
(a) IX 48 ditto
(b) I 8 | [Tangut] 3286
(c) I 113 | [Tangut] ~~honey-bee~~ 4805
(d) V 132 [Tangut] × by | [Tangut] × 4835 1728
(e) VI 104 [Tangut] | 2528
(f) IX A 156 [Tangut] × by | [Tangut] 3934
(i) ~~(a)~~ By itself W.I. 192² 216¹⁸ ~~siin. bu~~ worm B. 128¹ tr. 蛆
(ii) The dissyllable C.C.C. 17ᵃ 蛆蟲 "maggots & worms"
(iii) [Tangut] | W.I 134¹⁵ [Tangut] "silk worm"

4080 [Tangut] III A 68 [Tangut] | 6573
(a) VI 54 ditto
(b) VIII 3 | [Tangut] perfection 4145
(i) The dissyllable C.C.C. 34ᵃ 長大 "old & senior"

4081 [Tangut] VIII 6 "Family or clan name"
~~(a) IX 8 | [Tangut]~~
~~Presumably a double name~~

4082 [Tangut] VIII 52 [Tangut] | ? 0161
(a) I 1 ditto
(b) I 61 [Tangut] | 1944
(c) III 57 | [Tangut] 3018
(d) V 175 | [Tangut] 1165 (f) VI 99 | [Tangut] 1298
(e) VI 20 [Tangut] | 5127 (g) VII 52 | [Tangut] 3724
(h) IX 118 | [Tangut] 4598 (k) VIII A 57 [Tangut] 4502
(i) By itself C.C.C. 35ᵇ + passim 力 stobs "bala, strength"
(ii) (b) above C.C.C. 22ᵇ 体 工

4083 [Tangut] I 16 | [Tangut] 0056
~~(a) V 132 1728 × 4835~~
(i) The dissyllable C.C.C. 17ᵃ 鴛鴦 "mandarin drake & duck."

4084 [Tangut] IX 53 [Tangut] |
(a) IX 68 ditto

4085 [Tangut] VI 25 [Tangut] | 0235
(a) III A 119 ditto
(i) The dissyllable W.I 168⁸ II 28³·⁵ 34³ 何以故 why? 云何 why? B 231²

4086 5045 chain

4087 - 3039

4088 1785 chain

4089 1113 chain

4090 - 4581

4091 3026 chain

4092 4183 chain

4093 3089 chain

4094 3776 chain

4095 5133 chain

4096

4097 - 2001

4098 0249 chain

315

4086 [Tangut] III 63 | [Tangut] 3178

4087 [Tangut] IX 46 | [Tangut]
(a) III 68 ditto
(i) The dissyllable C.C.C. 20ª 兄弟 "elder brother & younger brother" W.I. 196² -spun "brothers".

4088 [Tangut] V 71 | [Tangut]

4089 [Tangut] IX 63 | [Tangut] 3181

4089A [Tangut] Err. for [Tangut] 4662

4090 [Tangut] IX 31 [Tangut] ||
(a) IX 8 ditto

?
4091 [Tangut] [VII 59-60] ~~4091~~
(a) III A 128 | [Tangut] 3304
(b) V 101 [Tangut] | 3026
(i) By itself C.C.C. 19ᵇ 弱 "weak" W.I. 32⁶ 劣 "weak" 46² ? B. 193⁵
(ii) (b) above C.C.C. 29ᵇ 淩 [?=淩] 弱 "strong & weak" (deep corrected to strong)

4092 [Tangut] VII 73 [Tangut] |

4093 [Tangut] III 170 [Tangut] | 3089
(a) V 171 ditto

4094 [Tangut] VIII 56 | [Tangut] 1017
(i) [Tangut] | W.I. 138¹⁴ 142¹⁸ 慙 愧 "ashamed" (in both cases)
B. 160²

4095 [Tangut] III 42 | [Tangut] 0860

4096 [Tangut] I 16 | [Tangut] 4072
(a) IX 53 ditto
(b) III 136 | [Tangut]

?
4097 [Tangut] V 112 | [Tangut] ? 2001
(a) V 15 ditto

4098 [Tangut] IX 153 | [Tangut] 0249
(a) I 67 [Tangut] | 4005
(b) II 35 | [Tangut] x(0237) 0668
(c) II 41 | [Tangut] 0232
(d) III 55 [Tangut] x by | [Tangut] 5397
(e) IX 42 [Tangut] | 0331

?

4099 2629 pair VII

4100 3123 chain

4101 0598 chain

4102 [5116] chain

4103 4029 chain I

4104
⊥ 1803 ┬ 2219 ┬ 1800
├ 3657 ├ 5049 – 3683
└ 5412 └ 5297

4105 independent

4106 1846 chain

4107 3160 chain

4108 independent

4109
⊥ 3049 – 5609

4110 4257 chain

4111 independent

4112 4183 chain

4113 5623 chain

4114 – 4953

4115 – 4958

4099
(a) IX 11

4100
W.I.138[13]

4101
C.C.C. 20[6]

4102
(a) VIII

4103
(a) IX

4104
(a) III

(i) The

"this" "tra

By itself

4105

Note. 410

4106

315

4099 [Tangut] I 36 [Tangut] |

(a) IX 115 ditto

4100 [Tangut] VII 115 [Tangut] | 3124

W.I.138[13]

4101 [Tangut] I 4 [Tangut] | 0598

CCC. 20[6] 寺 "hall, monastery" B. 261[2]

4102 [Tangut] VII A 21 [Tangut] |

(a) VIII A 59 [Tangut] | ? 0523

4103 [Tangut] IX 52 [Tangut] | 4029

(a) IX 51 ditto

4104 [Tangut] III 39 | [Tangut] [misspelt] x 1803

(a) III 101 ditto

(i) The disyllable W II 48[5] 彼此 "that & this"

By itself B. 186[5]

4105 [Tangut] V 72 Family or clan name

Note. 4104 + 4105 are barely distinguishable

4106 [Tangut] III 39 [Tangut] | 4412

4107 [Tangut] V A 63 [Tangut] | 3658 (3298A)

4108 [Tangut] V 35 Family or clan name

4109 [Tangut] VII 76 | [Tangut] 3049

(a) IX 16 ditto

? error for [Tangut] 4284/5

4109A [Tangut] x of IX 50 | [Tangut]

? an error for 4070

4110 [Tangut] II 1 [Tangut] [Tangut]

4111 [Tangut] IX 45 Family or clan name

4112 [Tangut] V A 59 | [Tangut] "grain"

(i) The disyllable B 101 cat. under "grain".

4113 [Tangut] III 42 [Tangut] | ? 4658

4114 [Tangut] I 12 | [Tangut]

(a) IX 79 ditto

? W.II.130[3] 吉 cf. 4115

4115 [Tangut] I 12 | [Tangut]

(a) IX 79 ditto

4116 5491 chain

4117 3144 chain

4118 2363 pair

4119 -3705

4120 3334 chain

4121 2793 chain

4122 5690 chain

4123
- 3247-4885
- 4212
- 5220 – [3734]
  - 3128
  - 5221

4124 5678 chain

4125 2377 chain

4126 2680 chain

4127
- 2289
- 3221
- 3455

4128 – 3330
- 3706
- 4465

4116
(a) I 44
(b) I 10
(c) V 13
(d) IX 5
C.C.C. 12b
W.II 32b 46
4117
C.C.C. 29a
4118
4119
(a) VIII
~~C.C.C. 26b~~
4120
4121
(a) I 13
(b) VIII
W.I. 138
4122

316

4116 [Tangut] b'i I 1 [Tangut] |
(a) I 44 ditto
(b) I 101 [Tangut] | 4585
[(c) V 132 [Tangut] × by [Tangut] | [Tangut]]
(d) IX 54 | [Tangut] 4667
C.C.C. 12b 下 "low" as opposed to "high". v.1985
W.II 32[6] 46[2] ditto. B.161[4] 下 'later' cf. 4117

4117 [Tangut] I 3 | [Tangut] "high"
C.C.C. 29a 下 "low" as opposed to "high". cf. 4116

4118 [Tangut] VII 19 [Tangut] |

4119 [Tangut] I 8 | [Tangut]
(a) VIII 6 ditto
~~C.C.C. 26b 毎又 (?)~~ ? B.194[1] 小

4120 [Tangut] V 64 [Tangut] |

4121 [Tangut] V 184 [Tangut] |
(a) II 133 ditto
(b) VIII A 13 | [Tangut]
W.I. 138[2,3] 私 "secret, private"

4122 [Tangut] III 3 | [Tangut]

4123 [Tangut] V 34 | [Tangut] × 4885 3247
(a) I 8 ditto
~~(aa) V A 76~~
(b) VII 123 [Tangut] | 4212
(c) VI A 39 | [Tangut] × 5220
(i) C.C.C. 10a ? 震 "to shake, quake"
(ii) C.C.C. 21a 杵 "pestle, to pound"
(iii) W.II. 122[2] 鳴 "to sound" B.168[2]

4124 [Tangut] III 44 [Tangut] | 5678
Rather an obscure word
W.II. 66[12] 慣 "accustomed to"
II 38[9] 40[7] ? C.C.C. 1a 6 B.160[4] 161[1] 鳥
B.187[1] q.v. 220[1]

4125 [Tangut] IX 33 [Tangut] | 2377

4126 [Tangut] VI 8 [Tangut] | precept 3311
律 S.H vinaya "rule, law" W.I 90[7] 268 2680 chain

4127 [Tangut] I 6 [[Tangut]] | [misspelt]
(a) I 19 ditto "elephant" 2289
(b) I A 48 | [Tangut] 3221
(c) VIII 9 | [Tangut] 3455
W.I. 224[11] ? c'e "great"

4128 [Tangut] VIII 27 × by self ||
(a) V 55 | [Tangut] 3706
(b) V 69 | [Tangut]

B. 232[5]

4129 3685 chain

4130 interpolated

4131 4262 chain

4132 0752 chain

4133 4926 chain

4134 -2352

4135 2149 chain

4136 5644 chain

4137 4357 chain

4138 5644 chain

4139 4208 chain

4140 [1095]

4140 中 | 薄伽梵

Bhagavan, "the Lord". W.II 2[4] B.199[3]

4141 ⊥1998-4146

中(ii) | 娑 菩

W.II 2[12]

中(iii) | 摩帝利 迦 W.II 4[1]

中(iv) W.II 76[9] (Brahman)

4128 com

(c) V 9

(d) IX

(i) B.186[3]

(ii) doubtful

(iii) W.II 88

4129

4130

(i)

4131

4132

(a) II 2

(b) VIII 8

Rather

W.I.96"

4133

4134

(a) IX

317

4128 cont.

~~(c) V 97 [Tangut] |~~ error for 4181

(d) IX 125 | [Tangut] 3330

(i) B 186[3] 重 (looks more like 'then') "heavy, important"

(ii) doubled to p. 23 重重 "very heavy" (?)

(iii) W. II 88[5] 更 "then"?

4129 [Tangut] III 44 [Tangut] | 4877

4130 [Tangut] III 1 Family or clan name

(i) | [Tangut] passim Phonetic 南無 namo

4131 [Tangut] VII 6 [Tangut] |

4132 [Tangut] II 18 | [Tangut] 0118

(a) II 2 [Tangut] | × 3752

(b) VIII 84 | [Tangut] × 1790

Rather an obscure word.

W I. 96[11] 138[7,10] B. 205[4]

4133 [Tangut] II 18 | [Tangut] 4926

4134 [Tangut] VI A 41 | [Tangut]

(a) IX 75 ditto

4135 [Tangut] III 43 | [Tangut]

4136 [Tangut] VI A 24 [Tangut] |

(a) IX 74 ditto

(b) I 14 | [Tangut] 5231

(c) III 64 | [Tangut] 4138

(d) V 18 | [Tangut] 4325

(e) VI 42 [Tangut] | 3365

B 344[3] 喻 to illustrate v. 4853 B 187[3]

4137 [Tangut] IX / III 33 [Tangut] | (a) IX 15 ditto

(b) V 19 | [Tangut]

4138 [Tangut] III 64 [Tangut] | 4136

4139 [Tangut] IX 13 [Tangut] | time 5688

(a) VII 71 | [Tangut] 5104

4139A [Tangut] ? error for [Tangut] 4153

Possibly the right form I 168[5]

4140 [Tangut] I 68 [Tangut] | [misspelt]

(a) III 85 ditto

4141 [Tangut] V 90 | [Tangut] new 1998

(a) VI A 43 ditto

B. 130[3] 舊 old

4142 –
⊥ 4364 – 4825

4143 0752 chain

4144 0251 pair

4149 4148 chain

4150 3446 chain

4145 4080 chain
4145 (i) W II 6[2] is an adjective

4151 3493 pair

4152 1431 chain

4146 4141 chain

4147 2167 chain

4153
┬ 0153
└ 1384

4148
┬ 4149
├ 0491
└ 2103

4142
(a) IX 12

4143

4144
(a) I 83
W. I. 90[14]
W. I. 136[13] I
W. I. 206[7]

4145
(a) III
1093
(i)
I 218[16]
perfect

4146

4147
(a) V 3

4148
(a) III 7
(a) III

318

4142 [Tangut] I 28 | [Tangut]

(a) IX 127 ditto

4143 [Tangut] II 3 | [Tangut] 1790

4144 [Tangut] V 157 [Tangut] |

(a) I 83 ditto

W. I. 90[14] 92[5] 濟 "to save, rescue" B. 188[2]

W. I. 136[13] II 70[8] 救 "to save, rescue" C.C.C. 1[a]

W. I. 206[7] II 84[9] ? B. 161[5]

4145 [Tangut] VIII 3 [Tangut] | 4080 *sumin*

(a) III 102 [Tangut] | ? 1780

(i) [Tangut] | W I 110[6] 118[2] II 32[10] 36[12] 成就 B 208[2] 109.3

I 218[16] *rnam grub. pa* "completion, perfection, *siddhi*." ✕

4146 [Tangut] I 24 | [Tangut] 1998 4080 chain new?

4147 [Tangut] III 7 | [Tangut] 'number' 2167

(a) V 34 ditto

4148 [Tangut] III 2 | [Tangut] 4149

(a) III 7 ditto

(b) III 166 | [Tangut] 0491

4148 cont.

(c) VIII A 2 | [Tangut] 2103

(i) *Passim* 善 "good"

(ii) (? a mistranslation) W II 18[5] 親 "relations"

4149 [Tangut] III 7 [Tangut] | "good" chain 4148

(a) III 2 ditto

4150 [Tangut] III 66 [Tangut] |

4151 [Tangut] VIII 3 [Tangut] |

(a) I 11 ditto

(i) The dissyllable B. 102 cat. under vegetables

4152 [Tangut] III 41 | [Tangut] 1431

(i) The dissyllable C.C.C. 11[a] 前年 "last year"

By itself B. 172[2] s.v. twice

4153 [Tangut] VII A 7 | [Tangut] 0153 chain 1431

(a) VIII A 22 ditto [[Tangut]]

(b) I A 86 | [Tangut] 1384

W. I. 168[5] II 84[6] [支 in both cases]

計 "to reckon, scheme"

B. 173[2] double (both 支)

4154 1844 pair

4155 4157 chain

4156
⊥1912–1913
The Hsi-hsia l. B.173³ 安靖 peaceful & quiet.

4157
+1438
-0912
-4155
L5338

4158 3575 chain

4159 2596 chain

4160 3772 chain

4161 independent

4162 3587 chain

4163 – 2270

4164
⊥4313 – 2682
L4321

4165 independent

4166 – 4354

4167 3226 chain

4154
(a) VII

4155

4156
(a) III 12
B.185 康
B.124⁵

4157
(a) II 4
(b) III
(c) VIII
(d) IX
B.168²

4158
?

4159
(a) VIII
C.C.C. 25ª

4160
(a) VI
(b) II
(i) The

319

4154 [Tangut] VII 103 [Tangut] | mis-spelt 1844
(a) VII A 120 [Tangut] | ditto

4155 [Tangut] III A 114 [Tangut] 支

4156 [Tangut] III 5 | [Tangut] 1912 contemplation
(a) III 124 [Tangut] ditto
B. 185 康 K'ang "repose"
B. 124⁵ Tr. 靖 quiet

4157 [Tangut] III 5 | [Tangut] 1438
(a) II 4 ditto
(b) III A 114 [Tangut] | (1345) 5338
(c) VIII 8 [Tangut] × by | [Tangut] 4155
(d) IX 79 [Tangut] | 0912
B. 168² (doubled) 168⁴

4158 [Tangut] III 66 | [Tangut]
?

4159 [Tangut] I 70 | [Tangut] 2596
(a) VIII 50 | [Tangut]
C.C.C. 25ᵃ 懷 "bosom"

4160 [Tangut] IX 52 [Tangut] |
(a) VI 38 ditto
(b) II 32 | [Tangut] 5335
(1) The dissyllable W.I. 112¹² 140⁸ II 16⁶

4160 cont.
恭敬 "respectful & reverent"

4161 [Tangut] I 70 Family or clan name

4162 [Tangut] III 1 [Tangut] | 3587
(a) III A 12 ditto

4163 [Tangut] III 28 | [Tangut]
(a) V 180 ditto

~~4164 [Tangut] I 55~~

4164 [Tangut] V A 33 | [Tangut]
(a) III 66 ditto

? ~~(a)~~

4165 [Tangut] VI 111 Family or clan (name)

Note 4164 & 4165 are barely distinguishable

4166 [Tangut] V 27 | [Tangut]
(a) IX 63 ditto

4167 ~~4168~~ [Tangut] IX 6 [Tangut] | 5062
(a) VI 67 | [Tangut] 1257

4168 1901 chain

W.I. 265[18] part of royal titles

義制 "making righteous regulations"

B.186[4] 旨 the purport?

4169 4529 chain

4170 1564 chain

4171 3598 pair

4172 3305 pair

4173 [1520] pair

4174 0322 chain

4175 1661 chain

4176 0157 chain

4177 2928 chain

4178 independent

4179-0648

4180 0394 chain

4181 3372 pair

4168

(a) I

(b) III

(c) V 4

(d) VI

(i) C.C.C. 20a

righteous

(ii) 理

4169

~~4170~~

4170

(a) IX

(b) I

(c) III

4171

~~4172~~

4172

(a) I

4173

(a) I

320

4168 [Tangut] II 42 [Tangut] | 1901

(a) I 118 [Tangut] × ly | [Tangut] 1192

(b) III 119 | [Tangut] 3622

(c) V 49 [Tangut] × ly | [Tangut] 5058

(d) VI A 21 | [Tangut] 3623

(i) C.C.C. 20[a] 義 "artha" the right, B 179[3] righteousness. W.I 90[7,11], 118[13] II 54[7] etc.

(ii) 理 "propriety" etc. W II 60[10] I 269[11]

4169 ~~4170~~ [Tangut] IX 59 | [Tangut]

4170 [Tangut] IX 7 | [Tangut] 1564

(a) IX 1 ditto

(b) I 17 [Tangut] |

(c) III 150 | [Tangut] 1412

4171 ~~4172~~ [Tangut] VIII 17 [Tangut] | 3598 ditto

4172 [Tangut] I 52 [Tangut] |

(a) I 71 ditto

4173 [Tangut] IX 56 [Tangut] |

(a) I 52 ditto

4174 [Tangut] V A 36 | [Tangut]

(a) I 57 ditto

W.I. 190[18] 218[8] mig "eye" Dict 1[a]2

4175 [Tangut] V A 68 [Tangut] | 1661

~~4176~~ [Tangut] VII A 10 | [Tangut]

(i) The dissyllable W.I. 134[2] 分離 "to tear asunder 168[14]"

(ii) | [Tangut] II 36[3]?

? two separate words. ~~Probably~~ an error for 4235 B [Tangut]

4177 [Tangut] I 55 [Tangut] 5320

W.I. 224[18] spen. pa ? Phonetic

4178 [Tangut] I 28 Family or clan name

4179 [Tangut] V 120 | [Tangut] 0648

(a) III 161 ditto

4180 [Tangut] I 130 [Tangut] | 0394

(a) I 78 ditto

4181 [Tangut] I.130 [Tangut] |

(a) V 97 ditto

4182 2928 chain

4183
- 0630
- 0692
- 0700
- 0808
- [0758]
- 2804
- 3063
- 3479
- 4092
- 4112
- 4283

4184 -5180

4185 0899 chain

4186 2765 chain

4187 3015 pair

4188 3836 pair

4189 2167 chain

321

4182 [Tangut] I 93 | [Tangut] 5320

4183 [Tangut] I 36 [Tangut] | 4474

(a) V 164 ditto

(b) II 4 [Tangut] | 0700

(c) III 2 [Tangut] | 2804

(d) III 29 [Tangut] | 0808

(e) III 47 [Tangut] | 3063

(f) III 47 [Tangut] | [0758]

~~(g) III 66~~ (see 4184)

(g) V 104 [Tangut] | 4283

~~(h) V 164 [Tangut] |~~

(i) V A 59 [Tangut] | 4112

(j) VII 73 [Tangut] | 4092

(k) VIII 6 [Tangut] | 0630

(l) IX 22 [Tangut] | 3479

(m) IX 41 [Tangut] | 0692

C.C.C. 13a 36a W.I.110 etc 果 I 216

hbras. bu "fruit".

4184 [Tangut] IX 4 [Tangut] | (misspelt)

(a) III 66 ditto

?

Note. 4183 + 4184 are often indistinguishable

4185 [Tangut] VI 41 [Tangut] | [Tangut] v. 3908 "to rise"

(a) II 41 | [Tangut] 1395

(b) V A 52 | [Tangut] 3702

(c) VI A 109 | [Tangut] 3728

(d) IX 41 | [Tangut] (0079) 0267 bis

C.C.C. 27b 28b W II 26 etc 坐 "to sit down"

W.I. 196 ndug. pa ditto

4184A [Tangut] x of VII 100 | [Tangut]

~~Probably~~ corrupt. error for 3685

4186 [Tangut] III A 136 [Tangut] |

(a) III A 9 | [Tangut]

B 185 燉 P.N. Tun(-huang)

B. 186 Phonetic.

4187 [Tangut] VII 20 [Tangut] | 3015 q.v.

(a) IX 23 ditto

B. 345 重 W.I. 266 | [Tangut]重祿 "very prosperous" (part of royal title)

4188 [Tangut] III 24 [Tangut] |

(a) III 113 ditto [[Tangut]

?

4188A [Tangut]

B. 100 | [Tangut] cat. under "camel"

4189 [Tangut] RI IX 4 [Tangut] | "ten thousand" 2167

W II 4 億 "myriad" 122 passim

4190 2496 pair

4191 4326 chain

4192 -2256 Family name probl.

4193 ~~2306~~ 2494 chain

4194 2154 chain

4194 [Tangut] | 不能 "not to be able W II 909

| [Tangut] = 能者 "able to W. II 92[5]

4195-3682 Double family name?

4196 3514 chain

4197 ~~4440 pair~~

4198 independent

4199 independent

4200
- 4605
- 3813-0281
- 5415

4201 0582 chain

B.167[1] 覆 to overthrow

4201 A 2925 pair

4190 [Tangut]

(a) IX

4191 [Tangut]

(a) VII

?

4192 [Tangut]

?

4193 [Tangut]

4194 [Tangut]

(a) V 15

A verbal

Often transl

C.C.C. 35[a]

224[6,10] II

or Chinese

4195 [Tangut]

(a) VI

A comm

4196 [Tangut]

C.C.C. 26[b]

321

4190 [Tangut] I 5 [Tangut] | 2496

(a) IX 9 ditto [[Tangut]]

4191 [Tangut] II 4 [Tangut] |

(a) VII 44 ditto

?

4192 [Tangut] VI 55 | [Tangut]

?

4193 [Tangut] I 55 [Tangut] 2544

4194 [Tangut] (ni) III 170 [Tangut] |

(a) V 152 ditto

A verbal affix participial or gerundive.

Often translates Chinese 能 "able to"

c.c.c. 35ª W. I. 100⁸ 108⁷ 110⁴ 140² 218⁹²

224⁶·¹⁰ II 2⁷ 12⁷ 18¹ 44¹¹ 50⁵ 76⁷

or Chinese 善 "good at" W. I 266²¹

4195 [Tangut] IX 44 | [Tangut]

(a) VI A 120 [Tangut] × by [Tangut] |

A common Phonetic.

4196 [Tangut] I 47 [Tangut] | 1463

c.c.c. 26ᵇ written [Tangut] B. 161⁵ tr. to 能

4197 [Tangut] IX A 12 | [Tangut]

(a) IX 88 ditto

(i) W II 44⁸ 受 "to receive" B. 161³ 128⁵

(ii) W I. 100³ ?

(iii) C.C.C. 28ᵇ: 承 "to receive"

(iv) C.C.C. 32ª³ ?

B 174⁵

4198 [Tangut] VII 4 "Family or clan name"

B 347³ 什 Shih [P.N.] 125⁵ 126¹

4199 [Tangut] IX 21 "Family or clan name"

4200 [Tangut] I 65 | [Tangut] 4605

(a) IX 109 ditto

(b) I 141 [Tangut] | × (0281) 3813

(c) IX 23 | [Tangut]

?

4201 [Tangut] IX 56 [Tangut] | 1292

~~(a) V 46~~

(a) VI 11 [Tangut] | 3692 ~~4884~~

~~(b) IX 109 (i) The disyllable~~

(i)(a) above 色顏 "colour" (in both cases)

V. 42 where it is ? an error of 4683

(ii) error for 4683

4201B [Tangut] error for [Tangut] 4216

c.c.c. 20ᵇ 外甥

4201A [Tangut] × of V 149 [Tangut] |

4202 – 2753 A

4208 chain
– 5265
– 0210 – 3697
 – 5688 – 0005
 – 4139 – 5104
 – 4942 – 0219
– 0944
– 2564
– 3295
– 4240

4203 1116 (Double Family name)

4204 1543 chain

4205 – 0980

4209 – 3779

4206 – 2123 B

4210 1596 chain

4211 2482 chain

4212 4123 chain

4212 'noise'? W.II 104[12]

4207
– 1454 – 4416
– 3972
– 5046

4213
– 1494
– 1514

4202
=3939A

4203

4204

4204A

4205
(a) VII 1
(i) The
'wild anim

4206
~~(a) I 12~~
(i) W.
(2968)

4207
(a) III 92
(b) I A 1
(c) III 157
(i) The
ceau, de

(no page 323)

322

4202 [illegible] VII 53 |[illegible]
(a) V 43 ditto
=3939A

4203 [illegible] IX 8 |[illegible]

4204 [illegible] IX 49 [illegible] |[illegible] 4545

4204A [illegible] see [illegible]

4205 [illegible] V 20 |[illegible]
(a) VII 14 ditto
(i) The dissyllable B.101 cat. under 'wild animals'

4206 [illegible] VI 12 |[illegible]
~~(a) I 123 |[illegible] [[illegible]]~~
(i) |[illegible] W.I.224[9] ngan.po "old" (?4213)
(2968)

cf. 4213
(4416)
4207 [illegible] III 123 |[illegible] 1454
(a) III 92 ditto
(b) IA 15 |[illegible] 5046
(c) III 157 |[illegible] 3972
(i) The dissyllable II 6[9] 休息 "to cease, desist."

4208 [illegible] IX 149 [illegible]|
(a) IX 43 |[illegible] ditto
(b) V 79 |[illegible] 0944
(c) VIII 78 |[illegible] 3295
(d) IX 13 |[illegible] 0210
(e) IX 17 [illegible]| 2564
(f) IX 160 |[illegible] 2999
(g) IXA 171 |[illegible] marrow 4240
C.C.C.19[a] W.I.134[2] II 24[3] 50[12] 骨 "bones"

4209 [illegible] III 11 |[illegible]
(a) VIII 1 ditto

4210 [illegible] IA 2 [illegible]| 5501

4211 [illegible] I 24 |[illegible] 0594

4212 [illegible] VI 123 |[illegible]
W.II.70[1] 諠 "clamour"

~~4212A [illegible] VII 59-60~~
~~error for 4669~~

4213 [illegible] III 53 |[illegible] 1494
(a) V 6 ditto
(b) I 123 |[illegible] 1514
cf. 4206

4214 3468 chain IX

4215 3011 chain

4216 1114 chain

4217 2416 pair III

4218 2539 pair

4219 independent

4220 1901 chain

~~Take out~~

4221 ~~0096 chain~~ III

4222 1992 chain VII

4223 3685 chain IX

| 繞 B.195[5] 覺了 to apprehend clearly

B229[3] 識

4224 3226 chain

4225 3929 chain VI

4226 ⊢0170 └1642

4214

4215

4216

(a) VIII 6

(b) I 5

(c) IX A

(i) The

4217

(a) I 14

4218

(a) VI

(i) The

4219

4220

4221

(ii) (a) VII

324

4214 [Tangut] III 37 | [Tangut] 3029

4215 [Tangut] IX 31 | [Tangut]

4216 [Tangut] IX 162 [Tangut] |

(a) VIII 62 ditto

(b) I 59 | [Tangut] 4731

(c) IX A 129 [Tangut] | 4799

(i) The dissyllable C.C.C. 20[b] [Tangut]

4217 [Tangut] VII 7 [Tangut] |

(a) I 142 ditto

4218 [Tangut] VIII 17 [Tangut] | 2539

(a) VI 51 ditto

(i) The dissyllable W.I.134[16]: B 221[2]

4219 [Tangut] IX 162 torn

4220 [Tangut] VIII 20 [Tangut] | 1901

4221 [Tangut] I 14 [Tangut] | 96

(a) VII 112 ditto unused

4222 [Tangut] III 7 [Tangut] | not 1992

4223 [Tangut] III 65 | [Tangut]

C 36[a2] W.I.112[7] 覺 "enlightenment, illumination, ~~bodhi~~": ~~176~~ B.260[2]

| [Tangut] W.I.176[6] 快覺 "swiftly enlightening"?

4224 [Tangut] VIII A 17 [Tangut]

"mystical sound, mantra"

B.94 [Tangut] ideogram, followed by [Tangut]. | is a [Tangut] [sacred word] used in mantras in [Tangut] [the sutras] B.216[5]

4225 [Tangut] V 16 [Tangut] | [Tangut] 4524

(i) W.I.130[4] 擇 "to decide"

(ii) The dissyllable W.I.162[8] 決斷 decisive, decided.

4226 [Tangut] IX 163 | [Tangut] 0170

(a) VII A 40

(b) IX A 35 [Tangut] | jealousy 1642

(i) By itself W.I 136[11] II 18[5]

(ii) The dissyllable C.C.C. 31[a] 淩 [淩] 持 "to grasp profoundly"

4227 4930 pair

B. 221[4] 惠

4227 A 3922 chain

4230 0627 chain

4228 2149 chain

4229 4276 chain

4231 - 4869

4232 0096 chain

4233 4276 chain

B. 221[2] tr. 生有

4234 4011 chain

B. 233[2] 皈 to return (? error) refuge

歸 to entrust (one's life etc.) S.-H. 'Sumati' śaraṇa S.-H. 69

4227

(a) V 17

(i) By i Cc

(ii) W.I. 124[11]

(iii)

or hurt:

4228

4229

(a) I 9

(b) I A

(c) III 11

(d) V 4

(e) V 4

(f) V 4

(g) V 10

(h) VI A

(i) VII

(j) VIII

(k) VIII

(l) IX

(m) IX

(i) C.C.C. 31

(ii) W.I. 21

(iii) The Hs

325

4227 [Tangut] VIII 53 [Tangut] |
(a) V 174 ditto
(i) By itself C.C.C. 6b 害 B 221[3] to injure
(ii) W.I. 124[11] 130[1] 142[9] etc. 礙chi to hinder
(iii) [Tangut] | C.C.C. 29b 傷害 "to injure & hurt".

4228 [Tangut] V 74 | [Tangut]

4229 [Tangut] III 9 | [Tangut] 4233
(a) I 95 | [Tangut] 1049
(b) I A16 | [Tangut] × 4959
(c) III 118 | [Tangut] × (2048) 2047
(d) V 41 | [Tangut] 4236
(e) V 42 | [Tangut] 5239
(f) V 44 | [Tangut] 4951
(g) V 100 [Tangut] × by | [Tangut] × (0397) 0289
(h) VI A106 | [Tangut] 4238
(i) VII 106 | [Tangut] × 4970
[(j) VIII 4 [Tangut] (5658) × by [Tangut] 3692 | [Tangut] 3922]
(k) VIII 84 | [Tangut] 4998
(l) IX 66 | [Tangut] 1749
(m) IX 95 | [Tangut] v. 3421 × 3421
(i) C.C.C. 31b 35b & passim 心 "heart, (mind etc.)"
(ii) W.I. 216[17]?
(iii) The disyllable C.C.C. 18b 心命 "mind life, longevity (of the Dharmakāya)".

4227A [Tangut] × of V 28 [Tangut] |

4230 [Tangut] VII A16 [Tangut] | 0627
(a) V 22 [Tangut] | 0449
(b) VIII 80 | [Tangut] [1107]
?

4231 [Tangut] III/IV 9 | [Tangut]
(a) III 37 ditto

4232 [Tangut] I 30 | [Tangut] 0096

4233 [Tangut] V 17 [Tangut] | 0252
(a) III 9 [Tangut] | "heart" v. 4229 ×
(b) VII 10 [Tangut] | [Tangut] 3978
(i) By itself passim 命 W.I. 216[3] srog "life"
(ii) (a) above C.C.C. 18b 心命 "mind life, longevity (of the Dharmakāya)"

4234 [Tangut] III 59 [Tangut] | head 4011
A common postposition, translating 至 "up to, to" 歸 "to" (?) W.I. 96[7,8] 98[1] 108[7] 134[5] 194[15] II 4[3] 16[6] 18[9] 44[8] 82[1]
W.I 168[12]? a verb 'to reach'! 4011 chain
B. 131[2,4]

4235 – 5620

| 𗌭 W.II.78[1] 恒河 Gaṅgā

(ii) B. 215[1]

4235A 5167 pair

B. 201[5]

4236 4276 chain

4236 欲 'to wish' verb W.II 84[7,12] B. 227[5]

II 78[10 1/2] 文 char B 217[2] (文 char) q.v.

B. 233[5]

4237 2335 pair

4238 4276 chain

4239 4966 pair

4240 4208 chain

4241 4330 chain

4242 3700 A chain

4243 1901 chain

𗋑 | W.I.266[21] part of royal title

cis. 法 古

4244 1456 chain

4245 – 4876 Double family name

4863

4246 3086 chain

4247 0304 chain

4248 independent

4235

(a) VI

V... as a

for Gaṅ[gā]

4235A

4235B

C35[b] ccc.

(i) W.I. 168[5]

224[9] spoi[...]

(ii) |

unounc[...]

4236

(a) IX

W.I. 100[1] 16

kāma

4237

C.C.C. 1[a] 3

4238

4239

(a) VI

4240

W.I. 216[3]

326

4235 [Tangut] V 39 | [Tangut]

(a) VI 24 ditto

?

Used as a Phonetic for 恒 hêng

for Gai[gā] W II 20^9 26^2 46^8 76^6

4235 A [Tangut] × of VII A 34 | [Tangut]

4235 B [Tangut], Correct form of 4176

C 35^b CCC. 1^a

(i) W I. 168^5 II 2^9 捨 to renounce, relinquish

224^9 spoṅ abstain from; upekṣā

(ii) | [Tangut] W II 18^4 捨離 "to renounce & abandon".

4236 [Tangut] V 41 [Tangut] | mind 4229 × 3316 2021

(a) IX 122 [Tangut] | greed

W.I. 100^1 168^2 etc. 欲 rajas "passion" kāma "love". 164^1 [Tangut] v. 1128

4237 [Tangut] III 154 [Tangut] | 3548

C.C.C. 1^a 3 (? error for 4236)

4238 [Tangut] VIII A 106 [Tangut] | mind 4229

4239 [Tangut] VI 36 [Tangut] |

(a) VI 120 ditto

4240 [Tangut] × IX A 171 [Tangut] | "bone" 4208

W.I. 216^3 rkaṅ "marrow (in bones)"

4241 [Tangut] V 15 | [Tangut]

4242 [Tangut] V A 43 | [Tangut] 3448

[(a) III 74 | [Tangut] error for 4256]

(b) III 91 | [Tangut] 5071

4243 [Tangut] VI 47 [Tangut] | 1901

(a) III 61 ditto

B. 345^1 ? 右 right hand

4244 [Tangut] IX 59 [Tangut] |

(a) IX 39 [Tangut] | 3129

W I 194^4 210^1 Phonetic lu

4245 [Tangut] VI 47 | [Tangut]

4246 [Tangut] III 44 [Tangut] | 4604

(a) III A 62 | [Tangut] 0189

W.I. 192^1 gtoṅ "to renounce, relinquish"

4247 [Tangut] VI 23 [Tangut] | 5383

4248 [Tangut] VI A 1 Family or clan name

B. 185 晉 Tsin (dynasty)

error for 4692
~~4249A 0125 pair~~

4250 independent (See 5204)

4251 independent

4252 5505 pair

4253 5540 chain

4254 0959 chain
4254 v.1637 / err. sh. 1k 餟 |

4255 2782 pair

4256 – 5198

4257 –
⊢4285–0220
⊢4110

4258 4544 chain

4259 5293 chain
縌 | B.195[2] W.I.265[18] 神謀 part of royal title "divinely planned"
v.0417

4260 3446 chain

4261 5462 chain

4262
⊢3475 ⊢3445 ⊢2425
⊢4131 ⊢5334
⊢3490 – 3083
⊢3713
⊢4263
⊢5335

4263 4262 chain

4264 3276 chain

4265 4027 chain

4249
4249A
~~4250~~
= 4606
4250
4251
4252
(a) VI 3
4253
W.I.168[4]
4254
W.I.100[14]
170[4] ditto
4255
(a) IX
? a doub
4256
(a
4257
(a) II 1
(a) IX

327

4249 [Tangut] VII 10 [Tangut] |

4249A ~~4250~~ [Tangut] × of IX 45 [Tangut] |

= 4606

4250 [Tangut] VIII 5 Family or clan name

4251 [Tangut] V 70 Family or clan name

4252 [Tangut] III 18 [Tangut] |

(a) VI 37 ditto [[Tangut]]

4253 [Tangut] IX 29 | [Tangut] 2447

W. I. 168[4] 忽 "suddenly, carelessly".

4254 [Tangut] VII 51 ~~[Tangut]~~ | [Tangut] |

W. I 100[14] 穢 "filthy, foul".

170[4] ditto but ? noun "filth"

4255 [Tangut] IX 43 "Family or clan name"

(a) IX 96 [Tangut] |

? a double name

4256 [Tangut] IX 31 | [Tangut]

(a) III 74 ditto

4257 [Tangut] VI 10 | [Tangut]

(a) II 1 [Tangut] × of [Tangut] [Tangut] 4110

~~(b)~~ (a) IX 9 ditto

4258 [Tangut] IX 56 [Tangut] |

4259 [Tangut] IX 9 [Tangut] | 5293

(a) I 23 ~~ditto ? v. 5293~~ 5290

(i) C.C.C. 27[6] W. II 67 樞 "pivot, axis". B. 191[2]

(ii) B. 179[3] 謀 "deliberate, plan, scheme"

Dict 1[a] 4 B. 195[2]

4260 [Tangut] VI 10 | [Tangut] 4515

W. I 96[13] 嘲 調 "to ridicule (or abuse) + excite.

4261 [Tangut] I 3 [Tangut] |

4262 [Tangut] IX 23 | [Tangut] "zaci" ×× 3476

(a) III 172 ditto

(b) VII 5 | [Tangut] 4131

4263 [Tangut] V A 112 | [Tangut] "zaci"

? W. II 70[3] 鏡 "mirror".

4264 [Tangut] VIII 55 | [Tangut] 2044

?

W. I 194[4] Phonetic hu

4265 [Tangut] V 62 [Tangut] 832 q.v.

(a) V 31 [Tangut] | 4900

(b) VI 41 | [Tangut] 4057

?

4266-1112

4267 5690 chain

4268-1529

4269 5690 chain

4270 3929 chain

4271 2278 chain (40 entries)

4276
- 0541-2238
- 4765-2400-2275
  - 2050
  - 2288
  - 5316
    - 0252-4233
      - 3978
      - 4229
        - 0289-0397
        - 1049
        - 1749
        - 2047-2048
        - 3421-3478
        - 4236-2021-3316
        - 4238
        - 4951
        - 4959
          - 1789
          - 4944
        - 4970-2409
        - 5239
        - 4998
    - 0792
    - 1301
    - 5600
- 5570
  - 0257
  - 0467
  - 1838-0454
  - 2798
  - 5393
  - 5607

4269 bis 2130 chain

~~4272 0599 chain~~

4272 居 'to dwell' W II 2[6]

4272
- 4010
- 2319

B.125[4] ? phon.

4273 5523 chain

4274 4889 chain

4275-3004

4266

(a) III 6

4267

(a) I 31

(b) III 8

(c) VI

(b) above

(i) II 38[10] 善

B.177[1]

W. I. 210[2]

4268

(a) III 31

W. I 176[4]

4269

(a) VIII

W. I 136[18]

II 14[11]

4270

C.C.C.[a] 電

4271

(a) V 2

4269 bis

I

4266 [Tangut] VIII 4 | [Tangut]

(a) III 66 ditto

4267 [Tangut] IX 17 [Tangut] | 1767

[(a) I 31 [Tangut] | error for 4818]

(b) III 83 [Tangut] | 1371

(c) VI A 77 [Tangut] | 4963

(b) above
(i) II 38[10] 善哉 good!

B.177[1] part of P.N. 125[4] to. Gs. 利

W.I. 210[2] Phonetic ra.

4268 [Tangut] V 37 | [Tangut] 1529

(a) III 31 ditto

W.I 176[4] 澤 "favour, kindness"? B.164[4] 172[1] q.v.

4269 [Tangut] III 21 | [Tangut] 5274

(a) VIII. 21 | [Tangut] 5675 ~~4269~~

W.I 136[18] 168[11] B.164[2] 171[3]

II 14[11] Phonetic [Tangut] da

4270 [Tangut] VI 53 | [Tangut] 4524

~~C.C.C. 9[a] 電 "thunder"~~

4271 [Tangut] V 27 | [Tangut] 2278

(a) V 2 ditto

4269 bis [Tangut] VII 37 [Tangut] | 2336

I 42 ditto

4273A [Tangut] error X VI.66 error for 4076

328

4272 [Tangut] VII A 135 | [Tangut]

(a) VI 5 ditto

(b) IX 133 [Tangut] | place 2319

(i) Passim 住 "sthiti to abide, stay" stand (still)

(ii) B.250 止 gnas.pa "to adhere to (a doctrine)" (iii) B 245[2] 居 dwell, live

4273 [Tangut] IX A 23 [Tangut] |

(a) I A 20 ditto

(b) V 1 | [Tangut] 5209

(c) V 2 | [Tangut] 3229

(d) IX 138 | [Tangut] 5466
B.230[5] orally.

C.C.C. 18[a] W.I 108[14] etc. 口 "mouth"

4274 [Tangut] I 47 [Tangut] | 4889

(a) I A 101 [Tangut] | 0509

(b) IX A 17 [Tangut] | 1008

(i) By itself II 80[3] 吹 "to blow (a pipe)" 94[9]

(ii) (b) above C.C.C. 32[b] 吹笛 "blowing flute" W.I. 98[5] q.v.

4275 [Tangut] V 1 | [Tangut] 3004

(a) IX 8 ditto

4276 [Tangut] VI A 23 [Tangut] | smells 541 市 甬

(a) IX 159 ditto 0541

[(b) II 1 [Tangut] × by [Tangut] |]

(c) V A 9 | [Tangut] grab 4765

4281
5000 — 5285

4276

[Tangut] | semi-labial sounds

Dict 1^6 Title of Ch. III

174^4 2.3
B.176 小 minor (priest)

4282 independent

4277
1575
1668
4678

4283 4183 chain

4284 0563 chain

4285 4257 chain

4278 – 2613

4279 4583 chain

4280 – 5480

4286
3041 chain

| [Tangut] B.216² 種族 kind of clan

4276 co…
(d) VI 7…
(i) (c) abov…
ccc. 20^b
small"…
4277 [Tangut]
(a) VIII…
(b) II.1…
(c) VI 5…
(i) CCC.16…
兎 rab…
ditto? B…
(ii) (b) …
W II 48^8 馬…
4278 [Tangut]
(a) VII 7…
(i) The …
"course"…
4279 [Tangut]
4280 [Tangut]
25/2/39 (a) I 25…

329

4276 cont.

(d) VI 72 | [Tangut] 5570 ~~'and'~~ 5570

(i) (c) above C.C.C. 20[b] B 187[2]

~~C.C.C. 20[b] 小 "small"~~ 大小 "great & small", by itself B 215[2] 小 215[3]

4277 [Tangut] IX 143 | [Tangut]

(a) VIII 84 ditto

(b) II. 11 [Tangut] wei

(c) VI 51 [Tangut] × by dissyllable 1668

(i) ~~C.C.C. 16[a]~~ The dissyllable C.C.C. 16[a] 兎 rabbit, or hare W II 48[4] 兎角 ditto? B. 101 cat. under "wild animals".

(ii) (b) above C.C.C. 16[a] 馿 "donkey" W II 48[8] 馿盧脣 donkey's lips!

4278 [Tangut] VII 11 | [Tangut].

(a) VII 74 ditto

(i) The dissyllable C.C.C. 17[b] 蟣虱 "louse" (in both cases)

4279 [Tangut] VII 11 [Tangut] | 4583

4280 [Tangut] VII 11 | [Tangut]

25/4/39 (a) I 25 ditto

4281 [Tangut] IX ~~31~~ 49 [Tangut]

(a) V 32 [Tangut] × by [Tangut] |

(b) VI 72 [Tangut] × by [Tangut] |

?

4282 [Tangut] V 60 "Family or clan name" B. 176[5] S.N.

4283 [Tangut] V 104 | [Tangut]

(d) The dissyllable C.C.C. 14[a] 橘子 "orange"

4284 [Tangut] ~~[illegible]~~ VIII 54 [Tangut] | 5144 "heavy"

v. 0563

4285 [Tangut] IX 9 [Tangut] |

(a) VI 10 ditto

(b) VII 64 [Tangut] | 0220

~~(c) IX 16 | [Tangut]~~ error for 4109

Either 4284 or 4285 must be [Tangut]. It is not clear to which (b) & (c) belong; or which is:–

(i) W. I. 120[13] [[Tangut]] ~~巖 "cliff"~~ error for 4702

(ii) W II 38[9] 利 "advantage" B. 171[4]

v. 3049

4286 [Tangut] I 11 [Tangut] | 3041 man

(a) I 77 ditto

(b) IX 79 | [Tangut]

4287 3829 chain

4288 independent

4289 3223 chain

4290 4011 chain

4291 3402 chain

4292 1559 chain

4293 3226 chain

4294 1584 chain

4295 5060 3518

4297 2906 chain

4298 -4048

330

4286 cont.

(i) By itself W.II 16[9] 氏 "family"

(ii) The dissyllable W.II 42[3] 姓 "family name" [See 3041]

Used as the explanation of a large number of characters representing family or clan names. For full list see App.x

4287 [Tangut] VII 6 | [Tangut] 3829

(i) The dissyllable C.C.C. 11[a] 正月 "first month". B.176[4]

4288 [Tangut] VIII A 14 "man's name" W.I 132[16]: B 126[1] P.N.

4289 [Tangut] I 53 [Tangut] | 3223

4290 [Tangut] I 56 | [Tangut] ruler 3760

(i) C.C.C. 6[a] 將 "the general" [name of a star].

(ii) C.C.C. 27[b] 28[a] 統 "governor, controller".

4291 [Tangut] III A 66 | [Tangut] glorious 4011 chain 3402

(i) C.C.C. 36[a] +passim 妙 "Su, sat mañju, sūkṣma" "wonderful, beautiful, supernatural" (Soot p.234)

(ii) W.I 190[8] mdzes "beautiful"

W.I 190[11] bzaṅ "beautiful".

W.I 265[19] 韶 B 179[3] brilliant B.195[3]

(ii) The dissyllable C.C.C. 13[a] 牡丹 "bull-red" (flower)

4292 [Tangut] I 28 | [Tangut] 1696

B.168[2] (doubled) + 1696! 168[3]

4293 [Tangut] IX 106 [Tangut] | 0577

4294 [Tangut] ṅga V 40 [Tangut] | 3394

C.C.C. 21[b] 呪 W.I.190[1] + passim sṅags "dhāraṇī, spell, curse"

?

4295 [Tangut] nu V 73 | [Tangut] 3518

(a) V 49 ditto.

? (b) III 40

4296 [Tangut] IX 47 "Family or clan name"

B.175[2] P.N.

4297 [Tangut] III 31 [Tangut] | 2906

(a) VIII 19 | [Tangut] ditto [~~ditto misspelt~~]

W.I 220[14] gre "name of a lunar mansion".

4298 [Tangut] VIII 10 | [Tangut] [misspelt]

?

4299 4814 chain

4300 2703 chain

4301-5010

4302 4011 chain

4303 4983 chain

4304 2278 chain

4304A 0638 chain

The Hsiyl. B 212[4] 破落 break + knock down

4305 2683 pair

4306 independent

4307 independent

4308 0271 chain

4309 1128 chain

4310 3443 chain

4308A [Tangut] × of [Tangut] | 5193
error for 3913

331

4299 ~~4298~~ [Tangut] VII 47 [Tangut] | 0661

4300 ~~4299~~ [Tangut] V 18 [Tangut] | 2226

4301 ~~4300~~ [Tangut] II 31 | [Tangut] 5010

(a) IX 2 ditto

4302 [Tangut] II 31 [Tangut] | ruler 3760

See 3760. It is very difficult to distinguish between the two characters. This is presumably the same as Chinese 王 wang. ~~The only~~ Clear instances of it are in II 20[2] 主 "ruler," B345[2] ditto I 266[21] II 128[12] translates 王 4011 chain

4303 [Tangut] I 51 [Tangut] |

(a) I 127 ditto
(b) I 47 × 3121

4304 [Tangut] IX 29 [Tangut] | × 2308 2918
(a) I 47

~~4305 [Tangut] VIII 84~~

~~4304A [Tangut] × of V 85~~

4304A [Tangut] : × of V 85 [Tangut]

? Probably authentic.

4305 [Tangut] VIII 84 [Tangut] |

(a) V 2 ditto

4306 [Tangut] V 2 [blank]

4307 [Tangut] VIII 84 "Family or clan name"

4308 [Tangut] IX 70 [Tangut] | "ear" 0271

(a) I 58 | [Tangut] 1351

(b) III 163 | [Tangut] "to listen" × 3700

(c) V 31 [Tangut] | 1430

(i) (b) above W. I. 128[14] II 22[2] [Tangut] 聽 聞 "to listen + hear"

Note. 4307 + 4308 are very difficult to distinguish. (a) or (c) may belong to the former + be a double name.

4309 [Tangut] IX A 127 [Tangut] | 1128

(a) VII A 80 | [Tangut] × 5646

4310 [Tangut] IX 110 [Tangut] | 3443

(a) IX 34 ditto × 5446

(b) VIII 71 [Tangut] | 1341

4316 (iii) | 𘅍 退轉 'to return'

W. II 94[4]

4311 2749 chain

4317 0148 chain

4311A 2027 chain

4318 4330 chain

4312 4773 chain

4313 4164 chain

4319 4014 chain

4314 1949 chain

4320 independent

4315 1457 chain

4321 4164 chain

4322 0271 chain

4323 2377 chain

4316 2749 chain

4324 4011 chain

4316 (ii) 𘅍 | 懺悔 'to repent' B 192[1] 同 193[3]

(? 'renounce') W. II 84[10]

B 208[1]

II. 150[2] | 𘅍 退轉

4325 5644 ~~2703~~ chain

4311 𘅍

4311A 𘅍

(? error)

4312 𘅍

4313 𘅍

(a) V A

(b) VI 9

(c) IX 9

4314 𘅍

4315 𘅍

(a) VIII

(b) VIII

(i) By itse

out'.

(ii) 𘅍 |

(2754)

cleanse' I

set rid

4316 𘅍

(a) IX 9

(b) I A

(i) W. II. 16[2]

(ii) II 126[9]

332

4311 [Tangut] I A56 [Tangut] |

4311A [Tangut] × of V 43 | [Tangut]

? error for 4061

4312 [Tangut] V 12 | [Tangut]

4313 [Tangut] III 66 [Tangut] |

(a) V A33 ditto

(b) VI 91 [Tangut] | 2682

(c) IX 92 | [Tangut] 4321

?

4314 [Tangut] IX 140 [Tangut] | 4413

4315 [Tangut] VIII 70 [Tangut] | 1457

(a) VIII 37 ditto

(b) VIII 12 | [Tangut] 4394

(i) By itself. W.I. 224[3] btkul ? 'to go out'.

(ii) [Tangut] | W I 200[2] sel. ba 'to remove, cleanse' II 38[11] 除去 'to remove, get rid of'.
(2754)

4316 [Tangut] IX A30 [Tangut] |

(a) IX 91 ditto

(b) I A56 | [Tangut]

(i) W.II. 16[2] 捨 'to give up, renounce'

(ii) II 126[9] 退 to recede, fall back'

(ii) | [Tangut] W II 80[8] 悔 惱 'repentance & sorrow'

4317 [Tangut] IX 92 | [Tangut] 0592

4318 [Tangut] VII 32 [Tangut] |

(i) C.C.C. 31[a] 肯 'to yield, consent, permit W.I. 168[8] do.

(ii) W.II 48[11] q.v. B.187[2] q.v. the 半 'half'

4319 [Tangut] VIII 83 [Tangut] | 4014

4320 [Tangut] VIII 83 × by itself [|] |

4321 [Tangut] IX 92 [Tangut]

4322 [Tangut] III 122 [Tangut] | 'to hear' 3092

4323 [Tangut] VII 44 | [Tangut] 3967 v. 1958 'virtue' passim

C.C.C. 20[a] 仁 'goodness' B.160[1] B 260

4324 [Tangut] V 2 [Tangut] | 'hear' 4011

(a) VIII A11 [Tangut] | 3742

C.C.C. 36[a] W.I 94[19] etc 等 'equal, universal' B 215[3] 4011 chain

4325 [Tangut] V 18 [Tangut] 4136

W.I. 224[13] mñam 'the same'

W II 128[10] 同 'the same' but cf. [Tangut]

4326
- 4191
- 0485 – 0310
- 0695 bis
- 4964
  - 0105
  - 0328 – 3709
  - 1935
  - 4075
  - 4587
  - 4779
    - 1437
    - 4753
      - 2393
      - 4751
  - 4959
    - 1789
    - 4944

4332 independent

4333 5423 pair

4334 4773 chain

4327 2750 pair

4335 independent

4328 5708 chain

4336 independent

4329 3864 chain

4337 1369 chain

B 94 | tone (?) 3

4330
- 4993
- 4241
- 4318

4338 2149 chain

4339 independent

4340 3226 chain

4331 3449 chain

4341–1029A

4326

(a) II 4

(b) III 13

(c) VI 1

(d) VI 9

(i) C.C.C. 33² W.I.

4327

(ii) W.I. 110⁴

4328

4329

W.I. 138²

4330

(a) IX 12

(b) V 15

(c) VII 3

W.I. 92¹ II 14

Used as

4331

(i) W.I. 214⁶

(ii) | W.

1649

333

4326 [Tangut] VII 44 | [Tangut] 4191 "noose"

(a) II 4 ditto

(b) III 131 [Tangut] | 0695

(c) VI 10 [Tangut] | 0485

(d) VI 95 | [Tangut] "man" 4964

(i) C.C. 33[2] W.I. 116[7] 人 W.I 194[2] mi "man"

4327 [Tangut] IX A 139 [Tangut] | 2750

(a) IX 167 ditto

(ii) W.I. 110[4] 仁 "goodness"

4328 [Tangut] IX 76 [Tangut] | misspelt? 1956

4329 [Tangut] VII 78 [Tangut] |

W.I. 138[2] 公 "public etc"

4330 [Tangut] V A 93 | [Tangut]

(a) IX 125 ditto

(b) V 15 [Tangut] | 4241

(c) VII 32 | [Tangut] 4318

W.I. 92[1] II 14[7] 樂 "joy"

Used as Phonetic W.II. 32[12]

4331 [Tangut] I 51 [Tangut] |

(i) W.I. 214[6] śi.ba "death"

(ii) | [Tangut] W.I. 208[13] 212[12] ʒags.pa "leash"

1649

4332 [Tangut] II 15 "Family or clan name"

B.347[2] 韋 Wei [uei] = P.N. B.174[4] Part of P.N.

4333 [Tangut] V 2 [Tangut] |

(a) V 23 ditto

4334 [Tangut] VIII 32 | [Tangut]

4335 [Tangut] III 17 "Family or clan name"

Used as Phonetic W.II 2[12], 152[10] 多

4336 [Tangut] VII 41 × by self [1] |

B 176[1]? B.166[1] (doubtful)

4337 [Tangut] II 2 [Tangut] 1369

B 98 [Tangut] [Tangut] Dictionary note on [Tangut] might mean "2nd tone" (doubtful)

4338 [Tangut] V 82 | [Tangut]

4339 [Tangut] III 76 "Family or clan name"

4340 [Tangut] VIII 60 [Tangut] | 5108

(a) V 169 [Tangut] × by [Tangut] |

4341 [Tangut] III 76 [Tangut] | 1029A

4342 1080 chain

4343 2635 chain

4344 independent

4345 1473 bis

4346 0159 chain

4347 4561 chain

4348 1552 chain

4349 4958 pair

4350 -3145

4351 3335 chain IV

4352 -1054 A

4353 4985 pair

4354 4166 pair

4355
3656-5093-5218
0942

4356 4911 pair

4357
4137-4584

4358 4913 pair

4359 1361 chain I

4342
(a) VIII
4343
4344
4345
(a) I 6
4346
4347
4348
globe, ba
4349
(a) IX
4350
(a) VIII

334

4342 VII 35 | 5665

(a) VIII 32 |

4343 IX 14 | and. 2013

4344 [VII 59-60]

4345 III 122 | 1755

(a) I 65 [ ] 4633

4346 VIII 16 |

4347 III 97 | 4561

4348 IX 146 |

(i) | C.C.C. 23b 燈毬 "lamp globe, ball."

4349 III 97 |

(a) IX 79 ditto

4350 III A101 |

(a) VIII 28 ditto

4351 III 97 |

4352 IX 51 | 1054A

4353 IX 146 blank

(a) V.32 |

4354 IX 63 |

(a) V 27 ditto

4355 IX A 147 | 0942

(a) I 9 ditto (b) V 79

C.C.C. 33a 乾 "dry (cake)".

4356 VII 7 |

(a) VII 39 ditto

? cf. 4358

4357 IX 15 | × 4589 4137

(a) IX 33 ditto misspelt

?

4358 VII 7 |

(a) VII 39 ditto

? cf. 4356

4359 VI A92 | 1373

B. 133' Ar. 善

4360 5678 chain III

[4367] 3196 pair VII

[4368] 4011 chain IX
4528A

4361 3685 chain IX

4369 0559 pair VII

4362 3210 chain

4370 1353 chain

[4371] 0741 chain VII

[4372] [4377] pair III

4363 independent VII

4364 4142 chain

[4373] 0731 chain

[4374] 4729 chain

4365 3026 chain VI

[4375] 2710 chain

4366 3467 chain

4360

(a) I

ccc. 36

W. I. 196

4361

B. 176 P.

4362

(i) By

(ii) The

樂. "prac

4363

4364

(a) I 28

(b) IX

4365

4366

W II 64 空

335

4360 [Tangut] VI 1 [Tangut] |

(a) I 17 ditto

C.C.C. 36[a] 他 "the other". W. II 86[4] C.C.C. 1[a]?

W. I. 196[8] p'a. rol "the other side"

4361 [Tangut] IX A 121 [Tangut] | "name"

B. 176[5] P.N. 任

Used as Phonetic W. II 42[3]

4362 [Tangut] III 66 | [Tangut]

(i) By itself W. II 10[12] 安 "peace" W. I. 102[3]?

(ii) The Dissyllable W. I. 136[4] II 76[10] 安樂 II 132[3] 安隱 "peace & happiness I 196[9]

bde. legs "happiness, well-being".

4363 [Tangut] VI 78 mistake

4364 [Tangut] IX 127 [Tangut] |

(a) I 28 ditto

(b) IX 139 | [[Tangut]] [Tangut] 4825

4365 [Tangut] VII 68 | [Tangut] 4398

4366 [Tangut] V 32 [Tangut] | 3464

W II 64[5] 空 "empty"

4367 [Tangut] IX 30 [Tangut] | 3196

(a) I 128 ditto

4368 [Tangut] V 17 [Tangut] | [Tangut] 4011

Dict. 54[a] 5 (i) Dissyll. D. 176[3,5] 頭監 chief superintendent 4011 chain

4369 [Tangut] IX 1[Tangut] |

(a) IX 4 ditto revised

4370 [Tangut] VII A 113 [Tangut] |

4371 [Tangut] III 105 [Tangut] | 0741

V. 4545 A

4372 [Tangut] VII A 17 [Tangut] |

(a) VII 66 ditto

4373 [Tangut] VI 75 [Tangut] | "wood"

4374 [Tangut] IX 17 [Tangut]

4375 [Tangut] IX 75 [Tangut] | 2702

(i) C.C.C. 5[b] 婁 W I 222[7] t'a "name of a constellation.

(ii) The Dissyllable C.C.C. 26[b] 子婁

[4376] 5690 chain IX

[4377] – [4372] VI 17

4378 3449 chain

4379 0760 chain VII

4380 3026 chain III

4381 2754 chain

4382 2279 chain

4383 1923 chain

4384 interpunct

4385 0609 chain VI

[4386] 2149 chain

4387 1254 chain

4388 · 3568 pair III

4389 3226 chain

4390 4454 chain

II.146 12 閑

4391 4775 chain V

4376

(a) IX

W. I 136 6

4377

(a) VII

4378

4379

4380

(a) III

4381

W. I. 134 10

pierce

4382

4383

(a) III

W. II 76 6

4384

A comm

336

4376 [illegible] I 66 [illegible] | 5274
(a) IX 59 [illegible] | 3023
W. I 136[6] 杖 a bamboo rod

4377 [illegible] VII 66 | [illegible]
(a) VII A 17

4378 [illegible] V 2 [illegible] | 1648

4379 [illegible] I 144 | [illegible] 1759

4380 [illegible] IX 93 [illegible] | 4398
(a) III 146 | [illegible] 1219

4381 [illegible] VII 97 | [illegible] 1716
W. I. 134[10] 斬 "to cut off" : W. I 168[15] 刺 "to stab, pierce".

4382 [illegible] V 103 [illegible] 2272

4383 [illegible] V 176 [illegible] | q.v. 1923
(a) III 145 [illegible] | 4849
W. II. 76[6] 校 "compare, compare with"

4384 [illegible] III 109 "man's name"

A common Phonetic

4385 [illegible] V 176 [illegible] | 0609
(a) V 18 | [illegible]
C.C.C. 7[a] 秤 B. 205[1] q.v. "balance, scales" B 174[1]

4386 [illegible] V 50 | [illegible]

4387 [illegible] VII A 127 [illegible] | 4400
B. 169[2] 帛 silk

4388 [illegible] V 17 [illegible] |
(a) I 65 ditto [illegible]
W. I. 194[18]

4389 [illegible] VIII A 27 | [illegible] 4760
(a) IX 88 [illegible] |

4390 [illegible] III 108 [illegible] | 4454
(a) I 35 | [illegible]
~~(b) VI A 28 | [illegible] 0380~~
W. I. 134[11] 塞 "to block up, stop up obstruct" I 170[?] ditto

4390A [illegible] x of III 16 | [illegible]
Error for 4707 or vice versa

4391 [illegible] II A 12 | [illegible] 3154
(i) By [illegible] B. 180[4] 下 "downwards"
(ii) The bisyllable W. I. 192[2] kp'yai. ba "hanging down"

4392 indeterminate

4393
- 3649
- 3926

4398 3026 chain

4394 1457 chain

4395 - 1348

4399 3086 chain

4396
- 3208 - 3209
- 1961
- 2731
- 5224
  - 1075
  - 1729
  - 3348 - 2439 - 2890
    - 2891
    - 5518
  - 4855

4400 1254 chain

4401 4506 chain

4402 1340 chain

4397 0214 chain cf. 2687

337

4392 III 160 "Family or clan name"

~~4393~~ Note 4391 + 4392 barely distinguishable

4393 V 38 | 3649

(a) V A 25 ditto

(b) VI 45 | 3926

4394 VIII 12 | 4315

?

4395 VIII 29 |

(a) I 8 ditto

4396 IX A 86 | ×3209 3208

(a) VIII A 38 ditto

(b) III 66 | 2731

(c) III 102 | "pearl" ×5224

(d) VIII 34 | 1461

(i) By itself passim = 寶 "jewel"

W.I. 216[8] rin.chen "jewel"

(ii) The disyllable C.C.C. 12[b] 寶物

W.I. 136[17] 財寶 "property & jewels."

B. Coin plate. The standard inscription on coins; translated 寶錢

4397 IX A 85 |

(a) IX 101 | (nil) 5103

(b) IX 126 | intercalary (3363 error) ×4864 ?

v. 0573

C.C.C. 36[a] 加 "to add, increase"

W II 80[10] 增 "to add." 90[9] ditto

W.I. 192[15] 222[16] ?

C.C.C. 7[b] W.I 271[6] 添 "additional"

4398 VII 28 | 2043

(a) VII | 1573

(b) VII 57 | 1480

(c) VII 68 | 4365

(d) IX 93 | ×(1219) 4380

? W.II 152[3] 術 magic

4399 VI A 82 | 3768

B. 186[2] 隋 Sui

B. 186 隋 Sui (dynasty) ? Phonetic.

4399A ~~4400~~ Error for 4414

W.I. 108[10,12] 144[17] 生 "to be born, birth."

4400 VII A 20 |

(a) VII A 127 |

W II 48[6] 去 "to send out" etc.

4401 ~~4402~~ III 56 |

4402 VI 98 |

(a) VI 73 | ×(5039) 3409

(b) VI A 118 × by | 1011

4403 4427 chain

4404 2027 chain

4405 1488 chain

4406 3685 chain

4407 2207 pair

4408 + 3248 A) 3291 } pair

4409 4428 chain

4410 – 4441A 4468 chain

4411 2909 pair

4412 1846 chain

4412A 4529 chain

4413 1949 chain

B.231[4] 生 to create

4414 – 1823

4415 0148 chain

4403

(a) VII 9

4404

4405 ~~4406~~

(a) VIII

4406

A phone

4407 ~~4408~~

(a) III

4408

W.I.134[3]

4408A ~~4410~~

4409 ~~4410~~

(a) VI

4410

4411 ~~4412~~

(a) V.3

B.168[5]

4403 [Tangut] III 91 [Tangut] | 0652 ?

(a) VII 91 | [Tangut] 3021

4404 [Tangut] VI A 87 | [Tangut] 0946

4405 ~~4406~~ [Tangut] IX 172 [Tangut] | 1488

(a) VIII 38 [Tangut] | 4647

4406 [Tangut] VIII A 103 [Tangut] [Tangut]

A Phonetic character

4407 ~~4408~~ [Tangut] V 29 [Tangut] |

(a) III 15 ditto

4408 [Tangut] III 42 [Tangut] |

W.I.134^3 錯 "to ~~cut~~, destroy"

4408A ~~4410~~ [Tangut] Error for [Tangut] 3528

4409 ~~4410~~ [Tangut] III 112 [Tangut] |

(a) VI A 48 ditto

4410 [Tangut] IX 170 [Tangut] |

4411 ~~4412~~ [Tangut] I 115 [Tangut] |

(a) V 30 ditto

B.168^5

338

4412 [Tangut] III 12 [Tangut] |

(a) VII A 114 ditto

(b) III 39 | [Tangut] |

(c) IX A 60 | [Tangut] 0209

(i) By itself W.I.134^15; B.126^2 出 put forth

(ii) | [Tangut] W.I.134^13 II 80^1 發露 give forth revelation S.-H 384 "~~to shut down upon~~"

~~4414~~ [Tangut]

4412A [Tangut] x of VIII 96 | [Tangut]

4413 [Tangut] wi II 27 [Tangut] | ? 1949

(a) I 11 ditto

(b) III 142 | [Tangut] 4888

(c) V 25 | [Tangut] x (2703) 3961

(d) VII 40 | [Tangut] 1810

(e) IX 140 | [Tangut] 4314

W.I.100^2,14 & passim 生 "to be born, creature" W.I.190^11 skyes "creature"

W.I.216^3 btsas.pa ? "harvest"

4414 [Tangut] III A 56 | [Tangut]

(a) III A 22 ditto

4415 [Tangut] IX 73 | [Tangut] 0149

4416 4207 chain III

4417 - 1546 A

4418 3685 chain

4419 1438 chain x

4420 2522 pair

4421 2485 chain

4422 2027 chain

4423 - 4424

4424 4423 pair

4425
┬2386 ┬2919 - 2922
└0932 └3287

4426 - 3991 A

4426 (a) IX2 x by 3955 Song

4427
┬4536
└0652 - 4403 - 3021

4428
┬4409
└0931 - 4429

4429 4428 chain

4416

4417

~~4418~~

4418

B. 174[5]

4419

? (a) VII

~~4420~~

4419

4420

4421

4422

B. 18

4423

(a) VII

339

4416 [Tangut] VI 83 | [Tangut]

4417 [Tangut] II 32 [Tangut] |

~~4418~~ Used as a Phonetic W.I. 192[6] for 210' bha.

4418 [Tangut] II 22 [Tangut] | "name"
B. 174[5] part of P.N.

4419 [Tangut] V 9 [Tangut] 1438A
?(a) VII A 109 | [Tangut] [Tangut] 2487

Used as Phonetic W.I. 210' ki

~~4420~~ [Tangut] Note. 4418 + 4419 are practically indistinguishable.
4419 perhaps has [Tangut]

4420 [Tangut] KI V 116 (~~106~~) [Tangut] | Family name B.126[1]
Yinki ?= Agni Karashahr B177[3] part of P.N.

4421 [Tangut] V 180 [Tangut] | 1458 (?9)

4422 [Tangut] III 94 | [Tangut] 1409
B. 180[3] 飾 adorn 168[3] tu 莊

4423 [Tangut] VII 64 | [Tangut]
(a) VII 13 ditto
(i) The dissyllable W II 24[6] 閒 飾 "to divide (?) + adorn"

Note 4422 + 4423 are barely distinguishable.

4424 [Tangut] VII 13 [Tangut] |
(a) VII 64 ditto

4425 [Tangut] I 119 | [Tangut] 2396
(a) VI 32 ditto
(b) II 15 | [Tangut] 0932

4426 [Tangut] IX 155 | [Tangut] 3991A

4427 [Tangut] V A 53 | [Tangut] 4536
(a) VII A 138 ditto
(b) VI 46 | [Tangut] 0652
W.I. 136[6] ?蹻 to kick or tread on.

4428 [Tangut] VI A 48 | [Tangut]
(a) III 112 ditto
(b) III 81 | [Tangut] 0931
C.C.C. 28[b] 農 田 "agricultural land (name of a temple)"

4429 [Tangut] VI 11 | [Tangut] 0931
(i) The dissyllable C.C.C. 23[a] [Tangut]

4430 A 3569 pair

4430 2179 chain

4431 0406 pair

4431 W II 84[6] |[illegible] |[illegible]一日一夜 ? = if for one day & one night.

The common usage is |[illegible] which is just = if ° W. II 84[6, 11] 86[3]

4432 0464 chain

4433 4497 pair

4434 0444 chain

4435
- 1279
- 1275 – [1270]

4436 independent

4437 – 5376

4438 2928 chain

? |[illegible] B 200[5] 菩薩 Bodhisattva

4439 |[illegible] [illegible] [illegible] B. 248[3]

byaṅ. č'ub. sems. dpa "Bodhisattva"

a curiously composite phrase

φ.i. |[illegible] 菩提 Bodhi B. 227[2] W. I. 164[2]

φ ii |[illegible] 波羅蜜 Pāramitā

W. II. 120[1]

4439
- 5291
- 3219
- 1082 ~ 2654

4440 + 4197

4441 – 3007

4442 3685 chain

4441 A 4410 pair (error for 4468)

4430 A

4430

(a) VI A

A mantr

V. set as c

4431

(a) III 8

A very el

(i) C.C.C. 11

(ii) The diso

II 46" 或

II 46[12] ?

4432

(a) IX A

W. I. 168[9]

4433

(a) III

4434

(a) II

4435

(a) IX

(b) VII

?

4430A [Tangut] X of 3569 (IX A185)

340

4430 [Tangut] NA V A128 "sacred word"
(a) VI A115 | [Tangut]
A mantra
Used as a Phonetic W.I.192[7] 214[4] na

4431 [Tangut] III 176 | [Tangut] "if" 0406
(a) III 83 ditto v. 406
A very elusive word
(i) C.C.C. 11[a] — "one" (day).
(ii) The disyllable W.II 20[6] 若 "if"
II 46[11] 或 "if" B 233[1]
II 46[12] ?

4432 [Tangut] IX 74 | [Tangut] misspelt 0464
(a) IX A101 [Tangut] | ? 1970
W.I.168[9] 賚 "to give, offer".

4433 [Tangut] III 141 [Tangut] |
(a) III 6 ditto

4434 [Tangut] VI 32 [Tangut] | 0444
(a) II 17 ditto

4435 [Tangut] IX 78 | [Tangut] 1279
(a) IX 72 ditto
(b) VIII 39 | [Tangut] 1275
?

4436 [Tangut] VI A108 Family or clan (name)

4437 [Tangut] V A57 | [Tangut]
(a) VII 112 ditto

4438 [Tangut] IX 18 [Tangut] | 4532

4439 [Tangut] I 22 | [Tangut] 5291
(a) II 3 ditto
(b) I 16 | [Tangut] ×2653 1082
(c) III 135 [Tangut] | 3219
? B.176[5] part of P.N. tr. 遇 B. 215[4] phon. iii
Used as a Phonetic.
(i) W.I 92[7] 108[17] etc | [Tangut] 菩提
bodhi

4440 [Tangut] IX 88 | [Tangut] 4197
(a) IX A12 ditto
Dict 56[4]5 II 154[3] 觀 S.H. 489 to contemplate etc.

4441 [Tangut] III 180 | [Tangut]
(a) IX 8 ditto

4442 [Tangut] VIII A102 [Tangut] cf. 2033
A Phonetic character

4441A [Tangut] X of IX 170 4410

4443 0157 chain

4449 ~~4454 chain~~

4450 = 2987

4444 2143 chain

4451 1343 chain

4452 1891 series

4453 2725 pair

4445 1891 chain

4446 1834 pair

4454
- 0676
- 1714
- 2035
- 2165
- 3512
- 3531
- 4449
- 4390 – 5534

4447 0655 chain

4448 0752 chain

4443

(a) I 7

(b) II A

(c) VI

4444

(a) II 9

B.94

| is

written

遣 'to

B.132³

W.II 2¹²

4445

W II 2¹ B.

bam.po

4446

(a) VI A

4447

4448

341

4443 [Tangut] I A12 |[Tangut] 0157

(a) I 7 |[Tangut] 1465

(b) II A33 |[Tangut][Tangut] 3184

(c) VI A11 [Tangut] | 0494

4444 [Tangut] VII 18 | [Tangut] 2143

~~(a) II 9 |[Tangut]~~

B.94 [Tangut] on one side; [Tangut] (3218 aux. verb) follows. | is [Tangut][Tangut] [translated 策畧 "a written plan"]; or [Tangut] [translated 遣 "to send"]; also the word for [Tangut][Tangut] [translated 分行

B.132^3

W.II 2^{12} used as Phonetic. B.126^1: do.

4445 [Tangut] – IX A25 |[Tangut] 5611

W II 2^1 B.218 卷 "volume" B.248^1 passim ✓

bam.po ditto.

4446 [Tangut] VI 73 [Tangut] | 1834

(a) VI A62 ditto

4447 [Tangut] IX 129 [Tangut] | 0653

4448 [Tangut] V 25 |[Tangut] 0118

4449 [Tangut] VIII 45 [Tangut] |

Note. 4448 & 4449 are indistinguishable

4450 [Tangut] III 94 |[Tangut] 2987

(a) II 9 ditto misspelt

(i) The dissyllable CCC.25^b 鋪帛 ? "silk broadstuff".

4451 [Tangut] V 17 [Tangut] | 1343

4452 [Tangut] VII 14 |[Tangut] 5705

4453 [Tangut] II 25 [Tangut] |

(a) II 11 ditto

(i) W II.26^1 放 "to diffuse (light)" verb ✓ 76^5 do.

(ii) W I $132^{13,16}$ spread (fire)

B.122^3 tr. 出 127^1 170^2

4454 [Tangut] VI A9 |[Tangut] ~~4392~~

(a) VI 124 ditto 0676

(b) II 1 |[Tangut] 1714

(c) III 40 |[Tangut] 3525

(d) III 57 |[Tangut] 2165

(e) III 108 |[Tangut] × 4390

(f) VI A18 |[Tangut][Tangut] 3631

(g) VIII 45 |[Tangut] 4449

4458 4550 chain

4459 5204 chain

4460 0464 chain

4261 4659 chain

4462 2027 chain

4455
4525
1329
1444

4463 2027 chain

4456 2751 pair VI

4457 4512 chain

4464 2754 chain IX

4465 4128 chain V

342

4454 (cont)

(h) VIII 57 | [Tangut] 2035

B.93 [Tangut] ideogram; [Tangut] follows. | is [Tangut] [translated 盈 "abundant, complete"] or [Tangut] [transl. 富 "rich"] or [Tangut] [溢 ? this] or [Tangut] [贏 "profit, surplus"] or [Tangut] [足 "enough"]

(i) W.I.108[8] 滿 "whole, complete". II.118[20] to complete

(ii) W.II 10[1] 充 "full, ample".

(iii) W.II.34[7] 盈 "complete"

(iv) W.I.190[7] rgyas "complete" B.250[2] rgya.

4455 [Tangut] V 123 | [Tangut]

(a) V.A 19 ditto

(b) V A 141 | [Tangut] 1329

(c) VII 81 | [Tangut] 1444

4456 [Tangut] IX 128 [Tangut] |

(a) IX 82 ditto

4457 [Tangut] P'A I 27 [Tangut] |

(a) VII 21 ~~ditto~~ [Tangut] | 2745

?Lo Handbook p.20 translates 番 'aboriginal, ? i.e. Hsi Hsia'. B.174[5] | [Tangut] 羌 漢 ?

Barbarian & Chinese B165[2] · B126[1]: pl.

4458 [Tangut] I 136 [Tangut] |

4459 [Tangut] V A 110 | [Tangut]

4460 [Tangut] IX 155 [Tangut] |? 1970

4461 [Tangut] VI 80 [Tangut] |

(a) VI 41 ditto [Tangut]

4462 [Tangut] III A 71 | [Tangut] 4463

(a) II 9 | [Tangut] 1409

(b) III 16 | [Tangut] × 4061

(c) VI 15 | [Tangut] 2914

4463 [Tangut] VIII 13 [Tangut] | 2027

(a) VI 17 ditto

(b) I 57 | [Tangut] sand? 946

(c) III A 50 | [Tangut] place 1467

(d) III A 71 [Tangut] | × 4462

4464 [Tangut] III 60 [Tangut] | 2754

(a) III 25 ditto

4465 [Tangut] V 69 [Tangut] |

4466 – 5014

4467 1540 pair

4468 4471 chain

4469 2707 chain

4470 – 1893

4471
⊥ 4468 – 4410

4472 4473 chain

4473
┬ 4472
├ 0653
├ 3744
└ 3928

4474 4183 chain

4475 0985 chain

4476 0809 chain

4477 3993 chain

4466
(a) I 18

4467
(a) V 11

Note 446

4468
(a) III 11
(b) IX 1
W.I.134[14]

4469

4470
(a) V 1

4471
(a) IX

4472
(a) IX 4
?

343

4466 [Tangut] VA58 | [Tangut]
(a) I 18 ditto

4467 [Tangut] VA72 [Tangut] |
(a) V 118 ditto

Note 4464–67 are barely distinguishable

4468 [Tangut] IX 88 [Tangut] |
(a) III 113 ditto
(b) IX 170 | [Tangut] 4410
W.I.134[14] 破 to break

4469 [Tangut] VII 40 [Tangut] |

4470 [Tangut] VA114 | [Tangut]
(a) V 165 ditto

4471 [Tangut] III 113 | [Tangut]
(a) IX 88 ditto

4472 [Tangut] IX 72 [Tangut] | .
(a) IX 4 ditto
?

4473 [Tangut] IX 4 | [Tangut]
(a) IX 72 ditto
(b) III 120 | [Tangut] 0653
(c) V 68 | [Tangut] 3928
(d) VII 94 [Tangut] | 3744
W.I.136[6]? 拉 to pull, drag

4474 [Tangut] V 164 | [Tangut]
(a) I.36 ditto
C.C.C.9[b] 辛 "the 8th stem"

4475 [Tangut] III 7 [Tangut] |
(a) V 185 ditto
| [Tangut] C.C.C.23[a] 杓 笊 籬 "spoon, ladle, bamboo fence." [? error for 4477]

4476 [Tangut] I 27 [Tangut] [Tangut] 1942
(a) VI 26 | [Tangut] 0870
| [Tangut] C.C.C.14[b] 蘿 蔔 "carrots, turnips"

4477 [Tangut] VII 84 | [Tangut] 2510
(a) IX 6 | [Tangut] 3458 ~~4477~~
(b) IX 20 | [Tangut] 5711
See 4475

4478 2298 chain

4478 v. 5094

4483 5690 chain

4484
3159
4961

~~W. II 124~~

B.159[1,2] | 衣 as. 碑文 inscription monumental
173[5,4]
B122 記 'to record'

4485
0092 A
3225

4479-0682
1201-4904

4480-3101

4486 4651 chain

4487 4027 chain

4481 3086 chain

4482 2596 chain

4488 3801 chain

4478

(a) IX

(i) By itself

(ii) W.I.122

W.I.136

(iii) W.II 18

disperse

(iv) |

'to chain

Spoir. ba

4479

(a) IX 6

4480

(a) IX

4481

4482

(i) W II 72[3] 肩

(ii) The

肩背

344

4478 [Tangut] I 84 | [Tangut] 2298

(a) IX 54 ditto

(i) By itself W II 72³ 失 to lose B.188³

(ii) W.I.122⁹ ? B 200¹ s.v. 237² 出

W.I.136² ? 2209

(iii) W.II 18⁶ | [Tangut] 散 失 to scatter, disperse & lose.

(iv) | [Tangut] W.I.198¹⁰ bsal.bar gyur.ba "to cleanse, atone for": W I 206⁸² spon.ba "to avoid, shun

4479 [Tangut] III 94 | [Tangut] 0682 ~~086~~

(a) IX 62 ditto

4480 [Tangut] VII 112 | [Tangut]

(a) IX 64 ditto

4481 [Tangut] III 64 | [Tangut] 5723

4482 [Tangut] wa II 38 死 | "back" 0055

(i) W II 72³ 肩 "shoulder".

(ii) The dissyllable reversed C.C.C. 18⁶ 肩 背 "shoulder breast, back".

4483 [Tangut] VIII 5 | [Tangut] 3809

4484 [Tangut] ?

(a) VII 112 | [Tangut] 4961

(b) IX 108 | [Tangut] 3169

(ii) | [Tangut] W II 8⁷ 授 記 II 42⁴ do. B.187⁴ 受記 124⁸ to receive a Buddha predestination. I 108¹¹ 授 決 "to give decisions

(i) ~~B.159¹ 碑 monument~~

4485 [Tangut] I.136 | [Tangut] 4092A

(a) I A62 [Tangut] | 3225

4486 [Tangut] I.118 [Tangut] "land"

C.C.C. 29⁶ 傷 "to injure" [metaphorically]

4487 [Tangut] V A32 [Tangut] | 0832 q.v.

(i) | [Tangut] C.C.C. 29⁶ 傷 害 "to injure & harm"

(ii) | [Tangut] C.C.C. 31ᵃ 毁 傷 "to destroy & harm" W.I. 134² do. 134¹⁵ takes 誅 傷殺

(iii) | [Tangut] W.I. 220³ gnod.pa "to hurt, harm". 0170

4488 [Tangut] IX 33 | [Tangut] 5551

W.I.138⁵ ?

4494 4027 chain

4489 = 2148

4494 W.II 100[11] 置 ~~a word of various meanings.~~ to set up, arrange B.216[1]

W.I.132[15] 抗 ~~to erect (a trap)~~

4490 2149 chain

4491 of 0741 chain

4492 2928 chain

(?)

4493 B 246[7] 何 to be able to (follows verb) 4495 2193 chain

4493 0899 chain

W.II 78[3] 從 'from' [Tangut] | 坐 |'from his seat'

W.I.135[-15] verbal affix 4496 1559 chain

4497 = 4433

345

4489 [Tangut] V.167 | [Tangut]
(a) V A 106

4490 [Tangut] ga V 167 | [Tangut]
W.I.166[18] II 56[12] B.237[2] 次 "for the second time". B.248[2] yai "again"

4491 [Tangut] VI 128 [Tangut] 0741

4492 [Tangut] II A 13 [Tangut] | 4591

4493 [Tangut] sti III 59 [Tangut] | 3908
A particle of obscure & various (?) uses. CCC.32[a] W.I.132[15,18] 168[11] 224[8]
II 2[6] 20[5] 24[4] 46[3] 46[11] 76[7] B.164[2]
(i) Verbal noun affix [Tangut] "to dwell"
[Tangut] [Tangut] "dwelling place" W II 2[6]
(ii) Participial? I 174[7] B.192[5]
(iii) | [Tangut] verbal affix II 76[7]
(iv) Auxiliary verb "to be able [Tangut] |
B.233[4]
[Tangut] 不可說 "cannot be said" W II 88[8]

4494 [Tangut] III 59 [Tangut] | 832
(a) I 70 [Tangut] | 2117
(b) VI 12 [Tangut] | 3456
[(c) VIII 91 [Tangut] x by [Tangut] [Tangut] |] 1180 0625
(d) IX 124 [Tangut] 2578
(i) W.I.190[8] bjog.po P.N. of a Khu
(ii) W.I 132[15]? B.164[5]
(iii) W.II.46[5] [Tangut] | 恭敬 "to respect & revere"
(iv) [Tangut] | 分散 "to scatter"

4495 [Tangut] III 43 [Tangut] | 3474
~~W.I.134[11]~~

4496 [Tangut] II 17 [Tangut] | I'E.w2
(a) III 11 ditto
~~W.I.168~~ (i) The 4 syllable W.I.168[1] 今 "now" II 44[4] 今從 "now & henceforward (?)" B.165[4]
B.230[4] [[Tangut]]

4497 [Tangut] III 6 | [Tangut]
(a) III 141 ditto
W.I.134[11][2]? B.161[1] (ornithic) 165[3] (Jou)
apparently 推 to push, shove takes [Tangut] or [Tangut]: 沈溺 to drown

4498 3685 chain

4499 -1698

4500 0754 chain

4501 0148 chain

4501 | [Tangut] 開闌 "to open or expound" W.II 4[9] 講宣 'to expound'.

4502 4083 chain

4502B [Tangut] | W.I 172[12] 結髮 'top-knot, uṣṇīṣa.'

4503 5678 chain

4504 2906 chain

4505 Φi | [Tangut] 修羅 Asura W.I 170[8]

4505-2175.

B.227[4] 秀 Hsiu ? phon.

4506 ┬ 1829
└ 4401

4507 — 4401

4508 - 2259

4509 0356 chain

4498 [Tangut]

A Phone…

4499 [Tangut]

(a) VI…

4500 [Tangut]

4501 [Tangut]

(a) V 9…

(b) IX…

C.C.C. 13[a]…

open, ex…

(ii) W II 3…

4502 [Tangut]

(a) V 2…

(b) VI…

W.I 136[18] 13…

"power…

4502A…

4502B [Tangut]

= ?= 4507…

4503 [Tangut]

W II 44[2]…

語…

B.176[5] 左…

346

4498 □ VIII A 105 □ □

A Phonetic character

4499 □ VII 31 | □

(a) VI 36 ditto

4500 □ I 84 | □ 3119

4501 □ I 144 □ | 0148

(a) V 90 | □ 1160

(b) IX 26 □ | × 0172

C.C.C. 13[a] W.I.134[17] II 4[9] 開 "to open, explain" B.186[5]

(ii) W II 34[2] 解 "to explain" 104[10]

4502 □ VIII A 67 | □ 4083

(a) V 2 □ | 3807

(b) VI 78 | □ ×0080 3186

W.I.136[18] 138[9] II 14[10] 勢 I.218[10] B.171[3] *dbain* "power, influence" B.176[5] (part of P.N.)

4502A □ = □ 3579

4502B □ IX 9 □ × by | □ 1304 2331

? = 4507 v. 2439

4503 □ V A 31 | □ "I". 3983

W II 44[2] translates 能 "can", translated by 語 "say" which seems right.

B.176[5] 左 "as follows"

4504 □ VII 112 □ | 2906

4505 □ VI 77 | □

(a) I 22 ditto [□] misspelt

(i) The dissyllable B.100 cat. under "horse"

4506 □ III 78 □ | 1829

(a) I 147 ditto [□]

(b) III 56 | □ 4401

(i) By itself W II 30[4] 析 "to divide" B.163[2] B.122[2] 分

(ii) □ | W.I.134[5,9,10,12,13] ? 2143 (138, ?)

4507 □ VII 59 blank. (a) III 56 4401

might be 4502B or 4510A

On the edge of a tear, possibly misspelt.

4508 □ I 34 | □

(a) I 55 ditto

?

4509 □ III 176 | □

(a) VIII 28 ditto

(i) The dissyllable B.101 cat. under "wild animals".

4515 3446 chain

4515 (ii) 宣 "to proclaim, promulgate

W. II 134[6]

4510 ┼4831 └2108–5313

4510A 4688 pair

4511 2485 chain

4516 ┼5238 └1906

4512 ┼3560 └4457–2745

4513 3011 chain

4517 4620 pair

4514 4026 chain

4518 ┼5266 └1004

~~4510~~

4510

(a) III 13

(b) IX

4510A

? = 450

4511

~~4512~~

(i) The

帕 han

4512

(a) VIII

(b) I

?

4513

(a) IX

4514

(i) The

"to make

(ii)

the hai

(iii) by its

347

~~4510~~ III 90

4510 VI.32 | 4831

(a) III 13 ditto

(b) IX 42 | ×(5313) 2108

4510A × of IX 143 | 4888

? = 4507
4511 ~~4512~~ III 90 | 1458

(i) The dissyllable C.C.C. 25[b] 手帕 handkerchief.

4512 I 136 | 3560

(a) VIII 18 ditto

(b) I 27 | 4457 q.v. above ×2745 4457

?

4513 I 84

(a) IX 8 × by |

4514 VI 67 | 2426

(i) The dissyllable W.I. 108[7] 作禮 "to make reverence" 170[5] B.128[4]

(ii) (1060) | W.II. 4[4] 頂禮 "to bow the head"

(iii) By itself B. 346[3] 禮 'reverence, to revere'

4515 Tsê VI 76 | misspelt 3446

(b) I 10 | 2738 ?

(a) III A 30 ditto 3446

(c) VI 10 |

(d) VI A 95 | ×3482 3485

(i) By itself Passim 說 "to say, speak" W.I. 198[13] gsuis. pa "to speak" B.254 bśad. pa exposition [noun] ~~"to preach"~~

(ii) | C.C.C. 6[b] 句陳 (name of a constellation) ? phonetic

4516 V 97 | (misspelt)

(a) IX A 42 ditto 5238

(b) VIII 13 | 1906

4517 V 6 |

(a) I 27 ditto

[(b) VIII 87 × of |] 5649 2895 4622

4518 VI A 88 | 5266

(a) III 115 ditto

(b) VI 19 | 1004

?

4519 – 4519A (? = 4521)

4519A 4519 pair

4520 1826 chain

4521 ~~1222 chain~~

4522 3685 chain

4523 0809 chain

4524 3929 chain

4524 (c) V.16

(ii) (c) above W.I.162[8] 決斷

decided, decisive

4525 4455 chain

4526 5462 chain

4527 1891 chain

4528 1891 chain

4529
- 4412A
- 0513
- 3499
- 4169

4530 independent

4519

4519A

? = 452

4520

(a) III

4521
~~4522~~

(a) VIII

(b) I

(c) VIII

(i) C.C.C. 21

(ii) W.I. 13

(iii) B.180[4]

(iv) W.I. 21

4522
~~4523~~

(a) VIII

(b) VIII

(c) VIII

(a) – (c)

4524

(i) |

wick" (

16) 決斷

348

4519 [Tangut] III 68 [Tangut] |

4519A [Tangut] See 4519

? = 4521

4520 [Tangut] III 111 [Tangut] |

(a) III 121 ditto

4521 ~~4522~~ [Tangut] IX 34 [Tangut] | to respect 1222

(a) VII 32 ditto

(b) I 28 | [Tangut] ? 5324

(c) VIII 96 | [Tangut] 5329

(i) C.C.C. 21a 鬘

(ii) W.I. 138[13] 鬟 "top-knot"

(iii) B. 180[4] 纓 "tassel, fringe"

(iv) W.I. 216[4] hp'ren.ba "garland"

cf 4519A

4522 ~~4523~~ [Tangut] VIII 38 [Tangut] | "name" 4368

(a) VIII A 102 [Tangut] x by | [Tangut]

(b) VIII A 103 [Tangut] x by | [Tangut] 1709

(c) VIII A 108 [Tangut] x by | [Tangut]

(a)–(c) are phonetic characters

4523 [Tangut] III 180 | [Tangut] 5271

(i) | [Tangut] C.C.C. 23b 燈草 "lamp wick" (?)

(aa) V 16 4225

4524 [Tangut] VI 78 | [Tangut] 3929 x 5406

(a) V 24 | [Tangut]

(b) VI 52 [Tangut] | 4270

← V. 3603

W. I 176[13] 快 swift, keen

4525 [Tangut] V A 19 [Tangut] |

(a) V 123 ditto

4526 [Tangut] III 180 | [Tangut]

C.C.C. 21a W. I 136[1] 燒 "to burn"

W. II 100[1] 燃 "to lik(?)e, burn"

4527 [Tangut] III 108 [Tangut] | 4891

~~(a) II~~

(a) V 113 | [Tangut] 2768

(b) VIII 27 | [Tangut] [[Tangut] 4528

4528 [Tangut] VIII 27 [Tangut] (?) |

4529 [Tangut] VIII 96 [Tangut] 4412A

(a) III 172 [Tangut] | 3499

(b) VII A 24 | [Tangut] 0513

(c) IX 59 [Tangut] | 4169

(i) W. II 24[9] 敷 [? to clothe / to make known]

4530 [Tangut] IX 79 Family or clan name

(ii) W. I. 132[16] 罾 large square net

4531 1822 — 1819 / 2281

4540 1424 pair

4532 2928 chain

4539 0731 chain

4533 0671 pair

4541 — 4542 — 0654 / 2220 / 3164

4535 3663 chain

4542 4541 chain

4536 4427 chain

4537 - 2031

4538 0908 pair

4531

(a) IX 8

4532

(a) IX 1

B.185[2] ?

4533

(a) VIII

4534

4535

(a) VI 9

Dict 1b 3

4536

(a) V.

4537

(a) IX

W.L. 218

4538

(a) V

349

4531 [illegible] V.166 | [illegible] × 1822

(a) IX 84 ditto

4532 [illegible] IX 171 | [illegible] 847

(a) IX 18 | [illegible] ?meaning 4438

B.185² ? B.164²

4533 [illegible] V 166 [illegible] |

(a) VIII 40 ditto

4534 [illegible] V A28 | [illegible]

4535 [illegible] V A71 [illegible] | 3663

(a) VI 9 | [illegible]

Dict 1ᵇ3 54ᵃ5

4536 [illegible] VII A138 [illegible] | 4427

(a) V A 53 ditto

4537 [illegible] VI 2 | [illegible] ? 2031

(a) IX 79 ditto

W.L.218⁹ Phonetic ɪe

4538 [illegible] II 9 [illegible]

(a) V 87 [illegible] |

4540 ~~4539~~ [illegible] V 6 [illegible] | 1424

(a) VI 113 ditto

4539 ~~4540~~ [illegible] VI A114 [illegible] | "wood"

(i) The dissyllable C.C.C. 22ᵇ 木檻 "wooden railing"

4541 [illegible] V 6 | [illegible]

(a) V 45 ditto

(i) The dissyllable C.C.C. 23ᵃ 器皿 "vessel, dish"

4542 [illegible] ngu V 45 [illegible] |

(a) V 6 ditto

(b) V 3 | [illegible] 2220

(c) VI 1 [illegible] | 0654

(d) IX A124 [illegible] | 3164

(i) By itself W.L.150¹ 器 "vessel, utensil" W.L.98³ ? B.169¹

(ii) The dissyllable C.C.C. 23ᵃ 器皿 "vessel, dish"

(iii) (c) above C.C.C. 23ᵇ 茶曰 "tea-pot"

4543 2579 chain

4544
- 4654
- 0849
- 0885–0922
- 2712
- 4258
- 4563 – [1330]
- 4571
- 4594
- 4608
- 5134

4545 1543 chain

4545A 0741 chain

4545B ~~5496 pair~~ error for 4555 q.v.

4546 3655 chain

[4547] 1272 chain

4548 1283 chain

4549 4550 chain

4550
- 4549
- 0496
- 1400
- 4458

4551 3626 chain

4545AA

4543

4544

(a) IX

(b) III

(c) V

(d) V

(e) V

(f) V

(g) VII

(h) VII

(i) IX

(ii) IX

(i) By itse

W.I.134

(ii) (e) ab

"leather

4545

(a) IX

4545A

4545B

W.I.168

4545AA [Tangut] B.132[17] 蜆 mussels hsien ? loan-word

350

4543 [Tangut] VI A113 [Tangut] | vinegar? 693

4544 [Tangut] nja VII 117 | [Tangut] 4654

(a) IX 94 ditto

(b) III 102 [Tangut] |

(c) V 53 | [Tangut]

(d) V 104 [Tangut] |

(e) V A42 | [Tangut] 4594

(f) V A137 | [Tangut] 2712

(g) VII 49 | [Tangut] x[1330] 4563

(h) VIII 17 | [Tangut] x(0922) 0885

(i) IX A43 [Tangut] | 0849

(k) IX 56 4258

(i) By itself W.I.214[9] hp'ags.pa

& W.I.134[2] ? ?B.131[1] 皮.

(ii) (e) above C.C.E. 25[a] 皮 裘 "leather garments."

4545 [Tangut] V 104 | [Tangut] 3673

(a) IX 49 | [Tangut]

4545A [Tangut] x of V 5 [Tangut] |

Error for 4371

4545B [Tangut] x of VII A51 | [Tangut]

W.I.168[15] 斫 "to amputate"

4546 [Tangut] VI 73 [Tangut] | 3655

(a) IX 34 | [Tangut] 3652

(i) W.I.132[17]? ?B176[3] P.N.

(ii) [Tangut] | B.101 cat. under "sheep" 1481

4547 [Tangut] IX A138 [Tangut] | 1272

(a) IX 180 ditto

4548 [Tangut] V 104 | [Tangut]

(a) V 116 ditto

4549 [Tangut] II 44 [Tangut] | 4550

(a) VI 83 ditto

4550 [Tangut] tu VI 83 | [Tangut] 4549

(a) II 44 ditto

(b) I 136 | [Tangut] 4458

(c) III 19 | [Tangut] (misspelt) 0496

(d) IX 154 | [Tangut] 1400

W.I.216[3] sag "fat"?

4551 [Tangut] VI 119 [Tangut] |

4552 2033 chain

4553 2906 chain

4554 2991 chain

4555
- 5496
- 4592
- 4593

4556 1449 chain

4558 5632 chain

4557 0655 chain

4559 3449 chain

4560 1992 chain

4561 W II 4[4] apparently "to" of motion to a place.

W. II 84[6] to 乃 then

W. II 88[10] 於 [to speak] "about"

W. II 90[4] practically meaningless, indicates object or quasi-inst.

"he said (in) a gāthā"

4561
- 3271
- 0074 — 1968 — 1872
- 0463 — 0465 2317 — 2318, 2322
- 0468
- 1230
- 1231
- 1244
- 3758
- 4056 — 1969 —, 2795
- 4347

4552

(a) IX

c.c.c. 29

4553

4554

(i)

strings

4555

(a) I

(b) III

W. I. 134[1]

Note. The

4556

(a) IX

4559

4557

(a) IX

351
352

? 2033

4552 [Tangut] IX A128 [Tangut] |

(a) IX 43 ditto

C.C.C. 29a chain 2033

4553 [Tangut] IX 35 [Tangut] | 2906

4554 [Tangut] III 118 | [Tangut] 2996

(i) | [Tangut] C.C.C. 32a "絃" "(having) strings" (of an instrument) v. 3530.

4555 [Tangut] VII 106 | [Tangut] misspelt 5496 'VII A 51 ditto

(a) I 76 | [Tangut] [Tangut]

(b) III A 100 | [Tangut] [Tangut]

W.I. 134[1,2] ? 烹 "to cook" or "kill"?

Note. The last component sh'd be [Tangut].

4556 [Tangut] III 55 [Tangut] | flesh 1449

(a) IX 79 [Tangut] | 4747

4558 [Tangut] VI 25 | [Tangut]

4557 [Tangut] VI A 123 [Tangut] | 0655

(a) IX A.16 ditto

4559 [Tangut] I 2 [Tangut] | 3449

(a) VII 15 ditto

4560 [Tangut] II 43 [Tangut] [Tangut] not to go (in haste) 1992

4561 [Tangut] Ri IX 22/22 | [Tangut] 3271

(a) IX 17 ditto [[Tangut]]

(b) II 5 | [Tangut] xxx 0074

(c) III 46/47 | [Tangut] 3758

(d) III 51 | [Tangut] "to reach" x 4056

(e) IX 97 | [Tangut] 4347

(f) V A 38 | [Tangut] 1231

(g) VII A 77 | [Tangut] x 0463

(h) VIII 71 | [Tangut] 1230

~~(i) IX 22~~ Rather an uncertain ~~(j) IX 22~~ particle, very common. On the whole it seems to represent an instrumental postpos"; but this does not always fit very well. v. 1968

C.C.C. 36b W.I. 96[10] 98[2] 100[7] 136[2] 198[12]

II 4[4] 10[5] 16[8] 22[11] 24[3] 32[7] (36[5]) (34[1]) 38[4,6]

50[9] 82[2] B211[2] ("to") 234[1] 所

125[2] tr. 從

I 269[13] (instr.) B.124[3]

B. 192[2] tr. 所 192[4]

4562 2395 chain

4563 4544 chain

4564 3549 chain

4565 3765 chain

4566 – 4008

4567 3086 chain

4568 5356 chain

4569 – 1768

4570 3226 chain

4571 ~~4544 chain~~

4572 – 4049

4573
⊥ 2797 – 2171

4574 3462 pair
~~⊥ 2797 – 2171~~

4575 0471 ~~pair~~

W.I 270[20] 行 row, line
error for 3632

4562

4563

(a) VII

W.I.134

4564

(a) V

4565

4566

(a) I

(i) |

4566A

4567

4568

4569

(a) IX

?

352

353

4562 [Tangut] II 33 [Tangut] | 2530

4563 [Tangut] VII 49 [Tangut] |

(a) VII 16) [Tangut] | [1330]

W.I.134³? 屠 "to kill, butcher".

4564 [Tangut] VI 19 [Tangut] | 3549

(a) V 65 ditto

4565 [Tangut] VI 15 [Tangut] | 3703

4566 [Tangut] III A 39 | [Tangut]

(a) I A 4 ditto

(i) | [Tangut] W.I.198³ su, ba "a sort of ulcer".

4566A [Tangut] error for 4561

4567 [Tangut] V 26 [Tangut] |

4568 [Tangut] IX A 107 | [Tangut] 3289

4569 [Tangut] VIII 7 | [Tangut] 1768

(a) IX 2 ditto

4570 [Tangut] VII 29 [Tangut], [Tangut] 2342

"auxiliary word".

C.C.C. 34⁶ 方 W II 22⁴ B. 228² q.v. 229²

而 W II 4¹² B. 187⁴ 186⁵ tu 故 (? wrong)

To complete since W II 32¹⁰ 40² 88¹⁰

A conjunction "and, then, now".

4571 [Tangut] V 53 [Tangut] |

[(a) III A 115 [Tangut] (2214) x by [Tangut] (2211) |]

4571A [Tangut] x of VIII A 110 | [Tangut]

4572 [Tangut] V 25 | [Tangut]

(a) V 3 ditto

4573 [Tangut] V 104 | [Tangut]

(a) IX 107 ditto

4574 [Tangut] V 2 [Tangut] |

(a) I 34 ditto

4575 [Tangut] IX 115 | [Tangut] 0471

(a) I 130 ditto

4576 0233 chain

4577 + 3027
2977

4578 4027 chain

4579 4651 chain

4580 0148 chain

4581 4090 pair

4581 bis 0258 chain

4582 5578 chain

4583 + 4571 A
4279

4584 0809 chain

4585 5491 chain

4586 2596 chain

4587 4326 chain

4588 - 3316 A

4589 4357 chain

4590 5394 pair

4576
(a) VIII
?(b) III
?

4577
(a) II
(b) VI
ccc. 31b

4578
(a) V
?

4579
ccc. 30b ?
Note. 4
Distingu

4580
(a) II
(b) IX
?

4581
(a) IX

353

4576 [Tangut] I 14 [Tangut] | 0233
(a) VIII 4 ditto
?(b) III 118 [Tangut] x by [Tangut] | 1408 (5159)
?
4577 [Tangut] II 4 | [Tangut] 3027
(a) II A 4 ditto
(b) VIII 83 | [Tangut] 2977
C.C.C. 31b 曉 "to understand" or "dawn"

4578 [Tangut] VIII 12 | [Tangut] 3095 ? 3098
(a) V 138 | [Tangut] x (1097) 3035
?
4579 [Tangut] VIII 95 [Tangut] | 4070
C.C.C. 30b ? 問 "to ask"
Note. 4576–4579 are barely distinguishable.
4580 [Tangut] IX 8 | [Tangut] 4042
(a) II 17 [Tangut] | x 5159
(b) IX 22 | [Tangut] 3894
?
4581 [Tangut] IX 8 [Tangut] |
(a) IX 31 ditto

VIII 21
4581 bis [Tangut] | 3028 (v. 3627) 354
4582 [Tangut] V 104 | [Tangut]
4583 [Tangut] VIII A 110 [Tangut] | 4571A
(a) VII 11 | [Tangut] 4279
4584 [Tangut] V 104 | [Tangut] 5043
(a) V 160 [Tangut] x by [Tangut] |
(i) The trisyllable C.C.C. 15a 吃兜芽

4585 [Tangut] I 101 | [Tangut]
W. II. 132² 輕 'light' (not 'heavy')
4586 [Tangut] IX 36 | [Tangut] 3308
4587 [Tangut] V 135 [Tangut] | 4964
4588 [Tangut] I 75 | [Tangut]
(i) [Tangut] | C.C.C. 18b 耳塞 "ear plug"
4589 [Tangut] V 19 [Tangut] | 4137
4590 [Tangut] VII 117 [Tangut] |
(a) IX 123 ditto

4591 2928 chain

4592 4555 chain

4593 4555 chain

4594 4544 chain

4595 - [1542]

4596 - 3624

4597 3086 chain

4598 4083 chain

4599 4607 chain

4600 - 2119

4601 0271 chain

4602 3086 chain

4603 0741 chain

4604 3086 chain

4591

4592

W. I. 134

4593

4594

4595

4596

4597

4598

4599

354

355

4591 [Tangut] V 171 [Tangut] | 0446
(a) II A 13 | [Tangut] 4492

4592 [Tangut] III A 100 [Tangut] |
W. I. 134³ ? 割 injure

4593 [Tangut] I 76 [Tangut] |

4594 [Tangut] V A 42 [Tangut] |
(i) The disyllable C.C.C. 25ª 皮裘 "leather garments".

4595 [Tangut] I 13 | [Tangut]
(a) I 82 ditto

4596 [Tangut] IX 16 | [Tangut]
(a) IX 109 ditto

4597 [Tangut] I 50 [Tangut] |

4598 [Tangut] IX 118 [Tangut] | 4083

4599 [Tangut] II 30 [Tangut] | 3625 q.v.

4600 [Tangut] IX A 122 | [Tangut]
(a) IX 168 ditto

4601 [Tangut] I A 49 [Tangut] | ear 0271
(a) VIII 51 | [Tangut] 3819
W. II. 26⁶ 聾 "deaf".

4602 [Tangut] III 17 [Tangut] |
D. 164¹

4603 [Tangut] V. 5 | [Tangut]

4604 [Tangut] kyi V 104 [Tangut] | 3086
(a) I 50 | [Tangut] 4597
(b) III 3 | [Tangut] ×(2542) 0940
(c) III 10 | [Tangut] 3112
(d) III 14 | [Tangut] ×(0431) 3885
(e) III 17 | [Tangut] 4602
(f) III 44 | [Tangut] × 4246
(g) III 73 | [Tangut] 0059
(h) V 26 | [Tangut] 4567
(i) V 102 | [Tangut] 0910
(k) V 163 | [Tangut] 2549
[(k) V A 13 [Tangut] × by [Tangut]]
(l) V A 115 | [Tangut]
(m) VI 86 | [Tangut] 1416

4604. B.185[3] 所 'which'
B.220[4] 227[3] q.v.

W.I.268[8] (q.v.) 所 'which'

4605 4200 chain

4606 2601 chain

4607
3625 - 4599
5298
5508

W.I.267[13] 云 'to be called' (certain)
B.185[5], 186[2,3] 195[5] to name (q.v.)
B.216[51] to utter, cry, call, 呼
B.220[5] 名 to be named.

4608 4544

4609 - 1607

4610 0609
| B.171[5] tr. 舉 to raise

4610A 1938 pair

4604 co
(n) VI
(o) VI
(p) VI
(q) VI
(r) IX
A-part
various
(i) C.C.C. 34[6]
(ii) W II 4[4]
(vii)
(iii) W II 16
(iv) W II 18[4]
(v) |
(vi)
"what i

4605
(a) I 6

4606
(a) IX 6
C.C.C. 19[a]

355

356

4604 cont.

(n) VI 132 | 4756

(o) VI A6 | ×5085

(p) VII 27 | 3211

(q) VII 95 | ×4399 3768

(r) IX 177 | ×1468

A particle of obscure & probably various meanings.

(i) CCC.34[b] 巳 (i) "already" W.I.206[7] to.

(ii) W II 4[11] : I 172[3]

(vii) 雖 although W.II 104[8]

(iii) W II 16[5] 既 already

(iv) W II 18[4] 將 "will" 124[9]

(v) | W II 20[8,11] 當 "must" 44[6], 104[2]

(vi) | W II 22[11] 60[11] 云何爲 "what is?"

4605 IX 109 |

(a) I 65 ditto

4606 IX 113 | "blood"

(a) IX 60 | [? ditto] 3451 V. 4249A

CCC. 19[a] 脈 "vein"

4607 VIII 7 | ×4599 3625

(a) VIII 7 ditto

~~(b) II 30~~

(b) III 3 | 5308

(c) VII 70 | 5298

CCC. 31[b] [? might be] 謂 "to be called" [uncertain, might be 乎?]

W.I.108[1] final particle or 名 "name"

W II 16[3] 28[3] 44[7]

See 3265. Clearly ends quotations. On the whole this looks more like a final particle than a verb.

I.168[4] clearly final particle.

4608 V 104 |

4609 I 11 | 1607

(a) II 9 ditto [

4610 III 34 |

(a) VI 34 ditto

(b) VII A73 | 3030

(i) The dissyllable CCC. 33[a] 34[a] 准備 B.164[4]

(ii) dissyl. unnecl B 170[3]

4610A x of I 20 |

4611 -5054 pair

4612 3206 pair

4613 -2155

B.172 tr. 成 'completely'

4614 - 4616

4615
2072
0474

4616 4614 pair

4617
4685 - 4698
5619

4618 1130 chain

4619
5408
0475
3185

4620 3665

4620 A
4621 - 5469

4611

(a) VII

46

4612

(a) I 1

(i) The

産 "pro

4613

(a) VII

B

4614

(a) IX

4615

(a) V 2

(b) V

ccc. 9

4616

(a) IX

356

357

4611 [Tangut] III.34 [Tangut] | 凡

(a) VII 64

~~46~~

4612 [Tangut] III 34 [Tangut] |

(a) I 1 ditto

(i) The dissyllable C.C.C. 26b 財産 "property & patrimony"

4613 [Tangut] III 18 | [Tangut]

(a) VII 42 ditto

~~[illegible]~~ B 171[1] [Tangut] | tr. 一閃 ? moment one flash

4614 [Tangut] IX 22 | [Tangut]

(a) IX 152 ditto

4615 [Tangut] III A 121 [Tangut]

(a) V 24 ditto

(b) V A 99 | [Tangut] 0474

C.C.C. 9a ~~W.I.~~ W.I. 92[2] etc 雷 W.I. 190[14] tbrug. "thunder"

4616 [Tangut] IX 152 [Tangut] |

(a) IX 22 ditto

4617 [Tangut] VII 44 | [Tangut]

(a) IX A 83 ditto [but X has [Tangut]]

(b) I 36 | [Tangut]

(i) (b) above C.C.C. 7b 霹靂 "thunder clap"?

(ii) By itself B 221[1] 靂

4618 [Tangut] VII 17 [Tangut] | 1130

W.I. 220[14] mechu ~~[illegible]~~ "name of lunar mansion"

4619 [Tangut] I 8 | [Tangut]

(a) VIII 11 ditto

(b) I 58 | [Tangut] 3185

(c) VII 33 | [Tangut] 0475

C.C.C. 10b 曉 "dawn"

4620 [Tangut] ~~[illegible]~~ VII 4 | [Tangut]

(a) VI 95 ditto

(i) By itself B.187[1] B 217[3] etc. W.I. 120[4] 140[12] 仙 "sage"

(ii) The dissyllable W.I. 224[5] etc. drai sroi "sage"

4620 ~~4619~~ A [Tangut] X of V 133 [Tangut] |

4621 [Tangut] V 133 | [Tangut]

(a) IX 138 | [Tangut]

?

4622 - 4517

4623 independent

4624 0016 chain

4625 0434 chain

4626 2716 chain

4627
⊥ 5176 ┬ 1496
├ 4657
└ 5151

[4628] 2158 chain

[4629] 0970 chain

[4630] ~ 1613 Double name

4635 4651 chain

4631 2485 chain

4632 4651 chain

4633 1473 bis chain

4634 independent

4636 4773 chain

4637 4651 chain

4638 4651 chain

4639
├ 0991
└ 4702

4640 2353 chain

4641 4651 chain

4622
(a) V

4623

4624
W.I. 132

4625

4626

4627

4628
(a) V

4629
(a) V
B 176

~~4630~~

4630
(a) IX
Presumab

4622 [Tangut] I 27 | [Tangut] 4517
(a) V 6 ditto

4623 [Tangut] V 165 Name of country

4624 [Tangut] IX A 48 [Tangut] |
W.I. 132[15] ? 168[5] & 塗 'mud'
~~? pitfall~~ pitfall for catching game

4625 [Tangut] V A 105 [Tangut] | 434

4626 [Tangut] IX 152 [Tangut] |

4627 [Tangut] III 59 | [Tangut] 5176
(a) VI 17 ditto

4628 [Tangut] VI 86 [Tangut] | 2158
(a) V 71 ditto

4629 [Tangut] VIII 6 [Tangut] |
(a) VI 33 | [Tangut] 3059
B 176[4] 瓦 tile, brick

~~4630 [Tangut] III~~
4630 [Tangut] III 54 Family or clan name
(a) IX A 95 | [Tangut] 1613
Presumably a double name

357 358

4635 [Tangut] I 56 [Tangut] |

4631 [Tangut] III 54 [Tangut] [Tangut] 2485

4632 [Tangut] III 94 | [Tangut] cultivated land 1941 4638
(a) I 29 [Tangut] ?

4633 [Tangut] I 65 | [Tangut] 4345

4634 [Tangut] IX 63 x by self [|] |

4636 [Tangut] IX 9 | [Tangut]

4637
~~4636~~ [Tangut] III 13 | [Tangut] 2182
(a) VII 15 [Tangut] | [[Tangut]] 0659
Dict. 1[a]6 [[Tangut]] B. 169[5] [[Tangut]] B 191[2] [[Tangut]] q.v.

4638 [Tangut] I 29 | [Tangut] ? 4632

4639
~~4638~~ [Tangut] VII 57 – [tone]
(a) I 85 | [Tangut] 4702
(b) III 71 [Tangut] x by (a) 0991
(i) 穴 'cave, burrow' W.I. 134[11]
(ii) 孔 ~~'hole'~~ pore (in the skin) / W II 76[5]
(iii) 竅 '(ear) hole' C.C.C. 18[b]

4640
~~4639~~ [Tangut] V 59 [Tangut] | 2371

4641
~~4640~~ [Tangut] VII A 78 [Tangut] |

4642 1713 chain

4648 – 1764

4643 4701 chain

4649
┬ 5709 – 5595
└ 4670 – 4534

4644 2278 chain

4650 independent

4645 4651 chain

4646 independent

4651
┬ 2504
├ 0473 – 1124
├ 0477
├ 1629
├ 1902
├ 1941 – 4632 – 4638
├ 2182 ┬ 4637 – 0659
│ └ 4682
├ 2686
├ 3194
├ 4070 ┬ 3939
├ 4486 └ 4579
├ 4635
├ 4641
├ 4652
├ 4645
├ 4668
├ 4671
└ 5130

4647 1488 chain

359

4642 VI 14 | 4774
(a) I 86 | 4867
(b) VII 51 | 5243
(i) By itself C.C.C. 22b W.I. 134 11,15 土 W.I. 192 9 s.a. "earth, soil".
(ii) (a) about C.C.C. 12a 土 沙 "earth or sand".

4643 II 24 | [misspelt]
(a) IX 31 ditto

4644 V 72 | temple 1939

4645 VI 103 | earth 4651
C.C.C. 26b 頃 to bow the head

4646 III A 26 "Name of country"
(a) III A 19 x by | 1511 3845

Note. (a) is a Phonetic?

4647 VIII 38 | 4405
(i) | B. 160 2 C.C.C. 28a 内 宿 "inner star" (name of temple) v. 3846

4647 A See 4635

4647 B VI 33 See 4701
(a) I 28

4648 I 16 |
(a) III 6 ditto
(i) The dissyllable W.I. 138 7 B. 159 1,2 塔 temple pagoda [not found separately?]

4649 IX A 27 | 5709
(a) IX A 41 ditto
(b) II 10 | × 4534 4649
(i) C.C.C. 13a 鑿 "to dig (a well)"
(ii) W.I. 132 15, 134 15 dig up / to dig (a pitfall)

4650 V A 74 Name of country

4651 IX 143 | 2504
(a) I 16 | 0477
(b) I 38 | ditto
(c) I 56 | 4635
(d) I. 118 | 4486
(e) II 44 | 2686
(f) III 61 | 1962
(g) III 128 | 4652
(h) V 135 | 4671
(i) V A 49 | × 3939 4579 4070

4652 4651 chain

4653
+1961
0733

4654 4544 chain

4655 independent

4656 1667 chain

4657 4627 chain

4658 5623 chain

4659
+4261
4677

4660 5152 chain

4661
+2260-1977
2948

4662 1406 chain

4651 (c

(j) VI

(k) VI

(l) VII

(m) VI

(n) VI

(o) IX

(p) IX

(q) IX

(r)

X of I

(i) 土也

c.c.c.

(ii)

4652

4653

(a) I

(b) VI

(i) c.c.c. 23

(ii) c.c.c.

4654

(a) VII

359

360

4651 (cont.)
(j) VI 24 | [Tangut] x(1124) 0473
(k) VI 29 | [Tangut] 1629
(l) VII 33 | [Tangut] diligent 4668
(m) VI 103 | [Tangut] to bow 4645 4668
(n) VII A 78 | [Tangut] 4641 xx 4638 x (4632)
(o) IX 75 | [Tangut] 1941
(p) IX 96 | [Tangut] (pp) 2182 IX 98 [Tangut]
(q) IX 129 | [Tangut] snore 3194
(r) | [Tangut] name of a country
x of I A 8 [Tangut] etc.
(i) 地 "earth" (as opposed to "heaven")
C.C.C. passim
(ii) | [Tangut] B 246[3] 地方 'place'

4652 [Tangut] IX 128 [Tangut] | 4651 earth

4653 [Tangut] VI A 26 | [Tangut] ? 1961
(a) I 20 ditto
(b) VI A 117 [Tangut] x [Tangut] | [Tangut] 1013 0733 Phonetic character
(i) C.C.C. 23[a] 土 "earth, soil"
(ii) C.C.C. 9[b] 己 "sixth stem"

4654 [Tangut] IX 94 [Tangut] |
(a) VII 117 ditto

4655 [Tangut] VIII A 48 name of country

4656 [Tangut] V 89 [Tangut] | 1667

4657 [Tangut] III A 94 | [Tangut]

4658 [Tangut] I A 95 | [Tangut] 0372
(a) III 42 | [Tangut] ? 4113

4659 [Tangut] VI 41 | [Tangut] 4261
(a) VI 80 ditto [misspelt]
(b) I 70 [Tangut] |
(i) W.I. 132[15] 戟 halberd
(ii) [Tangut] | B. 100 cat. under "camel"

4660 [Tangut] VIII 12 [Tangut] | 5152
(a) IX 16 [Tangut] | 1503

4661 [Tangut] III A 23 | [Tangut] chain 5152 x 1977 2260
(a) III 15 ditto
(b) III 57 [Tangut] 2948

4662 [Tangut] V 109 [Tangut] 1406
(a) IX 57 misspelt

4663 3685 chain
4671 4651 chain

4664 [1521] pair

4672 1536 chain

4673-3674A
4665 1781 chain
4673 Phonetic v. 虎

4674 3795 chain

4666 3174 pair

4675 1985 chain

4667 5491 chain

4668 4651 chain
4676 0752 chain

4669 4703 chain
4669 Φ(i) | 剎那 *kṣaṇa*
"a moment" W.II. 84[5]
Φ(ii) | 剎帝利 *kṣatriya* 4677 4659 chain
W.II 86[1]

4670 4649 chain

4663
4664
(a) III
(i) The ...
"wild ...
4665
(a) V A
(b) VII
4666
(a) VI
4667
4668
(a) I
C.C.C. 26[6]
4669
Frequently
4670
(a) V

360

361

4663 [Tangut] VIII 10 [Tangut] | "name"

4664 [Tangut] III 86 [Tangut] |

(a) III 103 ditto

(i) The dissyllable B.100 cat. under "wild animals".

4665 [Tangut] IX 150 | [Tangut] 1689

(a) V A 77 | [Tangut] 0948

(b) VII A 76 | [Tangut] 4679

4666 [Tangut] VIII A 33 [Tangut] | 3174

(a) VI A 89 ditto [Tangut]

4667 [Tangut] IX 54 [Tangut] | [Tangut]

4668 [Tangut] VI 33 [Tangut] | earth 4651

~~(a) I 28~~ ~~Error see~~ 4701

CCC. 26b 敏 diligent

4669 [Tangut] VII 36 [Tangut] |

Frequently used as a Phonetic.

4670 [Tangut] II 10 [Tangut] |

(a) V A 28 [Tangut] | 4534

4671 [Tangut] V 135 [Tangut] | [Tangut]

[(a) VII A 132 [Tangut] × by [Tangut] |]

4672 [Tangut] [Tangut] V. 135 | [Tangut] 1536

4672A [Tangut] × of V A 50 [Tangut] |

4673 [Tangut] VII 112 | [Tangut]

4674 [Tangut] VI 13 | [Tangut] ocean 2221

(i) The dissyllable B.103 cat. under 'rivers & seas'.

4675 [Tangut] NAN III A 65 [Tangut] [Tangut] 1985 P.N. of mountain 4697A ?4268

4675A ~~4676~~ [Tangut] See 468~~1~~ 4184

4676 [Tangut] VII 34 | [Tangut] 0118

4676A [Tangut] × of II 34 [Tangut] [Tangut]

4677 [Tangut] I 70 | [Tangut]

4678 4277 chain

4685 4617 chain

W.II 126[2] 閃

4679 1781 chain

4680 3685 chain

4681 0838 chain I.134[15] ?

4681 植 "to plant" (a root) W.II 104"

B.169[4] | 官作 (door)-keepers?

4682 4651 chain

4686 2427 pair

take over
4683 0042 chain

4687 independent

4684 3931 chain

4688 – 4510 A

361
362

4678 [Tangut] II 1 [Tangut] |

4679 [Tangut] VII A 76 [Tangut] | 4665

4680 [Tangut] VII 9 [Tangut] | "name"

4681 [Tangut] IX 3 [Tangut] |
(a) IX 67 [Tangut] × by | [Tangut] 1156
(b) IX 84 [Tangut] × by ditto 1814
A rather obscure word.
(i) By itself W.I. 134[15] II 6[4] 22[8]:
B.176[2] part of P.N. B 213[1] 結? to form
(ii) | [Tangut] c.c.c. 26[b] 農器 "agri-cultural implement".
(iii) | [Tangut] c.c.c. 27[a] 耕牛 "plough ox".

4682 [Tangut] I 122 [Tangut] |

4683 [Tangut] IX A 93 | [Tangut] 0042
(a) V 46 | [Tangut] 5373

4684 [Tangut] III 88 | [Tangut] 3931

4685 [Tangut] IX A 83 [Tangut] |
(a) VII 44 ditto [[Tangut]]
(b) VI 104 | [[Tangut]] [Tangut]
B. 89 [Tangut] ideogram [Tangut] ideogram.
| is [Tangut] | [Tangut], which is the word for
[Tangut] [Tangut] [shining brightly].
(i) By itself W.I. 218[2] glog "lightning"
W II 38[1].
(ii) (b) above c.c.c. 9[a] 閃電
W.I. 190[14] (194[14]) glog tshyin "lightning flash".
(iii) | [Tangut] W.I. 110[10] 大燈 "the great (sky) lantern".
Note. 4684 & 4685 are indistinguishable & troublesome. It is possible that the latter begins [Tangut] & the former [Tangut]. There is danger of confusion with 4681.

4686 [Tangut] VI 96 [Tangut] | 2427
B. 200[5] P.N. B 215[4] do.

4687 [Tangut] III 53 Family or clan (name)

4688 [Tangut] IX 143 | [Tangut]

4689 4868 chain

4691 independent

4692 4868 chain

4693 5204 chain

4694 5204 chain

4695 0464 pair

4696 0953 chain

4697 independent

4697 A = 4268 III

4698 4617 chain

4699 3685 chain

4700 1674 pair

4701
┼4643
└2171

?B.161² tr. 竅 'intelligence'

4702 4639 chain

W.I.270¹⁹

4703 (infinitely) B.341² 山谷 gully

4703
┼1295–4704
└4669

4690

4691

4692

4693

4694

4695

(a) III

4696

(a) III

(i) c.c.c.

4697

4697 A

(ii) W.I.

363

~~4689 IX 143~~

4690 III 106 |

4691 IX 49 Name of country.

4692 III A 15 | 0125
(a) IX 45

4693 VIII A 24 |

4694 VIII 10 |

4695 III 60 |
(a) III A 82 ditto

4696 IX 92 | "1st stem"
(a) III 86 ditto
(i) CCC. 9b 乙 2nd stem.

4697 VIII 15 Family or clan (name)

4697A X of III A 65 x by | 1985 4675

(ii) W.I. 216[5] ? to. tog "harvest"

4698 VI 104 |
(i) The dissyllable CCC. 9a 閃電 W.I. 190[14] 194[14] glog tly in "lightning flash" B 221[1] ro.
By itself B 227[5] 奉 ? phon?

4699 VI 77 | "name"

4700 IX 152 | 1674
(a) V 158 ditto

4701 IX 31 | 4643
(a) II 24 ditto
(b) I 28 | 伎 [misspelt] 2177
(i) By itself W.I. 100[5] 塵 "dust, 227[2] this world, illusion" B. 228[5] ditto
(ii) (a) above CCC. 13a 塵土 "dust & soil"

4702 I 85 | 4639
(a) III 71 x by dissyllable
(i) W.I. 144[6] 巖 "precipice" ~~B 341 岩 ditto~~ ? sh. be 4704 3 岩
(ii) W.I. 190[7] 216[17] brag "rock"
(iii) W.I. 216[8] stor. k'un "gutter" valley

4703 V 27 | 1296
(a) V 83 ditto X (4704) 1295
(b) VII 36 | 4669

4712A 4809 pair

4710–1986

4711 3812 chain

4704 4703 chain
4704. B.260[2] 巖 cliff, precipice
W.I 270[19] 岩 same as

4712
4832

4705 3259 chain

4713 – 4818

4706 independent

4707 (4390A) – 3358

4714 3694 pair

4708 1667 chain

4715 4775 chain

4716–1952

4709 1667 chain

4703
Note. 4
4702
4704
(i) The
"cliff
4705
(a) III
4706
4707
4708
(a) III 1
(i) The
B 221[3]
C.C.C. 16[a]
4709
(i) The
"wilt an

4703 cont.

?

Note. 4702 + 4703 are barely distinguishable. It is apparently 4702 which means 'rock' etc. + 4703 which means 'gully'.

4704 [Tangut] V 58 | [Tangut]

(i) The dissyllable C.C.C. 12[a] 崖谷 "cliff & valley".

4705 [Tangut] V 51 [Tangut] | 3259

(a) II 1 ditto

4706 [Tangut] [VII 59-60]

4707 [Tangut] VI 81 | [Tangut]

(a) III 16 ditto (misspelt)

4708 [Tangut] II 6 [Tangut] |

(a) III 173 ditto

(i) The dissyllable B.100 catalogue heading "wild animals".

B 221[3]

C.C.C. 16[a] 野獸 "wild animal"

4709 [Tangut] I 139 [Tangut] |

(i) The dissyllable B.101 cat. under "wild animals".

4712A [Tangut] × of VII 21 [Tangut] 3673

364

4710 [Tangut] II 6 | [Tangut]? 1986

(a) IX 103 ditto (badly spelt)

4711 [Tangut] I 139 | [Tangut]

4711

4712A [Tangut] See 53

4712 [Tangut] [VII 59-60]

(a) V 129 | [Tangut]

(i) By itself C.C.C. 19[a] 腰 "waist"

(ii) | [Tangut] C.C.C. 24[b] 腰 [Tangut] "waist band". B.103 cat. under "clothing".

4818

4713 [Tangut] I 31 | [Tangut] misspelt.

(a) II 16 ditto [[Tangut]]

4714 [Tangut] IX 53 [Tangut] |

(a) V 23 ditto

3700 V. 4739

V. 83

4714A [Tangut] Error for [Tangut]

4715 [Tangut] III A 135 [Tangut] |

4716 [Tangut] V 52 | [Tangut] 1952

(a) VII 1 ditto

W. I, 222[13] name of a planet? khag.pa

4717 3765 chain
4717 (iii) ~~...~~ (b) v. 3703

4723 independent

4724 5110 chain

4725 [3909] chain

[4726] 3134 pair

4718 3771 chain

4719 4775 ~~chain~~

4727 4734 ~~chain~~
B 223[2] (+ many others) 'once upon a time'

4720 1507 ~~chain~~ ~~troubled~~ B 227[2]

4721 3771 chain

4722
0587
1068 – 1164

4728 – 1854

4717
(a) VI
(i) C.C.C. 8
(ii) W.I. 21
B.
(iii)
drug" (
4718
(a) III
(i) By
(ii) The
4719
4720
4721
(a) I 2
4722
(a)
(b) IX
C.C.C. 29
W.I. 196
58

364

365

(b) VI 52 [Tangut] | ×3703

4717 [Tangut] VI 11 [Tangut] |

(a) VI 36 ditto

(i) C.C.C. 8[b] 膏 "unguent"

(ii) W.I. 210[3] sman.pa II 8[5] 藥 "drug"

B. 128[3] B. 216[2]

(iii) | [Tangut] C.C.C. 13[a] 芍藥 "peony drug" (name of a flower).

4718 [Tangut] VIII 7 | [Tangut] 3771

(a) III 137 | [Tangut] 0425

(i) By itself C.C.C. 34[a] (torn)

(ii) The dissyllable C.C.C. 34[b] (torn)

4719 [Tangut] V 151 [Tangut] |

4720 [Tangut] III 75 [Tangut] |

4721 [Tangut] I 6 | [Tangut] 3771

(a) I 22 ditto [干]

4722 [Tangut] nčê VII 40 | [Tangut] 0587

(a) VII A 143 ditto

(b) IX A 33 | [Tangut] ×(1164) 1068

C.C.C. 29[b] (W.I. 132[10] to exist) 有 "to have, having"

W.I. 196[1] 224[6] ldan.pa "having".

4723 [Tangut] II 26 Name of country.

4724 [Tangut] I 126 | [Tangut] Water

Dict. 1[a].1 B. 188[2] ? tr. 遠 distant

4725 [Tangut] I 20 [Tangut] | [3906] see 3905

4726 [Tangut] [VII 59-60]

(a) IX 39 [Tangut] | (error for [Tangut])

(i) The dissyllable C.C.C. 12[b] W.I. 92[10] 琥珀 "amber" B. 102 cat. under "precious things".

B 215[1] [Tangut] tr. 黄 yellow

4727 [Tangut] VI 87 [Tangut] | 4734

(a) I 8 | [Tangut] ×4730

(c) IX 41 [Tangut] | 4851

(b) V A 123 | [Tangut] B 220[5] 0255

(i) By itself C.C.C. 8[b] 9[b] & passim 時 in all its meanings "time, timely, at the time when...."

(ii) | [Tangut] W. I. 194[13] etc. dus. dus. su "sometimes".

4728 [Tangut] IX 39 | [Tangut]

(a) IX 109 ditto

(i) The dissyllable C.C.C. 9[b] 卓 [=朝?]

4734
- 5416
- 1091
- 2979
- 4727
  - 0255
  - 4730 – 3425
  - 4851

4729 ± 3173 / 4374

4730 4734 chain

4735 2724 pair

4731 1114 chain

4732 3504 pair

(4736 same as 4749)

4733 2253 chain

4737 independent [?]

4738 3144 chain

4734
- 5416
- 1091
- 2979
- 4727
  - 0255
  - 4851
  - 4730 – 3425

365

366

4728 cont.

午 "morning & noon".

4729 [Tangut] IX 115 | [Tangut] 3173

(a) III 141 ditto.

(b) IX 17 | [Tangut]

4730 [Tangut] I 8 [Tangut] | 4727

(a) IX 89 | [Tangut] 3425

4731 [Tangut] I 59 [Tangut] | 4216

(i) The dissyllable C.C.C. 20b

外男 生男

4732 [Tangut] I 43 [Tangut] |

(a) VII 44 ditto

4733 [Tangut] III A 24 [Tangut] |

(a) III 84 ditto

4734 [Tangut] nê III 131 | [Tangut] night

(a) V 27 ditto

(b) I 14 | [Tangut] 2979

(c) VI 87 | [Tangut] time × 4727

(d) VIII 38 | [Tangut] day (after numerals) 1091

(i) By itself 日 in all its meanings

(a) Specifically ~~day~~ "the sun" C.C.C. 10b

(b) ñin, ñi.ma "day" W.I. 198^6

[4374] (ii) 晝 "by day" II 20^4 78^11

(iii) | [Tangut] C.C.C. 10b 白日 0151

4735 [Tangut] II 13 [Tangut] | 2724?

(a) IX A 110 ditto

(i) 昊 "vast" C.C.C. 4a

(ii) W.I. 110^{8,18} etc. 廣 "vast, wide"

(iii) 弘 "vast" B. 185, 186^1

(iv) rgyas "wide" W.I. 214^6 216^18

(v) The dissyllable 廣博 "vast & wide" W.II 24^6

4736 [Tangut] VI 3 [Tangut] |

? Duplicate of 4749

4737 [Tangut] VIII A 56 "Family or clan name"

~~4736 A [Tangut] × of VII 21 | [Tangut]~~

4738 [Tangut] VI 4 [Tangut] 2367

4739 0023 pair

4740 3829 chain

4741 4775 chain

4742 2758 chain

4743 5110 chain

4744 4775 chain

4745 0194 chain

4746 1055 chain

4747 1449 chain

4748 3685 chain

4749 3891 chain

4750 2758 chain

4751 4326 chain

4752 3393 chain

4753 4326 chain

4739

4740

(i) The

"to-mo

4741

(i) The

鶴

4742

Phonet

4743

4744

4745

(a) V

4745A

4746

(ii) The

昴 W.T.L.

Pleiad

(i) By

367

4739 [Tangut] VI 74 [Tangut]

4740 [Tangut] VI 74 | [Tangut] 3326

(i) The dissyllable C.C.C. 10b 後日 "to-morrow"

q. 4744

4741 [Tangut] V 47 | [Tangut] 3008

(i) The dissyllable C.C.C. 16b 鸞鷟鶴

4742 [Tangut] VIII A 101 [Tangut]

Phonetic character

4743 [Tangut] VI 101 [Tangut] |

4744 [Tangut] VII 93 [Tangut] |

q. 4740

4745 [Tangut] I 29 [Tangut] | 194

(a) V 86 ditto

4745A [Tangut] Err. for [Tangut] 4844

4746 [Tangut] VI 101 [Tangut] [|]

(ii) The dissyllable C.C.C. 8a 欃昴 (W.I. 220⁹ smin. drug) "the Pleiades"

(i) By itself ditto

4747 [Tangut] IX 79 | [Tangut] ? 4556

chain 1449

4748 [Tangut] II 1 [Tangut] | ! 2438

(a) I 90 [Tangut] | "name" 3685

B. 271

4749 [Tangut] ? VI 3 [Tangut] | 3891

(a) VI 59 [Tangut] | "to think" 1950

(b) VI A 25 [Tangut] | "to think ? ditto" 3891

(c) IX A 92 | [Tangut] "to meditate on" 2039

(d) VI 3

(i) By itself. 想 "thoughts W.I. 98⁴ "to think" W.I. 136"

(ii) (b) above 思惟 "to think & consider" W.I. 112¹⁷

(iii) (c) above 思惟 ~~C.C.C. 31~~ "to think & consider" C.C.C. 31b W.II 28⁵ etc.

q. 4740

4750 [Tangut] VIII A 111 [Tangut]

Phonetic character

4751 [Tangut] II 20 | [Tangut] 4753

(i) | [Tangut] B. 100 cat. under "camel"

1650

4752 [Tangut] I 14 [Tangut] | "to laugh"

(a) I 73 ditto (misspelt)

4753 [Tangut] I. 14 | [Tangut] 4779

(a) II 20 [Tangut] | 4751

(b) IX 22 | [Tangut] 2393

4754-4817

4755 3776 chain

4756 3086 chain

4757 1992 chain

4758 4775 chain

4759 4824 pair

4760 3226 chain

4761 4819 chain

4762 0133 chain

4763 1781 chain

4764 2366 chain

4765 4276 chain

4766 2375 pair

4767 0556 pair

4768 0557 pair

4769 4039 chain

4754

(a) V

4755

(a) VI

4756

4757

4758

4759

(a) I

4760

(a) VIII

c.c.c. 10b

4761

4762

(a) V 2

(i) The ...

owl"

368

4754 [Tangut] V 112 | [Tangut]

(a) V 90 ditto [[Tangut]]

4755 [Tangut] VII 37 [Tangut] | 3776

(a) VI 77 ditto

4756 [Tangut] VI 132 [Tangut] | 4604

4757 [Tangut] VI 132 [Tangut] [Tangut] 1992 (not as go on leave)

4758 [Tangut] III A 85 [Tangut] |

4759 [Tangut] II 9 [Tangut] |

(a) I 11 ditto

4760 [Tangut] III 7 [Tangut] | 0577

(a) VIII A 27 [Tangut] |

C.C.C. 10^b 降 "abundant (rain)"

4761 [Tangut] III 66 [Tangut] |

4762 [Tangut] VII 19 [Tangut] | 0133

(a) V 2 ditto

(i) The dissyllable C.C.C. 17^a 老鴟 "old owl"

4763 [Tangut] I 29 | [Tangut] 1364

4764 [Tangut] VII 3 | [Tangut] ×(5504) 1471

(a) I 68 [Tangut] |

4765 [Tangut] V A 9 [Tangut] | × 2400

(a) I 36 | [Tangut]

(i) The dissyllable C.C.C. 20^b 大 小 "great & small"

(ii) By itself Dict 1^b 2 "principal"

4766 [Tangut] V 41 [Tangut] |

(a) VIII 2 ditto

4767 [Tangut] IX 146 [Tangut] |

(a) III 17 ditto but [Tangut]

cf. 4768

Note. [Tangut] is probably correct

4768 [Tangut] IX 146 [Tangut] |

(a) III 17 ditto

(i) The dissyllable C.C.C. 17^a 鶴鶉 ". . . & quail."

4769 [Tangut] V 51 [Tangut] |

(a) VI 39 ditto

4770 4793 pair

4771 0273 chain

4772 4775 chain

4773
- 3773
- 2968
  - 0428
  - 2396
  - 4312
  - 4334
  - 4636
  - 5582

4774 1713 chain

4775
- 0776
- 1307
- 1556
- 2537
- 2653
- 2657
  - 0419
  - 2534
  - 2656
  - 2661–3435
  - 3068–3067–5429
  - 3405
  - 3581
  - 3614
  - 3826
  - 4784
- 2992
- 3003
- 3008 / 4741
- 3009
- 3591
- 4715
- 4719
- 4744
- 4772
- 4758
- 4778–5597
- 4781
- 4782
- 4821–2995
- 4826
- 5153

(bb) B.221[3] C.C.C.16[b] v.2657

4770 [Tangut] V A104 [Tangut] |

(a) I 107 ditto [[Tangut]]

(i) The dissyllable [Tangut] CCC.16b W.I.132[18]

鵝 "goose".

4771 [Tangut] I 84 [Tangut] [Tangut]

(a) III 96 [Tangut] x by | [Tangut]

4772 [Tangut] IX 122 [Tangut] |

4773 [Tangut] V A20 | [Tangut] 3773

(a) V 19 ditto

(b) VIII 3 [Tangut] | 2968

(i) 君 "prince, nobleman" CCC.18a 29b 35a ~~+ passim~~.

(ii) 男 "male" W.I.98[3] etc.

(iii) 雄 a cock B.215[2]

4774 [Tangut] VI 51 [Tangut] |

(a) III 1 ditto

(b) VI 14 | [Tangut] 4642

CCC.8a 土 "the earth (star)"

4775 [Tangut] [VII 59-60]

(a) I 35 [Tangut] x by | [Tangut] 2537

(b) I 129 | [Tangut] (lunar mansion) 3009

(bb) II 1 [Tangut] |

(c) II 15 | [Tangut] 2657 3154

(d) III 72 [Tangut] x by | [Tangut] 0776

(e) III A85 | [Tangut] 4758

(f) III A135 | [Tangut] 4715

(g) V 4 | [Tangut] 3591

(h) V 8 | [Tangut] 2996

(i) V 21 | [Tangut] 4782

(j) V 48 | [Tangut] mag-pie 1556

(k) V 151 | [Tangut] 4719

(l) V 179 | [Tangut]

(m) VI 125 | [Tangut] fuan 3003

(n) VII 15 | [Tangut] 4781

(o) VII 93 | [Tangut] 4744

(p) VII 109 | [Tangut] 4741 3008

(q) VIII 9 | [Tangut] 4826

(r) VIII 20 | [Tangut] 4778

(s) VIII A82 | [Tangut] 1307

(t) IX 122 | [Tangut] 4772

(u) IX 145 | [Tangut] 4821

(v) ? VII A79 2653

飛 "to fly" CCC.16b W.I.132[15]

䲢 CCC.6b

B.167[5] 酉酉 10th branch

4776 – 4776

4777 2357 pair

4778 4775 chain

4779 4326 chain

4780 2635 chain

4781 4775 chain

4783 0043 chain

4784 4775 chain

4785 2327 chain

4786 1914 chain

4787 3438 chain

4788 2027 chain

4776

(a) V 6

(i) By

(ii) (a) abo

goose, d

4777

(a) VII

4778

(a) III

(i) By

(ii) (a) ab

4779

(a) I 11

(b) V

4780

4781

4782

c.c.c. 17a

369

370

4776 VI 42 [illegible]
(a) V 6 | ditto
(i) By i Ccy W.I. 134¹ 甲鳥 "duck"
(ii) (a) above C.C.C. 16ᵇ 鴈鴨 "wild goose, duck".

4777 VIII 11 | 2357
(a) VII 87 ditto

4778 VIII 20 |
(a) III 109 |
(i) By i Ccy 烏 "crow C.C.C. 4ᵃ 17ᵃ by a. rog. 'crow' W.I. 218¹¹
(ii) (a) above 鷰 "swallow" C.C.C. 17ᵃ

4779 VIII 67 | 4964
(a) I 14 | 4753
(b) V A 139 × by | 皮 1437

4780 II 12 | 2635

4781 VII 15 |

4782 V 21 |
C.C.C. 17ᵃ 鵓鴿 "dove"

4783 I A 92 | 0043

4784 VI 18 |
(i) C.C.C. 17ᵃ 雀子 "sparrow".

4785 VIII 5 |
(a) I 19 ditto
(b) V 77 | 3132
W II 40¹⁰ 請 "to request, invite" 92¹ do.
B. 125² 召 "to call" 128⁵ do. B 187⁵ 217²

4786 V 130 | ? 3733
(a) V 140 | ? 2576

4787 V 130 |

4788 IX A 106 | 3530
(i) | C.C.C. 25ᵇ 衲袋 "a pocket in a ceremonial robe"?

4788A × of III 37 |
? err for 4856

4779A × of VIII 111 |
err for 3315

~~4789 2183~~

2183 4789 — 1221 - 1175 — 4803

4795 3974 chain

4796 1245 chain

4790 1114 chain

4791 3959 pair

4798 3806 pair

4799 2208 chain

4792 0475 chain

4800 5465 chain

4793 - 4770

4801 5465 chain

4794 3829 chain

4802 5696 pair

370

4789 [illegible] I 24 | [illegible] (3664A) 2183

(a) I 5 | [illegible]

(b) V 91 | [illegible] ×(1175) 1221

(i) 賢 "virtuous" C.C.C. 17ª B.179⁴

(ii) 神 "divine, spirit" W.I. 112¹⁸ 142¹⁵

(iii) rdzu hp'rul "magical" W.I. 194¹⁸ 196¹ 222¹⁸

4790 [illegible] IX A 129 | [illegible] + 4216

4791 [illegible] III 96 [illegible] |

(a) VI 6 ditto

(i) The disyllable W.I. 206⁸ 224⁵ mts'on c'a "weapon".

4792 [illegible] III 37 | [illegible] 0416

4793 [illegible] mbâ I 107 | [illegible]

(a) V A 104 ditto

(i) The disyllable C.C.C. 16ᵇ / W.I. 132¹⁸

鵝 "goose" | 鵝 鴨 geese + ducks

B 94 dictionary explanation ...

4794 [illegible] I 37 | [illegible] "moon"

(a) IX 88 ditto

日 "sun" C.C.C. 4ᵇ W.I. 92¹ 118⁵ etc.

ñi "sun" W.I. 190¹³

C.C.C. 4ᵇ The disyllable

ñi. ma "sun" W.I. 222¹³

晝 "by day" W.II 78¹¹

4795 [illegible] IX 4 [illegible] | 3974

(a) IX 31 ditto

4796 [illegible] I 43 [illegible] |

4797 [illegible] IX 4 [illegible] | 1195

Hsyl. B. 192⁴

4798 [illegible] III 171 [illegible] |

(a) I 17 ditto

4799 [illegible] II 4 [illegible] | 2208

4800 [illegible] VIII 5 [illegible] | 0972

(a) III 8 | [illegible] 4801

(b) III A 61 | [illegible] × 5213

C.C.C. 8ᵇ 煙 "smoke"; [illegible]?

4801 [illegible] III 8 [illegible] | 4800

4802 [illegible] IX 4 [illegible] |

(a) I 24 ditto

4803 4789 chain
4803 (iii) | 〔Tangut〕 感應 "reward + punishment" B.159[1,2] (prof. mistrans[?])
(i) B185[3] 靈 "spirit" 186[5] q.v.

4804 ÷2997

4805 4079 chain

4806 5110 chain

4807 4005 chain

4808 4819 chain

4809 –4712 A
4810 – 2950
4811 1212 pair
4812 – 2248
4813 independent
4814
+ 5076 – 0661 – 4299
4815 0043 chain
4816 3477 pair

4803 〔Tangut〕
(i) sem "...
(iii) The ...
...
(ii) By itse...
4804 〔Tangut〕
(a) Ⅵ ...
(i) The ...
male + ...
4805 〔Tangut〕
(i) | 〔Tangut〕 cc...
4806 〔Tangut〕
c.c.c. 19[a] ...
4807 〔Tangut〕
4808 〔Tangut〕
(a) ...
(b) Ⅲ ...
(i) (a) abo...
"yellow...

371

4803 [Tangut] I 5 [Tangut] |

(i) sem "spirit" W.I.222[16] 224[5,6]

(iii) The dissyllable 神通 "ubiquitous supernatural power". [W.II.4[9] 122[12]]

(ii) By itself 通 W.I.176[8] ubiquitous II 86[10]

4804 [Tangut] V 83 | [Tangut] 2997

(a) V 19 ditto

(i) The dissyllable C.C.C.15[b] 鳳凰 "male + female phoenix"

4805 [Tangut] I 113 [Tangut] |

(i) | [Tangut] C.C.C.17[a] 蜜蜂 W.I.192[17] 210[1] "honey-bee" bui.bu

4806 [Tangut] V 102 [Tangut] |

C.C.C.19[a] 骨髓 "marrow"

Note. In C.C.C. [Tangut], possibly correct.

4807 [Tangut] I 113 [Tangut] |

4808 [Tangut] III 37 | [Tangut] | 4819

(a) ~~III~~ I 19 ~~[Tangut]~~ ditto

(b) III 66 | [Tangut] 4761

(i) (a) above C.C.C.17[a] 黄鵬子 "yellow cuckoo"

4809 [Tangut] VII 21 [Tangut] |

4810 [Tangut]. III 75 | [Tangut]

(a) IX 66 ditto

(i) The dissyllable W.I.134[12] 踐踏 "to trample down" takes 依

4811 [Tangut] III 171 [Tangut] | 1212

(a) III 27 ditto

4812 [Tangut] VI 77 | 枝 2248

(a) VI 27 ditto

4813 [Tangut] IX 32 × by itself | [|]

4814 [Tangut] I 108 [Tangut] | [Tangut] 5076

(a) VIII 24 ditto

W.I.218[15] smyo "mad".

4815 [Tangut] VII 75 | [Tangut] 0056

4816 [Tangut] I 108 [Tangut] |

(a) VI 107

371

4817 4754 pair

4818 4713 pair

4819. ⊥ 4808-4761

4820 0345 chain

4821 4775 chain

4822 2758 chain

4823 2758 chain

4824 - 4759

4825 4142 chain

4826 4775 chain

4827 0148 chain

4828 2193 chain

4829 - 2257

4830 ~~independent~~

4831 4510 chain

4832 4712 pair

4817 (a) V

4818

4819 (a) I

(i) The

"yellow

4820

Note. 48

4821

(a) IX

4822

Phonetic

4823

(a) VI

(b) VIII

(c) VIII

(d) VIII

(a)-(d) a

372

4817 [Tangut] V 90 [Tangut] | misspelt
(a) V 112 ditto [[Tangut]]

4818 [Tangut] II 16 [Tangut] | 4713
(a) I 31 ditto

4819 [Tangut] I 19 | [Tangut]
(a) III 37 ditto
(i) The dissyllable C.C.C. 17ª 黄鵬子 "yellow cuckoo"

4820 [Tangut] II 12 [Tangut] | 0347

Note. 4819 + 4820 are indistinguishable

4821 [Tangut] IX 145 [Tangut] | 4775
(a) IX 160 | [Tangut] 2995

4822 [Tangut] VIII A 100 [Tangut] [Tangut]
Phonetic character

4823 [Tangut] VIII 98 | [Tangut]
(a) VI 126 | [Tangut] 5622
(b) VIII A 100 [Tangut] × by | [Tangut] 4822
(c) VIII A 101 [Tangut] × by | [Tangut] 2760 4742
(d) VIII A 111 [Tangut] × by | [Tangut] 4750

(b) - (d) are Phonetic characters.

4824 [Tangut] I 11 | [Tangut]
(a) II 9 ditto
?

4825 [Tangut] IX 139 [Tangut] | 4364
B. 159¹ 勅 imperial decree B 260? 詔 mandate
W.I. 271¹ 詔

4826 [Tangut] VIII 9 [Tangut] |

4827 [Tangut] V A 85 [Tangut] | 5159
(a) III A 98 | [Tangut] 2984

4828 [Tangut] III 120 [Tangut] | 2193
(a) VIII A 77 | [Tangut] 1899

4829 [Tangut] VIII 82 | [Tangut] 2257
(a) VII 5 ditto

4830 [Tangut] VIII 82 Family or clan name
~~2(a)~~ B. 234³ 武 Wu

4831 [Tangut] III 13 [Tangut] |
(a) VI 32 ditto
~~B. 162⁵~~
A common Phonetic.
B. 162⁵
Φ.1. | [Tangut] 涅盤 Nirvāṇa C.C.C. 36ᵇ etc.

4832 [Tangut] V 129 [Tangut] |

372

4833 2279 chain

4837-2015

4838-0115 stand ~~chain~~

4839-2406

4840 2415 pair

4834 2492 chain

4841 ~~0022~~ chain

4835 4079 ~~3343~~ chain

4842 2411 chain

4836-5381-5398

4833

(a) III 9

(b) III

(c) V

(d) V

(e) V

(f) V

(g) VI

(h) VI

(i) VI

(j) VII

(i) (h) ab

whip:

(ii) (j) ab

saddle

(iii)

(iv) (b)

4834

occ. 24

4835

4836

(a) IX

(i) The di

"deer"

373

4833 [Tangut] RÂ IX 151 [Tangut] | 2279
(a) III 99 | [Tangut] 2301
(b) III A 41 | [Tangut] 3463
(c) V 137 | [Tangut] 2313
(d) V 166 | [Tangut] 1604
(e) V 180 | [Tangut] ×2455 2268
(f) V A 136 | [Tangut] 5341
(g) VI 49 | [Tangut] 0837
(h) VI 65 | [Tangut] ×5576 2424
(i) VI 100 | [Tangut] × 2272
(j) VIII 27 | [Tangut] ×{[3268] [3487]} [0811]
(i) (h) above C.C.C. 33b 馬鞭 "horse whip."
(ii) (j) above C.C.C. 33b 馬鞍 "horse's saddle."
(iii) | [Tangut] C.C.C. 33b 馬𩌏
(iv) (b) above cat. under "horse" B99

4834 [Tangut] IV A1 | [Tangut] 3480 "trousers" C.C.C. 24b 裙 "skirt"

4835 [Tangut] IX 151 | [Tangut] 1728

4836 [Tangut] V 34 [Tangut] | 5398
(a) IX 123 ditto
(i) The dissyllable C.C.C. 16a 鹿 麢 "deer" (in both cases)

4837 [Tangut] III 99 | [Tangut] 2015
(a) IX 107 ditto
B. 163[4] 167[5]

4838 [Tangut] VII 59-60
(a) III 15 × of | [Tangut]

A common Phonetic.

4839 [Tangut] V 157 | [Tangut]
(a) IX 58 misspelt 2406
(i) 瑞 auspicious C.C.C. 9a B175[1]
(ii) dpal blessedness W.I. 190[10]
(iii) | [Tangut] dpal blessedness W.I. 192[2] bkra.śis maṅgala
happiness W.I. 192[8], 220[9]
bde. legs ditto W.I. 210[4]
dge. ba ditto W.I. 196[6]
吉祥 ditto W II 69
(iv) | [Tangut] 萱草 a kind of lotus flower C.C.C. 13b

4840 [Tangut] V 157 [Tangut] |
(a) I 142

4841 [Tangut] V 157 [Tangut] [Tangut]
snake

4842 [Tangut] V 52 [Tangut] | 2411
(a) III 17 ditto
(b) V 173 | [Tangut] 3373
(c) VI 63 | [Tangut] 2759 spider

4843 2411 chain

4844 -3310 | [Tangut]

4845 2167 chain

4846-2915

4847 4858 pair

4848 2406 chain

4849 1923 chain

4850 3930 chain

緣 pratyaya a secondary cause

H-S. p. 440

Prepn. 'because of W.I.132" [Tangut] | "because of greed"

4851 4734 chain

4852 2482 chain

4858 1923 chain

4853 比 "like" W.I 104[4] II 116[8]

do. | [Tangut] 譬喻 'for instance' 'a simile,' } B.344[3]

B.160[1] | [Tangut] cs. 喻者 to illustrate, know

B.192[1] [Tangut] parable

4854 1583 pair

4842

4843

蟻 "a

gros.m

4844

(a) IV

4845

百 "10

bagya

4846

(a) V

4847

(a) I

(i) The

"wild a

4848

Used a

4849

374

4842 cont.

4843 V 47 | 承
蟻 "ant" C.C.C. 17a W.I. 136 2,6
grog.ma ditto W.I 194 10 224 8

4844 IX 33 |
(a) IV 5 ditto

4845 VIII 37 | "number" 2167
百 "100" C.C.C. 35a + passim
brgya ditto W.I 190 12 216 14

4846 VII/VIII 59 |
(a) V 30 ditto

4847 III 66 |
(a) I 67 ditto
(i) The disyllable B100 cat. under "wild animals"

4848 IX 41 |
Used as a Phonetic. W.II 14 10

4849 III 145 | 4383

4850 III 145 | because 3930
(a) VIII 58 ditto
(i) By itself. A terminal particle
故 "because (of)" C.C.C. 29b etc.
由 "because (of)" W.I. 100 2 etc.
B.161 1 tr. 緣
(ii) The disyllable 因緣 "because of" W.I. 100 8 etc.

4851 IX 41 | time 4727
C.C.C. 9a 季 "season".

4852 I 71 | 2482

4853 VI A 17 | 1923
(a) I 128 ditto
(i) By itself 譬 "like" W.II 76 6 B.344 3
如 "like" W.II 84 8 B.187 3 t.v. B 232 2
(ii) "as if" W.II 34 6

4854 IX 136 |
(a) III 11 ditto
(i) By itself C.C.C. 7a 蝎 "worm"
(ii) The disyllable W.I. 210 3 sdig.pa "a scorpion".

4855 4396 chain

4856 ~~3010~~
+ 3010
+ 4879

4857 1076 chain

4858 -4847

4859 5314 chain

4860 2538 pair

4861 2384 pair

4862 1720 pair

4863 4245 chain

4864 0214 chain

375

4855 V 29 | "pearl"
(i) | ["white"] C.C.C. 12b 鷰珠
"swallow pearl" B.102 cat. under "precious things"

4856 I 11 | 3010
(a) VI 23 ditto
(i) The dissyllable 蠅 "fly" C.C.C. 17a
蚊蚋 (W.I. 134[16] II 46[1/6]) "mosquitos & gnats" (B. 221[2])
abbrev. for "fly" W.I. 210[2]

4857 V 143 | "gold" 1076
(a) V A 54 ditto
(b) III 13 × by dissyllable
(c) VI 90 | (misspelt) 3538
(i) By itself 銀 "silver" C.C.C. 12b
(ii) The dissyllable B. 102 cat. under "precious things".

4858 I 67 |
(a) III 66 ditto
(i) The dissyllable B. 100 cat. under "wild animals".

4859 V 52 | 2962
A particle of obscure meaning
W.I. 100[10] 196[4] 226[12] 172[2] [tr. 同]
Dict. 1b 4 B. 125[1] 173[2] (tr. 經) 189[a]
B. 189[2] 猷 plan, counsel

(ii) | C.C.C. 27b 經略 "summary (?) of the scriptures" [name of temple].

4860 V 33 | 2538
(a) V 104 ditto
?

4861 VI 107 | 2384
(a) VI A 36 ditto
?

4862 III 37 | 1720
(a) V 13 ditto
(i) The dissyllable B. 103 cat. under "silk"

4863 III 145 — Same as

4864 [IX 126] | 3363
(a) VI 129 | (nil) 2188
C.C.C. 11a 閏 "intercalary (month)"
B. 345[2] 盛 abundant

4865 3472 pair

4866 0582 chain

4867 1713 chain

4868
- 0544 – 0739
- 1159 – 1178
- 2553
- 3253 – 0657
- 4689
- 4692 – 0125
- 4894 – 2032
- 4875

4869 4231 pair

4870 0809 chain

4871 3516 pair

4872 0249 chain

4873 2861 chain

4874 indepndent

4875 4868 chain

4876
4245 chain

4865

4866

4867

4868

376

4865 [Tangut] III 37 [Tangut] |
(a) III 172 ditto

4866 [Tangut] VIII A 107 [Tangut] | 3692
(i) W.I. 190[17] ?
(ii) [Tangut] | B. 100 cat. under "horse"

4867 [Tangut] I 86 [Tangut] | 4642
(a) VII 26 | [Tangut] ×1012
沙 "sand" C.C.C. 12[a] W.I. 170[9]
bye ma ditto W.I. 224[16]

4868 [Tangut] NE III 37 [Tangut] | "yellow" ×(0739) 0544
(a) III 117 ditto
(b) III 106 [Tangut] | 4689
(c) III A 15 | [Tangut] ×0125 4692
(d) III A 79 | [Tangut] 2553
(e) III A 108 [Tangut] × by | [Tangut] nyin Phon. 4894 [Tangut]
(f) VII 89 [Tangut] | ×(0657) 3253
(g) VII A 99 | [Tangut] 4875
[(h) VIII 4 [Tangut] × by [Tangut] | [Tangut]]
(i) IX 86 [Tangut] | ×(1178) 1159
朱 "vermilion" C.C.C. 6[b] W.I. 98[3]
赤 "red" W.II 46[9]
dmar "red" W.I. 192[12,13]
B. 176[2] 緋 "dark red" (tr.) B 175[1]

4869 [Tangut] III 37 [Tangut] |
(a) III 9 ditto

4870 [Tangut] V 134 [Tangut] | 0383

4870A [Tangut] Possibly correct form of [Tangut]

4871 [Tangut] III 37 [Tangut] |
(a) I 17 ditto

4872 [Tangut] III 37 [Tangut] | 1389

4873 [Tangut] III 37 [Tangut] | ~~misspelt~~ 2816
(a) V 89 ~~ditto~~ [[Tangut]] | 2822

4874 [Tangut] [? VII 59-60]
(i) 紅 "red" C.C.C. 13[b] W.I. 98[2]
dmar "red" W.I. 224[16]
(ii) [Tangut] | "mallow flower" C.C.C. 13[b]

4875 [Tangut] VII A 99 [Tangut] |

4876 [Tangut] NE III 37 Family or clan name TU
(a) III 145 [Tangut] × by | [Tangut]
(b) VI 48 [Tangut] |

(a) + (b) are very obscure. ? (a) is a Phonetic; if so very irregular.

376

4877 3685 chain

4884 1873 chain

4885 4123 chain

4878 – 0517

4886 – 2961

4879 4856 chain

4887 4889 chain

4880 0192 pair

4889
- 4887 – 5713
- 4274 – 0509 – 5532 – 5434 – 1590 – 0297 / 2651 / 3859 – 2469 / 4020
- 4274 – 1008 – 2126 – 3667
- 5661

4881 – 2037

4882 5248 chain

4888 1949 chain

4889 v. above ↑

4883
- 1422 – 4955
- 5662

4877 (a) III

4878 (a) V

Possibly

4879

4880 (a) I (b) V

?

4881 (a) IX

4882 (a) VII (b) II A

(i) The Hsi

WI 98

畜養

養

4883 (a) IX

377

4877 [Tangut] VII 100 [Tangut] | 'name' 3685

(a) III 44 | [Tangut]

Common Phonetic

4878 [Tangut] VIII 35 Family or clan (name)

(a) V 54 | [Tangut] [[Tangut]]

Possibly a double name?

4879 [Tangut] III 37 [Tangut] |

[var. [Tangut]]

4880 [Tangut] III A 80 [Tangut] | 0192

(a) I 11 ditto [[Tangut]] 0192

(b) V 132 [Tangut] × by [Tangut] | [[Tangut]]

?

4881 [Tangut] III 83 | [Tangut] 2037

(a) IX 79 ditto

4882 [Tangut] V 21 [Tangut] |

(a) VIII 25 [[Tangut]]

(b) II A 15 [Tangut] | [[Tangut]] 3106

(i) The disyllable 滋養 "to feed" W.I. 98[10]

畜養 "to feed" W.I. 134[1]

養 "to feed" W.I. 134[15] N.B. [Tangut] right.

4883 [Tangut] I 16 | [Tangut]

(a) IX 17 ditto

4884 [Tangut] I A 26 [Tangut] | to tie ~~seat~~ (misspelt) 2032

?(a) VIII 57

~~B.160[1] [Tangut] to assent?~~

4885 [Tangut] V A 76 [Tangut] [Tangut]

4886 [Tangut] VI 2 | [Tangut] 2961

(a) IX 43 ditto

(i) The disyllable cat. under "rivers & seas" √B.172[2]

4887 [Tangut] IX A 115 [Tangut] |

(a) V 29 ditto ~~name~~

(b) VII 31 [[Tangut] |] 5713

烝 (C.C.C. 8[a] vapour)

氣 vapour C.C.C. 9[a]

蒸 C.C.C. 15[b] steam

(ii) | [Tangut] B.101 cat. under "grains" (X.7.16)

(? steamed rice)

4888 [Tangut] III 142 [Tangut] | 4413

?

4889 [Tangut] V 29 [Tangut] | ~~4413~~

(a) IX A 115 ditto ← (b) I 47 [Tangut] 4274 5661

(c) VI 116 | [Tangut]

C.C.C. 33[a] 蒸 "steam" (cake)

B126[1] ? Hm.

4890 0322 chain

4891 5433 chain

4892 1217 pair

4893 – 5565

4894 4868 chain

4895 independent

4896 independent

4897 3597 chain

4898 3584 pair

4899 – 3364

4900 4027 chain

4901 – 3370

4902 ⊥3808 – 3987

4903 3795 chain

[4904] 4479 chain

[4905] – 3060

[4906] 0271 chain

[4907] 2928 chain

4890 'eye

4891

4892

(a) V

4893

(a) I

4894

(a) V

Phoneti

4895

B.346

4896

4897

(i) The

W.I.226

童子

4898

A comm

378

4890 VIII 51
'eye-water' i.e. tear

4891 VIII 51 |

4892 V 80 |
(a) V 77 ditto reversed

4893 I 46 |
(a) I 33 ditto [in both]

4894 III A108
(a) VIII 57 | ? ← N.B. 2032
Phonetic character NZIN

4895 VIII 20 × by self |
B.346[5] 李 Li

4896 IX 49 Family or clan name

4897 IX 49 | 2627
(i) The Dissyllable byis.pa 'child'
W.I.226[4]
童子 'youth, kumāra' W.II 10[7] 42[12] etc.

4898 IX 49 |
(a) III 44 ditto

A common Phonetic. 利 B.163[1]

4899 V 32 | misspelt
(a) III 109 ditto
Nevski I 254 'puppy' cf. 4901

4900 V 31 | 4265

4901 V 32 | 3370
(a) III 109 ditto
cf 4899

4902 V 149
(a) VI 44 ditto
Nevski I 254 'window'

4903 VIII 75 | ocean 2221
(i) | [tis. 土 海 'land + sea']
(1534)
B.102 cat. under 'rivers + seas'
Nevski I 253 'sea'

4904 IX A163 | 1201

4905 III 162 | 3068
(a) VI 33 ditto

4906 III 162 | tear 3087

4907 VIII A73 | 0446

4908 2395 chain

4909 1130 chain

4910 4933 chain

4911 – 4356

| W.I.178 爲無 "existence + non-existence".

4912 3566 pair

4913 – 4358

4914 3824 chain

4915 0058 chain

4916 5094 chain

4917 4924 chain

4918 0059 chain

takeover

4919 0058 chain

4920 2121 chain

4921 5086 chain

4922 3824 chain

4923 5094 chain

379

4908 I 18 | 2395

4909 I 18 | "star" 1130
(i) The Hsi-syllable
C.C.C. 7[1] 遜 "to yield, modest (star!)"

4910 I 18 | 1401
B.160[5] tr. 浪 wave v. 2168 232[2] ditto

4911 VII 39 |
(a) VII 7 ditto
爲 "existence W II 64[3,4] cf. 4913
B.198[1]

4912 IX A 170 | 3566
(a) IX A 108 ditto reversed

4913 VII 39 |
(a) VII 7

4914 I A 22 | "snow"
霄 "hail (storm) C.C.C. 9[a]

4915 I 61 |

4916 VII 40 5088

4917 V 47 |
(a) V 4 ditto
(b) IX 9 |

4918 V 174 | 5860(?)

4919 VII 92 | 58 'cold'
(a) VII A 11 ditto

4920 II 32 | misspelt
(a) IV 2 ditto [ ] 'frost' v 2121
(b) IX 61 | 2266
(c) IX 73 | 5680
露 "(white) dew, or frost C.C.C. 9[a]

4921 II 32 |

4922 II 4 |
(a) I A 22 | "hail" v. 4914
雪 "snow" C.C.C. 9[a2]
gains ditto. W. I. 216[14] 224[16]

4923 V 151 |

4924
⊥ 4917-5174

4932 0151 chain

4925-0178 pair

4933
┬ 2435
└ 1401 - 4910

4926
├ 0179
├ 4133
└ 5605

4934 3226 chain

4927 0159 chain

4928 3829 chain

4929 5094 chain

4935 independent

4930 - 4227

4936 0148 chain

4937 0148 chain

4931 0156 chain

4924
(a) V

4925
(a) V

4926
(a) V
(b) II
(c) V
?W.II 36[3]

4927

4928
(1) The
"the eas

4929
(a) V

4930
(a) VI

4931

380

4924 [Tangut] V 4 | [Tangut] 4917

(a) V 47 ditto

4925 [Tangut] V 119 [Tangut] | 0178

(a) V 92 ditto incorrect

4926 [Tangut] V 159 | [Tangut] 0179 ~~0224~~ ~~0177~~

(a) V 152 ditto

(b) II 18 [Tangut] | 4133

(c) V 60 [Tangut] | 5605

?W.II 36[3] [Tangut] "remiss" 156[8] [Tangut] to Nevski I 434

4927 [Tangut] V 159 [Tangut] | 0159

4928 [Tangut] IX A 123 | [Tangut] 3829

(i) The dissyllable C.C.C. 11[a] 臘月 "the last month (of the year)"

4929 [Tangut] III A 55 [Tangut] |

(a) V 151 | [Tangut] 4923

4930 [Tangut] V 174 [Tangut] | [Tangut]

(a) VIII 53 ditto

4931 [Tangut] VIII 13 [Tangut] |

4932 [Tangut] VIII 43 [Tangut] | 0176

(a) III 58 [Tangut] | 5250

(b) VIII 77 | [Tangut] 5712A

Nevski I 434 "ici"

4933 [Tangut] II 32 | [Tangut] 2435

(a) IX 11 ditto

(b) II 28 | [Tangut] 1401

(i) The dissyllable 脊背 "the spine" C.C.C. 18[b]

(ii) | [Tangut] 腎 "kidneys" C.C.C. 18[b]

4934 [Tangut] W.I II 4 [Tangut] [Tangut] "auxiliary word".

An obscure particle W.I. 100[3,14] 108[16] 198[11] 214[2] 170[15] [? accusative suffix] 170[17] [[Tangut] | so ? verbal prefix] 170[18] ? v.p.

~~4934A~~ [Tangut] [? VII 59-60]

error for 3314

4935 [Tangut] VI 16 "Family or clan (name)"

4936 [Tangut] VI A 69 | [Tangut] 4937

4937 [Tangut] VI A 15 | [Tangut] 1441

(a) VI A 69 [Tangut] | 4936

4939 bis – 4940

4938 3195 pair

4939 – [1094]

4940 4939 bis pair

4941 2071 chain

4942 4208 chain

4943 0322 chain

4944 4276 chain

4945 4972 chain

4946 3089 chain

4947 2482 chain

4948 independent

4949 1891 chain

4949. B 347[1] 心 heart, (metaph.)

In B.122,3,4 etc. this is often written [illegible]

B. 283[5]

W. I 136[9] (I wish)

[4950] 0453 pair

[4951] 4276 chain

4952 0965 chain

4953 4114 chain

4954 4326 chain

4939

4938

(a) I

Dict.

4939

(a) I

4940

(a) VI

4941

4942

(a) VII

W. II 24

Dict 1

4943

4944

4945

4946

4939 bis [illegible] VI 40 (39) | [illegible] balanced by 5018 vacant
(a) IX 70 ditto

381

4938 [illegible] III 172 [illegible] |
(a) I 11 ditto
Dict. 1a 5 B.168³ 170³

4939 [illegible] VII 9 | [illegible]
(a) I 1 ditto

4940 [illegible] IX 70 [illegible] |
(a) VI 40 (39) ditto

4941 [illegible] III 155 [illegible] |

4942 [illegible] VI 40 [illegible] | 5688
(a) VIII 52 | [illegible] 0219
W.II 24¹⁰ 28⁷ 量 "measure"?
Dict 1a 7

4943 [illegible] IX 169 [illegible] | etc

4944 [illegible] IX 169 | [illegible] forgot 4959

4945 [illegible] VI 116 | [illegible] to stir 5694

4946 [illegible] II 14 [illegible] | 3089

4947 [illegible] I 145 | [illegible] 2482

4948 [illegible] I 69 "Family or clan name"

4949 [illegible] III 60 (39) | [illegible]
願 "praṇihita praṇidhāna
resolve, will desire W.I.100¹, 136⁹ II 8⁵ 42¹⁰ B.166¹
誓 "to take an oath" W.I.152¹⁵

4950 [illegible] IX 79 [illegible] | 0453
(a) V 3 ditto

4951 [illegible] V 44 [illegible] | 4229

4952 [illegible] VII A 91 [illegible] | 965
(a) III 61 | [illegible] 'seal' 1211
(b) IV 4 | [illegible] report, statement' 4995
信 "faith, truth" C.C.C.20a W.I.96⁴
108⁵ II 12¹ 36⁸
B.191³ 193¹

4953 [illegible] IX 79 [illegible] |
(a) I 12 ditto

4954 [illegible] VIII A 37 | [illegible] 1921
~~(a) V 151 ditto (misspelt)~~

4955 4883 chain

4956 5871 chain

4963 5690 chain

4964 4326 chain

4957 5690 chain

4958 – 4349 invert / remember

4959 ~~4326~~ 4276 chain

4965 +0230 +2245

4960 4011 chain

4966 – 4239

4961 4484 chain

4962 5030 chain

4967 3891 chain

382

4955 [Tangut] VI 36 [Tangut] 1422

4956 [Tangut] VII 17 [Tangut] | 5671

(a) VI 10 ditto [[Tangut]] reversed

(i) | [Tangut] 驚 畏 zum. par Zgyur. ba "to be alarmed & despondent" 1984[2] B.252.

W.II 142[10] 驚 恐 ditto

4957 [Tangut] V 23 [Tangut] | virtue 5675

D 246[3] 公 'Duke'

4958 [Tangut] IX 79 | [Tangut]

(a) III 97 [[Tangut]] ditto

Nevski I 257 ([Tangut] is correct)

4959 [Tangut] I A 16 [Tangut] | 4229

(a) IX 96 | [Tangut] 1789

(b) IX 169 [Tangut] | 4944

忘 "to forget" W.I.138[10] II 112[2]

brjed "to forget" W.I. 212[16] 218[16]

[compound of [Tangut] mind + [Tangut] not]

4960 [Tangut] IX 79 [Tangut] | head 4011

4961 [Tangut] VII 112 [Tangut] | ? 4484

4962 [Tangut] II 18 [Tangut] | 0242

(i) 孝 "filial piety, to respect" [noun & verb] C.C.C. 20[c] 31[a,b] B.191[2]

(ii) | [Tangut] ["red piety"] = 葵 "mallow flower" C.C.C. 13[b]

4963 [Tangut] VI A 77 | [Tangut] 4267

4964 [Tangut] ndzu VI 95 [Tangut] | 4326

~~(a) I A 24 | [Tangut]~~ × 4957

(b) III 30 | [Tangut] 4075

(c) V 135 | [Tangut] 4587

(d) V 139 [Tangut] | ? ×(1622) 1955

(e) V 151 | [Tangut] [might be mean (×4954)] ×(4954) 1921

(f) VI A 7 | [Tangut] 0105

(g) VII 41 | [Tangut] 0328

(h) VIII 67 | [Tangut] × 4779

人 "man" passim

mi "man" W.I. 210[3]

4965 [Tangut] VI A 76 [Tangut] 0230

(a) VI A 37 ditto

(b) I A 23 | [Tangut] 2243

4966 [Tangut] VI 120 | [Tangut]

(a) VI 36 ditto

4967 [Tangut] VIII 12 | [Tangut]

(i) The disyllable 憂 愁 "sadness & anxiety" I.168[12] W.II 18[7] B 251[1] mya. ṅan "misery, affliction"

4968 4115 ~~chain~~ pair

4977 – 3935 A

4969 2889 chain

4978 3226 chain

4970 4226 chain

4979 [2208] chain

4971 4972 chain

4980 – 0131 ~~[illegible]~~

chain 4972 – 5694

4972 (ii) ~~The disyllable~~ (c) above v. 脩

4972
┬ 5694 ┬ 4945
├ 1994 └ 4971
└ 2102

4981 1903 chain

4982 3846 chain

4974 independent W.I.265' Queen (Rom.) 梁 Liang 梁

4983
┬ 4203 – 3121 ┬ [1119]
└ 1280 └ 2718

4975 independent

4976 – 0743A or 0908

4976 負 'to carry on back W.I.170⁹

擔 burden, load B.200¹ W.I.132¹⁶ | pron. glossed as Chinese word

4973 5038 chain

4968
(a) I
4969
4970
(a) V
4971
4972
(a) V
(b) I
(c) IX
施 'to
byin,
stsol
40
4974
B.159²
4975
4976
(i) By i C.
4973
(a) IX
?

383

4968 [Tangut] [Tangut] IX 79 [Tangut] |

(a) I 12 ditto

4969 [Tangut] III 177 [Tangut] | 2559

4970 [Tangut] VII 106 [Tangut] | 4229

(a) VII A 118 [Tangut] | 2409

4971 [Tangut] VI 104 [Tangut] | to give 5694

4972 [Tangut] I 58 | [Tangut] to give 5694

(a) V 101 ditto

(b) I 56 [Tangut] | q.v. 2102

(c) IX 16 [Tangut] | alms q.v. 1994

施 "to give" W.I. 94[7] + passim

byin, sbyin "gift" W.I. 214[12] 226[5]

stsol "to give" W.I. 198[7]

~~4974~~ 4973 [Tangut] IX 120 "Family or clan name"

B.159[2] 涼 Liang (chou) B345[1] 梁 Liang (family)

~~4975~~ 4974 [Tangut] I 145 "Family or clan name"

4976 [Tangut] VIII 89 | [Tangut]

(i) By itself W.I. 132[16] ? Nevski I 247 to carry

4973 [Tangut] VII A 44 | [Tangut]

(a) IX 146 ditto (misspelt)

?

(ii) | [Tangut] 重擔 "heavy load" W.II 2[9]

~~4976~~ 4977 [Tangut] II 13 [Tangut] |

~~4977~~ 4978 [Tangut] V 49 [Tangut] | 0577

~~4978~~ 4979 [Tangut] III 34 | [Tangut] 3528

~~4979~~ 4980 [Tangut] III 34 | [Tangut] 0131

(a) III 44 ditto

~~4980~~ 4981 [Tangut] IX 131 | [Tangut] 1903

~~4981~~ 4982 [Tangut] I 127 | [Tangut] 5686

(i) By itself k'an "house" W.I. 194[17] B.163[4] 168[4] 127[5]

(ii) | [Tangut] 殿前 "front palace, hall or temple" [name of temple] CCC. 28[a]

~~4982~~ 4983 [Tangut] I 127 | [Tangut] 4303

(a) I 51 ditto

(b) VIII 39 [Tangut] | 1280

(i) By itself 冠 "cap" CCC. 25[a]

(ii) [Tangut] | [top-knot cap] 冠子 "cap" CCC. 25[b]

(iii) [Tangut] | 雞冠 "cock's comb" (flower) CCC. 13[b]

(iv) [Tangut] | 戴花 "head flower(?)" CCC. 33[a]

4984 3846 chain

4985 4353

4986 ?3980 chain

4987 0457 chain

4988 2335 chain

4989 0457 chain

4990 2710 chain

4991 3143 pair

4992 4997 pair

4993 4330 chain

4994 2204 chain

4995 0965 chain

4996 5637 chain

4997 4992 chain

4985A. [Tangut] B.p.96 2nd half of fan-tsie of [Tangut] P'A
Probably error for 5056

384

4984 [Tangut] III 177 [Tangut] |

4985 [Tangut] V 32 | [Tangut]

4986 [Tangut] IX 1 | [Tangut]

4987 [Tangut] II A 11 [Tangut] | 1127
(a) I A 69 | [Tangut] 4989

4988 [Tangut] IX 118 [Tangut] | 2335
(a) V 34 ditto
(b) V 53 | [Tangut] x(4237) 3548
(c) IX A 151 | [Tangut] 1784
(i) By itself 畏 "fear" W.I.90[15] 92[3] 122[2].
W.I.136[15]?
(ii) [Tangut] 4956 驚 畏 zum. par tsgyur. ba
"to be alarmed & despondent" B.252

4989 [Tangut] I A 69 [Tangut] | 4987
(a) V A 130 [Tangut] x by [Tangut] |

4990 [Tangut] V 57 [Tangut] | food 5440
(i) The disyllable chag. ma "offals, remains" W.I.216[6]
(ii) By itself B.189 餘 surplus chain 5440

4991 [Tangut] IX 4 [Tangut] |
(a) IX 52 ditto
(ii) The disyllable C.C.C. 29[a]
B.188[5] 152[10]
(i) 遺 "to leave behind" W.II 88[4]

4992 [Tangut] IX 4 [Tangut] |
(a) I 24 ditto v. 4997
cf. 4997

4993 [Tangut] IX 125 [Tangut] |
(a) V A 93 ditto

4994 [Tangut] VIII 8 [Tangut] | to tie? 2204
(a) IX 8 ditto

4995 [Tangut] IV 4 [Tangut] | "truth" 4952 5021
(a) III A 51 | [Tangut] ~~[struck]~~ "in form"
C.C.C. 30[a2] 32[a] 狀 "report, statement"?

4996 [Tangut] I 24 | [Tangut] 2197
(a) IX 4 | [Tangut] 3261
cf. 4997

4997 [Tangut] I 24 | [Tangut]
(a) IX 4 ditto
cf. 4996

4998 4276 chain

4999 2229 pair

5000 4281 chain

5001 1891 chain

B 233^3

[5002] 1080 chain

5002 is really [Tangut] i.e. 5071 bis

B.174^4

5003 3226 chain

5004 0214 chain

5005 4030 chain

| [Tangut] B.188^2 tr. 示悟 (S.H.199-325)

to indicate or apprehend

5006 4027 chain

5007 - 3508

5008 3685 chain

5009 0322 chain

5010 4301 pair

4998

W.I.168

W.I.216'

4999

(a) IX

5000

(a) VI

(b) IX

5001

(a) VII

— "a"

42^{3,12}

[5002]

(i) The

B179'24

W.I 265

5002

5004

(a) VI

(b) IX

385

4998 [Tangut] VIII 84 [Tangut] | "heart"
W.I. 168[4] 稱 "to be pleased"
W.I. 216[17] sdug.pa "pleased"?

4999 [Tangut] VIII 84 [Tangut] | 2229
(a) IX 95 ditto

5000 [Tangut] V 32 [Tangut] [Tangut]
(a) VI 72 [Tangut] x by | [Tangut]
(b) IX 49 [Tangut] x by | [Tangut]
?

5001 [Tangut] V 27 [Tangut] | 1891
(a) VIII 66 ditto
一 "a" (rather than "one") W.II 22[6]
42[3,12] etc. B 245[1] (follows noun) 126[5] 161[3]

[5002 [Tangut] IX 40 | [Tangut]
(i) The dissyllable [W.I. 108[1] 138[7]
B 179[1] 248[1] etc. 經 "sutra".]
W.I 265 經典 Sutra (correct)

5003 [Tangut] VII 68 [Tangut] | 2342

5004 [Tangut] V A 90 [Tangut] | 02.14 [illegible]
(a) VI A 13 ditto
(b) IX A 85 [Tangut] | 4397 [illegible]
?

5005 [Tangut] III 91 [Tangut] | 2344
(a) III A 87 [Tangut] | 3178
(i) The dissyllable 教 授 "to instruct" W.I. 146[12], 147[1]
(ii) (a) above 指 示 "to point out & indicate CCC 36[6]

5006 [Tangut] III 8 [Tangut] | 832 q.v.

5007 ~~5006~~ [Tangut] VIII A 89 | [Tangut]
(a) VIII A 90 ditto
Used as Phonetic.
Φ.1. | [Tangut] e.la "cardamom"
W.I. 192[4] 194[4]

5008 [Tangut] III 47 | [Tangut]
(i) The dissyllable 讀 誦 "to read & recite" W.I. {266[8] 108[5] II 16[3] 18[10] 34[1]
B 245[2] by itself 讀 "to read"

5009 ~~5008~~ [Tangut] VIII A 93 [Tangut] |

5010 ~~5009~~ [Tangut] IX 2 [Tangut] | 4301
(a) II 31 ditto
?

5011 3773 pair

5012 5387 pair

5013
┬ 5402
├ 0794
└ 5135

5014 4466 pair

5015 3226 chain

5016 2167 chain

5017
┬ 3410
├ 0493
├ 2779
├ 4038
└ 5147 – 3634 – [0879]

5017 [illegible] | W.I.265[18] part of royal title 天奉 : indicates to God

| [illegible] B.193[3] tr. 和親

W.I.134[10]

5019 ~~0604 chain~~
┬ 1248
└ 1874

5020 3226 chain

5021 0965 chain

5011 [illegible]
(a) VI

5012 [illegible]
(a) VI

5013 [illegible]
(a) II
(b) VI
(c) IX

5014 [illegible]
(a) V

5015 [illegible]

5016 [illegible]

Note. 5

5017 [illegible]
(a) VII
(b) IA
(c) IA
(d) III
(e) VII

386

5011 [Tangut] IX 59 [Tangut] |
(a) VI 20 ditto reversed

5012 [Tangut] III 37 [Tangut] |
(a) VIII 46 ditto

5013 [Tangut] VIII 65 | [Tangut] 5402
(a) II 15 ditto
(b) VIII 35 [Tangut] |
(c) IX 146 [Tangut] | 0794

5014 [Tangut] I 18 [Tangut] |
(a) V A 58 ditto

5015 [Tangut] V 41 [Tangut] | 3677

5016 [Tangut] VI 9 [Tangut] | 5069

Note. 5015 + 5016 are barely distinguishable

5017 [Tangut] mBu I 18 | [Tangut] 3410
(a) VII 3 ditto
(b) I A 72 | [Tangut] 0493
(c) I A 106 | [Tangut] 4038
(d) III 100 [Tangut] | 5147
(e) VII A 128 [Tangut] × by | [Tangut] 2779

A very common nominal postposition
(i) 因 "because of" C.C.C. 27[b]
(ii) 依 "according to" C.C.C. 29[a]
(iii) 由 "by" C.C.C. 35[b]
(iv) The dissyllable B 237[1] trans 自然 "naturally"

~~5018 [Tangut] III 131~~

5019 [Tangut] VII 15 | [Tangut] (misspelt) 1248 [~~0927~~]
(a) VII 69 ditto
(b) VII 50 [Tangut] | 1874
賤 "money" W. II 26[8]

5020 [Tangut] VII 28 [Tangut] | 2342

5021 [Tangut] III A 51 [Tangut] | 4995
(a) III A 31 [Tangut] × by | [Tangut] 1522
(i) 告 "to inform" C.C.C. 28[a] 30[b]
(ii) W. I. 108[14] II 80[6] B 220[3] 投 "to throw" surrender?

Note. Falsely written [Tangut] at III A 51.

5022–1009 A

5023 3086 chain

5024 –1184

5025 0180 chain take over

5026 2101 pair

5027 1599 chain

5028 1891 chain

5029 4775 chain

5030
–1203
–0242 –1947
–4962

(b) W.I.266 [19] 慈悲 compassion + pity (Hoffmann 399)

5031 0271 chain

5032 3685 chain

5033 1781 chain

5034
–2122
–0183
–2114

5022

5023

CCC 31

5024

(a)

5025

(a)

(b)

(ii) The

W.I.22

(i) By

5026

(a)

5027

(a) V

(b) V

(i) The

oath".

5022 [Tangut] V 47 [Tangut] |

5023 [Tangut] V 44 [Tangut] | 0205

CCC 31^{a} 招 "to call, summon".

5024 [Tangut] V 79 | [Tangut] misspelt

(a) IX 53 ditto [[Tangut]]

5025 [Tangut] IX A 99 | [Tangut]

(a) III 131 ditto

(b) V 177 | [Tangut] 2062

(ii) The Disyllable dmod.pa "to curse" W.I.226^{7}: 罵 "to curse" W.II 68^{8}

(i) By itself 罵 "to curse" W II 80^{8}

5026 [Tangut] VII A 110 [Tangut] |

(a) VIII 73 ditto

5027 [Tangut] III A 40 [Tangut] |

(a) V 19 ditto

(b) V A 46 | [Tangut] × 5501

(i) The Disyllable dmod.pa "curse, oath". W.I.224^{5}

387

5028 [Tangut] IX 35 [Tangut], [Tangut]

5029 [Tangut] VII A 43 [Tangut] | 1461

5030 [Tangut] III 96 | [Tangut] 1203

(a) VII 33 ditto

(b) II 8 | [Tangut] 0242

(i) By itself 旻 "compassionate" CCC 4^{a}

(ii) The Disyllable 慈悲 "pity" W II 20^{12} 42^{7}

(iii) | [Tangut] 哀 愍 "to pity the miserable" W. II 78^{10} 94^{10}

5031 [Tangut] IX 62 [Tangut] | to know 1958

5032 [Tangut] VII 57 [Tangut] | "name"

B 245^{2} 仲 "the younger, second", "junior".

5033 [Tangut] VII 57 [Tangut] | 1364

5034 [Tangut] III 70 | [Tangut] 2122

(a) III 106 ditto

(b) I 17 [Tangut] | 2114 ~~0 18~~

(c) VI 36 [Tangut] | 0183

5035 4027 chain

5036–5037

5037 5036 pair

5038
┬ 4973
└ 1432

5039 1340 chain

B. 224[3] 中 |[Tangut][Tangut]拘留孫 S:H. 261

Krakucchanda.

5040 3226 chain

5041 5290 chain

5042 0271 chain

5043 0809 chain

5044 0379 pair

5045
┴ 3179 ┬ 4086
└ 5053

5046 4207 chain

5047 3795 chain

5048 5647 pair

388

5035 [Tangut] V 48 [Tangut] |

5036 [Tangut] VIII A 87 | [Tangut]
(a) VIII A 88 ditto ~~ditto~~

5037 [Tangut] VIII A 88 [Tangut] |
(b) VIII A 87 ditto

5038 [Tangut] IX 146 | [Tangut] 4973 misspelt
(a) III A 102 | [Tangut] 1432
(b) VII A 44 [Tangut] | ie ditto unused

5039 [Tangut] V 160 [Tangut] | 3409
[(a) VIII A 102] irrelevant]
(B. 212[1])
Used as Phonetic W. II 22[7]

5040 [Tangut] I 128 [Tangut] | 3600
(a) III 25 | [Tangut] 2663
(i) Normal, & very common meaning, 尊 "to honour"; "honourable" passim B 260
(ii) | [Tangut] W. I. 118[12] 薩梨 "sa.li sarira"

5041 [Tangut] Sa. VI 17 [Tangut] |
(i) | [Tangut] C.C.C. 6[b] 句陳 name of constellation chü ch'ên ? phonetic

5042 [Tangut] V 160 [Tangut] | year 0271

5043 [Tangut] V 160 [Tangut] [Tangut] 1942
(a) V 104 [Tangut] | 4584
(i) The trisyllable C.C.C. 15[a] 吃兜芽

5044 [Tangut] VI 17 [Tangut] |
(a) VI 30 ditto

5045 [Tangut] III 94 | [Tangut] 3179
(a) III A 58 ditto

5046 [Tangut] I A 15 [Tangut] |

5047 [Tangut] VI 130 [Tangut] |

5048 [Tangut] V 93 [Tangut] |
(a) V 36 ditto

5049 4104 chain

5050 – 3369

5051 3144 chain

5052 3226 pair

5053 5045 chain

5054 – 4611

5055 – 1856

5056 – 5721

5057
⊥ 3205 – 3272

5058 1901 chain

5059 1105 chain

5059 頌 'poem' W. II. 134[4]

(ii) the dissyl. B. 124[1] 'song of praise'?

5060 4295 chain

5061 3226 chain

5062 3226 chain

5049

(a)

(i) By i C

(ii) (a)

and so

5050

(a) I

?B. 174[5]

5051

5052

(a) I

昔 'fo

nin '

5053

W.I. 212

B. 195[5] Ph

5054.

(a) III

5055

(a) IX

389

5049 VI 81 |
(a) III 16 | 3683
(i) By itself [Zach who?]
(ii) (a) above W.I. 212" tr. 某甲 "so and so."

5050 III A52 |
(a) I 36 ditto
?B.174[5]

5051 VI 35 | 3144

5052 III 91 | 3220
(a) I 92 ditto
昔 "former" W.II 66[3]: I 168[14]? B.187[1]
ṅin "ancient, former" W.I. 224[3]

5053 VII 64 |
W.I. 212[12]? p'o.ña "messenger"
B.195[5] Phon. 師

5054 VII 64 |
(a) III 34 ditto

5055 VII 64 |
(a) IX 109 ditto

5056 III 94 |
(a) VI 131 ditto
v. 5985A

5057 III 94 | ×3205
(a) III 38 ditto

5058 V 49 (4168 "light") (2412 "like") 4168

5059 IX 100 | 5431
(aa) I A11 2498
(a) IV 3 | 3377
W.II 16[8] 偈 "gāthā". B.248' not in Tibetan orig. but tr. 頌 "song". B.186[4]

5060 | V 49 |
(a) V 73 ditto
(i) The disyllable W.I 208[7]
(ii) By itself B.228[3] q.v. tr. 日

5061 V 47 | "woven" 5062

5062 IX 6 | "to set up" 1654
(3621)
(a) I 123 | ? 2007
(b) V 47 | 5061
(c) V 57 | 1845
(d) IX 6 | ×(1257) 4167
W.I. 218 t'ag "rope"
W.II 46[12] 織 "woven"

5063
- 3650
- 1225
- 1322

B.216[4] 點 dot

5067 2167 chain

5068 5708 chain

5064 1891 chain

5069 2167 chain

15065 3820 pair

5066–0969

B.187[5] 揚 "to raise"

B.195[2] 惇 to consolidate

5070 5281 chain

5071 3700A chain

390

5063 [Tangut] IX 59 | [Tangut] 3650
(a) II 13 [Tangut] | (aa) IX 46 ditto 1225
(b) V 98 | [Tangut] 1322
B.132²? 散 to scatter B 217²

5064 [Tangut] IX 59 [Tangut] | 1891
(i) The dissyllable 都 案 "all law cases? table??" B.174¹ C.C.C. 28ᵇ 30ᵃ

5065 [Tangut] III 170 [Tangut] |
(a) V 97 ditto

Note. Distinguish from 5001

5066 [Tangut] V 156 | [Tangut] 0969
(a) III 93 ditto
The dissyllable
(i) W.I. 98⁵ ? See 0838
(ii) [Tangut] | C.C.C. 32ᵇ 琵琶 "guitar"
(iii) [Tangut] | C.C.C. 32ᵇ 琴 "lute" 5066
(iv) [Tangut] | C.C.C. 32ᵇ 箏 "harpsichord"
(v) [Tangut] | C.C.C. 32ᵇ 箜篌 "guitar"
(3008)

5067 [Tangut] VI 130 [Tangut] |
W.I. 138⁶ 268⁸ 僧 "priest" [sangha]
B.126²

5068 [Tangut] VI 81 | [Tangut] 也 2153
(a) IX 115 | [Tangut] family? 1026
[Zach "who?"] B.122² tr 卒 Phonetic? to crush out
B. 205⁴ φ stupa

5069 [Tangut] nwi V 94 | [Tangut] 3719
(a) III A 78 [Tangut] | 1051
(b) VI 9 | [Tangut] 5016
(c) VI 33 [Tangut] | 2095
(d) VI 130 | [Tangut] 5067
(e) VIII 34 | [Tangut] 0451
(i) 合 in all its senses "friendly, united etc." C.C.C. 6ᵃ 1ᵃ8 174⁴ tr B.176³ 僧
(ii) mdza.ba "friendliness W.I. 196⁷ 214¹⁰ W.I. 265¹⁸ B 179³ 睦 friendly
(iii) (c) above 和合 "union & concord" C.C.C. 19ᵇ

5070 [Tangut] III 6 | [Tangut] 5001

5071 [Tangut] III 91 [Tangut] | 4242

5071 bis v. 5002

5072 0572 chain

5073 0680 chain

5074 4011 chain

5075 1488 chain

5076 4814 chain

5077 = 5312

5078
⊢ 0119
└ 5080

5079 2038 chain

5080 5078 chain

5081 3493 pair

5082 3226 chain

5083 3226 chain

hon, de terminates one question & adds another "do they?- Or do they? B. 250'

[5084] [3743] chain

5085 3086 chain

5086
⊢ 1735
└ 4921

5087 5094 chain

5088 5094 chain

[5080A]

[Tangut] B.201[5] 急 remiss 233[1] do. ? correct form of 5079

391

5072 [Tangut] VI 32 | [Tangut] 0118
B187[1] s.v. lis. 吹 to blow, praise

5073 [Tangut] III 90 [Tangut] | 0686

5074 [Tangut] V 94 [Tangut] | fire & bow 1403

5075 [Tangut] V 50 [Tangut] | 1488
(i) [Tangut] | C.C.C. 22[a] 厨庵 "kitchen building".

5076 [Tangut] VIII 24 [Tangut] | 4814
(a) I 108 ditto
(b) VIII 41 | [Tangut] 0661

5077 [Tangut] III 93 [Tangut] |
(a) III 75 ditto

5078 [Tangut] VIII A40 [Tangut]
(a) VIII A86 | [Tangut]

5079 [Tangut] IX 99 [Tangut] | 2033
v ↗ (5080A) chain 2033

5080 [Tangut] VIII A86 [Tangut] |

5081 [Tangut] IX 99 [Tangut] |

5082 [Tangut] [Tangut] I 59 [Tangut] [Tangut] auxiliary word.
An interrogative final particle, 乎 ? C.C.C. 31[b] B 197[4] 麼 4011 chain
hon. de 取 ~~ditto~~ B.250[1]

5083 [Tangut] III 155 [Tangut] | 2442

5084 [Tangut] VIII 99 [Tangut] |

5085 [Tangut] VI A6 [Tangut] | 4604
(a) VI A105 [Tangut] | 5561
B.124[2]

5086 [Tangut] I A36 | [Tangut] 1735
(a) V 136 ditto to ...
(b) II 32 | [Tangut] 4921

5087 [Tangut] VII 56 [Tangut] | (5094)

5088 [Tangut] VII 96 [Tangut] |
(a) VII 40 | [Tangut] 4916

5089 independent

5095 5677 chain

5096
┬ 5471 – 0171
0171

5090 independent

5091 independent

5097 5531 chain

5098 1891 chain

5092 0970 chain

5099 2136 pair

5093 4355 chain

5100
┴ 5217 ┬ 0691
└ 3175

5094
┬ 1132 ┬ 1133
│ └ 2040
├ 4929 – 4923
├ 5087
└ 5085 – 4916

5101 [1130] chain

| W.I.136^2 瀉湯 to boil (water) 5102 3824 chain

5089
青
(2716
C.C.C. 15

5090
as

5091
(a) I

(a) is a

5092
(a) I
(b) II

5093
(a) V

5094
(a) IX
(b) III
(c) VII
(d) VI
W.I. 118^3
W.I. 136^2
Note. A

392

5089 [Tangut] [VII 59-60]
(i) [Tangut] 炒米 "cooked rice" (2716)
C.C.C. 15[b]. B.101 cat. under "grain".

5090 [Tangut] [IX gap]
灰 "ashes" C.C.C. 13[a]

5091 [Tangut] I 106 "Family or clan name"
(a) I A35 [Tangut] × by [Tangut] |

(a) is a phonetic character?

5092 [Tangut] I 120 | [Tangut] | 0970
(a) I 106 ditto
(b) II 36 | [Tangut] 3321

5093 [Tangut] VI 110 [Tangut] | 3656
(a) VI A110 | [Tangut]

5094 [Tangut] VI 48 | [Tangut] ×{1133, 2040}
(a) IX 43 ditto 1132
(b) III A55 | [Tangut] ×4923, 4929
(c) VII 56 | [Tangut] [Tangut] 5087
(d) VII 96 | [Tangut] ×4916, 5088
W.I. 118[3] [Tangut] "heat" II 86[7] do.
W.I. 136[2] B. 204[4]
Note. Also used as Phonetic.

5095 [Tangut] III 83 | [Tangut]
燈 "lamp" C.C.C. 23[b3] etc. W.I 136[1] B.165[1]
燭 "candle" W.I. 138[12]

5096 [Tangut] VIII 99 | [Tangut] 5471
(a) VIII A47 ditto
煮 "to boil" W.I. 134[16]
W.I. 134[3] ditto

5097 [Tangut] VI 48 | [Tangut]

5098 [Tangut] VII 18 [Tangut] 1891

5099 [Tangut] V 66 [Tangut] | 2136
(a) III 12 ditto

5100 [Tangut] III 167 | [Tangut]
(a) III A17 ditto reversed
W.I. 98[11] 滑 "slippery".

5101 [Tangut] III 167 [Tangut] | [1150]
C.C.C. 24[b] 熨 "flat iron".

5102 [Tangut] II A30 [Tangut] |
(a) VI 35 ditto
(b) II 4 [Tangut] | 4922
(i) 澤 "to soak, downpour" C.C.C. 7[b]. B. 221[5] cat. 水
(ii) The dissyllable 雨 "rain-storm" W II 48[11]

5103 bis – 3688

5103 0214 chain

5108 3226 chain

B 217' 溺 to drown

5104' 4208 chain

5109 2519 chain

5105 5106 chain

5106
- 0216 – 0101, 0694, 5214
- 0363
- 2985
- 5105
- 5172
- 5263
- 5460

5110
- 5183
- 0695
- 1580
- 2168
- 3368
- 3403
- 4724
- 4743
- 4806
- 5111
- 5120
- [5122]
- 5173
- 5195
- 5226
- 5236 – 5219
- 5241
- 5257

5107 0214 chain

5103 bis [illegible] Dict. 1 27. VII 71 | [illegible]
(a) VII 24 do

393

5103 [illegible] IX 101 [illegible] | 4397

5104 [illegible] VII 71 [illegible] | ? 4139

5105 [illegible] IX A 31 [illegible] |
慳 "sparing, stingy" W.I. 138[4]

5106 [illegible] IX 101 | [illegible] ×0216
(a) IX A 68 ditto
(b) I 11 [illegible] | 5263
(c) V 114 | [illegible] 2985
(d) VI 104 | [illegible] 5460
(e) VII A 74 | [illegible] 0363
(f) IX 116 | [illegible] 5784
(g) IX A 31 | [illegible] 5105 ~~0363~~
(h) IX A 148 | [illegible] 5172
(i) The dissyllable B. p. 99 cat. under "sheep" (+ tis. 蘇 油 "harvest grease"??)

5107 [illegible] II 9 [illegible] |
(i) [illegible] | B. 99. cat. under "sheep".

5108 [illegible] III 75 [illegible] | 0577
(a) VIII 60 | [illegible]
B. 188[1] 墜 S.-H. 431 to fall, sink 188[3] 沉

5109 [illegible] I 65 [illegible] vinegar? 693
(i) [illegible] | 甘 W.I. 214[9] bu. ram. sin "sugar cane"

5110 [illegible] IX 159 | [illegible] 5183
(a) III 175 ditto
(b) I 68 | [illegible] - 5111
(c) I 96 | [illegible] 1240 - 2168
(d) I 126 [illegible] | - 4724
(e) II 22 | [illegible] - 3368
(f) III 134 | [illegible] "flood" - 5120
(g) III 138 [illegible] | - 5173
(h) III 180 | [illegible] - 5236
(i) III A 35 [illegible] × by | [illegible] - [5122]
(j) III A 93 | [illegible] - 5226
(k) V 44 [illegible] | camel - 1580
(l) V 102 | [illegible] - 4806
(m) V 147 | [illegible] ? - 5195
(n) V 178 | [illegible] 5257
(o) VI 101 | [illegible] - 4748
(p) VII 30 [illegible] | - 3403
(q) VII 33 | [illegible] - 0695

5118 - 5491A

5119 1778 chain

5120 5110 chain

5111 5110 chain

5121 0822 chain

5112 0151 chain

~~5112 0151 chain~~

5122 5110 chain

[5113] 2710 chain

5114 3918 chain

[5115] 2865 chain

[5116] +[1909] 4102-0523

5117 0022 chain

5123 independent

394

5110 (cont.)

(2) VII 86 | [illegible] 5241

[(3) VIII 51 [illegible] x by [illegible] |]

(i) 水 "water" W.I. 132[17] etc.

c'u "water" W.I. 214[7]

(ii) |[illegible] pa.wa.śaiś "the planet Venus" W.I. 224[17]

5111 [illegible] I 68 [illegible] |

5112 [illegible] VIII 77 [illegible] | 4932

[5113 [illegible] VIII 65 [illegible] | 2710

(i) [illegible] | B.101 cat. under "grains" (2536)

5114 [illegible] III 75 [illegible] | 3918

5115 [illegible] I 68 [illegible] |

5116 [illegible] III 75 [illegible] | [1909]

(a) I 27 ditto x (0523)

(b) VII A 21 | [illegible] 4102

5117 [illegible] IX 116 [illegible] |

(a) VI 73 | [illegible] "turtle" 5121

(i) 魚 "fish" C.C.C. 7[a] 17[b] etc. B 219[5]

(ii) | [illegible] ["fish pipe"] 七星 "seven stars" [? a kind of musical instrument] C.C.C. 32[b].

5118 [illegible] VIII 67 [illegible] |

5119 [illegible] IX 106 [illegible] |

5120 [illegible] III 134 [illegible] | "water" C.C.C. 12[b] 洪 "flood"

5121 [illegible] VI 73 [illegible] | "fish" 龜 "turtle" C.C.C. 17[a]

5122 [illegible] III A 35 [illegible] "in the middle of water." B.92 [illegible] in succession. | is the word for | in the middle of the water."

B 215[3] 檀 sandal wood

Used as a Phonetic. In [illegible] W.I 126[9] = 檀 dan used to mean dāna "gift"

5123 [illegible] III A 4 Family [illegible]

5125 0214 chain

5126 3587 chain

5127 4083 chain

5132 independent

5124 3226 chain

5133
0860-4095

5128
3872 bis
3192 (3145A)
5410

B 221[2] v. 4233

5134 4544 chain

5129 independent

5135 5013 chain

5130 4651 chain

5136 1869 chain

5131 3587 chain

5137 5202 pair

395

5125 [Tangut] VI 20 | [Tangut]

5126 [Tangut] IX A125 [Tangut] | 5131

(i) W.I. 216[14] *riad. ldan* "fragrance"

(ii) [Tangut] | W.I. 196[5] *myos. pa* 0139

Nevsky I 329

5127 ~~5126~~ [Tangut] VI 20 | [Tangut] 4083

5124 [Tangut] V 66 [Tangut] | 3600

5128 [Tangut] VII 71 | [Tangut]

(a) VII 24 ditto

(b) V A108 [Tangut] |

(c) VII 26 [Tangut] | [Error for [Tangut]] 3192 3195A

(i) (c) above 衆生 "all creatures"

W.I. 98[9] 108[16] 134[12]

(ii) By itself Dict 1[a] 7

5129 [Tangut] VIII 35 "Family or clan (name)"

B176 P.N.

5130 [Tangut] IX 96 [Tangut] |

5131 [Tangut] VIII 84 [Tangut] | 0955

(a) I 65 | [Tangut] 5165

(b) III 59 | [Tangut] 0456

(c) III 67 | [Tangut] 0469

5131 cont.

(d) V 134 | [Tangut] 2698

(e) IX 66 [Tangut] x by | [Tangut] 0114

(f) IX A125 | [Tangut] 5126

(i) 酒 "wine" C.C.C. 32[a] II 48[6]

5132 [Tangut] VI 100 "Family or clan name"

5133 [Tangut] IX 59 | [Tangut] "bowl" 0860

(a) III A122 ditto

(i) [Tangut] "bottle" C.C.C. 23[b]

(ii) | [Tangut] name of constellation

C.C.C. 7[b] 奎宿 W.I. 222[7] *nam. gru*

5134 [Tangut] III 102 | [Tangut]

5134A [Tangut] x of VI 35 | [Tangut]

5135 [Tangut] VIII 35 | [Tangut]

5136 [Tangut] III 99 [Tangut] | 1194

5137 [Tangut] VIII 35 [Tangut] |

(a) VII 72 ditto

(0977 5740) pair

5138 2485 chain

5139 2485 chain

(ii) 渡 Pāramitā W.I.178[2]

5147 5017 chain

5140 2765 chain

5141 –3466

5142 – 3507

5143 5237 chain

5144 0563 chain

[illegible] 祀 | "full labial sounds"

Dict 1[b]6 Title of Ch. I

W.I.168[13] possibly 重 "heavy". III 90[8] do.

5148 – 5234
└ 5247

5145 – 5253

5139 B.12 (a) (i) 度 Vub II 6[1] 5140 5141 (a) B 245[2] 5142 5143 5144 (a) I (b) V (i) By it ~~514~~ (ii) W II 29 5145 (a) I

396

5138 [Tangut] VII 46 [Tangut] | 5139
B.121[2] (?) tr. 度 pass over
5139 [Tangut] V 44 | [Tangut] 3234
(a) VII 46 | [Tangut]
(i) 度 "to pass over" B.170[2] q.v. W.I.126[14] 148[15]
Var. II 6[1]: Pāramitā W.I.178[2] II 122[11]
5140 [Tangut] V 44 | [Tangut] 3816
v. 5134 A
5141 [Tangut] III A 36 | [Tangut] misspelt
(a) VII 10 ditto
B 245[2] ? Proper name 董 Dong
5142 [Tangut] IX 73 | [Tangut]
(a) I 20 ditto
5143 [Tangut] V 13 [Tangut] |
5144 [Tangut] IX 90 | [Tangut] q.v. tone 0563
(a) IX A 76 ditto
(b) VIII 54 | [Tangut] 4284
(i) By itself W.I.98[13]? Dict 1[b]5 II 118[5]
(ii) [Tangut] | 重 擔 "heavy load" 4976
W.II.29 B.200[1]
5145 [Tangut] I A 17 | [Tangut]
(a) I 41 ditto

5146 [Tangut] VI 38 [Tangut] |
(a) VI 58 ditto
(i) The dissyllable 船 舶 "boat" W.II.48[12]
(ii) By itself B.219[5] 船 boat
5147 [Tangut] III 100 | [Tangut]
(a) IX 97 | [Tangut] 3634
B.97 [Tangut] ideogram & the whole of [Tangut]. | is [Tangut] [去 to go out] & [Tangut] [於 "to"] & [Tangut] [Tangut] [彼 所 "that which"] & [Tangut] [之 "of"]. It is an auxiliary word: [Tangut] [Tangut] i.e. I[c]-A
此 "this" C.C.C. 29[b] W.I.138[1]
彼 "that" C.C.C. 31[b] B 219[5]
C.C.C. 32[a]? W.I.100[2]?
B.245[7] 其 "that"
5148 [Tangut] VII A 50 | [Tangut]
(a) III 103 ditto
(b) III 8 | [Tangut]
(i) | [Tangut] 汗衫 "sweat shirt, sweater (lit. "sweat protector")
C.C.C. 24[b] B.103 cat. under "clothing"

5151 4627 chain

5149 – 5150

5150 5149 pair

5158 i suppl

5152 0492 chain

5159 0148 chain

5152 Φi 𗧓 薾 沙門 *śramana* 𗧓 𗦈 過去 "past" W.I 178[12] 267[11] S.-H.J.414 B 344[4] W.I.967 過

W.II 130[12] 268[8]

5152
├ 0492
└ 4660–1503

5153 4775 chain

5154 3918 chain

5155
├ 0225
└ 1655–1656

5156 0488 pair

5157 0078 chain

397

5151 [Tangut] VII A 19 | [Tangut]

5149 [Tangut] III 104 | [Tangut]
(a) III 79 ditto misspelt

5150 [Tangut] III 79 [Tangut] | misspelt.
(a) III 104 ditto

44[4] 12 I.178 26[7] [11]

5152 [Tangut] VII 55 [Tangut] | 0492
(a) IX A 90? ditto [[Tangut]]
~~(b) VIII 12? ditto [Tangut]~~
(b) VIII 12 | [[Tangut]] [Tangut] (1503) 4660

chain?

B.186 Used as a phonetic 沙

5153 [Tangut] V 179 [Tangut] | 4775

5154 [Tangut] VI 66 [Tangut] | 3918

5155 ~~5154~~ [Tangut]
(a) III 31 [Tangut] | 1655
(b) IX 80 | [Tangut] 6225

W.I. 138[10] ? 亂 "confused"

Dict 1[a] 3 1 [Tangut]

5156 [Tangut] VIII 28 [Tangut] | 0488
(a) IX A 152 ditto (misspelt)

5157 ~~5156~~ [Tangut] III 58 | [Tangut] jade 590

(i) 瑠 "glass" C.C.C. 13[a]

(ii) 琉 "crystal" W II 24[6]

See 0078

(iii) The dissyllable 瑠璃 "crystal"

B.181[2] B.102 cat. under "precious things"

5158 [Tangut] II 17 Family or clan name

5159 ~~5158~~ [Tangut] II 17 [Tangut] | [Tangut] 4580 ~~Family or clan name~~
(a) III 4 | [Tangut] 3323
(b) III 113 | [Tangut] ×× 0592
(c) III 118 | [Tangut] × by [Tangut] |
(d) V 2 [Tangut] × by | [Tangut] ×× 0134
(e) V 34 | [Tangut] to calculate 4013
(f) V 140 | [Tangut] × 1611
(g) V A 85 | [Tangut] × 4827
(h) V A 111 | [Tangut] 3279
(i) V A 120 | [Tangut] × 2543
(j) IX 150 | [Tangut] 3022

A rather obscure word

C.C.C. 29[a] 31[a] 34[a] W.I. 98[7] 100[5] 222[2]

II 2[7] 7[8] 24[9] 32[6] 38[5] 74[1] B 185[4] 161[5], 163[1]

Possibly 已 "already" W II 2[7] B.169[4] q.v.

W.II 2[8]

(ii) (b) above 已畢 "already completed"

~~B 344[4]~~ 過: W.II 122[12] 已盡

B 223[4] q.v. tr. 猶 yet, still 230[2]

5160 2149 chain

5165 3587 chain

5166 2149 chain

5161 0159 chain

5166 A W II 4[10] 盡 'to exhaust'

By itself B.215[4] 尞 sacrificial fuel

5167 – 4235 A

5168 0489 pair

5169 2149 chain

5162 1550 A

5170 – 2507

5163 4027 chain

5164 0159 chain

5171 1842 pair

5172 5106 chain

398

5160 [illegible] VI 47 | [illegible] 3955
(a) V 57 | [illegible] 5166
(b) VI 128 | [illegible] 3104

5161 [illegible] — [VII A 56 ~~VII 59-60~~] [illegible] | 5164 V.5164A
(i) | 菱 棗 "date or jujube tree"
C.C.C. 14[a]
(ii) [illegible] | 蜜 蜂 "honey-bee"
C.C.C. 17[a] bun.ba ditto W.I. 192[17]
210[2]
(iii) | [illegible] sbran.rtsi "honey" 0216
W.I. 214[8]
(iv) | [illegible] 苷 bu.ram.śin
5109
"sugar-cane" W.I. 214[9] See 5164A

5162 [illegible] VIII 12 [illegible] |

5163 [illegible] III 71 [illegible] | 832 q.v.

5164 [illegible] III A 70 | [illegible] 2227
(a) VII A 56 [illegible] | 5161
(b) IX A 172 | [illegible] 1141
甜 "sweet" C.C.C. 33[b] W.I. 98[8]

5164A [illegible] Possibly the correct form of 5161

5165 [illegible] I 65 [illegible] | 5131

5166 [illegible] V 57 [illegible] |

5166A [illegible] See [illegible] 5205

5167 [illegible] VII A 34 [illegible] |
B 246[3] 川' ~~[illegible]~~ stuan (Phonetic)

5168 [illegible] VII A 63 [illegible] | 0489
(a) VII 83 ditto

5169 [illegible] III A 120 [illegible] |

~~5170 [illegible]~~ IX

5169A [illegible] Error for [illegible] 5180

5170 [illegible] IX 159 | [illegible] 2507
(a) VIII 84 ditto

5171 [illegible] V 113 [illegible] | 1842 misspelt
(a) VII 38 ditto [[illegible]]
Nevski I 387

5172 [illegible] IX A 148 [illegible] | 5106

5173 5110 chain

5173 B.98 | [illegible] is one rendering of [illegible] in dictionary

5180 4184 pair

5174 4924 chain

5181 independent

5175 | 2989 chain

5182 3160 chain

5176 4627 chain

5183 5110 chain

5177 2601 chain

5184 5106 chain

5178 2618 pair

5185 2716 chain

5179 independent

5174

5173

5174

5174

5175

(a)

C.C.C.

B.188³

5176

(a)

(b)

(c)

(d)

5177

5177.

5178

(a).

W.I.13

B245²

5179

? authentic cf. 4775

5174B [Tangut] x of VII A 79 | [Tangut]

B reads [Tangut] perhaps rightly cf. [Tangut]

399

5173 [Tangut] III 138 | [Tangut] water

[Tangut] "liquid mud" W.I. 160[7]

5174 [Tangut] IX 9 [Tangut] |

5174A [Tangut] Error for [Tangut] 5128

5175 [Tangut] I 50 | [Tangut] 0139

(a) VIII A 41 [Tangut] | 2989

C.C.C. 12[a] 泊 "mooring, anchorage"

B. 188[3] tis. 昏 "dusk" Nevski I 350

5176 [Tangut] VI 17 [Tangut] | ? misspelt v. (b) 4627

(a) I 140 [Tangut] | 1496

(b) III 59 [Tangut] | ? ? ditto

(c) III A 94 [Tangut] |

(d) VII A 19 [Tangut] | 5151

5177 [Tangut] III 74 [Tangut] |

5177A [Tangut] Error for [Tangut] 5197

5178 [Tangut] V A 97 [Tangut] | 2618

(a) V 106 ditto

W.I. 138[5] ?

B 245[2] 舒 shu ? part of P.N.

5179 [Tangut] V 57 Family or clan name

5180 [Tangut] III 66 | [Tangut]

(a) IX 4 ditto

5181 [Tangut] VIII 65 Family or clan name

B. 125[5] 185[2]

~~5182~~ B. 185[2] ? Phonetic 繞 jao

5182 [Tangut] VIII 86 [Tangut] | 3160

(a) IX 66 [Tangut] 0736

(i) The dissyllable W.I. 218[7] ? h k'ou "entwine" B. 165[3] 223[3] tis. 環繞 encircle

(ii) [Tangut] | mu. k'yud "circumference, rim" W.I. 216[16]

~~By itself B. 165[3] 環 encircle~~

5183 [Tangut] III 175 [Tangut] | "water"

(a) IX 159 ditto

C.C.C. 10[a] ? 坎 "pit" B. 160[5]

5184 [Tangut] IX 114 [Tangut] | 5106

5185 [Tangut] VII 72 | [Tangut] 2716

(i) The dissyllable 糯米 "glutinous rice" C.C.C. 15[b] B. 101 cat. under "grains".

5186-1649

5191 ~~chain~~ 5190 chain

5192-2561

5187 2027 chain

5188 chain
- 3319
- 1271—0061
- 5188 1143

Tr... B.169[2] tr. 衣着

5193 1596 chain

5194 5190 chain

5195 5110 chain

5189 2519 chain

5196 0322 chain

5190
- 2184
- 3280
- 0175
- 5191
- 5194

5197 2601 chain

B.189[2] 窮 weak, exhausted

5198 4256 pairs

5186
(a)

5187

5188
(a) I
(b)
(c)
(i) (c)
"ein
B.103
(ii) By
128[10]
5189

5190
(a)
(b)
(c)
(d)
(i) 盡
W.I.96
(ii) 終
(iii) 畢

400

5186 [Tangut] V 9 | [Tangut] 1649

(a) IX 41 ditto

5187 [Tangut] III A 44 [Tangut] | 2027

5188 [Tangut] V 11 | [Tangut] 3319 outside

(a) III 81 ditto

(b) VIII 50 [Tangut] | ?

(c) IX 43 [Tangut] | 1143

(i) (c) above (misspelt) 襖子 "lined jacket, robe" C.C.C. 24[b] B.103 cat. under "men's clothing"

(ii) By itself W.II 50[4] 答 "reply" 128[10] ditto

5189 [Tangut] S- VI A 129 [Tangut] | 693

5190 [Tangut] SI VI 24 [Tangut] | 3280

(a) VI A 44 ~~ditto~~ [Tangut] | 0175

(b) I A 88 [Tangut] | 2484

(c) VI A 116 [Tangut] x by | [Tangut] 5194

(d) IX 65 | [Tangut] 5191

(i) 盡 "end, finish, [complete, entirely] W.I. 96[8] 142[9] II 30[7] 2[9] 4[11] B 180[5]

(ii) 終 "end, finish W.I. 112[14]

(iii) 畢 "end, finish W.II 46[11]

5191 [Tangut] IX 65 [Tangut] |

5192 [Tangut] VI 32 | [Tangut] 2561

(a) VI 61 ditto

W.II. 34[12] 貧 "poor"

5193 [Tangut] 30- VII A 25 | [Tangut] ?

[(a) III 78 [Tangut] x by [Tangut] [Tangut] |] 928

(b) VII 65 | [Tangut] 5293

C.C.C. 1[a] 4 B 246[1] 用 use (vert)

5194 [Tangut] SYAN VI A 116 [Tangut] [Tangut]

Phonetic character

5195 [Tangut] V 147 [Tangut] | water 5110

Nevski I 333

B 246[3] 管 Gwan (Proper name) (means "pipe")

5196 [Tangut] IX 154 [Tangut] | 0322

5197 [Tangut] VI 2 [Tangut] | "pus" 2601

(a) I 80 ditto

(b) I A 33 | [Tangut] 1052

(c) IX 113 | [Tangut] 4606

血 "blood" C.C.C. 19[a] W.I. 98[8] II 24[3]

~~[illegible]~~ krag ditto W.I. 216[2]

5198 [Tangut] III 74 [Tangut] |

(a) IX 31 ditto

Nevski I 353 "cream"

5202 bis 2865 chain

5199 – 2800

5200 2193 chain

5201 2896 pair

5202 – 5137

5203 1596 chain

5204
- ~~4469~~ 4693
- 4459
- 4694
- 5233

5205 2167 chain

5206 3492 chain

5207 0322 chain

5208 2485 chain

5209 5523 chain

5210 4776 pair

5211 3213 chain

5212 5690 chain

5202 bis I 68 | 3133
=5115

401

5199 III 105 |
(a) IX 51 | [i.e. ditto]

5200 V 110 | 2193

5201 IX A 6 |
(a) I 29 ditto
(i) The dissyllable 蒲葦 "rushes & reeds" C.C.C. 16[a] water vegetable

5202 VII 72 |
(a) VIII 35 ditto

5203 VII 65 | 5193

5204 VIII 5 | ? error
(a) V A 110 | 4459
(b) VIII 10 | 4694
(c) VIII A 24 | ? ditto 4693
(d) IX 52 | ~~? ditto~~ 5235
溝 "ditch, drain" C.C.C. 12[a]

5205 VIII 5 | (9)
(i) The dissyllable B. 102 cat. under "rivers & seas" tr. 九井 "nine wells".

5206 V 115 |
~~(a) IX A 141~~ 井 "well" C.C.C. 12[a]
B. 188[1] do.

5207 V 161 | 3387
(i) 眶 "eye-socket" C.C.C. 18[b]
(ii) | ~~w~~ tag "the star Orion"
W.I. 220[9]

5208 V 161 | 3486
靴 "boot" C.C.C. 25[a]

5209 V 1 |
Nevsky T Φ I 337 "mouth"

5210 V 6 |
(a) VI 42 ditto
(i) The dissyllable C.C.C. 16[b] 鴈鴨 "wild goose, duck"
? water bird

5211 V 11 |
(a) V A 64 ditto

5212 III. 160 | 1367
(ii) The dissyllable 天 陰 "dark sky"? C.C.C. 10[b]
(i) By itself W II 14[5] 怒 "anger" [but see passage]

5213 5465 chain

5221 4123 chain

5222 5677 chain

5214 5106 chain

5223 0878 pair

5215 2765 chain

5216 0322 chain

5224 4396 chain

5217 5100 chain

[Tangut] | [Tangut] B.221[5] 滑 潤 slippery

5218 4355 chain

5219 5510 chain

5220 4123 chain

5225 3685 chain

402

5213 [Tangut] III A 61 [Tangut] | 4800

(a) V 95 | [Tangut] black 3051

(b) IX A 140 | [Tangut] × 2975 ⊘

雲 "cloud" W.I.92[11] II 8[7] B 260[2]

<u>sprin</u> ditto W.I. 208[18] B 221[1]

5214 [Tangut] VII A 137 [Tangut] |

5215 [Tangut] VI 33 [Tangut]

B.172[1] q.v.

5216 [Tangut] I 81 [Tangut] |

Nevski I 347 "tieri"

5217 [Tangut] III A 17 | [Tangut]

(a) III 167 ditto unerrat

(b) I A 58 [Tangut] | 3175

(c) IX 41 | [Tangut] (v) 0691

5218 [Tangut] VI A 110 [Tangut] | 5093

(i) | [Tangut] C.C.C. 23[b] 急 隨 鉢子

(2798)

5219 [Tangut] III 118 [Tangut] |

5220 [Tangut] VI A 39 [Tangut] | 4123

(a) VII A 53 | [Tangut] 5221

(b) VIII A 75 | [Tangut] 3128

(c) IX 81 | [Tangut] [0734]

Nevsky I 852 "to make a noise"

5221 [Tangut] VII A 53 [Tangut] |

5222 [Tangut] III 103 [Tangut] |

5223 [Tangut] I 50 [Tangut] |

(a) III 3 ditto

5224 [Tangut] III 103 [Tangut] | 4396

(a) V 3 [Tangut] | 1729

(b) V 7 [Tangut] | 1075

(c) V 29 [Tangut] | 4855

(d) VIII 2 | [Tangut] xx 3348

(i) By itself 珠 "pearl" C.C.C. 3[a]

W.I. 108[8] <u>nor. bu</u> "jewel" I 192[11]

(ii) (b) above 碧 珊瑚珠 "green

jade . . . . pearl" C.C.C. 12[b]

B. 102 cat. under "precious things"

(iii) | [Tangut] C.C.C. 8[a] 計都星

name of star

5225 [Tangut] VI A 73 [Tangut] |

a name W.I 271[1] q.v.

5226 5710 chain

5227 3687 pair

5228 2360 chain

5229 -1669

5230 5237 chain

5231 5644 chain

5232 1778 chain

5233 5204 chain

5234 5148 chain

5235 2716 chain

5236 5110 chain

5237
- 0665
- 5143
- 5230

5238 4516 chain

5239 4276 chain

5240 independent

403

5225A [illegible] Error for [illegible] 5238

5226 [illegible] III A93 [illegible] | water

(i) | [illegible] me. dbal "a sort of disease" W.I. 208"

5227 [illegible] VIII 25 [illegible] |

(a) I 31 ditto

5228 [illegible] IX 101 [illegible] | white 2360

5229 [illegible] IX 159 | [illegible] 1669

(a) II 1 ditto

5230 [illegible] VI A128 [illegible] [illegible] 5237 1709

Phonetic character

5231 [illegible] I 14 [illegible]

少 "slight" W II 40[32]

Nevski I 334

5232 [illegible] IX 153 [illegible]

5233 [illegible] IX 52 [illegible] | 5204

[illegible] 'ditch' C.C.C.12[a] Tϕ II 335

5234 [illegible] III 103 [illegible] |

(a) VII A50 ditto

5235 [illegible] I 47 [illegible] | 2705

~~(a) VII 51 [illegible] | [[illegible]]~~

W.I. 218[8] sku ? "body image [[illegible]]

Distinguish from 5244

Note. [illegible] is no doubt correct.

5236 [illegible] III 180 [illegible] |

(a) III 118 | [illegible]

5237 ~~5238~~ [illegible] VI 23 | [illegible] 0665

(a) IX 8 ditto

(b) V 13 | [illegible] 1709 5143

(c) VI A128 [illegible] x by | [illegible] 5230

5238 [illegible] IX A42 [illegible] |

(a) V 97 ditto

5239 ~~5240~~ [illegible] V 42 [illegible] | 4229

5240 [illegible] VIII 93 "Family or clan" (name)

[(a) III A109 [illegible] x by [illegible]]

W.I. 98[8]: [possibly phonetic]

Used as Phonetic II 2[12]

5241 5710 chain

5242 2405 pair

5243 1713 chain

5244 5245 chain

5245
+ 5244
+ 5256

5246 1930 ~~do~~ pair

5247 5148 chain

5248
+ 4882-3106
+ 2939

5249 ? 2485 chain

5250 0151 chain

5251 3685 ~~chain~~

5252 3973 pair

5253 5145 pair

404

5241 [illegible] VII 86 [illegible] | "water"
B.95 [illegible] ideogram, plus the whole of [illegible]. | [cf. 沫 "froth, ~~| [froth, saliva]~~ is "water |, or [illegible]."
B215² 沫 froth 232² 浪 wave

5242 [illegible] VIII 93 [illegible] | 2405
(a) III 21 ditto

5243 [illegible] VII 51 [illegible] | 4642
(i) | [illegible] c.c.c. 22ᵇ 和 [illegible]
(ii) By itself 泥 "mud" W.I.160⁷

5244 [illegible] III 58 [illegible] |
(a) VII 51 ditto
W.I.218⁸ skin body, image?

5245 [illegible] VII 51 | [illegible]
(a) III 58 ditto
(b) III 58 | [illegible]
(i) [illegible] | [illegible] c.c.c. 22ᵇ [illegible] 舍 ? mud house.

5246 [illegible] VI 23 [illegible] | misspelt
(a) V 3 ditto

5247 [illegible] III 8 [illegible] |

5248 [illegible] VIII 25 | [illegible] ×3106 4882
(a) V 21 ditto
(b) VIII A6 [illegible] | 2939
(i) The disyllable W.I.134¹ c.c.c. 21ᵇ 畜養 "to rear & feed"; W.I.98¹⁰ 滋養 "to feed"; W.I.134¹⁵ 養 "to feed".
By itself B.162³ 204¹

5249 [illegible] VIII 25 [illegible] | 9.8 1458

5250 [illegible] III 58 | [illegible] 4932

5251 [illegible] VI 26 | [illegible]
(i) The disyllable c.c.c. 31ᵇ 分折 "to divide & separate".

5252 [illegible] I 11 [illegible] |
(a) IX 1 ditto
(i) The disyllable 泉原 "spring" c.c.c. 12ᵃ B.102 cat. under "rivers + seas"

5253 [illegible] I 41 [illegible] |
(a) I A17 ditto

5254 — 5698

5262 — 5261

5263 5106 chain

~~5264 Phonetic in 4255~~

5255 2091 chain

5264
⊢1579
└1498

| [Tangut] W.I 266[21] part of royal title tr. 口主

5256 5245 chain

5257 5110 chain

5265 4208 chain

5258 5424 pair

5266 4518 chain

5259 3354 chain

[5267] 3929 chain

5260 5517 pair

[5268] 5300 chain

5269 3835 chain

5261 5262 pair

525… (i) Th… "brig… spur…
5255
5256
5257
5258
(a) …
(i) The …
~~kind~~
5259
壬 '9
5260
(a) V
5261
(a) III

405

5254 [Tangut] VI 96 | [Tangut]
(a) IX 69 ditto
(i) The dissyllable W.I.100[3] 皎潔 "bright & pure" II 18[8] 鮮潔 "fresh & pure" II 26[9] 清潔 "pure".

5255 [Tangut] VIII 36 [Tangut] | 3956

5256 [Tangut] III 58 [Tangut] | 5245

5257 [Tangut] V 178 [Tangut] |

5258 [Tangut] III A 131 [Tangut] |
(a) I 27 ditto
(i) The dissyllable 乳頭 [presumably a kind of food "milk-head"?] nipple C.C.C. 33[a]

5259 [Tangut] III 140 | [Tangut] 11th stem 1531
壬 "9th stem" C.C.C. 9[b]

5260 [Tangut] IX 72 [Tangut] |
(a) VII 45 ditto

5261 [Tangut] III 136 [Tangut] |
(a) III 45 ditto

5262 [Tangut] III 45 | [Tangut] ~~ditto~~
(a) III 136 ditto
Nevski I 353 "drink"

5263 [Tangut] I 11 | [Tangut] 5706

5264 [Tangut] IX 43 | [Tangut] 1579
(a) V 44 ditto
(b) IX 47 | [Tangut] | country 1498
(i) | [Tangut] 3832 "increase" B.102 cat. under "rivers & seas".
(ii) By iCoy Dict. 1[b]3 B.345[2]

5265 [Tangut] IX 43 [Tangut] | 4208 [illegible]
(a) IX 149 ditto
5264 Phonetic + [Tangut]

5266 [Tangut] III 115 [Tangut] | 4578
(a) VI A 88 ditto

5267 [Tangut] VII 111 [Tangut] [|] ?error 5406
(a) V 24 | [Tangut] 5407

5268 [Tangut] V 46 [Tangut]

5269 [Tangut] VII 116 [Tangut] |

5270 3109 chain III

5271 0809 chain I 11

5273 0532 pair VI

5274 5690 chain VIII

5275 4011 chain

5276 ~~interpunct~~ III

5277 2217 chain

5278 0233 chain

5279 3382 pair

5272 ~~interpunct~~

5280 5281 chain

406

5270 [Tangut] I 23 [Tangut] | 3109

(a) V 37 ditto

5271 [Tangut] VII A 12 [Tangut] | 0889

(a) VI 30 ditto

(b) I 110 | [Tangut] 0778

(c) I A 14 [Tangut] | 2836

(d) I A 52 [Tangut] | × 3131 / 5649 2895

(e) III 132 | [Tangut] 1639

(f) III 180 [Tangut] | 4523

~~(g) VI 30~~

(g) VI 97 [Tangut] | 5388

(h) VII 58 | [Tangut] 2860

(i) (j) VII A 32 | [Tangut] 2802

(j) (k) VII A 38 | [Tangut] 0761

(k) (l) IX 7 [Tangut] | × 2855 2835

(l) (m) IX 61 [Tangut] | 2810

(m) (n) IX 124 [Tangut] | 2803

(n) (o) IX 139 | [Tangut] 2898

草 grass, leafy vegetable C.C.C. 13b

W. I. 134[17] ?

5272 [Tangut] [VII 59-60]

?

YAN

5273 [Tangut] VIII A 42 | [Tangut]

(a) I 98 ditto

(i) The disyllable B. 100 cat. under "wild animals"

5274 [Tangut] VI 57 [Tangut] | 3203

(a) I 66 | [Tangut] × 4376

(b) III 21 [Tangut] | × 4269

5275 [Tangut] VII 20 [Tangut] | first born 1103

4011 chain

5276 [Tangut] [VII 59-60]

5277 [Tangut] VIII 22 [Tangut] | 2217

5278 [Tangut] V A 41 [Tangut] |

5279 [Tangut] VII 27 [Tangut] |

(a) I 32 ditto

(i) The disyllable cat. under "camels"

5280 [Tangut] VII A 103 [Tangut] |

5281
- 3001 – 2983 – 0597
- 5280 – 5070
- 5378

5286 2482 chain

5287 – 3494

5288 1876 chain

5282 2231 ~~chain~~

5289 5610 pair

5283 – 2271 [VIII 39]

5290
- 4259
- 2189
- 5041
- 5666
- 5308

5284 2385 chain

5285 ~~2...~~
- 2241
- 1399

5291 4439 ~~chain~~ [VI...]

407

5281 [Tangut] IX A135 | [Tangut] "3001"

(a) III 121 ditto

(b) VII A62 [Tangut] | 5280

(c) VII A103 | [Tangut] 5280

(ii) The dissyllable 煩 惱 "trouble ~~anguish~~ anguish" ~~& trouble~~ C.C.C. 35[b] W.II.2[8]

(i) 煩 "trouble" W.I.118[3]

(ii) 惱 "anguish" W.I.136[8] II 118[6]

B.251[1] zug "pain"

5282 [Tangut] I24 [Tangut] | 2231

5283 [Tangut] VII 111 [Tangut] | [Tangut] 2271

(a) VI 69 ditto

5284 [Tangut] III 40 [Tangut] | [Tangut]

(a) III 52 ditto

5285 [Tangut] VII 16 | [Tangut]

(a) IX 41 ditto

(b) IX 94 | [Tangut] 1399

5281 A [Tangut] x of V 130 | [Tangut]

Error for 5300

5286 [Tangut] III 50 | [Tangut] "black"

(i) The dissyllable B.101 cat. under "wild animals"

5287 [Tangut] IX A150 [Tangut]

(a) IX A149 ditto

5288 [Tangut] I 87 | [Tangut]

5289 [Tangut] I A50 [Tangut] |

(a) I 88 ditto

B.186[4] q.v. tr. 自

5290 [Tangut] I 23 | [Tangut] 4259

(a) III 15 | [Tangut] 5666

(b) V 61 | [Tangut] 2189

(c) VI 17 | [Tangut] 5041

(d) VII 52 | [Tangut] 5308

意 manas "mind, intellect" (Soothill p.400) passim.

yid ditto W.I.194[1]

blo ditto W.I.194[7]

5291 [Tangut] II 3 [Tangut] | 4439

(a) I 22 ditto

5292 & 2990 pair

5298 4607 chain

5293
├ 1102
└ 4259 — 5290 —

5300 } — { 3315
5281A } { 4779 A

5294 1594 chain

5299 5301 chain

5301 ~~2445 chain~~
┬ 2445 — 0429
└ 0840 ├ 1569
├ 2326 — 4249
│ └ 5299
├ 3633
├ 3827
└ 5306

5295 0741 chain

B 121²? [illegible] ko. 嗚乎 alas!

5296 0258 chain

5297 4104 chain

5302 1128 chain

未 408

5292 [Tangut] VII A 6, [Tangut] | 2990
(a) VII A 93 ditto
W II 66[2] 倒 "inverted, upside down" perverted
I 172[14]

5293 [Tangut] [VII 59-60]
(a) IV 4 | [Tangut] ? 1102
(b) IX 9 | [Tangut] plan 4259

5294 [Tangut] I 106 [Tangut] | 1694
(a) I 46 ditto
(b) VI 28 [Tangut] 1640
(i) The dissyllable 蝴蝶 "butterfly" C.C.C. 17[a]

5295 [Tangut] VII 30 [Tangut] |

5296 [Tangut] VI 69 [Tangut] B. 125[1]
C.C.C. 35[b] 争 "to wrangle, dispute"
W.I. 134[8] 諍 "to dispute, remonstrate"

5297 [Tangut] VII 111 | [Tangut] "of"
A rather elusive particle.
(i) | [Tangut] 爾 時 "at that time W II 22[6] 16[7].
(ii) [Tangut] | W.I. 108[5] 不 "not"

W.II 16[6] 未 "not yet". In this case the word is practically meaningless.
II 114[10]

5298 [Tangut] VII 70 | [Tangut]

~~5299~~ 5300 [Tangut] VII 111 | [Tangut]
(a) V 130 ditto
v. 5281 A

5299 [Tangut] I 11 | [Tangut] 2326

5301 [Tangut] V 105 | [Tangut] 2445
(a) VIII 82 ditto
(b) III 70 | [Tangut] 0840
(ii) The dissyllable 遊戲 "vikrīḍita" "to roam for pleasure; sport" W.I 110[18]
(i) [Tangut] By itself 遊 "bhrāmya- to ramble, wander" W.I. 144[5]
(iii) | [Tangut] ditto, ditto W.I 148[11] II 4[10]
(i) rtse "play, amuse oneself" W.I. 226[4]
(iv) | [Tangut] rgyags.pa (1569)
W.I. 224[17]

5302 [Tangut] V 46 [Tangut] |
(a) III 60 [Tangut] |
祠 "ancestral hall" W.I. 92[15]
詞 W.I. 160[4]

5303 1781 chain

5304 3086 chain

5305
3256
2017 – 2152

5311 – 2240

5312 5077 pair

5306 5301 chain

5313 4510 chain

5314
1962 – 1032
1050
1278
1139
4039
4059

5307 1182 chain

5308 5290 chain

5309 1438 bis chain

5310
1835
1475
1695
2947
3047

5306AA [Tangut] B.171² ? err for 5309 or 5323

409

5303 [Tangut] VI 135 [Tangut] | 3111

5304 [Tangut] VA115 [Tangut] | 4604
(a) V 73 [Tangut] | 3239

5305 [Tangut] V 107 | [Tangut] 3256 ~~2017~~
(a) VII 36 ditto
(b) V 6 | [Tangut] × 2152 2017
(i) (b) above *參差
C.C.C. 30ᵇ

5306 [Tangut] V 40 [Tangut] |
W II 26¹² 52⁵ 踊躍 "to leap, jump" B.171¹

5306A [Tangut] Err for [Tangut] 3364
5307 [Tangut] VA101 | [Tangut] 2694
C.C.C. 26ᵇ 鋤 "a hoe".

5308 [Tangut] VII 52 [Tangut] |

5309 [Tangut] VII 30 | [Tangut] 3555

5310 [Tangut]
(a) I 60 [Tangut] | 1835
(b) V 82 [Tangut] | 3047

5310 cont.
(c) V A18 [Tangut] | 2947
(d) VIII 3 [Tangut] | 1695
(e) VIII 15 [Tangut] | 1475
B.159² 中 州 chou.

5311 [Tangut] VII 16 | [Tangut] 2240
(a) IX 41 ditto

5312 [Tangut] III 75 [Tangut] |
(a) III 93 ditto reversed

5313 [Tangut] V 6 | [Tangut] misspelt 2108

5314 [Tangut] VII 116 | [Tangut] × (reversed) 1962
(a) VI 103 ditto
(b) I 143 | [Tangut] 4039
(c) II 39 | [Tangut] 1278
(i) 聚 'samāsa' to assemble, collect (Soot. p. 427) W.I.90⁵
(ii) 積 "accumulation, gathering together" W.I.92¹³ 100¹³
(iii) dpuṅ "army" W.I.194¹⁸
(iv) ts'ogs "assembly" W.I.196⁸
B.195¹ 集 kūṭa accumulation

409

5315-2140 2194

B.122 singl. 郎刻 instantly

5316 4276 chain

5321 0322 chain

5322 0322 chain

5323-0650

5317 1889 chain

5324 1222 chain

5325 0322 chain

5318 2928 chain

5326 3931 chain

5319 2485 chain

5327 1957 pair

5320 2928 chain

410

5315 VII 111 |

(a) IX 151 ditto

(i) The dissyllable C.C.C. 30b W.I. 168[6] immediately

II 46[7] 64[1] 立 便 84[10] B.246[9] 疾速 immediately

~~[very obscure] Probably merely~~ 便 "then"

B.245[2] 忽然 suddenly 248 立 immediately

5316 VI 27 | 2275

(a) II 1 | 0792

(b) VI 99 | 1301

(c) VII 49 | 5600

(d) VIII 3 | 0252

(i) | B.103 cat. under "silk" 2007

5317 I 57 | 1889

(a) VI 70 ditto

(b) I A 63 | 1286

(c) III 49 | 2359

5318 I 49 | 5320

5319 I A 41 | 2485

see 4th. 5319. II. 428

5320 I 41 | 2928

(a) VII A 117 ditto

(b) I 49 | 5318

(c) I. 55 | 4177

5320 cont.

(d) I 93 | 4182

(e) IX 179 | 0915

邊 "limit, end" W.I. 96[15] B.180 II 94[8]

際 ditto W.I. 142[17] 邊 B.131[2] 際 juncture

mt'a ditto W.I. 192[3] B.249

5321 V 83 | 5322

The dissyl. B.128[2] 盲 瞽 "blind"

5322 I A 89 | "eye"

(a) V 83 |

盲 "blind" W II 26[6]

5323 I 49 |

(a) VII 15 ditto

5324 I 28 | garland 4521

5325 III 147 |

5326 III 89 |

5327 V 83 | misspelt 1967

(a) I 29 ditto [in both]

B.171[5] 昏 confused, dusk, dark

5328 1131 pair

5329 1222 chain

5330 3905 chain

[5331] 1357 chain

5332 3829 chain

5333 – 5345 A

5334 4262 chain

5335 4262 chain

5336 (vi) | [Tangut] 現前 'manifest' before on W II 4[9]

W. II. 118[8] 前

5336 ⊥ 5340 – 2645 – 2623

5337 – 3407

5338 4157 chain

5339 1686 chain

5340 5336 chain

5328

(a)

5329

5330

[5331

5332

5333

5334

5335

(i) The

'the m

5336

(a) IX

A very

(ii) The

appoin

wrt.

(of pla

411

5328 [Tangut] V 83 [Tangut] |

(a) VII 18 ditto

5329 [Tangut] VIII 96 [Tangut] | garland 4521

5330 [Tangut] III 142 | [Tangut] 3905

5331 [Tangut] VI 25 [Tangut] |

5332 [Tangut] IX 146 [Tangut] | 3829

5333 [Tangut] VII 97 [Tangut] |

5334 [Tangut] IX 4 [Tangut] | 3445

5335 [Tangut] III 52 | [Tangut]

(i) The dissyllable c.c.c. 29^{a} 人情 "the nature of man"?

5336 [Tangut] VIII 8 | [Tangut]

(a) IX 4 ditto

A very obscure word

(ii) The dissyllable W.I. 98^{16} 136^{8} apparently not representing any Chinese word. W II 52^{9}: 於 … 前 "before" (of place I 170^{12}; ditto? B 243^{2} 216^{1}

5336 cont.

(i) By itself mdun-du "in front of"

(iii) | [Tangut] c.c.c. 22^{a} 枙 栿

(iv) | [Tangut] c.c.c. 29^{a} 棹 "table"?

(v) [Tangut] | c.c.c. 28^{a} 殿前 "front hall or temple"?

5337 [Tangut] VI A 122 | [Tangut]

(a) IX 107 ditto

W.I. 98^{4} 態 "behaviour"

5338 [Tangut] VIII 8 | [Tangut] 4157?

(i) [Tangut] | c.c.c. 23^{a} 毛 柵 "hair screen"? 3464

5339 [Tangut] VIII 8 [Tangut] | .1686

(a) III 35 ditto

(b) VIII 33 | [Tangut]

W.II 128^{8}

(ii) (b) above 守護 "to protect, guard"

5340 [Tangut] IX 4 [Tangut] | 5336 fin?

(a) IX 4 ditto ×2623 2645

(b) VIII 19 [Tangut] [Tangut] | ?

A very obscure word v. 5336 (ii).

5341 2309 chain

5342 0010 pair

B. 231³ [Tangut character] (3 or 4 times)

5343 2278 chain

5344 - 1073

5345 - 5419

5345A 5333 pair

5346 3226 chain

B. 187¹ lis. 發 emit etc. 192³

5347 0899 chain

5348 2558 pair

5349 - 3102

5350 - 0737

5351 1239 pair

5352 interjection

412

5341 [Tangut] VA 136 [Tangut] | 4833

5342 [Tangut] wei II 14 | [Tangut] 0010
(a) IX A 11 ditto
~~(a) IX A 1~~ (i) By itself 愚 "stupid" C.C.C. 17^6 31^6 W.II 26^7 B.132^1
(ii) The disyllable 愚蒙 "stupid" C.C.C. 31^a 愚惑 ditto W.I. 168^8 愚癡 "foolish & doting" II 60^4

5343 [Tangut] IX 29 | [Tangut] 1036
(i) The disyllable B.101 cat. under "wild animals".

5344 [Tangut] IX 29 | [Tangut]
(a) IX 52 ditto
~~(i) [Tangut] grib. non "filth-spouting" name of devil. W.I 212^17 218^15~~

5345 [Tangut] VI 32 [Tangut] | ~~|~~
(a) III 3 ditto
~~(b) I 55~~ (i) The disyllable grib. non "filth-spouting" a sort of devil. W.I. 212^17 218^15

5345A [Tangut] × of | [Tangut] VII 97
? might be [Tangut]

5346 [Tangut] VI 24 "auxiliary word"
(a) III 45 ~~[Tangut]~~ | [Tangut] × (3893) 3327
W.II 66^3 ? Dict. 1^a 2 152^7 II. 140^6 所 B.168^5 B.162^1

5347 [Tangut] V 62 | [Tangut] 3908
(i) | [Tangut] W.II 66^3 ~~2~~ 今生 "to bring into existence?" : II 80^11 起 "to bring forth" B.187^5 發開
(i) the disyl. B.164^5 trs. 發起

5348 [Tangut] I 64 [Tangut] | 2558

5349 [Tangut] V 62 | [Tangut] 3102
(a) VII 47

5350 [Tangut] V 62 | [Tangut]
(a) IX 85 ditto
(Variant 5404 a)

5351 [Tangut] I 64 [Tangut] |
(a) VII 64 ditto

5352 [Tangut] V 96 Family or clan name

5353 5356 chain

5354 2500 pair

5357 5356 chain

5358 4027 chain

5355 (ii) The disyllable 飢 "hungry"

W.I.170[2]

5355
5506
5516

5359 0233 chain

5360 1402 pair

5361 – 5363

5356
5357
2591
2639
3289 — 3333
5353 4568

5362 2511 pair

413

5353 [Tangut] IX 107 [Tangut] |

5354 [Tangut] III 35 [Tangut] | 2500

(a) IX 5 ditto

(i) ~~(a)~~ The disyllable 駱駝 "camel" C.C.C. 16^{a}. B.100 Chapter heading.

cf. 5362

5355 [Tangut] VIII A 43 | [Tangut]

(a) VII A 89 ditto

(b) I 88 | [Tangut] thirsty 5516

B.91 [Tangut] ideogram plus the centre of [Tangut]. | [tr. 飢 "hungry, famine"] is [Tangut]. It is the word for [Tangut] [tr. 食未得 "~~to~~ not to obtain food"].

~~飢 "hungry" W.I.170^{2}~~

5356 [Tangut] VIII 85 | [Tangut]

(a) IX 13 ditto

(b) I 45 | [Tangut] × 3289

(c) I 141 | [Tangut] 2591

(d) III 82 | [Tangut] 2639 5353

(i) (e) mnal "womb" W.I.216^{2}

eto "belly" W.I. 218^{14}

胞胎 "placenta or womb" W.I 100^{3}

(ii) (b) above 腹肚 "belly" C.C.C. 19^{a}

(iii) (d) above 脖臍 "navel" C.C.C. 19^{a}

5357 [Tangut] IX 13 [Tangut] |

(a) VIII 85 ditto

(i) 胄 "helmet" C.C.C. 5^{b} bra. ñe W.I 222^{7} name of a lunar mansion.

5358 [Tangut] III 22 [Tangut] |

(i) The disyllable B.100 cat. under "camel"

5359 [Tangut] VI 38 [Tangut] |

5360 [Tangut] VII 21 [Tangut] | 1402

(a) I.16 ditto

5361 [Tangut] V A 79 | [Tangut]

(a) IX A 19 ditto

(i) The disyllable 飽滿 "full, replete" W.II 24^{4}

5362 [Tangut] III 35 [Tangut] | 2511

(a) IX 5 ditto cf. 5354

5363 ~~3299 pair~~ 5361 pair

5369 3417 ~~chain~~

(iii) (c) above W.I 172[9] 下 "lower (quarter)"

5364 3299 pair

5370 1453 pair

5365 3400 pair

5371 1572 chain

5366 — 3696

5372 ~~independent~~

5367 — 3718

5373 0042 chain

5368 5467 pair

5374 3402 ~~chain~~

414

5363 [Tangut] IX A 19 [Tangut] |

(a) V A 59 ditto

(i) The Dissyllable 飽滿 "full, replete" W.II.24[4]

5364 [Tangut] III 6 [Tangut] |

(a) I.16 ditto

(i) The Dissyllable C.C.C. 24[b] 袜 肚

5364A [Tangut] Error for [Tangut]?

5365 [Tangut] III 6 [Tangut] |

(a) I 79 ditto

(i) The Dissyllable C.C.C. 24[b] 袩

5366 [Tangut] VI 96 | [Tangut]

(a) VI A 29 ditto

[Tangut] ? correct

5367 [Tangut] VIII A 34 | [Tangut]

(a) VIII A 31 ditto

5368 [Tangut] IX A 74 [Tangut] |

(a) IX A 2 ditto [[Tangut]]

Note. The form in IX A 2 may well be correct.

5369 [Tangut] V 131 [Tangut] | "bottom"

(a) II 3 ditto ×3417

(b) I 14 [Tangut] | 3266

(c) VII 67 [Tangut] | 2235

(d) VIII 56 [Tangut] | ×(0711) 1500 (e) IX 85 [Tangut] | 1756

(i) 間 "during" C.C.C. 9[b] B 164[5]

下 "in" C.C.C. 31[b] B 163[2], 174[2] 內 "within" W.I 168[17]

(ii) | [Tangut] (1817) B.103 cat. under "clothing"

[tr. 下著 "inner clothing"]

5370 [Tangut] III 128 [Tangut] | 1453

(a) VI 96 ditto reversed

5371 [Tangut] IX A 5 [Tangut] |

(i) The Dissyllable B.101 cat. under "wild animals."

5372 [Tangut] VII A 139 Family (name or clan)

5373 ~~5376~~ [Tangut] V 46 [Tangut] | 4683

(a) IX 132 [Tangut] | 2337

5374 [Tangut] V 69 [Tangut] | shrine 3402

5375 ⊢1975 ⊢0298

5376 4.437 pair

5381 -4836 pair

5377 1891 chain

5382-5383

5378 5381 chain VII

5383 5382 pair

5379 1313 chain V

5384 (i) 同 'same' W.II 128^{10}

5380 0233 chain V

5384 3922 chain

| W.II 128^{10} 同 時 'at the same time'

B.234^{4} 同

415
~~405~~

5375 [Tangut] VI 101 | [Tangut] 1975
(a) VIII 82 ditto
(b) VII 39 [Tangut] × by Dissyllable 0297
(i) The Dissyllable C.C.C. 15[a] 塩
W.I. 138[11] 鹽 "salt"

A word of doubtful meaning, in some places apparently 各 "each", in others 處 "place" W.I. 100[2] II 4[3], 10[4], 22[9] 38[7] 50[2]
(i) 各 "each" W.II 4[3] [clear case] I 170[15] (probably) II 116[10] 所 q.v. B. 122[2] 170[4] ~~186~~ 220[2] 231[3] B. 186[4] tr. 互 "to dovetail together". 237[2]

5376 [Tangut] VII 112 [Tangut] |
(a) V A 57 ditto
(i) | [Tangut] [Tangut] (2448) bcom. ldan. ḥdas "Bhagavan, lord" W.I. 190[4] B. 248[2] = "victoriously consummated"
(ii) | [Tangut] ḥjoms. pa "to attack, conquer W.I. 196[8]

5381 [Tangut] IX 123 | [Tangut] 4836
(a) V 34 ditto
(b) VIII 88 | [Tangut] 5398
(i) The Dissyllable C.C.C. 16[a] 鹿麕 "deer".

Note. 5380 & 5381 are indistinguishable.

5377 ~~[Tangut]~~ [Tangut] III 181 [Tangut] | 3898

5382 [Tangut] III 72 | [Tangut]
(a) III 83 ditto

5378 [Tangut] VII A 62 [Tangut] |

5383 [Tangut] III 83 [Tangut] |
(a) III 72 ditto

5379 [Tangut] VI 97 [Tangut] | 1313
(a) V 80 | [Tangut] 5612

5384 [Tangut] III 181 [Tangut] |
(i) By itself 同 "close, thick (rain) C.C.C. 9[a] B. 172[3]
(ii) 侵 "to invade, usurp" W.II 18[6]
(iii) The Dissyllable 同共 "all together W.II 48[9]

5380 [Tangut] III 126 [Tangut] | 0233
(a) VI 90 [Tangut] | 0156
(b) VIII 1 [Tangut] | (5 times) 1137
[(c) VIII 88 | [Tangut]]

5394-5385 1584 chain

5386 4027 chain

5387 5399 pair

5388 0809 chain

5389 3402 chain

5390 independent

5391 3089 chain

5392 1929 chain

5393 5708 chain

5394 -4590

5395+4018 chain

5396 - 0975

5397 0249 chain

5398 4836 chain

5399 - 5387

5400 盛 abundant W.III 112[5] B.165[4]

+ (ii) (c) above 强盛 powerful W.II 130[8]

III 144[3] 熾盛 effulgence

5400 1398 chain B.193[2]

絥 | W.I. 265[14] part of royal title

德盛 "(promoting) great virtue"

(c) B.221[5] 盛繁 luxurious + abundant

416
~~406~~

5385 [Tangut] I A100 | [Tangut] 3394

5386 [Tangut] VIII A61 | [Tangut]

(a) III 22 | [Tangut]

(i) (a) above B.100 cat. under 'camel'.

5387 [Tangut] IX 87 [Tangut] |

(a) IX 172 ditto

5388 [Tangut] VI 97 | [Tangut] 5271

5389 [Tangut] I 104 | [Tangut] 3402

5390 [Tangut] I A37 family or clan (name)

5391 [Tangut] VII 92 [Tangut] 3089

5391A [Tangut] Probably error for [Tangut]

5392 [Tangut] TSanVI 97 | [Tangut] 3338

5393 [Tangut] IX 172 [Tangut] | ? 1099

5394 [Tangut] IX 123 [Tangut] (|)

(a) VII 117 ditto

5395 [Tangut] III 76 [Tangut] |

(a) I 89

B.168[5] (Tangut)

5396 [Tangut] II 16 | [Tangut] misspelt

(a) VII A 26 ditto

5397 [Tangut] III 55 [Tangut] 4098

5398 [Tangut] VIII 88 [Tangut] |

(i) The Hsyllable B.101 cat. under "wild animals"

5399 [Tangut] IX 172 | [Tangut].

(a) IX 87 ditto

W.I.132[13] 捕 "to catch (fish)"

W.I.136[6] ? 壓 to repress

5400 [Tangut] II A7 [Tangut] | 1398

(a) V A139 ditto

(b) II 23 [Tangut] | 3792 × {1769 2074}

(c) IX 92 | [Tangut] 2687

(d) IX 178 [Tangut] | 2509

榮 "glorious, flourishing" C.C.C.19[6]

5400 (ii) (c) above 熾盛 'splendid'

WⅡ144[3]

5401 2327 chain

5402 5013 chain

5403 5462 chain

5404 3741 chain

5405 3496 pair

5406 3929 chain

5407 3929 chain

5408 4619 chain

5409 5690 chain

5410 5128 chain

5411 - 4019

5413 - 0549

5412 4104 chain

540
豐
126[16]
茂
隆
興
540
540
540
(a)
(a)
(b)
(c)
(d)
5404
W.I.98
B 215
5404
5405
(a)
(i)

417 ~~406~~

5400 cont.

豐 luxurious, abundant W.I.124[2] 126[16] 178[1]

茂 "luxuriant" B.181[1]

隆 (lung) "abundant" B.186[1] q.v.

興 "prosperous B.186, 272[2] W.I 271[10]

5401 [Tangut] IX 123 [Tangut] |

5402 [Tangut] II 15 [Tangut] |

(a) VIII 65 ditto

5403 [Tangut] VII 46 [Tangut] | 5462

(a) III 129 ditto

(b) I 3 | [Tangut] 4261

(c) III 74 | [Tangut] 1535 ~~540~~

(d) III 180 [Tangut] | 4526

5404 [Tangut] VIII 40 | [Tangut] 3741

W.I.98[7]

B 215[2] 鬱 | [Tangut] | 金 'saffron' & phon. kunkuma

5404A [Tangut] Error for [Tangut] 5350

5405 [Tangut] V 123 [Tangut] |

(a) I.14 ditto

(i) The disyllable 革登

C.C.C. 33[6]

5406 [Tangut] V 24 [Tangut] | 4524

(a) VII 111 ~~ditto~~ [Tangut] | 5267

B.126[2]

5407 [Tangut] V 24 [Tangut] | 5267

5408 [Tangut] VIII 11 [Tangut] |

(a) I 8 ditto

5409 [Tangut] III 139 [Tangut] | 1367

(i) The disyllable C.C.C.10[4] 天晚 "the sky gets dark"?

5410 [Tangut] V A 108 | [Tangut]

5411 [Tangut] IX 122 | [Tangut]

(a) VIII 1 ditto

晚 "evening" C.C.C.9[4]

5412 [Tangut] III A 59 | [Tangut]

(a) V 121 ditto

(i) By itself W.I.98[4]? B 171 tr. 察察 (examine)

B.123[5] tr. 緣 (? error) pratyaya cause, reliance

(ii) [Tangut] | 觀 察 "to examine"

W. II 16[8]

5412 [Tangut] VIII A 51 [Tangut] | 1803

5414 2187 pair

5415 4200 chain

5416 4734 chain

[5417] 2234 pair

5418 3473 pair

5419 5345 pair

5420 – 0162 ~~pair~~

5421 5477 chain

5422 0970 chain

5423 – 4333

5424 – 5258

5425 1140 chain

5426 independent

5427 4037 chain

418
~~408~~

5414 [Tangut] IX 23 [Tangut] |

(a) VIII 79 ditto

Note. Written [Tangut] in IX 23, but in error considering VIII 79 & 5415.

5415 [Tangut] IX 23 [Tangut] |

5416 [Tangut] V 27 [Tangut] | 4734 [illegible] (sun)

(a) III 131 ditto

B127[3] 夜 ✓

(i) mts'an.mo ~~[illegible]~~ night W.I. 212[12]

(ii) |[Tangut] 朝夕 "morning & evening"; ~~[illegible]~~ early & late CCC 29[6] 34[6]

5417 [Tangut] I 53 [Tangut] |

(a) VI 7 ditto

夢 "dream" W I 100[7] II 18[7]

5418 [Tangut] III 3 [Tangut] |

(a) VI 12

5419 [Tangut] III 3 [Tangut] |

(a) VI 32 ditto

(i) The dissyllable gzib.non "filth-spreading" a sort of devil W.I 212[17] 218[15]

5420 [Tangut] VII 35 |[Tangut] 0162

(a) IX 9 ditto

B.127[5] [illegible] 夜 (~~[illegible]~~ for 5416) 229[4]

5421 [Tangut] VIII 58 [Tangut] | fragment 1021

5422 [Tangut] VIII 97 [Tangut] |

5423 [Tangut] V 23 |[Tangut]

(a) V 2 ditto

5424 [Tangut] I 27 |[Tangut]

(a) III A 131 ditto

(i) The dissyllable 乳頭 [~~presumably~~ nipple ~~a kind of food "milk head"(?)~~] CCC 35[a]

5425 [Tangut] III 7 |[Tangut] 1140

(a) VI A 3 [Tangut] | 5724

5426 [Tangut] [VII 59-60]

5426A [Tangut] x of V 43 |[Tangut]
error for 5428

5427 [Tangut] III 178 |[Tangut]

5428
⊥ 2742-2192

5429 4795 chain

5433
⊥ 5439-4891
3126

[5430] - 1249

5434 4889 chain

5435 2003 pair

5431 1105 chain

5431 (ii)(c) 讚嘆 "to praise & admire"

W.II 94[5]

5436 5500 chain

5437 3160 chain

5438 5645

5439 5433 chain

5432 - [5524]

5324 sh^d come here

419

5428 VII 85 | 2742 W.I. 226[2]
(a) V 43 ditto misspelt

5429 VII 85 | 3067

5430 I 39 | 燮
(a) V A 60 ditto
(i) The dissyllable 分 別 (Soot. p. 139) vibhajya, vibhāga, parikalpana, vikalpa "division, discrimination discernment, reason" W.II 62[2] 152[2] B. 19

5431 VIII 20 | 0979
(a) IX 100 | 5059
(i) By itself 讚 "to praise" W.II 18[9] B. 160[1]
(ii) The dissyllable (a) 讚 "to praise" W.II 22[4] B. 233[3] 讚 嘆
(b) 讚 歎 ditto W.II 68[9] 116[6]
(c) 稱 揚 "to publish & display" W.II. 12[12]
(d) 嘆 譽 "to admire & praise" C.C.C. 27[b]

5432 III 170 |
(a) III A 32 ditto
(i) 1700 k'yur. mid "to swallow"
5661

1/3/39

5433 VI A 30 |
(a) II A 10 ditto
(b) V 122 | 3126
riar phlegm W.II 216[7]

5434 VI A 32 | 5532
(a) VI 4 | 1590

5435 IX 27 | to eat 2003
(a) V 15 ditto

5436 III A 132 5468 1700 PI YA
Phonetic character

5437 VII 36 | 3153

5438 IX 163 |

5439 II A 10 |
(a) VI A 30 ditto
(b) VIII 51 | 3126
skyugs. pa "vomit" W.I. 216[8]

5440 long chain excluding (m)

5440 2710 chain

5441 3218 pair

5442 – 5445

5443 5671 chain

5444 – 3437

5445 5442 pair

5446 3443 chain

5447 – 5502

5448 0043 chain

420

5440 [Tangut] III 60 | [Tangut] q.v. 1120

(a) I 20 | [Tangut] gruel 1083

(b) I 43 | [Tangut] ? 5457

(c) I 79 | [Tangut] ? ? (4036) 0373

(d) III 60 | [Tangut] (2004) 5452

(e) III 158 | [Tangut] ? 5521

(f) V 57 | [Tangut] offal 4990

(g) V A 61 | [Tangut] ? 3932

(h) VI 31 [Tangut] | ? jar (2078) 2076 5530

(i) VI 127 | [Tangut] ? 5474

(j) VII 116 | [Tangut] ? 2606

(k) IX 61 [Tangut] | flour 2216

(l) IX A 32 | [Tangut] (2412) 3122

[(m) IX A 90 | [Tangut] ? (possibly error) 0492]

(i) By itself 食 "food" passim

zas "food" W.I. 216[2] & passim

(ii) The disyllable C.C.C. 33[a] 食饌

(iii) (a) above C.C.C. 33[a] 粥 "gruel, congee".

(iv) | [Tangut] C.C.C. 22[a] 廚庖 "kitchen".

(v) | [Tangut] [Tangut] W.I. 216[4] g-tor.ma "a strewing oblation".

N.B. noun, not verb

5441 [Tangut] I 39 ↑ [Tangut]

(a) I 23. ditto reversed

B. 170[3] Ch. 令

5442 [Tangut] ← I 64 | [Tangut]

(a) I 109 ditto

5443 [Tangut] 'I A 26 | [Tangut] 2198

Note 5442 & 5443 are indistinguishable

5444 [Tangut] V 65 | [Tangut]

(a) IX 1 ditto

5445 [Tangut] I 109 [Tangut] |

(a) I 64 ditto

5446 [Tangut] VI 37 [Tangut] | 1341

5447 [Tangut] IX 130 | [Tangut]

(a) IX 158 ditto

5448 [Tangut] VIII 76 [Tangut] | 0056

(i) By itself 鶏 "cock" C.C.C. 13[b] W.I. 132[18]

(ii) The disyllable ditto C.C.C. 17[a]

5449 5486 chain

5450 2327 chain

5451-5522

5452 2710 chain

5453 5523 chain

5454 3226 chain

5456 3213 chain

5457 2710 chain

5458 - 1040

5459 0666 pair

5460 5106 chain

[5461] 2569 chain

5462
⊥ 5403 ┬ 1535
├ 4261
└ 5425

5463 5465 chain

5464 5096 chain

421

5449 [Tangut] VIII 76 [Tangut] | 5486
(a) I 1 ditto
(b) IX 64 [Tangut] |

5450 [Tangut] III 15 | [Tangut] 1376

5451 [Tangut] V 24 | [Tangut]
(a) V 2 ditto

5452 [Tangut] III 60 [Tangut] | part 5440
(a) III 67 | [Tangut] ? 2004

5453 [Tangut] VI A 33 [Tangut] |

5454 [Tangut] I 76 [Tangut] |

5455 [Tangut] [C.II. t'ai, ta]
Error for ? (→ 5456)

5456 [Tangut] III 147 [Tangut] | 3227

5457 [Tangut] I.43 [Tangut]. | part 5440

5458 [Tangut] VI 37 | [Tangut]
(a) VII 96 ditto
飲 "drink, beverage" [noun] W.II 22[12] 132[5]

5459 [Tangut] IX 119 | [Tangut]
(a) IX 132 ditto

5460 [Tangut] VI 104 [Tangut] | 5106

5461 [Tangut] III 129 | [Tangut] 2569

5462 [Tangut] III 129 | [Tangut] 5403
(a) VII 46 ditto
(i) [Tangut] | nbar. ba "blaze" W.I.224[4]
(ii) | [Tangut] W.I.198[3] a sort of ulcer.

5463 [Tangut] IX 140 [Tangut] | 0972
(i) By itself C.C.C. 9[b] 火 "[illegible] fire"
(ii) The Disyllable B.253. me. t'ar. pa

5464 [Tangut] ?
(a) IX 26 | [Tangut] 0171
W.I.132[13] 燒 "fire (noun)" ~~"to burn"~~
~~Probably an error for 5471~~
quite clear

5465 chain
- 2664?
- 0972 — 0012 ; 0187 ; 0851 ; 4800 — 4801 ; 5213 — 2975–1843 ; 3051 ; 5463 ; 5494 ; 5367

5466 5523 chain

5467–5368

5468
- 1149
- 2611

5469 4620 A chain

5470 2864 chain

5471 5096 chain

5472

5473 – 3034

5474 2710 chain

5475 5300 chain

5476 [0424 chain]

5477
- 2904
- 0642
- 1021–5421
- 1104
- 2994
- 4062

422

5465 [Tangut] I 6 | [Tangut] 2664
(a) II 1 ditto
(b) I 47 | [Tangut] × 0972
(i) [Tangut] | C.C.C. 10a 巽离 "mild ?ghost bogey"?

5466 [Tangut] IX 138 [Tangut] | [Tangut] |

5467 [Tangut] IX A 2 | [Tangut]
(a) IX A 74 ditto.
滅 "extinguish, exterminate, destroy W.L. 122[9] II 84[9]

5468 [Tangut] II A 20 | [Tangut] 1149
(a) I 20 ditto
(b) V 16 | [Tangut] 2641

5469 [Tangut] IX 138 [Tangut] |

5470 [Tangut] II 6 [Tangut] | 2864

5471 [Tangut] VIII A 47 [Tangut] | boil 5096
(a) VIII 99 ditto
(b) v. 5464

5472 [Tangut] YAN VIII 59 "Family or clan name"
[(a) VII A 131 [Tangut] × by [Tangut] |]
B. 92 Name of a city + country
Note. (a) is a Phonetic character.

5473 [Tangut] I 3 | [Tangut] "4 ... "
(a) II 1 ditto
B. 92 "One side of [Tangut] + [Tangut] ideogram. | is the ~~name of a~~ word for the name of a [Tangut] [the 城 city] + the name of a country."
C.C.C. 9b 丙 "the 3rd stem."

5474 [Tangut] VI 127 [Tangut] | 5440 foot

5475 [Tangut] VI A 16 [Tangut] |
(a) VI 119 ditto

5476 [Tangut] I 114 | [Tangut] ?537
(a) VIII A 96 [Tangut] |

5477 [Tangut] IX 49 [Tangut] | 2904
(a) III 66 ditto
(b) I 24 [Tangut] × by Disyllable 4062
(d) V 49 [Tangut] | 0642
(e) VII 14 [Tangut] × by | [Tangut] 3420 sort (5121) fragment × 1021
(f) VIII 80 | [Tangut] 1164
(c) I. 80 [Tangut] | 2994 54

5478 1891 chain

5478 薰 fragrance, perfume W. I 154[3] B. 239[2] 174[16]

5479 0809 chain

5480 4280 pair

5481 ~~interpretant~~

5482 5708 chain

5483 3033 pair

5484 = 5495

5485 - 3458 ~~3398 chain~~

5486 = 4032

5487
⊥ 5449 - 2433 (2103A) } - 1936

5488 5300 chain

5489 4030 chain

5490 3144 chain

5491
⊥ 4116 - 4585
└ 4667

423

5477 (cont)
香 fragrance W.I 98[7] III 10[2] 24[7]
dri fragrant food W.I. 190[15] 194[11] 216[4] 218[13]
B.170[3]

5478 [Tangut] V 113 [Tangut] |
~~W.I.174[16] 董 to rule, direct?~~

5479 [Tangut] IX 49 | [Tangut] 0383
(i) The disyllable 香菜 "fragrant vegetable" B.101 cat. under "vegetables"

5480 [Tangut] I 25 [Tangut] |
(a) VII 11

5481 [Tangut] I 25 blank.
W.II 24[7] 芬 "fragrant"

5482 [Tangut] III 57 [Tangut] | 1099

5483 [Tangut] V A 8 [Tangut] | 3033
(a) V 120 ditto

5484 [Tangut] I 15 | [Tangut]
(a) I 30 ditto reversed

5485 [Tangut] III 104 | [Tangut]
(a) III A 43 | [Tangut] 3453

5486 [Tangut] III 104 | [Tangut]
(a) VII 94

5487 [Tangut] I 1 | [Tangut]
(a) VIII 76 ditto

5488 [Tangut] III 128 | [Tangut]
(a) III A 132 [Tangut] x by | [Tangut] 5436
(b) V 66 | [Tangut]
飲 "to drink" CCC.32[a] W.I 134[8] 170[4]
ht'ui, ba ditto. I 216[2] B.128[1]
Used as a phonetic W.II 4[2] B.180

5489 [Tangut] I 1 [Tangut] | 2344
(i) The disyllable CCC.28[b] 30[a] 31[a]
指揮 "to point & wave"? 2680 chain

5490 [Tangut] I 44 | [Tangut]
B.160[4]?

5491 [Tangut] I 44 | [Tangut] 4 III 6
(a) I 1 ditto

5491A 5418 pair

5492 – 2084

5493 2087 pair

~~5493 [Tangut] | W.I.170² [Tangut] "hungry" Buddha W.II.112²~~

5494 5465 chain

5495 5484 pair

5496 – 4545 B ~~[illegible]~~

5497 3226 chain φ v. B.215³

5497 φ(i) | [Tangut] 阿羅漢

Arhan W.II 2⁷ 86⁹

φ(ii) | [Tangut] 阿若橋陳如 W.II 2¹¹ B.224³ (but [Tangut])

φ(iii) | [Tangut] 阿說侍多

W.II 2¹²

φ(iv) | [Tangut] 阿難陀

W.II 4²

φ(v) W.I.269¹¹

(vi) II 122⁷ asaṅkhya H.S. 285

5498 2917 pair (vii) B 163¹

(viii) B.237²

5499 – 1439

5497 φ(vi) | [Tangut] 阿耨多羅三藐三菩提 ~~Anuttarasamyaksambodhi~~

W.II 78⁵

φ(vi) | [Tangut] 阿閦 ~~Name of a~~

5500

5475

5488 – 5436

5268 5527

5379

5501 1597

5502 5447 pair

5503 ~~[illegible]~~

5504 2366 chain

5505 – 4252

424

5491 A [Tangut] x of VIII 77 | [Tangut]

5492 [Tangut] VII 93 | [Tangut]

(a) VI 85 ditto

5493 [Tangut] V 119 [Tangut] |

(a) V 81 ditto [misspelt]

cf. 5506

5494 [Tangut] III 178 [Tangut] |

W.I. 136' 138" [樵 薪] "(to use as) fuel" 燃 burn as fuel

5495 [Tangut] I 30 | [Tangut]

(a) I 15 ditto revised

5496 [Tangut] VII A 51 [Tangut] | 4555 misspelt

(a) VII 106 ditto misspelt

5497 [Tangut] VIII A 36 [Tangut]

(a) VIII A 85 | [Tangut] 5529

A mantra or sacred sound.

A very common Phonetic

5498 [Tangut] I A 104 [Tangut] |

(a) VI 22 ditto

5499 [Tangut] III 158 | [Tangut]

(a) III 154 ditto

5500 [Tangut] — VI 119 | [Tangut] 5475

(a) VI A 16 ditto

(b) III 128 [Tangut] | "to drink" × 5488

(c) V 46 | [Tangut] 5268

(d) VII A 131 [Tangut] × by | [Tangut] 5579

食 "to eat" passim.

3a ditto W.I. 216² + passim

N.B. Verb, not noun.

5501 [Tangut] V A 46 [Tangut] | 5027

(a) I A 2 | [Tangut] 4210

誓 "oath" vow W.I. 132¹² II 6³

5502 [Tangut] IX 158 [Tangut] |

(a) IX 130 ditto

5503 [Tangut] V 2 × by self [ ] |

5504 [Tangut] I A 110 [Tangut] | 1471

5505 [Tangut] VI 37 | [Tangut]

(a) III 18 ditto

5506 (ii) The disyllable 飢 "hungry".
W.I.170[2]
5506 5355 chain
5507 1678 pair
5508 4607 chain
5509 0159 chain
5510 4027 chain
5511 0731 chain
5511 中(i) | 龍 跡 迦 攝 波
Kāśyapa W.II 4' B.200[3]
中(ii) | 龍 ditto W.II.4'[1,2]
5513 1715 pair

5514 5569 chain
5515 – 2905
5516 5355 chain
5517 – 5260
5518 4396 chain
5519 5500 chain
5520 0180 chain
5512 2680 chain

425

5506 [Tangut] VII A 89 [Tangut] |
(a) VIII A 43 ditto
~~(b) V 81 | [Tangut]~~
"B.95 [Tangut] follows [Tangut] ideogram.
| is [Tangut] [飢 "hungry"], [i.e.] not having food or drink." [Tangut]"
[fan. ts'ie njwi – (?)]
(i) 飢 "hungry" W.II 24² 38"

cf 5493
5507 [Tangut] IX 20 [Tangut] | 1678
(a) V 73 ditto

5508 [Tangut] III 3 | [Tangut]

5509 [Tangut] V 60 [Tangut] |
餅 "cake, pastry" c.c.c. 33 a⁷ b²

5510 [Tangut] III 111 [Tangut] 832 q.v.

5511 [Tangut] KYA V A 86 [Tangut] |
p III B. 215¹ (... phonetic)
A common phonetic.

5513 [Tangut] VIII 29 [Tangut] | 1715
(a) II 1 ditto

5514 [Tangut] V 77 [Tangut] |
(a) V 146 ditto [Tangut]
(b) VII 96 [Tangut] | to swallow 1700

5515 [Tangut] (ti) III 149 | [Tangut] 2905
(a) III A 14 ditto
唾 "spittle" c.c.c. 19 a
me'il ditto W.I. 216⁷

5516 [Tangut] I 88 [Tangut] |
餓 "thirsty" (?) W.II. 24²
饉 ditto W.II 38"

5517 ~~5516~~ [Tangut] VII 45 | [Tangut]
(a) IX 72 ditto

5518 ~~5517~~ [Tangut] III 149 [Tangut] | 2890

5519 ~~5518~~ [Tangut] VII A 131 [Tangut] [Tangut]
5580 5472
to eat phonetic
V.47 ? Phonetic

5520 ~~5519~~ [Tangut] VIII 49 [Tangut] | 0180
(i) [Tangut] | c.c.c. 31 b 謀知

5512 [Tangut] VI 107 | [Tangut] to attach 2680 chain

5521 2710 chain

5522 5451 pair

5523

| [Tangut] 'labial sounds' Dict 1^6 6^2

5523
- 4273 – 3229
  - 5209
  - 5466
- 1115
- 5453
- 5643

| [Tangut] B.221^2 ('long lips') [Tangut] mosquito

5524 5432 pair

5525 independent

5526 – 4069

5527 5500 chain

5528 independent

5529 3226 chain

5530 2710 chain

5531
⊥ 3502 – 5097

5532 4889 chain

5533 4064 chain

5534 4454 chain

5535 4027 chain VIII

426

5521 III 158 | food 5440

5522 V 2 |
(a) V 24 ditto

5523 mo I A 20 | lya × 4273 "mouth"
(a) IX A 23 ditto
(b) I A 45 | 5645
(c) III 148 | 1115
(d) VI A 33 | 5453
~~(e) VII 106 | []~~
唇 "lips" C.C.C. 18[a]
mc'u "lips" W.I. 218[6]
觜 "beak" W.II. 50[1]

5524 III A 32 |
(a) III 170 ditto

5525 IX A 3 "Family or clan name"

5526 I 45 |
(a) III 6 ditto

5527 V 66 |

5528 V 66 "Family or clan name"

5529 VIII A 85 | A

Note. 5528 & 5529 are indistinguishable & the translation of the latter is a mantra.

5530 VI 31 | food 5440
(a) VIII 53 | jar 2078
B. 170[1] tr. 齋 to fast

5531 V 2 | 3502
(a) IX 165 ditto

5532 I 86 | 0509
(a) VI A 32 | × 5434

5533 II 15 | 2426

5534 I 35 |

5535 V A 56 | 8329 ×

5536 – 2104

5537 5540 chain

5538 5540 chain

5539 – 5602

5540
- 2443 – 4253
- 1274
- 3976
- 5537
- 5538

(c) opposite III 142'' 㾌速疾 'to hurry, hasten'

B. 189² tr. 速 'to hurry'

[5541] 0970 chain

5542 0741 chain

[5543] – [1268]

B. 124²

5544 0752 chain

5545 – 1504

5546 – 5557

5547 interjection

5548 1891 chain

5549 2562 chain

5550 3812 chain

速

迅

馬史

5541

B. 122¹

5536 VII A 98
(a) VII A 97 ditto

5537 VII 49 |

5538 VIII 73 |
速 "swift, urgent" W. II 52[10] 34[1]
& passim.
B 126[1] ? phon. 189[1] 早 early

5539 VIII A 84 |
(a) VIII A 52 ditto.

5540 VI 118 | ×4253 2443
(a) I 74 ditto
~~(b) VII 22~~
(b) VII 49 | 5537
(c) VIII 39 | 1274
(d) VIII 73 | 5538
(e) IX 2 | 3976
迅 "swift" W. I. 112[13]
mzyogs ditto W. I. 194[8]
駛 "swiftly flowing" W. II 12[10]

5541 VII A 94 |
B. 122[1] tr. 焦 to harass

B. 161[4] tr. 辛 ~~bitter pungent~~ 427

5542 IX 64 |

5543 I 46 | PAn
(a) I 93 ditto Pu
(i) The dissyllable 爹爹 "father" - vs. ar. arithmetic

5544 IX 44 |

5545 IX 4 | 1504
(a) VI 34 ditto

5546 I 46 |
(a) I 33 ditto

5547 VIII A 45 × by itself |
緊 "violent" C.C.C. 10[6]
drag. pa ditto W. I. 208[14]
W. I. 134[3] ? 楚 grievous

5548 V 138 | 1891

5549 V 122 | 2602

5550 I 33 |
(i) The dissyllable W. I. 134[16] 136[6]

5551 3801 pair

5552 – 3498

5553
5554 – 0764
3444 – 5560

W.II.132[2] 重

B.187[4] 崇 to reverence

B.188[5] B.193[1] 尊

5554 | [Tangut] hjigs.pa "to fear B.252[4] II 118[7]

5534 to 5553 chain 怖畏 fearful

5555 3772 chain

5556 – 1505

5557 5546 pair

5558 0604 chain

5559 1889 chain

5560 5553 chain

5561 3086 chain

5562 5690 chain

5563 – 3856

428

5551 [Tangut] VII A 6 [Tangut] | 3801

(a) V 7 ditto reversed (b) IX 33 4488

C.C.C. 28b 納 "to give, present"

5552 [Tangut] II 4 | [Tangut]

(a) IX 115 ditto

5553 [Tangut] I. 146 | [Tangut] 5554

(a) V A 87 ditto

(b) V 90 [Tangut] | 3444

貴 "honourable" C.C.C. 19b 32a 35b W. II 16[6]

敬 "to respect" C.C.C. 29b W. I. 142[8]

奉 "respect" W. I. 112[15] II 34[6]

慙 causing shame W. I. 138[14] 142[18] 152[18] W. I 265[19]

B. 179[4] 恭 respected

5554 [Tangut] V A 87 [Tangut] | (5541)

(a) I 146 ditto

(b) V A 44 | [Tangut]

[(c) VI 34 | [Tangut] [? error for [Tangut]] 1505]

(d) VII 22 [Tangut] | 0764

畏 "fear" W. I. 122[12]

憎 "to hate, dislike" W. I. 136[11]

skrag "fear" W. I. 192[6]

bsñig.pa "fear" W. I. 194[16]

W. I. 186[15] ?

5555 [Tangut] II 32 [Tangut] | 4062

5556 [Tangut] IX 4 | [Tangut] 1505

(a) VI 34 ditto misspelt

5557 [Tangut] I 33 [Tangut] |

(a) I 46 ditto

B. 204[3] tr. 來往

5558 [Tangut] IX 64 [Tangut] |

5559 [Tangut] VIII 3 [Tangut] |

5560 [Tangut] V A 44 [Tangut] |

5561 [Tangut] VI A 105 | [Tangut] 5085

~~[Tangut] "flame, blaze" W. I. 110[4] 140[13]~~

~~(ii) [Tangut] "blaze" W. I. 224[4]~~

5562 [Tangut] VII 42 | [Tangut] 3809

(a) I 86 | [Tangut] 5568

(i) C.C.C. 25b 釵 "hair-pin"

(ii) B. 104 cat. under "woman's clothing"

5563 [Tangut] V 1 | [Tangut]

(a) I. 13 ditto [[Tangut]]

5564 3226 chain

5564. B 246^5 preposition 方尺 in

B 180^2 所

5565 4893 pair

5566 4096 chain

5567 ·5465 chain

W.II 138^4 [illegible] 火留

5568 5690 chain

5569 ⊥ 5514 : 1700

5570 4276 chain

5570 亦 meaning "then" after "if"

W.II 84^12 86^5

5571 1460 pair

5572 [3905] chain

5573 2954 chain

5574 1891 chain; W.I. [illegible]

429

5564 [Tangut] *nu* V 1 / VI [Tangut] [Tangut] 2342
"auxiliary word".
A nominal suffix corresponding primarily to the instrumental.
以 "with, by" <u>passim</u> W.I. 132^{12}
<u>-kyis</u> W.I. 208^{8} etc.

5565 [Tangut] I 33 [Tangut] |
(a) I 46 ditto
W.I. 132^{17}?

5566 [Tangut] III 136 [Tangut] |

5567 [Tangut] IX 102 [Tangut] |
(i) [Tangut] "flame, blaze" W.I. 110^{4} 140^{13}
W.II 112^{4} B 217^{1}
(ii) |[Tangut] <u>h.bar.ba</u> "blaze" W.I. 224^{4}

5568 [Tangut] I 86 [Tangut] | 5562
C.C.C. 25^{b} 金車

5569 [Tangut] V 146 |[Tangut] x 1700 5514
(a) V 77 ditto

5570 [Tangut] *tsi* VI 72 [Tangut] | 4276 small?
(a) I 34 [Tangut] | 467? 0467
(b) V A 126 [Tangut] | 2798 here ? affix
(c) VI 48 [Tangut] | 1838 here an affix?
(d) VI 115 |[Tangut] 5607?
(e) VI A 84 [Tangut] x by | [Tangut] Phonetic 5593
(f) VII 77 [Tangut] | 257 'if' 0257
A conjunction meaning apparently "also" & ? other things. cf 5559 b.
亦 "also" W.I. 108^{1} 267^{13} ('also' certain)
<u>yaṅ</u> 'also' B 255^{2}
雖 "although" W.I. 168^{5}
To complete sense W.I. 100^{7}

5571 [Tangut] IX 125 [Tangut] |
(a) IX 67 ditto wound
W.I. 132^{15}? to wound or 彈射 bullet & shot

5572 [Tangut] VI 109 |[Tangut] [3905]
C.C.C. 19^{b} 賤 "mean, low, cheap"

5573 [Tangut] VI 55 |[Tangut] 2501

5574 [Tangut] VI A 86 [Tangut] | 3157
W.II. 18^{4} 減 "to reduce, diminish"
W.I. 222^{17} <u>ne.zad</u> (? hurt, injury)

5575 2278 chain

5576 2309 chain

5577 1891

5578 Family name double?
├ 4774
└ 4582

5579 – 2832

5580 2085 chain

5581 unimportant

5582 4773 chain

5583 0304 chain

5584 1929 chain

5585 4281 chain

5586 1929 chain

5587 – 5012

5588 1713 chain

5589 2245 chain

430

5575 [Tangut] V 155 [Tangut] |

A nominal suffix corresponding broadly to the locative.

間 "during, in" C.C.C. 27[a] W.I. 168[4] B.128[2]

中 "in" C.C.C. 31[a] W.I. 108[11] 116[9]

-la "in" W.I. 224[5]

-du "in" W.I. 222[17]

B 245[2] ends a temporal clause "while"

5576 [Tangut] I 71 [Tangut] | 2424

5577 [Tangut] I A 51 [Tangut] | "cai"

5578 [Tangut] IX 110 Family or clan name.

(a) V 104 [Tangut] | 4582

(b) [Tangut] VI 94 [Tangut] | 1774

Very puzzling; possibly corrupt.

5579 [Tangut] VI 55 | [Tangut]

(a) IX 32 ditto

5580 [Tangut] VI A 126 [Tangut] "a sound"

5581 [Tangut] I A 25 Family or clan (name)

5582 [Tangut] IX 43 | [Tangut] 2968

5583 [Tangut] IX 43 | [Tangut] 1775

(a) VI 23 | [Tangut] 4247

(b) VIII 6 | [Tangut] 3970

5584 [Tangut] I 7 [Tangut] | 1929 (sort of sheep)

(a) IX 109 | [Tangut]

(i) (a) above B. 99 cat. under "sheep"

5585 [Tangut] VI 72 [Tangut] [Tangut]

(a) V 32 [Tangut] x by | [Tangut]

5586 [Tangut] IX 109 [Tangut] |

(i) The disyllable B. 99 cat. under "sheep"

5587 [Tangut] VIII 46 | [Tangut]

(a) III 37 ditto

5588 [Tangut] VII 93 | [Tangut] 1012

5589 [Tangut] IX 138 | [Tangut] 2245

(a) I A 103 | [Tangut] 2332

C.C.C. 7[a] 雙 "a pair, couple"

5590 2593 chain

5591 – 0920

5592 0364 chain

5593 4276 chain

5594 0582 chain

5595 4649 chain

5596 0604 chain

5597 4775 chain

5598 1935 chain

5599 3685 chain

5600 4276 chain

5601 independent

5602 5539 pair

5603 – 5604

5604 5603 pair

431

5590 [Tangut] VII 33 [Tangut] |

(a) I 17 ditto

5591 [Tangut] lau IX 6 | [Tangut]

(a) IX 5 ditto

[(b) III A 99 [Tangut] x by [Tangut] | Phonetic]

~~(c) V 32 [Tangut] |~~

B. 253³ 而 "and". W II 84 ^9,12^ ~~ditto~~?

A pretty clear conjunction

5592 [Tangut] III A 6 [Tangut] | 3817

5593 [Tangut] TSYO VI A 84 ~~[Tangut]~~ [Tangut]

5594 [Tangut] VII 33 [Tangut] | 1566

(i) The disyllable B. 100 cat. under "horse"

5595 [Tangut] III 43 [Tangut] | 5709

B. 122¹ 126²

5596 [Tangut] IX 20 [Tangut] | 0604

(a) V 32 ditto

(b) III A 5 [Tangut] x by [Tangut] |

5597 [Tangut] III 109 | [Tangut]

(i) The disyllable [Tangut] "swallow"

C.C.C. 17ᵃ

5598 [Tangut] rya IX 104 [Tangut] |

C.C.C. title & 15ᵃ 漢 "Chinese"

5599 [Tangut] xan VIII 41 [Tangut] | "name"

(a) IV A 4 | [Tangut] 3505

B. 89 The whole of [Tangut]; [Tangut] follows. [Tangut] | is the name of a family or clan & of a country. The word for | Lo Fu ching translates 漢 China

5600 [Tangut] VII 49 [Tangut] |

5601 [Tangut] I 88 x by self | [|]

5602 [Tangut] VIII A 52 [Tangut] |

(a) VIII A 84 ditto

5603 [Tangut] V 60 | [Tangut]

(a) V 122 ditto

5604 [Tangut] V 122 [Tangut] |

(a) V 60 ditto

5605 4926 chain

5606 3587 chain

5607 4275 chain

5608 3240 chain

5609 4109 chain

5610-5289

5611 1891 chain

5612 1313 chain

5613 2710 chain

5614 2524 chain

5615 1538 chain

5616 1992 chain

5617 2309 chain

5618 2710 chain

?B.194' ?土

5619 4617 chain

432

5605 [Tangut] V 60 | [Tangut]

5606 [Tangut] IX 110 | [Tangut] 3587
(a) V 7 | [Tangut] 0984
(b) V 91 | [Tangut] 2320
(c) VI 11 [Tangut] | × 0955

5607 [Tangut] VI 115 [Tangut] | 5570

5608 [Tangut] VII 100 [Tangut] | 0193

5609 [Tangut] IX 60 | [Tangut] 3049

5610 [Tangut] I 88 | [Tangut]
(a) I A 50 ditto

5611 [Tangut] kyuan V A 16 [Tangut] |
(a) IX A 25 [Tangut] | 4445
~~(b) VIII A 100~~
[(b) VIII A 100 [Tangut] × by [Tangut] |
(c) VIII A 104 [Tangut] × by [Tangut] |] [[Tangut]
B. 90 | [Tangut], [Tangut] follows.
| is a Chinese word, juanr the equivalent of the foreign word [Tangut] [scroll]

This word is one of the few clear cases of a loan word 卷 "küan, scroll".

Note. 5610 & 5611 are barely distinguishable

5612 [Tangut] V 80 [Tangut] | 5379

5613 [Tangut] II 2 [Tangut] | 2710

5614 [Tangut] VII 111 [Tangut] | 2524

5615 [Tangut] VII 27 [Tangut] |

5616 [Tangut] II 2 [Tangut] [Tangut] not to go, or behave 1992

5617 [Tangut] III 61 [Tangut] | 1057

5618 [Tangut] II 2 [Tangut] | [cf. 5613 [?error]]
~~(a) VII 67~~ W II 22 熱 "hot"
104 do. B. 125 173

5619 [Tangut] I 36 [Tangut] |
~~(a) IX A 152 [Tangut] | [[Tangut]]~~
(i) the disyllable 霹靂 "thunder-clap" C.C.C. 7th

5620 4235 pair

5621 3395 pair

5622 2758 chain

5623 chain
- 4016 – 3804
- 0372 – 2713 – 1144 – 0506 – 2041 – 1855, 3828
- 2713 – 4658
- 1144 – 2019, 2706, 2711, 4034 – 2628, 4113
- 2247
- 3717

5624 5678 chain

| [Tangut] W.I.132[10] 自從 'from'

| [Tangut] with 至於 'up to'

5625 independent

5626 5632 chain

5627 1849 pair

5628 3041 chain

5623 chain
- 4016 – 3804 – 3831
- 0372 – 2713

5629 1766 pair

5630
- 3071 – 0177
- 1740
- 3071 – 3071

5631 3595

433

5620 [Tangut] VI 24 [Tangut] |
(a) V 39 ditto

5621 [Tangut] VI 32 [Tangut] | 3395
(a) IX 108 ditto

5622 [Tangut] VI 126 [Tangut] |

5623 [Tangut] VI 24 [Tangut] | "year" 4016
(a) VII 15 ditto
(b) I 16 [Tangut] | ? 3717
(c) I 132 [Tangut] | ? 0372
(d) V A22 [Tangut] x by [Tangut] | 2604 "time" 3871
(e) IX 63 [Tangut] |, 2247
?

5624 [Tangut] VIII 11 [Tangut] | 2523
A nominal postposition corresponding apparently to the locative?
在 "in" C.C.C. 31b
自從 "from" W.I. 96^10 132^10 10^2
| [Tangut] 至於 "up to" W.I. 96^10

Note. 5623 & 5624 are indistinguishable & (b)–(e) may belong to the latter.

5625 [Tangut] VII 59 (~~58~~) torn
Possibly not complete.

5626 [Tangut] IX 26 [Tangut] |
(a) VII 99 [Tangut] |

5627 (~~5628~~) [Tangut] VIII 71 [Tangut] | misspelt 1849

5628 [Tangut] IX 79 [Tangut] |
(i) [Tangut] | dpal "blessedness" W.I. 192^2
bkra.śis maṅgala "happiness"
W.I. 192^8 220^9
bde.legs ditto W.I. 210^4
dge.ba ditto W.I. 196^6
吉祥 ditto W.II 6^9

5629 (~~5630~~) [Tangut] IX A134 [Tangut] |
(a) VI 17 ditto [illegible]

5630 [Tangut] IX 74 | [Tangut] 3071
(a) IX 17 ditto
The disyllable W.I. 168^11 苦 "pain distress".

5631 (~~5632~~) [Tangut] II 37 | [Tangut] short [[Tangut]]
(a) II 12 ditto
"long" v. over B. 130^5 [Tangut] "long"

5632
+3968
-1016
-2495
-4558
└5626
form checked
(i) Disyllable W.II.130[3] 延長 'to be prolonged'

5633 5636 chain

5634 2178 chain

5635 1891 chain

5636
-5633
└3594

5637 ~~2197 chain~~
┴2197 ┬0244
└4496-3261

5638 4071 chain

5639 2934 chain

5640 -3081

5641 1891 ~~chain~~

5642 5678 chain
B 215[4] 兼 also

434

5632 [Tangut] VII A136 | [Tangut] 3968
(a) IX 11 ditto
(b) V 15 | [Tangut] 1016
(c) VI 25 [Tangut] | 4558
(d) VI A 111 | [Tangut] 2495
(e) IX 26 | [Tangut] 5626
[長 "long" passim — belongs to 5631
rin. ba "long (life)" W.I.194[17]]

Note. 5631 + 5632 are indistinguishable + (b) – (e) may belong to the former" B.204[1]

5633 [Tangut] IX 41 | [Tangut]

5634 [Tangut] VIII 71 [Tangut] | 3137

5635 [Tangut] IX 34 [Tangut] |
[(a) VI 18 [Tangut] × [Tangut] |]
(b) VI 99 | [Tangut] 5641
(i) C.C.C. 25[b] 條 "strip (of cloth)".
(ii) [Tangut] | B.103 cat. under "silks".
(iii) [Tangut] | (bright streak) 2131
skya.rins "morning twilight" W.I.198[9]

5636 [Tangut]
(b) IX 41 [Tangut] |
(a) VII A 104 [Tangut] (|) 3594

5637 [Tangut] IX 74 | [Tangut] misspelt
(a) IX 4 ditto [Tangut] 2197

5638 [Tangut] IX 74 | [Tangut]
(i) | [Tangut] 云何爲 "what are?" W.I.138[5], W.II 22[11], 54[11] 88[12] 何者是

5639 [Tangut] VII 58 | [Tangut]
(a) VI 89 ditto

5640 [Tangut] V 86 | [Tangut] 3081
(a) VIII A 70 ditto

5641 [Tangut] VI 99 [Tangut] |

5642 [Tangut] IX 74 [Tangut] | 2523
A common conjunction?
C.C.C. 35[a] 雖然 "although
| [Tangut] sʒan. yan "moreover" W.I.194[4].
W.I 102[3], 222[7,17], 224[3], 196[1] II 20[8], 28[2,7] 44[9].
II 92[5] = "and" to complete sense
B 180[5]! and B.160

5643 5323 chain

5644
4136 — 3365
4138
4325
5231

5645
1682
5438

5646 1128 chain

5647 — 5048

5648 independent

B.176[2] P.N. 175[5] do.

5649 0809 chain

5650 1813 pair

5651 1426 chain

5652 1537 pair

5653 1815 pair

5654 3975 chain

5654 | 圓滿 "complete circle globe"

W.II 124[4]

| 國土 "country" W.II 128[11] B164[2] 178[3]

| 地方 'place' B246[3]

| W.I 266[21] part of royal title

B.186[5] q.v.

435

5643 [Tangut] I A 45 | [Tangut]

W.I. 220[9] mgo name of constellation [tr. 觜 "beak]

5644 [Tangut] IX 74 | [Tangut] 4136

(a) VI A 24 ditto

W.II. 60[3] 論 "to discuss, converse"

C.C.C. 1[a]5 B. 121[2]? B. 123[1]?

5645 [Tangut] V A 11 | [Tangut] 1682

(a) III 143 ditto

(b) IX 163 | [Tangut] 5438

C.C.C. 18[b] 咽 "throat"

5646 [Tangut] VII A 80 [Tangut] | 4309

(a) III 33 [Tangut] | 2134

(b) III 174 [Tangut] | 2739

(c) III A 67 | [Tangut] 0376

~~(d) VII A 80 [Tangut] |~~

(d) VI 59 | [Tangut] [0770]

(i) By itself C.C.C. 34[a] W.II 42[11]?

B. 127[1] 128[2] tr. 求

(ii) (b) above 供 "to borrow" [offer, worship] W.I. 138[9]

5647 [Tangut] V 36 | [Tangut]

(a) V 93 ditto

5648 [Tangut] čo VII A 5 Family or clan (name)

Lo Handbook p. 20 | [Tangut] 張天錫 Chang T'ien Hsi ? Proper name

5649 [Tangut] VIII 87 [Tangut] 2895

5650 [Tangut] III 107 [Tangut] |

(a) III 110 ditto

5651 [Tangut] VIII 4 [Tangut] (all) 1426 ×2053

(a) VI 51 [Tangut] [sic!] [Tangut] 2535

B. 165[2]

5652 [Tangut] VII 6 [Tangut] |

(a) VII 10 ditto

5653 [Tangut] III 107 [Tangut] | misspelt

(a) III 110 ditto

5654 [Tangut] VIII 87 [Tangut] | 3795

(a) I 14 [Tangut] | +0670

(b) V A 83 | [Tangut]

(i) By itself 院 "hall, college" C.C.C. 28[a2]

(ii) See 2102

(iii) [Tangut] | mu. k'yud "circumference, rim" I. 192[9]

5662 4883 chain

5655 2237 chain

5663 2085 chain

5664 2167 chain

5656 - 2176

5657 0271 chain

5665 1080 chain

5666 5290 chain

5658 0582 chain

[5667] 1713 chain

5659 1864 chain

5668 0249 chain

5660 independent

B 224³ φ v. 5039

5669 3066 chain

5661 4889 chain

VII 59-60 ф.B.186[3]

436

5655 VIII 4 | 2237
(a) VIII 68 ditto
相 lakṣana external appearance, form, phenomenon
C.C.C. 3[a] I 92[27] 98[4] 100[3] 108[13] II 16[12] 18[4]
B 245[7] n. B. 180[3]

5656 VI 72 | 2176
(a) VIII A18 ditto

5657 I 14 |
B. 97 ideogram, follows.
| is the word for the dissyllable.
(i) The dissyllable 耳 環 "earring"
C.C.C. 25[a]

5658 VIII 4

5659 I 37 | 5717

5660 IX 65 Family or clan (name)

5661 VI 116 | 4889

5662 IX 17 |

5663 IX 139 | "a sound"

5664 VIII 32 |
(a) I A 34 | [?error for 5665] ×1806 2316
(b) VI 93 × by |
八 "eight" C 36[b] + passim
brgyad ditto W.I 224[6]

5665 III 121 | 4068
(a) VII 35 |
(i) The dissyllable B. 100 cat. under "horse"
N.B. used as Phonetic.

5666 III 15 |

5667 III A1 | | 1012

5668 III 168 | 1389

5669 I 83 | 3066

5676 3428 pair

5676 ф(i) | 䋼 䃔 聣 摩 訶 那 摩 Kahānama W.II 2[12]

ф.2 | 殺 摩 尼 mani B.180[3] W.I.178[7]

ф.3 B.161[1] Nagarta ф.iv B.219[4]

5670 5677 chain

5671 |
+4956
└2198–5473

5677 ┌1157 ┌2132 └5095
├2138
├1090–0223–5222 └3651
├5682
├3660
└5670

5672–0640

disyllable reversed W.I.270[18] 光明 prabhāsa

5673 2115 chain

5674 3907 chain

5678 chain
├4360
├2523 ─ 2932
└4124 ┬3574
├3983 ── ┬0240
├5624-q.v. ├2789
│ └4503
└5642

5675 5690 chain

B.189[1] 勳 merit

5679 –3226 chain

5679. B.245[7] 爾 嚴 水 "(you) must be" 是 料

B.234[1]

437

5670 [Tangut] I A78 [Tangut]
Phonetic character

5671 [Tangut] VI 10 [Tangut] | 4956
(a) VII 17 ditto reversed
(b) I A96 [Tangut] | 2198

5672 [Tangut] VI 10 | [Tangut]
(a) V 98 ditto
(i) The disyllable 虛空 'ākāśa ether' C.C.C. 4b & passim B.125[2] 230[4]

5673 [Tangut] III 168 [Tangut] | 2115

5674 [Tangut] III 168 | [Tangut] 3907

5675 [Tangut] VIII 21 [Tangut] | 4269
(a) I 13 [Tangut] | 3860
(b) V 23 | [Tangut] 4957 'Duke'
(c) IX 2 | [Tangut] 1767
(i) 功 'merit' puṇya, ~~virtue~~, achievement passim
(ii) 用 "useful things" C.C.C. 3b
(iv) [Tangut] | 德 virtue W.I. 90[2]
(iii) 感 "influence" W.I. 122[18]

5676 [Tangut] I 59 [Tangut] | 3428
(a) I 74 ditto
B.234[2] 磨
A common Phonetic.

5677 [Tangut] I 3 [Tangut] | 2133
(a) VI 71 ditto reversed
(aa) I A 79 (ab) I A 82 3651 3660
(b) IX 9 | [Tangut] 5682
(c) IX 174 | [Tangut] 1090 ~~5677~~
(i) 光 prabhā light, brightness, splendour: passim
2a hod ditto I 190[13] 216[15]
hod.zer ditto I 224[7]

5678 [Tangut] I 17 | [Tangut] 4360
(a) VI 1 ditto
(b) III 44 | [Tangut] 4124
(c) III 121 [Tangut] | 2523
(i) 他人 ?another "that man" C.C.C. 29b
(ii) 他 "that" W.I 96[11] "another" 138[9]
Used as Phonetic W.I. 192[14]

5679 [Tangut] NA III 121 [Tangut] 2342
(a) V 104 [Tangut] × by [Tangut] | ? 1971
C.C.C. 31b untranslated. Imperative affix W.II 54[6] ditto. W.II 40[4] The verb seems to be surrounded by [Tangut] — | 130[6] do. (v. 3674) B 129[1]. B 197[2] (you ... must)

5680 2121 chain [5688] 4208 chain

5681 independent

5682 5677 chain

B.123[4] | 赫明 fiery & bright

5683 independent 5689 0582 chain

5684 0262 chain 5690 | 皇太后 "Empress" W.I.265

B.223[1] 天 specifically 'heaven'

5685—0211

5690 | Regnal period on coin.

B. Coin plate translated 天慶

n. | Handbook p.20 Divine virtue (b) 皇帝 W.I.265

5686 - 3846 chain 5690 chain

2527 — 0370, 2356

0430 — 3544, 4122

1367 — 2931

2402 — 3171, 3848 — 0688, 5212, 5409

3747

3203 — 3136 — 4267 — 1371, 4963; 4483

3809 — 5562 — 5568

5274 — 4269 — 5675 — 1767, 3860, 4957

4376 — 3023

3576 — 0081

5691 1784 chain 3761

5687 - 3582 5691 See 2783 (iii)

5690 | B.164[4] 皇太后 165[5]

5691 B.131[5] 全 complete

438

5680 [Tangut] IX 73 | [Tangut] 4920

(i) By itself [2227] 露 "dew" C.C.C. 7[a] B.194[2]

(ii) | [Tangut] 甘露 "sweet dew", amṛta ambrosia" C.C.C. 7[b] W.I. 90[2] etc.

5681 [Tangut] IX 73 Family or clan (name)

5682 [Tangut] IX 9 [Tangut] [Tangut] |

B.168[3] doubtful + Hsiyl!

5683 [Tangut] VIII 21 Family or clan name

5684 [Tangut] V 99 | [Tangut]

5685 [Tangut] V 63 | [Tangut]

(a) V 16 ditto

5686 [Tangut] II 3 [Tangut] |

(a) V 11 ditto

(b) I 127 [Tangut] | 4982

(c) III 177 | [Tangut] 4984

C.C.C. 28[a] 城 "city"

5687 [Tangut] VIII 6 | [Tangut]

(a) I 43 ditto

5674 A

5688 [Tangut] Ka V 10 | [Tangut] "body" 0210

(a) V A 12 | [Tangut] ? 0005

(b) VI 40 | [Tangut] measure? × 4942

(c) IX 13 | [Tangut] × 4139

體 "limb, (heavenly) body". C.C.C. 3[a] etc.

身本 "limb" C.C.C. 19[a]

dnos "body, bhava, varta W.I. 214[11]

B.165[2]

5689 [Tangut] V 12 [Tangut] | 3692

(a) III 125 | [Tangut] banner 3609

W.I. 224[12] ? sño "green vegetable"

B. 215[2] 青 green

5690 [Tangut] ngu V 12 [Tangut] | 2527 celestial

(a) VI 104 ditto

(b) I. 13 | [Tangut] 1357 heaven

(c) V 49 | [Tangut] 430 word, speak

(d) V 64 | [Tangut] × 3203

(e) VI 33 | [Tangut] 2492 empress

(f) VI 56 | [Tangut] × 3576 emperor

Specifically "divine" not "celestial"?

皇 "supreme" C.C.C. 4[a] B.179 Dict. 1[a]6

天 "divine" C.C.C. 6[a] W.I. 122[6]

5691 [Tangut] no V 14 [Tangut] | (misspelt) 3843 ×(0824)

(a) VI 34 [Tangut] | 2622

(i) By itself rgyas "ample" W.I. 190[8]

具 "all, complete" W.II 2[11] etc.

P.T.O.

5697 – 3662

5698 5254 pair

5693 3226 chain

chain 4972–5694

5694 4972 chain

5699 1891 chain

5700 1478 pair

中(ii) B.223² | [Tangut] 舍衛 śrāvasti
5701 – 0766

5701 中(i) | [Tangut] Śariputra

5695 2570 pair

WII 4²

中(ii) | [Tangut] B.122² 238⁵ 舍利 śarīra

5702 – 3862

5696 – 4802

5703 3041 chain

5692 3583 chain

5697A [Tangut] B 347[2,5] 施 'to bestow'

439

5691 (cont.)

(ii) [Tangut] | 盡 皆 "all" C.C.C. 27[a] 28[b] 34[a,b]

(iii) | [Tangut] 具足 "all, complete" C.C.C. 32[a] W.I. 92[12], 108[13], 150[6] & passim.

全 備 ? the same C.C.C. 20[a]

(iv) | [Tangut] pʻun. sum. tsʻogs. pa "perfect" W.I. 220[9]

5693 [Tangut] III 136 [Tangut] | 3327

5694 [Tangut] V 101 [Tangut] | to give 4972

(a) I 58 ditto

[(b) III 38 [Tangut] × by [Tangut] |] 1099 0100

(c) VI 104 | [Tangut] ? 4971

(d) VI 116 [Tangut] | ? 4945

與 "to give" W.I. 138[6,12] II 18[2] 108[3] B.170[4]

5695 [Tangut] VIII 6 [Tangut] |

(a) V 21 ditto

5696 [Tangut] I 24 | [Tangut]

(a) IX 4 ditto

cha "divine" W.I. 208[13] 218[1]

5692 [Tangut] VIII 6 [Tangut] |

(a) I 43 ditto

(b) IX 177 [[Tangut] |] 3005

5697 [Tangut] ? 146 | [Tangut]

(a) III 44 ditto

Note 5695 (6) & 5696 (7) are indistinguishable & it is not clear which means cha

5698 [Tangut] IX 69 [Tangut] |

(a) VI 96 ditto [[Tangut]]

(ii) The disyllable W.I. 100[3] 皎 潔 "bright & pure": II 18[8] 鮮 潔 "fresh & pure": II 26[9] 清潔 "pure"

(i) by itself B.176[1]

5699 ~~5698~~ [Tangut] II 7 [Tangut] | 1891

5700 ~~5699~~ [Tangut] II A 9 [Tangut] |

(a) II 10 ditto

5701 ~~5700~~ [Tangut] VII 14 | [Tangut] "to carry"

(a) II 13 ditto

B.176[1] part of p.N.

5702 [Tangut] VII 14 | [Tangut]

(a) III 140 ditto

5703 [Tangut] I 5 [Tangut] | 3041 man

5704 5708 chain

5705 1891 chain

5706 0673 chain

5707 interpunct

5707 v. 3137

5708 chain
- 5704
- 0044 — 2153
  - 0292
  - 1099
    - 0100
    - ~~0238~~
    - 3693 — 0238
    - 5393
    - 5482
  - 3725
  - 3937
  - 5068 — 1026
- 1956
  - 1109 — 3998
  - 4328
- 3909

B.192² ? one type

5709 4649 chain

5710 0673 chain

5711 3993 chain

5712 1903 chain

5713 4889 chain

5715 0959 chain

5716 3139 pair

5717 1864 chain

440

5704 [Tangut] IX 24 [Tangut] | 5708
(a) III 24 ditto
B246[5] (part of name)

5705 [Tangut] V 144 [Tangut] | 1891
(a) VII 14 [Tangut] |
滴 "drop" W II 30[3] B.194[2]
t'igs.pa ditto L 192[17]
II 44[4] 46[4] ?

5706 [Tangut] III 157 | [Tangut] 2630
(a) VIII A 81 | [Tangut]

5707 [Tangut] IX A 10 "Family or clan name"
v 5137 B.176[4]

5708 [Tangut] 8te III 24 [Tangut] |
(a) IX 24 ditto
(b) V 69 | [Tangut] 3909
(c) VIII 45 | [Tangut] × 1956
(d) IX 148 | [Tangut] × 0044
(i) 一 one, a single W.I. 136[12], 168[9 2]
獨 "solitary, alone" W.I. 128[18]
(ii) | [Tangut] ran. sans. rgyas
Pratyekabuddha W.I. 208[8] B.249[4]
II 86[10] 獨覺 do

5709 [Tangut] IX A 41 [Tangut] |
(a) IX A 27 ditto
(b) III 43 | [Tangut] 5595

5710 [Tangut] VIII A 81 [Tangut] | 5706

5711 [Tangut] IX 20 [Tangut] | 4477
C.C.C. 23[a] 盔 "vessel, bowl, helmet"

5712 [Tangut] VII A 18 [Tangut] | 3604
(i) | [Tangut] 琴 "lute" C.C.C. 32[4]

5713 [Tangut] VII 31 [Tangut] | 4887

5714 [Tangut] V 78 "Family or clan name"

5715 [Tangut] V 78 [Tangut] |

5716 [Tangut] V 78 [Tangut] |
(a) IX 39 ditto

5717 [Tangut] VII A 92 [Tangut] | 1864
(a) VI A 63 ditto
(b) I 37 [Tangut] | 5657
(c) VI 136 [Tangut] | 3501

5717 (i) By itself 輪 "wheel" W.II 86[1] 80[3] 5723 3085 chain

| [Tangut] B.213[1] 輪 轉 samsāra S.H.444.

5724 1140 chain

5718 3142 pair

5719 3213 chain

5720 3226 chain

5721 5056 pair

5722 3240 chain

5722 | [Tangut] "dental sounds" i.e. actually gutturals Dict 2[a] 1 Ith of Ch V

441

5717 cont.

(d) VI A 57 [illegible] | 0784

(e) VII A 27 | [illegible] 0923

(i) The dissyllable 車輪 迴 "the return of the wheel (cakra" C.C.C. 37[a]

(ii) | [illegible] hk'or.lo "disk" W.I.208[12]

(iii) | [illegible] mu.k'yud "circumference rim" W. I 192[9]

(iv) | [illegible] ditto W. I. 216[16]

5718 [illegible] V 57 [illegible] |

(a) VI 89 ditto

(i) The dissyllable 旋 風 "whirl-wind" C.C.C. 7[b]

5719 [illegible] VI 131 [illegible] |

5720 [illegible] VII 79 [illegible] | 2342

5721 [illegible] VI 131 [illegible] |

(a) III 94 ditto

5722 [illegible] V 106 [illegible] | back teeth 3240

(a) VII 105 ditto

(b) VII 39 | [illegible] eye-tooth 1959

牙 "front teeth" C.C.C. 18[a]

5723 [illegible] VIII A 64 [illegible] |

(a) III 64 [illegible] | [[illegible]]

5724 [illegible] VI A 3 | [illegible] 5425

W.I.168[18] 唆 B.128[1].

The End.

27/3/39

Cross references finished 14/9/46

INDEX

The index of radicals listed on pages 894–895 presents the 500 radicals according to which the characters are indexed. The number against each radical is the page number where the section of the index covering this radical starts.

The index of characters is given on pages 896–936. Within each radical, characters are ordered by stroke count and Unicode code point sequence. For each radical entry, the character is followed by its entry number in the dictionary, and then the folio number on which the entry is found. Some characters have more than one entry, in which case each entry and folio number is given on a separate line. All of the folio entries are to be understood to be on the recto side of the folio, since this accounts for the overwhelming majority of the entries. An asterisk * following three of the folio numbers indicates that the entry is to be found on the facing folio (verso of the preceding folio); thus 1* refers to *f.* ii v, 96* refers to *f.* 95v, and 149* refers to *f.* 148v.

Where a character given in the dictionary is written incorrectly, it is indexed under the standard Unicode form of the character. However, if the incorrect form used in the dictionary is also encoded as a Unicode character then it is indexed under both the incorrect form and the corresponding standard form. In cases where the character form used in the dictionary correctly follows the form given in *Homophones* Edition A, but the corresponding Unicode character is based on a slightly different form given in *Homophones* Edition B, then it is indexed under both forms if they are in different places in the index, but only under the form given in the dictionary if both forms have the same radical and stroke count.

Index of radicals

Index of characters

[illegible]	1934	146
[illegible]	1925	146
[illegible]	1950	148
[illegible]	2037	155
[illegible]	1965	149
[illegible]	1954	148
[illegible]	1974	150
[illegible]	1997	152
[illegible]	1943	147
[illegible]	1917	145
[illegible]	1953	148
[illegible]	2049	156
[illegible]	1937	147
[illegible]	1914	145
[illegible]	1971	150
[illegible]	1957	148
[illegible]	1902	144
[illegible]	1901	143
[illegible]	2020	154
[illegible]	2021	154
[illegible]	1961	149
[illegible]	1903	144
[illegible]	1959	149
	1998A	152
[illegible]	1936	147
[illegible]	1935	147
[illegible]	1933	146
[illegible]	1928A	146
	1929	146
[illegible]	2004	153
[illegible]	2047	156
[illegible]	2002	153
[illegible]	2008	153
[illegible]	1975	150
[illegible]	1960	149
[illegible]	1940	147
[illegible]	2007	153
[illegible]	1923	145
[illegible]	1920	145
[illegible]	1921	145
[illegible]	1963	149
[illegible]	2019	154
[illegible]	2024	154
[illegible]	2017	154

[illegible]	2016	154
[illegible]	2029	155
[illegible]	1991	151
[illegible]	1930	146
[illegible]	1932	146
[illegible]	1969	150
[illegible]	2003	153
[illegible]	2033	155
[illegible]	1999	152
[illegible]	1973	150
[illegible]	1978	150
[illegible]	1941	147
[illegible]	1907	144
[illegible]	1946	148
[illegible]	2040	156
[illegible]	1919	145
[illegible]	2027	155
[illegible]	2023	154
[illegible]	2025	155
[illegible]	1987	151
[illegible]	1922	145
[illegible]	1966	149
[illegible]	1982	151
[illegible]	1926	146
[illegible]	2035	155
[illegible]	1967A	149*
	1980	151
[illegible]	1976	150
[illegible]	1977	150
[illegible]	1998	152
[illegible]	1944	148
[illegible]	1909	144
[illegible]	1947	148
[illegible]	2039	155
[illegible]	1900	143
[illegible]	2022	154
[illegible]	1931	146
[illegible]	1970	150
[illegible]	1928	146
[illegible]	2009	153
[illegible]	2034	155
[illegible]	1981	151
[illegible]	1942	147
[illegible]	2042	156

[illegible]	1967	149
[illegible]	2032	155
[illegible]	2026A	155
[illegible]	1956	148
[illegible]	2038	155
[illegible]	1904	144
[illegible]	2026	155
[illegible]	1915	145
[illegible]	1908	144
[illegible]	1913	144
[illegible]	1916	145

Radical [illegible]

[illegible]	2030	155
[illegible]	1996	152

Radical [illegible]

[illegible]	2418	186

Radical [illegible]

[illegible]	1605	121
[illegible]	1608	121
[illegible]	1606	121
[illegible]	1609	121

Radical [illegible]

[illegible]	115	10
[illegible]	118	10
[illegible]	88	8
[illegible]	171	15
[illegible]	117	10
[illegible]	169	14
[illegible]	147	12
[illegible]	148	12
[illegible]	150	13
[illegible]	134A	11
	135	11
[illegible]	149	13
[illegible]	172	15
[illegible]	173	15

Radical [illegible]

[illegible]	2899	223
[illegible]	4881	377
[illegible]	5602	431
[illegible]	1157	87

Radical [illegible]

[illegible]	5603	431
[illegible]	184	16
[illegible]	121	10
[illegible]	162	14
[illegible]	3093	238
[illegible]	178	15
[illegible]	153	13
[illegible]	127	11
[illegible]	185	16
[illegible]	109	9
[illegible]	1153	87
[illegible]	164	14
[illegible]	166	14
[illegible]	122	10
[illegible]	134	11
[illegible]	128	11
[illegible]	182	16
[illegible]	112	10
[illegible]	110	10
[illegible]	177	15
[illegible]	179	15
[illegible]	165	14
[illegible]	168	14
[illegible]	146	12
[illegible]	151	13
[illegible]	108	9
[illegible]	142	12
[illegible]	1264	95
[illegible]	186	16
[illegible]	119	10
[illegible]	1154	87
[illegible]	1152	87
[illegible]	131	11
[illegible]	126	11
[illegible]	208A	18
	242	20
[illegible]	154	13
[illegible]	156	13
[illegible]	180	16
[illegible]	113	10

[illegible]	5177A	399
	5197	400
[illegible]	5104	393
[illegible]	5228	403
[illegible]	5174	399
[illegible]	5169A	398
	5180	399
[illegible]	5225A	403
	5238	403
[illegible]	5181	399
[illegible]	5148	396
[illegible]	5163	398
[illegible]	5216	402
[illegible]	5099	392
[illegible]	5151	397
[illegible]	5168	398
[illegible]	5262	405
[illegible]	5193	400
[illegible]	5190	400
[illegible]	5125	395
[illegible]	5155	397
[illegible]	5207	401
[illegible]	5166A	398
	5205	401
[illegible]	5209	401
[illegible]	5200	401
[illegible]	5202	401
[illegible]	5233	403
[illegible]	5243	404
[illegible]	5259	405
[illegible]	5218	402
[illegible]	5221	402
[illegible]	5258	405
[illegible]	5103bis	393
	5128	395
	5174A	399
[illegible]	5213	402
[illegible]	5171	398
[illegible]	5170	398
[illegible]	5164	398
[illegible]	5147	396
[illegible]	5210	401
[illegible]	5192	400
[illegible]	5208	401
[illegible]	5158	397
[illegible]	5161	398
[illegible]	5159	397
[illegible]	5236	403
[illegible]	5230	403
[illegible]	5232	403
[illegible]	5100	392
[illegible]	5178	399
[illegible]	5185	399
[illegible]	5157	397
[illegible]	5186	400
[illegible]	5200	401
[illegible]	5229	403
[illegible]	5107	393
[illegible]	5172	398
[illegible]	5102	392
[illegible]	5182	399
[illegible]	5219	402
[illegible]	5115	394
	5202bis	401
[illegible]	5108	393
[illegible]	5161	398
	5164A	398
[illegible]	5143	396
[illegible]	5166	398
[illegible]	5150	397
[illegible]	5119	394
[illegible]	5195	400
[illegible]	5189	400
[illegible]	5127	395
[illegible]	5246	404
[illegible]	5231	403
[illegible]	5234	403
[illegible]	5257	405
[illegible]	5215	402
[illegible]	5241	404
[illegible]	5110	393
[illegible]	5117	394
[illegible]	5248	404
[illegible]	5113	394
[illegible]	5116	394
[illegible]	5141	396
[illegible]	5265	405
[illegible]	5194	400
[illegible]	5203	401
[illegible]	5124	395
[illegible]	5175	399
[illegible]	5101	392
[illegible]	5177	399
[illegible]	5242	404
[illegible]	5173	399
[illegible]	5112	394
[illegible]	5114	394
[illegible]	5227	403
[illegible]	5245	404
[illegible]	5214	402
[illegible]	5123	394
[illegible]	5187	400
[illegible]	5139	396
[illegible]	5198	400
[illegible]	5106	393
[illegible]	5212	401
[illegible]	5118	394
[illegible]	5183	399
[illegible]	5121	394
[illegible]	5120	394
[illegible]	5244	404
[illegible]	5122	394
[illegible]	5134A	395
	5140	396
[illegible]	5105	393
[illegible]	5109	393
[illegible]	5111	394
[illegible]	5249	404
[illegible]	5174B	399
[illegible]	5235	403
[illegible]	5196	400
[illegible]	5226	403

Radical [illegible]

[illegible]	1291	96
[illegible]	1292	97

Radical [illegible]

[illegible]	1517	114
[illegible]	1514	114
[illegible]	1515	114
[illegible]	1513	114
[illegible]	1512	114

Radical [illegible]

[illegible]	1669	125
[illegible]	1686A	126
	1691	127
[illegible]	1663	124
[illegible]	1701	128
[illegible]	1683	126
[illegible]	1667	125
[illegible]	1662	124
[illegible]	1664	124
	1995A	152
[illegible]	1687	126
[illegible]	1685	126
[illegible]	1681	126
[illegible]	1692	127
[illegible]	1670	125
[illegible]	1689	126
[illegible]	1682	126
[illegible]	1695	127
[illegible]	1684	126
[illegible]	1658	124
[illegible]	1657	124
[illegible]	1665	125
[illegible]	1675	126
[illegible]	1680	126
[illegible]	1696	127
[illegible]	1671	125
[illegible]	1700	128
[illegible]	1668	125
[illegible]	1688	126
[illegible]	1698	127
[illegible]	1673	125
[illegible]	1674	126
[illegible]	1699	127
[illegible]	1660	124
[illegible]	1659	124
[illegible]	1666	125
[illegible]	1694	127
[illegible]	1697	127
[illegible]	1676	126
[illegible]	1679	126
[illegible]	1690	127

[illegible] 3296 253
[illegible] 3264 251
[illegible] 3298 253
[illegible] 3271 251
[illegible] 3275 252
[illegible] 3292 253
[illegible] 3271bis 251
[illegible] 3274 252
[illegible] 3270 251
[illegible] 3307 254
[illegible] 3273 252

Radical 夂
[illegible] 3293 253
[illegible] 3309 254
[illegible] 3282 252
[illegible] 3257 250
[illegible] 3286 253
[illegible] 3265 251
[illegible] 3305 254

Radical [illegible]
[illegible] 1280 96
[illegible] 1277 96
[illegible] 1270 95
[illegible] 1268 95
[illegible] 1276 95
[illegible] 1282 96
[illegible] 1281 96
[illegible] 1274 95
[illegible] 1265 95
[illegible] 1271 95
[illegible] 1273 95
[illegible] 1269 95
[illegible] 1272 95
[illegible] 1266 95
[illegible] 1267 95
[illegible] 1279 96
[illegible] 1278 96
[illegible] 1275 95

Radical 广
[illegible] 91 8
97 9
[illegible] 107 9
120 10
[illegible] 90 8
[illegible] 86 8
[illegible] 106 9
[illegible] 85 8
[illegible] 84 8
[illegible] 87 8
[illegible] 103 9
[illegible] 100 9

Radical [illegible]
[illegible] 1518 114
[illegible] 1519 114

Radical [illegible]
[illegible] 289 24
[illegible] 5533 426
[illegible] 501 40
[illegible] 360 29
[illegible] 392 32
[illegible] 290 24
[illegible] 2328 179
[illegible] 498 39
[illegible] 479 38
[illegible] 300 25
[illegible] 271 22
[illegible] 374 30
[illegible] 313 26
[illegible] 319 26
[illegible] 324 27
[illegible] 382 31
[illegible] 3606 277
[illegible] 4536 349
[illegible] 485 38
[illegible] 305 25
[illegible] 500 39
[illegible] 499 39
[illegible] 358 29
[illegible] 480 38
[illegible] 350 29
[illegible] 3211 247A
[illegible] 393 32
[illegible] 308 25
[illegible] 307 25
[illegible] 310 25
[illegible] 322 26
[illegible] 293 24
[illegible] 291 24
[illegible] 434 35
[illegible] 433 35
[illegible] 379 31
[illegible] 497 39
[illegible] 2417 186
[illegible] 493 39
[illegible] 359 29
[illegible] 514 40
[illegible] 187A 16
510 40
[illegible] 404 33
[illegible] 314 26
[illegible] 311 26
[illegible] 312 25
[illegible] 326 27
[illegible] 292 24
[illegible] 283 23
[illegible] 315 26
[illegible] 268 22
[illegible] 334 28
[illegible] 440 35
[illegible] 447 36
[illegible] 432 35
[illegible] 451 36
[illegible] 507 40
[illegible] 328 27
[illegible] 469 37
[illegible] 458 37
[illegible] 457 37
[illegible] 511 40
[illegible] 477 38
[illegible] 494 39
[illegible] 496 39
[illegible] 301 25
[illegible] 375 30
[illegible] 395 33
[illegible] 255 21
[illegible] 455 37
[illegible] 398 33
[illegible] 351 29
[illegible] 274 23
[illegible] 317 26
[illegible] 277 23
[illegible] 316 26
[illegible] 325 27
[illegible] 279 23
[illegible] 278 23
[illegible] 286 24
[illegible] 430 35
[illegible] 438 35
[illegible] 441 35
[illegible] 426 34
[illegible] 425 34
[illegible] 446 36
[illegible] 435 35
[illegible] 437 35
[illegible] 439 35
[illegible] 296 24
[illegible] 512 40
[illegible] 363 30
[illegible] 408 33
[illegible] 482 38
[illegible] 481 38
[illegible] 303 25
[illegible] 416 34
[illegible] 471 38
[illegible] 344 28
[illegible] 337 28
[illegible] 503 40
[illegible] 502 40
[illegible] 352 29
[illegible] 355 29
[illegible] 353 29
[illegible] 478 38
[illegible] 487 39
[illegible] 299 25
[illegible] 327 27
[illegible] 383 31
[illegible] 376 30
[illegible] 515 40
[illegible] 357 29
[illegible] 280 23
[illegible] 509 40

[illegible]	240	20
[illegible]	196	17
[illegible]	200	17
[illegible]	237	20
[illegible]	195	17
[illegible]	193	17
[illegible]	218	19
[illegible]	241	20
[illegible]	227	19
[illegible]	236	20
[illegible]	199	17
[illegible]	217	19
[illegible]	232	19
[illegible]	239	20
[illegible]	230	19
[illegible]	207	18
[illegible]	197	17
[illegible]	209	18
[illegible]	194	17
[illegible]	119	10
	201	17
[illegible]	222	19
[illegible]	223	19
[illegible]	221	19
[illegible]	204	17
[illegible]	229	19
[illegible]	225	19
[illegible]	190	16
[illegible]	212	18
[illegible]	220	19
[illegible]	222	19
[illegible]	206	17
[illegible]	228	19
[illegible]	234	20
[illegible]	198	17
[illegible]	219	19
[illegible]	205	17
[illegible]	238	20

Radical [illegible]

[illegible]	5076	391
[illegible]	5074	391
[illegible]	5032	387
[illegible]	5045	388
[illegible]	5058	389
[illegible]	5048	388
[illegible]	5063	390
[illegible]	5034	387
[illegible]	5039	388
[illegible]	5030	387
[illegible]	5016	386
[illegible]	5051	389
[illegible]	5020	386
[illegible]	5065	390
[illegible]	5072	391
[illegible]	5024	387
[illegible]	5035	388
[illegible]	5046	388
[illegible]	5077	391
[illegible]	5053	389
[illegible]	5049	389
[illegible]	5001	385
[illegible]	5059	389
[illegible]	5015	386
[illegible]	5052	389
[illegible]	5014	386
[illegible]	5011	386
[illegible]	5031	387
[illegible]	5013	386
[illegible]	5027	387
[illegible]	3427A	263
	5021	386
[illegible]	5047	388
[illegible]	5071	390
[illegible]	5044	388
[illegible]	5041	388
[illegible]	5078	391
[illegible]	5057	389
[illegible]	5012	386
[illegible]	5019	386
[illegible]	5066	390
[illegible]	5069	390
[illegible]	5056	389
[illegible]	5005	385
[illegible]	5025	387
[illegible]	5050	389
[illegible]	5003	385
[illegible]	5029	387
[illegible]	5080	391
[illegible]	5028	387
[illegible]	5010	385
[illegible]	5038	388
[illegible]	5073	391
[illegible]	5022	387
[illegible]	5006	385
[illegible]	5033	387
[illegible]	5009	385
[illegible]	5002	385
[illegible]	5036	388
[illegible]	5103	393
[illegible]	5062	389
[illegible]	5061	389
[illegible]	5017	386
[illegible]	5068	390
[illegible]	5070	390
[illegible]	5060	389
[illegible]	5042	388
[illegible]	5040	388
[illegible]	5079	391
	5080A	391
[illegible]	5007	385
[illegible]	5083	391
[illegible]	5054	389
[illegible]	5055	389
[illegible]	5082	391
[illegible]	5037	388
[illegible]	5064	390
[illegible]	5026	387
[illegible]	5067	390
[illegible]	5023	387
[illegible]	5008	385
[illegible]	5004	385
[illegible]	5043	388
[illegible]	5075	391
[illegible]	5081	391

Radical [illegible]

[illegible]	251	21
[illegible]	252	21
[illegible]	253	21
[illegible]	254	21

Radical [illegible]

[illegible]	2220	171
[illegible]	2226	171
[illegible]	2229	172
[illegible]	2223	171
[illegible]	2218	171
[illegible]	2227	171
[illegible]	2219	171
[illegible]	2221	171
[illegible]	2230	172
[illegible]	2217	171
[illegible]	2225	171
[illegible]	2216	170
[illegible]	2222	171
[illegible]	2228	172
[illegible]	2224	171
[illegible]	2207	170

Radical [illegible]

[illegible]	1876	140
[illegible]	1881	141
[illegible]	1745	131
	1884A	141
[illegible]	1883	141
[illegible]	1870	140
[illegible]	1744	131
[illegible]	1888	141
[illegible]	1885	141
[illegible]	1879	140
[illegible]	1874	140
[illegible]	1878	140

Radical [illegible]

[illegible]	3349	257
[illegible]	3357	257
[illegible]	3375	259
[illegible]	3352	257
[illegible]	3372	258
[illegible]	3359	258
[illegible]	3338	256
[illegible]	3350	257
	3351	257
[illegible]	3358	257
[illegible]	3368	258

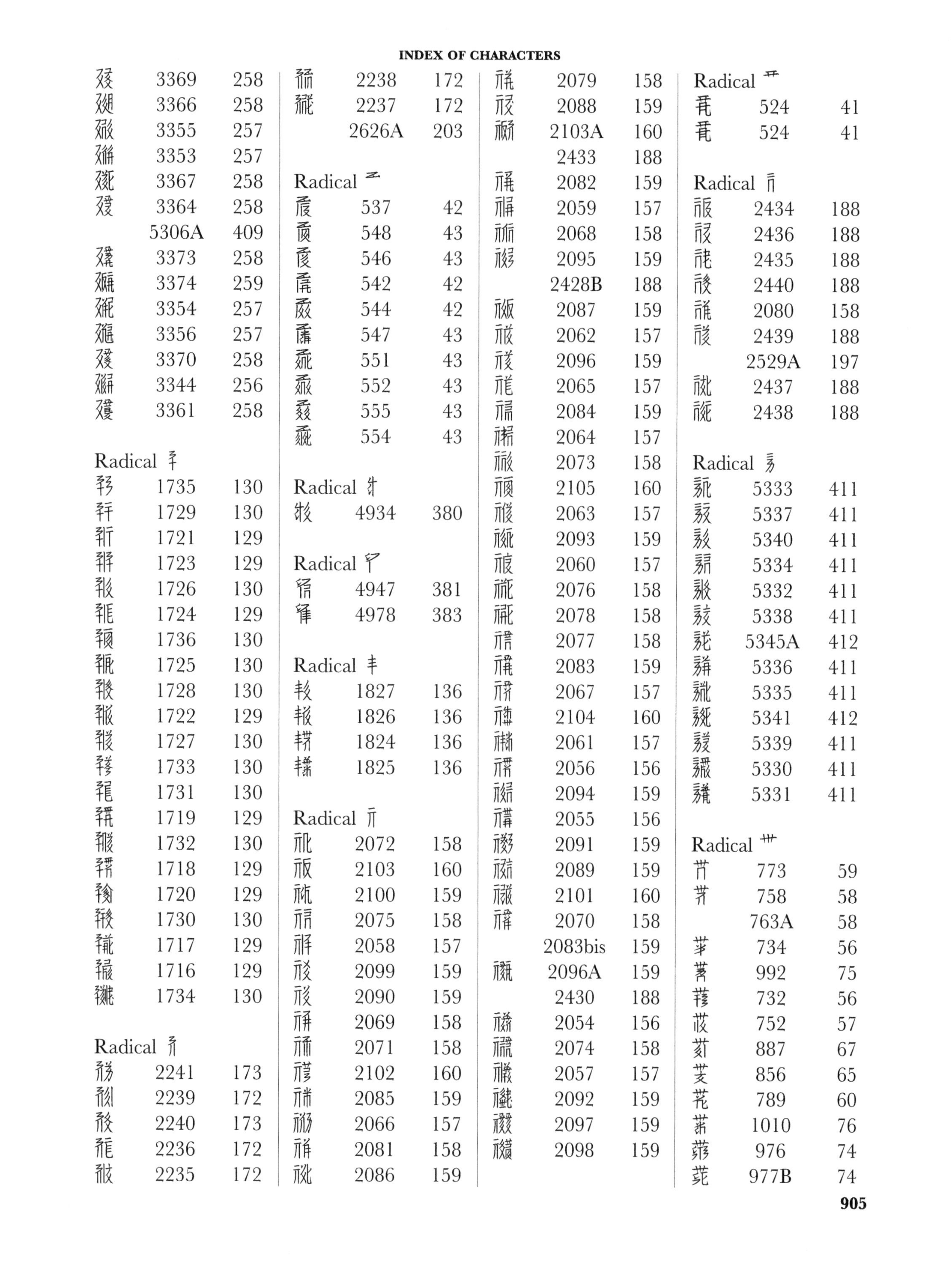

Character	No.	Page
[illegible]	728	56
[illegible]	696	54
[illegible]	711	55
[illegible]	775	59
[illegible]	752A	58
	774	59
[illegible]	919B	70
	952	72
[illegible]	838	64
[illegible]	845	64
[illegible]	1005	76
[illegible]	795	60
[illegible]	927	70
[illegible]	767	59
[illegible]	970	73
[illegible]	994	75
[illegible]	1015	77
[illegible]	983	75
[illegible]	984	75
[illegible]	695bis	54
	753A	58
[illegible]	1006	76
[illegible]	997	76
[illegible]	1019	77
[illegible]	776	59
[illegible]	714	55
[illegible]	897	68
[illegible]	833	63
	834A	63
[illegible]	960	73
[illegible]	703	54
[illegible]	720	55
[illegible]	761	58
	789A	60
[illegible]	1011	77
[illegible]	735	56
[illegible]	1000	76
[illegible]	772	59
[illegible]	857	65
[illegible]	925	70
[illegible]	996	75
[illegible]	993	75
[illegible]	1009A	76
[illegible]	975	74
[illegible]	988	75
[illegible]	698	54
	783A	60
[illegible]	733	56
[illegible]	782	59
[illegible]	815	62
[illegible]	779	59
[illegible]	1009	76
[illegible]	853	65
[illegible]	854	65
[illegible]	751	57
[illegible]	749	57
[illegible]	757	58
[illegible]	754	58
	773A	59
[illegible]	905	68
[illegible]	916	69
[illegible]	910	69
[illegible]	835	64
[illegible]	837	64
[illegible]	802	61
[illegible]	717	55
[illegible]	794	60
[illegible]	742	57
[illegible]	971	74
[illegible]	995	75
[illegible]	705	54
[illegible]	963	73
[illegible]	967	73
	977A	74
[illegible]	974	74
[illegible]	987	75
[illegible]	977	74
[illegible]	986	75
[illegible]	981	75
[illegible]	731	56
[illegible]	730	56
	849C	64
[illegible]	724	56
[illegible]	726	56
[illegible]	780	59
[illegible]	855	65
[illegible]	831	63
[illegible]	778	59
[illegible]	779A	59
[illegible]	964	73
[illegible]	829	63
[illegible]	753	58
[illegible]	710	55
[illegible]	713	55
[illegible]	814	62
[illegible]	906	68
[illegible]	890	67
[illegible]	911	69
[illegible]	899	68
[illegible]	893	68
[illegible]	892	67
[illegible]	915	69
[illegible]	902B	68
[illegible]	953	72
[illegible]	920	70
[illegible]	898	68
[illegible]	901	68
[illegible]	902A	68
	921	70
[illegible]	835	64
[illegible]	834	63
[illegible]	848	64
[illegible]	842	64
[illegible]	844	64
[illegible]	844A	64
[illegible]	790	60
	801A	61
[illegible]	873	66
[illegible]	735A	56
	739	56
	832bis	63
	872	66
[illegible]	760	58
[illegible]	1017	77
[illegible]	864	65
[illegible]	879	66
[illegible]	929	71
[illegible]	1023	77
[illegible]	998	76
[illegible]	741	57
[illegible]	945	72
[illegible]	764	58
[illegible]	765	58
[illegible]	824	62
[illegible]	870A	66
	926	70
[illegible]	747	57
[illegible]	972	74
[illegible]	704	54
[illegible]	978	74
[illegible]	979	74
[illegible]	822	62
[illegible]	729	56
[illegible]	757A	58
	768	59
[illegible]	797	60
[illegible]	798	60
[illegible]	710A	55
[illegible]	849	64
[illegible]	849A	64
	1240	93
[illegible]	962bis	73
[illegible]	708	55
[illegible]	748	57
[illegible]	750	57
[illegible]	1018	77
[illegible]	763	58
[illegible]	889	67
[illegible]	891	67
[illegible]	962	73
[illegible]	950	72
[illegible]	893A	68
	946	72
[illegible]	922	70
[illegible]	913	69
[illegible]	956	72
[illegible]	848A	64
	883	67
[illegible]	841	64
[illegible]	846	64
[illegible]	847	64
[illegible]	788	60
[illegible]	803	61
[illegible]	761A	58
	791	60
[illegible]	800	61

Radical 卌

Radical [illegible]

[illegible]	2752	213
[illegible]	2753	213
[illegible]	2749	213
[illegible]	2748	213
[illegible]	2754	213
[illegible]	2741	212
[illegible]	2743	212
[illegible]	2750	213
[illegible]	2742	212
[illegible]	2739	212
[illegible]	2751	213
[illegible]	2746	212
[illegible]	2744	212
[illegible]	2740	212
[illegible]	2745A	212
[illegible]	2747	213

Radical [illegible]

[illegible]	3214	247A
[illegible]	3226	248
[illegible]	3228	248
[illegible]	3213	247A
[illegible]	3216	247A
[illegible]	3223	248
[illegible]	3220	248
[illegible]	3229	248
[illegible]	3215	247A
[illegible]	3219	248
[illegible]	3225	248
[illegible]	3218	247A
[illegible]	3219	248
[illegible]	3221	248
[illegible]	3217	247A
[illegible]	3212	247A
[illegible]	3222	248
[illegible]	3224	248
[illegible]	3227	248

Radical [illegible]

[illegible]	5515	425
[illegible]	5522	426
[illegible]	5451	421
[illegible]	5445	420
[illegible]	5440	420
[illegible]	5475	422
[illegible]	5523	426
[illegible]	5519	425
[illegible]	5437	419
[illegible]	5439	419
[illegible]	5518	425
[illegible]	5444	420
[illegible]	5514	425
[illegible]	5482	423
[illegible]	5483	423
[illegible]	5490	423
[illegible]	5476	422
[illegible]	5441	420
[illegible]	5436	419
[illegible]	5520	425
[illegible]	5442	420
[illegible]	5527	426
[illegible]	5498	424
[illegible]	5455	421
[illegible]	5435	419
[illegible]	5487	423
[illegible]	5497	424
[illegible]	5432	419
[illegible]	5496	424
[illegible]	5521	426
[illegible]	5491	423
[illegible]	5443	420
[illegible]	5457	421
[illegible]	5446	420
[illegible]	5510	425
[illegible]	5452	421
[illegible]	5528	426
[illegible]	5517	425
[illegible]	5495	424
[illegible]	5489	423
[illegible]	5506	425
[illegible]	5493	424
[illegible]	5513	425
[illegible]	5434	419
[illegible]	5488	423
[illegible]	5450	421
[illegible]	5499	424
[illegible]	5492	424
[illegible]	5529	426
[illegible]	5516	425
[illegible]	5438	419
[illegible]	5430	419
[illegible]	5485	423
[illegible]	5512	425
[illegible]	5502	424
[illegible]	5456	421
[illegible]	5447	420
[illegible]	5503	424
[illegible]	5433	419
[illegible]	5484	423
[illegible]	5507	425
[illegible]	5509	425
[illegible]	5508	425
[illegible]	5453	421
[illegible]	5458	421
	5491A	424
[illegible]	5500	424
[illegible]	5504	424
[illegible]	5429	419
[illegible]	5449	421
[illegible]	5532	426
[illegible]	5524	426
[illegible]	5505	424
[illegible]	5454	421
[illegible]	5477	422
[illegible]	5481	423
[illegible]	5531	426
[illegible]	5480	423
[illegible]	5424	418
[illegible]	5426	418
[illegible]	5501	424
[illegible]	5425	418
[illegible]	5426A	418
	5428	419
[illegible]	5448	420
[illegible]	5486	423
[illegible]	5431	419
[illegible]	5530	426
[illegible]	5479	423
[illegible]	5478	423
[illegible]	5511	425

Radical [illegible]

[illegible]	3340	256
[illegible]	3336	256
[illegible]	3339	256
[illegible]	3341	256
[illegible]	3365	258
[illegible]	3360	258
[illegible]	3362	258
[illegible]	3348	257
[illegible]	3343	256
[illegible]	3342	256
[illegible]	3371	258

Radical [illegible]

[illegible]	3386A	260
[illegible]	3407	262
[illegible]	3397	260
[illegible]	3401	261
[illegible]	3394	260
[illegible]	3381	259
[illegible]	3409	262
[illegible]	3376	259
[illegible]	3403	261
[illegible]	3392A	260
	3453	265
[illegible]	3410	262
[illegible]	3377	259
[illegible]	3379	259
[illegible]	3378	259

Radical [illegible]

[illegible]	2738	212
[illegible]	2735	212
[illegible]	2736	212
[illegible]	2737	212
[illegible]	2734	211

Radical [illegible]

[illegible]	2926	225
[illegible]	2927	225

Radical [illegible]

[illegible]	1397	106
[illegible]	1396	106

Character	No.	Page
[illegible]	4091	315A
[illegible]	4288	330
[illegible]	4123	316
[illegible]	4021	309
[illegible]	4061	312
[illegible]	3788	290
[illegible]	3896	299
[illegible]	3911	300
[illegible]	3946	303
[illegible]	4259	327
[illegible]	4260	327
[illegible]	4286	329
[illegible]	3958A	304
	4119	316
[illegible]	4230	325
[illegible]	4229	325
[illegible]	4233	325
[illegible]	4249	327
[illegible]	4250	327
[illegible]	4253	327
[illegible]	3859	296
[illegible]	3889	298
[illegible]	4087	315A
[illegible]	4055	312
[illegible]	4281	329
[illegible]	3964	304
[illegible]	3854	296
[illegible]	3763	288
[illegible]	3782	290
[illegible]	3861	296
[illegible]	3837	294
[illegible]	4086	315A
[illegible]	4075	313
[illegible]	4294	330
[illegible]	4274	328
[illegible]	4214	324
[illegible]	4120	316
[illegible]	4121	316
[illegible]	3819	293
[illegible]	4045	311
[illegible]	4046	311
[illegible]	3925	301
[illegible]	3918	300
[illegible]	3780	289

Character	No.	Page
[illegible]	3790	290
[illegible]	3812	292
	3929	301
[illegible]	3793	291
[illegible]	4293	330
[illegible]	3942	302
[illegible]	4219	324
[illegible]	4208	322
[illegible]	4088	315A
[illegible]	3682	283
[illegible]	4144	318
[illegible]	4026	309
[illegible]	3681	283
[illegible]	3915	300
[illegible]	4118	316
[illegible]	4037	310
[illegible]	3699	284A
[illegible]	3343A	256
	3870	297
[illegible]	4011	308
[illegible]	3706	284B
[illegible]	4269bis	328
[illegible]	3936	302
[illegible]	4285	329
[illegible]	4284	329
[illegible]	4025	309
[illegible]	3949	303
[illegible]	4268	328
[illegible]	3680	283
[illegible]	4195	321B
[illegible]	3696	284A
[illegible]	3979	305
[illegible]	3976	305
[illegible]	4282	329
[illegible]	3686	283
[illegible]	4244	326
[illegible]	4201	321B
[illegible]	3956	304
[illegible]	3948	303
[illegible]	4295	330
[illegible]	3953	303
[illegible]	3906	300
[illegible]	3959	304
[illegible]	4166	319

Character	No.	Page
[illegible]	4200	321B
[illegible]	4224	324
[illegible]	4227	325
[illegible]	4239	326
[illegible]	3710	284B
[illegible]	4237	326
[illegible]	4228	325
[illegible]	4248	326
[illegible]	3674	282
[illegible]	3898	299
[illegible]	3746	287
[illegible]	3748	287
[illegible]	3862	296
[illegible]	3890	298
[illegible]	3885	298
[illegible]	3971	305
[illegible]	3970	305
[illegible]	4215	324
[illegible]	4264	327
[illegible]	4263	327
[illegible]	3735	286
[illegible]	3738	286
[illegible]	3835	294
[illegible]	3842	295
[illegible]	3838	294
[illegible]	3847	295
[illegible]	3839	294
	3884A	298
[illegible]	4073	313
[illegible]	4077	314
[illegible]	4085	314
[illegible]	4299	331
[illegible]	3965	304
[illegible]	3851	295
[illegible]	4133	317
[illegible]	4220	324
[illegible]	4136	317
[illegible]	4093	315A
[illegible]	3794	291
[illegible]	3805	292
[illegible]	4101	315B
[illegible]	3921	301
[illegible]	3924	301
[illegible]	3920	301

Character	No.	Page
[illegible]	3930	301
[illegible]	3922	301
[illegible]	3787	290
[illegible]	3784	290
[illegible]	3877	297
[illegible]	3878	297
[illegible]	4189	321A
[illegible]	3760	288
[illegible]	4211	322
[illegible]	4127	316
[illegible]	3865	296
[illegible]	3990	306
[illegible]	3683	283
[illegible]	4043	311
[illegible]	3675	282
[illegible]	3685	283
	4184A	321A
[illegible]	4199	321B
[illegible]	4162	319
[illegible]	3712	285
[illegible]	4177	320
[illegible]	3937	302
	4018A	309
[illegible]	3873	297
[illegible]	3698	284A
[illegible]	3705	284B
[illegible]	4163	319
[illegible]	3866	296
[illegible]	4004	307
[illegible]	3714	285
[illegible]	3876	297
[illegible]	4160	319
[illegible]	4158	319
[illegible]	3694	284A
[illegible]	3899	299
[illegible]	3688	283
	3782bis	290
[illegible]	4050	311
[illegible]	3986	306
[illegible]	3988	306
[illegible]	3983	306
[illegible]	4031	310
[illegible]	4169	320
[illegible]	3754	287

[illegible]	4115	315B
[illegible]	3674A	282
	4201B	321B
	4216	324
[illegible]	4261	327
[illegible]	3901	299
[illegible]	3902	299
[illegible]	3856	296
[illegible]	3758	287
[illegible]	3736	286
[illegible]	3733	286
[illegible]	3853	296
[illegible]	3846	295
	3887A	298
[illegible]	3806A	292
	3857	296
[illegible]	4084	314
[illegible]	4076	313
	4273A	328
[illegible]	4074	313
[illegible]	3762	288
[illegible]	3994	307
[illegible]	3996	307
[illegible]	4156	319
[illegible]	3678	282
[illegible]	3289A	253
	3654	280
[illegible]	3872	297
[illegible]	4094	315A
[illegible]	4015	308
[illegible]	4019	309
[illegible]	4017	309
[illegible]	4014	308
[illegible]	3868	296
[illegible]	4092	315A
[illegible]	4001	307
[illegible]	4279	329
[illegible]	3951	303
[illegible]	4196	321B
[illegible]	3993	307
[illegible]	3992	307
[illegible]	3987	306
[illegible]	4152	318
[illegible]	4146	318
[illegible]	3743	286
[illegible]	3721	285
[illegible]	3718	285
[illegible]	4110	315B
[illegible]	4246	326
[illegible]	3751	287
[illegible]	3888	298
[illegible]	3969	305
[illegible]	3731	286
[illegible]	4083	314
[illegible]	4210	322
[illegible]	3713	285
[illegible]	4039	310
[illegible]	4042	311
[illegible]	4040	311
[illegible]	4041	311
[illegible]	3715	285
[illegible]	3701	284B
[illegible]	4161	319
[illegible]	3711	284B
[illegible]	4002	307
[illegible]	4278	329
[illegible]	4024	309
	4056A	312
[illegible]	4027	310
[illegible]	3756	287
[illegible]	4176	320
[illegible]	3950	303
[illegible]	4198	321B
[illegible]	3687	283
[illegible]	3689	284A
[illegible]	3695	284A
[illegible]	4149	318
[illegible]	3740	286
[illegible]	3755	287
[illegible]	3719	285
[illegible]	3741	286
[illegible]	3742	286
[illegible]	3834	294
[illegible]	4078	314
[illegible]	3795	291
[illegible]	3991A	306
[illegible]	4151	318
[illegible]	4010	308
[illegible]	4159	319
[illegible]	3702	284B
	3948A	303
[illegible]	4056	312
[illegible]	3757	287
[illegible]	3693	284A
[illegible]	4147	318
[illegible]	3697A	284A
[illegible]	4030	310
[illegible]	3700A	284B
	3709	284B
[illegible]	4223	324
[illegible]	4235B	326
[illegible]	3900	299
[illegible]	4102	315B
[illegible]	3954	303
[illegible]	4155	319
[illegible]	4203	322

Radical [illegible]

[illegible]	3944	303
[illegible]	4063	312
[illegible]	3943	303
[illegible]	4183	321A
[illegible]	4179	320
[illegible]	4124	316
[illegible]	4129	317
[illegible]	4128	316
[illegible]	3875	297
[illegible]	4272	328
[illegible]	4059	312
[illegible]	4205	322
[illegible]	4277	329
[illegible]	4141	317
[illegible]	4098	315A
[illegible]	4207	322
[illegible]	4053	311
[illegible]	4052	311
[illegible]	4165	319
[illegible]	4099	315B
[illegible]	4067	313
[illegible]	4065	313
[illegible]	3895	299
[illegible]	3704	284B
[illegible]	3769A	289
	4048	311
[illegible]	4298	330

Radical [illegible]

[illegible]	3934	302
[illegible]	1294	97

Radical [illegible]

[illegible]	4676	360
[illegible]	4636	357
[illegible]	4686	361
[illegible]	4673	360
[illegible]	4687	361
[illegible]	4698	362
[illegible]	4204A	322
	4685	361
[illegible]	4190	321B

Radical [illegible]

[illegible]	3259	251
[illegible]	3260	251

Radical [illegible]

[illegible]	3650	280
[illegible]	3657	281
[illegible]	3334	256
	3661A	281
[illegible]	3661	281
[illegible]	3649	280
[illegible]	3289B	253
	3652	280
[illegible]	3656	281
[illegible]	3653	280
[illegible]	3660	281
[illegible]	3651	280
[illegible]	3655	280

Radical [illegible]

[illegible]	3313	254
[illegible]	3322	255
[illegible]	3326	255
[illegible]	3324	255
[illegible]	3321	255

	2585	200
	2593	201
	2610	202
	2567	199
	2599	201
	2571	199
	2590	201
	2581	200
	2565	199
	2595	201

Radical

	4936	380
	4935	380
	4937	380

Radical

	1749	131
	1739	130
	1741	131
	1743	131
	3248	250
	1746	131
	1740	130
	1747	131
	1748	131

Radical

	3247	250
	3249	250
	3248A	250
	3248	250
	3250	250

Radical

	519	41
	2796	216
	517	41
	518	41

Radical

	5380	415
	5382	415
	5387	416

	5396	416
	5402	417
	5384	415
	5383	415
	5370	414
	5404	417
	5393	416
	5395	416
	5369	414
	5376	415
	5390	416
	5374	414
	5385	416
	5399	416
	5397	416
	5403	417
	5389	416
	5371	414
	5400	416
	5377	415
	5391	416
	5386	416
	5375	415
	5373	414

Radical

	5381	415
	5401	417
	5372	414
	5394	416
	5392	416
	5379	415
	5388	416
	5378	415
	5398	416

Radical

	246	20
	245	20

Radical

	1738	130

Radical

	2443	189
	2477	192
	2470	191
	2478	192
	2490	193
	2445	189
	2467	191
	2476	191
	2448	189
	2494	193
	2444	189
	2482	192
	2468	191
	2457	190
	2452	190
	2463	191
	2449	189
	2481	192
	2469	191
	2483	192
	2491	193
	2479	192
	2464	191

Radical

	2455	190

Radical

	3245	250
	3246	250

Radical

	243	20
	244	20

Radical

	5344	412
	5352	412
	5347	412
	5343	412
	5349	412
	5350	412
	5404A	417

Radical

	1778	133
	1776	133
	1774	133
	1783	133
	1784	134
	1777	133
	1781	133
	1780	133
	1775	133
	1790	134
	1793	134
	1782	133
	1786	134
	1792	134
	1788	134
	1795	134
	1787	134
	1785	134
	1789	134
	1779	133
	1794	134
	1791	134

Radical

	2674	207
	5534	426
	3096	238
	625	49
	629A	49
	661	51
	568	44
	3628	278
	659	51
	663	51
	571	44
	599	47
	598	47
	116	10
	593	46
	645	50
	633	50
	582	45
	595	47

Radical 丰

Radical 艹

Radical 礻

Radical 衤

Radical 糸

Radical 歹

Radical 耒

Radical [illegible]

[illegible] 2371 183
[illegible] 2361 182
[illegible] 2362 182
[illegible] 2367 183
[illegible] 2363 183
[illegible] 2360 182
[illegible] 2365 183
[illegible] 2375 184
[illegible] 2368 183
[illegible] 2357 182
[illegible] 2358 182

Radical [illegible]

[illegible] 5286 407
[illegible] 5288 407
[illegible] 5287 407

Radical [illegible]

[illegible] 5611 432
[illegible] 5609 432

Radical [illegible]

[illegible] 557 43
[illegible] 556 43

Radical [illegible]

[illegible] 5561 428
[illegible] 5547 427
[illegible] 5549 427
[illegible] 5554 428
[illegible] 5545 427
[illegible] 5544 427
[illegible] 5546 427
[illegible] 5552 428
[illegible] 5557 428
[illegible] 5560 428
[illegible] 5558 428
[illegible] 5550 427
[illegible] 5551 428
[illegible] 5542 427
[illegible] 5556 428
[illegible] 5543 427
[illegible] 5617 432
[illegible] 5548 427
[illegible] 5553 428
[illegible] 5555 428
[illegible] 5559 428

Radical [illegible]

[illegible] 1287 96
[illegible] 1290 96
[illegible] 1289 96
[illegible] 1293 97
[illegible] 1286 96
[illegible] 1283 96
[illegible] 1288 96
[illegible] 1285 96
[illegible] 1284 96

Radical [illegible]

[illegible] 1148 87
[illegible] 1119 84
[illegible] 1106 83
[illegible] 1073 81
[illegible] 1101 83
[illegible] 1103 83
[illegible] 1025 78
[illegible] 1067 80
[illegible] 1108 83
[illegible] 1113 84
[illegible] 1133 86
[illegible] 1098 83
[illegible] 1068 80
[illegible] 1071 80
[illegible] 1128 85
[illegible] 1127 85
[illegible] 1075 81
[illegible] 1143 86
1131A 86
[illegible] 1064 80
[illegible] 1063 80
[illegible] 1059 80
[illegible] 1062 80
[illegible] 1093 82
[illegible] 1081 81
[illegible] 1078 81
[illegible] 1079 81
[illegible] 1117 84
[illegible] 1102 83
[illegible] 1121 84
[illegible] 1125 85
[illegible] 1069 80
[illegible] 1100 83
[illegible] 1074 81
[illegible] 1076 81
[illegible] 1144 86
[illegible] 1142 86
[illegible] 1082 81
[illegible] 1145 86
[illegible] 1092 82
[illegible] 1080 81
[illegible] 1116 84
[illegible] 1066 80
[illegible] 1126 85
[illegible] 1105 83
[illegible] 1132 86
[illegible] 1120 84
[illegible] 1139 86
[illegible] 1099 83
[illegible] 1136 86
[illegible] 1146 86
[illegible] 1060 80
— 82
[illegible] 1061 80
[illegible] 1122 85
[illegible] 1123 85
[illegible] 1135 86
[illegible] 1131 85
[illegible] 1131A 86
[illegible] 1110 84
[illegible] 1130 85
[illegible] 1147 87
[illegible] 1124 85
[illegible] 1129 85
[illegible] 1072 80
[illegible] 1070 80
[illegible] 1140 86

Radical [illegible]

[illegible] 2755 213
[illegible] 2759 214
[illegible] 2756 213
[illegible] 2757 213
[illegible] 2747 213
2758 213

Radical [illegible]

[illegible] 3188 245

Radical [illegible]

[illegible] 3187 245

Radical [illegible]

[illegible] 3398 261
[illegible] 3391 260
[illegible] 3402 261
[illegible] 3400 261
[illegible] 3387 260
[illegible] 3405 261
[illegible] 3399 261
[illegible] 3408 262
[illegible] 3399A 261
3466 266
[illegible] 3382 259
[illegible] 3383 259
[illegible] 3411 262
[illegible] 3396 260
[illegible] 3384 259
[illegible] 3395 260
[illegible] 3380 259
[illegible] 3389 260
[illegible] 3388 260
[illegible] 3392 260
[illegible] 3386 260
[illegible] 3390 260
[illegible] 3393 260
[illegible] 3404 261
[illegible] 3406 261

Radical [illegible]

[illegible] 2741A 212
2924 225

Radical [illegible]

[illegible] 1356 102

Radical [illegible]

[illegible]	2558	199
[illegible]	2544	198
[illegible]	2551	198
[illegible]	2552	198
[illegible]	2548	198
[illegible]	2553	198
[illegible]	2550	198
[illegible]	2555	198
[illegible]	2556	198
[illegible]	2549	198
[illegible]	2561	199
[illegible]	2560	199
[illegible]	2546	198
[illegible]	2545	198
[illegible]	2547	198
[illegible]	2557	199
[illegible]	2543	198
[illegible]	2559	199
[illegible]	2554	198

Radical [illegible]

[illegible]	2376	184
[illegible]	2370	183
[illegible]	2364	183
[illegible]	2374	184
[illegible]	2377	184
[illegible]	2369	183
[illegible]	2378	184
[illegible]	2373	183
[illegible]	2366	183
[illegible]	2359	182
[illegible]	2372	183

Radical [illegible]

[illegible]	61	5
[illegible]	62	5

Radical [illegible]

[illegible]	1363	103
	3161	243
[illegible]	1369	103
	2929A	225

Radical [illegible]

[illegible]	1370	104
[illegible]	1358	102
[illegible]	1373	104
[illegible]	1361	102
[illegible]	1362	103
[illegible]	1366	103
[illegible]	1360	102
[illegible]	1365	103
[illegible]	1367	103
[illegible]	1359	102
[illegible]	1364	103
[illegible]	1374	104
[illegible]	1372	104
[illegible]	1371	104
[illegible]	1357	102

Radical [illegible]

[illegible]	3144	242
[illegible]	3148	242
[illegible]	3168	244
[illegible]	3160	243
[illegible]	3158	243
[illegible]	3150	242
[illegible]	3166	243
[illegible]	3156	243
[illegible]	3163	243
[illegible]	3149	242
[illegible]	3151	242
[illegible]	3162	243
[illegible]	3167	244
[illegible]	3157	243
[illegible]	2730	211
[illegible]	3165	243
[illegible]	3153	242
[illegible]	3152	242
[illegible]	3147	242
[illegible]	3164	243
[illegible]	3159	243
[illegible]	3154	243
[illegible]	3145	242

Radical [illegible]

[illegible]	3175	244

Radical [illegible]

[illegible]	5661	436

Radical [illegible]

[illegible]	1839	137

Radical [illegible]

[illegible]	2261	174
[illegible]	2260	174

Radical [illegible]

[illegible]	1841	137
[illegible]	1840	137
[illegible]	1842	138
[illegible]	1843	138
[illegible]	1845	138
[illegible]	1848	138
[illegible]	1844	138
	3083A	237
[illegible]	1846	138
[illegible]	1847	138

Radical [illegible]

[illegible]	2186	168
[illegible]	2184	168
[illegible]	2185	168
[illegible]	2188	168

Radical [illegible]

[illegible]	2889	223
[illegible]	2814	217
[illegible]	2824	218
[illegible]	2829	218
[illegible]	2863	221
[illegible]	2849	220
[illegible]	2850	220
[illegible]	2892	223
[illegible]	2877	222
[illegible]	2890	223
[illegible]	2887	223
[illegible]	2815	217
[illegible]	2813	217
[illegible]	2842	219
[illegible]	2864	221
[illegible]	2895	223
[illegible]	2893	223
[illegible]	2826	218
[illegible]	2869	221
[illegible]	2888A	223
[illegible]	2851	220
[illegible]	2845	220
[illegible]	2862	221
[illegible]	2843	219
[illegible]	2812	217
[illegible]	2859	221
[illegible]	2823	218
[illegible]	2885	222
[illegible]	2883	222
[illegible]	2866	221
[illegible]	2830	218
[illegible]	2840	219
[illegible]	2848	220
[illegible]	2878	222
[illegible]	2803	217
[illegible]	2854	220
[illegible]	2835A	219
	2844	219
[illegible]	2870	221
[illegible]	2828	218
[illegible]	2825	218
[illegible]	2891	223
[illegible]	2897	223
[illegible]	2868	221
[illegible]	2853	220
[illegible]	2894	223
[illegible]	2871	221
[illegible]	2872	221
[illegible]	2861	221
[illegible]	2884	222
[illegible]	2831	218
[illegible]	2818	218
[illegible]	2855	220
[illegible]	2856	220
[illegible]	2896	223
[illegible]	2832	219
[illegible]	2888	223
[illegible]	2846	220
[illegible]	2835	219

[Tangut]	4658	359
[Tangut]	4682	361
[Tangut]	4630	357
[Tangut]	4704	363
[Tangut]	4628	357
[Tangut]	4631	357
[Tangut]	4622	357
[Tangut]	4620A	356
[Tangut]	4647	358
[Tangut]	4654	359
[Tangut]	4680	361
[Tangut]	4621	356
[Tangut]	4672	360
[Tangut]	4624	357

Radical [Tangut]

[Tangut]	1299	98
[Tangut]	1297	97
[Tangut]	1301	98
[Tangut]	1298	98
[Tangut]	1295	97
[Tangut]	1300	98
[Tangut]	1302	98
[Tangut]	1296	97

Radical [Tangut]

[Tangut]	4712	363
[Tangut]	4814	371
[Tangut]	4789	370
[Tangut]	4812	371
[Tangut]	4819	372
	4820	372
[Tangut]	4758	367
[Tangut]	4818	372
[Tangut]	4769	367
[Tangut]	4817	372
[Tangut]	4759	367
[Tangut]	4790	370
[Tangut]	4731	365
[Tangut]	4761	367
[Tangut]	4728	364
[Tangut]	4794	370
[Tangut]	4802	370
[Tangut]	4773	368
[Tangut]	3385	259
	4750	366
[Tangut]	4780	369
[Tangut]	4821	372
[Tangut]	4792	370
[Tangut]	4760	367
[Tangut]	4736	365
[Tangut]	4788	369
[Tangut]	4734	365
[Tangut]	4735	365
[Tangut]	4747	366
[Tangut]	4805	371
[Tangut]	4784	369
[Tangut]	4738	365
[Tangut]	4785	369
[Tangut]	4740	366
	4744	366
[Tangut]	4798	370
[Tangut]	4824	372
[Tangut]	4822	372
[Tangut]	4811	371
[Tangut]	4736	365
	4749	366
[Tangut]	4826	372
[Tangut]	4808	371
[Tangut]	4729	365
[Tangut]	4732	365
[Tangut]	4791	370
[Tangut]	4746	366
[Tangut]	4763	367
[Tangut]	3315	254
	4779A	369
[Tangut]	3406A	262
	4823	372
[Tangut]	4762	367
[Tangut]	4816	371
[Tangut]	4756	367
[Tangut]	4730	365
[Tangut]	4796	370
[Tangut]	4797	370
[Tangut]	4795	370
[Tangut]	4774	368
[Tangut]	4771	368
[Tangut]	4716	363
[Tangut]	4715	363
[Tangut]	4786	369
[Tangut]	4718	364
[Tangut]	4764	367
[Tangut]	4741	366
[Tangut]	4782	369
[Tangut]	4800	370
[Tangut]	4714	363
[Tangut]	4783	369
[Tangut]	4809	371
[Tangut]	4815	371
[Tangut]	4813	371
[Tangut]	4757	367
[Tangut]	4737	365
[Tangut]	4765	367
[Tangut]	4788A	369
[Tangut]	4806	371
[Tangut]	4779	369
[Tangut]	4770	368
[Tangut]	4745	366
[Tangut]	4743	366
[Tangut]	4787	369
[Tangut]	4742	366
[Tangut]	4793	370
[Tangut]	4755	367
[Tangut]	4776	369
[Tangut]	4720	364
[Tangut]	4724	364
[Tangut]	4726	364
[Tangut]	4723	364
[Tangut]	4825	372
[Tangut]	4803	371
[Tangut]	4751	366
[Tangut]	4753	366
[Tangut]	4717	364
[Tangut]	4719	364
[Tangut]	4781	369
[Tangut]	4739	366
[Tangut]	4754	367
[Tangut]	4713	363
[Tangut]	4721	364
[Tangut]	4810	371
[Tangut]	4766	367
[Tangut]	4725	364
[Tangut]	4712A	363
[Tangut]	4727	364
[Tangut]	4807	371
[Tangut]	4777	369
[Tangut]	4772	368
[Tangut]	4722	364
[Tangut]	4748	366
[Tangut]	4778	369
[Tangut]	4801	370
[Tangut]	4804	371
[Tangut]	3993A	307
	4775	368
[Tangut]	4752	366
[Tangut]	4799	370

Radical [Tangut]

[Tangut]	3662	281

Radical [Tangut]

[Tangut]	1280A	96*
	3324A	255
	3331	256
[Tangut]	3323	255
	3330A	255
[Tangut]	3332	256

Radical [Tangut]

[Tangut]	4841	373
[Tangut]	4839	373
[Tangut]	4840	373

Radical [Tangut]

[Tangut]	2513	195
[Tangut]	2501	194
[Tangut]	2532	197
[Tangut]	2534	197
[Tangut]	2540	198
[Tangut]	2503	194
[Tangut]	2539	197
[Tangut]	2523	196
[Tangut]	2520	196
[Tangut]	2529	197
[Tangut]	2524	196
[Tangut]	2537	197

[illegible] 5581 430

Radical [illegible]

[illegible] 4939 381

Radical [illegible]

[illegible] 3520 270
[illegible] 3526 271
[illegible] 3530 271
[illegible] 3522 270
[illegible] 3525 271
[illegible] 3545 272
[illegible] 3546 272
[illegible] 3542 272
[illegible] 3538 272
[illegible] 3524 271
[illegible] 3523 270
[illegible] 3536 272
[illegible] 3548 272
[illegible] 3528 271
4408A 338
[illegible] 3541 272
[illegible] 3537 272
[illegible] 3544 272
[illegible] 3529 271
[illegible] 3540 272
[illegible] 3527 271
[illegible] 3532 271
[illegible] 3531 271
[illegible] 3539 272
[illegible] 3535 272
[illegible] 3534 272
[illegible] 3521 270
[illegible] 3547 272
[illegible] 3533 271

Radical [illegible]

[illegible] 2232 172
[illegible] 2231 172
[illegible] 2234 172
[illegible] 2233 172

Radical [illegible]

[illegible] 3555 273
[illegible] 3568 274
[illegible] 3581 275
[illegible] 3585 275
[illegible] 3561 273
[illegible] 3580 275
[illegible] 3567 274
[illegible] 3565 274
[illegible] 3558 273
[illegible] 3578 275
[illegible] 3554 273

Radical [illegible]

[illegible] 2138 163
[illegible] 2141 163
[illegible] 2140 163
[illegible] 2156 166
[illegible] 2143 163
[illegible] 2153 165
[illegible] 2157 166
[illegible] 2147 164
[illegible] 2149 164
[illegible] 2150 165
[illegible] 2142 163
[illegible] 2146 164
[illegible] 2144 164
[illegible] 2145 164
[illegible] 2148 164
[illegible] 2139 163
[illegible] 2159 166
[illegible] 2155 165
[illegible] 2158 166
[illegible] 2151 165
2153A 165
[illegible] 2154 165
[illegible] 2152 165

Radical [illegible]

[illegible] 1753 131
[illegible] 1752 131
[illegible] 1751 131
[illegible] 1755 132

Radical [illegible]

[illegible] 1750 131
[illegible] 1756 132
[illegible] 1754 132
[illegible] 1757 132

Radical [illegible]

[illegible] 2687 208
[illegible] 2686 208

Radical [illegible]

[illegible] 2506 195
[illegible] 2522 196
[illegible] 2511 195
[illegible] 2542 198
[illegible] 2505 195
[illegible] 2500 194
[illegible] 2499 194
[illegible] 2538 197
[illegible] 2510 195
[illegible] 2508 195
[illegible] 2530 197
[illegible] 2512 195
[illegible] 2503A 194
2504 194
[illegible] 2526 197
[illegible] 2507 195
[illegible] 2496 194
[illegible] 2509 195
[illegible] 2497 194
[illegible] 2502 194
[illegible] 2517 196
[illegible] 2519 196
[illegible] 2531 197
[illegible] 2518 196
[illegible] 2498 194

Radical [illegible]

[illegible] 250 21
[illegible] 249 21

Radical [illegible]

[illegible] 5366 414
[illegible] 5365 414
[illegible] 5359 413
[illegible] 5364A 414
5367 414
[illegible] 5360 413
[illegible] 5364 414
[illegible] 5368 414

Radical [illegible]

[illegible] 2731 211
[illegible] 2733 211
[illegible] 2732 211

Radical [illegible]

[illegible] 2771 214
[illegible] 2769 214
[illegible] 2765 214
[illegible] 2772 215
[illegible] 2766 214
[illegible] 2767 214
[illegible] 2762 214
[illegible] 2770 214
[illegible] 2760 214

Radical [illegible]

[illegible] 3236 249
[illegible] 3235 249
[illegible] 3230 248
[illegible] 3234 249
[illegible] 3231 248
[illegible] 3232 249
[illegible] 3233 249

Radical [illegible]

[illegible] 3430 263
[illegible] 3420A 263
3460 266
[illegible] 3434 264
[illegible] 3470 267
[illegible] 3481 268
[illegible] 3495 269
[illegible] 3496 269
[illegible] 3433 264
[illegible] 3463 266
3464 266

Radical [illegible]

[illegible]	2918	225

Radical [illegible]

[illegible]	2329	180
[illegible]	2331	180
[illegible]	2333	180

Radical [illegible]

[illegible]	2330	180
[illegible]	1649A	123
	2332	180

Radical [illegible]

[illegible]	1654	124
[illegible]	1655	124
[illegible]	1656	124

Radical [illegible]

[illegible]	5306	409

Radical [illegible]

[illegible]	1758	132
[illegible]	1759	132
[illegible]	1762	132
[illegible]	1761	132
[illegible]	1760	132
[illegible]	1763	132

Radical [illegible]

[illegible]	2385	184
[illegible]	2384	184
[illegible]	2386	184
[illegible]	2387	184
[illegible]	2383	184

Radical [illegible]

[illegible]	5608	432
[illegible]	5610	432
[illegible]	5618	432
[illegible]	5619	432
[illegible]	5616	432
[illegible]	5614	432
[illegible]	5613	432
[illegible]	5612	432
[illegible]	5615	432

Radical [illegible]

[illegible]	3618	277
[illegible]	3620	278
[illegible]	3619	277
[illegible]	3616	277
[illegible]	3617	277
[illegible]	3613	277
[illegible]	3615	277
[illegible]	3614	277
[illegible]	3621	278
[illegible]	3612	277
[illegible]	3611	277
[illegible]	3609	277
[illegible]	3610	277

Radical [illegible]

[illegible]	4986	384
[illegible]	4972	383
[illegible]	4971	383

Radical [illegible]

[illegible]	1259	94
[illegible]	1260	94
[illegible]	1261	94

Radical [illegible]

[illegible]	3039	233
[illegible]	3043	234
[illegible]	3038	233
[illegible]	3041	234
[illegible]	3040	234
[illegible]	3042	234
[illegible]	3037	233

Radical [illegible]

[illegible]	4342	334
[illegible]	4337	333
[illegible]	4338	333
[illegible]	4336	333
[illegible]	4341	333

Radical [illegible]

[illegible]	1603	121

Radical [illegible]

[illegible]	5416	418
[illegible]	5419	418
[illegible]	5418	418
[illegible]	5420	418
[illegible]	5417	418

Radical [illegible]

[illegible]	7	1
[illegible]	7A	1*
	2768	214
[illegible]	5	1
[illegible]	6	1

Radical [illegible]

[illegible]	39	4

Radical [illegible]

[illegible]	3177	244
[illegible]	3179	244
[illegible]	3178	244

Radical [illegible]

[illegible]	44	4
[illegible]	45	4

Radical [illegible]

[illegible]	4830	372
[illegible]	4831	372
[illegible]	4829	372

Radical [illegible]

[illegible]	2775	215
[illegible]	2777	215
[illegible]	2776	215
[illegible]	2774	215
[illegible]	2778	215

Radical [illegible]

[illegible]	2392	185
[illegible]	2389	185
[illegible]	2391	185
[illegible]	2393	185
[illegible]	2395	185
[illegible]	2394	185
[illegible]	2390	185

Radical [illegible]

[illegible]	3172	244
[illegible]	3170	244
[illegible]	3171	244
[illegible]	3173	244

Radical [illegible]

[illegible]	3186	245
[illegible]	3185	245
[illegible]	3174	244
	3186A	245

Radical [illegible]

[illegible]	2382	184
[illegible]	2380A	184
[illegible]	2381	184
[illegible]	2379	184
[illegible]	2380	184

Radical [illegible]

[illegible]	1910	144
[illegible]	1911	144

Radical [illegible]

[illegible]	5664	436
[illegible]	5680	438
[illegible]	5677	437
[illegible]	5673	437
[illegible]	5672	437
[illegible]	5675	437
[illegible]	5678	437
[illegible]	5676	437
[illegible]	5670	437
[illegible]	5674	437
[illegible]	5682	438
[illegible]	5669	436
[illegible]	5683	438
[illegible]	5681	438

[illegible] 2625 203
2791A 216

Radical [illegible]
[illegible] 3189 245
[illegible] 3190 245
[illegible] 3194 245
[illegible] 3195 245
[illegible] 3191 245
[illegible] 3192 245
[illegible] 3193 245
[illegible] 3195A 245

Radical [illegible]
[illegible] 3584 275
[illegible] 3566 274
[illegible] 3572 274
[illegible] 3576 275
[illegible] 3574 274
[illegible] 3559 273
[illegible] 3556 273
[illegible] 3575 274
[illegible] 3557 273
[illegible] 3562 273
[illegible] 3564 274
[illegible] 3577 275
[illegible] 3579 275
4502A 346
[illegible] 3571 274
[illegible] 3550 272
[illegible] 3560 273
[illegible] 3583 275
[illegible] 3570 274
[illegible] 3563 274
[illegible] 3582 275
[illegible] 3586 275

Radical [illegible]
[illegible] 2256 174
[illegible] 2258 174
[illegible] 2253 173
[illegible] 2252 173
[illegible] 2257 174
[illegible] 2254 174
[illegible] 2251 173
[illegible] 2255 174

Radical [illegible]
[illegible] 2692 208
[illegible] 2697 209
[illegible] 2700 209
[illegible] 2706A 209
2724 211
[illegible] 2699 209
[illegible] 2717 210
[illegible] 2703 209
[illegible] 2695 208
[illegible] 2713 210
[illegible] 2704 209
[illegible] 2698 209
[illegible] 2710 210
[illegible] 2716 210
[illegible] 2715 210
[illegible] 2712 210
[illegible] 2714 210
[illegible] 2705 209
[illegible] 2696 208
[illegible] 2711 210
[illegible] 2701 209
[illegible] 2709 209
[illegible] 2706 209
[illegible] 2702 209
[illegible] 2694 208
[illegible] 2693 208

Radical [illegible]
[illegible] 2708 209

Radical [illegible]
[illegible] 2919 225
[illegible] 2920 225
[illegible] 2922 225
[illegible] 2921 225

Radical [illegible]
[illegible] 1572 118
[illegible] 1543 116
[illegible] 1571 118
[illegible] 1547 117
[illegible] 1544 116
[illegible] 1573 118
[illegible] 1554 117
[illegible] 1565 118
[illegible] 1574 118
[illegible] 1549 117
[illegible] 1568 118
[illegible] 1561 118
[illegible] 1555 117
[illegible] 1550A 117
[illegible] 1552 117
[illegible] 1570 118
[illegible] 1562 118
[illegible] 1546A 117
[illegible] 1557 117
[illegible] 1553 117
[illegible] 1559 117
[illegible] 1550 117
[illegible] 1558 117
[illegible] 1569 118
[illegible] 1546 116
[illegible] 1551 117
[illegible] 1560 117
[illegible] 1545 116
[illegible] 1567 118
[illegible] 1566 118
[illegible] 1548 117
[illegible] 1556 117
[illegible] 1563 118
[illegible] 1564 118
[illegible] 1542 116

Radical [illegible]
[illegible] 1575 118

Radical [illegible]
[illegible] 3074 236

Radical [illegible]
[illegible] 3071 236
[illegible] 3075 236
[illegible] 3076 237
[illegible] 3078 237
[illegible] 2254A 174
3079 237
[illegible] 3081 237
[illegible] 2251A 173
3073 236
[illegible] 3080 237
[illegible] 3077 237
[illegible] 3072 236

Radical [illegible]
[illegible] 5649 435
[illegible] 5654 435
[illegible] 5656 436
[illegible] 5653 435
[illegible] 5651 435
[illegible] 5658 436
[illegible] 5652 435
[illegible] 5659 436
[illegible] 5650 435
[illegible] 5655 436
[illegible] 5657 436

Radical [illegible]
[illegible] 4522 348
[illegible] 4442 340
[illegible] 4467 343
[illegible] 4406 338
[illegible] 4510 347
[illegible] 4498 346
[illegible] 4434 340

Radical [illegible]
[illegible] 3256 250
[illegible] 3255 250

Radical [illegible]
[illegible] 2662 206
[illegible] 2652 205
2655A 205
[illegible] 2659 206
[illegible] 2656 205
[illegible] 2663 206
[illegible] 2654 205
[illegible] 2651 205

[illegible]	4476	343
[illegible]	4436	340
[illegible]	3543	272
[illegible]	4512	347
[illegible]	4426	339
[illegible]	4478	344
[illegible]	4504	346
[illegible]	4407	338
[illegible]	4376	336
[illegible]	4386	336
[illegible]	4473	343
[illegible]	4470	343
[illegible]	4495	345
[illegible]	4410	338
[illegible]	4445	341
[illegible]	4427	339
[illegible]	4500	346
[illegible]	4383	336
[illegible]	4415	338
[illegible]	4379	336
[illegible]	4367	335
[illegible]	4374	335
[illegible]	4377	336
[illegible]	4372	335
[illegible]	4378	336
[illegible]	4531	349
[illegible]	4471	343
[illegible]	4472	343
[illegible]	4363	335
[illegible]	4497	345
[illegible]	4533	349
[illegible]	4513	347
[illegible]	4412A	338
	4528	348
[illegible]	4517	347
[illegible]	4534	349
[illegible]	4469	343
[illegible]	4441A	340
	4468	343
[illegible]	4479	344
[illegible]	4369	335
[illegible]	4447	341
[illegible]	4366	335
[illegible]	4370	335
[illegible]	4381	336
[illegible]	4375	335
[illegible]	4380	336

Radical [illegible]

[illegible]	2801	217
[illegible]	4620	356

Radical [illegible]

[illegible]	1828	136

Radical [illegible]

[illegible]	189	16

Radical [illegible]

[illegible]	3503	269
[illegible]	3506	269
[illegible]	3507	269
[illegible]	3517	270
[illegible]	3516	270
[illegible]	3511	270
[illegible]	3513	270
[illegible]	3514	270
[illegible]	3519	270
[illegible]	3508	269

Radical [illegible]

[illegible]	83	8
	3233A	249

Radical [illegible]

[illegible]	1532	115
[illegible]	1525	115
[illegible]	1530	115

Radical [illegible]

[illegible]	3053	235

Radical [illegible]

[illegible]	3051	234

Radical [illegible]

[illegible]	3047	234
[illegible]	3057	235
[illegible]	3049	234
[illegible]	3044	234
[illegible]	3056	235
[illegible]	3045	234
[illegible]	3046	234

Radical [illegible]

[illegible]	5648	435

Radical [illegible]

[illegible]	4348	334
[illegible]	4353	334
[illegible]	4350	334
[illegible]	4360	335
[illegible]	4359	334
[illegible]	4355	334
[illegible]	4357	334
[illegible]	4341	333
[illegible]	4339	333
[illegible]	4352	334
[illegible]	4343	334

Radical [illegible]

[illegible]	4349	334
[illegible]	4354	334
[illegible]	4351	334
[illegible]	4347	334

Radical [illegible]

[illegible]	3442	264

Radical [illegible]

[illegible]	2108	160

Radical [illegible]

[illegible]	1055	79
[illegible]	1029A	78
[illegible]	1030	78
[illegible]	1048	79
[illegible]	1138	86
[illegible]	1031	78
[illegible]	1032	78
[illegible]	1036	78
[illegible]	1034	78
[illegible]	1054	79
[illegible]	1057	79
[illegible]	1037	78
[illegible]	1040	78
[illegible]	1065	80
[illegible]	1052	79
[illegible]	1046	79
[illegible]	1051	79
[illegible]	1050	79
[illegible]	1029	78
[illegible]	1043	79
[illegible]	1047	79
[illegible]	1056	79
[illegible]	1049	79
[illegible]	1035	78
[illegible]	1058	80
[illegible]	1045	79
[illegible]	1033	78
[illegible]	1044	79

Radical [illegible]

[illegible]	1149	87
[illegible]	1083	81

Radical [illegible]

[illegible]	1864A	139
	2342	180
[illegible]	2337	180
[illegible]	2343	181
[illegible]	2339	180
	3105B	239
[illegible]	2338	180
[illegible]	2341	180
[illegible]	2344	181
[illegible]	2340	180

Radical [illegible]

[illegible]	1820	136
[illegible]	1816	136
[illegible]	1822	136
[illegible]	1814	135
[illegible]	1817	136
[illegible]	1815	135
[illegible]	1823	136

[Tangut] 4888 377
[Tangut] 4885 377
[Tangut] 4892 378
[Tangut] 4886 377
[Tangut] 4891 378
[Tangut] 4883 377
[Tangut] 4889 377

Radical [Tangut]
[Tangut] 4850 374
[Tangut] 4849 374

Radical [Tangut]
[Tangut] 4767 367
[Tangut] 4768 367

Radical [Tangut]
[Tangut] 4861 375

Radical [Tangut]
[Tangut] 3169 244

Radical [Tangut]
[Tangut] 92 8
1457A 110
[Tangut] 92A 9
[Tangut] 93 9
[Tangut] 95 9
[Tangut] 94 9

Radical [Tangut]
[Tangut] 96 9

Radical [Tangut]
[Tangut] 159 14
[Tangut] 160 14

Radical [Tangut]
[Tangut] 3202 246

Radical [Tangut]
[Tangut] 264 22

Radical [Tangut]
[Tangut] 275 23
[Tangut] 273 23
[Tangut] 269 22

Radical [Tangut]
[Tangut] 2723 211
[Tangut] 2718 211
[Tangut] 2726 211
[Tangut] 2720 211
[Tangut] 3201 246
[Tangut] 2727 211
[Tangut] 2725 211
[Tangut] 2722 211
[Tangut] 2719 211
[Tangut] 2721 211

Radical [Tangut]
[Tangut] 1597 120
[Tangut] 1596 120
[Tangut] 1592 120
[Tangut] 1590 120
[Tangut] 1594 120
[Tangut] 1595 120
[Tangut] 1591 120
[Tangut] 1593 120

Radical [Tangut]
[Tangut] 3086 237

Radical [Tangut]
[Tangut] 2794A 216
3084 237
[Tangut] 3083 237
[Tangut] 3085 237
[Tangut] 3082 237

Radical [Tangut]
[Tangut] 1894 143

Radical [Tangut]
[Tangut] 2335 180
[Tangut] 2336 180
[Tangut] 2334 180

Radical [Tangut]
[Tangut] 1584 119

Radical [Tangut]
[Tangut] 3114 240
[Tangut] 3117 240
[Tangut] 3116 240
[Tangut] 3120 240
[Tangut] 3118 240
[Tangut] 3119 240
[Tangut] 3121 240
[Tangut] 3115 240

Radical [Tangut]
[Tangut] 1576 119
[Tangut] 1577 119
[Tangut] 1580 119
[Tangut] 1578 119
[Tangut] 1581 119
[Tangut] 1579 119

Radical [Tangut]
[Tangut] 4938 381

Radical [Tangut]
[Tangut] 5624 433
[Tangut] 5623 433
[Tangut] 5622 433

Radical [Tangut]
[Tangut] 4836 373

Radical [Tangut]
[Tangut] 2646A 205
2665 206

Radical [Tangut]
[Tangut] 3549 272

Radical [Tangut]
[Tangut] 2688 208

Radical [Tangut]
[Tangut] 520 41
[Tangut] 521 41
[Tangut] 522 41

Radical [Tangut]
[Tangut] 2795 216

Radical [Tangut]
[Tangut] 3596 276
[Tangut] 3599 276
[Tangut] 3597 276
[Tangut] 4448 341
[Tangut] 3595 276
[Tangut] 3598 276
[Tangut] 3603 276
[Tangut] 3600 276
[Tangut] 3592 276
[Tangut] 3602 276
[Tangut] 3594 276
[Tangut] 3601 276
[Tangut] 3593 276
[Tangut] 3604 276

Radical [Tangut]
[Tangut] 1867 140
[Tangut] 1868 140

Radical [Tangut]
[Tangut] 1203 90
2397A 185

Radical [Tangut]
[Tangut] 1160 87
[Tangut] 1164A 88
[Tangut] 1164 88
[Tangut] 1175 88
[Tangut] 1165 88
[Tangut] 1167 88
[Tangut] 1166 88
[Tangut] 1179 88
[Tangut] 1198 90
[Tangut] 1199 90
[Tangut] 1215 91

Character	No.	Page
	4563	352
	4558	351
	4572	352
	4591	354
	4564	352
	4560	351
	4562	352
	4567	352
	4582	353
	4545	350
	4579	353
	4556	351
	4597	354
	4592	354
	4557	351
	4585	353
	4569	352
	4583	353
	4603	354
	4549	350
	4561	351
	4566A	352
	4609	355
	4571	352
	4552	351
	4553	351
	4604	354
	4580	353
	4550	350
	4599	354
	4547	350
	4588	353
	4593	354
	4554	351
	4584	353
	4573	352
	4596	354
	4548	350
	4600	354
	4565	352
	4566	352
	4568	352
	4606	355
	4586	353
	4587	353
	4601	354
	4545B	350
	4555	351
	4595	354
	4581	353
	4545AA	350
	4546	350
	4594	354

Radical

	2347	181
	2345	181
	2346	181

Radical

	1811	135

Radical

	2411	186
	2413	186
	2414	186
	2415	186
	2412	186
	2416	186

Radical

	5632	434
	5631	433
	5636	434
	5645	435
	5641	434
	5635	434
	5633	434
	5629	433
	5634	434
	5627	433
	5626	433
	5643	435

Radical

	545	43
	543	42

Radical

	4605	355

Radical

	4945	381
	4946	381

Radical

	1088	82
	1089	82
	1084	81
	1090	82

Radical

	1115	84
	1109	84
	1111	84
	1107	83
	1104	83

Radical

	4880	377

Radical

	3143	242

Radical

	908	68
	1252A	94
	903	68

Radical

	759	58

Radical

	999	76
	1004	76
	1001	76

Radical

	743A	57
	1225	92

Radical

	1479	112

Radical

	2963	228
	2961	228
	2962	228

Radical

	3004	231
	2994	230
	2998	230
	3011	232
	3015	232
	3012	232
	3007	231

Radical

	10	1
	11	1

Radical

	5717	440
	5718	441

Radical

	5427	418

Radical

	5525	426
	5526	426

Radical

	4895	378

Radical

	3140	241
	3136	241
	3129	241
	3128	241
	3130	241
	3127	241
	3133	241
	3134	241

Radical [illegible]
[illegible] 2168 167
[illegible] 2161 166
[illegible] 2162 166
[illegible] 2167 166
[illegible] 2169 167
[illegible] 2165 166
[illegible] 2163 166
[illegible] 2164 166
[illegible] 2166 166
[illegible] 2160 166

Radical [illegible]
[illegible] 2684 208

Radical [illegible]
[illegible] 2355 182
[illegible] 2354 182

Radical [illegible]
[illegible] 550 43
[illegible] 551 43
[illegible] 553 43

Radical [illegible]
[illegible] 5537 427
[illegible] 5540 427
[illegible] 5538 427
[illegible] 5539 427
[illegible] 5535 426
[illegible] 5536 427

Radical [illegible]
[illegible] 1039 78

Radical [illegible]
[illegible] 4340 333

Radical [illegible]
[illegible] 1233 92
[illegible] 1235 92

Radical [illegible]
[illegible] 888 67

Radical [illegible]
[illegible] 811 61
[illegible] 813 62
[illegible] 812 62

Radical [illegible]
[illegible] 2398 185
[illegible] 2407 186
[illegible] 2400 185
[illegible] 2401 185
[illegible] 2405 186
2406 186
[illegible] 2399 185
[illegible] 2403 185
[illegible] 2402 185
[illegible] 2404 185

Radical [illegible]
[illegible] 3013 232
[illegible] 3014 232
[illegible] 2992 230
[illegible] 2997 230
[illegible] 2999 230
[illegible] 3009 231
[illegible] 2991 230
[illegible] 3002 231
[illegible] 3010 231
[illegible] 2996 230
[illegible] 2990 230
[illegible] 3005 231
[illegible] 3006 231
[illegible] 3000 231
[illegible] 2995 230
[illegible] 2989 230
[illegible] 3003 231
[illegible] 2993 230
[illegible] 3016 232
[illegible] 2987 230
[illegible] 3008 231

Radical [illegible]
[illegible] 3146 242

Radical [illegible]
[illegible] 3728 285
[illegible] 3725 285
[illegible] 3724 285
[illegible] 3727 285

Radical [illegible]
[illegible] 98 9
[illegible] 101 9
[illegible] 102 9
[illegible] 99 9

Radical [illegible]
[illegible] 3182 244

Radical [illegible]
[illegible] 3123 240
[illegible] 3124 240
[illegible] 3125 240

Radical [illegible]
[illegible] 294 24
[illegible] 295 24

Radical [illegible]
[illegible] 1583 119

Radical [illegible]
[illegible] 5541 427

Radical [illegible]
[illegible] 1262 94
[illegible] 1263 95

Radical [illegible]
[illegible] 3633 279
[illegible] 3632 278
[illegible] 3641 279

Radical [illegible]
[illegible] 1192A 89
3634 279
[illegible] 3638 279
[illegible] 3639 279
[illegible] 3635 279
[illegible] 3640 279
[illegible] 3637 279

Radical [illegible]
[illegible] 3647 280
[illegible] 3643 280
[illegible] 3644 280
[illegible] 3642 279
[illegible] 3646 280
[illegible] 3645 280

Radical [illegible]
[illegible] 233 19
[illegible] 235 20

Radical [illegible]
[illegible] 203 17
[illegible] 202 17

Radical [illegible]
[illegible] 5700 439
[illegible] 5699 439

Radical [illegible]
[illegible] 5714 440
[illegible] 5715 440
[illegible] 5716 440

Radical [illegible]
[illegible] 4896 378
[illegible] 4898 378
[illegible] 4897 378

Radical [illegible]
[illegible] 3100 238

Radical [illegible]
[illegible] 1042 79
[illegible] 1041 78
[illegible] 1038 78

Radical [illegible]

[illegible]	583	46
[illegible]	584	46

Radical [illegible]

[illegible]	4079	314
[illegible]	4082	314

Radical [illegible]

[illegible]	1158	87

Radical [illegible]

[illegible]	1211	91

Radical [illegible]

[illegible]	1194	89
[illegible]	1195	90
[illegible]	1196	90

Lightning Source UK Ltd.
Milton Keynes UK
UKOW07f1816221117
313154UK00001B/1/P

9 781782 01167